ALL
SHOOK
UP

ROCK&ROLL REMEMBRANCES SERIES

TOM SCHULTHEISS, Series Editor

pierian
press
1985

All Shook Up

ELVIS

Day-By-Day, 1954-1977

by Lee Cotten

ISBN 0-87650-172-2
L   1

Copyright ©1985
by Lee Cotten

All Rights Reserved

PIERIAN PRESS
P.O. BOX 1808
ANN ARBOR, MI 48106

Contents

APPENDIXES

Introduction

As the reader might suspect, the amount of specific information on Elvis' childhood is very limited. This is, of course, true of most people born into this world having parents with only the normal expectations for their children. Only royalty, either blooded or popularly elevated, has offspring whose every movement is a matter of public record. Most of us do not. The Presleys in Tupelo and Memphis, prior to 1954, were just another hard working family, struggling to overcome the effects of being born and raised in a location ravaged by the Depression. Certainly, they must have had lowered expectations. Their movements during Elvis' childhood are shadowy, recalled only dimly by the few remaining relatives and friends who actually knew them well. In this area, I am indebted to Janelle McComb of Tupelo for her gracious assistance and for her comments.

Then came the explosion: Elvis' first professional recording was issued in July 1954. It was only a matter of months before he was being acclaimed as the biggest thing ever to come down the pike — at least the pike between Memphis and Shreveport. Within eighteen months, Elvis was on the verge of breaking out of the South and into the national spotlight. Barely six months after his first coast-to-coast television exposure, Elvis was a full-blown phenomenon who was loved and hated with equal passion throughout the country. Along with this new-found teenage fad came a media explosion. Elvis' name sold magazines and newspapers, and the amount of coverage devoted to Elvis doubled monthly during 1956. Everyone around Elvis was eager to promote this popularity, but Elvis' manager, Colonel Parker, took the reins and the amount of hard, inside information slowed to a trickle. Elvis was prevented from talking to the press in any setting other than a formal news conference, and the answers he gave to reporters' questions were invariably shallow or flippant. No hard facts to confuse the issue. No hard facts to obscure the legend. Elvis found himself surrounded by an entourage of cousins and bodyguards

Elvis over breakfast in 1956 . . . cantaloupe and a cigar.

whose sole purpose was to keep the public from approaching the superstar.

By the time Elvis left the Army in March 1960, the curtain surrounding him was complete. He commuted between Graceland and Hollywood, making three movies a year. He virtually stopped all personal appearances (only two shows in seven years). He retreated behind high walls where his comings and goings were kept under a complete cloak of secrecy. There might be a glimpse of Elvis in Memphis at a midnight movie. Or entering a recording studio in Nashville or Hollywood. Or riding through the neighborhood on a motorcycle accompanied by the starlet of the week. But the information on Elvis' personal life had been reduced to level zero.

Then, in 1968, Elvis' career took another turn with the broadcast of the NBC-TV special, "Elvis." The years of movie contracts were over, and it was decided to take to the road again in a return to the live performances that Elvis said he missed. Starting in Las Vegas in July 1969 and continuing through to his death in August 1977, Elvis criss-crossed the United States in an ever growing number of live concerts. While this increased the amount of information on Elvis' whereabouts, it also meant that I was faced with a mountain of basically repetitive information. This became especially true toward the end of Elvis' life. The concerts in the early 1970s were marked by high spirits on the part of both Elvis and the audiences who came to see him. Seven years later, Elvis was walking through many of these shows, even though most of the fans in the audience were still mesmerized by the very presence of such a legendary performer. Meanwhile, away from the concert stage, Elvis remained as reclusive as ever. The wall of friends and management surrounding him had grown to monumental proportions. Only a select few ever entered the private domain of the King of Rock 'n' Roll. And no information ever leaked out until almost the end. I am sure that this is the main reason that news of Elvis' drug habits came as such a shock to those were proud to be called Elvis' fans. By 1977, Elvis stood for more than just the name of an entertainer. It stood for a way of life that had begun more than twenty years earlier. The music of rock 'n' roll had changed, and many performers were into hard drugs which had killed off more than a few of the superstars. But the image of Elvis remained above all of this. A product of more modest times, Elvis remained the gentleman until the end. The private Elvis was kept completely under wraps. The public was not even allowed to know that Elvis smoked. Although it had been mentioned that Elvis liked an occasional cigar, almost all private photos show him holding a thin stogie. The public did not know that Elvis wore reading glasses.

Many people did not know that Elvis tinted his naturally sandy brown hair and eyebrows black. But, if these little details about Elvis could have been so easily hidden behind a screen of friends and relations, what other truths were being withheld? Was Elvis a mindless drug addict? A homosexual? A perverted womanizer? A self-destructive, wimpering, pampered, mama's boy who never matured beyond the impotent age of twelve? Or maybe he was from outer space? Or a reincarnation of Jesus? Or the physical puppet of his dead twin brother? Once the walls of secrecy that surrounded Elvis until his death began to crumble, almost any half-truth was fodder for the scandal sheets and "quicky" biographers eager to stand in the falling star's limelight.

In the end, what we know about Elvis is the sum of the facts about a very public man whose life had been the center of continuous controversy for all of his more than twenty public years, but who's private life remained just that, private.

Work on this book began more than ten years ago. My primary motivation at that time was my disillusionment with all the existing books on the life of Elvis Presley, so many of which contained a great deal of conflicting information, not to mention outright falsehoods. Many of these books received such widespread distribution that the misstatements, errors and lies they contain became part of the growing legend surrounding Elvis' life. My frustration with the genre of journalistic pop biography reached a climax when, in the hectic days following Elvis' death, almost all news reports stated that he and his mother were the same age, forty-two, when they died. In fact, only Elvis was forty-two; Gladys Presley was forty-six. This type of error is the sloppiest sort of journalism. Any reporter, and there were literally thousands in Memphis in August 1977, could have checked this seemingly minor detail by walking the short distance from the mausoleum first used as Elvis' final resting place to the gravesite of his mother. To my mind, the failure to check such facts was unforgivably careless.

When I first began my research, I gathered information on a haphazard basis and kept it in a spiral notebook. My goal at the time was simply to keep the basic facts surrounding Elvis' career straight. As more books and articles were published, I continued to add notations and, by 1980, it was obvious that the material in the notebook was ready for publication. *Elvis: His Life History,* which ran a scant sixty-four pages, filled an immediate need. It has been interesting, over this past year, to discover just how inadequate it was. And, just how full of errors. Yet, *Elvis: His Life History* was an invaluable source in itself, representing hundreds of hours of personal research, and I referred back to this slim volume time and again when newly discovered facts did not fit the ones already on file. Although limited to 200 copies (which quickly sold out), it established to my satisfaction the need for a larger and more complete work along the same lines. The result is now in your hands.

In January 1983, after sending in the manuscript for *Jailhouse Rock* (Pierian Press, 1983), I began again the process of locating and organizing all the illuminating and verifiable facts I could find about Elvis' life. In compiling such facts, every conceivable type of source material was checked thoroughly. Newspapers, weekly news magazines, fan magazines, music trade journals, movie magazines, newsreels, Elvis' movies, interviews, press releases, biographies of Elvis and other music personalities, and volumes that covered the history of music over the past thirty years were all meticulously picked apart for any bit of useful information about Elvis. The many pieces were finally amassed into an enormous chronological card file which formed the nucleus for *All Shook Up*. This project became an all-consuming passion during the last few months of 1983, and research continued into the middle of 1984.

Much of the news of Elvis' recording career was gathered from back issues of *Billboard* magazine, the national music trade journal which has had the reputation for being the most complete and accurate source of information on the music business. Many of the items about Elvis' movie career came from *Variety*, another national trade journal with an equally impressive reputation for its coverage of the film industry and what was generally known as vaudeville even in the mid-1950s (i.e., live performing). All references to record chart positions were derived from the various charts in *Billboard*; complete *Billboard* charts on Elvis' recording career are included in the back of this volume. All of the references to chart positions for Elvis' films were derived from the film charts in *Variety*, another appendix to this work. In each case, all available issues, numbering over 2000 between the two journals, were scrutinized for material relating to Elvis' career.

Movie magazines, those intended for the casual movie fan, proved to be a less reliable sources of factual information. It is the stock-in-trade of these magazines to "hype" the career of a show business personality in the beginning, and then to attempt to destroy the image they helped to create at the end of that career. Facts play little part in the process. As one might expect, these magazines frequently printed totally fictitious stories under the guise of truth.

Fan magazines devoted to Elvis, on the other hand, proved to be an invaluable source of news clippings and firsthand accounts of Elvis' concerts and his movements throughout his career. The

A young Elvis as pictured on a vending machine arcade card from the late fifties.

purpose of these fanzines, as one might expect, is to present Elvis in an almost perfect light while ignoring the bad press. This means that the researcher must wade through much gushing and fawning to discover the hard facts. However, after the tinsel was trimmed away, these magazines were still of enormous help.

My research included reviewing as many of the nation's daily newspapers as time would allow. Most thoroughly covered were the papers from Memphis, Los Angeles, New York, San Francisco, Seattle, St. Louis, and Atlanta. It is an unfortunate fact of life that most newspapers do not have a complete index to aid in this work. The *Los Angeles Times* does not even have a clipping file on Elvis because, in the words of their reply to my inquiry, "the clips have been missing for years." *Elvis Presley Reference Guide And Discography,* by John A. Whisler, was a great help in this area, even though its coverage of newspapers extended only to the two Memphis dailies and *The New York Times.* On the other hand, Whisler's book provided fine access to periodical articles, including most of the national magazines and music and movie trade journals.

The many biographies of Elvis each presented a different problem based on the perspective of the author. Each successive book should have benefitted from the research of those that came before, but most did not. Many authors approached Elvis' life strictly as a means to cash in on Elvis' fame, producing poorly written biographies to make a quick buck. This was especially true after Elvis' death. Even those books which attempted to present themselves as "serious" works on the life of Elvis often were less than useful due to their author's preoccupation with destroying the myth and legend that completely surrounded Elvis during his life. It seems a part of human nature to want to belittle that which is larger than yourself, to bring the superstar down to a common level. The fact that Elvis' remarkable career and his personal lifestyle were so much bigger than those of the people who were closest to him must have grated on many nerves over the years, judging by the number of "tell all" books which have come out following his death. Each of these books, on the other hand, did offer a slightly different perspective on Elvis' complex personality. Elvis' ex-wife, Priscilla, is writing a book which will reportedly appear at about the same time as *All Shook Up,* and which may clear up some of the questions which are raised in my book. This leaves only three people still alive who have not been heard from in one way or another: Colonel Parker, Charlie Hodge, and Linda Thompson.

Elvis' movies were a constant source of amazement to me; I marveled at the contrast between how bad they could be at times

Even RCA can't get Elvis' story straight. A recently released *That's All Right* single gives a 1955 recording date for the song recorded July 5, 1954 . . .

. . . and the latest promotional literature celebrates a 50th Anniversary birth date that is a year too early!

and yet how entertaining most remained as a whole. I was often reminded of how awful many of the songs were, and yet how fine the performances were at the same time. Picking each movie apart allowed me to confirm specific locations where Elvis worked.

Newsreels gave me a chance to see the real Elvis at work on the one-nighter circuit in the 1950s. But it was the newsreel footage of Elvis in the Army that was an eye-opening marvel. Here was the "real" Elvis, unadorned by the trappings of stardom, in an unnatural situation, caught off guard.

Despite all of the research that has gone into this book, though, it is my sad duty to report that it is not now, nor will it ever be, complete. As I mentioned at the beginning of this introduction, specific information about Elvis' childhood apparently does not exist in a form which would add hard facts to this type of research. Even Elvis' professional career is difficult to track. While *All Shook Up* offers the most complete listings of Elvis' shows and concerts ever published, there are gaps which may never be filled. The earliest shows were advertised only on radio; there were no newspaper ads for the many schoolhouse performances in 1954 and 1955. Even after Elvis came under the guidance of Colonel Parker, the tours were not announced nationally, so the first shows of 1956 have been impossible for me to follow. On the other hand, by the time Elvis went back on the road in the 1970s, there were numerous books which listed Elvis' many concerts. Every one of them has errors which had to be cross-checked and resolved. Even RCA Victor cannot get Elvis' story straight. Promotional information issued by Elvis' recording company contains several errors as to specific concert dates. RCA erred on the date that Elvis opened at the International Hotel in Las Vegas in 1969 in the booklet that accompanied the album *Elvis-A Legendary Performer, Volume 1* in 1973, and more recently got Elvis' birth date wrong on a promotional fiftieth anniversary flyer (pictured opposite). RCA Victor, after about 1960, stopped using specific "release" dates for their records, which has led to some confusion. Even the earlier release dates may not be absolutely accurate.

Frankly, I hope that I never have the impulse to work on this type of book again, other than to leisurely update this work over a period of years. The amount of general information on Elvis' career is staggering. The amount of specific, reliable information is much more limited. Add to this the fact that no author has yet published a complete, accurate story of Elvis' life — most have relied on interviewed sources (many having their own personal ax to grind), hearsay, or, worst of all, other published works — and you have all the makings of a nightmarish biographical jigsaw

xvii

puzzle. The research for this book was often akin to a detective's job, in that much of the real story was hidden between the lines of prose and had to be extracted with great care to insure accuracy. Frequently, one item would lead my research off in an unexpected direction. Just as frequently, days of investigations would lead to a dead end.

John McNab wrote, "After you've heard two eyewitness accounts of a motor accident, you begin to worry about history." Two humans just do not see the same event in the same way.

So, after all the research, who did I believe?

First, I usually preferred the first-hand accounts of reporters and fans which were written at the time of an event rather than most other, later accounts, no matter how profound the later work might appear to be on the surface. As I said above, most recent works have relied on interviews with people who were trying to recall events as long ago as twenty years in the past, and many of these memories have by now become tainted with personal ambition, egotism, or protracted ill will.

Second, if there were a variety of stories about one event, each with only minor conflicting details but with most of the facts the same, I combined them into what I felt was the most probable scenario. Again, each story was judged against a variety of factors, including the passage of time, in determining its credibility.

Third, where there were two stories with facts which were in total conflict, and where it was impossible to determine which story might be the more accurate, I usually discussed both versions in the book. This was most often done when I felt that the differing stories would affect the reader's view of Elvis' character; fortunately, the majority of discrepant accounts could be resolved with some investigation. In most cases, I found that the version which had received the widest distribution was the one which was most damaging to Elvis' personal life, while the conflicting story had received little or no attention.

Finally, several stories which were so exaggerated that I felt they could not have possibly occurred were omitted from the main text altogether. Those that dealt with Elvis' musical life before his first professional recording session in July 1954 are covered in Appendix 1. Also, many of the stories which concerned Elvis' reported addiction to prescribed drugs appear to be the result of poor research or outright slander. Typical of these was the story of Elvis' apparent drug overdose on the morning following his closing performance in Las Vegas in February 1975. Several books refer to this story, but each seems to have copied from another which in turn may have been basing its account on an ill-founded rumor. I have read first-hand accounts, published at the time,

Another arcade card portrait from the late fifties.

On stage in early 1956.

that place Elvis and Linda Thompson in attendance at cabaret shows in Las Vegas on the very night of the alleged overdose, and for several nights thereafter. I do not think that this is the behavior of someone near death.

Touching on the subject of Elvis' drug habits, I must add that when there was specific information, I used it. Reviews of Elvis' concerts which hinted at his possible misuse of drugs were included, right along with the more laudatory variety. Information from dated prescriptions which were admitted as evidence in the legal actions against Dr. George Nichopoulos, Elvis' personal physician, were also included. On the other hand, I did not want to join in the character assassination that has been typical of most "serious" biographies of Elvis published after his death by repeating the unsubstantiated or highly questionable tattletale memories of his "friends." The depth of Elvis' addiction to prescribed medication will, in all likelihood, never be fully known. Everyone close to Elvis had their own version of this side of his life. From my own standpoint, the subject has been covered to the point of overkill by other authors with credentials no better than mine.

I discovered an interesting facet of human nature while involved in the research for this book: authors tend to believe the "last fact found." No matter where a given fact originated or how tenaciously I would cling to the accuracy of that fact, I had to constantly fight the urge to pencil it out in favor of a new and contradictory "last fact," or "latest account." A wonderful example of this dilemma involves the date of Elvis' only appearance on the "Grand Ole' Opry." I held on to September 4, 1954, for years, until several new books in succession reported the date as September 25. I was just beginning to waver in my conclusions when further research in a primary source revealed the undeniable fact that Elvis was in Memphis on September 25, 1954. So much for the last fact found! The mystique of the "just revealed" must be weighed against the inherent shortcomings of accounts which are "far removed," and it is my hope that *All Shook Up* strikes a satisfactory balance.

Whatever the difficulties, the reader can rest assured that no page has been left unturned in my quest for every useful piece of information on Elvis' life. There is, however, still much work to be done to make future editions of *All Shook Up* even more complete and accurate. If Elvis ever appeared in your town, I'd greatly appreciate a visit to your library for a review of back issues of the local newspapers available on microfilm. If you find any pertinent data, please send it to me c/o Golden Oldies, 809 K Street Mall, Sacramento, California 95814.

Now, that's enough about me and my methods of researching

the material for this book. I trust the reader will appreciate the amount of time and hard work involved, and feel that it was all worthwhile. Writing a book is not unlike the birth of a child. They take too long from germination to public debut, contain more than a little of the author's own personality, and are seldom perfect. The reader is cautioned to keep in mind that *All Shook Up* is not 100 percent perfect, either.

Lee Cotten
Sacramento, CA
November 1984

Acknowledgements

This book could not have been written without the generous help of some dedicated fans of Elvis Presley:

In Sacramento, Barry Dallas and Darrell Theobald. In Hollywood, Joan Deary of RCA Victor Records. In Tupelo, Janelle McComb. And worldwide, the many people who submitted thousands of newspaper articles and reminiscences to the many hundreds of fanzines which found their way into my hands over the years.

My editor and publisher at Pierian Press, Tom Schultheiss, also is in line for special praise for his patience and the talent that he brought to this project. Without him, *All Shook Up* would have been an infinitely more difficult book to bring to completion.

Also, special thanks to Howard DeWitt, my co-author on *Jailhouse Rock,* a close personal friend, and a dedicated historian of the rock 'n' roll scene.

And, finally, special thanks to my wife, Patty, and my children, Nicole and Sean, who have put up with less from me than a husband and father ought to give his family. Over the years it has taken this book to reach completion, they stood right by my side. Without their support, this book would have fallen by the wayside long ago.

Thank you all.

Gimmie the beat, boys,
And free my soul.
I wanna get lost in
    your rock and roll,
And drift away.

DAVID PRESSLEY
(Arrived New Bern, NC, circa 1745
from Scotland or Ireland)

ANDREW PRESSLEY
(Arrived with father, circa 1745;
blacksmith; lived in Anson County, NC)

ANDREW PRESSLEY, JR. ———————— **ELIZABETH** ?
(1754-1855)   (4 children)
(Blacksmith; lived in
Lancaster County, SC)

1st wife ——————— **DUNNAN PRESSLEY** ———— 2nd wife
(2 sons)   (b. 1780,   (3 sons)
                                     Lancaster County, SC;
                                     d. 1850, Georgia)

DUNNAN PRESSLEY, JR. ————— **MARTHA JANE WESSON**
(b. 1827, Madison, TN;   (2nd wife; 2 daughters;
d. 1900, Barry County, MO)   m. 1861, Itawamba County, MS)
(deserted wife about 1864)

ROSELLA ("ROSIE") PRESSLEY
(b. 1862, Fulton, MS;
d. 1924, Fulton, MS)
(sharecropper, never
married, had 9-10 children)

MINNIE MAE HOOD ——————— **JESSIE D. (J.D.) PRESSLEY**
(b. 1893, Fulton, MS;   (b. 1896, Fulton, MS;
d. 1980, Memphis, TN)   d. 1973, Louisville, KY)
(m. 1913, divorce 1947)

VERNON ELVIS PRESSLEY ———
(b. 1916, Fulton, MS;
d. 1979, Memphis, TN)
(Brothers and Sisters:
Vester, Delta Mae,
Gladys Erlene, Nashville
Lorene)

ELVIS

THE PRESSLEY/PRESLEY FAMILY TREE

JOHN SMITH
(From Atlanta, GA)

ANN MANSEL ——— **OBE SMITH**
(Alabama widow)   (Lived in Saltillo, MS)

OCTAVIA LAVINIA ——— **ROBERT LEE SMITH**
("DOLL") MANSELL   (d. 1932, Springhill, MS)
(d. 1935, Spring Hill, MS)

— **GLADYS LOVE SMITH**
(b. 1912, Lee County, MS;
d. 1958, Memphis, TN)
(Brothers and Sisters:
Tracy, Travis, Johnny, Lavelle,
Cletis (wife of Vester Presley))
(Cousins: Carroll ("Junior") and Gene
by Lavelle, Bobby and Billy by Travis)

Prologue

BEFORE THE STORY BEGINS . . .

Gladys Love Smith was born on April 25, 1912, in Lee County, Mississippi, outside of Tupelo. She was the fifth girl of nine children. She left school after the eighth grade. In 1932 , her father moved to East Tupelo so that the family could look for employment. Gladys found a job with the Tupelo Garment Company as a sewing machine operator. She worked twelve hours a day, five or six days a week. She was paid by the piece and could earn up to thirteen dollars a week.

Vernon Elvis Presley was born on April 19, 1916, in Fulton, Mississippi. About 1932, his father moved the family to East Tupelo. He and Gladys met and fell in love. They eloped by hitchhiking the twenty miles to Ponotoc, Mississippi, where they purchased a marriage license on June 17, 1933. On the license, Vernon added four years to his age, making it twenty-one. Gladys deducted two years from her age, making it nineteen. (In 1958, and again in 1977, this added to the confusion about her true age when she died. Most reports read that she was forty-two when she was actually forty-six.) Vernon and Gladys were married later that day in Verona, Mississippi. The couple's first home was with his parents on Old Saltillo Road in East Tupelo. Vernon worked as a carpentry foreman for the WPA (Works Progress Administration) building outhouses. By 1934, he was employed by Orville S. Bean as a milkman on Bean's dairy farm near Tupelo. In 1934, the couple moved in with Gladys' grandmother, "Doll" Smith, on Berry Street in East Tupelo. When Gladys quit her job with the Tupelo Garment Company in late summer because she was pregnant, the couple changed homes again, this time moving in with Dan and Nora Greenwood, who apparently were distant cousins. Vernon borrowed $180 from Orville Bean to build a home for Gladys and his coming children. He, his father and his brother Vester, who was employed at Long's Laundry and Dry Cleaners in Tupelo, built a two-room house on Old Saltillo Road next door to J.D. Presley's home, on land owned by J.D. In December 1934, Vernon and Gladys moved into their new home.

AND THE REST IS HISTORY . . .

1

The house where Elvis was born and where he lived until 1938, built by Elvis' father, Vernon.

Elvis' birth certificate; both Vernon and Gladys again used their "adopted" ages (as they had when they were married).

Stranger In My
Own Home Town

ALL
SHOOK
UP
ELVIS
Day-By-Day,
1935-53

1935
JANUARY

JAN 8   (Tues.) Shortly after 4:30 a.m., in the house at 306 Old Saltillo Road, Elvis Aron Presley was born. He was the second twin born to Gladys. The first-born, Jesse Garon, was stillborn. Dr. William Robert Hunt was the attending physician. His fee of fifteen dollars was paid by the local welfare agency.

JAN 9   (Wed.) After laying in state in the Presley house, Jesse Garon Presley was buried in an unmarked grave in Priceville Cemetery, located three miles northeast of Tupelo on Feemster Lake Road.

During the years in East Tupelo, the Presleys attended the Assembly of God church at 206 Adams Street. Services and church school took up most of the mid-day on Sundays, and there was always a service on Wednesday nights. The services featured much singing, which in the Tupelo area Assembly of God churches was accompanied by a guitarist, not a pianist or organist.

Another diversion for the Presleys and other families in East Tupelo were the almost weekly "excursions" planned by J.D. Presley's brother, Noah (who was probably Elvis' most notable relative, owning a grocery store in East Tupelo, later becoming a law officer and mayor of East Tupelo). These excursions took place almost every Saturday or Sunday afternoon. Families would pay a dollar, and Noah would ferry them to various places, such as Memphis or the Shiloh Battlefield, in his converted yellow school bus.

1936
APRIL

APR 6   (Mon.) A tornado destroyed fifteen residential blocks of Tupelo, but it missed the Presley's home by about a mile. It was reported that 212 people were killed and over 500 were injured.

1937
NOVEMBER

NOV 17   (Wed.) The *Tupelo Journal* reported that "three men, Travis Smith, Luther Gable, and Vernon Pressley [were] indicted for forgery and placed under bonds of $500 each." (Travis was Gladys' brother, Luther's real name was Lether, and Pressley should read Presley.) Allegedly, the forgery involved changing the amount on a check issued by Orville S. Bean to his employee, Vernon Presley. One account has the amount being a change from three dollars to eight dollars for the sale of a cow. By all accounts, the amount was very small.

1938
MAY

MAY 25   (Wed.) In the Lee County Circuit Court of Judge Thomas H. Johnston, Vernon and the two other accomplices pleaded guilty. Each man was sentenced to a term of three years in the state penitentiary at Parchman, Mississippi. They were remanded to the custody of the Lee County sheriff for safekeeping in the county jail in Tupelo, until transportation could be arranged to the penitentiary.

Although much has been made of the harshness of the sentence versus the minor amount of the forgery, it must be kept in perspective, based on the times. In East Tupelo, there was never any stigma attached to the prison term. Much has also been written about the terrible conditions at Parchman Farm. The prison had a work relief program, which allowed inmates to spend time at home, and families often visited the prison on weekends.

Gladys, Elvis and Vernon.

Standing beside Vernon's father's house on Old
Saltillo Road.

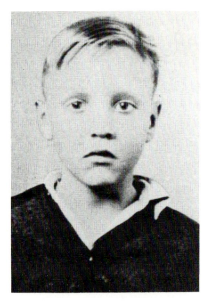

Elvis' first school photo.

Possibly taken at the Tupelo fair on the day that Elvis sang *Old Shep*.

In fact, visiting Parchman Farm was one of the most
eagerly awaited events of the week.

Shortly after Vernon pleaded guilty, Orville S. Bean
called in his note on the $180 that Vernon had bor-
rowed in 1934 to build the house that the Presley's
called home, and the house where Elvis had been born.
Gladys and Elvis moved next door to stay with Vernon's
parents, J.D. and Minnie Presley. Gladys was forced to
find employment as a seamstress, again, this time at
Reed's Garment Company.

1941
JANUARY

JAN 4   (Sat.) Vernon was released from Parchman State Penitentiary. The last five months of his three-year sentence
had been commuted by the Governor of Mississippi.
Vernon found work as a handyman for the Leake and
Goodlet Lumberyard in Tupelo.

MARCH
Elvis had a severe case of tonsillitis with a high fever, but he suffered no long-term ill effects.

SEPTEMBER
In the fall, Elvis entered the East Tupelo Consolidated School System, attending Lawhorn School on Lake Street. At this time,
the Presleys were still living on Old Saltillo Road, probably with
Vernon's parents.

1942
The Presleys moved to a larger house "in the valley," on Kelly
Street, when Elvis was seven. They were living in this house
when Elvis entered second grade at Lawhorn School.

During the year, Elvis had his first sweetheart, Caroline Ballard,
daughter of Rev. James Ballard, pastor of the First Assembly of
God Church in East Tupelo.

Vernon worked for a few months at a war materials plant in Memphis, 105 miles northwest of Tupelo. He lived in a rooming
house and commuted to Tupelo on the weekend. Grandmother
Minnie moved in with Gladys to help her in the raising of Elvis.

1943

When Vernon returned to Tupelo after working in the Memphis war materials plant, he was unable to find work for a time, so the Presleys moved in with Gladys' parents on Berry Street. This was the address used when Elvis entered the third grade at Lawhorn School.

1944

During the year, the Presleys moved into a small house on Adams Street, near the Assembly of God Church in East Tupelo. They rented the house from a local doctor. It was from this house that Elvis walked to and from Lawhorn School during the fourth grade.

1945

MAY

MAY 24   (Thurs.) Priscilla Ann Wagner was born in Brooklyn, New York. Her father, James Wagner, was a Navy pilot. He was killed about October 1945 in an air crash. In 1949, Priscilla's mother, Ann, married Joseph Beaulieu, a lieutenant in the Air Force, who adopted Priscilla.

SEPTEMBER

The Presley's were living with a relative on Old Saltillo Road when Elvis enrolled in the fifth grade. His teacher was Mrs. J.C. (Oleta) Grimes. According to Mrs. W.K. (Jewel) Webb of Tupelo, Elvis and two school friends sang in a Tupelo cafeteria, and Elvis sang *God Bless America* in a chapel program in school. It was Mrs. Grimes who suggested to the school principal, J.D. Cole, that Elvis be entered in the upcoming talent contest at the local fair.

OCTOBER

OCT 3   (Wed.) Elvis made his first public appearance as a singer during "Children's Day" at the Mississippi-Alabama Fair and Dairy Show, held in Lee County (Tupelo). Vernon had to work, so Gladys accompanied Elvis. For his part in the talent contest, Elvis stood on a chair and sang *Old Shep*, unaccompanied, into a microphone. The

"Radio Talent Show" was broadcast over WELO radio, which had studios in the Lee County Courthouse. The contest was part of the station's "Black And White Jamboree." Elvis won second prize of five dollars, which included free admission to all the carnival rides for the rest of the day. (Some accounts place this appearance in 1943 or 1944, and according to Vernon Presley in a CBS-TV interview broadcast on October 3, 1977, Elvis won third place. However, authentication of the date and the second place finish comes from the winner of the competition, Becky Harris of Bissell, Mississippi.)

1946
SPRING

Lack of work forced the family to take an apartment on Commerce Street, on the east side of Tupelo, in an area of low income families.

When Vernon found work driving a truck for wholesale grocer L.P. McCarty for twenty-two-dollars-and-fifty-cents a week, the family moved into a house on Mobile Alley near the fairgrounds, then to a house on North Green Street in the northeast corner of Tupelo.

SUMMER

Another tornado lashed Tupelo, and Elvis and Gladys hid in a storm shelter to escape injury. While in the shelter, they discussed Elvis' desire to have a bicycle. Gladys talked him into accepting a twelve-dollar-and-ninety-five-cent guitar instead of a fifty-five dollar bicycle.

The guitar was subsequently bought at the Tupelo Hardware Company from employee F.L. Bobo. The store was owned by George Booth, whose son Billy still owns the store.

SEPTEMBER

Elvis enrolled in Milam Junior High School, located at the corner of Gloster and Jefferson Streets. His sixth grade teacher was Mrs. Quay Web Camp.

1947
DECEMBER

DEC 25   (Thurs.) Elvis received a bicycle for Christmas.

1948

East Tupelo merged with Tupelo proper.

SEPTEMBER

SEP 12   (Sun.) Vernon loaded the family's possessions into his
                 1939 Plymouth coupe, and they left their final Tupelo
                 home on North Green Street to move to Memphis.
                 Apparently Vernon had lost his job with McCarty, and
                 the family was almost destitute. The move to Memphis,
                 it was hoped, would open the doors to a better life.
                 Two of Gladys' brothers, Johnny and Travis, were al-
                 ready in Memphis, employed at Precision Tool.
          The Presleys moved into a first-floor, one-room apartment
                 at 572 Poplar Avenue, which cost thirty-five dollars a
                 month. The apartment was owned by Clifton and
                 Mallie Johnson.
SEP 13   (Mon.) Elvis enrolled in L.C. Humes High School, located
                 at 659 North Manassas Street.

LATE 1948

Vernon worked at Precision Tool for a short time, and then he
drove a truck for a wholesale grocer. Gladys worked as a sewing
machine operator for Fashion Curtains in Memphis. Vernon was
reported to be making eighty-three cents an hour (thirty-three
dollars and fifty cents per week).

NOVEMBER

Elvis first met George Klein, a classmate at Humes High, who
would become one of Elvis' closest friends.

1949

FEBRUARY

Vernon started working at the United Paint Company at 446 Con-
cord Avenue. He was paid a dollar an hour to pack cans of
paint into crates for delivery.

FEB 17   (Thurs.) Vernon applied for assistance from the Memphis
                 Public Housing Authority. The case worker assigned to
                 the Presleys was Mrs. James Richardson.

MAY

MAY 1   (Sun.) The Presleys moved into a two-room (living room/
              bedroom and kitchen) apartment on the ground floor
              at 185 Winchester Street, Apartment 328. The housing
              was known collectively as Lauderdale Courts, and it was
              one of several public-assistance housing projects in Mem-
              phis. The Presley telephone number was 37-4185, and
              the apartment cost thirty-five dollars a month. After
              moving to Lauderdale Courts, Elvis' grandmother,
              Minnie Mae Presley, moved in with the family. One of
              their neighbors was Mrs. Ruby Black, the mother of Bill
              Black, who would later play bass for Elvis.
          The Presleys attended church at the First Assembly of God,
              960 South Third Street. Their pastor was Rev. James
              Hamill. Elvis joined the Sunday School, where other
              members of his class included three members of the
              Blackwood Brothers Quartet, and the members of the
              Stamps Quartet (both nationally famous gospel groups).

1950

SEPTEMBER

One of Elvis' school jobs during his tenth grade year was as Library
Assistant at Humes High; his picture appeared in the yearbook
along with a group of other assistants.

NOVEMBER

To help make ends meet, Elvis got a job as an usher at Lowe's
State Theater at 152 S. Main. He was paid $12.75 a week, and
he worked from 5:00 to 10:00 p.m. week nights. He was
forced to quit by his mother when he fell asleep in class.

DECEMBER

During the annual Christmas talent show at Humes High, Elvis
sang *Cold Icy Fingers*; due to the enthusiastic response, Elvis
was allowed the only encore in the show. He sang *Til I Waltz
Again With You*.

Elvis had two more girl friends during the year. Betty McCarran
lived on the third floor of Lauderdale Courts. The second girlfriend was Billie Wardlow. Neither romance lasted very long.

1951

JANUARY

Following his sixteenth birthday, Elvis took his driver's test and received his driver's license.

In January, Elvis joined the Army R.O.T.C. program at Humes High.

SUMMER

Elvis returned to work at Lowe's State Theater. After a few months, he was fired by theater manager Arthur Groom following a fight with another usher over the affections of a candy-counter girl.

AUGUST

Elvis tried out for the football team at Humes High. According to the coach, Rube Boyce, Elvis kept bringing his guitar to the locker room. When he was told to either play football or sing, Elvis quit the team. (According to legend, Elvis quit rather than submit to a haircut, which would have shortened his hair to a more conventional length.)

1952

SPRING

Elvis passed the eleventh grade with marginal grades. His best grade was a "B" in Advanced Woodwork. In math, he received a "C" even though he had an "F" in both conduct and academic for the third quarter, and an "F" on the final exam. He received a "C" in American History. In English, Elvis had three straight "As" for conduct, but an "F" in the academic portion for the first quarter, and an "F" on the final exam, which brought his grade down to a "C." In Speech, Elvis got a "C" after failing the final exam. He had been absent eleven days, and tardy once. There were no grades for R.O.T.C. or study hall. His homeroom teacher was Virginia Alexander.

SUMMER

Elvis reportedly started attending all night gospel sings at the Memphis Auditorium. J.D. Sumner, who later backed Elvis while on tour, was with the Sunshine Boys at this time, and he remembered Elvis hanging around backstage. One of Elvis' close friends from Sunday School at the First Assembly of God was Cecil Blackwood, younger brother of R.W. Blackwood, of the famed Blackwood Brothers Quartet.

AUGUST
The Public Housing Authority reported that Vernon's weekly salary was $53.22 ($2,767.44 per year).

FALL
Elvis participated in an auto "Road-E-O," sponsored by the local Jaycees. His photo appeared in the local paper, showing him watching as a tire was being changed. He was named "Mr. Safety."

Gladys started working at Britlings, a downtown Memphis cafeteria.

SEPTEMBER
Elvis started the twelfth grade. He met Marty Lacker, who would become a close friend. Lacker had just moved to Memphis from New York.

Elvis began work at MARL Metal Company at 208 Georgia Avenue. He worked as a sweeper on the evening shift, from 3:00 to 11:00 p.m., in the fabricating division of the plant which manufactured kitchen furniture. He was paid a dollar an hour.

NOVEMBER
Gladys forced Elvis to stop working at MARL Metal because his grades began to suffer from the late evening hours.

Gladys got a job as a nurses' aide at St. Joseph's Hospital.

NOV 28   (Fri.) The Presleys were notified that they had to move out of Lauderdale Courts within ninety days because their combined income was above the limit allowed for public assistance housing.

1953
JANUARY

JAN 7   (Wed.) The Presley family moved to 398 Cypress Street. Their new home was a seven-room house, which was occupied by four families. It cost fifty-two dollars a month for their two rooms.

Elvis' twelfth grade school portrait.

MARCH

Vernon bought a 1942 Lincoln Zephyr for Elvis. It cost fifty dollars, and was light green in color.

APRIL

The Presleys moved into the lower half of a two-story brick apartment building at 462 Alabama Street, owned by Mr. Dubrovner. The rent was fifty dollars a month.

JUNE

JUN 3   (Wed.) In the morning, Elvis applied for job placement at the Tennessee Employment Security Office at 122 Union Avenue. He was given the "General Aptitude Test Battery" by Mrs. Weir Harris, and sent to M.B. Parker Machinists on the north edge of Memphis for an interview.

That evening, graduation ceremonies for the Humes High School Class of 1953 were held at Ellis Auditorium. Speakers included Principal T.C. Brindley, Memphis School Superintendent Ernest C. Ball, and Class President George Klein. Elvis' major was listed as shop, history, and English. He had been active in R.O.T.C., the Biology Club, the English Club, the History Club, and the Speech Club. The Class Prophecy, published in Humes High's yearbook, *The Herald*, said of Elvis, "We are reminded not to forget to invite you all to the Silver Horse on Onion Avenue to hear the singing hillbillies of the road, Elvis Presley, Albert Teague, Doris Wilburn, and Mary Ann Propst." The Class Will read, "Donald Williams, Raymond McCraig, and Elvis Presley leave hoping there will be someone to take their places as 'teacher's pets'????"

JUN 4   (Thurs.) Elvis started work at Parker Machinists Shop.

JULY

JUL 14   (Tues.) Elvis received a thirty-three dollar salary advance to make a car payment. (Since his car had been paid for in full, this was a strange request.)

JUL 18   (Sat.) On this Saturday morning, Elvis may have dropped by the Memphis Recording Service, a division of Sun

Records, 706 Union Avenue, telephone number 37-7197. (The company mottos: "We record anything — anywhere — anytime. A complete service to fill every recording need. Combining the newest and best equipment with the latest and finest sonocoustic studios."

Elvis paid his $3.98 (plus tax) to Marion Keisker, secretary to owner Sam Phillips. Elvis, accompanied only by his own guitar, recorded *My Happiness* and *That's When Your Heartaches Begin* directly on a ten-inch acetate disc. Ms. Keisker, as an afterthought, taped half of the first song and all of the second. By Elvis' own admission, the record was to be a surprise for his mother.

SEPTEMBER

Elvis stopped working at Parker Machinists and started working at Precision Tool, at the corner of McLemore and Kansas Streets. He was paid a dollar-sixty-five cents an hour, and he worked the 7:00 a.m. to 3:30 p.m. shift. Precision Tool made .90 and .101 millimeter artillery shells for the U.S. Army, and Elvis was involved in the assembly line production of shell casings. Elvis and his cousin Gene Smith obtained their jobs through Elvis' uncles, Travis and Johnny Smith, who had been employed at Precision for several years.

FALL

Elvis auditioned at a local recording studio for a gospel quartet sponsored by the Assembly of God Church and led by Jim Hamill, the son of Elvis' pastor in his neighborhood church. He was not asked to join the quartet.

NOVEMBER

Elvis started work at Crown Electric Company, 353 Poplar Avenue, owned by James R. Tipler. Elvis started at a dollar an hour, thirty-five dollars a week. His first job was as stock clerk, but he later drove the Dodge delivery truck and studied at night to be an electrician.

I Got Lucky

JANUARY

JAN 4   (Mon.) Elvis visited the Memphis Recording Service again. This time, Sam Phillips had a chance to meet and talk to him. Elvis recorded *Casual Love Affair* and *I'll Never Stand In Your Way* on a ten-inch acetate disc for his own enjoyment. He paid his $3.98 (plus tax) and left. Phillips made a note to contact Elvis if the need arose for a singer.

FEBRUARY

Elvis met Dixie Locke, age sixteen, at the Rainbow Rollerdome. During the next few years, she would be one of Elvis' steadiest dates. They both attended the First Assembly of God Church at 1085 McLemore Avenue.

MAY

MAY 25   (Tues.) Doug Poindexter and his Starlight Wranglers had a recording session at Sun Records. The songs *My Kind Of Carrying On* and *Now She Cares No More For Me* were released as Sun 202. The Starlight Wranglers featured Winfield Scott (Scotty) Moore, III (born December 27, 1931 in Gadsden, Tennessee) on guitar, and William (Bill) Black, age 27, on bass. Scotty was working days blocking hats at his brother's dry cleaners, and Bill worked at the local Firestone store. Scotty Moore had started his musical career in Washington, DC, on WBRO radio. He moved to Memphis in 1951 and had previously been featured on Eddie Hill's recording of *Hot Guitar* on Mercury Records.

JUNE

During the month, Sam Phillips, owner of Sun Records, received a demonstration record of a song titled *Without You*, sent by Peer Music, a Nashville music publisher. Phillips tried in vain to locate the singer on the demo. Marion Keisker, Phillips' secretary, suggested that he call Elvis in to see if he could sing the song.

JUN 26   (Sat.) Phillips called the Presley home, and Elvis rushed to Sun Studios. He was unable to sing *Without You* to Phillips' satisfaction.

When asked what he could sing, Elvis ran through a series of currently popular songs, including *Rag Mop* (a 1950 hit for the Ames Brothers). Phillips was sufficiently impressed to call Scotty Moore, who had been working with Phillips to develop local talent. (Moore had been a frequent visitor at Sun Studios, and he hung around Miss Taylor's cafe, next door to the Sun Studios.)

JUN 30   (Wed.) R.W. Blackwood (baritone) and Bill Lyles (bass) of the Blackwood Brother's Quartet were killed in a light plane crash outside Clanton, Alabama, following a gospel show. R.W.'s younger brother, Cecil, was Elvis' classmate at the Assembly of God Sunday school.

JULY

JUL 2   (Fri.) A funeral was held at the Ellis Auditorium for the two members of the Blackwood Brothers. Elvis reportedly was so upset that he and Dixie Locke grieved all night on a park bench. (Less than two weeks later, Cecil Blackwood was chosen to join the quartet, and he asked Elvis to fill his vacancy in the Songfellows, a subsidiary of the Blackwood Brothers. By then, Elvis had a contract "to sing the blues.")

JUL 4   (Sun.) Elvis first met Scotty Moore at Scotty's apartment on Belz Street. Elvis was dressed in a pink shirt, pink pants with a white stripe down the legs, and white shoes. Scotty recalled that he had "lots of hair." Bill Black was called, and together the trio rehearsed several songs, including *I Don't Hurt Anymore* (a song by Hank Snow), *I Apologize* (a 1951 hit for Billy Eckstine), and *I Really Don't Want To Know* (a country success for Eddy Arnold). Scotty telephoned Sam Phillips and said that with the right song, he thought Elvis would do all right in the studio.

(NOTE: For an in-depth look at Elvis' place in the Memhis music scene prior to cutting his first record, please see Appendix 1.)

JUL 5   (Mon.) Memphis was in the grips of a record-breaking summer heat wave with highs above a hundred degrees and humidity near ninety percent. About 8:00 p.m., Elvis, Scotty, and Bill started their first recording session at Sun Record's studio at 706 Union Avenue. Their first attempt to record a song was apparently the standard *Harbor Lights*. Several times the trio ran through the song, actually completing it two times out of five attempts. This was followed by an attempt to record Leon Payne's 1949 country hit, *I Love You Because*. After several takes, they had completed two versions of the song, one with a spoken bridge in the middle and one without. During a break in the session, Elvis was clowning around to relieve the tension, and he broke into a sped-up version of *That's All Right*, originally written and recorded by Arthur "Big Boy" Crudup for RCA Victor Records in 1946. Sam Phillips, who was engineering the session, liked what he heard, and he asked the group to run through it again so he could set the levels on the microphones. Elvis, Scotty, and Bill appear to have recorded the song at least nine times before completing a successful "take." Elvis, excited over finally completing a song which all present agreed had the potential of being a hit, then attempted to record two more songs, the names of which have been lost with time. These songs might have included *Tennessee Saturday Night*, which is unreleased to date. The session lasted until midnight. (See Appendix 2.)

JUL 6   (Tues.) At 8:00 p.m., the trio was back in Sun Record's studio attempting to come up with another song which could be paired with *That's All Right* for release as a single. Again, after attempting several songs, the band took a break. Some clowning, this time by Bill Black, resulted in a fast version of Bill Monroe's 1946 country hit, *Blue Moon Of Kentucky*. As an idication of how hard the trio was trying to come up with a "different" sound, at one point during an attempt to sing *Blue Moon Of Kentucky* with a rockabilly beat, Sam Phillips emerged from the control room and exclaimed, "That's a pop song now, nearly 'bout!" One of the songs that may have been attempted during the early hours of this session was *Blue Moon*, a 1949 hit for Mel Torme. The session broke up around midnight. (See Appendix 2.)

JUL 10   (Sat.) During the week, Sam Phillips had demonstration discs of *That's All Right* and *Blue Moon Of Kentucky* pressed (possibly on the Presto lathe at Sun Records which was used for making the custom records of the Memphis Recording Service). These demos were delivered to two local Memphis disc jockeys. On WMPS, Uncle Richard was the first to play Elvis' record, spotlighting *Blue Moon Of Kentucky*. At WHBQ, Dewey Phillips (no relation to Sam Phillips) played *That's All Right* and *Blue Moon Of Kentucky* on his 8:00 to 11:00 p.m. "Red, Hot and Blues" show about 9:30 p.m. Listener reaction was so strongly in favor of *That's All Right* that Phillips was prompted to call the Presley home only to discover that Elvis had gone to the Suzore's No. 2 Theater at 279 North Main to see Red Skelton and Cara Williams in "The Great Diamond Robbery" and Gene Autry and Slim Pickins in "Goldtown Ghost Riders." Friends and relatives located him, and he was rushed to the studios of WHBQ, located on the mezzanine of the Old Chiska Hotel on Main Street. Phillips interviewed Elvis on the air. By the end of the show at 11:00 p.m., the station had received fourteen telegrams and forty-seven telephone calls. Dewey Phillips had played the record a total of seven times. Later that night, Phillips took a copy of the demonstration disc to radio station WHHM, where Sleepy-Eyed John (Lepley) played *Blue Moon Of Kentucky* on his country-oriented show.

JUL 12   (Mon.) Elvis signed a managerial contract with Scotty Moore. Scotty was to receive ten percent of all royalties in addition to being paid as a regular member of Elvis' band. In the beginning, Elvis received fifty percent of any booking, with Scotty Moore and Bill Black getting twenty-five percent each.

mid-JUL During the week, Sam Phillips arranged for *That's All Right/ Blue Moon Of Kentucky* to be pressed as a 78 and 45 r.p.m. single by Plastic Products Co., 1746 Chelsea Avenue in Memphis.

In a 1956 photo, Elvis picks a song for disk jockey
Dewey Phillips.

Elvis' first press photo: a bad haircut, a bowtie and
an oversized coat.

Advertisements for Elvis' very first two performances, the second of
which (bottom) misspelled his name.

JUL 19   (Mon.) Elvis' first single record, *That's All Right/Blue Moon Of Kentucky*, was released. Fifteen-year-old Eldene Beard purchased a copy at Charles Records on Main Street in Memphis. This was probably the first Elvis record ever sold.

JUL 23   (Fri.) The first large order for *That's All Right* came from Big State Record Distributors in Dallas, Texas. The order was probably for 200 to 500 copies.

JUL 28   (Wed.) The *Memphis Press-Scimitar* published an interview with Elvis by Edwin Howard in his "The Front Row" column. The article reported that Elvis' first single was "getting an amazing number of plays on all Memphis radio stations." Accompanying the story was a photo of Elvis sporting a longish flat-top haircut with sideburns and a ducktail. He was wearing a plaid, western-style suit and a bow tie. The *Press-Scimitar* also published the first ad for an appearance by Elvis. He was listed as one of the performers on the July 30th Slim Whitman show in Memphis.

late JUL   In late July, Elvis made several guest appearances as an "added attraction" with Doug Poindexter and his Starlight Wranglers at the Bon Air Club, 4862 Summer Avenue in Memphis. Scotty and Bill were still members of the Poindexter band.

JUL 30   (Fri.) A second ad for that night's Slim Whitman show in the *Memphis Press-Scimitar* misspelled Elvis' name. He was listed as "Ellis Presley." That night, Elvis made his first billed appearance, being listed third to Whitman and Billy Walker for the 8:00 p.m. show at Memphis' outdoor Overton Park Shell. Also on the bill were Curly Harris and Sonny Harville. Tickets for the show were $1.00 advance and $1.25 at the door. Although not known for certain, Elvis probably sang both sides of his recently released single.

AUGUST

AUG 7   (Sat.) *The Billboard*, the national music trade weekly magazine, in its "Review Spotlight" section, critiqued Elvis' first single, calling Elvis a "potent new chanter [who] comes thru with a solid performance." (Hereafter, *The Billboard* will be referred to simply as *Billboard*.)

Elvis was the headline attraction at Sleepy-Eyed John's

An early Sun Records promotional photo.

Elvis headlines only a month after
his first recording session.

Eagle's Nest Club in Memphis, located at Clearpool on
Lamar Avenue. The house band for the evening was
Tiny Dixon's Band. Admission was a dollar twenty
cents. The doors opened at 8:30 p.m., with dancing
from 9:00 p.m. to 1:00 a.m. The club's motto was
"don't wear a tie unless your wife makes you."

AUG 21   (Sat.) Elvis, Scotty, and Bill performed in Gladewater,
Texas.

AUG 22   (Sun.) Elvis and his band appeared at Magnolia Gardens
in Houston, Texas.

AUG 27   (Fri.) Elvis appeared at the Eagle's Nest Club in Memphis
for their Friday ladies' night. Admission was fifty cents
for ladies and a dollar twenty cents for men.

AUG 28   (Sat.) *Billboard* reported in its chart of "C&W Territorial
Best Sellers" that *Blue Moon Of Kentucky* was number
3 in Memphis for the week ending August 18th. By this
time, Sun Records was back-ordered 6,000 copies.

AUG 31   (Tues.) Elvis probably attended the S.E.J. Fan Club Dance
at the Eagle's Nest Club sponsored by Bob Neal.

In August Elvis appeared at the Bel Air Club, 1850 South Bellvue
Boulevard with the Poindexter band. Although Scotty and
Bill were still members of the band, there was growing dissen-
sion among other members because Scotty and Bill appeared
with Elvis in the "guest" spot and at night clubs which featured
Elvis without the Poindexter band.

Elvis also appeared with the Jack Clement Band at the Bel Air
Club and may have appeared during Clement's performance at
the Eagle's Nest on August 16th. Clement was an engineer at
Sun Records. In most instances, Elvis was paid ten dollars for
his appearances.

Elvis also made an appearance at the Kennedy Hospital's entertainment benefit show, sponsored by the B'nai B'rith Society.

SEPTEMBER

SEP 4   (Sat.) Elvis, Sam Phillips and Marion Keisker, in one car,
followed by Scotty Moore, Bill Black and the instruments in another car, drove to Nashville for Elvis' only
appearance on the "Grand Ole Opry" radio show,
broadcast over WSM from 8:00 to 11:00 p.m. The
"Opry" originated from Ryman Auditorium. Elvis appeared on the Hank Snow segment, sponsored by Kel-

logg's cereals. Also in this segment were Eddie Hill and the Davis Sisters. Elvis wanted to sing a new song, *Good Rockin' Tonight*, but he was persuaded by Jim Denny, head of "Opry" talent, to sing both sides of his first release. Following Elvis' guest appearance, Denny told Elvis that he ought to consider going back to driving a truck. Elvis was so upset that he left his show clothes in a service station restroom on the way back to Memphis.

SEP 8   (Wed.) Elvis' photo was part of a twenty-page supplement to the *Memphis Press-Scimitar* announcing the next day's opening of the Lamar-Airways Shopping Center, Memphis' first. The photo's caption read, "Memphis Newest Hit In The Recording Business."

SEP 9   (Thurs.) Elvis was paid ten dollars to perform at the grand opening of the Lamar-Airways Shopping Center at 2256 Lamar Avenue. About 300 people attended the 9:00 p.m. performance. Elvis performed with Sleepy-Eyed John and the Eagle's Nest band from a flat-bed truck parked in front of the new Katz Drug Store, the shopping center's central store.

SEP 10   (Fri.) Elvis started his second series of recording dates at Sun Records. He evidently began the session by trying another rhythm and blues song, *Tomorrow Night*, which had been a hit by Lonnie Johnson in 1948. (The version that Elvis recorded for Sun was never issued. On March 13, 1965, the original Sun master tape was overdubbed, and the "pure" Sun version was lost forever.) Elvis then tried to record *I'll Never Let You Go*, a country hit for Jimmy Wakely in the early 1940s. Then he switched to *Just Because*, a polka hit for Frankie Yankovic in the late 1940s. He apparently worked on these last two songs for several hours. Next, Elvis attempted *Satisfied*, a gospel number previously sung by Martha Carson. The results were apparently so bad that the song was abandoned after only one attempt. So far, none of the songs had met the expectations of either Elvis or Sam Phillips. The trio then attempted *Good Rockin' Tonight*, a rhythm and blues hit in 1948 for both Roy Brown and Wynonie Harris. There must have been more problems, because Elvis went back to *Just Because*. After completing a successful take, he returned to *Good Rockin' Tonight*. Finally, everything

fell into place, and Elvis waxed one of his finest rocka-
billy performances. *I Don't Care If The Sun Don't
Shine*, which was to be the flip side of *Good Rockin'
Tonight* was also recorded during the evening. (See
Appendix 2.)

SEP 18 (Sat.) Elvis appeared at the Eagle's Nest Club in Memphis.
He headlined the 9:00 p.m. show, which featured Sleepy-
Eyed John and Tiny Dixon's Band. Admission was one
dollar.

SEP 24 (Fri.) Elvis performed at the Eagle's Nest Club with Tiny
Dixon's Band. It was a special ladies' night at the club
with admission fifty cents for ladies and a dollar for
men.

SEP 25 (Sat.) Elvis' second single *Good Rockin' Tonight/I Don't
Care If The Sun Don't Shine* was released.
Elvis appeared again at the Eagle's Nest Club from "9 til?"
He performed with the Tiny Dixon Band.

OCTOBER

OCT 1   (Fri.) Elvis appeared at the Eagle's Nest Club in Memphis
with Tiny Dixon and the Eagles Band.

OCT 6   (Wed.) Elvis performed on "ladies night" and "fan club
night" at the Eagle's Nest Club in Memphis.
Admission for ladies was fifty cents.

OCT 9   (Sat.) Elvis and Sleepy Eyed John were the performers
at the Eagle's Nest in Memphis.

OCT 13 (Wed.) It was ladies night again at the Eagle's Nest as
Elvis performed at the Memphis night club.

OCT 15 (Fri.) Elvis appeared in Memphis at the Eagle's Nest Club.

OCT 16 (Sat.) *Billboard*, in the "Folk Talent & Tunes" column,
reported that Bob Neal of WMPS in Memphis was planning a fall tour with Elvis, the Louvin Brothers, and Jim
Ed and Maxine Brown. Bob Neal (Hopgood) was a local
promoter of country acts, in addition to being one of
Memphis' most popular disk jockeys.
Elvis made his first appearance on the "Louisiana Hayride"
radio show, broadcast from the Shreveport, Louisiana,
Municipal Auditorium over KWKH radio. The show
was also carried over 190 radio stations in thirteen states.
Elvis appeared during the Lucky Strike cigarette segment
of the show which featured new talent. Elvis was intro-

In late 1954, Elvis performs a series of one-night stands.

duced by Frank Page, emcee for the "Louisiana Hayride." He performed *That's All Right* and *Blue Moon
Of Kentucky*. The booking had been done through Sam
Phillips, and Elvis was paid eighteen dollars. The total
budget for each "Hayride" show was $1,500. Admis-
sion was sixty cents for adults and thirty cents for children.

Elvis, Scotty and Bill stayed at the Al-Ida Motel in Bossier
City, across the Red River from Shreveport. According
to Scotty Moore, while the trio was in Shreveport, some
play dates booked by Tillman Franks, a local agent, did
not materialize, and the trio was stuck in the motel and
could not pay their bill. Another agent, Pappy Covington, booked a couple of dates in East Texas for the
group so that they could leave town. It is known that
during this time Elvis appeared on the "Old Texas Cor-
ral" in Houston, and a KSIJ radio concert in Gladewater.
Elvis, Scotty and Bill also appeared at the Lake Cliff
night club in Shreveport as "special guests" of Hoot
(Rains) and Curly (Herndon), who performed at the
club one night a week and were regulars on the "Louisiana Hayride."

OCT 22   (Fri.) Elvis was booked on "The Old Barn Dance" in New
Orleans by Keith Rush.

OCT 23   (Sat.) *Blue Moon Of Kentucky* was number 6 in Nashville and number 3 in New Orleans, according to *Billboard*'s C&W territorial chart for the week ending
October 13th. This was the first time Elvis had charted
a song outside the Memphis area.

Elvis made his second appearance on the "Louisiana Hayride" in Shreveport.

OCT 29   (Fri.) Elvis returned to the Eagle's Nest Club in Memphis,
where he shared the bill with Chuck Reed, Tiny Dixon
and Herb Jeffries.

OCT 30   (Sat.) Elvis was back at the Eagle's Nest in Memphis.

In October, Elvis reportedly had a recording session at the studios
of KWKH in Shreveport. He supposedly recorded *Always Late
(With Your Kisses), Blue Guitar, Give Me More More More
(Of Your Kisses)*, and *That's What You Gotta Watch*. (Although it was common practice for artists to use radio stations
for recording purposes, there is no further substantiation for
this story. See Appendix 2.)

On the road with the "Louisiana Hayride," Elvis sports his new leather guitar cover.

NOVEMBER

NOV 6   (Sat.) *Billboard*, in its "Review Spotlight" section, called *I Don't Care If The Sun Don't Shine/Good Rockin' Tonight* a "solid record that could easily break loose."

Billboard reported that Colonel Thomas Parker, of Jamboree Attractions, had signed a contract with Hank Snow to handle Snow's personal appearances. This move would have significant consequences on Elvis' future career.

Elvis signed a contract with the "Louisiana Hayride" which called for him to appear on the show for fifty-two consecutive Saturday nights between 8:00 and 11:00 p.m., whenever the International Broadcasting Corporation designated. He would be paid eighteen dollars a night, and Scotty and Bill would receive twelve dollars each.

Elvis made another appearance on the "Louisiana Hayride." As part of his duties as a regular performer, he sang a short commercial ditty for Southern Donuts which described them as "pipin' hot." Also guesting on the show was Willie Jones, "The Singing Emcee" of the "Texas Jamboree" in Corpus Christi.

NOV 13   (Sat.) Elvis was voted the eighth "Most Promising" C&W vocalist in *Billboard*'s annual disc jockey poll. (Others, in order, were Tommy Collins, Justin Tubb, Jimmy & Johnny, Maxine and Jim Ed Brown, Rita Robbins, Skeeter Bonn, Jimmy Newman, Elvis, Willie Jackson, and Faron Young.)

Good Rockin' Tonight peaked at number 3 in Memphis for the week ending November 3rd, according to *Billboard*.

Elvis made another appearance on the "Louisiana Hayride."

NOV 15   (Mon.) Elvis received a check for $82.50 from Sun Records, which was probably a payment for an earlier recording session and an advance against future royalties.

NOV 17   (Wed.) Elvis, along with "Louisiana Hayride" artists Jimmy and Johnny, appeared in Memphis at the Eagle's Nest Club. Admission was one dollar for the show.

NOV 20   (Sat.) *Billboard* mentioned Elvis' appearance on the "Louisiana Hayride" on October 16th and 23rd. The short article also mentioned that Elvis had signed a con-

tract with the "Louisiana Hayride." There was also a
list of the roster for the Hayride: Slim Whitman, Red
Sovine, Johnny Horton, Elvis, Jimmy Newman, Tibby
Edwards, Jimmy and Johnny, Hoot and Curley, Jim Ed
and Maxine Brown, Jimmy and Dido, Rowley, Jeanette
Hicks, Betty Amos, the Circle 6 Ranch Boys, Ginny
Wright, Carolyn Bradshaw, Jack Ford, Buddy Attaway,
and the Lump Lump Boys.

Elvis appeared on the "Louisiana Hayride."

NOV 27 (Sat.) Elvis made another appearance on the "Louisiana
Hayride."

Elvis stopped working for Crown Electric in November because
his increasing popularity was demanding more and more of his
time.

Among the places that Elvis and his band played late in 1954 were
Sweetwater, Lufkin, Longview, Boston, and Odessa, all in Texas.

DECEMBER

EARLY DECEMBER

Early in December, Bob Neal booked Elvis on a short tour of
school house auditoriums and gymnasiums in Arkansas, including Helena, North Little Rock and Texarkana; and Mississippi.
Also sharing the bill were Jim Ed and Maxine Brown and the
Louvin Brothers.

DEC 4 (Sat.) Elvis performed on the "Louisiana Hayride."

DEC 7 (Tues.) Marty Robbins recorded his version of *That's All
Right*, which was issued by Columbia Records (21351).
This was the first cover version of a song recorded by
Elvis. Although Robbins' version is more country-
oriented than Elvis', it is closer to Elvis' record than to
the original by Arthur "Big Boy" Crudup. Robbins version also outsold Elvis' record by a large margin.

DEC 8 (Wed.) According to a Sun Records "session sheet," Elvis
apparently attempted to record *Tomorrow Night* and
Uncle Pen during a session on this date. No other information is available, and the tape from this session was
not transferred to RCA Victor in December 1955. (See
Appendix 2.)

DEC 11 (Sat.) In the "Folk Talent & Tunes" column in *Billboard*,
it was reported that "the hottest piece of merchandise

on the 'Louisiana Hayride' at the moment is Elvis Presley, the youngster with the hillbilly blues beat."

Elvis made another appearance on the "Louisiana Hayride." He was also a guest on the "Red River Roundup"
record show, which followed the "Hayride" on KWKH
radio at 11:00 p.m., the latter hosted by "Balin'-wire"
Bob Strack.

DEC 18   (Sat.) Elvis again appeared on the "Louisiana Hayride."

DEC 20   (Mon.) Elvis had another recording session at Sun Studios.
He recorded *Milkcow Blues Boogie*, originally recorded
by Kokomo Arnold in 1935 as *Milkcow Blues*, and
You're A Heartbreaker, the first song which Elvis was
the first to record. It is also possible that Elvis attempted
to record *I'm Left, You're Right, She's Gone*. Of all of
the songs recorded by Elvis for Sun Records, this appears
to have been the most difficult to achieve an acceptable
take. Two complete reels of tape were used by Sam
Phillips, indicating that many attempts were made before
the session was completed. This song was also the first
to feature a drummer, Johnny Bonnero of the Dean
Beard Band (who recorded for Memphis' Fox Records
in 1955 and had a minor hit with *Rakin' And Scrapin'*
for Atlantic Records in 1956). An earlier take of *I'm
Left, You're Right, She's Gone*, which did not feature
the drummer and which was very slow and bluesy compared to the released version, has surfaced on several
bootlegged records with the title *My Baby's Gone*. The
guitar lick on *My Baby's Gone* by Scotty Moore was
taken from the Delmore Brothers' 1949 recording of
Blues Stay Away From Me. (See Appendix 2.)

DEC 25   (Sat.) Elvis spent Christmas with his family in their new
home at 2414 Lamar Avenue in Memphis. Their tele-
phone number was listed as 37-4185. (In 1968, this
house was converted into the Tiny Tot Nursery.)

DEC 28   (Tues.) Elvis headlined at Cook's Hoedown club in
Houston, Texas, as part of the "Yuletide Jamboree."
The show was booked by Pappy Covington, and included
Floyd Tillman among others. Tickets were $1.25 at
the door, and about 150 persons attended.

In December, a paternity suit was filed against Elvis by a Mississippi teenager, but the case was later dismissed.

In December, Elvis' photo appeared in the souvenir program from
the "Louisiana Hayride," which sold for only a dollar.

Elvis signs a managerial contract with Bob Neal (right) as Sam Phillips (left) looks on.

Guitar Man

ALL
SHOOK
UP

ELVIS
Day-By-Day,
1955

JANUARY

JAN 1   (Sat.) Elvis signed a managerial contract with Bob Neal, who took over completely from Scotty Moore. Neal was to receive fifteen percent off the top, with another twenty percent going for promotion. Dominic Joseph (D.J.) Fontana, resident drummer for the "Louisiana Hayride," was to join Elvis' band for the salary of a hundred dollars a week. The remainder of any monies would be split between Elvis (fifty percent) and Scotty Moore and Bill Black (twenty-five percent each).

Elvis headlined a sell-out show at the Eagle's Hall in Houston as part of the "Grand Prize Saturday Night Jamboree," broadcast over KNUZ radio from 8:00 to 11:00 p.m. The show was sponsored by Grand Prize Beer, and the regulars were Jerry Jerico, Tommy Sands, George Jones, emcee Biff Collie, and announcer Ken Grant. The show's producer was Buddy Covington. Emcee on this date was Gabe Tucker.

JAN 8   (Sat.) An article in *Billboard*'s "Folk Talent & Tunes" column reported that Bob Neal had taken over the personal management of Elvis, "who in a few short months has catapulted to a top spot on the 'Louisiana Hayride.' "

Sun Records released Elvis' third single, *Milkcow Blues Boogie/You're A Heartbreaker.*

Elvis resumed his weekly appearances on the "Louisiana Hayride."

EARLY JANUARY

Early in January, Elvis was interviewed by Lynn McDowell, WBIP radio, in Booneville, Mississippi in a promotion plugging his upcoming personal appearance in that town. Booneville was twenty-five miles north of Tupelo.

JAN 12   (Wed.) Elvis started a short tour with a show in Clarks-
         dale, Mississippi. Appearing with Elvis were Texas Bill
         Strength, Jim Ed and Maxine Brown, and members of
         the "Louisiana Hayride."
JAN 13   (Thurs.) Elvis performed in Helena, Arkansas, for a
         twelve dollar guarantee, singing from the back of a flat-
         bed truck.
JAN 15   (Sat.) Elvis made another appearance on the "Louisiana
         Hayride."
JAN 16   (Sun.) Elvis appeared in Booneville, Mississippi. Also on
         the show were Jim Ed and Maxine Brown.
JAN 17   (Mon.) Elvis traveled to Sheffield, Alabama, for a personal
         appearance.
JAN 18   (Tues.) The tour continued with a show in Leachville,
         Arkansas.
JAN 19   (Wed.) Elvis traveled just over the Missouri border for a
         show in Sikeston.
JAN 22   (Sat.) Elvis performed on the "Louisiana Hayride."
JAN 23   (Sun.) During this week, Elvis toured East Texas in a
         series of dates booked by Tom Perryman of Gladewater,
         Texas. Dates probably included Midland with Billy
         Walker (1600 paid attendance); Boston; Gladewater; the
         Cotton Club in Lubbock (with Jimmie Rodgers Snow);
         and the Creole Club in Mobile, Alabama.
JAN 29   (Sat.) *Billboard* reviewed *Milkcow Blues Boogie*, giving it
         a rating of eighty, while saying "Presley continued to
         impress." *You're A Heartbreaker* received a rating of
         seventy-six, and *Billboard* said it was a "slick country-
         style reading."
         Billboard reported that Bob Neal had flown to Shreveport
         to confer with A.M. (Pappy) Covington and other
         "Louisiana Hayride" officials regarding future bookings
         for Elvis.
         Elvis appeared at the Eagle's Hall in Houston, Texas.

In January, Elvis was interviewed on the "Milkman's Jamboree"
radio show broadcast from 10:30 p.m. to 5:00 a.m. over WMPS
in Memphis. The host was Dick ("Uncle Richard") Stuart.

FEBRUARY

FEB 4   (Fri.) Elvis and the "Blue Moon Boys," as Scotty and Bill
         were now being booked, made a personal appearance in

New Orleans. Also on the show, which probably took
place at the Lake Ponchartrane amusement area, were
Bud Deckelman, Ann Raye, Bill Cason, the Daydream-
ers, and the Arkansas Troopers. The show was promoted
by Red Smith of WBOK.

FEB 5   (Sat.) Back in Memphis, Elvis had a recording session at
Sun Records. He recorded *Baby Let's Play House*, a
1954 r&b hit for Arthur Gunter. He also attempted a
song which was now a regular part of every live show,
I Got A Woman, which was a current hit for Ray
Charles. He also tried unsuccessfully to record *Tryin'
To Get To You*, a 1954 r&b hit for the Eagles. (See
Appendix 2.)

FEB 6   (Sun.) Elvis performed two shows, at 3:00 and 8:00 p.m.
at the Memphis Auditorium. The show was headlined
by Faron Young and featured Martha Carson, Ferlin
Huskey, and the Wilburn Brothers. (Huskey dropped
the "e" in his last name in 1956.)

FEB 12   (Sat.) Elvis returned to the "Louisiana Hayride."

FEB 14   (Mon.) Elvis, Scotty and Bill, after driving almost 1,000
miles, performed for a sell-out crowd in Carlsbad, New
Mexico. Over a hundred people were turned away at the
door.

FEB 15   (Tues.) It is probable that Elvis performed in Albuquerque,
New Mexico, with Faron Young.

FEB 16   (Wed.) Elvis joined a Hank Snow tour for a jamboree in
Odessa, Texas. The tour had been on the road for a
couple of weeks without Elvis, playing dates in California,
Arizona, New Mexico, and Colorado. Also touring with
Snow were his son, Jimmie Rodgers Snow, Charlene
Arthur and Whitey Ford (known professionally as "The
Duke Of Paducah"). Emcees for the show were Lee
Alexander and Bill Myrick of KECK, Odessa, and Keith
Ward of KJBC, Midland.

FEB 18   (Fri.) Hank Snow wound up his tour with a show in
Monroe, Louisiana.

FEB 19   (Sat.) A brief mention of Elvis appeared in *Billboard*.
According to the report, he was "hot" in Eldorado, Ar-
kansas. "His style really pleases the teenagers."
Elvis performed his regular Saturday night show with the
"Louisiana Hayride."

FEB 22   (Tues.) Elvis played Hope, Arkansas. Also on the bill
were The Duke Of Paducah, Mother Maybelle and the

Carter Sisters, Jimmy Rodgers Snow, Charley Stewart, and Uncle Dudley.

FEB 24   (Thurs.) Elvis appeared in Bastrop, Louisiana.

FEB 26   (Sat.) *Billboard* reported that Elvis was "currently on tour with the Browns in Miss., Ala., Mo., and Ark." This item apparently refers to the short tour beginning January 12th.

Elvis played the "Circle Theater Jamboree" in Cleveland, Ohio. The show was from 8:00 to 11:00 p.m., and was broadcast over WERE radio.

MARCH

MAR 5   (Sat.) Elvis appeared on that portion of the "Louisiana Hayride" which was televised for the Shreveport area. This was Elvis' first TV performance, and he was introduced on the show by Horace Logan. (Elvis' previous "Louisiana Hayride" shows were broadcast on radio only.)

MAR 6   (Sun.) Elvis was booked on a five-day tour with Jimmy Work, the Duke Of Paducah, and Betty Amos. The tour swung through Tennessee, Arkansas, Mississippi, Louisiana, and Missouri.

MAR 12   (Sat.) Elvis appeared on the "Louisiana Hayride."

MAR 14   (Mon.) Elvis made an appearance on the "Town And Country Jubilee" in Washington, DC, hosted by Jimmie Dean and broadcast over WMAL-TV (the local ABC-TV affiliate) at 5:30 p.m. Elvis was interviewed by Dean, but he did not perform.

MAR 15   (Tues.) Elvis may have renewed his contract with Bob Neal on this date. Apparently, it ran for a year, until March 1956.

mid-MAR In mid-March, Elvis traveled to New York to audition for "Arthur Godfrey's Talent Scouts" TV show. His performance did not impress the producers, and Elvis was not accepted for the show. While in New York, Elvis is reported to have gone to Harlem to see Bo Diddley perform at the Apollo Theater.

Also in mid-March, Elvis stopped his regular weekly appearances on the "Louisiana Hayride" to concentrate on spreading his popularity outside of the South and Southwest. However, since his contract with the Hayride lasted until October 1955, it cost $400 a week to get

Elvis backed by **Scotty Moore** on guitar and **Bill Black** on bass.

him out of a contract which only paid him eighteen dollars a show.

MAR 19 (Sat.) Elvis appeared in Houston, Texas, at the Eagle's Hall for the "Grand Prize Jamboree." The show was broadcast simultaneously over KPRC-TV and KNUZ radio. Also on the bill were Hoot Gibson (not the film star, but a DJ on KGRY, Gary, Indiana), Sonny Burns, the Brown Brothers, Tommy Sands, James O'Gwynn, Coye Wilcox, the Dixie Drifters, Ernie Hunter, and Herbie Remington. The show ran from 8:00 to 11:00 p.m. (The April 2nd issue of *Billboard* mentioned that Elvis may have had other dates in the Houston area.)

MAR 26 (Sat.) Elvis returned to Shreveport for an appearance on the "Louisiana Hayride."

MAR 28 (Mon.) Elvis returned to the "Circle Theater Jamboree" in Cleveland. He was paid $350. Following the show, promoter Tom Kennedy took Elvis to meet Cleveland's reigning rock 'n' roll disc jockey, Bill Randle (also spelled Randall in some texts). Randle interviewed Elvis over WERE radio.

APRIL

APR 1 (Fri.) Elvis appeared in Odessa, Texas. Along with Scotty and Bill were D.J. Fontana and Floyd Cramer. Attendance was reported at 850.

APR 2 (Sat.) According to a brief article in *Billboard*, Elvis was booked solid through April. It was mentioned that Onie Wheeler would be working a number of dates in Arkansas with Elvis. (During April, Elvis appeared at a jamboree in El Dorado, which drew a full house to the local high school auditorium. Appearing with Elvis were Onie Wheeler, Betty Amos, and T. Tommy and his band. Elvis was also reported to have played Texarkana with Chessie Smith, and Helena late in April.)

Elvis performed on the "Louisiana Hayride" in Shreveport.

APR 9 (Sat.) Elvis was back on the "Louisiana Hayride."

APR 16 (Sat.) Elvis headlined the "Big D Jamboree" in Dallas, Texas. The show was held in the sportatorium at 8:00 p.m., and featured Sonny James, Hank Locklin, Charlene Arthur, the Bellew Twins, Jimmie Collie, Doug Bragg, LeFawn Paul, Orville Couch, Riley Crabtree, Joe Bill and others, including three bands. Admission was

> sixty cents for adults and thirty cents for children. According to promoter J.F. Dolan, Elvis "pulled a terrific crowd."

APR 23 (Sat.) Elvis appeared on the "Louisiana Hayride," which was being broadcast "remote" from the Heart O'Texas Coliseum in Waco. More than 5,000 attended. Also on the show were Jim Ed and Maxine Brown, Jim Reeves, and Slim Whitman.

APR 30 (Sat.) Elvis' fourth single, *Baby Let's Play House/I'm Left, You're Right, She's Gone* was released. This was the first of Elvis' singles to be pressed outside of Memphis, with several thousand copies produced at Monarch Records in Los Angeles.

Elvis performed on the "Louisiana Hayride," which was broadcast "remote" from Gladewater, Texas. He was late for the show, and he had time to sing only one song. He chose *Tweedle Dee*, a recent hit for LaVerne Baker in the r&b field, Georgia Gibbs in popular music, and Bonnie Lou in the country market. Scotty and Bill were also late for the show, so Elvis was backed by members of Ray Price's band, the Cherokee Cowboys, including James Clayton Day on steel guitar.

MAY

MAY 1 (Sun.) Elvis, Scotty, and Bill joined "Hank Snow's All Star Jamboree" for a show in New Orleans. The twenty-one-day/twenty-town tour was booked by Colonel Tom Parker. For three weeks, thirty-one performers appeared throughout the South. Each show was set up in two parts. On the first half of the show, Jimmie Rodgers Snow, the Davis Sisters, and the Wilburn Brothers performed, with Elvis coming on right before intermission. The second half of the show opened with the Carter Family, followed by Slim Whitman, and Hank Snow closed the show. Other entertainers who were also on several of the shows were Faron Young, Martha Carson, and Onie Wheeler.

MAY 4 (Wed.) The tour stopped for two days in Mobile, Alabama.

MAY 5 (Thurs.) Elvis and the Hank Snow package entertained for a second day in Mobile.

MAY 6 (Fri.) Elvis performed with the Hank Snow Jamboree in Birmingham, Alabama.

MAY 7   (Sat.) The tour traveled to Daytona Beach, Florida.

MAY 8   (Sun.) Remaining in Florida, Elvis and Hank Snow appeared in Tampa.

MAY 9   (Mon.) The Hank Snow tour performed in Macon, Georgia.

MAY 10   (Tues.) It was back to Florida for Elvis, as he appeared in Ocala with Hank Snow, Faron Young and the Wilburn Brothers, in a show which brought in an overflow crowd of 2,700.

MAY 13   (Fri.) The Hank Snow tour stopped for a show in a ball park in Jacksonville, Florida, before 14,000 fans. At the close of his set, Elvis told the crowd, "Girls, I'll see you all backstage." About half the audience broke through the police barricade and made for the stage. Elvis ran for the dugout which led to the dressing rooms, but about a hundred girls made it into the dressing room. Elvis was almost stripped of all of his clothes. In the parking lot, Elvis' Lincoln Continental was covered with names, telephone numbers, and notes to Elvis written in lipstick or scratched into the paint.

MAY 14   (Sat.) *Billboard*, in its review of *Baby Let's Play House* gave it a rating of seventy-seven and called the song a "distinctive country effort." *I'm Left, You're Right, She's Gone* was rated seventy-one and described as an "unusual, rhythmic country chant."

MAY 16   (Mon.) Elvis closed the Hank Snow show during their stop at the Mosque Theater in Richmond, Virginia. Also on the bill were Martha Carson and Slim Whitman.

MAY 17   (Tues.) In two performances in Norfolk, Virginia, the Hank Snow jamboree drew 6,000 paid attendance. Appearing with Snow and Elvis were Slim Whitman, the Davis Sisters, Onie Wheeler, and Jimmie Rodgers Snow.

MAY 18   (Wed.) The Hank Snow tour stopped for two shows at the American Legion Auditorium in Roanoke, Virginia. Shows were at 7:00 and 9:00 p.m., and tickets were a dollar advance, a dollar-fifty reserved seats, and fifty cents for children. The performers spent the night in the Hotel Roanoke. The show was sponsored by the Roanoke Record Shop. It was reported that Elvis did not have his own back-up band but used members of other performers' bands (it is probable that Scotty and Bill played as part of other performers' bands, thereby confusing the issue).

MAY 19 (Thurs.) It is probable that Elvis and the Hank Snow
            package, featuring the Davis Sisters and Martha Carson,
            played New Bern, North Carolina.
MAY 20 (Fri.) The last show of the Hank Snow Jamboree tour was
            held in Chattanooga, Tennessee.
MAY 21 (Sat.) As part of *Billboard*'s annual review of country and
            western music, Elvis ran a quarter-page ad which touted
            him as the "freshest, newest voice" in that field.
            Elvis, along with Onie Wheeler, returned to the "Louisiana
            Hayride."
MAY 22 (Sun.) Elvis appeared at the Magnolia Gardens in Houston,
            Texas. Onie Wheeler continued to perform with the
            Elvis show.

   According to a May 28 report in *Billboard*, Elvis had appeared in
      Kilgore, Texas, with the Browns and a "Louisiana Hayride" unit,
      and he was a guest on KOCA radio. Also in the May 28 issue of
      Billboard, it was mentioned that Elvis had played a ball park in
      Gainesville, Texas, with Scotty and Bill, Onie Wheeler, Frank
      Starr and the Rock-a-way Boys. This show was staged by Jerry
      O'Dell of KGAF radio. Elvis may have also appeared at the
      American Legion Hall in Breckinridge, Texas, at this time. He
      was paid $300 and attendance was over 1,000.

MAY 25 (Wed.) Elvis appeared as part of the second annual "Jimmie
            Rodgers Memorial Celebration" in Meridian, Mississippi.
            Others who appeared during the two-day event were
            Jimmie Davis, Slim Whitman, Ernest Tubb, Jimmy New-
            man, Jim Reeves, Johnny Horton, and Dizzy Dean.
MAY 28 (Sat.) Elvis appeared on the "Big D Jamboree" radio
            broadcast from Dallas. Other guest artists were Arlie
            Duff and Texas Bill Strength.
MAY 29 (Sun.) Elvis played a "round robin" with two shows in two
            separate locations. At 7:30 p.m., he appeared at the
            Northside Coliseum in Fort Worth. At 8:30 p.m., Elvis
            and the rest of the troupe opened at the Sportatorium
            in Dallas, twenty miles away. Appearing on this tour
            were Martha Carson, Bill Carlisle and the Carlisles, Ferlin
            Huskey, Jim Ed and Maxine Brown, Chuck Lee, and
            Onie Wheeler. The tour had been booked by Bob Neal,
            who was "currently working with Colonel Tom Parker
            on promotion."

MAY 30 (Mon.) Elvis and the rest of his show performed at the Fair Park Auditorium in Abilene, Texas.

MAY 31 (Tues.) Elvis played another "round robin" with a matinee in Midland and an evening performance in Odessa, Texas. Appearing with Elvis was Billy Walker.

JUNE

JUN 1 (Wed.) The tour continued with an appearance in Guymon, Oklahoma.

JUN 2 (Thurs.) Back in Texas, the show stopped in Amarillo at the City Auditorium.

JUN 3 (Fri.) The final show of this week-long tour was held in Lubbock, Texas. A capacity crowd of 6,000 was on hand to see Elvis, Ferlin Huskey, Martha Carson, the Carlisles, the Browns, Onie Wheeler, and George and Earl.

JUN 4 (Sat.) In the "Folk Talent & Tunes" column in *Billboard*, it was reported by Cecil Holifield, owner of record shops in Midland and Odessa, Texas, that Elvis "continues to gather speed over the South. West Texas is his hottest territory to date and he is the teenagers' favorite wherever he appears. Our sales of Presley's records have beat any individual artist in our eight years in the record business."

Elvis returned to the "Louisiana Hayride" in Shreveport.

JUN 6 (Mon.) During the week, it is probable that Elvis and fellow Sun Records performers Johnny Cash and Carl Perkins appeared in Marianna, Arkansas.

JUN 9 (Thurs.) Elvis joined a Hank Snow tour for a show in Lawton, Oklahoma. The other performers on this road show included Ferlin Huskey, Marty Robbins, Sonny James, the Maddox Brothers and Rose and Rhetta, the Bellew Twins, and the Texas Stompers.

JUN 10 (Fri.) The Hank Snow Jamboree remained in Lawton for a second night.

JUN 11 (Sat.) Elvis returned to Shreveport and the "Louisiana Hayride."

JUN 13 (Mon.) Elvis started a short tour with a show in Bruce, Mississippi.

JUN 14 (Tues.) The tour moved on to Tupelo, Mississippi.

JUN 15 (Wed.) Elvis traveled north to Gobler, Missouri, for another show.

JUN 16   (Thurs.) Elvis appeared in El Dorado, Arkansas.
JUN 17   (Fri.) During the early morning hours, as Elvis and his
         date traveled south on Highway 69 between Hope and
         Texarkana, Arkansas, a wheel bearing went out on his
         new pink Cadillac, and the car caught fire and burned.
         Scotty and Bill were following Elvis in a second car, but
         by the time they arrived, the only items which could
         be salvaged were the musical instruments. They char-
         tered a light plane and flew to Stamford, Texas, for
         that evening's performance.
JUN 18   (Sat.) Elvis appeared on the "Big D Jamboree," broadcast
         from Dallas.
JUN 19   (Sun.) Elvis performed at the Magnolia Gardens in Hous-
         ton, Texas.
JUN 20   (Mon.) Elvis had two shows in Beaumont, Texas, which
         also featured Marty Robbins, the Maddox Brothers and
         Rose, Sonny James, the Bellew Twins, the Texas Stomp-
         ers, and Charlene Arthur. The shows were a benefit for
         the Beaumont Police Department. Over 2,400 people
         attended each show. The admission was only a dollar.
JUN 21   (Tues.) Elvis and the other performers gave three more
         shows in Beaumont.
         Elvis and his show remained in Beaumont for another
         three shows.
JUN 22   (Wed.) Elvis performed in Vernon, Texas.
JUN 23   (Thurs.) Elvis traveled to Lawton, Oklahoma, for the
         night's performance. Also on the bill were Leon Payne,
         Cecil Lee (a DJ at KSWO), Joe Carson, and Chuck Lee.
JUN 24   (Fri.) Remaining in Oklahoma, Elvis appeared in Altus.
JUN 25   (Sat.) Elvis returned to the "Louisiana Hayride" for his
         regular spot.
JUN 26   (Sun.) Elvis, along with Marty Robbins and Sonny James
         performed in Biloxi, Mississippi. Elvis met, and started
         dating June Juanico. (See mid-June 1956.)
JUN 27   (Mon.) Elvis appeared at the NCO Club at Keesler AFB,
         Mississippi.
JUN 28   (Tues.) Keesler AFB played host to Elvis' show again.
JUN 29   (Wed.) Elvis, along with Marty Robbins and Sonny James,
         Played the Radio Ranch Club in Mobile, Alabama. This
         club was owned by Curtis Gordon, a c&w performer.
JUN 30   (Thurs.) Elvis stayed at the Mobile night spot for another
         evening's performance.

SUN'S NEWEST STAR

Elvis Presley

Lucky Elvis Presley — "Sun's Newest Star" — at 19 is already enjoying the first reality of his life's dream: to sing for people and hear the spontaneous applause that means he's made a hit! When Elvis was a youngster down in Tupelo, Mississippi, folks used to stop him on the street and say, "Sing for us, Elvis." And he would . . . standing on the street corners, in the hot Mississippi sun . . . or in church . . . or at school . . . anywhere someone wanted to hear him, he'd sing.

Now the same thing is happening all over again. When he's recognized on the street or at any public place, people call out: "Sing for us, Elvis!" And it's all because of a tremendous new record he waxed on the Sun label — a record that was a "first" in several ways.

"That's All Right" and "Blue Moon Of Kentucky" were Elvis' first professional work of any kind. He's a self-taught musician and worked out his unique style while listening to records and picking out the tunes on a cheap ($2.98) guitar. One day he drifted into a Memphis recording studio to make a personal record — just to get an idea how he sounded — and was heard by Sam Phillips, prexy of Sun Record Company, who thought that with a little work and polish the boy might made as a commercial artist.

song which must be put into just one category. "That's All Right," for example, was a tremendous hit with teen-agers — and in Memphis, where the record broke first, the current greeting among the teen-agers is still a rhythmical line from the song: "Ta dee da dee dee da!"

Elvis, of course, is a teen-ager, too. Just 19, he's been out of high school but one year — and the big (6-footer) blonde guy likes nothing better than to spend an afternoon practicing football with some of the youngsters in the neighborhood. Other hobbies of Elvis' include movies, listening to records — and eating!

Stories of the singer's appetite are many. His girl friend, Dixie, declares that recently at one sitting he ate 8 Deluxe Cheeseburgers, 2 bacon-lettuce-tomato sandwiches — and topped it off with three chocholate milk shakes.

Since the release of the two-sided hit, Elvis has been making personal appearances and bringing the house down every time. As the featured entertainer at the grand opening of a new business arcade, he played to a wildly enthusiastic audience of more than 3,000 — who couldn't restrain themselves and started dancing and jitterbugging when Elvis sang "That's All Right." Incidentally, the latest pairing by the boy features "You're A Heartbreaker," backed with "Milk Cow Blues Boogie" — both fine offerings. . . . the fact that . . . "sure

Elvis' first national magazine article.

The first national magazine article on Elvis appeared in the June issue of *Cowboy Songs* magazine. Entitled "Sun's Newest Star," the article was comprised of equal parts pure fiction and publicity hype.

SUMMER
The Presleys moved from 2414 Lamar Avenue to 1414 Getwell Street.

JULY

JUL 1   (Fri.) Elvis continued his tour with an appearance in Baton Rouge, Louisiana, at Lou Millet's club.

JUL 2   (Sat.) *Cashbox*, another national music trade weekly, voted Elvis the "Up and Coming Male Vocalist" in country music. Elvis placed an ad in the magazine thanking all of the disc jockeys for voting for him while plugging his latest release, *I'm Left, You're Right, She's Gone/Baby Let's Play House.*
Elvis made a non-singing radio appearance in Corpus Christi, Texas, to promote his upcoming show.

JUL 3   (Sun.) Elvis appeared with the Statesmen and the Blackwood Brothers Quartet in Corpus Christi.

JUL 4   (Mon.) Elvis performed as part of a day-long Fourth of July celebration at the City Recreational Building in Stephenville, Texas. Elvis headlined the country and western segment, which also featured Slim Willit and the Farren Twins. Also appearing at the all-day event were the Blackwood Brothers, the Statesmen Quartet, the Deep South Quartet, the Stamps Quartet and the Stamps Ozark Quartet, all of which performed during the afternoon gospel show. (Some confusion surrounds the location of this show. One source lists DeLeon, Texas, as the play date. DeLeon is only twenty-five miles from Stephenville, and apparently was erroneously listed in the pre-show publicity. Stephenville was mentioned in an article *after* the date. However, it is also possible that this was another round-robin with performances simultaneously in both towns.)

JUL 5   (Tues.) Elvis returned to Memphis for a two-week vacation. He had been on the road constantly for the past several months. His summer and fall schedule was being arranged by Colonel Parker and it looked very busy.

JUL 11   (Mon.) Elvis had another recording session at Sun Records. The first song attempted was *Mystery Train*, a 1953 hit for Junior Parker on Sun Records. The song, as sung by Elvis, owed more to the flip of Parker's single, *Love My Baby*, than to *Mystery Train*, especially in Scotty Moore's guitar work. This was followed by a pair of songs that used a drummer who sounds as though he might be different from the drummer used on the December 20, 1954 session. *I Forgot To Remember To Forget* was an Elvis original, while *Tryin' To Get To You* was a rhythm and blues hit for the Eagles in 1954. *Tryin' To Get To You* also was the only song that Elvis recorded for Sun to feature a piano. The pianist might have been Elvis, and according to Malcom Yelvington, it could have been Frank Tolley, a member of Yelvington's Star Rhythm Boys.

      Elvis also apparently attempted to record *When It Rains It Pours*, which had been recorded for Sun Records by Billy "The Kid" Emerson the previous January. Elvis attempted the song several times, and only one "take" had any commercial potential. Carl Perkins was on hand in the studio but did not participate in Elvis' session. This song remained unissued until 1984's **Elvis — A Legendary Performer, Vol 4**. (See Appendix 2.)

JUL 16   (Sat.) Elvis had his first nationally ranked single as *Baby Let's Play House* entered the *Billboard* "Music Popularity Charts" at number 15 on the "Country And Western Best Sellers In Stores" list for the week ending July 6th. The single stayed on the chart for fifteen weeks, reaching a high of number 10.

JUL 22   (Fri.) Elvis performed in the "Pioneer Jamboree" in Odessa, Texas, with Ferlin Huskey, the Browns, Tibby Edwards, and Sonny James. The show was booked by Lee Alexander of radio station KECK.

JUL 23   (Sat.) Elvis was the guest artist on the "Big D Jamboree" in Dallas.

JUL 25   (Mon.) During a tour of Florida, Elvis appeared on the same bill with Andy Griffith, Ferlin Huskey, Jimmie Rodgers Snow, Marty Robbins, Tommy Collins, Frank Evans, and Glenn Reeves. The opening night's show was held in Tampa at the 116th Field Artillery Armory and was sponsored by the Seratoma Club.

JUL 26   (Tues.) Elvis and the other performers traveled to Orlando for two days.

JUL 27   (Wed.) Elvis stayed in Orlando with the tour for a second day's performances. *Billboard* reported that "Elvis stole the show."

JUL 28   (Thurs.) The tour moved on to Jacksonville for shows in the Gator Bowl.

JUL 29   (Fri.) During a second day's show in Jacksonville, the crowd broke through the police barriers in a replay of the previous May's riot. By the time Elvis could be rescued, he had lost his tie, handkerchief, belt and the better part of his coat and shirt. While loading equipment on the car in the parking lot, Elvis fainted. He was taken to a hospital; before morning, however, he was back in the hotel room.

JUL 30   (Sat.) The tour with Andy Griffith moved on to Daytona Beach, Florida, for a performance.

JUL 31   (Sun.) Elvis started a new tour with an appearance in the Community Center in Sheffield, Allabama. Also on the bill were Webb Pierce, Johnny Cash, Bud Deckelman, and Wanda Jackson. Both performances were "Standing Room Only."

AUGUST

AUG 1   (Mon.) The tour continued with a show in Little Rock. Elvis' parents were on hand for this show. They had driven to Little Rock specifically to meet with Colonel Parker at Elvis' insistence. However, they did not sign a contract with Colonel Parker at this time, even though Elvis wanted very much to do so.

AUG 2   (Tues.) Elvis continued to perform in Little Rock.

AUG 3   (Wed.) Elvis returned to his hometown of Tupelo for a show.

AUG 4   (Thurs.) There were two shows in Camden, Arkansas.

AUG 5   (Fri.) Elvis appeared as part of Bob Neal's "Eighth Anniversary Jamboree" at the Overton Park Shell in Memphis. Also on the bill were Webb Pierce, Red Sovine, Sonny James, Jim Wilson, Johnny Cash, Wanda Jackson, Texas Bill Strength, Bud Deckelman, and Charlie Feathers. (Both Cash and Feathers were signed to Sun Records at this time.) This three-hour show was reported to be the biggest country jamboree ever held in Memphis, pulling

Elvis meets backstage with Bill Haley in Cleveland.

in over 4,000 fans despite the threat of rain.

AUG 6   (Sat.) Elvis' fifth and final single for Sun Records, *Mystery Train/I Forgot To Remember To Forget* was released.

A brief article in *Billboard* mentioned that Elvis and the Browns had just returned from a West Coast trek and would appear in Detroit on September 2nd and 3rd. (Both pieces of information are wrong.)

AUG 8   (Mon.) Elvis started a week's tour of the Gladewater, Texas, area with Jim Ed and Maxine Brown. Elvis was interviewed on KSIJ radio in Gladewater.

AUG 11   (Thurs.) Elvis appeared at the Texas State Fair in Dallas.

AUG 12   (Fri.) Elvis traveled on to San Antonio for another show.

AUG 13   (Sat.) Elvis appeared in Houston, Texas.

AUG 15   (Mon.) Colonel Tom Parker, acting on behalf of Hank Snow Attractions (Parker and Snow were equal partners) signed Elvis to a one-year contract, with Bob Neal to act as an advisor. The contract allowed for two one-year options. Parker was to be paid $2,500 in five $500 installments, and he was to be reimbursed for any expenses. The contract also stipulated: "As a special concession to Colonel Parker, ELVIS PRESLEY is to play 100 personal appearances within one year for the special sum of $200 including musicians."

AUG 20   (Sat.) *Billboard*, in its "Review Spotlight" section, examined *I Forgot To Remember To Forget*, predicting the single would be "certain to get strong initial exposure."

Elvis returned to Cleveland to do two shows, which were filmed by Universal Studios for a short subject featuring local DJ Bill Randle of radio station WERE. The working title for the "short" was "The Pied Piper of Cleveland, or A Day in the Life of a Famous Disk Jockey." The first show was at St. Michael's School Assembly Hall, and the second show was at Brooklyn High School. Elvis sang *That's All Right, Blue Moon Of Kentucky* and *I Forgot To Remember To Forget*. Also appearing on the shows were Pat Boone, Bill Haley and His Comets, and the Four Lads. The short subject was never released.

AUG 31   (Wed.) Elvis, Scotty and Bill were interviewed by Elvis' manager, Bob Neal, over WMPS as a plug for Friday night's shows in Texarkana.

SEPTEMBER

SEP 1   (Thurs.) Elvis performed in New Orleans.

SEP 2   (Fri.) While driving from New Orleans to Texarkana, Arkansas, Elvis was ticketed for speeding. Later, he had an accident outside of Texarkana. Over $1,000 damage was done to his 1955 Cadillac. That night, Elvis performed in Texarkana with Johnny Cash, Charlene Arthur, Floyd Cramer, and Jimmy Day at the Arkansas Municipal Auditorium. Shows were held at 7:00 and 9:00 p.m.

SEP 3   (Sat.) Elvis appeared on the "Big D Jamboree" in Dallas, Texas.

SEP 5   (Mon.) Elvis, along with Johnny Cash, Bud Deckelman and Eddie Bond, appeared in Forrest, Arkansas, at an outdoor jamboree.

SEP 6   (Tues.) In Bono, Arkansas, population 311, Elvis and his show drew 1,152 paid attendance.

SEP 7   (Wed.) Elvis and the rest of his troupe performed in Sikeston, Missouri.

SEP 8   (Thurs.) Elvis appeared in Clarksdale, Mississippi.

SEP 9   (Fri.) A receipt from Plastic Products Co., the pressing plant for Sun Records, to Binkley Distribution Co. in Jacksonville, Florida, shows the strength of Elvis' records. The Florida company ordered fifty 78s and a hundred-seventy-five 45s of *That's All Right*, fifty 78s and a hundred 45s of *Good Rockin' Tonight*, fifty 78s and a hundred 45s of *Milkcow Blues Boogie*, and a hundred 78s and three hundred 45s of *Baby Let's Play House.*

McComb, Mississippi, played host to another show by Elvis. Following the show, Scotty, Bill, and DJ Fontana left to drive with the instruments to Norfolk, Virginia.

SEP 10   (Sat.) *Billboard*, based on the intensive chart action of *Mystery Train* and *I Forgot To Remember To Forget*, placed the single in "This Week's Best Buys" section, reporting that "Presley has been coming more and more to the forefront. His current record has wasted no time in establishing itself."

Elvis returned to the "Louisiana Hayride" without the "Blue Moon Boys." Following his performance, he flew from Shreveport to Norfolk, Virginia.

SEP 11   (Sun.) Elvis started a tour with the "Hank Snow All Star Jamboree," which also featured Cowboy Copas, the Louvin Brothers, and Jimmie Rodgers Snow. The opening night's show was held in the auditorium in Norfolk, Virginia, and it was broadcast over WCMS radio. According to promoter Sheriff Tex Davis, the show "broke all attendance records for the town." Davis reported that "the teenagers went wild when he [Elvis] went into his act. The girls mobbed him afterward and literally tore his clothes apart for souvenirs."

SEP 12   (Mon.) The Hank Snow tour continued to pack the house in Norfolk.

SEP 14   (Wed.) The troupe moved on for a show in Ashville, North Carolina.

SEP 15   (Thurs.) The jamboree played the American Legion Auditorium in Roanoke, Virginia. Elvis was billed as "extra special by popular demand." Tickets were a dollar in advance and a dollar-fifty at the door. The show was sponsored by the Roanoke Record Shop.

SEP 16   (Fri.) A smaller unit of Elvis, the Louvin Brothers, and Cowboy Copas played New Bern, North Carolina.

SEP 17   (Sat.) Elvis had one of his biggest weeks on the *Billboard* charts for the week ending September 7th. On the "C&W Territorial Best Sellers," *I Forgot To Remember To Forget* was number 1 in Memphis; *Mystery Train* was number 4 in Dallas-Ft. Worth, 5 in Houston and 8 in New Orleans; *Baby Let's Play House* was number 4 in St. Louis and 8 in Richmond. On the national country and western charts, *Mystery Train* was number 14 and *Baby Let's Play House* was number 15 in sales, while *I Forgot To Remember To Forget* was number 10 and *Baby Let's Play House* was tied for number 15 (with Carl Smith's *There She Goes*) in radio airplay.
Elvis played Wilson, North Carolina.

SEP 18   (Sun.) There was a concert in Raleigh, North Carolina.

SEP 19   (Mon.) The tour moved on to Thomasville, North Carolina.

SEP 20   (Tues.) Elvis played Richmond, Virginia's "Old Dominion Barn Dance," heard over WRVA. There were two shows. at 2:30 and 8:30 p.m.

SEP 21   (Wed.) Elvis, the Louvins, and Cowboy Copas appeared in Danville, Virginia.

SEP 22   (Thurs.) The tour closed with a show in Kingsport, Tennessee. The Louvin Brothers opened the show and were

The star of the "Elvis Presley Jamboree."

followed on stage by Elvis, who reportedly opened his portion of the show with *Rock Around The Clock*, a big hit for Bill Haley and His Comets. Cowboy Copas closed the show. Following the show, Elvis returned to Memphis, arriving on the morning of the 23rd.

SEP 24   (Sat.) Elvis made a personal appearance on the "Louisiana Hayride."

SEP 26   (Mon.) Elvis started a West Texas tour with Johnny Horton, Betty Amos, David Houston, Sonny Trammell, Ray Gorman, Tillman Franks, and "Woody Birdbrain." The first show was in Wichita Falls.

SEP 27   (Tues.) The tour stopped for a show in Bryan at the Saddle Club.

SEP 28   (Wed.) Elvis and the troupe played Conroe.

SEP 29   (Thurs.) The tour played a show in Austin at the Sports Arena.

SEP 30   (Fri.) The week-long tour ended with a show in Gonzales, Texas.

Country Song Roundup magazine ran an article on Elvis titled "Folk Music Fireball" in its September issue.

OCTOBER

OCT 1   (Sat.) Elvis returned to Shreveport for an appearance on the "Louisiana Hayride."

OCT 8   (Sat.) Elvis was back on the "Louisiana Hayride."

OCT 9   (Sun.) Elvis may have performed in Lufkin, Texas.

OCT 10   (Mon.) It is probable that Elvis appeared in Brownwood, Texas.

OCT 11   (Tues.) Elvis headlined his own "Elvis Presley Jamboree" with guests Jimmy Newman, Jean Shepard, Bobby Lord, Johnny Cash, Floyd Cramer, Porter Wagoner, and Wanda Jackson. The opening show for the tour was in Abilene, Texas.

OCT 12   (Wed.) The "Elvis Presley Jamboree" moved on to Midland, Texas.

OCT 13   (Thurs.) Elvis played Amarillo, Texas.

OCT 14   (Fri.) The tour stopped for shows in Odessa, Texas.

OCT 15   (Sat.) Elvis performed at the Cotton Club in Lubbock, Texas, as a guest of the Western Swing Kings. The opening act was a local duo, "Buddy and Bob," featuring a young Buddy Holly in one of his first engagements. Also on the bill were Jimmy Newman, Floyd Cramer, and Jimmy Day.

OCT 16 (Sun.) Elvis, along with Buddy and Bob, made a personal appearance at Hub Motors, the local Ford dealer in Lubbock. They sang on a makeshift stage to attract customers to the used car lot. (Other reports put this at the Pontiac dealer for the opening of the dealer's showroom. Authentication goes to singer Mac Davis.)

OCT 17 (Mon.) The tour moved on to El Dorado, Arkansas, in a Jaycee-sponsored stage show.

OCT 19 (Wed.) Elvis opened for the Roy Acuff show in Cleveland's Circle Theater.

OCT 20 (Thurs.) The Roy Acuff show remained in Cleveland for a second night.

OCT 21 (Fri.) Roy Acuff's jamboree moved on to St. Louis for an evening performance.

OCT 22 (Sat.) There was a repeat engagement in St. Louis for Roy Acuff and Elvis.

OCT 26 (Wed.) Elvis performed at a local fair in Prichard, Alabama, for WAIP radio disc jockey, Jack Cardwell.

OCT 27 (Thurs.) Elvis continued to perform in Prichard.

OCT 28 (Fri.) Elvis wrapped up his three-day engagement at the Prichard fair.

OCT 29 (Sat.) Elvis was back in Shreveport for an appearance on the "Louisiana Hayride."

During October, the bidding for Elvis' recording contract became very heated. Mercury Records offered Sam Phillips $10,000. This was beaten by Columbia's bid of $15,000. Finally, Atlantic Records, a leader in the rhythm and blues field, offered $25,000.

NOVEMBER

NOV 2 (Wed.) Bob Neal was involved in an auto accident, but he was not seriously hurt.

NOV 4 (Fri.) RCA Victor entered the bidding for Elvis' contract with Sun Records, offering $35,000 to Sam Phillips and $5,000 as a bonus to Elvis, which would cover the back royalties due him.

NOV 5 (Sat.) *I Forgot To Remember To Forget/Mystery Train* appeared on all three of *Billboard*'s national country music charts. The single was number 7 in sales, number

9 on juke boxes, and number 12 in radio plays.

Elvis appeared on the "Louisiana Hayride" in Shreveport.

NOV 6   (Sun.) Elvis performed in Biloxi, Mississippi.

NOV 7   (Mon.) Elvis took his show to the NCO Club at Keesler AFB, Mississippi.

NOV 8   (Tues.) Elvis continued to perform at Keesler AFB.

It was reported that Elvis, Johnny Cash, and Carl Perkins played Amory, Mississippi, about this time. Perkins supposedly wrote *Blue Suede Shoes* while backstage.

NOV 10   (Thurs.) Elvis and Bob Neal traveled to Nashville for the annual Country Music Disk Jockey Convertion being held at the Andrew Jackson Hotel. While at the convention, they reached an agreement with Steve Sholes, head of Specialty Singles for RCA Victor, and Bill Bullock, Singles Division Manager for RCA Victor, concerning a contract for Elvis with the major record company.

NOV 11   (Fri.) Elvis left Nashville in the evening and drove almost 600 miles to Carthage, Texas.

NOV 12   (Sat.) Elvis did very well in *Billboard*'s annual disc jockey poll. He was ranked number 1 in the "Most Promising C&W Artist" category, number 13 in the "Most Played C&W Artist" listing, and number 16 in both the "Favorite C&W Artists" and "Favorite C&W Records" (for *Baby Let's Play House*) categories.

Elvis appeared in the afternoon in Carthage, and he was able to make his regular spot on the "Louisiana Hayride" that night since Carthage is only 100 miles from Shreveport.

NOV 13   (Sun.) Elvis performed two shows at Ellis Auditorium in Memphis. The shows were a "goodbye" to Texas Bill Strength of KWEM radio, who was leaving for Minneapolis. Also on the bill were Hank Thompson, Carl Smith, Charlene Arthur, and Carl Perkins.

NOV 14   (Mon.) Elvis appeared in Forrest City, Arkansas. He was accompanied by Hank Thompson, Charlene Arthur, and Carl Perkins.

NOV 15   (Tues.) Elvis performed in Sheffield, Alabama.

NOV 16   (Wed.) Elvis' tour rolled in to Camden, Arkansas.

NOV 17   (Thurs.) There was a show in Texarkana, Arkansas.

NOV 18   (Fri.) The week-long tour ended with a show in Longview, Texas.

NOV 19   (Sat.) Elvis appeared on the "Louisiana Hayride" which

Elvis is kissed by his mother, Gladys, flanked by (left) Colonel Tom Parker, (right) Vernon, Colman Tilly III, an attorney for RCA Victor, and Bob Neal.

was broadcast remote from Gladewater, Texas.

NOV 20   (Sun.) Elvis signed a three-year contract with RCA Victor
Records. The contract was the standard five percent
of royalties, with an option to renew at the end of three
years. Elvis also signed a "long term writing pact" with
Hill and Range Publishing Company, which was to set
up a separate publishing firm for "Elvis Presley Music,
Inc." The $40,000 paid to Sun Records gave RCA Vic-
tor all five of Elvis' Sun pressings as well as five unreleased songs, while Sun was allowed to press copies of
Mystery Train until the end of 1955. Hill and Range
also acquired Hi-Lo Music from Sun Records, which
gave the company the publishing rights to *Mystery
Train, I'm Left, You're Right, She's Gone* and *You're A
Heartbreaker*. In addition, Hill and Range acquired
That's All Right from Wabash Music.

NOV 21   (Mon.) An internal news release at RCA Victor announced
that Elvis had been signed to the company.

NOV 22   (Tues.) The *Memphis Press-Scimitar* reported that "Elvis
Presley, 20, Memphis recording star and entertainer who
zoomed into bigtime and big money almost overnight,
has been released from his contract with Sun Recording
Company of Memphis and will record exclusively for
RCA Victor."

NOV 25   (Fri.) Elvis appeared at the Woodrow Wilson Junior High
School Auditorium in Port Arthur, Texas. Also appearing were members of the "Louisiana Hayride." Proceeds
from the show went to the Port Arthur Fire Department.
Only a small crowd of about 100 attended, probably including a young Janis Joplin.

NOV 26   (Sat.) Elvis pulled a capacity crowd for his appearance on
the "Louisiana Hayride." Also on the show were Jim-
my Newman, Johnny Horton, Werley Fairburn, George
Jones, Betty Amos, Jeannette Hicks, Hoot and Curley,
Jack Ford, Buddy Attaway, Floyd Cramer, and the
Lump Lump Boys. Guests included Slim Rhodes and
Buddy Thompson.

DECEMBER

DEC 2   (Fri.) Less than two weeks after acquiring Elvis from Sun
Records, RCA Victor re-released the first of the singles
that came as part of the contract, *Mystery Train/*

I Forgot To Remember To Forget.

Elvis brought his show to Atlanta's Sports Arena. Elvis was reportedly paid $300 for his performance but, due to poor attendance, the gate was only $285.

DEC 3   (Sat.) Elvis' signing with RCA Victor made the front page of *Billboard* in an article entitled "Double Deals Hurl Presley Into Stardom." RCA Victor also ran a full page ad in the magazine touting Elvis as "The Most Talked About New Personality In The Last Ten Years."

Billboard also reported that Colonel Tom Parker had recently signed to represent Elvis for personal appearances.

Elvis appeared as part of the stage show for WBAM radio's annual "Talent Search Of The Deep South" at the State Coliseum in Montgomery, Alabama. Also on the bill were Roy Acuff, Kitty Wells, Johnnie and Jack, Jack Turner, Fred Wamble and Buddy Hawk. Over 15,000 attended this final night of the competition.

DEC 10   (Sat.) Elvis' first song folio was published by Hill and Range Publishing Company. The original issue contained the following song sheets: *Rag Mop, I Almost Lost My Mind, Cryin' Heart Blues,* and *I Need You So.* The folio was republished in the spring of 1956, and the above titles were changed for *Blue Suede Shoes, Mystery Train, I Was The One,* and *Heartbreak Hotel.* The original folio sold for one dollar and the re-issue sold for a dollar and twenty-five cents. In addition, several of the photos inside the folio were changed in 1956.

Elvis performed on the "Louisiana Hayride" in Shreveport.

DEC 17   (Sat.) CBS-TV and Jackie Gleason announced that Elvis had been signed to appear on "Stage Show" on four consecutive Saturday nights, starting January 28, 1956. NBC-TV had also been in the bidding for Elvis' first national TV appearance. (See January 28, 1956.)

Elvis performed on the "Louisiana Hayride." The show was a benefit for the local YMCA and originated from Hirsch Memorial Coliseum in Shreveport. This special show helped Elvis out of his contract with the "Louisiana Hayride," which was to run another six months.

DEC 20   (Tues.) RCA Victor re-released the remaining four singles acquired from Sun Records in November: *That's All Right/Blue Moon Of Kentucky, Good Rockin' Tonight/I Don't Care If The Sun Don't Shine, Milkcow Blues Boogie/You're A Heartbreaker,* and *Baby, Let's Play House/I'm Left, You're Right, She's Gone.*

During December, Elvis starred in a benefit show at his alma
   mater, Humes High School, in Memphis. Proceeds went to the
   "discretionary fund," which helped needy children purchase
   milk for lunch.

WINTER
   Elvis was featured in an article in *Country Song Roundup*'s winter
      issue. The article was titled "Rockin' To Stardom." In the
      same issue, Elvis was ranked ninth in a list of the top country
      artists in the nation.
   Country And Western Jamboree magazine, a trade publication,
      reported that Elvis had received 250,000 votes in a reader's poll
      for "New Star Of The Year."

Fame And Fortune

**ALL
SHOOK
UP
▬▬▬
ELVIS**
Day-By-Day,
1956

JANUARY

JAN 5   (Thurs.) Elvis traveled to Nashville to meet with Steve
         Sholes and Chet Atkins, RCA Victor's A&R (artist and
         repertoire) man for country music, as well as an RCA
         Victor recording star in his own right. Plans were made
         for Elvis' first recording session the next week.

JAN 7   (Sat.) RCA Victor ran a full page ad in *Billboard* pro-
         claiming their lineup of country artists to be "First in
         '56." Elvis' photo was included.
         Elvis made his first "Louisiana Hayride" appearance of
         1956.

JAN 10   (Tues.) Elvis had his first recording session for RCA Vic-
         tor. The session was held in a studio that RCA had con-
         verted from a building leased from the Methodist Tele-
         vision, Radio, and Film Commission at 1525 McGavok
         Street in Nashville. In addition to Scotty and Bill, D.J.
         Fontana was on drums for his first session with Elvis,
         even though he had been touring with Elvis throughout
         most of 1955. Chet Atkins played guitar, and Floyd
         Cramer was on piano. The first song recorded was *I Got
         A Woman*, a 1955 rhythm and blues hit for Ray Charles.
         Elvis had been performing the song for almost a year
         and had even attempted to record it for Sun Records in
         February 1955. Chet Atkins did not play guitar on *I
         Got A Woman*. The second song recorded was an Elvis
         original, *Heartbreak Hotel*, which he had picked up in
         Jacksonville from one of the composers, Mae Boren
         Axton, mother of country star Hoyt Axton and part-
         time publicist for Hank Snow. The next song recorded
         was *Money Honey*, a 1952 rhythm and blues hit for
         Clyde McPhatter and the Drifters. According to Chet
         Atkins, Elvis got so worked up during the session that

In a publicity photo for "Stage Show," Elvis is flanked by Tommy and Jimmy Dorsey.

he split the inseam of his new pink pants.

JAN 11   (Wed.) Sometime after midnight, three vocalists were
          added to the recording session: Gordon Stoker of the
          Jordanaires, and Ben and Brock Speer of the Speer
          Family, both well known gospel groups. Two more
          songs were recorded with the background vocalists: *I'm
          Counting On You* and *I Was The One*, neither of which
          had been hits for any other artists.

JAN 14   (Sat.) Elvis returned to Shreveport for an appearance on
          the "Louisiana Hayride."

JAN 20   (Fri.) Steve Sholes supervised the splicing of two takes of
          I Love You Because, originally recorded in July 1954
          for Sun Records. The two takes, both almost three-and-
          a-half minutes long, were combined into a smoother
          version which was shorter by almost a minute (2:39).

JAN 21   (Sat.) Elvis was back on the "Louisiana Hayride."

JAN 23   (Mon.) During the week, Elvis, Scotty, Bill and D.J. fre-
          quently rehearsed at Elvis' home for the upcoming tele-
          vision appearance on "Stage Show."

JAN 27   (Fri.) RCA Victor released the first of Elvis' singles con-
          taining material original to the label, *Heartbreak Hotel
          /I Was The One.* (Interesting note: There really was
          a Heartbreak Hotel, built in 1915 in Kenansville, Flori-
          da, on State Road 523 just off US 41, about fifty miles
          south of Orlando. The two-story brick building has
          been owned by James Wallace Webb, a local preacher,
          since 1959. There is no evidence that Mae Boren Ax-
          ton or Tommy Durden, the song's composers, were
          aware of the hotel's existence, even though they lived in
          Jacksonville, about 150 miles to the north.)

          Elvis performed in Austin, Texas. Following the show, he,
          Scotty, Bill, and D.J. drove to Dallas where they caught
          a flight to New York.

JAN 28   (Sat.) Elvis and his band arrived in New York in the morn-
          ing. They stayed at the Warwick Hotel. In the after-
          noon, there were rehearsals for that evening's show.

          Elvis made his first national television appearance on
          CBS-TV's "Stage Show," a Jackie Gleason production
          which featured Tommy and Jimmy Dorsey, famous big
          band leaders from the 1940s. (The 8:00 p.m. (EST)
          show served as a lead-in for Gleason's 8:30 p.m. show,
          which featured "The Honeymooners.") Elvis was listed
          as guest emcee for the show. Other guests included

singer Sarah Vaughn and comedian Gene Sheldon.
Elvis was paid $1,250 for each of the six "Stage Shows"
on which he appeared. On this show, he sang *Shake,
Rattle and Roll,* coupled with *Flip, Flop and Fly,*
and *I Got A Woman.* The show was broadcast
from CBS Television Studio 50 on Broadway, between
53rd and 54th Streets in New York. In the Nielsen
ratings for the week, "Stage Show" got 18.4% of
the national TV audience compared to 34.6% for
"The Perry Como Show," which had aired at the
same time.

JAN 29   (Sun.) Elvis performed in Richmond, Virginia.

JAN 30   (Mon.) Elvis returned to New York for his first recording
session at RCA Victor's studios, located at 155 East
24th Street. The only extra musician, other than
Elvis' usual trio, was Shorty Long on piano. Songs recorded during the session, which started at 11:00 a.m.
and ran into the night, included *Blue Suede Shoes*, recently released on Sun Records by Carl Perkins; *My
Baby Left Me*, a late 1940s rhythm and blues hit for
Arthur "Big Boy" Crudup; *One-Sided Love Affair, So
Glad You're Mine* and *I'm Gonna Sit Right Down And
Cry (Over You)*, which had not been hits for any other
artists; and *Tutti Frutti*, Little Richard's 1955 hit.

JAN 31   (Tues.) Elvis was interviewed by Fred Danzig at RCA's
studios.

FEBRUARY

FEB 3   (Fri.) Elvis returned to RCA Victor's New York studios
for another recording session. The personnel was the
same as the session on January 30--31. This session produced *Lawdy Miss Clawdy*, recorded in 1952 by Lloyd
Price, and *Shake, Rattle And Roll*, Bill Haley's smash
hit from 1954. Although not generally credited, Elvis
later said he played piano on *Lawdy Miss Clawdy*.

FEB 4   (Sat.) Elvis made his second appearance on "Stage Show."
He sang *Baby Let's Play House* and *Tutti Frutti*. Nielson
ratings for the show were down from the previous week at
18.2% against 38.5% for Perry Como's show. Other guests
on the show were comedian Joe E. Brown and comic chim-
panzees Tippy and Cobina.

FEB 5   (Sun.) Elvis appeared at the Montecello Auditorium in
          Norfolk, Virginia.
FEB 6   (Mon.) Elvis performed at the National Theater in
          Greensboro, North Carolina, at 8:00 p.m.
FEB 11   (Sat.) *Billboard* reviewed *Heartbreak Hotel/I Was The
          One* in its country and western "Spotlight" section,
          saying: "Presley's first Victor disc might easily break
          in both markets. 'Heartbreak Hotel' is a strong blues
          item wrapped up in his usual powerful style and a great
          beat."
          Elvis again appeared on "Stage Show" in New York. He
          sang *Blue Suede Shoes* and *Heartbreak Hotel.* Other
          guests on the show were Ella Fitzgerald and Jackie Miles.
FEB 18   (Sat.) *Billboard* again called attention to *Heartbreak Hotel*
          in its c&w "Best Buys" section, saying that the record
          had "snowballed rapidly in the past two weeks with pop
          and r&b customers joining Presley's hillbilly fans in de-
          manding the disc."
          Elvis made his fourth appearance on "Stage Show" in New
          York. He sang *Tutti Frutti* and *I Was The One.*
          Other guests on the show were George DeWitt and the
          Tokayers.
FEB 21   (Tues.) Elvis performed at the Florida Theater in Sarasota,
          Florida, with Justin Tubb, the Carter Sisters, and Benny
          Martin.
          During the week, the Madison, Tennessee, offices of Hank
          Snow Enterprises and Jamboree Attractions (Colonel
          Parker) were enlarged and new staff was hired to handle
          the booming business generated by Elvis' growing na-
          tional popularity.
FEB 25   (Sat.) Elvis had his first national number 1 record as *I For-
          got To Remember To Forget* topped *Billboard*'s c&w
          "Best Sellers In Stores" chart for the week ending Febru-
          ary 15th. The single remained at number 1 for two
          weeks.
          Elvis returned to the "Louisiana Hayride" in Shreveport.

     Also in February, *Country Song Roundup* magazine ran an article
       title "The Elvis Presley Story." The story offered readers little
       in the way of factual information, and only added to the grow-
       ing legend surrounding Elvis.

An early publicity photo shows a blonder-than-usual Elvis in 1956.

MARCH

MAR 3   (Sat.) *Billboard* ran an article entitled "Presley Hot As $1 Pistol On Victor" which said, in part, "The hottest artist on the RCA Victor label this week has been none other than the amazin', young, country warbler, Elvis Presley." The article reported that Elvis had six singles in the company's top 25 best sellers: *Heartbreak Hotel/ I Was The One*, number 2; *Mystery Train/I Forgot To Remember To Forget*, number 9; *Good Rockin' To-night*, number 14; *Baby, Let's Play House*, number 15; *That's All Right*, number 21; and *Milkcow Blues Boogie,* number 23.

        Elvis broke into the popular field in *Billboard* as *Heartbreak Hotel* entered "The Top 100" at number 68 for the week ending February 22nd. This list was a tabulation of dealer, disk jockey, and jukebox operator replies in popular music. *Heartbreak Hotel* stayed on the chart for twenty-seven weeks, eventually reaching number 1. The single also entered the c&w "Best Sellers In Stores" chart at number 9. It stayed on the country charts for twenty-seven weeks, reaching number 1.

        Elvis appeared on the "Louisiana Hayride" in Shreveport.

MAR 7   (Wed.) It was reported that *Heartbreak Hotel* had passed the 300,000 mark in sales after only three weeks on the market.

MAR 10   (Sat.) RCA Victor ran a half-page ad in *Billboard* touting Elvis as "The New Singing Rage." On "The Top 100," *I Was The One* entered the list at number 84. It stayed on the chart for sixteen weeks and peaked at number 23. *Heartbreak Hotel* was a runaway best seller, and along with *I Forgot To Remember To Forget*, Elvis had records in two of the top three positions on the c&w sales chart.

        Elvis made an appearance on the "Louisiana Hayride" in Shreveport.

MAR 13   (Tues.) RCA Victor released Elvis' first long play album, **Elvis Presley**. The company also released Elvis' first extended play, which featured *Blue Suede Shoes*, and a double EP, with eight songs. Both were titled **Elvis Presley**.

MAR 14   (Wed.) Elvis appeared at the Fox Theater in Atlanta. He performed three shows each day, at 4:30, 7:18, and

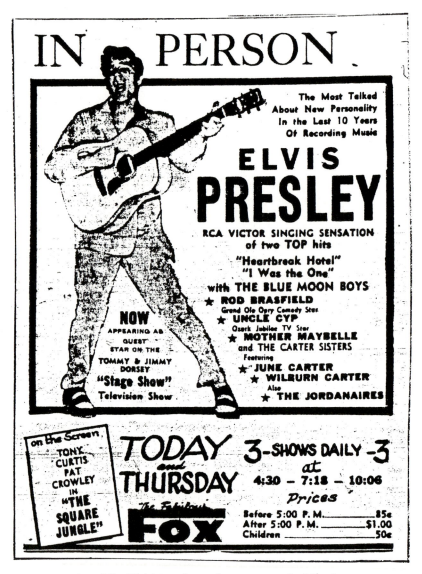

An ad for Elvis' two days of appearances in Atlanta.

10:06 p.m. with "Grand Ole' Opry" star Rod Brasfield, Uncle Cyp of the Ozark Jubilee, Mother Maybelle and the Carter Sisters with June Carter, the Wilburn Brothers, and the Jordanaires. Elvis' show alternated with the movie "The Square Jungle," which starred Tony Curtis and Pat Crowley. Admission was eighty-five cents before 5:00 p.m., a dollar after 5:00 p.m.; children were fifty cents.

MAR 15   (Thurs.) Elvis signed a long-term managerial contract with Colonel Tom Parker. Colonel Parker had been masterminding Elvis' career since August 1955, but he had not signed a managerial contract until Bob Neal's contract with Elvis expired. Although not publicized, it was assumed at the time that Elvis would receive seventy-five percent and the Colonel twenty-five percent of any profits.

The *Atlanta Constitution*, in a short review of the previous night's show, mentioned "turnaway throngs" for the "semi-hillbilly singing sensation."

Meanwhile, Elvis continued to play the Fox Theater for another night.

MAR 17   (Sat.) *Heartbreak Hotel* was number 1 in Seattle in the *pop* field for the week ending March 7th, according to *Billboard*. The single also topped the national c&w sales chart, while it came in number 2 to *I Forgot To Remember To Forget* in jukebox plays. Elvis held the number 1 spot on the country charts in Houston, Nashville, New Orleans, and Richmond. In Memphis, *I Was The One* was number 3.

Elvis returned to New York for his fifth appearance on "Stage Show." The show was now aired at 8:30 p.m. (EST), following "The Jackie Gleason Show." Also on the show were comedian Henny Youngman and eleven-year-old organist Glenn Derringer. Elvis sang *Blue Suede Shoes* and *Heartbreak Hotel*.

MAR 22   (Thurs.) Elvis appeared at the Mosque Theater in Richmond, Virginia, for two shows.

MAR 23   (Fri.) Elvis sent a telegram to Sun Records' star Carl Perkins, who had been hurt in an automobile accident in Dover, Delaware, on March 21st while enroute from Norfolk to New York for an appearance on Perry Como's TV show (which would have been opposite Elvis' sixth appearance on "Stage Show").

Elvis' screen test pitted him against veteran actor
Frank Faylen.

Elvis and Milton Berle on the deck of the U.S.S. Hancock.

MAR 24   (Sat.) *Billboard*, in highlighting the album **Elvis Presley** in
          its "Review Spotlight" section, said: "In view of his
          success on singles, the LP might well chalk up a healthy
          sales record."

          Elvis was interviewed in his room at the Warwick Hotel by
          Robert Carlton Brown.

          Elvis made his sixth and final appearance on "Stage Show"
          at 8:30 p.m. over CBS-TV. He sang *Money Honey* and
          Heartbreak Hotel. Ratings from the Nielsen Corp. gave
          "Stage Show" 20.9% of the national audience, compared
          to Perry Como's 31.8%. Over the past eight weeks, the
          ratings for "Stage Show" had not been affected signifi-
          cantly by Elvis' appearances. The other guest on the
          show was Glenn Derringer.

MAR 25   (Sun.) Elvis flew to Los Angeles for a meeting with Hal
          Wallis, producer for Paramount Pictures.

MAR 31   (Sat.) Elvis' album, **Elvis Presley**, entered *Billboard*'s
          "Best Selling Packaged Records — Popular Albums"
          chart at number 11. It reached number 1 and stayed
          on the chart for forty-nine weeks.

          RCA Victor ran a full-page ad in *Billboard* under the ban-
          ner "A Red Hot Star Is Born On RCA Victor Records."
          The ad announced Elvis' new album, as well as the single
          extended play **Elvis Presley** and the double EP **Elvis
          Presley**. According to a brief note, Elvis' album had
          already passed the 100,000 mark in sales.

In March, Elvis purchased a red-and-black, three-wheel Messerschmitt automobile, I.D. #56007.

APRIL

APR 1   (Sun.) At Paramount studios in Hollywood, Elvis had a
          screen test for Hal Wallis. He sang *Blue Suede Shoes* and
          performed a scene from "The Rainmaker," a film which
          was as yet unmade. Elvis acted opposite veteran actor
          Frank Faylen, who had been filming "Gunfight At The
          O.K. Corral" at Paramount.

APR 3   (Tues.) Elvis appeared on "The Milton Berle Show,"
          broadcast from 8:00 to 9:00 p.m. over ABC-TV. The
          show originated from the deck of the aircraft carrier,
          USS Hancock, which was docked at the San Diego Naval

Station. Elvis sang *Blue Suede Shoes, Shake Rattle And Roll,* and *Heartbreak Hotel,* and participated in a comedy skit with Berle. The show alternated on a weekly basis with Martha Raye's show and "The Chevy Show." Other guests on this show included actress Esther Williams, comedian Arnold Stang, and Harry James and his orchestra.

APR 4   (Wed.) In the afternoon, Elvis autographed copies of his album at a local San Diego record shop.

Elvis performed at the San Diego Arena. The U.S. Navy Shore Patrol had to be called out to protect Elvis from the over-enthusiastic crowd. Elvis temporarily stopped the show in an attempt to get the crowd to return to their seats. The show started at 8:15 p.m. Admission was a dollar twenty-five in advance, a dollar fifty at the door.

APR 5   (Thurs.) Elvis performed for a second day in San Diego's Arena. The total gross for the two days was $17,250, with 11,250 fans attending the shows.

APR 6   (Fri.) In Hollywood, Elvis signed a seven-year contract with Hal Wallis and Paramount Pictures. The initial contract called for three movies, with Elvis' salary to be $100,000 for the first film, $150,000 for the second and $200,000 for the third. (Because Wallis did not have a suitable picture for Elvis to star in, Elvis was loaned to 20th Century-Fox for a picture titled "The Reno Brothers" at this time.)

APR 7   (Sat.) In *Billboard*'s country charts, *Heartbreak Hotel* copped a "Triple Crown" for being number 1 on all three lists for the week ending March 28th. *Blue Suede Shoes* entered "The Top 100" at number 88, where it stayed twelve weeks and peaked at number 24. (*Blue Suede Shoes* was the first song on the **Elvis Presley** EP.)

Elvis made his last "regular" appearance on the "Louisiana Hayride" in Shreveport. He would have one final performance in December to terminate his contract.

APR 10   (Tues.) Within a month of its release, Elvis' first album had sold an astonishing 362,000 copies, making it RCA Victor's first $1 million album by a solo artist.

Robert Johnson's article in the *Memphis Press-Scimitar,* titled "Our Elvis Presley – In Vista Vision" told readers of Elvis' recent signing with Hal Wallis and Paramount

Pictures.

Returning to Memphis aboard an airplane, Elvis' flight had engine trouble and almost crashed in Texas. Elvis had a fear of flying for many years afterward, and traveled by train or motorhome for years as part of a promise to his mother, whenever possible.

APR 11   (Wed.) *Variety* reported that *Heartbreak Hotel* had gone over the million mark in sales.

Elvis traveled to Nashville for another recording session with RCA Victor, which ran from 9:00 a.m. to noon. Joining Elvis and his trio were Chet Atkins on guitar, Marvin Hughes on piano, and Gordon Stoker, Ben and Brock Speers on vocals. Only one song was recorded, the ballad *I Want You, I Need You, I Love You.* At the session, Elvis was awarded a gold record for a million copies sold of *Heartbreak Hotel*.

APR 13   (Fri.) It is probable that Elvis made a personal appearance at the Municipal Auditorium in Wichita Falls, Texas.

APR 14   (Sat.) In a *Billboard* article, it was reported that *Heartbreak Hotel* was selling between 25,000 and 30,000 copies a day.

APR 15   (Sun.) Elvis played the Municipal Auditorum in San Antonio, Texas at 8:00 p.m. Also on the bill were Hank Locklin, the Louvin Brothers, and Ray Price. Tickets were $2.00.

mid-APR In mid-April, RCA Victor released Elvis' second extended play record, **Heartbreak Hotel**, which featured both sides of Elvis' first RCA Victor release as well as *Money Honey* and *I Forgot To Remember To Forget.*

APR 16   (Mon.) Elvis appeared in Corpus Christi, Texas.

APR 17   (Tues.) It is probable that Elvis performed in Oklahoma City.

APR 18   (Wed.) Elvis appeared in Tulsa, Oklahoma.

APR 19   (Thurs.) It is probable that Elvis traveled to Amarillo, Texas, for that night's show.

APR 20   (Fri.) Elvis' concert at the Northside Convention Center in Fort Worth was sold out.

APR 21   (Sat.) *Billboard* reported that Elvis' record sales were $75,000 a day in retail record shops around the country. In Canada, Elvis had the first eight singles of Victor's top ten sellers. In the U.S., Elvis' LPs and EPs were selling at the rate of 8,000 a day, while the singles were selling 50,000 copies each day, accounting for fifty percent of RCA Victor's total pop business.

An ad for Elvis' opening night at the New Frontier Hotel.

The 24-foot promotional figure of Elvis greets guests outside the New Frontier Hotel in Las Vegas.

Heartbreak Hotel was reported by *Billboard* to be number
1 in record sales in pop music for the week ending April
11th.

Elvis' tour stopped for a show in Dallas.

APR 22   (Sun.) Elvis appeared at the San Antonio Municipal Auditorium for a matinee and evening performance. Over
6,000 attended each show with a total gross of $14,300.
During the matinee, Elvis barely escaped with his life as
3,000 fans stormed the stage.

APR 23   (Mon.) Elvis opened in Las Vegas at the New Frontier
Hotel's Venus Room. He was third on the bill to Freddy
Martin and His Orchestra, and comedian Shecky Greene.
Elvis was billed as an "Extra Added Attraction" and as
"The Atomic Powered Singer." On the first night (the
23rd), Elvis closed the show, but after that night, he
opened each show. There were two shows each night,
one at 8:00 p.m. (dinner) and at midnight (cocktails).
There was a two dollar minimum for each show. Elvis
was paid $12,500 per week for his two-week engagement.
(In the film "Hollywood Or Bust" starring Dean Martin
and Jerry Lewis, the large, twenty-four foot tall figure of
Elvis outside the New Frontier Hotel can be seen in the
background in several shots.)

APR 28   (Sat.) In *Billboard*'s regional popular charts for the week
ending April 18th, *Heartbreak Hotel* was number 1 in
Baltimore, Buffalo, Chicago, Cincinnati, Denver, Detroit,
Kansas City, Milwaukee, Minneapolis-St. Paul, New Orleans, St. Louis, Seattle and Toronto.

A special matinee was held for teenagers who could not
attend the regular nighttime performances at the New
Frontier. Teenagers were charged a dollar for a bottle
of soda pop and a chance to see Elvis perform. Proceeds from this special show went toward lights for a
baseball park for the youth of Las Vegas. About 700
attended the show.

APR 30   (Mon.) The first major article about Elvis appeared in a
national news magazine, *Life*. Titled "A Howling Hillbilly Success," the article mentioned Elvis' March tour
of Texas and his Las Vegas engagement.

MAY

MAY 2   *Variety*, in reviewing Elvis' debut in Las Vegas, said he "doesn't hit the mark. The loud braying of the tunes which rocketed him to the bigtime is wearing and the applause comes back edged with a polite sound. For the teenagers he's a whiz; for the average Vegas spender, he's a fizz."

MAY 4   (Fri.) RCA Victor released Elvis' second "original" single, *I Want You, I Need You, I Love You* b/w *My Baby Left Me*.

MAY 5   (Sat.) Elvis' long play album, **Elvis Presley**, was number 1 on *Billboard*'s LP chart. It remained number 1 for ten weeks. The single, *Heartbreak Hotel*, also made number 1 on "The Top 100," where it remained at the top of the chart for six weeks.

It was reported in *Billboard* that radio station WSLM of Salem, Indiana, had inaugurated a program called "Rockin' With Presley."

MAY 9   (Wed.) Elvis closed his two-week engagement at the New Frontier Hotel. It was reported in the Las Vegas daily newspaper that he was replaced on the bill by "starlet" Jana Mason. (According to a May 9th front-page article in *Variety*, Elvis closed on May 7th and was replaced by single Roberta Sherwood.)

MAY 11 (Fri.) The Presleys bought a home at 1034 Audubon Drive in Memphis for $40,000. This was the first time the Presleys had actually owned a house. The home was a green and white ranch-style house.

MAY 12 (Sat.) Elvis was voted the top new c&w artist and the favorite c&w artist in a poll conducted as part of *Billboard*'s annual review of the Music Operators Of America (jukebox owners). *Billboard* also reported in an article entitled "E.P. Is V.I.P. For Victor" that *I Want You, I Need You, I Love You* had the largest advance order of any RCA Victor release, with 300,000 copies ordered by April 3rd. Elvis was also the first RCA Victor artist to have two million sellers in a row. *Heartbreak Hotel* had sold 1,350,000, and was still selling at a pace of 70,000 a week. The LP, **Elvis Presley** was now the biggest selling album in RCA Victor's history.

Billboard, in a rare move, ran a review of *My Baby Left Me/I Want You, I Need You, I Love You* in all three "Review Spotlight" sections (pop, c&w, r&b). The journal called the single "another pair of exciting Presley sides."

On *Billboard*'s pop music charts for the week ending May 2nd, *Heartbreak Hotel* was number 1 in sales, jukebox play, and disk jockey plays, as well as number 1 on "The Top 100" and on the "Honor Roll Of Hits," which listed the nation's top songs (as opposed to strictly records). *Money Honey* (representing the **Heartbreak Hotel** EP) entered "The Top 100" at number 84. It stayed on the chart for only five weeks and peaked at number 76.

MAY 13 (Sun.) Elvis performed two shows in St. Paul, Minnesota. Ten extra policemen had to be hired by the promoter to protect Elvis during the afternoon and evening shows. However, it was reported that the turnout was "scanty."

MAY 14 (Mon.) Elvis was featured in two magazine articles. *Newsweek* ran an article titled "Hillbilly On A Pedestal," and *Time* covered Elvis' quick rise to national prominence in "Teener's Hero."

Elvis appeared at the Mary E.E. Sawyer Auditorium in La Crosse, Wisconsin. Four thousand fans attended the 7:30 p.m. show, but only 1,200 came to the 9:30 p.m. performance. In addition to his regular repertoire, Elvis sang *Only You*, a recent hit for the Platters. Elvis stayed at the Stoddard Hotel.

MAY 15 (Tues.) Elvis appeared as part of Memphis' Cotton Festival. He shared top billing with Hank Snow at Ellis Auditorium. At the same time, singer Eddie Fisher was performing at the Show Boat, but Elvis easily outdrew him. Reportedly, Fisher even closed his show early. At the Tent Theater, Mother Maybelle and the Carter Sisters, George Morgan and Hal and Ginger Willis held forth with a country show. Elvis' show attracted so many people that both sides of the auditorium were opened, and he had to turn back and forth to face each audience.

MAY 16 (Wed.) In Arkansas, Elvis appeared at the Little Rock Auditorium.

MAY 17 (Thurs.) Elvis played the Shrine Mosque in Springfield, Missouri at 7:00 p.m. Tickets were a dollar-fifty, two
MAY 18 dollars, and two-fifty.

(Fri.) Elvis appeared before 4,000 screaming fans in

While on the road, Elvis makes a backstage call to his mother.

Elvis listens to a demonstration copy of his next record.

Des Moines, Iowa. The girls from St. Joseph's Academy
were advised not to attend the concert.

MAY 19 (Sat.) In a full-page ad in *Billboard*, RCA Victor proclaimed that *I Want You, I Need You, I Love You* had
sold an astounding 213,000 copies in the first two days
after its release on May 4th. After six days, 389,000
copies had been sold, and by mid-May, the single had
sold 653,219 copies.

Billboard placed *My Baby Left Me/I Want You, I Need
You, I Love You* in the "Best Buys" section, saying:
"both sides have gotten generous deejay play." The
single placed number 5 on the "Coming Up Strong"
chart, with *My Baby Left Me* still the "A" side.

Elvis brought his show to the University of Nebraska's
Coliseum in Lincoln. Tickets were scaled up to $2.50,
and Elvis filled half the Coliseum.

MAY 20 (Sun.) Seven thousand fans filled two shows in Omaha
with gross receipts topping $14,000. Tickets were
$2.50 for the best seats.

MAY 23 (Wed.) *My Baby Left Me/I Want You, I Need You, I
Love You* entered *Billboard's* country and western
singles chart for May 25th at number 13. It reached
number 1 and stayed twenty weeks.

MAY 24 (Thurs.) At a Kansas City, Missouri show, 2,500 fans, out
of a possible 12,000 seats, made it a memorable day by
storming the stage after Elvis had sung only half a
dozen songs, ending the show at 10:00 p.m.

MAY 25 (Fri.) Elvis brought in $16,184 in Detroit's Fox Theater
with three shows. Attendance totaled 11,900 out of a
possible 15,000 seats. Admission was $1.50 to $2.50.

MAY 26 (Sat.) The cover of *Cashbox* had a photo taken at the
New Frontier Hotel in Las Vegas, with Elvis holding a
gold record. Along with Elvis were Colonel Tom Parker,
Freddie Martin, and several RCA Victor executives.

For contributing the most to c & w music, Elvis was voted
the "Jimmie Rodgers Achievement Award" during the
annual Jimmie Rodgers Memorial Celebration in Meridian, Mississippi. The voting was done by fan clubs
and members of the music trade. Elvis was not present.

In *Billboard, I Want You, I Need You, I Love You* was the
number 1 record on the "Coming Up Strong Chart."
Heartbreak Hotel held down the number 1 spot on the
"Honor Roll Of Hits," "The Top 100," and was number

1 in store sales, jukebox plays, and radio airplay in the pop field, and number 1 in sales and jukeboxes in the country field.

Rain kept the crowds down in Columbus, Ohio, where Elvis had two evening shows at the 3,964-seat Veteran's Memorial Auditorium. Tickets were $2.50 tops, and the gross receipts were $8,481.

MAY 27   (Sun.) Rain continued as Elvis performed two shows at the 4,000-seat Fieldhouse of the University of Dayton, Ohio. Elvis was an hour-and-a-half late for the afternoon show. About 1,800 attended each show. Tickets were pegged at $2.50, and Elvis was paid $1,800 per show. The shows reportedly grossed $7,208. (Many critics felt that the small crowds on this tour were a result of the $2.50 price for the best tickets.)

In May, *Country And Western Jamboree* magazine ran an article titled "Overnight Stardom Comes To Elvis Presley."

JUNE

JUN 2   (Sat.) In a *Billboard* article entitled "Elvis Presley Pacted For Day At Tupelo Fair," the details of Elvis' September 1956 appearance at the Mississippi-Alabama Fair in Tupelo were outlined.

On *Billboard*'s charts, three of Elvis' singles held down the number 1 spots on the three "Best Sellers In Stores" lists: *I Want You, I Need You, I Love You* in popular music, *I Forgot To Remember To Forget* in the c&w field, and *Heartbreak Hotel* in rhythm and blues.

JUN 3   (Sun.) Elvis performed at 3:00 and 8:00 p.m. at the Oakland Auditorium Arena. The first part of the show lasted an hour and a half; Elvis was on stage only twenty minutes. Three thousand fans made it to the afternoon show, and 2,500 paid $2.50 tops for the evening show. After the show, Elvis flew to Los Angeles, arriving at the International Airport about 4:00 a.m.

JUN 4   (Mon.) After a few hours' sleep at the Knickerbocker Hotel, Elvis went to the ABC-TV studios for a rehearsal of the upcoming Milton Berle television show.

In a front page article titled "This Is Elvis," the *San Francisco Chronicle* said Elvis "sent two crowds of teenagers into screaming hysteria." An Oakland policeman was

Elvis clowns with Milton Berle during his second appearance on Berle's TV show.

quoted as saying, "If he did that stuff on the street, we'd lock him up."

JUN 5   (Tues.) Elvis appeared on the final "Milton Berle Show" of the season, broadcast over ABC-TV from 8:00 to 9:00 p.m. (EDT). He sang *I Want You, I Need You, I Love You*, and clowned around with Berle during *Hound Dog*. The Nielson ratings for the show topped the popular "Sgt. Bilko Show" for the only time that season. During the show, which originated live from ABC-TV's studios in Los Angeles, Elvis was presented with two Triple Crown Awards from *Billboard* magazine for *Heartbreak Hotel*, which had topped the sales, juke box, and disc jockey lists in both pop and country music. Also on the Berle show were Debra Paget, Elvis' co-star in "Love Me Tender"; Irish McCalla, star of TV's "Sheena, Queen Of The Jungle"; comedian Arnold Stang; Barry Gordon, seven-year-old singer; and Les Baxter and His Orchestra. Elvis was paid $5,000.

JUN 6   (Wed.) Elvis appeared at the San Diego Arena at 8th and Harbor Drive at 7:30 p.m. With him were the Flaim Sextet, comedian Phil Maraquin, Frankie Conners, Miss Jackie Little, and the Jordanaires. The show was a sell out of all 2,500 seats priced at a dollar fifty advance, two dollars at the door. (Notice that the top ticket price has been reduced to two dollars after the small crowds during the May tour.)

JUN 7   (Thurs.) Elvis brought his show to the Long Beach Municipal Auditorium. General admission was a dollar fifty for the 7:30 p.m. show. Reserved seats were two dollars. The performance was standing room only as 3,300 listened as Elvis sang *Hound Dog, Blue Suede Shoes, Heartbreak Hotel, Long Tall Sally*, and *That's All Right*.

JUN 8   (Fri.) Elvis appeared at the Shrine Auditorium in Los Angeles at 7:30 p.m.

JUN 9   (Sat.) In *Billboard, Heartbreak Hotel* topped all three of the c&w charts again for the week ending May 30th.

JUN 11   (Mon.) During the week, Elvis and his parents vacationed at the Gulf Hills Dude Ranch in Ocean Springs, Mississippi. Elvis often dated his "Biloxi sweetheart," June Juanico.

JUN 13   (Wed.) *Variety*'s review of the previous weeks' "Milton Berle Show" said Elvis' appearance "certainly added no values to the program."

In New York, NBC-TV management said that Elvis would not be allowed to bump and grind on the Steve Allen TV show on July 1st. Allen said that there had been strong pressure to cancel Elvis' appearance altogether.

JUN 16   (Sat.) In a *Billboard* article entitled "Presley On Pan But Cash Keeps Rolling," the reaction to Elvis' recent appearance on the Milton Berle TV show was reviewed. The final analysis held that Elvis's popularity was unstoppable.

JUN 20   (Wed.) Elvis was interviewed by Wink Martindale on the Memphis TV show, "Dance Party," on KLAC-TV.

JUN 22   (Fri.) Elvis was mentioned in the popular "Peanuts" cartoon strip drawn by Charles Schulz. In the strip, Lucy confronted classical music-lover Schroeder with a photo of Elvis. Her exclamation of "Yes, sir, boy!" brought an agonized "Oh, good grief!" from Schroeder.

Elvis started another tour with three shows at the Paramount Theater in Atlanta, sharing the marquee with the movie "Fury At Gunsight Pass." Elvis performed at 2:00, 5:50 and 8:30 p.m. Tickets for both the movie and stage show were $1.25. The stage show consisted of the Carter Family; Rod Brasfield and Uncle Cyp, two comics from the "Grand Ole' Opry"; and the Jordanaires. Elvis' portion of the show started with *Heartbreak Hotel*. Other songs included *Long Tall Sally, I Was The One, Baby Let's Play House, I Want You I Need You I Love You, Blue Suede Shoes,* and *Hound Dog.*

JUN 23   (Sat.) An article in *America* magazine by Fr. Drinan, S.J., warned readers to "Beware Elvis Presley."

Elvis performed four shows in Atlanta, at 12:35, 3:15, 5:30, and 8:30 p.m.

JUN 24   (Sun.) Still at the Paramount in Atlanta, Elvis performed at 2:00, 5:30, and 8:30 p.m.

JUN 25   (Mon.) Elvis appeared at 7:00 and 9:30 p.m. at the Auditorium in Savannah, Georgia. Over 3,500 fans filled the Auditorium for each show.

JUN 26   (Tues.) Elvis performed only one show at the Coliseum in Charlotte, North Carolina.

JUN 27   (Wed.) It was reported in the press that production at RCA Victor was up twenty percent due to Elvis' sales, and that Elvis was responsible for twenty percent of

During rehearsals for Steve Allen's TV show, Elvis discusses clothes with music director Skitch Henderson.

Elvis sings *Hound Dog* **to Sherlock.**

RCA's singles business.

Over 6,000 fans filled Bell Auditorium in Augusta, Georgia, for one show.

JUN 28   (Thurs.) Elvis appeared at a baseball park in Charlotte, North Carolina, for one show. Following the personal appearance, Elvis and his cousin, Junior Smith, caught the train for New York while Scotty, Bill and D.J. traveled by car to Richmond, Virginia.

JUN 29   (Fri.) Elvis arrived in New York in the morning and went immediately to rehearsals for the upcoming Steve Allen TV show at a rehearsal in mid-town Manhattan. That night, Elvis caught the Richmond, Fredricksburg, and Potomac Railroad train to Richmond, Virginia, arriving the next morning.

JUN 30   (Sat.) After resting at the Hotel Jefferson, Elvis appeared at the Shrine Mosque Theater. He performed two shows, at 5:00 and 8:00 p.m. Also on the bill were Doris and Lee Strom, dancers; the Flaim Brothers, comedians; magician Phil Maraquin; and the Jordanaires. Following the show, Elvis, the band and the Jordanaires caught the 10:50 p.m. train back to New York.

The June issue of *Record Whirl* magazine ran an article titled "What's All The Shouting About?"

Country And Western Jamboree, in its June issue, ranked Elvis as the number one "Best New Male Singer." Others who made the list were (2) Sonny James, (3) Al Terry, (4) Johnny Cash, (5) Carl Perkins, (6) George Jones, (7) Justin Tubb, (8) Mitchell Torok, (9) Jerry Reed, and (10) Jimmy Dean.

JULY

JUL 1   (Sun.) Elvis arrived at Penn Station in New York at 6:15 a.m. He slept during the day at the Warwick Hotel. That night, he made his only appearance on "The Steve Allen Show," broadcast from the Hudson Theater on NBC-TV from 8:00 to 9:00 p.m. (EDT). He sang *I Want You, I Need You, I Love You* and *Hound Dog* (to a bassett hound named Sherlock), and he performed in his only comedy skit, "Range Roundup," with Allen, Andy Griffith, and Imogene Coca. Also on the Allen show was Milton Berle, who talked about Elvis' appearance on

Berle's show in June. Other guests on Allen's show in-
cluded singers Steve Lawrence and Edie Gorme, Skitch
Henderson and His Orchestra, and announcer Gene
Rayburn. Elvis was paid $5,500 for his appearance.
Trendex gave Allen's show a rating of 22.2% against
Ed Sullivan's 14.8% This was Allen's second show of
the season. He had started in June to get the jump
on Sullivan.

At 11:30 p.m., Elvis was interviewed from his hotel room
by Hy Gardner, a local *Herald-Tribune* columnist, who
had a show titled "Hy Gardner Calling!" over WRCA-
TV (channel 4). This show was re-broadcast in March
1958.

JUL 2   (Mon.) As reported in his book *1000 Sundays*, Ed Sullivan telephoned Colonel Parker to set up a meeting to
discuss Elvis' appearance on "The Ed Sullivan Show."
Previously, Sullivan had been very vocal about refusing
to even consider having Elvis on his show.

Elvis had another recording session at RCA Victor's studios in New York. The session started at 2:00 p.m. and
lasted until 9:00 that night. Along with his regular backup band, Shorty Long played piano and the Jordanaires
sang backup vocals. (This is the first session to use all
of the Jordanaires; previous sessions had used only
Gordon Stoker and two members of the Speer Family.
The Jordanaires included Stoker, Neal Matthews, Hoyt
Hawkins, and Hugh Jarrett.) Elvis recorded *Hound Dog*,
first recorded by Willie Mae "Big Mama" Thornton in
1953, although Elvis' version relies heavily on Freddy
Bell and the Bell Boys' 1955 recording on Teen Records.
Elvis also waxed *Don't Be Cruel* and *Any Way You Want
Me*, both originals.

JUL 3   (Tues.) Elvis and his entourage (Scotty, Bill, D.J., Colonel
Parker, Parker's assistant Tom Diskin, and Junior Smith)
boarded a train at Penn Station at 11:30 a.m. for the return trip to Memphis.

JUL 4   (Wed.) Shortly after 7:00 a.m., Elvis had breakfast in
Chattanooga while waiting to switch trains for Memphis.
He caught the 8:00 a.m. local and arrived in Whitehaven,
a suburb of Memphis, in mid-afternoon. The engineer
stopped the train to let Elvis off in a field near his Audubon Drive home.

During the afternoon, Elvis went motorcycle riding and ran

Time for a short ride on Elvis' new Harley-Davidson.

Elvis and June Juanico go horseback riding during Elvis' vacation.

out of gas.

That night, Elvis performed a benefit concert in Russwood Park at 8:00 p.m. for the *Memphis Press-Scimitar*'s milk fund and the Variety Club's home for convalescent children. As part of the benefit, Elvis' initial ring with fourteen diamonds was given away as a door prize. Over 14,000 fans attended, and Elvis made his entrance at 10:30 p.m. He was backed up by Bobby Morris and his orchestra, with Scotty, Bill, D.J. and the Jordanaires. Dewey Phillips of WHBQ radio was the emcee. Other performers who preceded Elvis on the bill were the Admiral's Band Of Navy Memphis, the Confederate barbership quartet, the dancing Dixie Dolls, and Helen Putnam. Members of Elvis' family were in the front row.

mid-JUL In July, following the Memphis concert, Elvis spent a couple of weeks at the Gulf Hills Dude Ranch in Ocean Springs, Mississippi. He swam at the Surf 'n Sand Motel in Biloxi daily. During his vacation, Elvis again dated June Juanico, and the story reached the press that they were engaged to be married. Elvis traveled to New Orleans and was interviewed on WNOE radio and another station in an attempt to quell the rumor. During the interviews, he said that he hoped to continue his vacation in Miami (a reference, possibly, to his upcoming Florida tour).

JUL 13 (Fri.) Less than two weeks after the recording session, RCA Victor released *Hound Dog/Don't Be Cruel.*

Ed Sullivan succumbed to teenage pressure and signed Elvis to three appearances on "The Ed Sullivan Show" for a fee of $50,000, the highest ever paid for a performer on a television variety show.

JUL 14 (Sat.) In an article entitled "You Can't Do That To Elvis," *Billboard* recounted the teenagers adverse reaction to Elvis' appearance on "The Steve Allen Show," which had Elvis performing in a tuxedo and singing to a bassett hound.

JUL 16 (Mon.) *Newsweek* magazine published an editorial titled "Devitalizing Elvis" by John Lardner, which covered Elvis' appearance on the "Steve Allen Show."

JUL 21 (Sat.) *Billboard* placed *Hound Dog/Don't Be Cruel* in the "Review Spotlight" sections in both popular and country music. The journal called *Hound Dog* "a highly charged rhythm opus in Presley's characteristic style & should enjoy heavy commercial acceptance."

JUL 25   (Wed.) In Redding, California, a KSDA disc jockey played
          Hound Dog and *Don't Be Cruel* hour after hour in pro-
          test to some listeners' protests that Elvis was "obscene"
          and "vulgar." The records were played at various speeds
          "to test the general trend of intelligence." One reaction
          came from the police, who showed up at the radio sta-
          tion fearing that the dee jay had dropped dead and the
          automatic player was going on without him.
JUL 28   (Sat.) RCA Victor placed two full-page ads in *Billboard*.
          The first cried "Here He Is! . . . The Most Talked About
          Singer In Show Business With The Song He Exploded
          On TV!", which was a plug for *Hound Dog*. The second
          ad, from Elvis, said "Thanks A Million To Everybody
          . . . You've Been Wonderful." *Hound Dog* was covered
          in the "Best Buy" section in both popular and c&w
          music, with *Billboard* saying "from first week reports
          it has become clear already that this will be one of the
          year's big grossers."
JUL 31   (Tues.) Eighteen days after its release, *Hound Dog* was
          certified as a million-seller.
          On the way back to Memphis from Ocean Springs, Elvis
          was ticketed for speeding in Hattiesburg, Mississippi, by
          Constable Charlie Ward.

   The July issue of *Folk And Country Songs* magazine featured a
   photo of Elvis on the cover.

AUGUST

AUG 3   (Fri.) Elvis opened a week-long series of Florida concerts
          with three shows at the Olympic Theater in Miami.
          Colonel Parker was on hand, selling fifty-cent photos of
          Elvis to the crowd, which numbered 7,000 for the shows.
          Elvis' lavender Lincoln Continental Mark II was spotted
          by fans outside the theater and it was duly covered
          with lipstick messages for Elvis. Elvis' companion on
          this tour was June Juanico of Biloxi, Mississippi.
AUG 4   (Sat.) *Hound Dog* entered *Billboard's* "Top 100" chart at
          number 24 for the week ending July 25th. The single
          stayed on the chart for twenty-eight weeks, reaching as
          high as number 2. *Hound Dog* also entered the c&w sales

chart at number 5, where it stayed twenty-nine weeks
and reached number 1.

Elvis appeared in Miami for three more performances.
Again, the attendance was estimated at 7,000 for the
shows.

AUG 5   (Sun.) Elvis appeared at 3:30 and 8:15 p.m. at the Fort
Homer Hesterly Armory in Tampa, sponsored by the
Seratoma Civic Club. Tickets were $1.50 for general
admission with reserved seats somewhat higher. Also on
the bill were the Jordanaires, Tampa's Frankie Connors,
who acted as emcee and sang Irish ballads, and Phil
Maraquin. Security for the shows was handled by six
policemen, a dozen National Guardsmen, and forty
members of the Seratoma Club. Total attendance for
the shows was above 10,000. More than 1,000 teenagers
were turned away at the door for the evening's performance. Elvis wore black pants, white suede shoes,
baby blue shirt, and maroon jacket.

AUG 6   (Mon.) Ed Sullivan, host of TV's "The Ed Sullivan Show,"
was injured in an automobile accident in Seymour,
Connecticut. He suffered several broken ribs. Although
it was initially reported that he would be well enough to
appear on the coming Sunday night's show, he remained
hospitalized for several days and was not well enough to
host the first appearance by Elvis on September 9th.

Elvis appeared at the Polk Theater in Lakeland for three
shows. He gave a tape-recorded interview to Paul Wilder
for an article which would appear in *TV Guide*
in September. Portions of the interview were also
issued as a promotional single by RCA Victor for use by
radio stations. Attendance at the three Lakeland shows
topped 5,500 total.

AUG 7   (Tues.) *Look* magazine published an article titled "Elvis
Presley . . . He Can't Be But He Is" which covered
Elvis' May show in Dayton and his home life in Memphis.
Look reported that "on-stage, his gyrations, his nose
wiping, his leers are vulgar." Elvis was quoted as saying,
"Without mah left leg, Ah'd be dead."

Elvis performed three shows in St. Petersburg's Florida
Theater. Attendance for the shows was estimated at
6,500. During the afternoon performance, fourteen
teenagers were stopped from climbing the theater's fire
escape ladder in an attempt to crash the show. Security
for the shows was handled by twenty-five police reserves

who augmenteed a force of forty-five regular policemen.

AUG 8   (Wed.) Elvis appeared for two shows in Orlando. Total
        attendance was pegged at 7,000.

AUG 9   (Thurs.) Elvis performed twice at the Peabody Auditorium
        in Daytona Beach. The total attendance was over 5,000.

AUG 10 (Fri.) Elvis packed the Florida Theater in Jacksonville,
        performing three shows a day, at 3:30, 7:30 and 9:00 p.m.
        to an average of 2,200 per show. Admission was a
        dollar-twenty-five-cents in advance and a dollar-fifty-
        cents at the door. Juvenile Court Judge Marion W.
        Gooding attended the first show and met with Elvis and
        the Colonel afterwards. He said that he felt Elvis' bumps
        and grinds were objectionable for the teenage audience, and
        he ordered Elvis to "quieten" his act. Warrants were
        made out for Elvis' arrest; but during subsequent shows,
        Elvis only wiggled his little finger. Also while in
        Jacksonville, Elvis was warned by Al Fast, a represen-
        tative of the American Guild Of Variety Artists, that
        his show would be closed unless Elvis joined the guild.
        Apparently the Colonel smoothed things as nothing
        else was heard about this problem.

AUG 11 (Sat.) *Don't Be Cruel* entered *Billboard's* "Top 100" chart
        at number 28 for the week ending August 1st. It stayed
        twenty-seven weeks, reaching number 1.

        Elvis continued performing three shows a day in Jackson-
        ville. The total attendance for Elvis' six Jacksonville
        shows topped 15,000. Estimated take for the week:
        between $100,000 and $200,000.

AUG 12 (Sun.) Elvis performed in the New Orleans Municipal
        Auditorium. Admission was $1.05 to $1.47. The crowd
        was estimated at 13,000.

AUG 13 (Mon.) The CBS-TV "Morning" show aired a report on
        British teenagers listening to Elvis' records.

AUG 18 (Sat.) *Hound Dog/Don't Be Cruel* reached number 1 on the
        Billboard chart for "Best Sellers in Stores" in pop mu-
        sic for the week ending August 8th. It stayed in the
        number 1 position on this chart for eleven weeks. *Hound
        Dog* also entered *Billboard's* "R&B Best Sellers In Stores
        Chart" at number 11. It, too, eventually reached number

Elvis gyrates on stage, just the type of wild abandon
that caused such a furor in Jacksonville.

Elvis relaxes off-camera on the set of "Love Me Tender."

1 and stayed eighteen weeks.

RCA Victor ran a double full-page ad in *Billboard* which read "History Making! Each Over A Million Already!" The ad referred to sales of *Hound Dog* and *I Want You, I Need You, I Love You. Billboard* also reported that WPGC radio in Washington had started a "Society For The Prevention Of Cruelty To Elvis Presley," while WBZ in Boston was offering six strands of Elvis' hair in a contest.

AUG 22 (Wed.) Elvis returned to Los Angeles and the 20th Century-Fox studios to begin filming "Love Me Tender," which was then known as "The Reno Brothers." He was accompanied by Cliff Gleaves, a Memphis disk jockey. Elvis took the entire top floor of the Knickerbocker Hotel in Hollywood for his entourage.

AUG 23 (Thurs.) Production started on "Love Me Tender." Outdoor scenes were photographed at the 20th Century-Fox movie ranch in the San Fernando Valley near Hollywood.

AUG 27 (Mon.) *Life* magazine published a nine-page article titled "Elvis – A Different Kind Of Idol." The article traced the reaction of his fans and civic leaders during the August tour of Florida, specifically the shows in Jacksonville and Miami.

Newsweek magazine ran an article entitled "Inextinguishable," which briefly covered Elvis' latest exploits. The article also stated that Elvis had been awarded the "Apollo," a "unique prize offered by a group of deluded newspapermen and disc jockeys."

AUG 28 (Tues.) RCA Victor secured exclusive rights to distribute "Elvis Presley Charm Bracelets," obtained from Elvis Presley Enterprises, Inc.

AUG 30 (Thurs.) A postcard to Elvis was mailed from Niagara Falls, New York, with the message, "If you don't stop this shit we're going to kill you." The card was intercepted by the Memphis Post Office and turned over to the F.B.I. Nothing more came of the threat.

AUG 31 (Fri.) RCA Victor, in an unprecedented move, released six singles at one time, made up of the twelve tracks off Elvis' first long play album: *Blue Suede Shoes/ Tutti Frutti, I Got A Woman/ I'm Counting On You, I'll Never Let You Go/I'm Gonna Sit Right Down And Cry (Over You), Trying To Get To You/ I Love You*

*Because, Blue Moon/Just Because, Money Honey/
One-Sided Love Affair*, and the previously unreleased
Shake, Rattle And Roll/Lawdy, Miss Clawdy.

In August, Elvis had a recording session in Hollywood for his first
film, "Love Me Tender." None of his regular musicians were
on hand, and the band was comprised of local studio musicians.
Ken Darby, a well-known arranger, wrote the four songs for the
film, but due to copyright problems, the composers's credit was
changed to Vera Matson (Darby's wife) and Elvis. Background
vocals for the songs were handled by The Ken Darby Trio.
Songs recorded included the title song, as well as *Let Me, Poor
Boy* and *We're Gonna Move.*

Modern Screen magazine's August issue contained the first full-
color pull-out photo of Elvis along with the article "Elvis Presley! Who Is He! Why Does He Drive Girls Crazy?"

SEPTEMBER

SEP 1   (Sat.) *Billboard* devoted almost all of its "Vox Jox" column to a review of Elvis' controversial popularity. At
WKMH in Detroit, the disk jockey received 500 letters
after refusing to play Elvis' records. Anti-Presley radio
stations included WCMC, Wildwood, New Jersey, and
WNIX, St. Johnsbury, Vermont. Pro-Presley DJ's included Shelia Owens, WEIC, Charleston, Illinois, and
Pete Barry, WGAW, Gardner, Massachusetts.

Elvis started three days of recording activity at Radio
Recorders, 7000 Santa Monica Blvd., in Hollywood.
Elvis' regular band — consisting of Scotty Moore on
guitar, Bill Black on bass and D.J. Fontana on drums —
was augmented by the Jordanaires singing backing vocals. During this session, which started at 1:00 p.m. and
ran until late at night, Elvis recorded *Playing For Keeps*,
an Elvis original; *Love Me*, first recorded by the rhythm
and blues duo Willie and Ruth in 1954, but owing much
to Georgia Gibbs' cover version; *How Do You Think I
Feel*, written by Webb Pierce and recorded by Jimmie
Rodgers Snow in 1956; and *How's The World Treating
You*, another original.

SEP 2   (Sun.) During sessions on this date. Elvis recorded *Paralyzed*, original to Elvis; *When My Blue Moon Turns To
Gold Again*, a 1940s ballad; *Long Tall Sally*, Little

96

Richard's 1956 hit; *Old Shep*, the song that Elvis had sung in 1945 at the Tupelo fair and which had been a hit for Red Foley in the early 1940s; and *Too Much*, another original Elvis song.

SEP 3 (Mon.) Elvis had another recording session at Radio Recorders. He recorded two Little Richard songs, *Ready Teddy* and *Rip It Up*, along with two originals, *First In Line* and *Anyplace Is Paradise*.

SEP 4 (Tues.) WSPT radio in Stevens Point, Wisconsin, banned all Elvis records from airplay. In retaliation, a fan threw a rock with a note attached through the station's window.

In early September, RCA Victor released two more extended plays by Elvis: **Elvis Presley**, featuring *Shake, Rattle And Roll*, and **The Real Elvis.**

SEP 5 (Wed.) *Variety* reported that filming on "Love Me Tender" was being rushed to meet an early November release date. It was expected that the film would be finished by late September. (Because the ending had to be re-shot, the film was completed October 8th.)

It was reported that Elvis was expected to sell over 10,000,000 records during his first year with RCA Victor. On that figure, Elvis would earn a royalty of $400,000, "a record breaking payoff for a disc performer." Elvis was reported to already have three gold records for *Blue Suede Shoes, Heartbreak Hotel* and *Hound Dog.* In addition, the seven singles released on August 31st were selling 12,000 copies a day. Due to the increase in the sales of Elvis' records, RCA Victor had been forced to use the pressing plants owned by Decca and M-G-M Records. It was understood that Elvis' discs accounted for approximately two-thirds of RCA Victor's total daily singles output.

Elvis bought a pink Cadillac for his mother.

SEP 8 (Sat.) Elvis' photo appeared on the cover of *TV Guide*, coinciding with his first appearance on "The Ed Sullivan Show." The magazine ran the first of a three-part article by Paul Wilder (the remaining two parts appeared in the September 22 and 29 issues). (See AUG 6, 1956)

Billboard placed its "Review Spotlight On" all seven of Elvis' new singles. The magazine said, "Fourteen tunes, formerly available on Presley's LP's and EP's now available on seven singles within reach of any kid with 89 cents."

Elvis scored another "Triple Crown" in *Billboard* as *Don't Be Cruel* topped the sales, jukebox, and disk jockey charts in country music for the week ending August 29th.

SEP 9   (Sun.) Elvis made his first television appearance on "The Ed Sullivan Show," broadcast on CBS-TV from 8:00 to 9:00 p.m. (EDT). This was the first Sullivan show of the season, but he had been hospitalized following an automobile accident on August 6th. Charles Laughton, the distinguished English actor, substituted for Sullivan as emcee. Because Elvis was working daily on "Love Me Tender" in Hollywood, he performed his portion of the show from CBS-TV studios in Los Angeles. Elvis sang *Don't Be Cruel, Love Me Tender, Ready Teddy,* and *Hound Dog.* Other guests on this show included the Vagabonds, Dorothy Sarnoff, Eddie Fisher, and Amru Sani. Nielson ratings for this show gave Sullivan 82.6% of all households (which works out to four out of every five) with a TV tuned in to watch Elvis. Over a third of all the people in the country (roughly 54 million) saw the show. These figures were the largest for any variety TV show up to that time, and they held until February 9, 1964, when the Beatles first appeared on the Sullivan show.

SEP 15   (Sat.) *Billboard* reported in its "Vox Jox" column that 300 irate rock 'n' roll fans had marched on WIEL radio station in Elizabethtown, Kentucky, when it was announced that the station was breaking Elvis' records. As a result, the station devoted fifteen minutes each day to a show playing nothing but Elvis, and fifteen minutes to a show "For All Those Who Don't Like Elvis Presley."

On the charts, *Don't Be Cruel* reached number 1 on "The Top 100" for the week ending September 5th. It stayed in the number 1 position for seven weeks.

During the week, RCA Victor presented Elvis with a second gold record for the same disc, as *Don't Be Cruel* joined *Hound Dog* in selling a million copies of the single on its own.

SEP 22   (Sat.) *Billboard* reported that all seven of Elvis' recent single releases had topped 100,000 in sales. In an article, "Presley Snaggs Pubbing Rights To His Pic 'Love Me Tender,' " it was reported that RCA was unhappy about

98

having to rush-release a single of *Love Me Tender*, but that there could be no other choice due to the heavy demand after Elvis sang the song on "The Ed Sullivan Show" on the 9th.

Billboard also reported that Elvis was scheduled to start his second movie, "Lonesome Cowboy," in December.

Billboard picked *Blue Moon/Just Because* as a "Best Bet," saying, "Of the seven singles released by Victor two weeks ago, this disk, with emphasis on *Blue Moon* is stepping out and starting to move."

Elvis and Nick Adams flew from Los Angeles to Memphis.

SEP 26 (Wed.) *Variety*, in a front-page article titled "Halo, Everybody, Halo: Latest Presley Pitch," reported that 20th Century-Fox was trying to get Colonel Parker to use Elvis to influence teenagers to stay away from juvenile delinquency."

"Elvis Presley Day" was proclaimed in Tupelo. Elvis received a scroll from Mississippi Governor J.P. Coleman and a citation from Tupelo Mayor James Ballard.

Elvis performed two shows, at 2:30 and 7:30 p.m. in Tupelo at the Mississippi-Alabama Fair and Dairy Show. Also on the bill were "Papa" John Gordy, Delores Watson, the Jordanaires, and the Blue Moon Boys (Scotty, Bill and D.J.). Elvis performed for forty-five minutes in each show, and more than 100 National Guardsmen surrounded the stage. At one point during the matinee, Elvis had to stop the show in order to get the crowd to cool down.

For his part in the shows, Elvis was paid $11,800 (a $5,000 guarantee, plus sixty percent of the grandstand receipts). Tickets were a dollar fifty and the grandstand held a capacity of 7,500.

SEP 28 (Fri.) RCA Victor released the title song from Elvis' first movie as a single, *Love Me Tender* b/w *Any Way You Want Me*. RCA Victor had received orders for 856,327 copies a week before its release.

SEP 29 (Sat.) *Billboard* reviewed a new facet in Elvis' career in an article entitled "Presley Juggernaut Rolls — Merchandising Campaign Expected To Top $20 Mil Sales By Year End." According to the article, H.G. Saperstein & Associates, in conjunction with Elvis and the Colonel had eighteen licensees producing thirty products, including hats, t-shirts, blue jeans (which were black), kerchiefs,

Elvis kisses Sarah Ann Patterson before taking the stage in Tupelo.

On stage before the Tupelo audience.

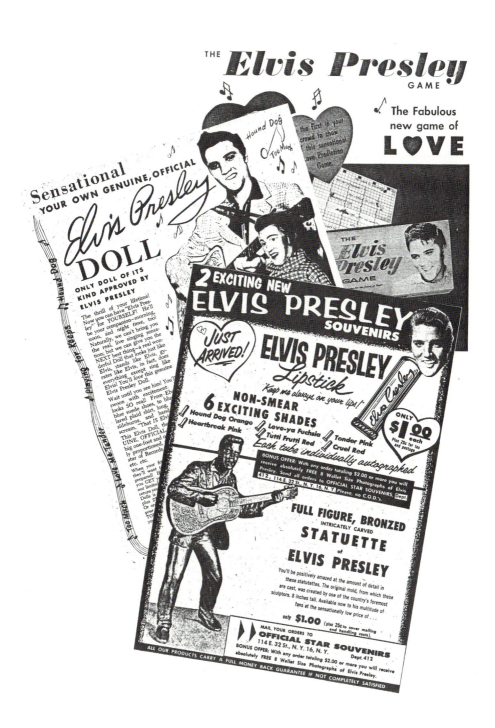

bobbysox, canvas sneakers, shirts, blouses, belts, purses, billfolds, wallets, charm bracelets, necklaces, magazines, gloves, mittens, a statue, bookends, a guitar, lipstick ("heartbreak pink," "hounddog orange," and "tutti frutti red"), cologne, stuffed "hound dogs" and dancing dolls, stationery, greeting cards, sweaters, and a soft drink. As of this date, sales were estimated at 4 million charm bracelets, 120,000 pair of blue jeans, and 240,000 t-shirts. The Elvis Presley Fan Club boasted 200,000 members. Finally, there was a new magazine, *Elvis Answers Back*, which would soon be released and carried by RCA distributors.

TV Star Parade's November cover carried photos of both Elvis and Pat Boone.

The September issue of *Rod Builder And Customizer* magazine carried an article with Elvis' byline titled "Rock 'N' Roll Drag." The article mentioned that Elvis had held a part-time job cleaning garages and that one of his earliest desires was to own a hot rod.

The September issue of *Coronet* magazine ran an article entitled "The Craze Called Elvis."

OCTOBER

OCT 1 (Mon.) Elvis returned to Los Angeles to complete filming "Love Me Tender." (There had been adverse reaction to the story's original ending which had Elvis' character being killed, so the studio decided to shoot an ending where he lived. The original ending was used, but Elvis could be seen singing a reprise of the theme song over the end credits.)

OCT 6 (Sat.) *Love Me Tender* was a "Review Spotlight" pick in *Billboard*: "Title tune from Presley's first flick has set a record for advance orders, which now exceed a million. Further comment unnecessary." On the charts, *Don't Be Cruel/Hound Dog* reached number 1 on the r&b sales list for the week ending September 26th.

OCT 8 (Mon.) *Newsweek* magazine published an article entitled "Mud On The Stars." The article mentioned an offer of $300,000 made by Colonel Parker to either NBC-TV or CBS-TV for the chance to have Elvis in his own TV special, along with two guest appearances during 1957.

Both networks declined the offer.

Elvis completed filming "Love Me Tender."

OCT 9   (Tues.) Associated Press reported that 20th Century-Fox
          planned to put Elvis together with Jayne Mansfield, a
          popular blonde "bombshell," in "The Love Maniac."
          According to Fox, the film would be a "comedy, taking
          advantage of his singing and her figure." The film might
          start production in early 1957. (No such film was ever
          made.)

          (NOTE: There is a fantastic story that concerns Mans-
          field's attempts to get Elvis included in the roster of
          rock 'n roll acts in her 1956 film, "The Girl Can't Help
          It." First, she approached Colonel Parker, who told her
          that Elvis' fee would be $50,000 for one song. Thinking
          that this was a bit steep, she traveled to Memphis, where
          she and Elvis spent several days in seclusion. Upon her
          return to Hollywood, she again called Colonel Parker,
          this time informing him that she and Elvis had worked
          everything out. The Colonel said that this was fine with
          him, but Elvis' fee was still $50,000 for one song. She
          was flabbergasted! Later she reflected, "I felt somehow
          that I'd been had." Reported by columnist Walter Scott
          in 1957.)

OCT 10   (Wed.) San Francisco disk jockey Bruce Vanderhoot of
          KYA, who objected to his station's ban on Elvis songs be-
          tween 10:00 a.m. and 4:00 p.m. (out of deference to
          children and housewives), took the issue to his listeners
          by playing *Love Me Tender* at various speeds fourteen
          times in a row. He was fired.

OCT 11   (Thurs.) Elvis appeared at the 71st State Fair of Texas in
          Dallas. His show was held in the 75,504-seat Cotton
          Bowl Stadium. Over 26,500 fans attended the 8:00 p.m.
          show. Tickets were $1.25 in advance and $1.75 at the
          door. Along with Elvis was Sherry Davis of the "Big D
          Jamboree." Elvis brought along his friend Nick Adams
          on this tour. Elvis sang *Heartbreak Hotel, Long Tall
          Sally, I Was The One, Blue Suede Shoes, I Got A Woman,
          Love Me, Don't Be Cruel*, and *Hound Dog.*

OCT 12   (Fri.) Elvis appeared at the Heart O' Texas Coliseum in
          Waco. Following the show, he had a midnight snack at
          the home of Eddie Fadal, a local disk jockey, who was
          to become one of Elvis' close friends during the next two
          years.

A shot from the photo session for the cover of Elvis' second album.

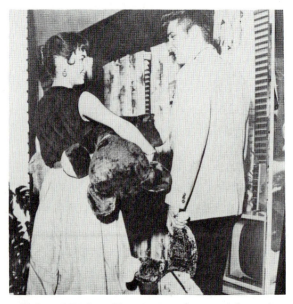

Elvis and Barbara Hearn return from a night at the fairgrounds.

OCT 13   (Sat.) *Billboard* listed *Love Me Tender* at number 1 in its
         "Coming Up Strong" chart. *Love Me Tender* also was
         in all three (pop, c&w, and r&b) "This Week's Best
         Buys" lists, with the magazine calling the record "A
         hit before it was ever released."
         Elvis took his show to San Antonio.

OCT 14   (Sun.) Elvis appeared in Houston.

OCT 15   (Mon.) Elvis performed in Corpus Christi. Following the
         show, Elvis returned to Memphis.

OCT 18   (Thurs.) Elvis was engaged in a short fist fight with Ed
         Hopper, forty-two, and Aubrey Brown, twenty-one, ser-
         vice station attendants in Memphis. Elvis had stopped
         by Hopper's gas station in his $10,000 Lincoln Contin-
         ental when a crowd of teenagers began to gather. Hop-
         per asked Elvis to leave three times, and then shoved
         him back into his car. Elvis emerged swinging, leaving
         Hopper with a black eye. All three men were charged
         with disorderly conduct and assault and battery, and
         each man posted a bond of fifty-two dollars.

OCT 19   (Fri.) In Memphis City Court, Elvis was acquitted by Judge
         Sam Friedman. Hopper and Brown were each fined
         twenty-five dollars for assault.
         The album **Elvis** and the EP **Elvis, Volume 1** were released
         by RCA Victor.

OCT 20   (Sat.) In an article entitled "Presley Busts Another Mark,"
         Billboard reported that Elvis had broken all records with
         Love Me Tender, which jumped onto the best selling pop
         singles chart at number 2, "the first time a disk has
         scored so high in its initial chart appearance." In addi-
         tion, *Love Me Tender* also entered the "Honor Roll Of
         Hits" (number 8), pop disk jockey (number 11), "The Top
         100" (number 12), country best sellers (number 9), and disk
         jockey (number 10), and the r&b sales chart (number 8).
         All charts were for the week ending October 10th.
         Elvis settled out of court with Miss Robbie Moore, who had
         objected to having her picture taken with Elvis. He gave
         her $5,500.

OCT 21   (Sun.) Elvis and Barbara Hearn, his nineteen-year-old date
         from Memphis, went to a local movie theater to see a
         clip from Elvis' appearance in Tupelo. Fans mobbed his
         Cadillac, jumping on the hood, ripping the upholstery,
         and denting the fenders. It took police ninety minutes
         to restore order.

The *Memphis Commercial Appeal* reported that Elvis wanted to premiere of "Love Me Tender" to be held in Memphis.

OCT 22   (Mon.) Elvis and his band, along with the Jordanaires, rehearsed at the Presley home on Audubon Drive for the upcoming appearance on the "Ed Sullivan Show."

OCT 24   (Wed.) *Variety*, in a front-page, banner-headlined story titled "Elvis A Millionaire In 1 Year," reported that his gross income was derived from record royalties ($450,000), movie deals ($250,000), TV appearances ($100,000) and personal appearances ($200,000). It was expected that Elvis merchandise would sell over $40 million in the next fifteen months. Other deals in the works included 18,000 ice cream locations and 30,000 hamburger stands selling "hounddogs" (large hot dogs) and "Presley burgers."

The Memphis Draft Board sent Elvis a Status Quesionnaire.

OCT 25   (Thurs.) RCA Victor issued **Perfect For Parties**, a promotional EP which featured Elvis introducing six songs from recent RCA Victor albums, including *Love Me* from **Elvis**. This special record could be purchased from record dealers for only a quarter.

OCT 26   (Fri.) *Colliers* magazine ran an article entitled "Boone vs Presley: The Rock 'n' Roll Battle," which attempted to compare the styles, fans, and backgrounds of Pat Boone and Elvis, who were locked into a "battle" for the top male vocalist at the time. *House And Garden* magazine also published an article, "The War Of The Generations."

OCT 27   (Sat.) *Billboard* ran an article on its front page titled "Army To Give Elvis Presley A G.I. Haircut." According to the article, which apparently originated with "Army officials," Elvis would report to Ft. Dix in early December. After a shortened basic training period, he would join the Special Services for an entertainment tour. According to the Army officials, high on Elvis' agenda would be extensive dental work. Elvis would be allowed to continue TV and recording dates, and he would be given a six-week early furlough to make a second film for Paramount. Finally, before his induction, Elvis would make his debut on the stage of the Paramount Theater in New York. (NOTE: Not one item in the article came to pass, except the part about the haircut.)

Billboard also reported that a law suit had been filed against

Elvis Presley Music and composers Lieber and Stoller by Valjo Publishing Company, a subsidiary of Lois Music, which was itself a subsidiary of King Records. In the suit, it was claimed that Johnny Otis was the co-author of *Hound Dog*, and that he had been under contract to Valjo Music since 1951. Otis had been credited as co-author on the recording of *Hound Dog* by Willie Mae "Big Mama" Thornton in 1953, and her recording featured Otis' band.

OCT 28   (Sun.) A forty-foot tall figure of Elvis was unveiled atop the marquee of the Paramount Theater in New York to publicize the upcoming premier of "Love Me Tender." Several hundred fans were on hand, and Colonel Parker had many printed placards stating "Elvis For President" to hand out to the crowd. (November 6th was national Election Day.)

Elvis received a Salk polio innoculation from Dr. Harold Fuerst.

In New York, Elvis held a press conference in the afternoon. The *New York Times* reported that Elvis was "polite, personable, quick witted, and charming." During the afternoon Elvis rehearsed for that night's appearance on the "Ed Sullivan Show."

Elvis made his second appearance on the "Ed Sullivan Show," broadcast from the Maxine Elliot Theater on 39th Street in New York by CBS-TV from 8:00 to 9:00 p.m. (EDT). Elvis sang *Don't Be Cruel, Love Me Tender, Love Me,* and *Hound Dog.* Other guests on the show included the cast of the Broadway show "Most Happy Fella," ventriloquist Senor Wences, and Joyce Grenfell. During the show, Elvis was presented with his fifth gold record for *Love Me Tender.* The Sullivan show received a Neilson rating of over eighty percent of the TV audience for the time slot.

OCT 30   (Tues.) It was reported in the press that Elvis had signed a new contract with RCA Victor calling for payment of $1,000 a week for twenty years in lieu of royalties (which for 1956 stood at around $430,000). Prior to this, Elvis had been receiving the standard five percent of ninety percent shipped in royalties as a singer. Colonel Parker's office quickly responded that the royalties would remain the same and that the only change in the new contract was in the length of time covered. As to how long the

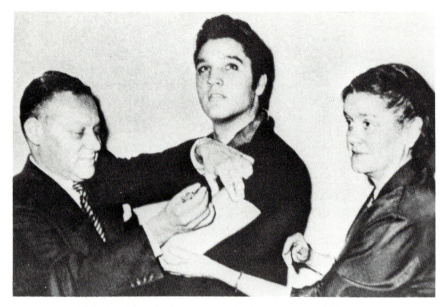

Elvis receives a polio vaccination from Dr. Harold Fuerst.

Joined by actor Nick Adams, Elvis and Natalie Wood
wait to go on Bob Neal's radio show.

contract would run, Colonel Parker was not saying.
The previous contract had another year to run with the
option for an additional year (which would surely be
picked up by Victor).

An insider reported that Elvis and the Colonel
wanted to spread the $430,000 royalties over a ten-year
period to amortize the earnings and thereby save them
from losing most if it in income taxes. The twenty-
year period came from changing the term of the contract from the two-year (plus one year option) to a five-
year contract with a five-year option. At the end of
the ten years, there was another ten-year option.

OCT 31   (Wed.) Movie starlet Natalie Wood flew in from Los Angeles to visit with Elvis for a week. She was met at the
Memphis airport by Elvis and Nick Adams. The trio
bought motorcycles for a tour of Memphis, which con-
cluded about 11:30 p.m. with an interview at WMPS
studios in the Chicksa Hotel on the Bob Neal show.

The premier issue of *Teenage Rock And Roll Review* magazine
featured Elvis on the cover. The accompanying article was titled
"Here's Elvis Presley" and reportedly was written by Elvis.
Elvis was featured in the October issue of *House & Garden* maga-
zine's article, "The War Of The Generations."
Elvis was featured on the covers of *Cowboy Songs, Country Song
Roundup*, and *Song Hits* magazines in their October issues.

NOVEMBER

NOV 1   (Thurs.) Elvis, Natalie Wood and Nick Adams were spotted
riding motorcycles in Memphis, again.

NOV 3   (Sat.) According to an article in *Billboard*, Elvis' hit single
Hound Dog/Don't Be Cruel was involved in its second
lawsuit in as many weeks. This time, song writer Otis
Blackwell was being sued by publisher Joe Davis, who
contended that he had Blackwell under contract when
he wrote *Don't Be Cruel*. According to Blackwell, the
contract was void after Davis stopped paying him in June
1955.

In *Billboard*'s pop music charts for the week ending October 24th, *Love Me Tender* was number 1 on all three
charts (sales, jukebox, and disk jockey), but it was only
number 3 on "The Top 100" listing.

In an article entitled "Victor To Plug Presley Portable," *Billboard* covered RCA's release of "Elvis Presley autograph models" in their line of portable record players. A four-speed model selling for $32.95 (75 cents down, 75 cents a week) would also come with a two-pocket EP containing eight of Elvis' songs from his first LP. An automatic 45 r.p.m. player selling for $44.95 ($1 down, $1 a week) would come with a 3-pocket EP containing twelve songs, eight from the LP and four of Elvis' hits.

In conjunction with the marketing of the phonographs, Elvis tape recorded several commercials for radio markets. The ads were prepared by Kenyon & Eckhardt, Inc., a New York advertising agency, on October 5th.

NOV 4   (Sun.) An interview in the *Los Angeles Times* with David Weisbart, producer of "Love Me Tender," quoted Weisbart as saying, "He [Elvis] will surprise a lot of people who go to see him because his presence is just a gimmick. Actually he plays an acting part in a legitimate story and does so very well."

NOV 7   (Wed.) In Syracuse, New York, housewives were circulating a petition to CBS demanding that Elvis be barred from television. The petition termed Elvis' "physical contortions . . . vulgar, suggestive and disgusting."

early NOV   Early in November, Natalie Wood and Nick Adams returned to Hollywood, and Elvis flew to Las Vegas for a vacation at the New Frontier Hotel. While there, he met and dated Marilyn Evans, a nineteen-year-old dancer in the New Frontier's floor show.

NOV 10   (Sat.) In *Billboard*'s "9th Annual DJ Poll," which covered the period January 1 – October 27, 1956, Elvis fared as follows: pop music, "Most Played Record," *Heartbreak Hotel* (number 5), *Don't Be Cruel* (number 7), *Hound Dog* (number 19); as an artist, Elvis ranked number one on the "Most Played" list. Elvis was not listed by the disk jockeys on either the "Most Favorite Record" or "Most Favorite Artist" chart.

Country and western disk jockeys ranked *Heartbreak Hotel* number 4, *Don't Be Cruel* number six, and *I Want You, I Need You, I Love You* number 12, as their most favorite record, while Elvis was only number fifteen as a favorite artist. In the "Most Played" category,

Heartbreak Hotel was number 1, *I Forgot To Remember To Forget* was number 13, and *Don't Be Cruel* was number 15. Elvis ranked number 1 in the "Most Played Artist" category. Rhythm and blues disk jockeys ranked *Don't Be Cruel* number 3, *Heartbreak Hotel* number 8, and *Hound Dog* number 9 as their "Favorite Records," yet none of the records made the "Most Played" chart. Elvis was number five as a favorite artist, but only number seventeen as "Most Played."

In *Billboard*'s "Top 100" for the week ending October 31st, *Love Me Tender* was number 1. It was number 1 for four out of the next seven weeks.

Billboard put its "Spotlight On . . . " **Elvis**, the second long play album, calling it a "top flight new package . . . "

NOV 13 (Tues.) *Look* magazine ran an article that analyzed "The Great Elvis Presley Industry." The article was generally condescending to both Elvis and the "industry," which was reported to be selling "between 9 and 12 million dollars' worth of junk" in the last six months of 1956.

NOV 14 (Wed.) Louisville, Kentucky, Police Chief Carl Heustis placed a "no-wiggle" ban on Elvis' upcoming appearance on the 25th. The Chief said he would not permit "any lewd, lascivious contortions that would excite the crowd."

NOV 16 (Fri.) "Love Me Tender" premiered at the Paramount Theater in New York City. The film eventually grossed $4.5 million in film rentals.

Elvis attended pianist-showman Liberace's show at the Riviera Hotel in Las Vegas. The pair were photographed backstage, with Elvis holding a candelabra (one of Liberace's trademarks) and Liberace strumming a guitar while Elvis sang *Blue Suede Shoes*. Elvis asked Liberace for his autograph for his mother.

NOV 17 (Sat.) **Elvis** entered *Billboard*'s "Best Selling Packaged Records" chart at number 7. It stayed on the chart for twenty-eight weeks, reaching number 1. *Love Me* from the extended play, **Elvis, Volume 1**, entered "The Top 100" in *Billboard* for the week ending November 7th at number 84. The song stayed on the chart for nineteen weeks and peaked at number 6.

NOV 21 (Wed.) "Love Me Tender" opened nationwide in over 500 theaters.

Variety's review said, "Appraising Presley as an actor, he ain't. Not that it makes much difference."

To coincide with the premier of Elvis' first movie, RCA Victor issued an extended play single containing the songs from the film, **Love Me Tender.**

NOV 22 (Thurs.) The *Los Angeles Examiner*'s review of "Love Me Tender" said, "Elvis can act. S'help me the boy's real good, even when he isn't singing."

The *Los Angeles Mirror-News* said, "Without Elvis, the film would be just an average, cheaply made western action movie . . . but with him it is a box office bonanza."

NOV 23 (Fri.) In its review, the *Beverly Hills Citizen* said, "Young Presley does a pretty good job and proves that today's kids are not so dumb. They know unusual talent when they see it."

Elvis performed two shows in the Sports Arena in Toledo, Ohio. He earned $16,000 and a total of 13,000 fans attended the shows.

Later that night, he was involved in a fist fight with nineteen-year-old Louis Balint at the Hotel Commodore Perry's Shalimar Room. Balint was fined $10 plus $9.60 court costs, which he could not pay. He was sent to the county work house for seven days. According to witnesses, Balint was upset because his wife carried Elvis' picture in her wallet but not a photo of Balint. The police reported that when they arrived, Balint was throwing Scotty Moore over a railing while Elvis was pounding him with his fists. Patrolman William Kina said, "Presley's no slouch. He was really working over that guy. He knows how to handle himself real fine."

NOV 24 (Sat.) The *New Yorker* magazine, in its review of "Love Me Tender" said, "Thick-lipped, droppy-eyed and indefatiguably sullen, Mr. Presley, whose talents are meagre but whose earnings are gross, excites a big section of the young female population as nobody has ever done."

Elvis performed in Cleveland, Ohio.

NOV 25 (Sun.) Elvis appeared in Louisville, Kentucky, where police imposed a "no wiggle" ban of the performance. Before the show, Elvis had lunch at the home of Jesse D. Presley, his grandfather, who had a small house in southern Louisville. When he left, he gave him a new car, a television set, and a $100 bill. A crowd of 500 had gathered in front of the elder Presley's home. Following the 8:00 p.m. show at the Armory, Elvis stayed at

A 1956 publicity photo.

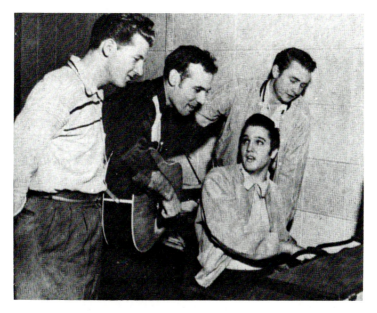

"The Million Dollar Quartet": (from the left) Jerry Lee Lewis, Carl Perkins, Elvis, and Johnny Cash.

the Seal Bark Hotel.

NOV 26   (Mon.) Elvis returned to Memphis.
Time magazine said of "Love Me Tender," "Elvis all but
steals the show from such better known players as
Richard Egan, Debra Paget and Mildred Dunnock."

NOV 27   (Tues.) It was reported that 20th Century-Fox wanted
Elvis to sign a contract to be in "The Way Of Gold,"
which would begin filming December 17th. The studio
offered $150,000 against fifty percent of the profits.
Colonel Parker turned them down, asking for $250,000
against fifty percent.

NOV 28   (Wed.) "Love Me Tender" entered *Variety*'s "National
Box Office Survey" at number 2 behind "Giant." The
film stayed on the chart for four weeks. *Variety* reported that "Love Me Tender" had grossed $540,000
during its first week of release.

NOV 30   (Fri.) Elvis was guest of honor at the E.H. Crump Memorial Football Game in Memphis, which was a benefit for
the blind.

In November, Elvis donated $900 to Humes High School for the
purchase of uniforms for the ROTC corps. (Elvis had been a
member of the ROTC while a student at Humes High.)

The November issue of *Dig* magazine featured a cover shot of Elvis
and a four-page story.

DECEMBER

DEC 4   (Tues.) Elvis and Marilyn Evans, the Las Vegas showgirl,
stopped by Sun Studios in Memphis. There they found
Carl Perkins in a recording session. Also on hand was
Jerry Lee Lewis, who had just had his first single, *End
Of The Road*, released by Sun Records. For the next
three hours, the three performers, later with the addition
of Johnny Cash, also a Sun recording artist, ran through
a succession of gospel and popular songs. Sam Phillips
called the *Memphis Press-Scimitar*, and a reporter and
photographer were dispatched to cover this impromptu
event. Later, this would be referred to as "The Million
Dollar Quartet."

DEC 8   (Sat.) RCA Victor ran a full-page ad in *Billboard* claiming
"over 500,000 sold in one month . . . and it's just taking
off" for the EP **Elvis, Volume 1**, which was represented
on the charts by the songs *Love Me, When My Blue Moon*

Turns To Gold Again, and *Paralyzed*.

"Presley Disks Set Canada Sales Mark" was the title of an article in *Billboard* that reported the sales of *Hound Dog/Don't Be Cruel* at 225,000 in fourteen weeks, *Love Me Tender* at 135,000 in six weeks, and the album, **Elvis**, at 30,000 in two weeks in Canada. Sales of 100,000 for a single were considered enough for a "gold" record in Canada. The article said that sales of **Elvis** in the U.S. had topped 150,000.

On the charts in *Billboard*, the album **Elvis** reached number 1, a position it held for the next five weeks.

The *Saturday Review* magazine, in reviewing "Love Me Tender," said, "The incomprehensible Presley is a triple-threat man in this one: he sings, he wiggles, he acts."

DEC 11   (Tues.) *Look* magazine published an article entitled "The Face Is Familiar," which compared Elvis' features with those of Michaelangelo's sculpture, "David."

DEC 12   (Wed.) It was reported in *Billboard* that Elvis had received requests for 1,400 different appearances during 1957. At that rate, he would have to do four shows daily just to fill the offers.

DEC 15   (Sat.) On *Billboard*'s chart for the week ending December 5th, *Love Me*, representing **Elvis, Volume 1**, entered the popular music list representing juke box plays. This was the first time an EP had ever been on this particular list.

Elvis left by car for Shreveport, Louisiana. Traveling in the car with him were his cousins, Gene and Junior Smith, and the director of "Loving You," Hal Kanter. Elvis' white Lincoln Continental was followed by the band in a Cadillac stretch-limousine.

DEC 16   (Sun.) Arriving before dawn, Elvis booked himself into the Captain Shreve Hotel.

That night, Elvis performed what was to be his final show for the "Louisiana Hayride" at the Louisiana Fairgrounds. Over 9,000 attended, and Elvis sang *Love Me Tender, I Was The One* and *Hound Dog* among others. The show was a benefit for the Shreveport YMCA and lasted from 8:30 to 11:30 p.m.

DEC 22   (Sat.) "Presley Top Hound Dog" was the title of a front-page article in *Billboard*, which reported that Elvis had the most records on the national popular retail sales chart for 1956 at six. He was followed closely by Pat Boone with five.

Elvis and Dottie Harmony spend Christmas opening presents.

Elvis made an appearance to lend support, but he did not sing at the WDIA "Goodwill Review" in Memphis. Performing were Junior Parker, Earl Malone, B.B. King, and Bobby "Blue" Bland. WDIA billed itself as "America's only 50,000 watt Negro radio station."

DEC 24   (Mon.) *New Republic* magazine published an article entitled "A Star Is Borne" [sic], which reviewed "Love Me Tender" in a tongue-in-cheek manner.

DEC 25   (Tues.) Elvis spent Christmas at home on Audubon Drive. He was visited by Las Vegas showgirl, Dottie Harmony. Barbara Hearn of Memphis gave Elvis a gold vest which Elvis wore on the Ed Sullivan TV show in January.

In Memphis, during the Christmas vacation, Elvis and some friends played a rough game of touch football at the Dave Wells Community Center. Along with Elvis was Red West, a bodyguard since 1954.

DEC 28   (Fri.) Elvis and Dottie Harmony rode around Memphis in his three-wheel Messerschmitt car.

DEC 29   (Sat.) Elvis had the largest number of songs on *Billboard*'s "The Top 100" of any artist up to that time: *Love Me Tender* (number 2), *Love Me* (number 7), *Don't Be Cruel* (number 26), *When My Blue Moon Turns To Gold Again* (number 38), *Old Shep* (number 47), *Hound Dog* and *Poor Boy* (number 54 tie), *Any Way You Want Me* (number 70), *Paralyzed* (number 78), and *Blue Moon* (number 93) for a total of ten, of which five represented extended play releases. The chart was for the week ending December 19th. (Elvis equaled this feat on January 20, 1957.)

In the year-end issue, *Billboard* ran a chart of "1956 Top Tunes" based on the weekly "Honor Roll Of Hits" listing. Elvis was represented by *Don't Be Cruel* (number 5), *Heartbreak Hotel* (number 9), *Love Me Tender* (number 16), *Hound Dog* (number 18), and *I Want You, I Need You, I Love You* (number 26).

DEC 31   (Mon.) Elvis' financial success made the front page of the *Wall Street Journal* in an article titled "Heartbreak, Hound Dogs Put Sales Zip Into Presley Products." The newspaper reported that Elvis merchandise had sold $22 million worth of Presley goods in the past few months. Included in the sales figure were 72,000 pairs of black jeans, 350,000 charm bracelets and 7,200 pairs of "Elvis Presley" shoes.

Elvis appeared on KLAC-TV's "Holiday Hop," hosted by Wink Martindale.

The December issue of *Cosmopolitan* magazine ran an article that asked, "What Is An Elvis Presley?"

Elvis was featured on the cover of the December issue of *TV And Radio Mirror* magazine, with a superimposed photo of Ed Sullivan looking over his shoulder.

Elvis was featured on the cover of the shortlived *Rock 'n' Roll Battlers* magazine, along with Bill Haley and Pat Boone.

The cover story on Elvis in *TV World* magazine asked the burning question, "Singer Or Sexpot?"

The cover photo of Elvis on the cover of *TV-Movie Fan* magazine was reversed and appeared to have Elvis playing the guitar left-handed.

In 1956, Elvis was the subject of many magazines devoted exclusively to his meteoric career. Among these were *The Amazing Elvis Presley, Elvis Presley, Elvis Photo Album, Official Elvis Presley Album, Elvis Presley Speaks,* and the mini-magazine *Elvis Presley In Hollywood.* Elvis was also featured prominently in the following annual magazines: *Rock 'N Roll Stars, Rock 'N Roll Jamboree* and *Elvis And Jimmy* (the late James Dean).

King Of The
Whole Wide World

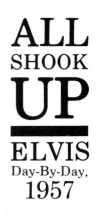

ALL
SHOOK
UP
━━━━
ELVIS
Day-By-Day,
1957

In January, according to a film industry press release, Elvis was supposed to start filming either of two films for Hal Wallis: "Rodeo," or "Sing, You Sinners." In the latter, the central character had been changed from a prize fighter to a singer.

JAN 2 (Wed.)-21 (Mon.) Elvis and others were featured on a sixteen-inch transcription which promoted the March Of Dimes over radio. Elvis spoke a few lines which preceded his recording of *Love Me Tender*.

JAN 2 (Wed.) In *Variety*'s annual review of the film industry, "Love Me Tender" ranked number 23.

JAN 4 (Fri.) RCA Victor released *Too Much* b/w *Playing For Keeps*.

Elvis arrived at the Kennedy Veterans Hospital in Memphis at 1:00 p.m. for his pre-induction physical given by Dr. (Capt.) Leonard Glick. He was driven to the hospital by Cliff Gleaves, and was accompanied by Dottie Harmony. They arrived in a cream-colored Cadillac. Elvis passed the physical and was given the Selective Service number 40 86 35 16, although no draft rating was given at this time.

After putting Miss Harmony on a plane for Los Angeles, Elvis left Memphis for New York by train, switching trains in Washington, D.C.

JAN 5 (Sat.) Elvis arrived in New York City at 6:20 a.m.

JAN 6 (Sun.) Elvis made his final appearance on "The Ed Sullivan Show," broadcast from 8:00 to 9:00 p.m. (EST) on CBS-TV. He sang *Hound Dog, Love Me Tender, Heartbreak Hotel, Don't Be Cruel, Peace In The Valley, Too Much*, and *When My Blue Moon Turns To Gold Again*. Other guests on the show included Arthur Worsley, Nanci Crompton, Leny Eversong, Carol Burnett, Lonnie Satin, and the Gutis. Following the show, Elvis returned to Memphis by train.

119

Elvis receives his pre-induction check-up from Capt. (Dr.) Leonard Glick.

Elvis' final appearance on "The Ed Sullivan Show."

Gladys and Vernon visit with Elvis in Hollywood.

Elvis on the set of "Loving You."

JAN 8   (Tues.) An Army press conference was held in Memphis to announce the results of Elvis' pre-induction physical exam. He had been rated 1-A. The announcement was made by Captain Elwyn "Rip" Rowan, Commander of the Memphis Recruiting Center.

JAN 10   (Thurs.) Elvis left Memphis by train for Hollywood to start work on "Loving You," his first film for Hal Wallis and Paramount Pictures under the contract signed in April 1956.

JAN 12   (Sat.) *Billboard* put its "Spotlight On" Elvis' latest release, *Playing For Keeps/Too Much*, saying "as heavily pre-ordered as this record is, not much description of it is necessary to sell the trade on it."

Elvis arrived in Los Angeles. To avoid the many fans waiting for him at the entrance to Union Station, he left the train while it was still in the railroad yards. He was briefly interviewed by a reporter from ABC-TV before he left in an Imperial convertible.

Elvis had a recording session at Radio Recorders in Hollywood. Members of the band included his regulars, Scotty Moore, Bill Black and D.J. Fontana, along with Dudley Brooks on piano and the Jordanaires with backup vocals. Songs recorded in this session included several for release on a religious EP: *I Believe, Peace In The Valley*, and *Take My Hand, Precious Lord*. Two songs from the soundtrack of "Loving You," *Got A Lot O' Livin' To Do* and *Mean Woman Blues*, were also recorded. During the session, Elvis recorded two songs for his next single release, *All Shook Up* and *That's When Your Heartaches Begin.* A version of *I Beg Of You* was attempted, but the released version was recorded on February 23rd. Finally, *Tell Me Why* was recorded, but the song remained unissued until 1965 for some unexplained reason. The session lasted into the early morning hours of the 13th.

mid-JAN Gladys spent two weeks in a hospital in Memphis for a checkup. Following her release, she and Vernon left Memphis via train for Hollywood. While in Hollywood, they stayed at the Knickerbocker Hotel with Elvis.

JAN 13   (Sun.) The *New York Times* ran a political cartoon with the caption, "The grapevine reports that Elvis Presley is joining the American Army as U.S. Ambassador to Cairo." Elvis, with guitar and microphone was holding

a note: "To Nasser From Ike." Nasser, seated on a
throne, was singing, "See you later, alligator; not in the
Nile crocodile."

JAN 16   (Wed.) *Variety* reported that Elvis had held the number 1
spot on the "Boxscore Of Top Talents And Tunes" chart
from April 18 through December 26, 1956, breaking all
previous records for a single artist with his eight-month
run.

JAN 19   (Sat.) *Playing For Keeps/Too Much* was a "Best Buy" in
Billboard. The trade journal said "advance orders put
this disk in the best seller class even before it was generally available."

Elvis had another recording session at Radio Recorders.
The band members were the same as the session on
January 12th. *It Is No Secret* was recorded to fill out
the religious EP. Also waxed were three songs which
appeared as fillers on the **Loving You** album: *Blueberry
Hill*, Fats Domino's smash from 1956; *Have I Told You
Lately That I Love You*, a 1930's hit for Gene Autry,
and an Elvis original, *Is It So Strange.*

JAN 21   (Mon.) Production started on "Loving You" for Hal B.
Wallis and Paramount Pictures. All of the scenes were
photographed at Paramount except for the visit to
Delores Hart's parents' farm, which was filmed in the hills
near Hollywood. Although most references give "Deke
Rivers" as the name of Elvis' character in the movie, the
true name of the character was "Jimmy Thompkins."

JAN 24   (Thurs.) Elvis had a recording session at Radio Recorders
on Santa Monica Boulevard. He waxed a short (1:45)
version of *Teddy Bear*, and a strong blues version of *One
Night* that closely followed the 1956 original version by
Smiley Lewis. No other information is available concerning the session.

JAN 26   (Sat.) *Too Much* entered *Billboard*'s "Top 100" at number
30 for the week ending January 16th. It stayed on the
list for seventeen weeks and peaked at number 2.

In *Billboard*'s "First Disk Jockey Quarterly," covering the
period from October 6 through December 29, 1956,
Elvis was number one on both the pop and c&w lists of
"Best Selling Artists On Singles." He was number two on
the r&b singles artist list. He was also number two on
the "Best Selling Artists On Albums" chart.

In the same issue, *Billboard* published its annual review. On the list of "1956's Top Popular Records," *Heartbreak Hotel* was number 1, *Don't Be Cruel* number 2, *Hound Dog* number 6, *I Want You, I Need You, I Love You* number 14, and *Love Me Tender* was number 15. On the c&w chart for top sellers for 1956, *Heartbreak Hotel* was number 2, *I Want You, I Need You, I Love You* number 6, *Don't Be Cruel* number 7, *I Forgot To Remember To Forget* number 9, *Hound Dog* number 11, *I Was The One* number 27, *Love Me Tender* number 31, *Mystery Train* number 33, and *My Baby Left Me* was number 49. On the "1956's Top Rhythm And Blues Records" chart *Don't Be Cruel* was number 14, *Heartbreak Hotel* number 19, *Hound Dog* number 21, *I Want You, I Need You, I Love You* number 36, and *Love Me Tender* was number 41.

Elvis and Debra Paget, his co-star in "Love Me Tender," were the cover story in the January issue of *Hit Parader* magazine.

Elvis was the cover story in *Rock And Roll Roundup* magazine's January issue. Elvis was also featured on the cover of *Dig* magazine, which carried scenes from "Love Me Tender." Elvis talked about teenagers in the cover story of *Movie Life.*

FEBRUARY

FEB 2 (Sat.) *Playing For Keeps* started up *Billboard*'s "Top 100" chart, entering at number 41. It stayed on the chart for nine weeks, peaking at 36.

FEB 3 (Sun.) The *New York Times* ran a story entitled "Presley Records A Craze In Soviet Union." The article reported that recordings of Elvis' songs had been cut on discarded X-ray plates and were selling in Leningrad for fifty rubles each (about twelve-and-a-half dollars).

FEB 14 (Thurs.) Elvis had a recording session at Radio Recorders. Both the slow and fast versions of *Loving You* were waxed. Musicians were Scotty, Bill and D.J., as well as Dudley Brooks on piano. The Jordanaires assisted on background vocals.

About this time, Elvis waxed the familiar version of *Teddy Bear*, as well as several other songs for "Loving You," *Got A Lot Of Livin' To Do, Mean Woman Blues, Hot Dog, Lonesome Cowboy,* and *Party.*

FEB 23   (Sat.) Two fifteen-year-old girls from San Francisco's
            Lincoln High School, Donna Dickson and Nancy Laity,
            along with their mothers, flew to Los Angeles with a
            San Francisco Chronicle reporter to have lunch with
            Elvis at Paramount Studios. (See November 11, 1972.)
         Elvis had a recording session at Radio Recorders in Holly-
            wood. Personnel was the same as the January 12th
            session. Elvis recorded *Loving You* for the film and al-
            bum. *True Love, I Need You So*, and *Don't Leave Me
            Now* also first appeared as fillers on the **Loving You**
            album. *When It Rains It Really Pours* was shelved until
            1965. *I Beg Of You* was held for release as a b-side in
            1958. *One Night* was held for release until 1959.
            Several other songs recorded during these sessions
            were background instrumentals (*Candy Kisses* and *Peter
            Cottontail*) or were those sung by Delores Hart (*Dancing
            On A Dare* and *Detour*). *We're Gonna Live It Up* was
            reportedly recorded by Elvis, but it remains unreleased.
FEB 24   (Sun.) In Washington, D.C. at a meeting of the National
            Association of Secondary School Principals, Orren T.
            Freeman, Principal of Senior High in Wichita Falls,
            Texas, (a town frequented by Elvis during 1954–56)
            said, "We do not tolerate Elvis Presley's records at our
            dances, or blue jeans, or ducktail haircuts."

      Elvis was featured on the cover of the first issue of *Hep Cats* maga-
         zine in February.
      Movieland magazine's February cover story looked at "The Lonely
         Private Life Of Elvis Presley."

MARCH

MAR 2   (Sat.) *Too Much* peaked at number 2 on *Billboard*'s "Top
            100" chart for the week ending February 20th. It re-
            mained in the number 2 position for a total of four
            weeks.
MAR 9   (Sat.) *Billboard* reported that Elvis had retained Henri
            Rene, band leader for RCA Victor, as an advisor for
            eight weeks. Rene was on the payroll of Elvis Presley
            Music Co., and would act as a liaison with 20th Century-
            Fox where Elvis was currently making a movie. (NOTE:
            At this time, Elvis was making a movie with Paramount
            and was scheduled to make his next film for M-G-M.)

In an article entitled "RCA '56 Sales 7% Over 1955," it was reported in *Billboard* that Elvis had sold 12.5 million singles and 2.75 million LPs in 1956. He was also the first artist to have an extended play sell more than 1 million (**Elvis, Volume 1**).

mid-MAR In mid-March, Elvis and his family returned to Memphis via train.

MAR 19 (Tues.) Elvis negotiated the purchase of Graceland, a large home located eight miles south of downtown Memphis, at 3764 South Bellevue Boulevard (U.S. Highway 51 South), in the Memphis suburb of Whitehaven. The home was built in the late 1930s, and named Graceland by its original owner, Dr. Thomas Moore. At the time Elvis purchased Graceland, it was being used by the Graceland Christian Church for services. Elvis paid $100,000 to Mrs. Ruth Moore, Dr. Moore's widow.

MAR 22 (Fri.) RCA Victor released *All Shook Up/That's When Your Heartaches Begin*, and the religious EP **Peace In The Valley**.

In Memphis, Private Hershal Nixon, eighteen, accused Elvis of bumping into his wife as they were leaving a restaurant two months earlier. Nixon claimed that Elvis pulled a gun on him which turned out to be a Hollywood prop. Elvis contended that Nixon had tried to start a fight. A hearing was scheduled for March 26th.

MAR 23 (Sat.) In *Billboard*'s "2nd Disk Jockey Quarterly," Elvis was listed as the best selling artist for the first quarter of 1957. On the chart of "Top Popular Records," Elvis had three songs on the list: *Too Much* (number 5), *Love Me Tender* (number 10) and *Love Me* (number 12).

Billboard placed its "Review Spotlight On . . . " the **Peace In The Valley** EP, saying "ex-choir singer Presley pulls a monumental switch, and warbles four sacred tunes with sincerity and commendable reverence." The "Spotlight" was also on *All Shook Up/That's When Your Heartaches Begin*, with the magazine saying "This coupling is so strong it can hardly miss."

MAR 26 (Tues.) Elvis and Private Nixon went to a private conference with a city judge. Later, both men said that "everything had been straightened out."

MAR 27 (Wed.) Elvis left Memphis by train for Chicago.

MAR 28 (Thurs.) Elvis held an afternoon press conference in Chicago at the Saddle and Sirloin Club at the Stockyards

Inn.

That night, he started a personal appearance tour with a
show at 8:00 p.m. in Chicago's International Amphi-
theatre. He performed in his famous gold suit. Tickets
were $2.00, $2.75, and $3.50, and the gross for the
show was $32,000 from the 12,000 attending.

Other acts on this tour included magician Rex Mar-
lowe, singer Patti Kelly, comic-emcee Jimmy James,
vocalist Frank Conners, dancer Frankie Trent, plus Al
Dvorin's twenty-piece orchestra.

During the Chicago engagement, thirteen girls had to be
carried off after "swooning upon viewing their idol."

MAR 29 (Fri.) Elvis packed the Kiel Auditorium in St. Louis.
Ticket sales topped $27,000.

MAR 30 (Sat.) A show in Fort Wayne, Indiana, also topped
$27,000.

MAR 31 (Sun.) More than 14,000 screaming fans turned out for
each of Elvis' two shows in Detroit's Olympia Stadium
at 2:00 and 8:00 p.m. Box office receipts totaled
$53,000 for the day. It was reported that 140 extra
policemen were on duty, including twelve special police
and ten patrolmen who were responsible for Elvis' personal security. Despite this, over a thousand fans
stormed the dressing room after each show.

TV Headliner magazine carried a photo of Elvis from "Love Me
Tender" on the cover. The accompanying article was "What
Elvis Wants On A Date!" *Movie Stars Parade* magazine's cover
article carried this one step further with "If You Were Elvis
Presley's Bride."

APRIL

APR 1   (Mon.) Elvis' show in Buffalo, New York, grossed $37,500.
Elvis stayed at the Statler Hotel.

APR 2   (Tues.) Elvis performed afternoon and evening shows in
Toronto's Maple Leaf Garden, grossing more than
$54,000. This was one of the few times that Elvis wore
the full gold suit. Usually he wore only the jacket with
a pair of black pants.

APR 3   (Wed.) In Ottawa, Elvis performed two shows in the 8,500
seat auditorium. There were 3,500 fans for the 5:00
p.m. show. Attendance had been kept down for this

matinee because of active opposition to Elvis by the local Catholic community. The evening show at 8:00 p.m. was played before a packed house. While singing *Blueberry Hill*, Elvis accompanied himself on piano. Ticket sales were $27,000. Thirty policemen had been hired to protect Elvis.

APR 5   (Fri.) In Memphis, Elvis was having Graceland repainted by C.W. Nichols. Because Nichols was not a member of the local painters' union, Graceland was picketed by Painter's Local #49.

Elvis appeared in the 6,500 seat Sports Arena in Philadelphia before half a house in a matinee and evening concert. Tickets were $2.00, $2.50 and $3.00.

APR 6   (Sat.) *All Shook Up* entered *Billboard*'s "Top 100" at number 25 for the week ending March 27th. It stayed on the chart for thirty weeks (Elvis' longest) and reached number 1.

Over 100 policemen were on hand in Philadelphia for Elvis' second day of performing at the Sports Arena. During the matinee, four students from Villanova University threw eggs at Elvis on stage, and although none of them hit him, one did land on his guitar.

The total take from this nine-day tour of the northeast was $308,000, plus an additional $20,000 in souvenir sales.

APR 9   (Tues.) Elvis took his show to the Municipal Auditorium in Wichita Falls, Texas.

APR 10   (Wed.) Elvis and his family moved into Graceland.

APR 13   (Sat.) *That's When Your Heartaches Begin* entered *Billboard*'s "Top 100" chart at number 59 for the week ending April 3rd. It peaked at number 58 two weeks later and only stayed on the chart for six weeks.

APR 20   (Sat.) *Billboard* reported that *All Shook Up* peaked at number 1 for the week ending April 10th. It remained at number 1 for a total of eight weeks.

APR 27   (Sat.) *All Shook Up* was awarded a "Triple Crown" by *Billboard* for topping all three of the charts for pop music, sales, disk jockey plays, and juke box plays.

APR 29   (Mon.) *Time* magazine ran an article advising its readers to "Combat The Menace!" In retaliation to Elvis' growing popularity, two students from Yale University were marketing "I Like Ludwig" (Beethoven) buttons.

late APR Late in April, Elvis took the train from Memphis to Los Angeles to begin work on "Jailhouse Rock" at the M-G-M Studios in Culver City, California.

In April, Elvis authorized installation of the world famous "Music Gate" at Graceland. Work on the gates was done by Doors, Inc. of 911 Baynor St. in Memphis.

Elvis was featured on the cover of the premiere issue of *Cool* magazine in April.

Elvis was also the cover story in the April issue of *Rock And Roll Roundup, TV Star Parade,* and *Teen Life* magazines.

Elvis shared the cover of April's issue of *TV And Movie Screen* magazine with singer Gisele McKenzie.

The April issue of *Harpers* magazine published an article entitled "Elvis, The Indigenous," which reviewed Elvis' popularity in Russia and Czechoslovakia.

Movie And TV Album magazine ran the cover story "Elvis Presley Has It All His Way!"

MAY

MAY 1 (Wed.) Elvis started pre-production work on "Jailhouse Rock" for M-G-M Studios in Culver City. He was paid $250,000 plus fifty percent of the royalties for this movie.

MAY 2 (Thurs.) Elvis had a recording session for "Jailhouse Rock" at the M-G-M Studios. Elvis' regular set of musicians, including Scotty Moore, Bill Black, and D.J. Fontana, were augmented by Dudley Brooks and Mike Stoller on piano, and the Jordanaires on backing vocals. Songs for the film included the title song, *Young And Beautiful, I Want To Be Free, Baby I Don't Care*, and a second version of *Don't Leave Me Now* (which had previously been recorded on February 23rd for the **Loving You** album). A version of *Treat Me Nice* was recorded for the film, but the version released on record was not recorded until September 1957. Another song, *One More Day,* was recorded for "Jailhouse Rock," but it was sung by Mickey Shaughnessey.

MAY 6 (Mon.) Elvis won his first "Triple Crown" in the rhythm and blues field as he was the first country-derived artist to top all three charts for r&b music: sales, juke box plays and airplay. (NOTE: *Billboard* changed from Saturday publication to Mondays effective April 29th.)

MAY 13 (Mon.) It was reported in the press that Elvis would have a return engagement in Tupelo as part of a benefit for an Elvis Presley Youth Center. The concert would be held in September 1957.

Principal photography for "Jailhouse Rock" started at M-G-M Studios in Culver City.

The **Peace In The Valley** EP was on both the LP chart and the "Top 100 Singles" chart in *Billboard* for the week ending May 8th. This was another first for Elvis' career. **Peace In The Valley** stayed on the LP chart for a total of nine weeks, peaking at number 3 on the chart for June 19th.

MAY 14   (Tues.) While filming a dance sequence for "Jailhouse Rock" at the M-G-M Studios in Culver City, Elvis swallowed a tooth cap. It lodged in a lung, and he was rushed to Cedars of Lebanon Hospital.

MAY 15   (Wed.) At the hospital, the tooth cap was removed without surgery by using a long forceps. Elvis was released from the hospital. Anne Neyland, an actress who had tried out for the lead in "Jailhouse Rock," visited Elvis in the hospital.

MAY 25   (Sat.) In a story copyrighted by Associated Press, and datelined May 24th in Mexico City, it was reported that the Mexican newspaper *Ultimas Norticas* had said that Elvis would marry Yvonne Lime, actress, in Acapulco "next week." Elvis and Yvonne would fly in on Monday.

MAY 26   (Sun.) The Associated Press interviewed Tom Diskin, Elvis' personal representative, who said that there was "absolutely nothing to the reports."

The first issue of *16* magazine, which came out in May, featured Elvis on the cover.

JUNE

JUN 10   (Mon.) Mae Boren Axton, teacher in one of the Jacksonville, Florida, high schools, was reported to be allowing her students class time to discuss Elvis or listen to his records if they completed the required work. According to Ms. Axton, the teenagers were able to accomplish more after an enthusiastic session of Elvis's influence. (Ms. Axton was co-composer of *Heartbreak Hotel*.)
         Billboard placed its "Review Spotlight On . . . " *Teddy Bear/Loving You*, saying the "special sleeve, spotlighting Elvis and a teddy bear, is powerful display material."

JUN 11   (Tues.) RCA Victor released *Loving You/Teddy Bear*. One week later, it was reported to have sold 1.25 million copies, and it became Elvis' eighth record to pass the million mark in sales.

JUN 14   (Fri.) The recording tapes from the "Jailhouse Rock"
         session were handed over to RCA Victor by M-G-M
         Studios.
JUN 24   (Mon.) *Teddy Bear* and *Loving You*, entered *Billboard*'s
         "Top 100" at number 47 and number 81 respectively
         for the week ending June 19th. *Teddy Bear* stayed on
         the chart for twenty-nine weeks and reached number 1.
         Loving You peaked at number 28, but it stayed on the
         chart for twenty-two weeks.
         Billboard reported in an article entitled "Victor Price Hike
         Body Blow To 78's," that of the 2 million copies of
         Heartbreak Hotel sold, less than ten percent were 78s.
         According to the article, the raise in price of 78s from
         98 cents to $1.15 was the death knell for that format.
         RCA Victor ran a double-page ad proclaiming "Presley
         Sings The Top Tunes From His New Smash Movie,
         'Loving You,' " which plugged both the single and the
         album from the movie.

   Filmland magazine's cover of Elvis was accompanied with Elvis'
   "own confession about girls! dates!"

JULY

JUL 1   (Mon.) In its search for a more accurate method of chart-
         ing records, *Billboard* enlisted the aid of New York
         School of Retailing. One result was a change from "The
         Top 100" to "The Top 100 Sides," a title which more
         accurately reflected the makeup of the chart. Another
         result was that *Hound Dog* was once again on the chart,
         at number 85, for the first time in twenty-one weeks.
early JUL In early July, Elvis returned to Memphis for a three-week
         vacation.
JUL 3   (Wed.) *Loving You* became Elvis' eighth gold single.
         Variety, in its movie review of "Loving You," said,
         "Though the rock 'n' roll craze perhaps passed its peak,
         there's little question that a sizeable part of the citizen-
         ry will welcome Elvis Presley back for his second appear-
         ance . . . Presley shows improvement as an actor."
         The *Hollywood Reporter* said, "Young girls, and some not
         so young, set up an ear-splitting scream almost every
         time Presley appeared on screen . . . [Elvis] would be
         attractive to a member of the older generation if the

Elvis and Anita Wood . . . love at first sight.

From a scene in "Loving You."

picture could be seen without the maddening female
chorus."

JUL 8 (Mon.) Elvis and Anita Wood visited the Strand Theater
in Memphis after hours to watch the construction of a
special front for the premiere of "Loving You." This
was their first date. She was the nineteen-year-old
hostess of the "Top 10 Dance Party" on Memphis TV.
They had been introduced by George Klein.

JUL 9 (Tues.) "Loving You" premiered at the Strand Theater.
Elvis did not attend. The film showed eight times on
the first day to accommodate the crowds.

JUL 10 Elvis, Anita Wood, and his parents attended a special midnight screening of "Loving You" at the Strand Theater.

JUL 13 (Sat.) Elvis picked Anita Wood up at her home in his white
Lincoln Continental and brought her to Graceland for
dinner with his parents.

JUL 15 (Mon.) *Teddy Bear* peaked at number 1 on *Billboard*'s
"Top 100 Sides" chart for the week ending July 6th.
It remained at number 1 for a total of seven weeks.

JUL 22 (Mon.) *Teddy Bear* was awarded a "Triple Crown." *Billboard* had changed its method of tabulating the "Triple
Crown" so it took a little longer for *Teddy Bear* to be
honored. A single now had to maintain its number 1
position on the "Best Sellers In Stores" chart for three
consecutive weeks. **Loving You** (LP) entered *Billboard*'s
LP chart at number 11 for the week of the 13th. It stayed
on the charts for twenty weeks, reaching number 1.

The press reported that Elvis would not be touring England
or Australia for the foreseeable future. According to
Colonel Parker, "We're so busy with pictures — we've
made three in seven months — that we can hardly make
any long-range commitments like that."

JUL 26 (Fri.) There was a midnight sneak preview of "Loving
You" at the Alhambra Theater in Sacramento, California.
The first twenty-five persons received a free LP and all
were given an "autographed" photo of Elvis.

JUL 30 (Tues.) "Loving You" opened in theaters across America.

JUL 31 (Wed.) "Loving You" entered the "National Box Office
Survey" in *Variety* at number 8. It stayed on the chart
for four weeks, peaking at number 7.

The *Los Angeles Times*, in its review of "Loving You,"
called the film, "A furtive step on Presley's part in a
screen career."

Elvis shared the cover of the second issue of *16* magazine with
  Harry Belafonte.
The July issue of *Photoplay* magazine carried a cover photo of
  Elvis.
Movieland's cover of Elvis was accompanied by the article "The
  Secret Of Presley's Power Over Women."

AUGUST

AUG 1   (Thurs.) The *Los Angeles Examiner*, in reviewing "Loving
         You," called Elvis, "The utter end, the living most, not
         alone if you belong to the passionate legions of Presley
         worshipers but also if sharp, tremendous personalities
         interest you."
AUG 2   (Fri.) The "Official Elvis Presley Fan Club Of Great
         Britain" was founded in London.
AUG 6   (Tues.) Arthur Berg, president of the National Association
         of Dance, predicted that both Elvis and rock 'n' roll
         would last a long time. He reported that dancing was
         enjoying its greatest popularity in history.
mid-AUG In mid-August, Elvis traded his three-wheel custom-built
         Messerschmitt for a two-and-a-half hour shopping spree
         at Lansky Brothers' clothing store in Memphis. Elvis
         had frequented the store, owned by Bernard and Guy
         Lansky, for several years, buying some of his more "out-
         landish" clothes there.
AUG 19   (Mon.) In *Billboard*'s "Disk Jockey Quarterly," Elvis was
         again the number one "Best Selling Artist" in pop music.
         All Shook Up was number 1 in sales for the second quar-
         ter of 1957, *Too Much* was number 13, and *Teddy Bear*
         was number 26.
AUG 27   (Tues.) Anita Wood was on hand as Elvis left Memphis for
         Spokane via train. She was wearing a new diamond and
         sapphire ring given to her by Elvis.
AUG 29   (Thurs.) After dark, Elvis and his bodyguards arrived in
         Spokane, Washington, to start his tour of the Pacific
         Northwest. The group stayed at the Randolph Hotel.
AUG 30   (Fri.) Elvis appeared at the Memorial Stadium in Spokane
         at 8:00 p.m. Tickets were $2.00, $2.50 and $3.50. The
         show grossed $22,400. Also appearing with Elvis on the
         first part of the show were emcee Howard Harlin, tap-
         dancing trio The Burns Twins and Evelyn, comedy

vocalist Joe Termini, acrobats Wells and the Four Fays, pantomimist Paul Desmond, and the Jordanaires. Elvis performed eighteen songs during his portion of the show. There were over 12,500 "mostly screaming, squealing young girls" in attendance, with 100 police and firemen required to contain the crowd.

AUG 31   (Sat.) Elvis took the Great Northern train from Spokane to Vancouver, B.C. The train stopped prior to arriving in Vancouver, and Elvis took a car to his hotel to elude the press and the fans who were waiting at the station.

There was a press conference in the Lions' dressing room during the late afternoon.

Elvis appeared at the Empire Stadium that night; 26,500 fans attended. He was on stage for thirty-five minutes. When a crowd of teenagers broke through the police barricade, a seaman was arrested for assaulting a cop. Later he was fined $250. The show grossed $44,000 on tickets priced from two to three-and-a-half dollars.

Elvis was the cover story in *Personalities* magazine which asked the question in the accompanying story: "Elvis Presley--True Or False?"

SEPTEMBER

SEP 1   (Sun.) The tour of the Pacific Northwest continued in Washington State, with a show in the Tacoma Stadium which grossed $11,000.

SEP 2   (Mon.) There were two shows in Sick's Seattle Stadium, also called the Ranier Ballpark, in Seattle. Elvis was on stage for thirty minutes during each show. A total of 30,000 fans attended, and the shows grossed $36,000. Tickets were two dollars and three-fifty.

SEP 3   (Tues.) Elvis performed two shows in the Multomah Stadium in Portland which grossed $34,000. After Elvis had been on stage for fifteen minutes, there was a riot, and Elvis was forced to stop his show.

SEP 4   (Wed.) Elvis returned to Hollywood by train. He was met by Anita Wood, who in the week since they had been apart, had won the "Hollywood Star Hunt" in New Orleans. They stayed at the Knickerbocker Hotel.

SEP 5   (Thurs.) Elvis had a recording session at Radio Recorders in Hollywood. This "double" session started at noon

Bill Black, playing electric bass guitar, leads his combo.

and ran until 8:00 p.m. Elvis recorded *Treat Me Nice* for release as the flip side of *Jailhouse Rock*. *My Wish Came True* was not released until 1959, and *Don't* was saved for release until December 1957. The remaining songs were recorded for a Christmas album: *Blue Christmas, White Christmas, Here Comes Santa Claus,* and *Silent Night.*

The usual group of Memphis/Hollywood musicians was on hand, as well as vocalist Mildred (Millie) Kirkham, who added a few high notes when needed. She was a part-time member of the Jordanaires and was called whenever a female voice was needed.

SEP 7   (Sat.) Elvis continued recording. Four more songs were recorded for the upcoming Christmas album: *Oh Little Town Of Bethlehem, Santa Bring My Baby Back To Me, Santa Claus Is Back In Town,* and *I'll Be Home For Christmas.*

SEP 16   (Mon.) It was reported that Marion Keisker, office manager at Sun Records, would join the U.S. Air Force. She had been instrumental in getting Elvis' audition with Sun Records' owner Sam Phillips. She would join the Air Force as a Captain, and she was scheduled to report to Lackland Field in San Antonio, Texas.

mid-SEP   During a vacation in September in Las Vegas, Elvis dated Kitty Dolen, a Vegas singer. He took her to see Sammy Davis, Jr.'s nightclub show.

SEP 21   (Sat.) The **Just For You** extended play entered *Billboard*'s album chart, staying only one week at number 16.

Scotty Moore and Bill Black resigned as regular members of Elvis' backing band. The trio had been together since Elvis' first recordings in July 1954. However, while Elvis had gone on to become immensely popular and richer than even his wildest dreams in 1954, Scotty and Bill were still being paid $100 a week at home and $200 a week on the road, plus a $1,000 Christmas bonus.

Bill Black formed the popular Bill Black's Combo, and he had a hit with *Smokie* in 1959. He continued to record with Elvis until Elvis went into the Army in 1958.

Scotty Moore founded Music City Recorders in Nashville, which he sold in 1963. He produced the hit recording *Tragedy* by Thomas Wayne (Perkins) on the Fernwood label out of Memphis in 1959. He continued to record with Elvis, when needed, until 1969, and he became a

successful freelance guitarist and record producer.
D.J. Fontana, who had been with Elvis since 1955, was
not affected by Scotty and Bill's decision. He had a
separate contract which allowed him greater leeway
with his career.

SEP 23 (Mon.) *Billboard* reported, in an article entitled "Victor
Pacts Lieber, Stoller To A&R Chores," that the hit
songwriting team had been hired by RCA Victor to
operate as independent A&R men and be responsible
for recording four artists, including Elvis. RCA at first
denied any deal, but by October 28th, it was official.

SEP 24 (Tues.) RCA Victor released *Jailhouse Rock* b/w *Treat
Me Nice.*

SEP 27 (Fri.) Elvis performed a benefit show for the "Elvis Presley Youth Recreation Center" in Tupelo at the Mississippi–Alabama Dairy Show and Fair stadium. He performed at 8:00 p.m. and the show netted $22,800.
Attendance was pegged at 12,000 and tickets were
priced at two dollars.

SEP 30 (Mon.) In a rare move, RCA Victor took out a full-page ad
to counter another record. The ad stated "The Big
Version Is By Elvis" and was an attempt to attract
buyers to Elvis' version of *Have I Told You Lately That
I Love You?* on the **Just For You** EP. The song had
recently been issued by Ricky Nelson on a single, an
album, and an EP. *Billboard* reported that for the week
ending September 21st, the **Just For You** EP was number
16 on the LP chart in its only appearance.

OCTOBER

OCT 3 (Thurs.) Elvis returned to Tupelo for a visit with some of
his friends and relatives.

OCT 7 (Mon.) *Billboard* instituted a new chart for extended play
records, thereby eliminating them from both the singles
and album charts. For the first week of the new chart,
which ended September 28th, Elvis had four of the ten
EPs listed: **Loving You, Vol. 1** (number 1), **Just For
You** (number 3), **Peace In The Valley** (number 9), and
Loving You, Vol. 2 (number 10).

OCT 10 (Thurs.) There was a press preview for the film "Jailhouse
Rock" at 8:30 p.m. at the M-G-M Theater located inside
M-G-M Studios, Culver City. Elvis did not attend.

OCT 14 (Mon.) *Jailhouse Rock* entered *Billboard*'s "Top 100 Sides" chart at number 15. It stayed on the chart for twenty-seven weeks and reached number 1.

OCT 16 (Wed.) *Variety*, in a review, said of "Jailhouse Rock": "Film is packed with type of sure-fire ingredients producers know Presley's followers will go for . . . Presley is still no great shakes as an actor, but [he] gets by well enough."

The *Hollywood Reporter* said, "The old Presley seems toned down to the extent that his distinctive mannerisms seem less florid."

OCT 17 (Thurs.) "Jailhouse Rock" premiered in Memphis. Elvis did not attend.

OCT 23 (Wed.) Elvis was interviewed by George Klein at a local Memphis radio station. Elvis discussed the possibility that he could be called to serve in the Army at any time.

OCT 24 (Thurs.) Elvis left Memphis for California via railroad.

OCT 26 (Sat.) Elvis performed two shows in the San Francisco Civic Auditorium which could seat 6,000 people. Shows were at 3:00 and 8:15 p.m. Tickets were $2.75 and $3.75. There was a press conference backstage at 8:15 p.m. while the other acts were performing.

The other acts on the bill were the same as the ones for the Northwest Pacific tour in August with the exception of Jerry Rosen's band, which augmented Scotty, Bill and D.J.'s playing. (Scotty and Bill had re-joined Elvis on a per-diem basis.)

Elvis wore a wine-red suit and sang fourteen songs.

OCT 27 (Sun.) Elvis traveled across the Bay for a show in the Oakland Auditorium at 8:15 p.m. Tickets were $2.75 and $3.75 again.

OCT 28 (Mon.) Elvis appeared at the Pan Pacific Auditorium in Los Angeles. There was a press conference at 7:00 p.m. in the auditorium prior to the 8:15 show. Nine thousand fans attended the show, and Elvis sang eighteen songs during his fifty minutes on stage. The police sent word to Elvis to clean up his act before the next night's show.

OCT 29 (Tues.) Elvis again appeared at the Pan Pacific Auditorium, and this time the police filmed the show. Nothing came of the police action. In the audience for the show were Ricky Nelson, Nick Adams, Carol Channing, Sammy Davis, Jr., Tommy Sands and many other Hollywood stars.

The total gross for the two days came to $56,000.

After the show on the 29th, Elvis had an open house at his suite in the Beverly Wilshire Hotel. Most of the stars mentioned above attended.

OCT 30   (Wed.) RCA Victor released the **Jailhouse Rock** extended play. This release went on to sell over a million copies.

NOVEMBER

NOV 4   (Mon.) *Jailhouse Rock* peaked at number 1 on *Billboard*'s "Top 100 Sides" chart. It remained at number 1 for a total of six weeks.

Elvis was awarded a "Triple Crown" by *Billboard* as *Jailhouse Rock* completed three weeks atop the pop music "Best Sellers In Stores" chart.

RCA Victor ran a full-page ad for "His Newest" EP, **Jailhouse Rock**. The ad mentioned that RCA was making a major push on the EP, including mailing 3,000 copies to DJ's complete with programming suggestions and plugs.

Time magazine, in an article entitled "Rock Is Solid," admitted that rock 'n' roll was here to stay. In the movie reviews, however, the magazine gave Elvis' performance in "Jailhouse Rock" a thorough going-over, calling Elvis' character a "slob."

NOV 5   (Wed.) Elvis left Los Angeles aboard the USS Matsonia.

NOV 8   (Fri.) "Jailhouse Rock" opened in theaters across the country. In many locations, the "B" feature was "Wayward Girl," with Marcia Henderson and Peter Walker.

NOV 9   (Sat.) Elvis had a press conference aboard the USS Matsonia after its arrival in Honolulu at 8:45 a.m. Elvis and his party stayed at the Hawaiian Village Hotel. Elvis' room was 14A.

NOV 10   (Sun.) Elvis performed a matinee at 3:00 p.m. at the Honolulu Stadium. He had a press conference after the show at his hotel in the Carousel Room. That night, at 8:15 p.m., Elvis gave a repeat performance at the stadium. A total of 14,963 fans attended the shows, which netted $32,000.

NOV 11   (Mon.) Elvis placed eighth in *Billboard*'s "10th Annual Disk Jockey Poll." None of his records, on the other hand, made the list of the DJ's most favorite.

RCA Victor ran a full-color ad for Elvis' **Jailhouse Rock**

EP on the NBC-TV show, "Tic Tac Dough."

In its quarterly review of music, *Billboard* noted that Elvis was the number 1 best selling artist on singles in the pop field.

Elvis performed for the men stationed at Schofield Barracks at Pearl Harbor. Ten thousand members of the armed forces attended the show.

NOV 13 (Wed.) "Jailhouse Rock" entered the *Variety* "National Box Office Survey" at number 4. It stayed on the chart for three weeks, peaking at number 3.

Elvis departed Hawaii aboard the USS Lurline.

NOV 17 (Sun.) Elvis arrived in Los Angeles.

NOV 19 (Tues.) RCA Victor released **Elvis' Christmas Album**. The album was a special package containing eight pages of full-color portraits of Elvis. RCA Victor also released a companion extended play, **Elvis Sings Christmas Songs**.

Reaction to **Elvis' Christmas Album** was legendary. In Portland, radio station KEX disk jockey Al Priddy was fired for playing *White Christmas* by Elvis over the air. Management said the "treatment of the song was in extremely bad taste." KMPC (Los Angeles) DJ Dick Whittinghill said, "No! I won't play it. That's like having Tempest Storm (a noted striptease artist) give Christmas presents to my kids." In Canada, the overwhelming reaction by radio stations was negative. CKXL radio in Calgary was the first Canadian station to ban Elvis' Christmas LP. This was followed by all six of Vancouver's stations. CFRB, Toronto's largest station was followed by CHNX, Halifax, and CKOY, Ottawa, in banning the album for airplay. Other stations who thought the album was in bad taste were CKCW, Moncton, and CJOB, Winnipeg.

NOV 25 (Mon.) **Elvis' Christmas Album** was a "Spotlight" pick in *Billboard*. The trade journal said, "Here's a packaging job that can hardly miss. The disk itself has great Presley treatments of Christmas songs and carols."

Billboard reported "Elvis Banned, Fans Picket" as radio station WCFL in Chicago banned all records by Elvis, probably as a stunt to tie in with the opening of "Jailhouse Rock." The station was picketed by a local fan club, but not before a press release had been sent out to the local news media.

late NOV Toward the end of November, Elvis caught the train for the trip back to Memphis and his Christmas vacation.

The twenty-fourth annual issue of *Movie Life Year Book* magazine featured Elvis on the cover, with an accompanying article
entitled "Elvis Presley's Search For Love."

DECEMBER

DEC 1   (Sun.) The *Memphis Commercial Appeal* reported that
Elvis had donated tickets to an upcoming football game
to Humes High students.

DEC 2   (Mon.) **Elvis' Christmas Album** entered *Billboard*'s LP
chart at number 23. Although it was only on the chart
for seven weeks, it was number 1 for four of those weeks.

DEC 19   (Thurs.) Memphis Draft Board #86 Chairman Milton
Bowers hand-delivered Elvis' draft notice to Graceland.
The order was signed by Grace F. Martin, Clerk of the
local board and dated the previous day. Elvis was ordered to report for induction at 7:45 a.m. on January
20, 1958 to Room 215, 198 South Main Street, Memphis.

DEC 20   (Fri.) Elvis drove to Madison, Tennessee, just north of
Nashville, to confer with Colonel Parker at the Colonel's
home. Asked about his upcoming military service by a
reporter, Elvis replied that he was looking forward to
the experience. "I might have been in uniform before
this if my mother hadn't wanted me to wait for the
draft."

DEC 21   (Sat.) As word of the draft notice circulated through
Memphis, Elvis was besieged by local reporters who had
him dress up in a pair of Army fatigues for photos.
Elvis also took delivery of an $1800 Isetta sports car,
which would be a Christmas gift for Colonel Parker.

DEC 23   (Mon.) In its annual report of the past year's music scene,
Billboard noted that among "1957's Best Selling Records" were *All Shook Up* (number 1), *Too Much* (number 9), *Teddy Bear/Loving You* (number 14), and *Jailhouse Rock* (number 16).

In articles in the nation's press, the full impact of Elvis'
draft notice was outlined: a loss of over $450,000 in
motion picture commitments, including a film for 20th
Century Fox scheduled for 1958 for which Elvis would
have received $200,000, and a commitment with M-G-M
for a film which would probably have been the biography
of Hank Williams, for which Elvis would have received

$250,000 plus fifty percent of the profits; plus loss of numerous personal appearances and a reduced recording schedule for RCA Victor.

Paramount Studios' President Y. Frank Freeman asked for an eight-week deferment for Elvis so that he could finish filming "King Creole," which was scheduled to start shooting January 13th. If cancelled, the studio would lose $350,000 in pre-production expenses. The draft board replied that such a request would have to come directly from Elvis.

DEC 24   (Tues.) Elvis personally wrote a letter to the draft board asking for an extension on the date he would be required to report for duty.

DEC 25   (Wed.) Elvis spent Christmas at Graceland with his family and relatives. He set off fireworks on the grounds.

DEC 26   (Thurs.) Elvis donated a truckload of teddy bears to the National Foundation for Infantile Paralysis.

DEC 27   (Fri.) The Memphis Draft Board granted Elvis a sixty-day deferment on his order to report for duty, rescheduling it until March 20, 1958.

DEC 30   (Mon.) *Billboard* placed its "Review Spotlight" on *Don't/ I Beg Of You*, calling the pairing "two sock performances, as usual, by the phenomenal artist."

DEC 31   (Tues.) Elvis performed a New Year's Eve concert in St. Louis.

Elvis was the cover story in December's issue of *Hep Cats* magazine.

Elvis and the late James Dean shared the cover of the sixth issue of *Movie Album* magazine.

In 1957, Elvis,continued to be the subject of many magazines devoted exclusively to his career. These included *Elvis – His Loves And Marriage, Elvis Presley: The Intimate Story,* and *Elvis Presley – Hero Or Heel?* Elvis was also featured in these one-time magazines, *Rock 'n' Roll Rivals, Teenage Rock And Roll Review,* and *Rock 'N Roll Stars #2.* During 1957, Elvis made his first appearance in a comic book, *Young Lovers* (number 18), with the story "The Real Elvis Presley Complete Life Story."

Mama Liked The Roses

ALL
SHOOK

UP
━━━

ELVIS
Day-By-Day,
1958

JANUARY

JAN 1   (Wed.) RCA Victor raised the price of its 45s from eighty-nine cents to ninety-eight cents. Most other record companies followed suit within a short time.

JAN 7   (Tues.) RCA Victor released *Don't/I Beg Of You.*

JAN 13   (Mon.) RCA Victor ran a full-page ad in *Billboard* claiming "Elvis Presley's First For '58 Already Over 1,000,000 Advance Sales" for *Don't/I Beg Of You.*
Elvis took the train from Memphis to Hollywood, where he would start filming "King Creole" for Hal Wallis and Paramount Pictures. He took a dozen friends with him, including Alan Fortas, Cliff Gleaves, Gene Smith, Freddie Bienstock and Tom Diskin.

JAN 20   (Mon.) Production started on "King Creole" at Paramount's studios in Hollywood.

JAN 23   (Thurs.) Elvis had a recording session at Radio Recorders in Hollywood. He recorded *My Wish Came True* and *Doncha' Think It's Time.* However, neither of these "takes" were satisfactory, and they remained unissued. Elvis used the usual musicians, Scotty, Bill, D.J., and the Jordanaires.

JAN 27   (Mon.) *Don't* and *I Beg Of You* entered the "Top 100" in *Billboard* at number 40 and number 46 respectively.

During January, Elvis had a recording session at Radio Recorders for "King Creole." The regular members of Elvis' band were on hand for this session, along with several Los Angeles studio musicians, adding a Dixieland touch. *Hard Headed Woman, Trouble, New Orleans, King Creole, Crawfish* (which featured the voice of Kitty White), *Dixieland Rock, Lover Doll, Don't Ask Me Why, As Long As I Have You, Young Dreams,* and *Steadfast, Loyal And True* were waxed. (See June 19, 1958.)

Another song recorded by Elvis was *Danny*, which was not released until 1978's **ELVIS: A LEGENDARY PERFORMER, VOL. 3**, but which was covered by Conway Twitty in 1958 with the title changed to *Lonely Blue Boy*. *Bananas, Turtles, Berries And Gumbo* was sung in the film by Lilliane Montevecchi in her part as a stripper. A version of *Dirty, Dirty Feeling* was attempted during these sessions, but it was apparently unsatisfactory and the song was shelved until the April 1960 session.

Harpers magazine published an article entitled "The Man In The Blue Suede Shoes." The cover photo of Elvis in *Hollywood Screen Parade* was accompanied by the article "The Girls That I Dig The Most!" *TV Headliner* magazine's cover article was "Why Hollywood Snubbed Elvis — And Welcomed Boone!"

FEBRUARY

FEB 1   (Sat.) Elvis had a recording session at Radio Recorders. For this session, Hilmer J. ("Tiny") Timbrell was added on guitar and Dudley Brooks sat in on piano. Again, *My Wish Came True* was unsatisfactory (the version released came from September 5, 1957). However, Elvis was able to complete an acceptable take on *Dontcha' Think It's Time*. Also recorded were Hank Williams' *Your Cheating Heart* and an original, *Wear My Ring Around Your Neck*.

early FEB   Elvis, along with his friend Nick Adams and the crew and cast from "King Creole," traveled via train from Los Angeles to New Orleans for location filming of "King Creole." In New Orleans, he reserved the entire tenth floor of the Roosevelt Hotel for his entourage.

Outdoor locations in New Orleans included the French Quarter, a local school (which was filmed on a Sunday), and Lake Ponchartrain (see March 8, 1958).

FEB 24   (Mon.) *Don't/I Beg Of You* was awarded a "Triple Crown" by *Billboard*, as it completed three successive weeks at number 1 on the "Best Sellers In Stores" chart.

MARCH
Filming continued in New Orleans for "King Creole."

MAR 8   (Sat.) Outdoor scenes for "King Creole" were filmed near
          Lake Ponchartrain outside New Orleans.
MAR 9   (Sun.) The film crew continued to film the lakeside scenes.
MAR 10   (Mon.) *Don't* reached number 1 on *Billboard*'s "Top 100
          Sides" chart for the week ending March 1st. It remained
          at number 1 for only one week.
          Elvis caught the train from New Orleans to Los Angeles.
          He had to return to Hollywood to be released from his
          commitment on "King Creole" by Hal Wallis and Para-
          mount Pictures. As soon as he received the release, he
          took the train from Los Angeles to Memphis. On the
          way, he became impatient, disembarked in Dallas and
          rented a fleet of Cadillacs for himself and his entourage,
          and they drove the rest of the way to Memphis.
MAR 14   (Fri.) Elvis arrived in Memphis. He rented the Rainbow
          roller skating rink for eight straight nights at sixty-five
          dollars a night, so he and his friends could have one last,
          long party.
MAR 15   (Sat.) Elvis appeared for two shows at Memphis' Russ-
          wood Baseball Park. Over 14,000 fans attended. During
          one of the shows, Elvis gave away his horseshoe diamond
          ring to a member of the crowd.
MAR 23   (Sun.) Elvis was awarded the "Pops-Rite Popstar Award"
          for being the star whose movies sold the most popcorn.
          The award was presented by Judy Spreckles, M-G-M
          starlet--president of Elvis' national fan club and daughter
          of the owner of Spreckles' sugar, and Joan Young of De-
          troit, on behalf of Jim Blevins, Mayor of Popcorn Village
          near Nashville.
          Elvis had an all-night party at Graceland, which included a
          trip to the Rainbow roller rink.
MAR 24   (Mon.) At 6:35 a.m., Elvis reported to the Memphis Draft
          Board #86. He was accompanied by Anita Wood, Judy
          Spreckles, Lamar Fike, Vernon, Gladys, Uncle Vester's
          family and Colonel Parker. At 7:14 a.m., he and the oth-
          er recruits took a bus to Kennedy Veteran's Hospital for
          a check-up and in-processing. At 4:00 p.m., Elvis arrived
          back at the draft board. Present when Elvis was sworn
          in as a member of the United States Army was Sgt.
          Walter Alden (father of two-year-old Ginger Alden, who

Elvis serenades Judy Spreckles.

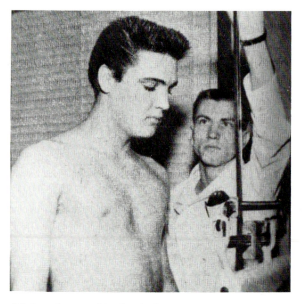

Elvis undergoes his physical examination at Kennedy
Veterans Hospital.

would be Elvis' last girlfriend). Elvis was given serial number 55310761, and he was put in charge of the other fourteen recruits as they boarded an Army bus for the ride to Ft. Chaffee, Arkansas, at 5:00 p.m. Enroute, Elvis was recognized when the bus stopped in West Memphis at the Coffee Cup diner so the soldiers could eat. There was a minor incident, but the recruits arrived at Ft. Chaffee at 11:15 p.m.

MAR 25 (Tues.) Elvis' first full day in the Army began with reveille at 5:30 a.m. He was met by Colonel Parker and seventy photographers and reporters who were on hand to cover the day's events. Elvis was paid seven dollars as part of his first month's military pay check, which would be $83.20 a month. In the morning, Elvis took a five-hour aptitude test. In the afternoon, he received his "G.I." haircut from civilian barber James B. Peterson at a cost of sixty-five cents.

MAR 26 (Wed.) Elvis received his uniform issue. At a press conference in the afternoon, it was announced that Elvis would be stationed on Ft. Hood, Texas, for both his basic training and his advanced tank training with the 2nd Armored Division.

MAR 27 (Thurs.) Elvis received various inoculations at the Ft. Chaffee dispensary.

MAR 28 (Fri.) Elvis and other recruits left Ft. Chaffee in the morning and traveled by bus toward Ft. Hood. At 1:30 p.m., lunch was a quick stop in Hillsboro, Texas, which avoided a crowd of 400 fans who were waiting at the regular lunch stop in Waxlahachie, Texas. The troops arrived at Ft. Hood at 4:34 p.m. Elvis was assigned to Company A, 2nd Medium Tank Battalion, 37th Armor, 2nd Armored Division for his eight-weeks of basic training. He would live in the barracks on the base with the rest of his Company during this time. The press was kept away from the base and Pvt. Presley was allowed some privacy after the past five days' circus atmosphere.

MAR 30 (Sun.) The "Hy Gardner Calling!" interview from July 1, 1956, was re-broadcast over WABD-TV (channel 5) in New York).

MAR 31 (Mon.) Elvis started his eight-weeks basic training. He was allowed to live in relative privacy. He still received 2,000 fan letters a week and hundred of fans even tried to reach Elvis by telephoning the base.

Movie Stars Parade magazine used a 1956 photo of Elvis for their March cover.

APRIL

APR 1   (Tues.) RCA Victor released *Wear My Ring Around Your Neck/Dontcha' Think It's Time.*

APR 7   (Mon.) *Life* magazine published an article entitled "Private Presley's Debut," which covered Elvis' induction into the Army.

Elvis' Golden Records was in the "Review Spotlight" in *Billboard*, where it was hailed as a "natural . . . it's a potent entry." Also in the "Spotlight" in all three music fields, pop-r&b-c&w, was Elvis' latest single, *Wear My Ring Around Your Neck/Doncha'* (or *Dontcha'*) *Think It's Time*, of which the magazines said, "both are likely clicks in all fields." RCA Victor ran a full-page ad for the single claiming "Over 1 Million Advance Sales Again!"

APR 14   (Mon.) The Army rejected a request from DeLeon Springs, Florida, for Elvis to perform at their Armed Forces Day celebration in May.

APR 21   (Mon.) *Wear My Ring Around Your Neck* entered "The Top 100 Sides" chart in *Billboard* at number 7, the highest for any of Elvis' singles in the first week. However, it peaked at number 3 and remained on the charts for only fifteen weeks. **Elvis' Golden Records** entered the album charts at number 9. It, too, was unable to reach number 1, peaking at number 3, but it remained on the chart for a total of fifty weeks. Both charts were for the week ending April 12th.

Elvis was the cover story in *Movie Life* magazine's April issue.

MAY

Elvis continued to train at Ft. Hood. During the last week in May, Elvis was appointed assistant squad leader for the fourteen-mile, full-pack march.

MAY 28 (Wed.) *Variety*, in its review of "King Creole," said the film "shows the young star as a better-than-fair actor."

Dig magazine's May cover had a photo of a civilian Elvis retouched to show him wearing an Army helmet and jacket.

JUNE

JUN 1   (Sun.) After completing the basic eight-weeks training,
           Elvis was granted a two-week leave. He was met by
           Anita Wood in a convertible outside Ft. Hood at 6:00
           a.m. They drove to Memphis, where he relaxed with
           Miss Wood, who was now considered a "Hollywood
           starlet." Many evenings, Elvis rented the Rainbow
           roller skating rink for all-night parties.

JUN 4   (Wed.) Elvis took his parents to a local Memphis theater
           to preview "King Creole."

JUN 10   (Tues.) RCA Victor released *Hard Headed Woman/Don't
           Ask Me Why*. This was the last of Elvis' singles to be
           issued as both a 45 r.p.m. and 78 r.p.m. record. All fu-
           ture single releases were issued as 45 r.p.m. records only.

           Elvis had a recording session at RCA Victor's studios in
           Nashville. The musicians for this session were Walter
           (Hank) Garland and Chet Atkins, guitar; Bob Moore,
           bass; D.J. Fontana, drums; Murray (Buddy) Harmon,
           bongos; Floyd Cramer, piano; and the Jordanaires, vo-
           cals. (Ray Walker had replaced Hugh Jarrett as bass sing-
           er in the Jordanaires.)

           Of the five songs recorded, only one had been a hit prior
           to Elvis' recording: *A Fool Such As I*, which was a
           country hit for Hank Snow in 1952 and a pop hit for
           Jo Stafford in 1953. All of the other songs were original
           to Elvis: *I Need Your Love Tonight, A Big Hunk O'
           Love, Ain't That Loving You Baby*, and *I Got Stung.
           Ain't That Loving You Baby* was not released until
           1964, and then it was spliced from two or more takes.

           The session lasted into the morning of the 11th, and then
           Elvis returned to Memphis.

JUN 13   (Fri.) During the week, Ed Sullivan had approached
           Colonel Parker in an attempt to have Elvis back on his
           TV show as soon as he was out of the Army.

           In Memphis, Elvis rented the Rainbow roller rink for a
           party.

JUN 14   (Sat.) Elvis returned to Ft. Hood.

JUN 16   (Mon.) He started eight weeks of advanced individual
           training as an armor crewman, followed by six weeks
           of training with his unit.

           Hard Headed Woman/Don't Ask Me Why was in *Billboard*'s
           "Review Spotlight," with the journal adding that the
           single "should score in all fields."

Home on leave, Elvis poses at the wheel of his convertible.

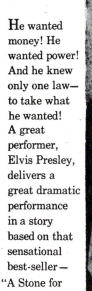

mid-JUN   Within a week after his return to Ft. Hood, Elvis requested that Vernon and Gladys join him while he completed training. The Presleys moved into a rented three-bedroom house-trailer parked just outside Ft. Hood, but it proved to be a problem because of the lack of security. The family moved into a three-bedroom rented house in Killeen. Grandma Presley and Lamar Fike also came from Memphis to live in Killeen. Elvis was allowed to move in with his family, since under Army regulations, they were his dependents.

One of the first visitors at the house was Anita Wood from Memphis.

Elvis often visited on weekends with Eddie Fadal and his family at Fadal's home, 2807 Laskar Avenue in Waco, Texas, forty-five miles from Ft. Hood. One Sunday at 8 p.m., Elvis and the Fadals went to the Waco Theater to see Nick Adams in "No Time For Sergeants." A curious crowd forced them to leave the theater at 9:00 p.m., so they returned to the Fadal home.

Elvis and his friends visited Dallas one weekend where they stayed in a motel with the Fadals.

JUN 19   (Thurs.) Chet Atkins produced a session in Nashville where vocals were overdubbed by the Jordanaires on *Steadfast, Loyal And True* and *Lover Doll* for release on the **King Creole** LP.

JUN 30   (Mon.) *Hard Headed Woman* entered *Billboard*'s "Top 100 Sides" chart at number 15 for the week ending June 21st. It remained on the chart for thirteen weeks and peaked at number 2.

The June issue of *Movie Stars Parade* magazine had a photo of Elvis on the cover and the accompanying article entitled "This Is The Story We Hoped We'd Never Have To Print," which attempted to correct some of the misinterpretations in an earlier article, "Ricky vs. Elvis — Hollywood's Hottest Feud."

JULY

JUL 2   (Wed.) "King Creole" opened in many theaters across the country. In many locations, the co-feature was "Bullwhip," with Guy Madison.

JUL 4   (Fri.) Elvis and his entourage visited the Fadals in Waco to celebrate Independence Day. They ate hamburgers at

Mrs. LaNelle Fadal's brother-in-law's house.

The *Los Angeles Examiner*, in reviewing "King Creole," said that the film had "such a profusion of music, I wonder whether Elvis' partisans will notice that he has improved somewhat as an actor."

The *Los Angeles Mirror-News* said, "[Elvis] is no longer depicted as the churlish, egotistical singing idol."

JUL 7   (Mon.) *Billboard* "Spotlighted" Elvis' extended play, **King Creole, Vol. 1**, saying it was "a natural to follow the smash sales pattern of his previous EP's."

Don't Ask Me Why entered the "Hot 100" at number 58 for the week of June 28th. It stayed nine weeks, peaking at number 28.

JUL 9   (Wed.) "King Creole" was number 5 on *Variety*'s "National Box Office Survey." The film remained on the list for four weeks.

The *Beverly Hills Citizen*, in its review of "King Creole," said of Elvis, "[He] does his best acting."

JUL 21   (Mon.) **King Creole, Vol. 1** entered *Billboard*'s EP chart at number 1; it remained number 1 for a total of twenty-three weeks.

Other than the success of the "King Creole" movie and records, July also was a busy month for Private Presley. He was sued for $5,000 by a Washington, D.C., secretary for damages suffered in 1956 when her car was struck by Elvis' car (sorry, no further details available). Elvis and his friends went to Temple, Texas, for a rhythm and blues show. Elvis stayed backstage with the performers. Elvis was ticketed in Ft. Worth for driving 95 m.p.h. in a 60 m.p.h. zone. And, he continued to train at Ft. Hood.

A photo of Elvis in his Army fatigues made the cover of *TV Star Parade* magazine's July issue.

TV And Movie Screen ran a 1956 photo of Elvis on its cover and asked the question, "Is Elvis Secretly Married?"

AUGUST

During the first of the month, Gladys became ill. She and Vernon were driven to Temple, Texas by Elvis, where she could be seen by a doctor.

AUG 4   (Mon.) In a new section titled "Spotlight Winners Of The Week," *Billboard* picked the extended play, **King Creole, Vol. 2**, saying "the first edition has proven a smash and this should do likewise."

AUG 8 (Fri.) Elvis drove Gladys and Vernon to the railroad station in Temple, where they boarded the train for Memphis.

AUG 9 (Sat.) Upon their arrival in Memphis, Gladys was taken to Methodist Hospital, where it was determined that she had acute hepatitis.

AUG 11 (Mon.) Gladys' doctors in Memphis asked the Army to allow Elvis to return to Memphis so he could visit his mother. Initially, the request was denied.

AUG 12 (Tues.) After urging by the Memphis doctors, Elvis was finally granted emergency leave. He drove to Waco and caught a plane to Memphis, arriving late in the afternoon. He visited Gladys at the hospital at 7:45 p.m. and stayed several hours.

AUG 13 (Wed.) Gladys' physical condition worsened. Elvis visited the hospital during the day and again at night. He returned to Graceland about midnight.

AUG 14 (Thurs.) Gladys passed away at 3:15 a.m. Vernon was at her side at the time, and he called Graceland where he talked to Elvis' cousin, Billy Smith, who was the person who relayed the news to Elvis.

About 10 a.m., Newton Thomas West, father of Red West, died in Memphis. Red was in the U.S. Marines at the time and was enroute from Norfolk, Virginia, on emergency leave when his father passed away.

That afternoon, Gladys' body was laid in state at Graceland.

AUG 15 (Fri.) Gladys' body was transferred to the Memphis Funeral Home for the 1:00 p.m. funeral service. Elvis' actor-friend Nick Adams and Anita Wood were on hand, along with 400 invited guests, to console Elvis and Vernon. Outside the funeral home, 3,000 fans grieved along with Elvis. Rev. James Hamill gave the eulogy, and the Blackwood Brothers, who had flown in from an engagement in North Carolina on a plane chartered by Elvis, sang *Precious Memories*, one of Gladys' favorite songs, and *Rock Of Ages*, her favorite hymn. Along the route to Forest Hills Cemetery, thousands of fans lined the street. The cemetery was three miles north of Graceland on Highway 51.

AUG 16 (Sat.) Elvis, Gene Smith, Alan Fortas, and Lamar Fike went to the funeral home to pay their respects to Red West's father.

Elvis and Vernon comfort each other over the death of Gladys Presley.

mid-AUG During the remainder of Elvis' leave, he stayed at Graceland. The Tennessee Highway Patrol took him on morning helicopter rides, and Elvis learned how to take off
and land the patrol's helicopter. Elvis also visited the
skating rink and movies, in an attempt to ease his grief.
He also bought a van and toured the Tennessee country-
side.

AUG 25 (Mon.) Elvis reported back to Ft. Hood.

SEPTEMBER

SEP 6 (Sat.) The **King Creole** album started up *Billboard*'s LP
chart. It peaked at number 2 and stayed only fifteen
weeks.

SEP 12 (Fri.) The Associated Press reported that Elvis had received
orders assigning him to the 3rd Armored Division in
Germany as a truck driver.

SEP 15 (Mon.) Kitty Dolen, whom Elvis had dated off and on
since September 1957, visited at the Presley home in
Killeen.

SEP 19 (Fri.) Elvis' unit boarded a troop train at 7:00 p.m.,
bound for the Military Ocean Terminal in Brooklyn,
New York. Elvis was seen off by Vernon, Grandma
Minnie, Red West, Lamar Fike, and Anita Wood.
Aboard the train to New Jersey, Elvis shared the same car
with Charlie Hodge, former singer with Red Foley's
Foggy River Boys. The night of the 19th, the train
made a short stop in the Memphis switching yard to
change train crews.

SEP 22 (Mon.) At 9:00 a.m., the train arrived at the Brooklyn
Army Terminal. One hundred fans waited patiently
at the gate, but they were too far away from the train to
see Elvis disembark. Elvis held a forty-minute press conference aboard the USS General Randall before he and
1,170 G.I.s departed for Germany.

late SEP Once aboard the ship, Elvis was transferred to the area
reserved for the NCOs, to protect him from autograph
seekers. His roommate again was Charlie Hodge. Both
participated in a serviceman's variety show on-board
ship. Elvis played piano and Charlie was the comedian/
emcee.

SEP 29 (Mon.) For the first time since February 1956, Elvis did
not have a record in *Billboard*'s listing of the top 100

1958

singles for the week ending October 5th. He remained "hitless" for a total of five weeks.

Elvis shared the cover of the September issue of *Movie Life* magazine with Ricky Nelson. The accompanying article was "Why Elvis And I Can't Marry Now" (which had nothing to do with Ricky, of course).

OCTOBER

OCT 1   (Wed.) The USS General Randall docked at Bremerhaven, West Germany, where over 1,500 fans were waiting. The troops marched down the gangplank and across a fifty-foot area to a waiting troop train, out of view of most fans. The train traveled through West Germany all day, finally reaching Ray Caserne, Friedberg, home of the U.S. 7th Army. At 1:00 a.m., as Elvis was leaving the train, ten girls broke through the guards to surround Elvis.

OCT 2-5   (Thurs.-Sun.) The base had an open house for the press. Elvis' father and grandmother arrived in West Germany to set up housekeeping at Ritter's Park Hotel in Bad Homberg. It was announced in a press conference at the Enlisted Men's Club that Elvis would be assigned to Company "D," 1st Battalion, 32nd Armor, 3rd Armored Division of the 7th Army, as a jeep driver for Lt. Col. Henry Grimm.

Also arriving with Vernon and Grandma Minnie were Lamar Fike and Red West.

OCT 5   (Sun.) As Elvis and his entourage walked in a local park, he was spotted by German photographers who suggested that he be photographed with sixteen-year-old Margrit Buergin. Elvis dated her off and on for the year-and-a-half he was stationed in West Germany.

OCT 6   (Mon.) *Life* magazine ran an article entitled "Farewell Squeal For Elvis," which covered Elvis' departure from the United States.

OCT 7   (Tues.) The *Memphis Press-Scimitar* reported that Elvis was telephoning Anita Wood from Germany.

early OCT   Elvis and his family and friends, including Vernon, Grandma Minnie, Lamar Fike and Red West, moved into a three-bedroom apartment in the Hotel Gruenwald in Bad Homburg for a short time, before settling into a

On his first Sunday in Germany, Elvis strolls with (from the left) Lamar Fike, Red West, Vernon, Margit Buergin, and some youthful fans.

Elvis takes target practice while on manuevers.

four-bedroom home at 14 Goethestrasse in Bad Nauheim which Elvis rented for $800 a month.

OCT 21   (Tues.) RCA Victor released *One Night/I Got Stung*. This
was Elvis' first single which was not released as a 78
r.p.m. record. All remaining singles appeared only as 45
r.p.m. records.

OCT 27   (Mon.) Elvis' new single was a "Billboard Pick" in the
"Spotlight Winner" section. *One Night* was called a
"rockaballad" and *I Got Stung* was a "rockabilly effort."
"Tri-market appeal" was predicted for the record.

OCT 29   (Wed.) Elvis attended a concert by Bill Haley and his
Comets in Stuttgart.

Elvis was the cover story of the October issue of *TV And Movie
Screen* magazine. The accompanying article entitled "The
Truth About My Love Affair With Elvis," was written by Elvis'
long-time girlfriend, Anita Wood.

The October issue of *Photoplay* magazine featured a cover
photo of Elvis in his Class A summer uniform in front
of Graceland, taken during his June leave, and ran an
article entitled "Please Don't Forget Me When I'm Gone."

The October issue of *Motion Picture* magazine featured a foldout
double-page color photo of Elvis in uniform.

Elvis was featured on the cover of the October issue of *Cool & Hep
Cats* magazine.

"Elvis' Only Faithful Girl" was the story accompanying the cover
picture of Elvis in *Movie Stars And TV Close-Ups Parade*.

NOVEMBER

NOV 3   (Mon.) *I Got Stung* entered *Billboard*'s "Hot 100" chart
at number 65. It remained on the chart for sixteen
weeks.

At Grafenwohr, West Germany, Elvis joined the 32nd Tank
Battalion for several weeks of maneuvers near the border
with Czechoslovakia. While stationed at Grafenwohr,
Elvis dated eighteen-year-old Elizabeth Stefaniak, a
German by birth and stepdaughter of Sgt. Raymond
McCormick.

NOV 15   (Mon.) *One Night* entered *Billboard*'s "Hot 100" at number 30 for the week ending November 16th. It remained
on the chart for seventeen weeks and peaked at number 4.

NOV 27   (Thurs.) Elvis was promoted to Private First Class (PFC).

In November, RCA Victor released a re-packaged **Elvis' Christmas Album**, with a different front cover and photos of Elvis in uniform on the back.

DECEMBER

DEC 15   (Mon.) In *Billboard*'s annual review of the year's music, Elvis' decline on the charts was apparent. On the "Chart Toppers of 1958" list, *Don't/I Beg Of You* was number 3, *Wear My Ring Around Your Neck/Doncha. Think It's Time* was number 22, and *Hard Headed Woman/Don't Ask Me Why* was 49. Only on the EP chart did Elvis retain his superiority: **Jailhouse Rock** (number 1), **King Creole, Vol. 1** (number 4), **Elvis** (number 6), **King Creole, Vol. 2** (number 8), **Loving You, Vol. 1** (number ten), **Peace In The Valley** (number 21), **Elvis Sings Christmas Songs** (number 25), and **Heartbreak Hotel** (number 30). On the LP chart for 1958, he only had one listed, **Elvis' Golden Records** at number eighteen.

DEC 20   (Thurs.) Elvis' unit returned to Friedberg. Elizabeth Stefaniak came to Bad Nauheim to be Elvis' secretary. Elvis was one of several men in his outfit to receive a three-day pass for excelling while on maneuvers. As soon as he arrived home, Elvis went to a local auto dealer and bought a used BMW 507 for $3,750. The two-seater was white-and-black with leather upholstery. Elvis was photographed in the showroom with Ursla Siebert in front of the car for a press release. Hedda Hopper, noted columnist, wanted to interview Elvis while she was touring through West Germany, but she was unable to meet with him.

DEC 23   (Tues.) *Look* magazine published an article entitled "Elvis And The Frauleins," which included photos of Elvis and Margrit Buergin.

DEC 25   (Thurs.) Due to the tragedies within Elvis' family, no one felt much like celebrating, and Christmas dinner was eaten at the base mess hall.

The Christmas card sent out by Elvis and the Colonel for 1958 showed Elvis in his summer Class A uniform, with Colonel Parker in a Santa Claus suit.

Elvis was featured on the one-time magazine *Who's Who In Rock 'N Roll* during 1958.

The First Time
Ever I Saw Your Face

ALL
SHOOK
UP

ELVIS
Day-By-Day,
1959

JANUARY

JAN 1   (Thurs.) While returning from a shopping tour of Frankfurt, Vernon and Elizabeth Stefaniak were hurt in an accident at night on the Frankfurt-Kassel autobahn five miles from Bad Nauheim. Elvis' BMW was totalled.

JAN 2   (Fri.) In Germany, following the wreck, there were rumors that Elvis had been killed.

JAN 3   (Sat.) In order to quiet the rumors, Elvis publicly donated a pint of blood to the local Red Cross.

JAN 7   (Wed.) "Love Me Tender" made the "All-Time Box Office Champs" list in *Variety*, with a total domestic gross of $4.5 million.

JAN 8   (Thurs.) Elvis was interviewed via trans-Atlantic telephone by Dick Clark on his "American Bandstand" show on ABC-TV as part of a celebration of Elvis' twenty-fourth birthday.

The January issue of *Movie Life* ran a cover picture of Elvis.

FEBRUARY

FEB 9   (Mon.) The album, **For LP Fans Only** was released by RCA Victor.

FEB 16   (Mon.) **For LP Fans Only** was a spotlight pick in *Billboard*, which said, "The chanter's genuine command for this type of material is displayed in full."

MARCH

MAR 2   (Mon.) Elvis sent a telegram of condolence to Eddie Fadal in Waco, Texas, whose mother had died recently.

MAR 10 (Tues.) RCA Victor shipped Elvis' new single, *(Now And Then There's) A Fool Such As I/I Need Your Love Tonight,* to dealers.

MAR 11 (Wed.) Elvis was awarded a gold record for *A Fool Such As I,* based on advance orders of over one million.

MAR 16 (Mon.) Elvis had one of his worst weeks on the charts in *Billboard.* He had no records on the "Hot 100," the "Best Selling LP's," the c&w best sellers, or the r&b best sellers. On the EP list, which Elvis had so long dominated, **King Creole, Vol. 1** was number 9, and **Elvis, Vol. 1** was number 10.

RCA Victor ran a full-page ad for *A Fool Such As I/I Need Your Love Tonight,* which noted that the record had already sold a million copies. *Billboard* picked the record for its "Spotlight" section, saying: "strong warbling on both [songs] adds up to a two-sided click."

MAR 23 (Mon.) *A Fool Such As I* entered *Billboard*'s "Hot 100" chart for the week ending March 29th at number 64. It stayed on the chart for fifteen weeks and peaked at number two. **For LP Fans Only** entered the "Best Selling LP's" list for the week ending March 14th at number 20. It only stayed on the chart for eight weeks, peaking at number 19.

MAR 24 (Tues.) The FBI investigated a letter postmarked March 12th from Canton, Ohio. In the letter, it was warned that Elvis was to be the subject of a murder attempt by a "Red soldier" from East Germany, who would slip into West Germany disguised as an American. The soldier was supposedly under orders to kill Elvis by any means possible, including blowing up the home in which Elvis was staying. Nothing came of the threat in the letter.

MAR 30 (Mon.) *I Need Your Love Tonight* entered the "Hot 100" in *Billboard* for the week ending April 5th at number 33. It stayed on the list for thirteen weeks, peaking at number 4.

Colonel Parker reported that he was turning down all TV offers for Elvis after he was released from the Army. Instead, he planned a 100-city closed-circuit television concert to re-introduce Elvis to the American fans.

APRIL

APR 10   (Fri.) Elvis was one of the hosts as Friedberg Army Base held an open house.

APR 13   (Mon.) While on leave in Germany, Elvis campaigned for the Salk vaccine by publicly receiving an inoculation.

APR 17   (Fri.) Private Presley supervised a crew of soldiers sent by the Army to Steinfurth to aid the town in moving its large memorial statue to World War I.

APR 27   (Mon.) *A Fool Such As I* peaked at number 2 on *Billboard's* "Hot 100" chart for the week ending May 3rd. It remained at number 2 for only one week.

Elvis was featured on the cover of *Movie World* and *TV Star Parade* magazine's April issue.

MAY

ABC-TV announced in New York that it would have an Elvis spectacular upon his return to the States. ABC said that they would finance the show at $100,000.

MAY 23   (Sat.) *Billboard* reported that as part of the **Touch Of Gold** EP, RCA Victor was enclosing a special fan club card from Elvis.

The May issue of *Movie Mirror* magazine featured Elvis on the cover. In *Movie World*, Elvis, dressed in fatigues, shared the cover with Debbie Reynolds.

JUNE

JUN 1   (Mon.) Elvis was promoted to Specialist 4th Class (Corporal). His pay increased to $99.37 a month.

JUN 3   (Wed.) Elvis was hospitalized for tonsillitis at the Army's 97th General Hospital in Frankfurt.

JUN 8   (Mon.) RCA Victor ran a full-page ad in *Billboard*, noting that Paramount had re-released a double package of Elvis' movies, "Loving You" and "King Creole."

JUN 9   (Tues.) Elvis was discharged from the hospital.

JUN 17   (Wed.) Elvis started a two-week leave with a visit to Munich. He stayed with Vera Tschechowa, a German actress, and her parents. Elvis had met her while doing

ELVIS PRESLEY
A TOUCH OF GOLD
Volume I

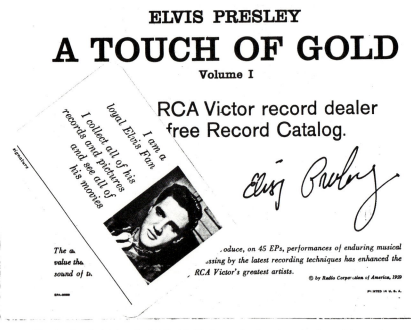

I am a loyal Elvis Fan I collect all of his records and pictures and see all of his movies

RCA Victor record dealer free Record Catalog.

The a. value tha. sound of t.

...oduce, on 45 EPs, performances of enduring musical ...ssing by the latest recording techniques has enhanced the RCA Victor's greatest artists.

© by Radio Corporation of America, 1959

PRINTED IN U.S.A.

The back of *A Touch Of Gold, Volume 1*, showing the fan club card.

One of Elvis' favorite photos of himself, taken during his time
in the Army.

some publicity photos in Friedberg. He and Vera,
accompanied by Elvis' bodyguards Red West, Lamar
Fike, and Cliff Gleaves, met Walter Brandin and his wife
and Toni Netzel, public relations for Polydor Records,
at the Operncafe before going to the Karne for dinner.
After dinner, the group went to the Moulin Rouge night
club, located in the Munzgasse district.

JUN 19   (Thurs.) Elvis and his group returned to the Moulin
          Rouge alone.

JUN 20   (Fri.) Elvis and his companions traveled to Paris, where
          they stayed in the Prince de Galles (Prince of Wales)
          Hotel. During his visit to Paris, Elvis visited the Lido de
          Paris night club.

JUN 26   (Fri.) Elvis returned to Friedberg with his friends.

The June edition of *Movieland And TV Time* magazine featured
a cover photo of Elvis in fatigues. Inside there were seven pages
of photos of Elvis from Germany.
Screen Stars' June issue had a cover photo of Elvis in his dress uniform, and wondered about "The Girl Elvis Will Come Home To."

JULY

JUL 6   (Mon.) *A Big Hunk O' Love* entered *Billboard*'s "Hot 100"
          for the week ending July 12th. It remained on the
          chart for fourteen weeks and reached number 1.

JUL 13   (Mon.) *My Wish Came True* started up the "Hot 100" at
          number 39 for the week ending the 19th. It peaked at
          number 12 and stayed eleven weeks.

AUGUST

AUG 3   (Mon.) *Billboard* reported that *A Big Hunk O' Love* had
          passed the million mark in sales, making it Elvis' four-
          teenth consecutive gold record and the fifth since Elvis
          entered the Army.

AUG 10   (Mon.) *Billboard* reported that *A Big Hunk O' Love*
          reached the number 1 spot on the "Hot 100" for the
          week ending August 16th. It was number 1 for two weeks.

In August, Paramount Pictures reported that Elvis' first film following his discharge from the Army would be titled "G.I. Blues."

SEPTEMBER

SEP 14   (Mon.) Elvis' album, **A Date With Elvis** was a "Spotlight" pick in *Billboard*, which said, "Strong showmanship is evidenced in packaging this elaborate double-fold LP."

SEP 21   (Mon.) **A Date With Elvis** entered *Billboard*'s LP chart at number 39 for the week ending September 20th. The album only stayed on the chart for eight weeks and peaked at number 32.

SEP 26   (Sat.) The *Saturday Evening Post* covered the current state of rock 'n' roll in an article titled "It All Started With Elvis."

OCTOBER

The 32nd Armored Division was shipped to Wildfliken to participate in the Army's "Winter Shield" war games near the Swiss border.

OCT 24   (Sat.) Elvis suffered from a recurrence of tonsillitis. He was shipped back to Frankfurt, where he was hospitalized in the 97th General Hospital.

OCT 29   (Thurs.) Elvis was discharged from the hospital, but he was confined to his quarters until Monday, November 2nd.

NOVEMBER

NOV 2   (Mon.) Fifteen enthusiastic Elvis fans in Leipzig, East Germany, were given prison terms ranging from six months to four-and-a-half years for marching through Leipzig shouting derogatory remarks about East German music and Communist party boss Walter Urich. The youths had also shouted, "Long live Elvis Presley."

NOV 9   (Mon.) For the first time since Elvis' records first started making the territorial charts in *Billboard* in August 1954, Elvis did not have a record on any chart in the journal. This situation would remain the same, with only a few exceptions, until April 1960.

NOV 19   (Thurs.) During a press conference in New York for RCA Victor's Rod Lauren, an RCA Victor executive said that Elvis would probably change his singing style when he returned to civilian life.

Elvis feeds Priscilla some cake during a holiday party.

The 1959 Christmas card from Elvis and the Colonel.

NOV 20   (Fri.) Colonel Parker's office was flooded with telephone
         calls from fans who protested any change in Elvis' style.

In November, Captain Joseph Beaulieu was transferred to Weis-
    baden Air Force Base near Friedberg. He was accompanied by
    his wife and daughters, including step-daughter Priscilla Ann,
    age fourteen. About a week and a half after their arrival,
    Priscilla was invited to meet Elvis by Curry Grant, a mutual
    friend. Their initial meeting took place in Elvis' home at 14
    Goetestrasse. (Peter Von Wechmar has also been mentioned as
    the person who introduced Elvis and Priscilla.)

DECEMBER
Elvis donated what was described as a "large check" to the Stein-
    muehle Orphanage near Friedberg.

DEC 14   (Mon.) In *Billboard*'s "12th Annual Disk Jockey Poll,"
         Elvis ranked as the twelfth "Most Played Artist." On
         the "Hot 100 For 1959," *A Big Hunk O' Love* was num-
         ber 30, *A Fool Such As I* was 34, *I Need Your Love To-
         night* was 44, and *My Wish Came True* was 93.
DEC 16   (Wed.) The Mississippi State Legislature passed a com-
         mendation for Elvis for the benefit show that he per-
         formed in Tupelo in September 1957.
DEC 21   (Mon.) The album, **Elvis Gold Records, Vol. 2** was "Spot-
         lighted" in *Billboard*, which said, "carrying out the
         theme of gold records is Presley himself in a crazy, gold
         lame suit." *Billboard* predicted that the LP would be
         "red hot."
DEC 25   (Fri.) Elvis hosted a Christmas party at his home in Bad
         Nauheim. Among the guests were Priscilla Beaulieu,
         Dee Stanley, and her husband Bill. Elvis gave Priscilla
         a gold wrist watch, which had a large diamond set into
         the face.
         The Christmas card from Elvis and the Colonel showed
         Elvis in uniform in two poses, with a German Shepherd
         and with horses. Colonel Parker was wearing a Santa
         suit on the card.

LATE 1959

Late in 1959, Colonel Parker had a make-believe newspaper front page printed with the banner headline, "Elvis To Re-Enlist." The Colonel then had the fake front page planted with a regular newspaper and delivered to producer Hal Wallis.

The December issue of *Starlife TV And Movies* magazine had a cover photo of Elvis while the accompanying article mused "Who's Waiting For Elvis?"

Elvis was the subject of the magazine *Elvis In The Army* during 1959.

Fools Fall In Love

JANUARY

JAN 20 (Tues.) Elvis was promoted to Sergeant. He commanded a three-man reconnaissance team for the 3rd Armored Division's 32nd Scout Platoon. He pay increased to $122.31 a month.

FEBRUARY

Early in the month, in anticipation of Elvis' impending discharge from the Army, Grandma and Aunt Delta along with some of Elvis' friends returned to Memphis.

FEB 15 (Mon.) **Elvis' Gold Records, Vol. 2** entered *Billboard*'s LP chart for the week ending February 19th at number 36. It was off the chart the next week and then reappeared for five weeks in April and May, never reaching higher than number 31.

FEB 17 (Wed.) East Germany's government banned Elvis' records and films. There were riots when teenagers were prohibited from crossing the border to West Germany.

FEB 29 (Mon.) "Elvis' Return Stirs Publicity Blitz" was the title of the front page article in *Billboard* by Bob Rolontz, which said: "Elvis' impact on the music world – thruout the world – has been greater than any single personality in the music business for the last, and perhaps two, decades. He shaped the course of American and European pop music, to a style that has now been absorbed into the mainstream of pop music."

Billboard also ran another front-page article on "The Legend Of Elvis Presley," which covered his early days.

Billboard also reported that Elvis had eighteen consecutive million selling singles, a mark which was unequaled by any other artist. This, added to his three million-selling

Sergeant Presley shows off his new stripes.

Elvis commands a reconnaissance jeep patrol during winter war exercises in Germany.

EPs and his album sales, had equaled to total sales of
$50,000,000 for Elvis' records.

LATE FEBRUARY

Late in February, Elvis started out-processing prior to his discharge from the U.S. Army.

Elvis was featured on the cover of the February issue of *Popular
Screen* magazine.

MARCH

MAR 1   (Tues.) A press conference was held at Friedberg Army
Base for Elvis to comment on his days in Germany.
Portions of the press conference were aired over the
U.S. Armed Forces Radio Network as a five-minute
interview.

MAR 2   (Wed.) Elvis boarded a Military Air Transport Service
(MATS) C-118, along with seventy-nine other G.I.s, at
Frankfort's Rhein-Main Airport for the trip back to the
United States. The plane made a brief stop at Prest-
wick Airport in Scotland for refueling.

The Air Force plane was followed by an airliner with two
dozen suitcases, Vernon, Lamar Fike, a female secretary (Elizabeth Stefaniak?), and 2,000 phonograph
records.

MAR 3   (Thurs.) Elvis' military transport arrived at McGuire AFB,
New Jersey, at 7:42 a.m. in a driving snow storm. Elvis
went to Ft. Dix, which is next to McGuire AFB, for
breakfast in the mess hall. Following his processing
through customs, Elvis held a two-hour press conference
in a ballroom full of reporters and cameramen. Attending the press conference were actress Tina Louise, who
represented a New York radio station, and Nancy Sinatra, daughter of singer Frank Sinatra, who presented
Elvis with two lace-front shirts, presents from her father.

Also very much in attendance at the press conference was
Colonel Parker. When asked how much Elvis' Army
salary was, he replied, "I don't know. I don't get a com-
mission on that." However, he did add that he wanted
the press to "please state that the government gets 91%
[of Elvis' earnings] in tax. Elvis is not a millionaire."
He added that Elvis' gross earnings in 1959 were $1.9

Elvis arrives home at McGuire AFB during
a driving snowstorm.

Leaving the Army, a happy Sergeant Presley holds
a press conference.

million.

Also on hand at the press conference were Gene Aberbach of Hill & Range Publishing, Co., Steve Sholes of RCA Victor, and Tom Diskin from Colonel Parker's office.

MAR 4 (Wed.) Harry Hunt, general manager of Hunt Brothers Circus, offered to have Elvis perform on April 15th at Palisades Park in New Jersey. Colonel Parker said Elvis was "not available," and suggested to the press that it was a publicity stunt.

Elvis continued out-processing at Ft. Dix. Meanwhile, outside, the weather continued to be a factor as the snowstorm virtually marooned the press corps at Ft. Dix. Tina Louise was reported to have gotten stuck in a snowbank while attempting to make the drive back to New York City.

MAR 5 (Sat.) Elvis was discharged from the Army. His final paycheck was $109.54 (less ninety-one percent = $9.86).

In Washington, Senator Estes Kefauver read a tribute of Elvis into the Congressional Record.

Elvis boarded "The Tennesseean" railroad train for the trip back to Memphis. Along the way, the train stopped several times and, at each siding, there were hundreds of fans waiting.

MAR 7 (Mon.) "Presley Return Sparks Wide Air Activity" was the title of *Billboard*'s front page story, which outlined the many radio tributes planned to take advantage of the increased attention to Elvis as he arrived back in the states. The article "Victor Distrib Machinery Oiled For Another Elvis Hit" said that Elvis' next single release, which had not yet been recorded, was already guaranteed a million sales. However, the article said, "In light of recent personnel changes at the exec level at Victor it has been strongly indicated that Colonel Tom Parker has insisted on increased recording responsibilities to the point where Presley becomes more isolated from direct Victor authority." The article went on to say, "Even now, certain revisions are being written into the Presley-Victor contract. These are known to deal to some extent with tax matters, but it is seen as likely that certain personal relationships with the artist may be spelled out in the pact."

Elvis arrived in Memphis. The waiting crowd numbered into the thousands. Colonel Parker had provided Elvis

Elvis and Frank Sinatra share a laugh during taping of the TV special
"Frank Sinatra's Welcome Home Party For Elvis Presley."

with a dress uniform, which accidentally promoted him
by displaying four stripes on the sleeve.

MAR 8   (Tues.) There was a press conference at Graceland in
         Elvis' office.
MAR 9   (Wed.) M-G-M re-released "Jailhouse Rock." The film
         had grossed $4 million in its original release in 1957.
MAR 12   (Sat.) Elvis attended a performance of "Holiday On Ice"
         in Memphis, and invited the cast back to Graceland.
MAR 14   (Mon.) *Life* magazine ran an article covering Elvis' depar-
         ture from Germany, which was titled "Farewell To
         Priscilla, Hello To U.S.A."
MAR 15   (Tues.) Elvis again played host to the "Holiday On Ice"
         cast at Graceland.
MAR 20   (Sun.) Elvis traveled to Nashville for his first post-Army
         recording session at RCA Victor's new Studio "B," and
         his first session in stereo. On hand were Scotty Moore,
         guitar; Bob Moore and Hank Garland, bass; D.J. Fontana
         and Buddy Harman, drums; Floyd Cramer, piano, and
         the Jordanaires, vocals. The session started at 8:00 p.m.
         and lasted until 7:00 the next morning.
         The songs recorded for this session included two for an
         immediate single release, *Stuck On You* and *Fame And
         Fortune*; three for a new album, *Make Me Know It,
         Soldier Boy*, and *It Feels So Right*; and *A Mess Of Blues*,
         which was held for release as a B-side later in 1960. (At
         the time of this session, RCA Victor had received ad-
         vance orders totalling 1,275,077 for a single which had
         not yet been recorded.)
         Following the session, Elvis returned to Memphis.
MAR 21   (Mon.) Elvis received his first degree black belt in karate.
MAR 22   (Tues.) Elvis departed from Memphis on the Missouri
         Pacific's "Texas Eagle" train for Miami. Colonel Parker
         arranged each whistle-stop along the way to resemble a
         Presidential campaign trip, with Elvis being introduced
         to the ever-increasing throngs from the train's rear plat-
         form. In Hollywood, Florida, it was reported that eggs
         were thrown at the train, but later, a contingent of fans
         apologized for the rudeness of their town.
MAR 26   (Sat.) Elvis was paid $125,000 for his first television
         appearance following his Army discharge, which was
         videotaped at 6:15 p.m. in the Grand Ballroom of the
         Fontainebleau Hotel in Miami Beach, Florida. The ap-
         pearance was part of the "Frank Sinatra —Timex Show,"

also billed as "Frank Sinatra's Welcome Home Party For Elvis Presley," which would air on May 8th over ABC-TV. Elvis sang *Fame And Forture* and *Stuck On You,* backed by the Nelson Riddle Orchestra, augmented by Scotty Moore, D.J. Fontana, and the Jordanaires. He closed his part of the show with a duet with Sinatra in which Elvis sang *Witchcraft*, and Sinatra sang *Love Me Tender*. Following the taping, Elvis and Sammy Davis, Jr., a guest on the show, appeared on stage to thank the audience, which numbered about 1,000, including 300 Elvis fan club members recruited by Colonel Parker to make sure that Elvis received a big homecoming welcome. Other guests on the TV show were Peter Lawford, Joey Bishop, and Nancy Sinatra.

MAR 28   (Mon.) *Billboard* placed the single, *Stuck On You/Fame And Fortune*, in its "Spotlight" section, saying, "Presley's back and he's as hot as ever."

(NOTE: The initial pressing run for this single was 1.3 million copies. During Elvis' heyday as a top selling artist (1956--1958), RCA Victor regularly pressed 1.3 million copies of each of his singles. During the lull, while he was in the Army, the run was cut back to 700,000. *Stuck On You* was also allocated in a quota system across the country with New York getting 72,000; Chicago 56,000; Detroit 42,000; Minneapolis 24,000; San Francisco 38,000; and Indianapolis 23,000. The figure shipped to Los Angeles was kept secret, but was estimated to be above 100,000.)

MAR 29   (Tues.) Elvis returned to Memphis by train.

The March issue of *TV Radio Mirror* magazine featured a 1956 photo of Elvis on the cover.

APRIL

APR 2   (Sun.) Elvis was named "Top Selling Male Vocalist" by the National Association of Record Merchandisers during their second annual convention, held at the Tropicana Hotel in Las Vegas. Elvis did not attend.

APR 3   (Mon.) Elvis returned to RCA's studios in Nashville for another recording session to complete enough tracks to fill the projected album. Songs for this LP were *Fever*, a 1956 hit for Little Willie John and a 1958 hit for Peggy

Lee; *Like A Baby; Girl Of My Best Friend; Dirty, Dirty
Feeling; Thrill Of Your Love; Such A Night*, a rhythm
and blues hit for Clyde McPhatter and the Drifters in
1954; *Girl Next Door Went A'Walking; I Will Be Home
Again*, which featured Charlie Hodge in a duet with
Elvis (Hodge had been a close friend of Elvis' from the
time they left Ft. Hood in September 1958); and *Reconsider Baby*, a hit for Lowell Fulson in the rhythm and
blues field in 1954. *It's Now Or Never* was held for release as a single later in 1960, and *Are You Lonesome
To-night?* and *I Gotta Know* were released as a single in
late 1960. *Are You Lonesome To-night* had been made
popular in the 1920s by Al Jolson, and had been popu-
larized again in 1959 by Jaye P. Morgan.
    Musicians were the same as March 20th with the
    addition of Homer "Boots" Randolph on tenor
    sax and Hank Garland back on guitar.

APR 4   (Mon.) *Stuck On You* entered *Billboard*'s "Hot 100" for
          the week ending April 10th at 84. It reached number 1
          in three weeks and stayed on the chart for sixteen weeks.

APR 11   (Mon.) *Fame And Fortune* started up the "Hot 100" at
          number 71 for the week ending the 17th. It stayed ten
          weeks, peaking at number 17.

APR 18   (Mon.) Elvis left Memphis in a private railroad car, which
          cost $2,500 to rent, for the trip to Los Angeles. His en-
          tourage numbered nine for the trip.

APR 19   (Tues.) During an hour-and-thirty-minute layover in El
          Paso, Elvis was greeted by over 2,000 fans.

APR 20   (Wed.) Elvis was mobbed in Los Angeles' Union Station
          upon his arrival aboard the Sunset Limited. He held a
          brief press conference and then, accompanied by Colonel
          Parker, he took a Yellow cab to the Beverly Wilshire
          Hotel, which would be his new headquarters while in Los
          Angeles.

APR 25   (Mon.) *Stuck On You* reached number 1 on *Billboard*'s
          "Hot 100" for the week ending May 1st. The single re-
          mained at number 1 for four weeks.
          Billboard "Spotlight"-ed the **Elvis Is Back** LP, saying:
          "Elvis is back — and singing better than ever in the rock
          and roll style he made famous."

APR 26   (Tues.) Elvis reported to Paramount Studios in Hollywood
          to begin filming "G.I. Blues."

APR 27 (Wed.) Elvis had a recording session at RCA Victor's studios in Hollywood. All of the songs were recorded for the film "G.I. Blues." Of the fifteen songs attempted during this long session, only seven were considered good enough to be released: *Didja Ever, Doin' The Best I Can, G.I. Blues, Tonight Is So Right For Love, What's She Really Like, Blue Suede Shoes*, and *Wooden Heart*.

Of the songs that were attempted and left unfinished, only *Whistling Blues* was never attempted again. The other uncompleted songs were *Shoppin' Around*, a different version of *Tonight Is So Right For Love, Frankfort Special*, a different version of *Wooden Heart, Big Boots* (both a fast and slow version), and *Pocketful Of Rainbows.*

The studio musicians for this session were Scotty Moore, Tiny Timbrell, and Neal Matthews (of the Jordanaires), guitar; Ray Siegel, bass; Dudley Brooks, piano; Frank Bode and D.J. Fontana, drums; Jimmie Haskell, accordian; Hoyt Hawkins (of the Jordanaires), tambourine, and the Jordanaires, vocals.

The session lasted into the early morning of April 28th.

(The large number of uncompleted songs might have been a result of the fact that this was Elvis' first session in RCA's Hollywood studios.)

The April edition of *Movie Stars TV Close-Ups* magazine featured a 1956 photo of Elvis on the cover.

MAY

MAY 2 (Mon.) Paramount started production on "G.I. Blues."

MAY 6 (Fri.) Elvis had another recording session at RCA's studios in Hollywood. He completed most of the songs which had been left unfinished on April 28th.

The musicians were the same for this session, except that Bernie Mattinson replaced Frank Bode on drums.

Successful songs included *Big Boots, Shoppin' Around, Pocketful Of Rainbows, Frankfort Special*, and *Tonight's All Right For Love*, which was used in European versions of the film due to copyright conflicts. It was originally recorded under the title *Vienna Woods Rock And Roll.*

MAY 7   (Sat.) A likeness of Elvis appeared on the cover of *TV
          Guide*, along with a smaller drawing of Frank Sinatra.
MAY 8   (Sun.) ABC-TV broadcast "The Frank Sinatra – Timex
          Show," also called "Frank Sinatra's Welcome Home
          Party For Elvis Presley," from 8:30 to 9:30 p.m. (EST).
          Guests included Sammy Davis, Jr., Joey Bishop, Peter
          Lawford, and Nancy Sinatra. This was the fourth Timex
          show of the season, and it received a 41.5% share of the
          national TV audience (compared to less than 21% for
          NBC and 4.2% for CBS). Elvis was paid $125,000 for
          his guest spot.
MAY 9   (Mon.) **Elvis Is Back** entered *Billboard*'s album chart for
          the week ending May 13th at 35. It stayed on the chart
          for fifty-two weeks and reached number 2.
MAY 12   (Thurs.) Elvis gave Anita Wood a diamond necklace.
MAY 16   (Mon.) *Life* magazine published an article titled "Idols To
          Team Up On T.V.," which covered Elvis' appearance on
          the Frank Sinatra TV special.
          Time magazine ran an article on "The Man Who Sold Pres-
          ley," which was a look at Colonel Parker.
MAY 30   (Mon.) *Newsweek* published an article entitled "Is This A
          New Presley?" in which a reporter interviewed Elvis on
          the set of "G.I. Blues."

The May issue of *TV And Movie Screen* magazine featured Elvis
   on the cover. The accompanying article, "Elvis' First Civilian
   Interview," was totally fictional.
The May issue of *Country Song Roundup* magazine had a photo of
   Elvis on the cover and an accompanying article entitled "Wel-
   com Home, Elvis."
Movie And TV Time magazine had a painting of Elvis on the cover,
   and wanted fans to "Meet The New Elvis Presley."
Movie World, on the other hand, ran a 1956 shot of Elvis on its
   cover.
Elvis and Elizabeth Taylor shared the cover of *Popular Screen.*

JUNE

JUN 6   (Mon.) **Elvis Is Back** peaked at number 2 on *Billboard*'s
          "Best Selling LP's" chart. The next week it was back to
          number 3, and then spent an additional two weeks at
          number 2 before starting a slow decline down the chart.

LATE JUNE

In late June, following completion of "G.I. Blues," Elvis and his entourage, which now included Charlie Hodge, Red and Sonny West, Lamar Fike, Joe Esposito, and Gene Smith, spent a week relaxing in Las Vegas.

The June edition of *Stardom* magazine featured a cover-shot of Elvis, and the story "Actually I'm Lonesome!"
Elvis shared the cover of *Movie Life* with Debbie Reynolds.

JULY

JUL 3   (Sun.) Vernon Presley married Davada ("Dee") Elliot Stanley in Huntsville, Alabama. The wedding took place at the home of her brother, Richard Neely. Elvis did not attend.

JUL 10   (Sun.) Elvis purchased a sixteen-foot fiberglass boat in Memphis. The boat had a seventy-five horsepower motor and Elvis inspected it at McKellar Lake. Elvis named the boat "Karate." Elvis took water skiing lessons from Dickie Waters.

JUL 11   (Mon.) RCA Victor ran a full-page ad in *Billboard* stating that Elvis' new single, *It's Now Or Never*, was "Backed By A Million Votes" (1960 was a Presidential election year). In its "Spotlight" review, *Billboard* said, "Both sides are potent."

JUL 18   (Mon.) *It's Now Or Never* entered *Billboard*'s "Hot 100" for the week ending June 24th at number 44. It would reach number 1 in five weeks, and stay on the chart for twenty weeks (the last of Elvis' singles to stay on the charts for twenty or more weeks).

The *Memphis Press-Scimitar* reported that Graceland was mortgaged for $134,000.

JUL 19   (Tues.) Paramount Pictures turned over the songs from the soundtrack to "G.I. Blues" to RCA Victor.

Modern Teen magazine's July issue featured a 1957 photo of Elvis on its cover.
Record Time TV Movies' cover of Elvis was accompanied by the article "How Elvis Treats His Enemies."

AUGUST

AUG 6　(Sat.)　East Germany declared Elvis to be an enemy of the people, after a riot by teenagers in Chemnitz.

AUG 12　(Fri.)　Elvis had a recording session in Hollywood for "Flaming Star." The musicians for this session were those that usually backed Elvis including the Jordanaires. Only four songs were recorded: *Flaming Star, Summer Kisses Winter Tears, A Cane And A High Starched Collar*, and *Britches*. Of the four, only *A Cane And A High Starched Collar* was actually sung by Elvis in the film. *Flaming Star* was used over the opening credits. *Summer Kisses Winter Tears* was released on a 33 1/3 EP with *Flaming Star* in April 1961, and *Britches* remains unissued.

AUG 15　(Mon.)　*It's Now Or Never* peaked at number 1 on *Billboard*'s "Hot 100" for the week ending August 21st. It remained at number 1 for a total of five weeks.

AUG 16　(Tues.)　Production started on "Flaming Star" at the 20th Century-Fox studios in Los Angeles. Outdoor locations for the film were shot at the Conejo Movie Ranch in the San Fernando Valley, near Los Angeles. The movie had a forty-two-day shooting schedule, lasting until mid-September.

AUG 18　(Thurs.)　A sneak preview of "G.I. Blues" was held in the Majestic Theater in Dallas. In a telegram from Raymond Willie, Vice President and General Manager of Interstate Circuit, Inc., to Paramount Pictures, he said, "We have never witnessed such marvelous reaction to any picture."

The August issue of *Movie Stars TV Close-Ups* magazine featured Elvis on the cover, along with the article "The Terrible Temptation In Elvis' Home." The temptation, it turned out, was for Elvis to tell Dee Stanley (who was not married to Vernon at the time the article was written) to start packing.

TV Film Stars' cover of Elvis was accompanied by the article, "Gabbing With Elvis."

Stardom's cover of Elvis was followed by the story, "When Will This Yearning Stop?"

SEPTEMBER

Elvis and his entourage moved out of the Beverly Wilshire Hotel and into an Oriental-style home at 565 Peruga Way in the Los Angeles suburb of Bel Air. The house had previously belonged to the Ali Khan and his wife Rita Hayworth. Elvis lived in the home until 1962.

Following the filming of "Flaming Star," Elvis returned to Memphis.

OCTOBER

OCT 3   (Mon.) *Billboard* placed its "Spotlight" on **G.I. Blues**, saying: "The album features the still hottest singer of them all in 10 brand new tunes, all of them showing new facets of the lad's talent."

OCT 10   (Mon.) *Life* magazine carried a one-page story on "G.I. Blues" titled "Rock-A-Bye Role For Presley."

OCT 16   (Sun.) Elvis was hospitalized in Memphis' Baptist Hospital for a fractured finger, suffered during a game of touch football at Graceland.

OCT 17   (Mon.) Elvis was discharged from the hospital. He was driven back to Graceland by his aide, Joe Esposito.

OCT 19   (Wed.) *Variety*, in reviewing "G.I. Blues," said the film "seems to be left over from the frivolous musicals of World War II."

OCT 30   (Sun.) Elvis traveled to Nashville for another night-long recording session at RCA Victor's "Nashville Sound" Studios. Most of the songs recorded were scheduled to be released on Elvis' first religious album, **His Hand In Mine**. Musicians for this date included Scotty Moore and Hank Garland, guitar; Bob Moore, bass; Floyd Cramer, piano; Boots Randolph, sax; D.J. Fontana and Buddy Harmon, drums; and the Jordanaires with Millie Kirkham on vocals. Charlie Hodge also accompanied Elvis, and his voice can be heard on a few tracks.

The religious songs recorded were *Milky White Way, His Hand In Mine, I Believe In The Man In The Sky, He Knows Just What I Need, Mansion Over The Hilltop, In My Father's House, Joshua Fit The Battle, Swing Down Sweet Chariot, I'm Gonna Walk Dem Golden Stairs, If We Never Meet Again, Known Only To Him* and *Working On The Building. Crying In The Chapel* was released in 1965.

Also recorded was a variation on the Italian love song, *Torma A Surriento*, called *Surrender*, which would be Elvis' first 1961 single release.

The session lasted into the morning of the 31st.

OCT 31   (Mon.) **G.I. Blues** entered *Billboard*'s album chart for the week of November 4th at number 6. It stayed on the list for 111 weeks (Elvis' longest charted record), and reached number 1 in six weeks.

The October issue of *Cosmopolitan* magazine published an article titled "Elvis And Juliet," which covered the making of "G.I. Blues."

NOVEMBER

NOV 5   (Sat.) Elvis rented the Rainbow roller skating rink for a late night skating party.

NOV 6   (Sun.) Elvis flew from Memphis to Los Angeles to start work on "Wild In The Country" for 20th Century-Fox. The opening scene of the movie featured a fist fight between Elvis and his bodyguard, Red West. The original ending of the film called for Elvis' character to commit suicide by running a car in a closed garage. The final ending had Elvis being saved by social worker Hope Lange.

NOV 7   (Mon.) *Billboard* picked *Are You Lonesome To-night?/I Gotta Know* for its "Spotlight" section, saying Elvis "turns in a warm, touching performance."

Elvis had a recording session in Hollywood for the film, "Wild In The Country." Musicians on this date were the same as those used on Elvis' Nashville sessions including Scotty Moore, D.J. Fontana, and the Jordanaires. The following songs were recorded in the studio: *Lonely Man, I Slipped I Stumbled I Fell, Wild In The Country, In My Way*, and *Forget Me Never*. Of these songs, *Wild In The Country* was used over the opening titles, and *Lonely Man* and *Forget Me Never* were cut from the film, leaving only two songs in the picture sung by Elvis.

Husky Dusky Day (which is actually sung in the film as *Husky Dusty Day*, which makes a little more sense) was a duet with Elvis and Hope Lange which was recorded on the film's sound stage, and it has not been officially released to date.

The session lasted into the early morning hours of the 8th.

NOV 9   (Wed.) The film crew from 20th Century Fox arrived in Napa, California, to start filming exterior locations for "Wild In The Country."

NOV 10   (Thurs.) After dark, Elvis, Tuesday Weld, and other members of the cast of "Wild In The Country" arrived in Napa. During the filming of "Wild In The Country," Elvis dated the wardrobe girl, Nancy Sharp. Elvis had first met Miss Sharp while he was working on "Flaming Star."

NOV 11   (Mon.) RCA Victor ran a full-page ad for *Are You Lonesome To-night?*, which read "Over 1,000,000 Copies Already Sold."

Filming started at the Victorian Ink House in St. Helena, about fifteen miles north of Napa.

NOV 12   (Sat.) Elvis was treated for a "minor infection" by a local physician. (The "minor infection," according to *Elvis: What Happened?* was boils on his posterior.)

NOV 14   (Mon.) *Are You Lonesome To-Night?* and *I Gotta Know* entered the "Hot 100" for the week ending the 20th at numbers 35 and 65 respectively. They stayed fifteen and eleven weeks and peaked at numbers 1 and 20 respectively

Filming continued in and around Napa.

NOV 16   (Wed.) The *Los Angeles Times*, in reviewing "G.I. Blues," said: "I wouldn't really call Elvis sophisticated in the picture, but he has grown up, for which we give thanks."

NOV 17   (Thurs.) Millie Perkins, co-star of "Wild In The Country," suffered a broken wrist when she slapped Elvis during a scene from the movie.

The *Los Angeles Examiner*, in its review of "G.I. Blues," said: "[Elvis] shorn of side burns comes through as a young man of great appeal, not only for his adoring bobby soxers, but for the maternal instinct in older women."

NOV 18   (Fri.) *Variety* reported that " 'Bootlegging' Presley Pic Soundtrack Sparks 20th Century-Fox Crackdown." The article said that a Denver disk jockey had taped two songs from "Flaming Star" while in a theater, and had transferred the songs to disk and played them over the air. The songs had also turned up on Pittsburgh and Los Angeles radio stations. RCA feared that the poor sound

Elvis and wardrobe girl Nancy Sharp had a movie-set romance during filming in Napa, California.

Elvis discusses a scene with director Phillip Dunne during the filming of "Wild In The Country."

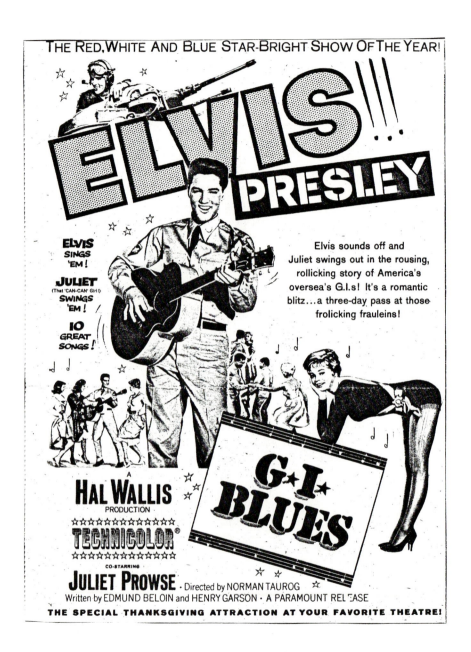

quality would hurt Elvis' image. 20th Century-Fox was
taking legal action, since RCA Victor had no plans to release the two songs.

Filming continued at a bridge and in the back woods near
Calistoga, twenty-five miles north of Napa.

NOV 19 (Sat.) Elvis, Nancy Sharp, and Red West drove to San
Francisco for a quick sightseeing visit.

NOV 21 (Mon.) Elvis returned to Hollywood to finish shooting
interior scenes for "Wild In The Country."

NOV 23 (Wed.) "G.I. Blues" opened in theaters across the United
States. In many locations, the co-feature was "Walk
Tall," with Willard Parker and Joyce Meadows.

NOV 28 (Mon.) *Are You Lonesome To-night?* peaked at number 1
on *Billboard*'s "Hot 100" for the week ending December 4th. It stayed at number 1 for a total of five weeks.

NOV 30 (Wed.) "G.I. Blues" was number 2 on *Variety*'s "National
Box Office Survey." The film remained on the list for
three weeks.

The *Los Angeles Mirror*, in an interview with Don Siegel,
director of "Flaming Star," quoted him as saying, "When
Elvis gets ready to do a serious scene he closes himself
in and is absolutely unapproachable to anyone but me
. . . Elvis has a very complex, but a very interesting personality."

Elvis was the cover story in *Song Hits* magazine's November issue.
The accomanying article was "The Elvis Legend."

Movieland Romances magazine featured a full-page color portrait
of Elvis on the back cover, along with an article entitled "Elvis
Unmasks Those Shocking Love Lies!"

DECEMBER
Early in the month, Elvis returned to Memphis for the holidays.

DEC 5   (Mon.) **G.I. Blues** reached number 1 on *Billboard*'s
"Best Selling LP's" chart for the week ending December
9th. It was back at number 2 the next week, and then
the album spent three weeks at number 1 before *Billboard* changed its LP charts. In April, the album was
back at number 1 for a week, as *Billboard* again changed
the makeup of its LP chart. In all, **G.I. Blues** remained
at number 1 for a total of five weeks.

Billboard "Spotlight"-ed Elvis' latest album, **His Hand In**

Mine, saying, "Elvis Presley finds himself in a new milieu for him in this altogether fascinating set of performances."

DEC 7 (Wed.) Colonel Parker read an editorial in the *Los Angeles Herald Examiner* which asked citizens to donate funds to a memorial to the USS Arizona, which had been sunk nineteen years earlier at Pearl Harbor. This was the germination of the idea for Elvis' benefit performance the next March in Honolulu.

DEC 8 (Thurs.) Pop singer, Fabian (Fabiano Forte), visited Elvis at Graceland. While Elvis was demonstrating karate, he tore his pants. Fabian kept them as a souvenir.

Elvis persuaded his father to invite Priscilla Beaulieu to visit Graceland for the holidays. Her parents agreed, and she flew from Frankfurt, West Germany, to New York where she was met by Vernon and Dee Presley. They escorted her back to Memphis. Priscilla stayed at Graceland with Elvis for about two weeks.

DEC 19 (Mon.) Elvis and the Colonel ran a full-page ad in *Billboard* which had the Colonel dressed as Santa Claus standing next to Elvis. In the holiday tradition, they wished "Everything Good To All Of You."

The *Hollywood Reporter* called "Flaming Star" "First-rate entertainment."

DEC 20 (Tues.) The Los Angeles Indian Tribal Council inducted Elvis in recognition "of his constructive portrayal of a man of Indian blood."

DEC 22 (Thurs.) "Flaming Star" opened in theaters in the United States. In many theaters, the co-feature was "Freckles."

The *Los Angeles Examiner* called "Flaming Star" an "extremely pleasant surprise . . . this picture should open up a whole new audience for [Elvis]."

DEC 25 (Sun.) Christmas was celebrated quietly at Graceland.

(One fan magazine reported that Elvis visited Nancy Sharp in St. Louis for Christmas. This is unlikely, considering that he had worked so hard to have Priscilla in Memphis for the holidays.)

The Christmas card from Elvis and the Colonel had three small shots of Elvis. Colonel Parker was wearing the usual Santa suit.

DEC 28 (Wed.) "Flaming Star" made its only appearance on *Variety*'s "National Box Office Survey" at number 12.

Elvis was the subject of two books published in 1960, *Operation Elvis* by Alan Levy, and *The Elvis Presley Story* edited by James Gregory. These were the first books devoted exclusively to Elvis.

Elvis' return to civilian life was the subject of the magazine *Elvis: The King Returns.*

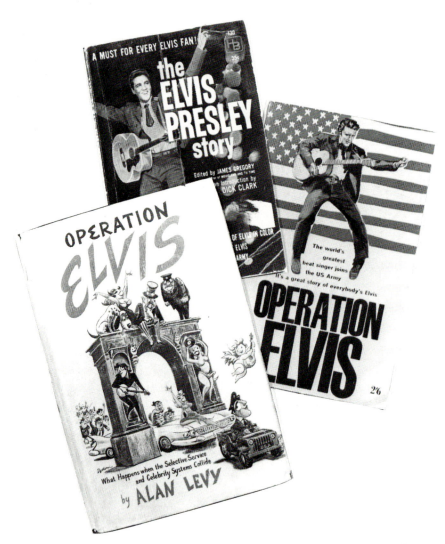

The first books about Elvis appeared in 1960. *The Elvis Presley Story* (paperback) reprinted earlier magazine articles, and *Operation Elvis* was issued in the U.S. (hardback) and the U.K. (paperback).

I'll Hold You
In My Heart
(Til I Can Hold
You In My Arms)

ALL
SHOOK
UP
━━━
ELVIS
Day-By-Day,
1961

JANUARY

Early in the month, Priscilla returned to West Germany.

JAN 4   (Wed.) "G.I. Blues" was the number 14 film in box office receipts for 1960, according to *Variety*'s year-end movie review. The film had grossed $4.3 million since its release in November.

JAN 6   (Fri.) *Time*, in an article titled "Same To You, Mac," noted that there were at least six different cover versions of *Are You Lonesome Tonight?* in response to Elvis' hit.

JAN 9   (Mon.) **His Hand In Mine** entered *Billboard*'s "Action Albums" chart for the week ending January 15th. It remained on the chart for twenty weeks, reaching number 13.

20th Century-Fox turned over the recording tapes from "Wild In The Country" to RCA Victor.

JAN 18   (Wed.) Elvis signed a five-year contract with Hal Wallis calling for a movie a year.

FEBRUARY

Elvis and some friends visited Tupelo during the first of the month. They tried to put up the "Elvis Presley Youth Center" sign, which had fallen over in a high wind.

FEB 5   (Sun.) RCA Victor released the single *Surrender/Lonely Man.*

FEB 9   (Thurs.) 20th Century-Fox turned over the recording tapes from "Flaming Star" to RCA Victor.

FEB 13   (Mon.) *Lonely Man/Surrender* was in *Billboard*'s "Spotlight," with the journal saying, "Elvis Presley will continue his million hit string with this fine pairing."

FEB 20   (Mon.) *Surrender* entered *Billboard*'s "Hot 100" at number 84 for the week ending February 26th. It stayed on the chart for twelve weeks and reached number 1.

FEB 25   (Sat.) "Elvis Presley Day" was proclaimed by the Governor of Tennessee, Buford Ellington.

At 12:30 p.m., Elvis was the host of a $100-a-plate luncheon in his honor at Memphis' Claridge Hotel, where he was honored for sales of 75 million records. RCA Victor gave Elvis a diamond-studded watch. The luncheon took in $17,200 for charity.

At 1:45 p.m., there was a press conference in the hotel's Empire Room.

There were two shows, one at 2:30 and one at 8:30 p.m. at Ellis Auditorium. Tickets were three dollars. The afternoon show took in $11,580 in ticket sales (3,860 attendance) and $2,100 in concession sales. The evening show brought $19,622 in tickets sales (6,540 attendance) and $1,075 in concession sales. A total of $51,607 was raised for the "Elvis Presley Youth Center" in Tupelo, and thirty-seven other Memphis charities.

George Jessel was the master of ceremonies. Also on hand were Governor Ellington and Memphis Mayor Henry Loeb.

The other acts on the bill were comedian Dave Gardner, impressionist N.P. Nelson, an acrobatic act, a tap dancer, and Larry Owens and His Orchestra, which was augmented by Scotty Moore, D.J. Fontana, Boots Randolph, and Floyd Cramer.

MARCH

MAR 8   (Wed.) Elvis drove to Nashville with Red West and Lamar Fike, where he attended a session of the Tennessee State Legislature. Elvis was the focus of a tribute by a joint session. He was made an honorary "Colonel" in the Tennessee Volunteers. Elvis returned to Memphis that night.

MAR 12   (Sun.) Elvis traveled to Nashville for a recording session at RCA Victor's studios. Most of the songs from this session were recorded for the album **Something For Everybody**: *I'm Comin' Home, Gently, In Your Arms, Give Me The Right, It's A Sin, I Want You With Me, There's Always Me, Starting Today, Sentimental Me* (a

1949 hit by the Ames Brothers), *Judy*, and *Put The Blame On Me. I Feel So Bad*, a 1954 rhythm and blues hit for Chuck Willis, was held for release as a single. The session lasted into the morning hours of the 13th.

MAR 18 (Sat.) Elvis purchased a Rolls Royce in Memphis prior to leaving for the West Coast.

MAR 20 (Mon.) *Surrender* reached number 1 on *Billboard*'s "Hot 100" for the week ending March 26th. It stayed at number 1 for two weeks.

MAR 21 (Tues.) Elvis started a three-day recording session at Radio Recorders in Hollywood. The fourteen songs recorded for "Blue Hawaii" were the most used in any of his films, or included on any of his single albums.

The musicians included Scotty Moore, Hank Garland, and Tiny Timbrell on guitar; Bob Moore on bass; D.J. Fontana, Hal Blaine, Bernie Mattinson on drums; Floyd Cramer and Dudley Brooks, piano; Boots Randolph, sax; Bernie Lewis, steel guitar; Fred Tavares and Alvino Ray, ukulele; George Fields, harmonica; and the Jordanaires and the Surfers, backing vocals.

On the 21st, the following were waxed: *Slicin' Sand, Aloha Oe, Ku-U-I-Po* (also referred to as *Hawaiian Sunrise*), *No More*, and *Hawaiian Sunset.*

MAR 22 (Wed.) Elvis recorded *Blue Hawaii, Ito Eats, Hawaiian Wedding Song, Island Of Love, Steppin' Out Of Line* (which was cut from the film and appeared on **Pot Luck**), *Almost Always True* and *Moonlight Swim.* There appear to have been two songs recorded during this session which have not been issued by RCA Victor. These may have included *Playing With Fire* (later recorded by Terry Stafford) and *La Paloma.*

(In the film, *Hawaiian Wedding Song* differs from the album version in that the opening portion of the song was a duet between Elvis and Joan Blackman in the movie.)

MAR 23 (Thurs.) Elvis recorded *Can't Help Falling In Love, Beach Boy Blues,* and *Rock-A-Hula Baby.* An additional three songs may have been recorded during this session, according to the RCA Victor matrix numbering system.

late MAR In late March, a film crew from Paramount Pictures arrived in Hawaii to begin filming locations to be used in "Blue Hawaii" at various places on Oahu and Kauai.

MAR 25 (Sat.) More than 3,000 fans were on hand to greet Elvis as he arrived at 12:20 p.m. at Honolulu's International

Airport via Pan American Airlines. That afternoon at 3:45 p.m., he hosted a press conference for newsmen, photographers, and a hand-picked group of twenty-seven high school reporters at the Carousel Room of the Hawaiian Village Hotel where he was staying.

Elvis' 8:30 p.m. show in the Bloch Arena that night was a benefit for the memorial to the USS Arizona, which had been lost during the Japanese attack on Pearl Harbor, December 7, 1941. Tickets were $10, $5, $3.50 and $3, with 100 ringside seats reserved for donations of $100. Elvis and the Colonel bought fifty of these seats for patients from Tripler Hospital. Over $62,000 was raised by Elvis.

MAR 27 (Mon.) Production started on "Blue Hawaii." Locations on Oahu included Waikiki Beach, the Punchbowl, Tantalus, the Ala Wai Yacht Harbor, Ala Moana Park, the Honolulu International Airport, the Waioli Tea Room, Hanauma Bay, the Honolulu Police Department's jail, and the pineapple fields in the middle of the island. On Kauai, locations included Lydgate Park, the Kauai Airport, the Wailua River, Anahola, and the Coco Palms Resort Hotel. Elvis stayed on the fourteenth floor of the Hawaiian Village Hotel on Waikiki, and in the bridal suite of the Coco Palms Resort while on Kauai. During this time, while flying in a private airplane, Elvis took the controls for a short time.

MAR 30 (Thurs.) The House of Representatives of the Hawaiian legislature passed a resolution "expressing gratitude and appreciation to Elvis Presley and Colonel Tom Parker on behalf of all Hawaii for their services in helping to raise the fund needed for the U.S.S. Arizona." (Resolution #105.)

APRIL

APR 10 (Mon.) RCA Victor ran a dual-purpose double-page ad in *Billboard*, claiming "Top Of The Compacts!" for the 33 1/3 Compact EP, **Elvis By Request**, which featured the title song from "Flaming Star." This ad also congratulated Elvis for a "Job Well Done" for his benefit concerts in Memphis and Honolulu.

APR 17 (Mon.) Elvis completed location filming for "Blue Hawaii" with the wedding scene at the Coco Palms Resort.

The wedding scene from "Blue Hawaii" was filmed at the Coco Palms resort on Kauai.

Another scene from "Blue Hawaii."

Shortly thereafter, Elvis and the movie crew returned to
Hollywood to continue filming indoor scenes at Para-
mount's studios.
Flaming Star from the **Elvis By Request** EP started up
Billboard's "Hot 100" for the week ending April 23rd.
It stayed on the chart for seven weeks, reaching number
16.

MAY

MAY 15   (Mon.) *I Feel So Bad* entered *Billboard*'s "Hot 100" at
         number 43 for the week ending May 21st. It peaked at
         number 5 and stayed on the chart for only nine weeks.
MAY 19   (Fri.) 20th Century-Fox ran a full-page ad in *Billboard*
         which said "Elvis Goes Wild In The Country."

JUNE

JUN 9   (Fri.) *Variety* said of "Wild In The Country": "Dramatical-
         ly, there isn't a great deal of substance, novelty or
         spring to this somewhat wobbly and artificial tale."
         The *Hollywood Reporter* called the film "a Southern
         'Peyton Place.' "
JUN 15   (Thurs.) "Wild In The Country" premiered in Memphis.
         Proceeds were donated to local charities. Elvis did not
         attend. As Colonel Parker put it, "Unless we can do our
         show, we don't go."
JUN 18   (Sun.) The *New York Times*, in its review of "Wild In The
         Country," said: "Even with Mr. Presley in the cast it
         should have been, at least, an honest drama, if not a
         particularly brilliant one. It isn't. It is shamelessly dis-
         honest. Indeed, it is downright gross in its social distor-
         tion of human values and social realities."
JUN 22   (Fri.) "Wild In The Country" opened in theaters in the
         U.S. In many locations, the co-feature was "The Right
         Approach," with Juliet Prowse and Frankie Vaughn.
JUN 25   (Sun.) Elvis had a recording session in RCA's studios in
         Nashville. *Kiss Me Quick, That's Someone You Never
         Forget*, and *I'm Yours* were scheduled for release on the
         Pot Luck album. *(Marie's The Name Of) His Latest
         Flame* and *Little Sister* were released back-to-back on
         a single in August. The musicians were the usual Nash-
         ville sidemen: Scotty Moore, Hank Garland, and Neal

Matthews (of the Jordanaires), guitar; D.J. Fontana
and Buddy Harmon, drums; Bob Moore, bass; Floyd
Cramer, piano and organ; Gordon Stoker (of the Jordanaires), piano; Boots Randolph, sax; and the Jordanaires,
vocals.
The session lasted into the morning of the 26th.

SUMMER
Elvis bought a larger boat to use on Lake McKellar in Memphis.
(See July 10, 1960.)

JULY

JUL 1   (Sat.) Red West, Elvis' longtime bodyguard, married Pat
          Boyd, one of Elvis' secretaries. The wedding took place
          in Memphis, and Elvis escorted Anita Wood.
JUL 5   (Wed.) Elvis returned to Nashville for another recording
          session at RCA Victor's studios. Most of the songs were
          recorded for the film "Follow That Dream": *Angel,
          Follow That Dream, What A Wonderful Life*, and *I'm
          Not The Marrying Kind. Sound Advice* was not released
          until 1965, and *A Whistling Tune* was unreleased. Elvis
          sang a single line from *On Top Of Old Smokey* in the
          movie, but it was recorded on the set and not in the
          studio.
          The musicians were Scotty Moore, Hank Garland and
          Neal Matthews, guitar; Bob Moore, bass; Floyd Cramer,
          piano; D.J. Fontana and Buddy Harmon, drums; and
          the Jordanaires with Millie Kirkham on vocals.
          This session was the only one set up specifically for a film
          soundtrack which was financed by RCA Victor.
mid-JUL   In mid-July, Elvis returned to Hollywood to start filming
          "Follow That Dream" at United Artists' studios. At
          this time, the movie was known as "Pioneer, Go Home."
JUL 24   (Mon.) **Something For Everybody** entered *Billboard's*
          "Top LP's" chart at number 136 for the week ending
          July 16th. It would remain on the chart for twenty-five
          weeks and reach number 1.
late JUL Elvis and the film company traveled to Clear River, Florida,
          on the Gulf of Mexico, about sixty-five miles north of
          Clearwater. Locations for "Follow That Dream" included
          Bird Creek, a bank in Ocala, the courthouse in Inverness,
          and the towns of Crystal River and Yankeetown. Elvis
          stayed at the Port Paradise Hotel.

JUL 30   (Sun.) Elvis was honored by the citizens of Weeki Wachee Springs, Florida, during an afternoon get-together. Elvis arrived about 4:00 p.m. and stayed two hours. Over 15,000 fans turned up for the event.

AUGUST

Filming on "Follow That Dream" continued around Crystal River.

AUG 14   (Mon.) *Billboard*, in "Spotlight"-ing *Little Sister/(Marie's The Name Of) His Latest Flame*, said they were "two sock sides."

AUG 21   (Mon.) *Little Sister* entered *Billboard*'s "Hot 100" at number 61 for the week ending August 27th. It reached number 5 and stayed on the chart for thirteen weeks.

AUG 28   (Mon.) *His Latest Flame* entered *Billboard*'s "Hot 100" at number 66 for the week ending September 3rd. It peaked at number 4 and stayed on the chart for eleven weeks.

SEPTEMBER

SEP 4   (Mon.) RCA Victor ran a full-page ad which claimed a "Big Two-Sided Hit," and showed a copy of *His Latest Flame* in the 33 1/3 Compact version.

SEP 20   (Wed.) Elvis was voted the "Top Male Singer" by *Melody Maker* magazine in England.

SEP 25   (Mon.) Paramount Pictures turned over the tapes from "Blue Hawaii" to RCA Victor.

OCTOBER

OCT 2   (Mon.) The **Blue Hawaii** album was in *Billboard*'s "Spot-light" section as the magazine predicted "this should be a big one."

OCT 15   (Sun.) Elvis had a recording session at RCA Victor's studios in Nashville. The purpose of the session was to produce a new single, and *Good Luck Charm* fit that need perfectly. For the flip-side, *Anything That's Part Of You* was waxed. *For The Millionth And Last Time* and *I Met Her Today* were released on the album **Elvis For Everyone**. *Night Rider* was scrapped and re-recorded in March 1962.

The musicians for this session included Scotty Moore and Jerry Kennedy, guitar; Bob Moore, bass; D.J. Fontana and Buddy Harmon, drums; Floyd Cramer, piano; Boots Randolph, sax and clarinet; Gordon Stoker (of the Jordanaires), accordian; and the Jordanaires with Millie Kirkham, vocals.

The session lasted through the night into the morning of the 16th.

OCT 23   (Mon.) **Blue Hawaii** entered *Billboard*'s "Top LP's" chart at 75 for the week ending October 29th. It stayed on the chart for seventy-nine weeks and reached number 1.

OCT 26   (Thur.) Elvis arrived in Hollywood to start production on "Kid Galahad" for United Artists. On this night, he is in the studios at Radio Recorders to cut the soundtrack for the movie. *A Whistling Tune* was completed satisfactorily this time (see July 5, 1961), as were *King Of The Whole Wide World*, *This Is Living* (original title, *Let's Live A Little*), *Riding The Rainbow*, *Home Is Where The Heart Is*, and *I Got Lucky*. One other song, *Love Is For Lovers*, was sung in the movie by Lola Albright. Other musicians included Scotty Moore, Bob Moore, and D.J. Fontana, with vocals by the Jordanaires.

NOVEMBER

Elvis began filming "Kid Galahad" for United Artists. Locations were filmed in Idyllwild, California, 100 miles east of Los Angeles, and interiors at the M-G-M Studios in Culver City.

NOV 6   (Mon.) Elvis traveled to Idyllwild, California, in the San Jacinto Mountains, for location filming on "Kid Galahad." He rented a house in which to live during the four weeks in Idyllwild. The rest of the United Artists crew stayed at the Idyllwild Inn. Scenes included Hidden Lodge, Idyllwild, and the backwoods area. During this time, Albert Hand, President of the Official Elvis Fan Club of Great Britain, visited Elvis.

Work was started on a new swimming pool at Graceland.

NOV 20   (Mon.) *Billboard*, in its "Spotlight" section, said of *Rock-A-Hula Baby*: "Here's a Presley twist special . . . ideal for the new dance craze."

NOV 22   (Wed.) "Blue Hawaii" opened in theaters across the country.

NOV 24   (Fri.) The *Hollywood Reporter* said that "Blue Hawaii" offered "a new setting to exploit the singer's appeal."

Elvis "surfing" in "Blue Hawaii."

Elvis greets British fan club president Albert Hand on
the set of "Kid Galahad" in Idyllwild, California.

The 1961 Christmas card from Elvis and The Colonel.

NOV 26   (Sun.) United Artists abandoned its efforts to complete
the location filming in Idyllwild after a snowstorm.
("Kid Galahad" was supposed to take place during the
summer.) The remainder of the film was shot at the
United Artists' studios in Hollywood.

NOV 29   (Wed.) "Blue Hawaii" was number 2 in *Variety*'s "National
Box Office Survey." The movie remained on the chart
for four weeks. In reviewing "Blue Hawaii" *Variety*
said the picture "restores Elvis Presley to his natural
screen element — romantic, non-cerebral film musical."
The *Motion Picture Herald* said that "box office insurance
of [this] kind [is] not often found these days."

DECEMBER

DEC 4   (Mon.) *Can't Help Falling In Love* entered the "Hot 100"
in *Billboard* at 57 for the week ending December 10th.
The single stayed on the chart for fourteen weeks, peaking at number 2. *Rock-A-Hula-Baby* started up the "Hot
100" at number 62, peaking at number 23 and staying
nine weeks.

DEC 11   (Mon.) **Blue Hawaii** reached number 1 on *Billboard*'s "Top
LP's" chart. It remained at number 1 for twenty weeks.

DEC 18   (Mon.) In *Billboard*'s "Chart Toppers of 1961," Elvis had
four singles: *Little Sister* (number 38), *Surrender* (number 51), *Flaming Star* (number 71) and *Are You Lonesome Tonight* (number 96).

mid-DEC In mid-December, work was still not complete on "Kid
Galahad" due to complications in late November on
location in Idyllwild.

DEC 25   (Mon.) Christmas was spent at Elvis' home on Perugia
Way in Bel Air. Due to extensions in the filming
schedule for "Kid Galahad," Elvis was not able to celebrate Christmas in Memphis. This was the first, and last,
time that this happened during Elvis' professional career.
The Christmas card from Elvis and the Colonel had a photo
of Elvis standing beside Colonel Parker, who was wearing
a Santa suit. The photo had been taken at the same time
as the one used on the 1960 card.

Take Me To The Fair

ALL
SHOOK
UP
——
ELVIS
Day-By-Day,
1962

JANUARY

By early January, Elvis had returned to Memphis for a much-needed vacation.

JAN 6   (Sat.) RCA Victor ran a double-page ad in *Billboard* which read "Happy New Year From All Of Us At RCA Victor And Thanks For Making 'Blue Hawaii' The Fastest Selling Album Of 1961."

JAN 8   (Mon.) Colonel Parker gave Elvis a car for his birthday. ABC-TV's "American Bandstand" had a special forty-five-minute tribute to Elvis, which featured a clip from a news conference that Elvis had held in Philadelphia (the home of "American Bandstand") in 1957. Elvis sent a telegram to the program, which was read over the air.

JAN 10   (Wed.) In *Variety*'s annual year-end review of the movie industry, "Blue Hawaii" ranked number 18 with a gross of $2 million since its release in November.

In January, Elvis rented a Mediterranean-styled home at 1059 Bellagio Way in Bel Air. However, he disliked the house so much that he shortly moved back to the house at 565 Perugia Way. He remained there until 1965.

JAN 20   (Sat.) **Blue Hawaii** became Elvis' first album to reach number 1 on the stereo charts in *Billboard*. It was in the number 1 position on the stereo chart for a total of four weeks.

JAN 21   (Sun.) The *Memphis Commercial Appeal* reported that Vernon had purchased a new home.

JAN 27   (Sat.) *Billboard* reported that Elvis would receive his twenty-ninth gold record for *Can't Help Falling In Love.*

FEBRUARY

FEB 3   (Sat.) *Can't Help Falling In Love* peaked at number 2 on
         Billboard's "Hot 100." By the next week, the song had
         started to slide back down the chart.

MARCH

MAR 9   (Fri.) In England, the *New Musical Express* reported that
         M-G-M was dickering for the rights to the Colonel Parker
         story as a starring role for Elvis. The film was to be
         called "Right This Way Folks," and was to be filmed at
         the Florida State Fair. The article said Elvis was set to
         star in "Mister, Will You Marry Me?" for M-G-M.

MAR 10   (Sat.) *Good Luck Charm/Anything That's Part Of You*
         was a "Spotlight Pick" in *Billboard*, which commented,
         "Presley has two more smash sides here."

MAR 17   (Sat.) *Good Luck Charm* entered the "Hot 100" in *Bill-
         board* at 51. It would eventually reach number 1, and
         stay on the chart for thirteen weeks.
         Elvis was the subject of no less than three front-page stories
         in *Billboard*. "New Presley Record Hypos Singles Mar-
         ket" reported from dealers "that this disk [*Good Luck
         Charm*] shapes up as one of his biggest — indicating that
         the chanter has lost none of his sales appeal, despite
         earlier reports to the contrary." Other articles were
         "Presley Leads Charmed Life," and " 'Charm' and 'Jam'
         Get N.Y.C. Action." The last article said, " 'Good Luck
         Charm' was starting to move [in the New York area]
         but not with impact dealers' had expected." (*The Jam*
         was the title of a single by Bobby Gregg on the Cot-
         ton label.)

MAR 18   (Sun.) In Nashville, Elvis had a recording session at RCA
         Victor's studios. In addition to the regular musicians,
         Grady Martin played vibes and guitar and Harold Brad-
         ley played guitar. The songs from this session were
         tagged for Elvis' next album, **Pot Luck**, and a new single.
         The songs for the LP were *Something Blue, Gonna Get
         Back Home Somehow, (Such An) Easy Question, Foun-
         tain Of Love, Night Rider* (attempted the past October),
         *Just For Old Time Sake, I Feel That I've Known You
         Forever,* and *Suspicion. Just Tell Her Jim Said Hello*
         and *She's Not You* were Elvis' next single. *You'll*

Be Gone was not released until February 1965, as the "B" side of a single.

The session lasted past midnight.

MAR 20 (Tues.) Elvis departed Memphis for Hollywood to begin work on "Girls! Girls! Girls!" for Paramount.

MAR 26 (Mon.) Elvis had a session at Radio Recorders for the film "Girls! Girls! Girls!" Two of the songs were released as a single prior to the release of either the film or the soundtrack album: *Return To Sender* and *Where Do You Come From.* All but one of the remaining songs first appeared in the soundtrack album: *I Don't Want To, We're Comin' In Loaded, Thanks To The Rolling Sea, Girls! Girls! Girls!* (A 1961 hit for the Coasters), *Because Of Love, The Walls Have Ears, Song Of The Shrimp, A Boy Like Me, A Girl Like You, Earth Boy, I Don't Wanna Be Tied* (original title, *Twist Me Loose*) and *We'll Be Together.* *Mama* was cut from the film and remained unreleased until it appeared on a Camden LP in 1970. *Plantation Rock* was also cut from the film, and it first appeared on a bootleg LP in the late 1970s. Other songs apparently recorded at this session which remain unreleased are *Potpourri, Dainty Little Moonbeams,* and *Girls, Girls, Girls (Of The World).*

Musicians for this session were the same as most Hollywood sessions from this period.

A version of *Mama* was sung in the film by the Four Amigos. Also, Stella Stevens is heard singing *Never Let Me Go, The Nearness Of You,* and *Take Me, Please.*

The session lasted until the early hours of the 27th.

MAR 27 (Tues.) In a survey by *Teen* magazine, 38,000 teenagers voted Elvis and Tuesday Weld the "Damp Raincoat Award" for "Wild In The Country." They were named the "most disappointing performers" of the year.

MAR 28 (Wed.) *Daily Variety*, in reviewing "Follow That Dream," called the film "a light romantic comedy with songs . . . [Elvis] delivers five songs with nary a wiggle."

The *Hollywood Reporter* said, "[Elvis] comes off with a disarming simplicity and sympathy."

APRIL

APR 7   (Sat.) Elvis arrived at the Honolulu International Airport at 12:50 p.m. via Pan American Airlines. He was

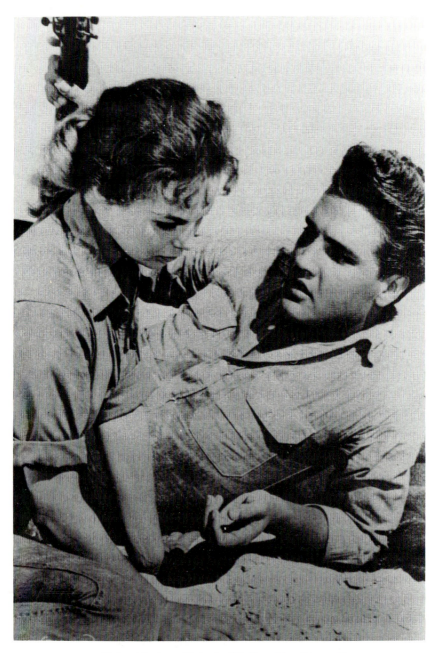

Elvis with Anne Helm in "Follow That Dream."

helicoptered from the airport to the Duke Kahanamoku Beach helipad next to the Hawaiian Village Hotel, where he arrived at 1:30 p.m. Over 5,000 fans were on hand to greet him, and Elvis lost his watch, a diamond ring and a tie clasp trying to negotiate the 300 yards from the landing pad to the hotel lobby. Elvis stayed there during filming on Oahu, and in a hotel at Kailua-Kona during filming on the island of Hawaii.

APR 9   (Mon.) Elvis started work on "Girls! Girls! Girls!" for Hal Wallis and Paramount Pictures. Locations included Ala Wai Yacht Harbor and the Bumble Bee Tuna Company's canning plant at Kewalo Basin, both near Waikiki Beach on Oahu; and Milolii on the Kona Coast of Hawaii. Red West, Elvis' bodyguard, can be seen strumming a guitar during the song *We're Comin' In Loaded.*

late APR   In late April, Elvis and the film company moved back to Hollywood to finish the interior scenes at Paramount Studios.

APR 20   (Fri.) In its review of "Follow That Dream," the *Los Angeles Times* said, "If Elvis will just ease up on the bread and potatoes, he can keep American girlhood in swoons for a while."

APR 21   (Sat.) *Good Luck Charm* reached number 1 on *Billboard*'s "Hot 100." It stayed at number 1 for only two weeks. This was Elvis' last number 1 single until *Suspicious Minds* in 1969.

MAY

MAY 12   (Sat.) The **Follow That Dream** EP entered "The Hot 100" in *Billboard* at 58. It stayed on the chart for ten weeks, peaking at number 15.

MAY 17   (Thurs.) Elvis was voted the top box office draw by the movie industry.

MAY 23   (Wed.) "Follow That Dream" opened in theaters in the United States. In many locations, the B-feature was "Errand Boy," starring Jerry Lewis.

MAY 30   (Wed.) "Follow That Dream" was number 5 in *Variety*'s "National Box Office Survey." The movie remained on the chart for two weeks.
     Blue Hawaii became Elvis' 30th gold disk.

In May, Elvis finished filming "Girls! Girls! Girls!" and returned to Hollywood and then to Memphis.

JUNE

JUN 3   (Sat.) Elvis donated a kangaroo to the Memphis zoo. The animal had been sent to him by an Australian fan.

JULY

JUL 14   (Sat.) **Pot Luck** entered *Billboard*'s "Top LP's" chart at number 116. It stayed on the chart for thirty-one weeks, peaking at number 4.

JUL 19   (Thurs.) In Memphis, Elvis visited the fairgrounds with a group of friends. He also frequently went to late night movies shown just for him at the Memphian Theater.

JUL 25   (Wed.) The *Memphis Press-Scimitar* reported that Elvis had purchased the land opposite Graceland.

Daily Variety, in reviewing "Kid Galahad," said, "Presley's acting resources are limited, but he has gradually established a character with which he doesn't have to strain too much for emotional nuance – the soft-spoken, unaffected, polite, unspoiled, forthright, and ultimately two-fisted country boy."

The *Hollywood Reporter* called the film "a good vehicle for the talents of Elvis Presley."

JUL 28   (Sat.) *Billboard* reviewed *Just Tell Her Jim Said Hello/ She's Not You* in the "Spotlight" section, saying the songs were "two pretty ballads by Elvis."

AUGUST

AUG 4   (Sat.) *She's Not You* started up *Billboard*'s "Hot 100" chart at number 57 where it peaked at number 5 and stayed ten weeks.

AUG 20   (Mon.) Elvis purchased a motorhome in Memphis prior to leaving for the West Coast. Since he had a fear of flying, the motorhome would allow Elvis the freedom to travel across country with his companions without the limitations of rail travel.

AUG 27   (Mon.) Elvis started filming "It Happened At The World's Fair" at M-G-M Studios in Culver City, California. Location filming was done at the World's Fair in Seattle.

AUG 29   (Wed.) "Kid Galahad" opened in theaters in the U.S. In many locations, the co-feature was "The Nun And The Sergeant," with Robert Webster and Ann Sten.

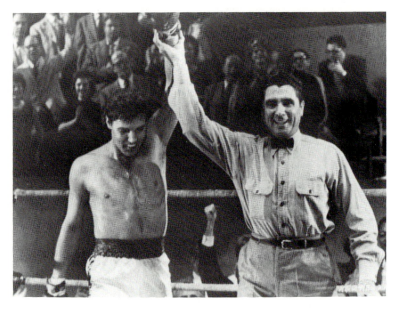

Elvis in "Kid Galahad."

Elvis signs autographs on location at the 1962 World's Fair in Seattle during filming for "It Happened At The World's Fair."

late AUG Late in the month, Elvis had a recording session at M-G-M
Studios for "It Happened At The World's Fair." Two of
the songs were released as a single prior to the release of
the film or the soundtrack album: *One Broken Heart
For Sale* and *They Remind Me Too Much Of You.* The
rest of the songs were released on the soundtrack LP:
*Happy Ending, Take Me To The Fair, I'm Falling In Love
Tonight, Cotton Candy Land, A World Of Our Own,
How Would You Like To Be, Beyond The Bend,* and
Relax. The musicians for this session were the usual
mixture of Hollywood and Nashville's finest. Backing
vocals were handled by the Jordanaires, who were assisted
by the Mello Men. It is rumored that another five songs
were recorded for the soundtrack to "It Happened At
The World's Fair," but they are unknown at this time.

In August, it was reported that Elvis would have the starring role
of Hank Williams in the film biography, "Your Cheating Heart."
(The film, "Your Cheatin' Heart," was produced in 1964 and
starred George Hamilton, with Hank Williams, Jr. singing the
soundtrack.)

SEPTEMBER

SEP 4 (Tues.) Elvis and a crew of 100 from Metro-Goldwyn-
Mayer arrived in Seattle to photograph scenes on location
at the World's Fair. Elvis and his entourage stayed at
the New Washington Hotel, in a fourteenth floor suite.
SEP 5 (Wed.) "Kid Galahad" was number 9 on *Variety*'s "Na-
tional Box Office Survey." The film remained on the
chart for only one week.
The first scenes photographed in Seattle for "It Happened
At The World's Fair" were those in and around the
Monorail Terminal at the fair site.
SEP 6 (Thurs.) Filming continued on the Gay Way (amusement
area), including a scene with Elvis winning a stuffed animal at the Lucky Strike Coin Pitch.
SEP 7 (Fri.) Filming on this date had to be postponed because
of rain.
SEP 11 (Tues.) After several days of inclement weather which
postponed production on the film, Elvis was back at the
World's Fair site for a scene with co-star Joan O'Brian
outside the Food Circus.
SEP 13 (Thurs.) Elvis gave a Tennessee ham to Washington Governor Albert D. Rosellini. The ham was a gift from

Priscilla at Graceland . . . sweet seventeen.

The 1963 Elvis calendar.

Tennessee Governor Buford Ellington. Another ham
was presented to Joe Gandy, President of the World's
Fair. In a mix-up, the Governor received the smaller
of the two.

Elvis filmed a scene outside the National Administration
exhibit with the fair's marching band.

SEP 14 (Fri.) The location of filming was moved to the NASA
exhibit. While Elvis was on location at the World's Fair,
he was protected by forty off-duty policemen.

SEP 17 (Mon.) Elvis returned to Hollywood to complete "It Happened At The World's Fair." In an interview with Sy
Devore. wardrobe man for the picture, Elvis' wardrobe
was said to cost $9,300. There were ten suits at $285
each, thirty shirts at ten dollars each, four sportcoats at
$200 each, two cashmere coats at $225 each, fifteen
pairs of slacks at $85 each, and fifty-five ties at seven
dollars each. There was no money budgeted for Elvis'
underwear, Devore disclosed, because Elvis did not wear
any.

SEP 22 (Sat.) In *Billboard*'s fifteenth annual DJ poll, Elvis ranked
number two as the most played artist, and number five
as the DJ's most favorite. **Blue Hawaii** was number 2 as
the DJ's most favorite album.

King Of The Whole Wide World from the **Kid Galahad** EP
entered the "Hot 100" at number 69, peaking at number
30, and staying seven weeks.

OCTOBER

OCT 13 (Sat.) In its review of *Return To Sender, Billboard* magazine said, "The amazing Elvis . . . offers another pair of
pic tunes. Another two sided sales dynamite from the
Prez."

OCT 20 (Sat.) *Return To Sender* entered *Billboard*'s "Hot 100"
at number 68, staying sixteen weeks, and reaching number 2.

RCA Victor's full-page ad for Elvis' "Autumn Special From
RCA Victor" (*Return To Sender*), also plugged the
1963 Elvis color calendar "available from your dealer."

In October, the Mexican government banned all of Elvis' movies
after a riot during an earlier showing of "G.I. Blues." It was reported that the theater had suffered torn seats, broken windows,
and other damage.

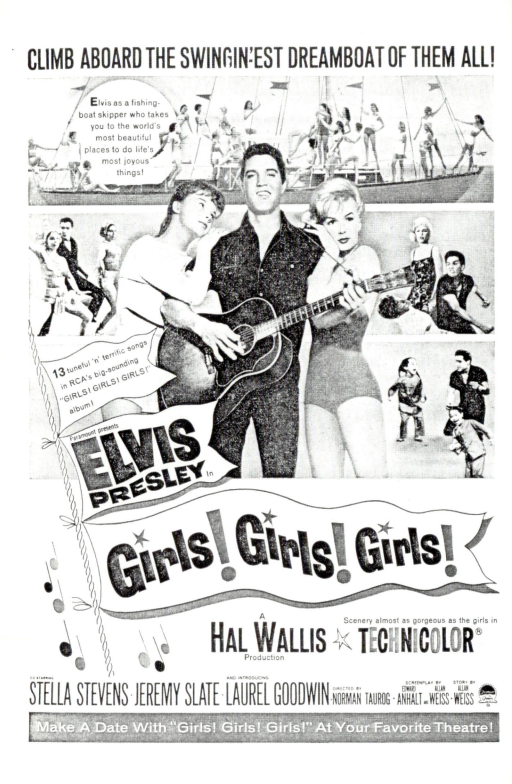

CLIMB ABOARD THE SWINGIN'EST DREAMBOAT OF THEM ALL!

late OCT Elvis and his buddies returned to Memphis in the motorhome.

After over a year of gentle persuasion, Elvis finally convinced
   Priscilla Beaulieu's father to allow her to stay in Memphis with
   Vernon and Dee, while she finished school at Immaculate Conception High School. She and her family arrived at Graceland
   while he was enroute to Travis AFB, California. Immaculate
   Conception is located on Central Avenue at Belvedere Boulevard. School Principal at the time was Sister M. Adrian Mully.

NOVEMBER

NOV 2   (Fri.) The *Hollywood Reporter*, in its review of "Girls!
          Girls! Girls!" said that Elvis "performs with his usual
          style and on some numbers demonstrates a growing ma-
          turity of voice."
NOV 6   (Tues.) The *Memphis Commercial Appeal* reported that
          Elvis planned to help the same charities that his bene-
          fit show in February 1961 had aided.
NOV 7   (Wed.) *Variety*, in reviewing "Girls! Girls! Girls!" said
          that Elvis "is given a plethora of songs regardless of
          whether or not they fit smoothly into the action . . . but
          [he] handles his role capably."
NOV 21   (Wed.) "Girls! Girls! Girls!" opened in theaters across the
          U.S. In many locations, the co-feature was "It Hap-
          pened In Athens," starring Jayne Mansfield.
NOV 23   (Fri.) In reviewing "Girls! Girls! Girls!" the *Los Angeles
          Times* said that the movie was "no better or worse than
          previous Elvis epics. It's just a question of whether you
          can take it."
NOV 28   (Wed.) "Girls! Girls! Girls!" was number 6 on *Variety*'s
          "National Box Office Survey." The movie stayed on the
          list for three weeks.

DECEMBER

DEC 1   (Sat.) *Billboard* reviewed the **Girls! Girls! Girls!** album,
          commenting, "Here's Elvis with another smash picture
          album, full of fine tunes that all fans will enjoy."
DEC 8   (Sat.) **Girls! Girls! Girls!** entered *Billboard*'s LP chart at
          number 27. It stayed on the chart for thirty-two weeks
          and reached number 3.

DEC 25   (Tues.) Elvis had a Christmas party at Graceland for thirty intimate friends. He introduced Priscilla and gave her a diamond ring.

DEC 31   (Mon.) Elvis hosted a New Year's Eve party at the Manhattan Club in Memphis. He attended with Priscilla.

That's Someone
You Never Forget

ALL
SHOOK
UP

ELVIS
Day-By-Day,
1963

JANUARY

It was reported that Elvis and his long-time girlfriend, Anita Wood, had parted company, presumably at Pricilla's request.

JAN 9   (Wed.) In *Variety*'s annual look at the past year's films' box office record, "Blue Hawaii" was number 14 with a gross of $4.7 million; "Girls! Girls! Girls!" was number 31 with receipts of $2.6 million; and "Kid Galahad" was number 37 with a take of $1.75 million.

JAN 11   (Fri.) M-G-M turned over the recording tapes from "It Happened At The World's Fair" to RCA Victor.

mid-JAN   In mid-January, Elvis and his Memphis Mafia, as his entourage of bodyguards was now referred to in the press, returned to Hollywood in the motorhome.

JAN 22   (Tues.) Elvis had a recording session at Radio Recorders in Hollywood for the soundtrack to "Fun In Acapulco." Songs included *I Think I'm Gonna Like It Here, Mexico, The Bullfighter Was A Lady, Marguerita*, and three versions of *Vino, Dinero Y Amor. Bossa Nova Baby*, which was also recorded, was released as a single prior to the release of the film or the soundtrack album.

The musicians were the usual group assembled for Elvis' mid-1960s' films, with the addition of Anthony Terran and Rudolph D. Loera on trumpet, and the Amigos on vocals to give a Mexican flavor to the music.

JAN 23   (Wed.) Elvis continued recording songs for the soundtrack to "Fun In Acapulco." *I Think I'm Gonna Like It Here* and *The Bullfighter Was A Lady* were re-recorded, but the versions released were the ones recorded on the 22nd. Other songs waxed included *Fun In Acapulco, No Room To Rhumba In A Sports Car, El Toro, Guadalajara,* and *You Can't Say No In Acapulco. Maleguena* was also recorded, but it was cut from the film and remains unreleased to date.

JAN 28 (Mon.) Production started on "Fun In Acapulco" for
        Paramount Pictures. Although set in Mexico, all of
        Elvis' scenes were filmed at the studio. A second movie
        crew traveled to Acapulco for background scenes to be
        used as "color."

FEBRUARY

FEB 9   (Sat.) *Billboard*, in its "Pop Spotlight" section reviewed
        *One Broken Heart For Sale/They Remind Me Too Much
        Of You*, calling the songs "two more smash hits from
        Elvis."
FEB 16 (Sat.) *One Broken Heart For Sale* entered the "Hot 100"
        in *Billboard* at 59. It stayed on the chart for nine weeks
        and peaked at number 11.

   The February issue of *Esquire* magazine ran an article about Elvis'
   career entitled "$10 Million Later."

MARCH

MAR 7   (Thurs.) The *New York Times* in a belated review of "Kid
        Galahad," said "Mr. Presley does not make a convincing
        pug."

APRIL

APR 1   (Mon.) *Variety*, in reviewing "It Happened At The World's
        Fair," said that the ten songs "upset the tempo of the
        yarn, frivolous as it is, and prevent plot and picture from
        gathering momentum."
APR 2   (Tues.) In its review of "It Happened At The World's
        Fair," the *Hollywood Reporter* said that Elvis "handles
        himself well."
APR 5   (Fri.) Elvis arrived back in Memphis.
early   In April, Elvis had minor surgery to remove several cysts.
APR   The operation was probably performed in the doctor's
        office.
APR 10 (Wed.) "It Happened At The World's Fair" opened in
        theaters across the country.
APR 13 (Sat.) *Billboard*, in reviewing the album, **It Happened At
        The World's Fair**, said it "should be a blockbuster."

Elvis as he appeared in "It Happened At The World's Fair."

MID-APRIL TO LATE MAY
    During his vacation in Memphis, Elvis frequently was seen riding
his motorcycle with a pretty new passenger, Priscilla Beaulieu.
He also rented the fairgrounds and the movie theaters for his
midnight fun. Films which he saw repeatedly were "Lawrence
Of Arabia" and "To Kill A Mockingbird."

APR 20   (Sat.) **It Happened At The World's Fair** entered *Billboard*'s
           LP chart at number 90. It reached number 4 and stayed
           twenty-six weeks.

    In April, RCA Victor announced that Elvis had sold over 100
million records worldwide.

MAY

MAY 26 (Sun.) Elvis traveled to Nashville for a recording session
          at RCA Victor's studios. Although it would appear that
          this session was set up to provide a new single and an al-
          bum, the songs appeared on several releases over the
          next few years. *Please Don't Drag That String Around*
          and *Devil In Disguise* were released back-to-back on a
          single in May 1963. *Never Ending* was released in 1964
          as a "B" side. *Witchcraft* was a "B" side on an October
          1963 release. *Echoes Of Love* appeared as a "Bonus
          Song" on the **Kissin' Cousins** soundtrack album. *What
          Now, What Next, Where To?* was a "Bonus Song" on the
          Double Trouble soundtrack LP, and *Finders Keepers,
          Losers Weepers* first appeared on **Elvis For Everyone**.
          Love Me Tonight was a "Bonus Song" on the **Fun In
          Acapulco** soundtrack album.
          Musicians included the usual group of sidemen along with
          Jerry Kennedy and Grady Martin on guitar, and Millie
          Kirkham and Joe Babcock joining the Jordanaires on
          vocals.
MAY 27 (Mon.) Elvis was back in the studios for another recording
          session. He started by attempting the Chuck Berry
          classic *Memphis, Tennessee,* but the takes were unsatis-
          factory. *Long Lonely Highway* first appeared as a "Bo-
          nus Song" on the **Kissin' Cousins** album. *Ask Me* proved
          to be less than satisfactory and was re-recorded in 1964.
          Western Union was a "Bonus Song" on the **Speedway**
          soundtrack LP. *Slowly But Surely* was placed on the

Fun In Acapulco album as a "Bonus Song," and *Blue River* was not released until 1965, when it appeared on a single.

The session lasted into the morning hours of the 28th.

JUNE

JUN 14   (Fri.) Priscilla graduated from Immaculate Conception High School. Following graduation, she enrolled in the Patricia Stevens Finishing School in Memphis.

JUN 29   (Sat.) *(You're The) Devil In Disguise* entered *Billboard*'s "Hot 100" chart at number 84, where it reached number 3 and stayed eleven weeks.

JULY

early JUL Elvis returned to Hollywood to start work on "Viva Las Vegas" for M-G-M.

JUL 7   (Sun.) At Radio Recorders Studio, instrumental tracks were recorded at a session for the soundtrack to "Viva Las Vegas."

The musicians for this session included Scotty Moore, Glen Campbell and possibly James Burton on guitar (Burton had played in the bands of Dale Hawkins and Ricky Nelson and would back up Elvis in concerts and recordings regularly starting in 1969). The rest of the musicians were the usual "Hollywood" group that backed Elvis. Vocals were handled by the Jordanaires, the Carole Lombard Trio, and the Jubilee Four.

JUL 9   (Tues.) At Radio Recorders Studio, Elvis had another recording session to complete the songs required for "Viva Las Vegas." Songs from both sessions included the title song, *Viva Las Vegas, What'd I Say, Today Tomorrow And Forever, I Need Someone To Lean On, If You Think I Don't Need You, C'Mon Everybody, Santa Lucia, Night Life, Yellow Rose Of Texas/The Eyes Of Texas,* and *Do The Vega.* The session lasted until the early hours of the 10th. One additional song is rumored to have been recorded during this session, *Yeah, Yeah, Yeah,* but little is known about it.

JUL 11   (Thurs.) Elvis and Ann-Margret recorded the duet *The Lady Loves Me.* The song was unreleased by RCA at the time, and it first appeared on a bootleg LP in the 1970s.

JUL 15 (Mon.) A crew of 227 from M-G-M arrived in Las Vegas to film locations for "Viva Las Vegas." The first scene filmed was a road race from Lake Mead Lodge to the intersection of U.S. 466 and 95, then to the water pump station at Boulder Dam and back to the lodge. Elvis was not involved in these scenes. That night, Elvis filmed his first scene at the Henderson, Nevada, Drag Strip, as the start of the race was enacted. Elvis stayed in the Presidential Suite at the Sahara Hotel during the next two weeks. He took most of the top floor for himself, his body guards, and his friends.

JUL 16 (Tues.) Locations included the Folies Bergere at the Tropicana Hotel. Elvis also filmed a scene at the Tropicana's skeet shooting range.
Additional scenes included the swimming pool at the Flamingo Hotel, a local park, and McCarran Airport.

JUL 18 (Thurs.) Elvis and Ann-Margret were filmed riding motorcycles in a parking lot at the airport. Even though both were accomplished cyclists, stand-ins were used during most of the scenes.
Other scenes which included Elvis were the towing of his race car along the Las Vegas Strip, and the "shootout" with Ann-Margret in the Old Vegas Amusement Park in Henderson.

JUL 20 (Sat.) The film crew sent out a call for dancers to be used in the next week's filming at the University of Nevada-Las Vegas.

JUL 22 (Mon.) Filming continued throughout this week. Early in the week, Elvis, Ann-Margret and the newly-hired dancers completed the gymnasium scene at the University.

JUL 27 (Sat.) The film company returned to Hollywood.

JUL 29 (Mon.) Elvis continued to film "Viva Las Vegas" at the M-G-M Studios in Culver City.

AUGUST

AUG 6 (Tues.) The *Memphis Press-Scimitar* ran a story with the headline, "It Looks Like Romance For Elvis And Ann-Margret."

AUG 14 (Wed.) The album **Elvis' Golden Records, Volume 3** entered *Billboard*'s LP chart, where it stayed forty weeks and reached number 3.

FALL

Elvis sponsored a football team in Memphis, the Elvis Presley
Enterprises.

OCTOBER

OCT 3   (Thurs.) Elvis had a recording session in Nashville at RCA
Victor's studios for the film soundtrack to "Kissin'
Cousins." Musicians for this session included the usual
Nashville group that backed Elvis, including Scotty
Moore, D.J. Fontana, Floyd Cramer, and Boots Randolph.
The title song, *Kissin' Cousins*, first appeared on a single,
but all the other material recorded was issued on the
soundtrack LP: *Barefoot Ballad, Catchin' On Fast,
Once Is Enough, One Boy, Two Little Girls, Smokey
Mountain Boy, Tender Feeling, There's Gold In The
Mountains,* and *Anyone* (which was originally titled
Anyone Could Fall In Love With You.)
Although most of Elvis' film soundtracks were recorded in
Hollywood, this one had a "country" theme, and there-
fore the producer thought it would sound better coming
out of Nashville.

EARLY-LATE OCTOBER

In October, Elvis started filming "Kissin' Cousins" for M-G-M
Studios. The budget for this film was only $800,000. Outdoor
scenes were filmed around Big Bear Lake, California, about
eighty miles east of Los Angeles. The shooting schedule called
for the film to be completed in two weeks, but it ran two days
over schedule.

OCT 7   (Mon.) Paramount Pictures turned over the recording tapes
from "Fun In Acapulco" to RCA Victor.
OCT 12   (Sat.) In the "Spotlight Winners Of The Week" section,
Billboard highlighted *Bossa Nova Baby/Witchcraft,* saying: "More Presley powerhouse wax."
OCT 19   (Sat.) *Bossa Nova Baby* started up *Billboard*'s "Hot 100"
chart at number 77, staying ten weeks.

NOVEMBER

NOV 8   (Fri.) The *Memphis Press-Scimitar,* following up its
story of August 6th, published an article with the headline, "Elvis Wins Love Of Ann-Margret."

A promotional gimmick from "Fun In Acapulco."

NOV 18 (Mon.) In England, Elvis was voted the "Top Male Singer" by *Melody Maker* magazine.

NOV 21 (Thurs.) In reviewing "Fun In Acapulco," *Variety* said: "Presley has come a long way and is deserving of better material."

Film Daily said: "In general, the film compares favorably with previous Presley pictures."

NOV 27 (Wed.) "Fun In Acapulco" opened in theaters in the United States. In many locations, the co-feature was "The Yellow Canary," starring Pat Boone.

The *Motion Picture Herald* said of "Fun In Acapulco," "The fans won't find many surprises in this new picture . . . but they won't be disappointed either."

DECEMBER

DEC 4 (Wed.) "Fun In Acapulco" was ranked number 5 in *Variety*'s "National Box Office Survey." It remained on the survey for three weeks.

DEC 7 (Sat.) In a full-page ad in *Billboard*, RCA Victor said that **Elvis' Christmas Album** was "heading for $2,000,000 in sales."

late DEC During the week before Christmas, Elvis was seen riding around Memphis in his new Rolls Royce.

DEC 21 (Sat.) **Fun In Acapulco** entered the *Billboard* LP chart, at number 63, where it peaked at number 3 and stayed twenty-four weeks.

late DEC Prior to Christmas, Elvis made several large donations to local Memphis charities.

DEC 25 (Wed.) Christmas was spent quietly at Graceland.

DEC 31 (Tues.) Elvis hosted a New Year's Eve party at the Manhattan Club in Memphis. He attended with Priscilla. It was reported that a girl did an impromptu strip tease and was taken away.

Elvis was the subject of a one-time magazine published by *Song Hits* in 1963 titled *Elvis Presley*.

Only The Strong Survive

ALL SHOOK UP

ELVIS
Day-By-Day,
1964

JANUARY

JAN 4   (Sat.) *Billboard* ran a picture of Elvis and RCA Victor's
           Steve Sholes with a caption stating that Elvis had re-
           ceived a gold record for sales of 100,000 copies of
           Elvis' Christmas Album since 1959.

JAN 8   (Wed.) In *Variety*'s annual year-end review of the movies
           of the past year, "Fun In Acapulco" was number 33 with
           a box office gross of $1.5 million and an estimated po-
           tential of $3.3 million; "It Happened At The World's
           Fair" was number 55 with $2.25 million.

JAN 10   (Fri.) A postcard was mailed from Huntsville, Alabama,
           on this date which threatened the lives of Elvis,
           Johnny Cash, President Johnson, and Governor George
           Wallace. The card was mailed to "Presdient [sic] Elvis
           Presley." Nothing came of this threat.

JAN 12   (Sun.) Elvis had a recording session at RCA Victor's
           studios in Nashville which started at 6:30 p.m. and ran
           to almost midnight. Only three songs were waxed:
           Memphis, Tennessee and *Ask Me* (both of which had
           turned out unsuccessfully during the March 27, 1963
           session) and *It Hurts Me*. The last two songs were to
           appear as "B" sides on singles, and *Memphis, Tennessee*
           appeared on the **Elvis For Everyone** LP.
           The musicians for this session were the same as most of the
           Nashville sessions. Chet Atkins was listed as the pro-
           ducer for the first time instead of Steve Sholes, even
           though Elvis did most of the actual producing of his own
           sessions.

JAN 23   (Thurs.) M-G-M Studios turned over the tapes from the
           soundtrack of "Kissin' Cousins" to RCA Victor.

JAN 30   (Thurs.) Elvis purchased President Franklin D. Roosevelt's
           165-foot long yacht, "The Potomac," at an auction by

Hydro-Capitol, Inc., for a bid of $55,000. He an-
nounced that he was going to donate it to the March
of Dimes to be used as a possible national shrine.
F.D.R. suffered from polio, the disease which was the
main concern of the March of Dimes Society.

FEBRUARY

FEB 6   (Thurs.) The March of Dimes announced, with much re-
           gret, that it could not accept "The Potomac." As a
           voluntary health agency, it was in no position to main-
           tain the yacht as a national shrine.
FEB 9   (Sun.) During the Beatles' first appearance on the "Ed
           Sullivan Show," a congratulatory telegram from Elvis
           and the Colonel was read by Sullivan.
FEB 11   (Tues.) Elvis attempted to turn "The Potomac" over to
           the 7th Coast Guard District Auxiliary in Miami. How-
           ever, the Coast Guard refused the gift when it was
           learned that the civilian auxiliary wanted to sell the
           yacht for scrap and use the money to build a clubhouse.
FEB 13   (Thurs.) In Long Beach, California, Elvis finally donated
           the Presidential yacht "Potomac" to the St. Jude's Hos-
           pital in Memphis. Actor Danny Thomas, founder of
           the hospital for children, accepted a bill of sale from
           Elvis during the ceremony aboard the yacht.
FEB 15   (Sat.) RCA Victor released *Kissin' Cousins/It Hurts Me.*
           Billboard, in "Spotlight"-ing *Kissin' Cousins/It Hurts Me*,
           said the songs were "two more contenders for chart honors."
FEB 22   (Sat.) *Kissin' Cousins* entered *Billboard*'s "Hot 100" chart
           at number 63, staying nine weeks and peaking at num-
           ber 12.
FEB 24   (Mon.) Elvis had a recording session at Radio Recorders in
           Hollywood for the soundtrack to "Roustabout."
           (Actual dates for this session are not known, as Para-
           mount Pictures booked studio time for the whole last
           week in February and the first week in March. It is
           possible that the backing tracks were recorded during
           the first week and Elvis' vocals during the second.)
           All songs were for the film, and all ended up on the sound-
           track album (except *I Never Had It So Good*, which was
           not in the film and remains unreleased to date): *Big Love
           Big Heartache, Carny Town, Hard Knocks, It's A Wonderful
           World, It's Carnival Time, Little Egypt* (which had

been a hit for the Coasters in 1961), *One Track Heart, Poison Ivy League, Roustabout, There's A Brand New Day On The Horizon,* and *Wheels On My Heels.*

In addition to the usual musicians used during Elvis' Hollywood sessions, Billy Strange was on guitar. The Mello Men actually recorded the backing vocals on *Roustabout*, but gave up their copyright claim and were paid on an hourly basis.

MARCH

MAR 4   (Wed.) *Variety* said of the movie "Kissin' Cousins," "This new Presley concoction is a pretty dreary effort . . . [Elvis] needs — and merits — more substantial material than this . . . Presley does as well as possible under the circumstances."

MAR 5   (Thurs.) The *Hollywood Reporter*, in its review of "Kissin' Cousins," said: "[The picture] gives the reliable singing star a fine showcase in an amusing double role . . . All of Presley's pictures are doing well, but this one should be outstanding."

MAR 6   (Fri.) *Viva Las Vegas* was issued as a single in England. This was the first time that any of Elvis' material had appeared in a foreign country before being issued in the United States. The movie also was shown in England before the United States, under the title "Love In Las Vegas."

"Kissin' Cousins" opened in theaters across the country.

MAR 9   (Mon.) Elvis started filming "Roustabout" for Paramount Studios in Hollywood. Locations were filmed at Hidden Hills and Thousand Oaks, California, about forty miles northwest of Los Angeles.

MAR 11 (Fri.) The *Memphis Commercial Appeal* reported that Elvis would be lauded for his patriotism by the Elks. The ceremony would take place on March 31st.

MAR 19 (Thurs.) The *Los Angeles Herald-Examiner*, in its review of "Kissin' Cousins," said: "Hollywood comes up with an answer to the Beatles by offering two, yes two, Elvis Presleys. [However], acting demands upon the singing personality are kept to a minimum."

MAR 31 (Fri.) The City of Memphis honored Elvis with its "First Americanism" award. The honor was bestowed by the local Elks Club. Elvis was not present at the ceremony.

APRIL

APR 1   (Wed.) "Kissin' Cousins" was ranked number 11 in *Variety*'s "National Box Office Survey." The film was only on the list for one week.

APR 9   (Thurs.) The Associated Press voted Elvis the "Performer of the Year."

APR 11   (Sat.) The **Kissin' Cousins** LP entered *Billboard*'s album chart at number 96 where it reached number 6 and stayed thirty weeks.

In reviewing the **Kissin' Cousins** album, *Billboard* said it represented "more fine work from the singer."

In April, Albert Hand, President of the Official Elvis Fan Club of Great Britain, met Elvis in Los Angeles after he had finished filming "Roustabout." Hand reported that Elvis had the flu and looked very pale.

MAY

MAY 2   (Sat.) *Kiss Me Quick* entered *Billboard*'s "Hot 100" chart at number 79 staying six weeks and peaking at number 34.

MAY 5   (Tues.) The "Shindig" TV show had a tribute to Elvis in celebration of his tenth year as a recording artist which starred Glen Campbell, Jimmy Boyd, The Blossoms, The Isley Brothers, and Linda Gail. Elvis did not participate.

MAY 9   (Sat.) In its review of the single, *Viva Las Vegas, Billboard* said: "Once again a Presley deck hits the wax mart and, once again, it means money in the bank for all concerned."

Viva Las Vegas entered *Billboard*'s "Hot 100" at number 87. It stayed on the chart for only seven weeks, peaking at 29.

MAY 18 (Mon.) *Variety* called "Viva Las Vegas" "a pretty trite, heavy-handed affair, puny in story development and distortedly preoccupied with anatomical oomph. [The picture] is designed to dazzle the eye, assault the ear and ignore the brain."

The *Hollywood Reporter*, on the other hand, said that "M-G-M has what will be one of Elvis Presley's biggest grossing pictures."

MAY 23 (Sat.) *What'd I Say* started up the "Hot 100" chart in *Billboard* where it stayed six weeks and reached 21.

JUNE

JUN 5   (Fri.) Elvis reported to M-G-M Studios in Culver City to begin pre-production on "Girl Happy." He was visited on the set by actor Sergio Franchi who was made an "honorary Colonel" by Colonel Parker as part of the promotion for "Kissin' Cousins."

JUN 16   (Tues.) Elvis started a recording session at Radio Recorders in Hollywood for "Girl Happy." Prior to his arrival in the studio, the musicians had laid down their backing tracks in a previous session. The musicians included most of the usual sidemen employed for Elvis' films. Joining the Jordanaires on background vocals were the Jubilee Four and the Carole Lombard Trio. All of the songs were recorded for the film, and most first appeared on the soundtrack album, except *Do The Clam* which was first issued as a single: *Girl Happy, Spring Fever, Fort Lauderdale Chamber Of Commerce, Startin' Tonight, Wolf Call, Do Not Disturb, Cross My Heart And Hope To Die, The Meanest Girl In Town, Puppet On A String,* and *I've Got To Find My Baby.* The session lasted three more evenings, until June 19th.

JUN 17   (Wed.) "Viva Las Vegas" opened in theaters across the country. In many locations, the co-feature was "Tamahine," starring Nancy Kwan.

JUN 20   (Sat.) *Billboard* reviewed the EP **Viva Las Vegas**, with the comment "potent one here." (The EP was on the "Hot 100" for only one week at number 92 on July 4th.)

JULY

JUL 1   (Wed.) "Viva Las Vegas" entered the "National Box Office Survey" in *Variety* at number 14. The film stayed on the list for two weeks.

JUL 3   (Fri.) The *Los Angeles Times*, in a review of "Viva Las Vegas" said: "Nothing is wrong with the motor in our boy. It's revved up as usual."

mid-JUL   In mid-July, Elvis and the M-G-M film crew traveled to Ft. Lauderdale, Florida, for location shooting on "Girl Happy."

JUL 18   (Sat.) *Billboard*, in its "Hot Pop Spotlight" section, reviewed *Such A Night*, calling it a "great tune, great performance."

JUL 25   (Sat.) *Such A Night* entered the "Hot 100" in *Billboard* at number 82, staying eight weeks and reaching number 16.

Elvis and Ann-Margret in "Viva Las Vegas."

AUGUST

AUG 15   (Sat.) *Billboard* reported that Elvis had received a gold record from A.G.J. McGrath, Director of Teal Record Company, RCA Victor licensee in South Africa, for sales of *Kiss Me Quick*. The award was presented to Elvis on the set of "Girl Happy."

AUG 25   (Tues.) Paramount Pictures turned over the recording tapes from "Roustabout" to RCA Victor.

LATE SUMMER

Elvis returned to Graceland after an eight month absence.

SEPTEMBER

In September, Brian Epstein, manager of The Beatles, had lunch with Colonel Parker in Memphis.

SEP 21   (Mon.) Elvis was made Deputy Sheriff of Shelby County, Tennessee (Memphis). Later that night, he went to a midnight movie at the Memphian Theater.

OCTOBER

OCT 3   (Sat.) In its "Hot Pop Spotlight" review of *Ask Me*, *Billboard* said the song was "one of his most powerful ballad performances."

OCT 10   (Sat.) *Ask Me* and *Ain't That Lovin' You, Baby* entered *Billboard*'s "Hot 100" at number 88 and number 76 respectively. *Ask Me* peaked at number 12 and stayed on the chart for twelve weeks. *Ain't That Loving You, Baby* stayed on the chart for ten weeks and reached number 16.

OCT 12   (Mon.) Production started on "Tickle Me," for Allied Artists Studios. It was well known that Allied was having financial difficulties, so even though they had Elvis under contract, Elvis' fee was cut back to $750,000 plus fifty percent of the profits (usually he received $1 million plus fifty percent). The film was budgeted at $1.48 million including Elvis' salary. To help cut other costs on the film, no new songs were recorded for the soundtrack. Musical numbers were culled from earlier Elvis LPs, such as **Pot Luck**.

NOVEMBER

NOV 7   (Sat.) The *Memphis Press-Scimitar* reported that Brigitte
        Bardot, French actress, might be Elvis' next co-star.
        Billboard, in reviewing the **Roustabout** album, said: "This
        one should do extremely well."
NOV 11 (Wed.) "Roustabout" opened in theaters in the United
        States.
        Variety, in its movie review of "Roustabout," said it was
        "a gaudily-staged, tritely-scripted film looming as a box
        office smash based on [the] lure of [the] Presley name.
        [The] good cast tries its best to cope with [the] non-
        sense, but it's a losing battle."
        The *Hollywood Reporter* said "the threadbare theme has
        been rewoven with skill . . . the trimmings are fancy and
        "Roustabout" should be a rousing success."
NOV 14 (Sat.) **Roustabout** entered *Billboard*'s album chart at
        number 100. It stayed on the chart for twenty-seven
        weeks and reached number 1.
NOV 22 (Tues.) The *New York Times* ran an interview with Colonel
        Parker in an article called "Hollywood: Money Man
        From Memphis." Colonel Parker said that Elvis was the
        highest paid movie star in history, receiving $600,000 to
        $1 million for each film, plus fifty percent of the profits.
        Elvis was filming "Tickle Me" at the time.
NOV 26 (Thurs.) The *Hollywood Citizen-News*, in its review of
        "Roustabout," said: "[Elvis] doesn't have to do much
        but he always manages to please his many followers with
        his easy going manner of acting and his (admittedly)
        sexy way of presenting a song."
NOV 27 (Fri.) In its review of "Roustabout," the *Los Angeles
        Herald-Examiner* called the film "the best Presley movie
        of his cinema career."

DECEMBER
        Early in the month, Elvis completed production on "Tickle Me."
        He and his Memphis Mafia returned to Memphis for the holidays.

DEC 2   (Wed.) "Roustabout" entered *Variety*'s "National Box
        Office Survey" at number 8. The movie stayed on the
        chart for two weeks.
DEC 5   (Sat.) In a full-page ad in *Billboard*, RCA Victor reported
        that **Elvis' Christmas Album** has sold 800,000 copies

and was available for the first time in stereo. Elvis'
single of *Blue Christmas/Wooden Heart* was also doing
well, with 150,000 copies shipped.

DEC 12   (Sat.) *Billboard*, in an article entitled "Elvis, Beatles,
Brenda [Lee] Top In Newspaper Poll" reported that
Elvis had been named "Top Male Singer for 1964" by
the *New Musical Express* in England. In another article,
"Elvis Over U.K. Pop: Aussies," *Billboard* reported that
Elvis' single, *Ain't That Lovin' You, Baby/Ask Me*
had topped the Australian charts. According to reports
from down under, this marked the "end to the British
beat boom."

DEC 14   (Mon.) Elvis personally delivered checks totaling $55,000
to charities in Memphis.

DEC 21   (Mon.) For the eighth year in a row, Elvis won the "American Bandstand" TV show's award as "Best Male Singer."
The announcement was made during the ABC-TV show's
broadcast from 3:00 to 5:00 p.m.

DEC 24   (Thurs.) The *Memphis Press-Scimitar* reported that Elvis
earned $1.75 million from his films in 1964.

DEC 25   (Fri.) Elvis spent Christmas at Graceland.

DEC 31   (Thurs.) New Year's Eve was celebrated at Graceland,
with a party for a few immediate friends.

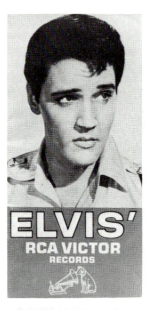

The 1965 "Elvis' RCA Victor Records" catalog
featured a cover photo from "Girl Happy."

Elvis also appeared on this five-cent arcade
card dispensed by vending machines.

Lonely Man

ALL
SHOOK
UP
ELVIS
Day-By-Day,
1965

JANUARY

JAN 2   (Sat.) **Roustabout** reached number 1 on *Billboard*'s "Hot LP's" chart, beating out such notables of the time as the Beach Boys, Beatles, and other "British invasion" groups. It would be his last number 1 album until 1973.

Elvis did not have any singles on *Billboard*'s "Top 100 Records Of 1964" list.

JAN 6   (Wed.) In *Variety*'s annual year-end review of movies, "Viva Las Vegas" was number 11 with a total gross of $4,675,000 and "Kissin' Cousins" was number 26 with a gross of $2.8 million.

JAN 21   (Thurs.) In reviewing "Girl Happy," the *Hollywood Reporter* said that the film "should do the customary brisk Presley business."

The *Motion Picture Daily* said, "With product like this, Presley's status . . . can't go anyway but up . . . he seems to enjoy it as much as his audiences will."

JAN 26   (Mon.) Paramount Pictures turned over the recording tapes from "Girl Happy" to RCA Victor.

JAN 27   (Wed.) *Variety* called "Girl Happy" "another winner . . . the type of pleasant fare which Presley's fans have come to expect."

JAN 30   (Sat.) It was reported in the entertainment press that Memphis City Commissioners Hunter Lane, Jr., and Thomas E. Sisson, had introduced a joint resolution "last week" calling for a public monument in the form of a building, roadway, park, or other institution to be named for Elvis, "thereby demonstrating the high esteem in which he is held by his fellow citizens."

In the current issue of the comic book, *Career Girl Romances*, Elvis was the subject of the story "Talent For Loving," in which the heroine couldn't decide among Elvis, Herman's Hermits or Johnny Rivers.

FEBRUARY

FEB 20 (Sat.) *Billboard*, in "Spotlight"-ing *Do The Clam*, called it a "swinging new dance."

FEB 24 (Wed.) Elvis had a recording session in Nashville for "Harum Scarum." All songs recorded were issued on the soundtrack LP and most appeared in the film. Musicians present for this date included the usual mix: Scotty Moore, D.J. Fontana, Floyd Cramer, Boots Randolph, and several other top Nashville sidemen. Backing vocals were handled by the Jordanaires.

Songs recorded included *Go East Young Man, Shake That Tambourine, Golden Coins, So Close Yet So Far, Harem Holiday* (which was the title of the film in its overseas release), *Mirage, Animal Instinct* (which was cut from the film), *Kismet, Hey Little Girl, Wisdom Of The Ages* (which was cut from the film), and *My Desert Serenade.*

FEB 27 (Sat.) *Do The Clam* entered *Billboard*'s "Hot 100" at number 68. It stayed on the chart for eight weeks and peaked at number 21.

late FEB Late in February, Elvis and his buddies traveled to Hollywood in an auto caravan.

MARCH

MAR 15 (Mon.) Production started on "Harum Scarum" (which was known at this time as "Harem Holiday") at M-G-M. The film was completed in eighteen days and was shot entirely at the Samuel Goldwyn studio in Culver City.

MAR 18 (Thurs.) *Tomorrow Night*, an original Sun Records recording from the September 10, 1954 session, was over-dubbed in Nashville's RCA studios. Chet Atkins produced the session and played guitar. Other musicians included Grady Martin, guitar; Henry Strzelecki, bass; Buddy Harmon, drums; Charlie McCoy, harmonica; and the Anita Kerr Singers, vocals. Unfortunately, the original tape containing the song was used for the remixing, so the "pure" Sun sound was lost forever. Elvis was not present for this session.

APRIL

Following work on "Harum Scarum," Elvis took a five-week holiday.

APR 7   (Wed.) "Girl Happy" opened in theaters nationwide. The co-feature in many locations was "Quick! Before It Melts," with George Maharis.

APR 17   (Sat.) **Girl Happy** was called "another winning package" in *Billboard*'s "Spotlight" section, as the album entered the chart at number 140. **Girl Happy** stayed on the chart for thirty-one weeks, reaching number 8. *Billboard* also "Spotlight"-ed a new single, *Crying In The Chapel*, noting, erroneously, that it came from Elvis' religious album, **His Hand In Mine**. The song was not on an LP until 1967.

APR 24   (Sat.) *Crying In The Chapel* started up the *Billboard* "Hot 100" chart at number 79, staying fourteen weeks and peaking at number 3. By the end of the year, *Crying In The Chapel* had sold 1,732,000 copies.

MAY

MAY 7   (Mon.) *Time* magazine ran an article entitled "Forever Elvis."

MAY 9   (Sun.) Many radio stations across the country aired the *Crying In The Chapel* single, and the **His Hand In Mine** album on this Mother's Day.

MAY 13   (Thurs.) Elvis had a recording session at the United Artists Recording Studios in Hollywood for the film "Frankie And Johnny." Musicians included the usual mix of Nashville/Hollywood sidemen. Background vocals were performed by the Jordanaires.

Two of the songs recorded, *Frankie And Johnny* and *Please Don't Stop Loving Me*, were released as a single prior to the album or film's release. All other songs were featured on the soundtrack LP and in the film: *Come Along, Petunia The Gardener's Daughter, Chesay, What Every Woman Lives For, Look Out Broadway, Beginner's Luck, Down By The Riverside/When The Saints Go Marching In, Shout It Out, Hard Luck,* and *Everybody Come Aboard.*

The sessions lasted two additional days, on the 14th and 15th.

Elvis in 1965's "Girl Happy," co-starring Gary Crosby (left).

A 1965 flyer for "Tickle Me."

MAY 24 (Mon.) Production started on "Frankie And Johnny" at the Goldwyn Studios for M-G-M. The film was shot entirely on the Culver City lot.

MAY 27 (Thurs.) The *Memphis Commercial Appeal* ran an article "Dedication of the Jesse Mahan Day Care Center Sunday to Honor Elvis." Elvis had included the center in his charity donations in December 1964.

JUNE

JUN 10 (Thurs.) The *New York Times* reported that *Crying In The Chapel* reached number 1 in the British hit parade. This was the first time that The Beatles had been topped by Elvis, and the first number 1 British hit for Elvis in three years.

JUN 12 (Sat.) *Billboard*, in reviewing *It Feels So Right/(Such An) Easy Question*, noted that the single had been "rushed into release." The songs were waxed in 1960 and 1962.

JUN 16 (Tues.) In reviewing "Tickle Me," *Variety* said, "Presley takes his character in stride, giving a performance calculated to appeal particularly to his following."

JUN 19 (Sat.) *(Such An) Easy Question* entered *Billboard*'s "Hot 100" at number 70. It stayed on the chart for only eight weeks and peaked at number 11.

JUN 21 (Sun.) *Box Office* magazine, in reviewing "Tickle Me," said, "While the story would hardly win an Oscar for originality, the great popularity of Presley will surmount that, as witness his strident success over the years."

JULY

JUL 3   (Sat.) **Tickle Me** was reviewed by *Billboard*, which said it was "a hot EP."

JUL 7   (Wed.) "Tickle Me" opened in theaters across the U.S. In many locations, the co-feature was "Stop Train-349," with Jose Ferrer.

JUL 10 (Sat.) The **Tickle Me** EP entered *Billboard*'s "Hot 100" at number 98. It only stayed on the chart for six weeks, peaking at number 70.

JUL 26 (Mon.) Backing tracks for "Paradise – Hawaiian Style" were recorded at Radio Recorders in Hollywood. Musicians included Scotty Moore, Barney Kessel, and Charlie McCoy on guitar; D.J. Fontana, Hal Blaine, and

Victor S. Feldman on drums; Ray Smith and Keith
Michell, bass; Larry Muhoberac, piano; Barnal K. Lewis,
steel guitar; and vocals by the Jordanaires and the Mello
Men. The session was continued on the 27th.

JUL 28 (Wed.) In a major article titled "Presley As Top-Money
Star," *Variety* told the story of Elvis' relationship
with Allied Artists and his involvement with "Tickle
Me." The film was reported to have earned $1,028,000
in eight weeks. It was expected to bring in a total of
$3 million, double the original cost, and enough money
to keep Allied Artists afloat for another year.

At a celebrity-filled ceremony, Elvis donated $50,000 to
the Motion Picture Relief Fund in Hollywood. This was
the largest single donation the fund had ever received.
On hand to accept the gift were Frank Sinatra and
Barbara Stanwyck, honorary heads of the fund.

JUL 31 (Sat.) In Hollywood, Elvis bought nine Harley Davidson
motorcycles for his friends, who were called "El's Angels."

AUGUST

AUG 2   (Mon.) Elvis began adding his vocals to the backing tracks
which had been recorded July 26th and 27th. Also in
the studio were the Mello Men. All songs recorded were
for the film "Paradise — Hawaiian Style," and all appeared on the soundtrack album: *Drums Of The Islands,
Datin', Scratch My Back, Stop Where You Are, A Dog's
Life, This Is My Heaven, Paradise — Hawaiian Style, A
House Of Sand, Queenie Wahine's Papaya*, and *Sand
Castles.* The backing tracks for *Sand Castles* were laid
down on this date, prior to Elvis' arrival.

In addition to the above songs, there appear to have been
two more songs recorded during these sessions which
remain unreleased by RCA Victor. They are rumored to
be *The Sands Of Time* (possibly *Sand Castles* under
another name?) and *Now Is The Hour.*

(The recording session lasted three days, probably for a
few hours each day, August 2nd, 3rd, and 4th.)

Several songs from the movie differ from those released on
the movie soundtrack album: *Queenie Wahine's Papaya*
and *Datin'* are sung by Elvis in duets with Donna Butterworth; *Scratch My Back* is a duet with Elvis and Marianna
Hill. Donna Butterworth also sings *Won't You Come
Home, Bill Bailey.*

AUG 5   (Thurs.) Elvis arrived at the Honolulu International Air-
         port at 11:55 p.m. via United Airlines. He stayed at the
         Ilikai Hotel, Room 2225, on Waikiki Beach. When he
         arrived, Elvis was suffering from a short-lived virus.

AUG 7   (Sat.) After a day's rest, Elvis started filming scenes for
         "Paradise – Hawaiian Style." The first location used
         was Hanauma Bay, and Elvis' character rescued James
         Shigeta and Donna Butterworth after their helicopter
         ran out of fuel and ditched.

AUG 9   (Mon.) Filming continued at a location known as China-
         man's Hat. Elvis, Donna Butterworth and Marianna Hill
         had a scene in which Miss Hill lost the key to Elvis'
         helicopter in the sand.

AUG 10   (Tues.) Production continued at Chinaman's Hat.

AUG 12   (Thurs.) Following a day off, Elvis returned to Chinaman's
         Hat for more movie making.

AUG 13   (Fri.) The film crew moved to a location at the Polynesian
         Cultural Center.

AUG 14   (Sat.) **Elvis For Everyone** entered *Billboard*'s album chart
         at number 149 where it peaked at number 10 and stayed
         twenty-seven weeks.
         Filming continued at the Polynesian Cultural Center.

AUG 15   (Sun.) During a Sunday lull in the filming schedule, Elvis
         and Colonel Parker visited the Memorial to the USS
         Arizona, which his 1961 concert in Honolulu had helped
         build. They arrived in the morning at CinCPac Head-
         quarters inside Halawa Gate, Pearl Harbor. The entour-
         age was taken by Navy launch to the memorial. Elvis
         laid two five-foot high wreaths at the memorial. One
         bell-shaped wreath was made from 1,177 carnations,
         the number of men lost on the Arizona. Elvis was pre-
         sented with the "Award Of Honor" by Tucker Gratz,
         chairman of the Pacific War Memorial Commission.
         Afterward, the group was given a tour of Pearl Harbor.

AUG 16   (Mon.) Filming resumed at the Polynesian Cultural Center.

AUG 17   (Tues.) Filming in Hawaii was wrapped up with some final
         scenes at the Polynesian Cultural Center. That night,
         Elvis signed autographs in his room from 5:30 to 10:00
         p.m.
         Other locations in the movie included the Maui Sheraton
         Hotel, the Hanalei Plantation Resort on Kauai (now
         known as the Hanalei Bay Colony Resort), and a country
         club on Kauai. Red West was one of the stuntmen

during the fight sequence at the steak house.

AUG 18   (Wed.) In the U.S. Senate, Hawaiian Senator Inouye requested that the August 16th article in the *Honolulu Advertiser* concerning Elvis' visit to the USS Arizona memorial be read into the Congressional Record.

Elvis was the guest of honor at a party given at the Polynesian Cultural Center. During the party, Elvis was interviewed by Peter Noone of the British rock group Herman's Hermits.

AUG 19   (Thurs.) Elvis flew back to Los Angeles. In Honolulu, radio station KPOI played the interview of Elvis taped at the Polynesian Cultural Center.

late AUG During the filming of "Paradise – Hawaiian Style," Elvis signed another contract with Hal Wallis for future films. The deal was confirmed between Colonel Parker and Wallis with a handshake.

AUG 21   (Sat.) *I'm Yours/Long, Lonely Highway* was a "Top 20" pick in *Billboard*, which said the songs were "both potential blockbusters.

AUG 24   (Tues.) Back in Los Angeles, Elvis continued filming scenes for "Paradise – Hawaiian Style" at the Torrance Airport, and at Paramount Studios in Hollywood.

AUG 27   (Fri.) During an American tour, the Beatles stopped to visit Elvis at his Perugia Way home in Bel Air. They arrived about 10:00 p.m., and they sang and talked with Elvis until 2:00 a.m.

AUG 28   (Sat.) *I'm Yours* entered *Billboard*'s "Hot 100" at number 83 where it stayed eleven weeks and reached number 11.

SEPTEMBER

SEP 11   (Sat.) The *Saturday Evening Post* published an article entitled "There Will Always Be An Elvis."

SEP 30   (Thurs.) M-G-M Studios turned over the recording tapes from "Harum Scarum" to RCA.

In September, Colonel Parker renegotiated Elvis' contract with RCA Victor, extending the basic pact for another ten years.

Before leaving Los Angeles, Elvis rented a ranch-style house at 10550 Rocca Place in Bel Air, about a mile from his Perugia Way home. He lived in the house when in Hollywood until mid-1967.

OCTOBER

OCT 2   (Sat.) *I'm Yours* reached number 1 on *Billboard*'s "Easy Listening" singles chart. It remained number 1 for three weeks.

OCT 7   (Thurs.) Elvis arrived back in Memphis about 11:00 p.m. driving his Dodge mobile home. He was followed by his entourage in five additional cars.

early   Once he was settled back at Graceland, Elvis bought a new
OCT   1966 Oldsmobile Toronado, one of the first of the front-wheel drive automobiles.

OCT 9   (Sat.) Elvis had fun riding a go-cart over the grounds at Graceland.

OCT 10   (Sun.) Elvis bought a new motorcycle and a new go-cart.

OCT 21   (Thurs.) Bill Black, long-time bass player with Elvis, and more recently, founder of the Bill Black's Combo, died of a brain tumor at age thirty-nine. He was a patient at Baptist Memorial Hospital in Memphis, where he had undergone three operations in the past six months. He left behind a wife, Evelyn, two teenaged children, Nancy and Lois, and Leigh Ann, twenty months.

OCT 22   (Fri.) The *Hollywood Reporter*, in reviewing "Harum Scarum," said that Elvis "continues to handle himself naturally, no different in manner or appearance than his earliest films."

OCT 27   (Wed.) *Variety*'s review of "Harum Scarum" said: "With anybody but Elvis Presley . . . this would be a pretty dreary affair. Elvis, however, apparently can do no wrong."

NOVEMBER

NOV 6   (Sat.) *Billboard*, in its "Pop Spotlight" section, picked *Puppet On A String* as a "Top 20" hit, calling the rendition a "smooth country ballad."

NOV 13   (Sat.) In the "Album Reviews" section of *Billboard*, **Harum Scarum** was reviewed with this statement: "Another sales giant from the latest of the long string of Presley's soundtrack hits."

         Puppet On A String started up *Billboard*'s "Hot 100" chart at number 30 where it peaked at number 14 and stayed ten weeks. **Harum Scarum** entered the *Billboard* LP chart at number 122 where it stayed twenty-three weeks and reached number 8.

NOV 16   (Mon.) In a belated review of "Tickle Me," the *Los Angeles Times* commented that the movie had "lousy color, cheap sets, hunks of stock footage, painted scenery and unconvincing process work, [but] who's to quibble when the movie is so much fun."

NOV 24   (Wed.) "Harum Scarum" opened in theaters across the United States. In many locations, the co-feature was "She," staring Ursula Andress.

NOV 27   (Sat.) The *Hollywood Citizen-News* said of "Harum Scarum" that "the cinematic farce just doesn't come off."

DECEMBER

DEC 1   (Wed.) "Harum Scarum" made a one-week appearance in *Variety*'s "National Box Office Survey" at number 11.

DEC 3   (Fri.) RCA Victor released *Blue Christmas/Santa Claus Is Back In Town.*

DEC 17   (Tues.) Elvis donated checks totaling over $50,000 to Memphis charities. The next day, the *Memphis Commercial Appeal* ran an article entitled "The Star Is A Little Nervous, But The Performance Is A Hit."

DEC 18   (Sat.) The *Memphis Commercial Appeal* ran an article praising Elvis for his annual donations to local charities.

late DEC   During the week before Christmas, Elvis read about an elderly black woman whose wheelchair had deteriorated with age. There was a fund being raised by her friends to buy her a new one. Elvis bought and personally delivered a new, electric wheelchair and gave her an additional $200.

DEC 24   (Fri.) Elvis opened Christmas presents with his family for about five hours in the evening.

DEC 25   (Sat.) *Billboard* picked *Tell Me Why* as a "Top 20" hit, and said the song was "a proven hit in England."
Christmas Day was celebrated quietly, and Elvis continued to open presents sent in from his many fans.

DEC 27   (Mon.) The *Memphis Commercial Appeal* reported that the Memphis city council wanted to name a fountain to honor Elvis.

DEC 31   (Fri.) Elvis hosted a New Year's Eve party at the Manhattan Club in Memphis from 9:00 p.m. to 5:00 a.m. Entertainment was provided by a local Memphis band led by Willie Mitchell, who had a hit with *20-75* in 1964.

During the Christmas season, **Elvis' Christmas Album** sold another 309,000 copies.

Elvis' career was matched with that of the Beatles for a one-time magazine published in 1965, *Elvis VS The Beatles.*

How Do You
Think I Feel

ALL
SHOOK
UP
ELVIS
Day-By-Day,
1966

JANUARY

JAN 1   (Sat.) *Tell Me Why* entered *Billboard*'s "Hot 100" at
         number 75. It stayed on the chart for seven weeks and
         reached number 33.
         Elvis and his buddies had a wild Roman candle fight on
         the grounds of Graceland at night, followed by a three-
         hour movie for his friends.

JAN 3   (Mon.) RCA Victor released Elvis' sales figures, showing
         that he had sold a total of 78 million records, up from
         49.3 million only two years ago.

early JAN Early in the month, Elvis had a slight cold.

JAN 5   (Wed.) In *Variety*'s list of "Big Rental Pictures Of 1965,"
         "Girl Happy" was number 25 with a gross of $3.1
         million, "Roustabout" was number 28 with a gross of
         $3 million, and "Harum Scarum" was number 40 with
         a gross of $2 million.

JAN 8   (Sat.) In a full-page ad, RCA Victor reported that
         525,720 copies of *Tell Me Why* had been shipped.
         Elvis spent a quiet birthday at Graceland, topped off with
         a midnight movie at a local theater. RCA Victor sent
         him a congratulatory letter which mentioned that 1965
         was "the biggest of all the ten years" he had been with
         the company.

JAN 18   (Tues.) The *Memphis Commercial Appeal* reported that
         the Memphis city council and other county officials had
         changed their minds about naming a fountain for Elvis.
         According to the article, they were in favor of building
         a monument.

JAN 25   (Tues.) Gary Pepper, a local Memphis fan and President
         of the Tankers Fan Club, presented the City Council
         with thousands of names gathered over the past months
         as a result of his efforts to re-name the Memphis

Coliseum to honor Elvis.

JAN 30   (Sun.) Elvis left Memphis in his moble home for Los
Angeles to begin filming "Spinout," which was known
at the time as "Never Say Yes/No," for M-G-M Studios.

FEBRUARY

FEB 15   (Tues.) United Artists turned over the recording tapes
from "Frankie And Johnny" to RCA Victor.
Musicians gathered at M-G-M's sound studios to begin recording the background tracks to the songs which would
be included in "Spinout."

FEB 21   (Mon.) Elvis had a session at M-G-M Studios to overdub
his voice on the songs for "Spinout." The title song,
Spinout, was issued as a single with *All That I Am* as
the flip side, but all of the other material appeared on
the soundtrack LP for the first time: *Stop, Look And
Listen, Adam And Evil, Never Say Yes, Am I Ready,
Beach Shack, Smorgasbord, I'll Be Back.*

Although the movie was set in Santa Barbara, California,
locations used in the filming of "Spinout" included the
Ascot Motor Car Racing Ground and Dodger Stadium
in Los Angeles. During the filming at Dodger Stadium,
a tour bus full of women stopped just as a racing sequence was in progress. Elvis was spotted and many of
the women ran across the street just as the race cars approached. No one was hurt, and work on the movie continued after Elvis shook a few hands and signed autographs. Two of Elvis' entourage, Red West and Joe Esposito, had small parts in the picture.

MARCH

MAR 12   (Sat.) The *Memphis Commercial Appeal* reported that
Memphis city officials planned to name a building,
possibly City Hall, for Elvis.
Please Don't Stop Loving Me/Frankie And Johnny was a
"Spotlight" pick in *Billboard*, which called the songs
"two exceptional Presley sides."

MAR 13   (Sun.) The United Press, in an article authored by Vernon
Scott, stated that Elvis was the highest paid entertainer
in the world, and also the largest single taxpayer on a
straight income in the United States.

MAR 15   (Tues.) The Memphis City Council was again petitioned by Gary Pepper to re-name the Memphis Coliseum for Elvis. He presented the council with 1,000 letters and petitions containing over 7,000 signatures from around the world. The matter was deferred to a meeting of the Coliseum Board on April 22nd.

MAR 19   (Sat.) *Frankie And Johnny* entered *Billboard*'s "Hot 100" at number 74. It stayed on the chart for eight weeks and reached number 25.

MAR 30   (Wed.) "Frankie And Johnny" opened in theaters in the United States.

           Variety, in a review of "Frankie And Johnny," said that Elvis "sings and acts, apparently doing both with little effort."

APRIL

APR 16   (Sat.) *Billboard*, in its "Album Reviews" section, said that the **Frankie And Johnny** LP represented a "power-packed sales explosion." Further, it added that the single of *Frankie And Johnny* was "racing like wildfire up the Hot 100 chart." (The album could not dent the top twenty. The single stalled at number 25.)

APR 22   (Fri.) At a meeting of the Coliseum Board in Memphis, the subject of re-naming the coliseum for Elvis was brought up by Gary Pepper. However, it was learned that the board had already voted to reject the proposal before it was brought up. The problem of a permanent municipal honor for Elvis was referred back to the Mayor and the City Commissioners.

APR 23   (Sat.) The album, **Frankie And Johnny** entered the *Billboard* LP chart at number 103, where it peaked at number 20 and stayed nineteen weeks.

           Elvis arrived back in Memphis driving a converted Greyhound bus. He drove all the way from Los Angeles, followed by a convoy of cars bringing the rest of his buddies.

late APR A few days after arriving back in Memphis, Elvis began attending his usual midnight movies. Some of the many movies (over forty) that Elvis viewed during his vacation were "The Ten Commandments," "Lady L," "The Magnificent Seven," "Chase," "Viva Marie," and "The Ghost And Mr. Chicken." Elvis also rented the Fair

Grounds Amusement Park for three late night parties
with Priscilla and his friends. Among his favorite rides
were the dodgem cars and the roller coaster, known as
the "Pippin'."

APR 27   (Fri.) In a review of "Frankie And Johnny," the
Los Angeles Times said the film was "pleasant, relaxing
entertainment . . . fast moving fun."

MAY

MAY 25   (Wed.) Elvis started a three-day recording session at 10:00
p.m. in RCA's Studio "B" in Nashville. Felton Jarvis
was the session A&R man (Elvis usually "produced" all
of his own songs), replacing Chet Atkins and Steve
Sholes. The number of musicians present during the
three-day session was much larger than usual for one of
Elvis' recording dates, but they included the usual nucleus of Scotty Moore, Bob Moore, Charlie McCoy, D.J.
Fontana, Buddy Harman, Floyd Cramer, Boots Randolph, Millie Kirkham, and the Jordanaires. In addition,
the following musicians contributed to the date: Chip
Young, guitar; Henry Strzelecki, bass; Henry Slaughter,
piano; David Briggs, organ; Pete Drake, steel guitar;
Rufus Long, Sax; Ray Stevens, trumpet; the Imperials,
vocals; and June Page, Dolores Edgin, and Sandy Posey,
vocals.

Two of the songs were recorded to be used as filler on the
Spinout album: *Down In The Alley* and *Tomorrow Is A
Long Time*. Another two songs were to be released as a
new single: *Love Letters* and *Come What May*. A final
song was released in 1967 as a single: *Fools Fall In Love.*

The remainder of the twelve songs recorded during the
three-day session were for Elvis' second religious album,
How Great Thou Art: *Run On, How Great Thou Art,
Stand By Me, Where No One Stands Alone, So High,
Farther Along, By And By, In The Garden, Somebody
Bigger Than You And I, Without Him, If The Lord
Wasn't Walking By My Side,* and *Where Could I Go But
To The Lord.*

One final song, *Beyond The Reef*, was waxed, but it sounds
more like a jam than a polished piece of material. It was
released in 1980 as part of the **Elvis Aron Presley** box set.

The sessions ran at night on the 25th, 26th and 27th, ending in the early morning hours of the 28th.

A scene from "Paradise, Hawaiian Style."

JUNE

JUN 2   (Thurs.) The *Memphis Commercial Appeal* reported that
          the movement to honor Elvis, first reported in Decem-
          ber 1965, was gaining support.

JUN 6   (Mon.) *Daily Variety* in its review of "Paradise – Hawaiian
          Style" said: "Presley delivers one of his customary
          ingratiating portrayals in usual voice and adept at
          comedy."
          The *Hollywood Reporter* said the picture was "not one
          of the best Presley films in incident and development,
          but it should satisfy his fans."

JUN 8   (Wed.) In its review, *Film Daily* said: "[The film followed]
          the successful formula of past Presley hits."

JUN 9   (Thurs.) "Paradise – Hawaiian Style" opened in Memphis
          at the Maslo Theater.

JUN 10   (Fri.) Elvis returned to RCA Victor's Studio "B" in Nash-
          ville for a recording session. Only three songs were
          finished: *Indescribably Blue*, which would be the "B"
          side of *Fools Fall In Love* from the May session; *I'll
          Remember You*, another filler for the **Spinout** album;
          and *If Every Day Was Like Christmas*, written by
          Elvis' bodyguard Red West. The last song prompted
          several of Elvis' friends to put a Christmas tree in the
          studio to get Elvis in the right frame of mind. The song
          was released as a single in late 1966.

late JUN Toward the end of June, several of Elvis' buddies left
          Memphis for Los Angeles in a caravan of autos, including
          Elvis' newest car, a black Eldorado Cadillac convertible,
          driven by Joe Esposito. Along with Esposito were Allen
          Fortas, Richard Davis, Mike Keaton, Ray Sitton, Sonny
          West, and Billy Smith, Elvis' cousin.

JUN 25   (Sat.) *Billboard* picked *Love Letters/Come What May* for
          its spotlight section, saying the "A" side was a "revival
          of a beautiful standard.

JUN 26   (Sun.) Elvis departed Memphis about 6:00 p.m. by airplane
          for Los Angeles, to start work on "Double Trouble"
          (which had the working title "You're Killing Me") for
          M-G-M. Accompanying Elvis was Red West, Marty Lacker,
          Jerry Schilling, Larry Geller, and Charlie Hodge. Although
          Elvis disliked flying, he felt it was necessary on this occa-
          sion so that he could spend more time with his grand-
          mother and uncle, who were ill.

That night, he had a recording session for "Double Trouble" at the M-G-M Studios in Culver City. The musicians included the usual group which backed Elvis in Hollywood. All of the instrumental tracks had been recorded before the 26th.

All songs except *It Won't Be Long* were featured in the film: *Double Trouble, Baby If You'll Give Me All Your Love, Could I Fall In Love, Long Legged Girl, Old McDonald, City By Night, I Love Only One Girl,* and *There Is So Much World To See.*

JUN 29   (Thurs.) Elvis' uncle, Travis Smith, died. He had been hospitalized for about six weeks. He was Gladys' brother and an employee of Elvis as a gatekeeper.

JULY

JUL 2   (Sat.) *Love Letters* entered the "Hot 100" in *Billboard* at number 87. It reached number 19 but stayed on the charts only seven weeks.

JUL 6   (Wed.) Paradise – Hawaiian Style" opened in theaters in the U.S. In many locations, the B-feature was "Get Yourself A College Girl," with the Dave Clark Five.

JUL 11   (Mon.) Production started on "Double Trouble" at the M-G-M Studios in Culver City. Although the movie was set in England and Belgium, all of Elvis' scenes were photographed on the sound stages and back lots of the Samuel Goldwyn Studios.

JUL 16   (Sat.) The album, **Paradise – Hawaiian Style**, entered the LP chart in *Billboard*. It stayed on the chart nineteen weeks, reaching number 15.

JUL 21   (Thurs.) The *Memphis Commercial Appeal* reported that Elvis' modesty had finally quashed any plans by the city council for a permanent monument in Elvis' name.

AUGUST

AUG 22   (Mon.) Elvis sent Joe Esposito to Memphis to drive the converted Greyhound bus back to Los Angeles.

SEPTEMBER

SEP 2   (Fri.) M-G-M turned over the recording tapes from "Spinout" to RCA Victor.

early SEP During the first week in September, Elvis finished work on "Double Trouble."

SEP 12   (Mon.) Elvis started filming "Easy Come, Easy Go" for
            Hal Wallis at Paramount Studios. Working titles for the
            movie included "Easy Does It," "Nice And Easy," "Port
            Of Call," and "A Girl In Every Port."
SEP 13   (Tues.) Vernon, his wife and stepsons, attended a special
            screening of "Spinout" at the Malco Theater in Memphis.
            "Blue Hawaii" was the opening movie on NBC-TV's
            "Tuesday Night At The Movies" for the fall season.
SEP 16   (Fri.) Vernon and Dee Presley flew from Memphis to
            Los Angeles to vacation with Elvis for a few weeks
            in Palm Springs.
SEP 24   (Sat.) *All That I Am/Spinout* was only a "Top 60" pick
            by *Billboard*, which said the records provided "two
            strong entries."
SEP 28   (Wed.) Elvis had a recording session at Radio Recorders in
            Hollywood for the soundtrack to "Easy Come, Easy
            Go." The usual musicians were on hand, as well as
            some new faces: Jerry Scheff, bass (he would tour with
            Elvis beginning in 1969); Emil Radocchia, drums; Michel
            Rubini, piano; Anthony Terran, Mike Henderson, Butch
            Parker, and E. Meredith Flory, horns. Although all of
            the songs were for the film "Easy Come, Easy Go," both
            She's A Machine and *Leave My Woman Alone* were
            omitted from the final cut of the film, and *Leave My
            Woman Alone* remains unissued.
            The other numbers included the title song, *Easy Come,
            Easy Go; Yoga Is As Yoga Does; You Gotta Stop; Sing
            You Children; I'll Take Love;* and *The Love Machine*.
            All six songs were issued on the soundtrack EP, while
            the versions in the film contained some overdubbing
            and editing. One final song, *Wheel of Fortune*, may have
            been recorded at this session, but it remains unreleased.

OCTOBER

OCT 8   (Sat.) RCA Victor, in a full-page ad, noted that all of
            Elvis' stereo 8 cartridges were being packaged with a
            color 3½ by 5-inch photo.
            Spinout and *All That I Am* entered the "Hot 100" in
            Billboard at number 78 and number 82 respectively.
            Spinout stayed on the chart for seven weeks and peaked
            at number 40, while *All That I Am* stayed eight weeks
            and peaked at number 41.

Elvis with Diane McBain in "Spinout."

OCT 17   (Thurs.) "Spinout" opened at the Lowe's State Theater
            in Memphis.
OCT 19   (Wed.) *Variety*, in a review, called "Spinout" "an enter-
            taining Elvis Presley comedy-turner."
OCT 29   (Sat.) The **Spinout** album entered *Billboard*'s LP chart
            where it stayed thirty-two weeks, reaching number 18.

NOVEMBER

NOV 11   (Fri.) *Time*, in reviewing "Spinout," said that Elvis "is
            pitching his act at some sort of adult audience –
            possibly adult chimpanzees."
NOV 23   (Wed.) "Spinout" opened in theaters across the U.S. In
            many locations the co-feature was "Maya," starring
            Clint Walker.
NOV 25   (Fri.) RCA Victor shipped *If Everyday Was Like Christ-*
            mas/How Would You Like To Be. The single would not
            appear on the "Hot 100," but on *Billboard*'s special
            Christmas music list.
NOV 29   (Tues.) After driving east across country in the converted
            Greyhound bus, Elvis stopped 130 miles short of Mem-
            phis in Little Rock to rest, and so that he could drive
            through the gates at Graceland after dark and view the
            Christmas lights, which had been in place for a week.
            About 9:30 p.m., the entourage led by "The Big Bus"
            came through the gates with horns blaring.

DECEMBER

DEC 12   (Mon.) Elvis donated checks totaling $105,000 to thirty-
            nine charities in Memphis. At the ceremonies, Elvis
            read a statement that said in part, "I am happy that I
            am in a position to give."
DEC 14   (Wed.) Elvis, Vernon, and Elvis cousin' Billy Smith paid a
            visit to Gary Pepper's home in Memphis. Elvis gave
            Pepper a new 1966 Chevrolet Impala convertible as a
            gift. Pepper was the president of the Tanker's Fan Club.
late DEC During Elvis' Christmas vacation at Graceland, he enjoyed
            many "midnight movies" including "Fantastic Voyage,"
            "Kaleidoscope," the re-make of "Stagecoach," "The
            Professionals," "The Appaloosa," and "What Did You Do
            In The War, Daddy?" However, the film that Elvis
            seemed to enjoy most was "After The Fox," starring
            Peter Sellers.

DEC 24   (Sat.) Elvis spent Christmas Eve with his friends and their families opening presents at Graceland. Later that night he and his friends attended a late showing of "Any Wednesday," starring Jane Fonda.

DEC 25   (Sun.) Elvis formally proposed marriage to Priscilla Beaulieu, and he gave her a diamond engagement ring as a Christmas gift. The Christmas card from Elvis this year showed Elvis and Priscilla in front of the Graceland nativity scene, and was signed "Elvis and Priscilla."
The Christmas card from Elvis and the Colonel showed Elvis in a red jacket, leaning on a chair. The card was dated 1966.

DEC 31   (Sat.) Elvis set up a large New Year's Eve party at the Manhattan Club in Memphis, but he did not attend. A local reporter had printed the information about the party in the Memphis newspapers, and a large crowd turned up to see Elvis. Reportedly, he drove up and down in front of the club, but could not find a parking space. He returned to Graceland in a bad mood.

In 1966, the Hollywood Women's Press Club awarded Elvis its "Sour Apple Award" as the "least cooperative male."

Can't Help
Falling In Love

ALL
SHOOK
UP

ELVIS
Day-By-Day,
1967

JANUARY

JAN 2   (Mon.) Colonel Parker and Elvis changed their contract to a fifty-fifty percentage. The previous contract allowed twenty-five percent to the Colonel. The new contract ran until January 22, 1976.

RCA Victor extended its option on Elvis as an exclusive recording artist through December 31, 1974.

JAN 4   (Wed.) In *Variety*'s annual year-end movie review, "Paradise – Hawaiian Style" was number 40 with a gross of $2.5 million; "Frankie And Johnny" was number 48 with $2 million; and "Spinout" was number 57 with $1.77 million.

Memphis Mayor William B. Ingram signed a local bill changing the name of the Mid-South Coliseum to the "Elvis Presley Coliseum." The arena was a 13,000-seat facility costing $4.3 million.

However, two city commissioners, Hunter Lane, Jr., and Pete Sisson, objected to the name change, as did County Commissioner Jimmy Moore. The name change never occurred, as Mayor Ingram lost his bid for re-election before the change could take place.

The original idea for naming the Mid-South Coliseum for Elvis came from Gary Pepper, long-time Elvis fan from Memphis, who had started the movement in 1965 in one of his columns in the British magazine, *Elvis Monthly*. Within a short time, he had received petitions from all over the world sent in by fan clubs thinking that something permanent should be named to honor Elvis.

JAN 6   (Fri.) RCA Victor released *Indescribably Blue/Fools Fall In Love.*

JAN 8   (Sun.) Elvis spent his thirty-second birthday quietly at Graceland.

early   Elvis bought seventeen horses for the stables at Graceland
JAN   during the first few weeks of 1967. He frequently
        could be seen riding his favorite, Rising Sun. The stable
        was aptly named "House of Rising Sun."

JAN 28 (Sat.) *Indescribably Blue* entered *Billboard*'s "Hot 100"
        chart at number 77 where it stayed eight weeks and
        peaked at number 33.

JAN 31 (Tues.) An M-G-M studio press release said that Elvis
        would star in "Bumble Bee, O' Bumble Bee" following
        work on "Pot Luck." His first films for M-G-M ("Jail-
        house Rock," "It Happened At The World's Fair,"
        "Kissin' Cousins," "Viva Las Vegas," "Girl Happy,"
        "Harum Scarum," and "Spinout") had grossed $76
        million; "Jailhouse Rock" was actually still in release,
        with a total of 30,000 play dates.

FEBRUARY

FEB 9   (Thurs.) Elvis purchased a 163-acre ranch near Walls,
        Mississippi from Jack Adams for $300,000. The pre-
        vious name of the ranch had been the Twinkletown
        Farm, but Elvis renamed it the Circle G (for Graceland).
        Later, the name was changed to the Flying Circle G be-
        cause there was already a ranch in Texas with the Circle
        G name.

FEB 10 (Fri.) Elvis' guitar with his name inlaid in mother of pearl
        in the fret board was presented to the U.S. pavilion to
        be displayed during Expo '67 in Montreal.

FEB 21 (Tues.) RCA Victor shipped a special 45 r.p.m. single, *How
        Great Thou Art/So High* to radio stations as an "air-play
        special."

        Elvis flew to Nashville in his Lear jet for a recording session
        at RCA Victor's Studio "B." This was the first Nash-
        ville session that did not feature Scotty Moore on guitar
        or D.J. Fontana on drums. The remainder of the mu-
        sicians were the usual group that appeared on Elvis'
        Nashville recording dates.

        All of the songs were recorded for the film "Clambake,"
        but *How Can You Lose What You Never Had* was cut
        from the final print of the film even though it was part
        of the soundtrack album. The other songs were *Clam-
        bake, Who Needs Money?, A House That Has Everything,
        Hey, Hey, Hey, The Girl I Never Loved, Confidence*, and

You Don't Know Me.
Following the session, Elvis returned to Memphis aboard
his chartered jet. Along the way, he had the pilot fly
over the Circle G Ranch so Elvis could get an aerial view.

MARCH

MAR 5   (Sun.) Elvis left Memphis for Hollywood to start filming
         "Clambake" for United Artists.
MAR 8   (Wed.) RCA Victor released the **How Great Thou Art**
         album.
MAR 10   (Fri.) Production started on "Clambake" for United
         Artists, but had to be delayed about three weeks after
         Elvis fell in his Rocca Place home in Bel Air and suf-
         fered a slight concussion. He had tripped over an elec-
         trical cord, and hit his head on the edge of the bathtub.
MAR 20   (Mon.) Elvis returned to Nashville for a recording session
         at RCA Victor's studios. Only one song, *Suppose*, was
         recorded, and this version was not released. The reason
         for the lack of finished tracks was not made public. The
         musicians on hand were the usual group, including
         Scotty Moore and D.J. Fontana.
MAR 22   (Wed.) "Easy Come, Easy Go" opened in theaters through-
         out the country. In many locations, the B-feature was
         "The Appaloosa," starring Marlon Brando.
         Variety, in its review of "Easy Come, Easy Go" said:
         "Elvis looks great and ageless."
MAR 24   (Fri.) The *Los Angeles Herald-Examiner*, in reviewing "Easy
         Come, Easy Go," called Elvis "a darn good actor."
late MAR During the last week in March, Elvis returned to Holly-
         wood to begin filming "Clambake." Although the film
         was set in Miami Beach, Elvis was not involved in any
         location work. All outdoor scenes were shot using a
         "double." The opening scene at a truck stop and the
         final scene on a road next to a beach were filmed in the
         Los Angeles area. Both Red West and Charlie Hodge had
         small parts in the picture.
MAR 24   (Fri.) RCA Victor released the **Easy Come, Easy Go**
         extended play. The record did not make any of *Bill-
         board*'s charts.
MAR 25   (Sat.) **How Great Thou Art** entered *Billboard*'s "Top
         LPs" chart at number 147 where it reached number 18
         and stayed twenty-nine weeks.

A scene from "Double Trouble."

Photo from a 1967 Easter postcard.

MAR 30   (Thurs.) M-G-M turned over the recording tapes from
          "Double Trouble" to RCA Victor.

APRIL

APR 1   (Sat.) The press ran a most unusual story: it was an-
          nounced "last week" in New Delhi, India, that Elvis
          and Louis Armstrong would share the bill for a single
          night's performance at the 600-seat auditorium of the
          All India Fine Arts and Crafts Society. The concert was
          organized by Dr. J.N. Tagore (M.A.), Secretary General
          of the World Association for Human Welfare. Tagore
          disappeared with 6000 rupees (about $800) in box
          office receipts and could not be located.
          At the time, Elvis was working on "Clambake" in Holly-
          wood and Louis Armstrong was performing in Long
          Island.
          Elvis' frequent guests on the set included Priscilla and her
          parents. Reportedly, the white suit with the black
          stitching used in the movie cost $10,000. This suit,
          along with many other pieces of Elvis' wardrobe, was
          cut into small patches for inclusion in the boxed record
          set, **Elvis: The Other Sides — Worldwide Gold Award
          Hits, Volume 2** in 1971.
          Billboard, in reviewing the **How Great Thou Art** LP said:
          "It's great!"
APR 5   (Wed.) "Double Trouble" opened in theaters in the
          United States.
          In reviewing "Double Trouble," *Variety* said that Elvis "as
          usual, gives a pretty fair account of himself despite
          what's handed him."
          The *Hollywood Reporter* called the movie "the most
          lavishly produced Elvis Presley film since 'Viva Las
          Vegas' . . . [the film] proves the singer's natural instinct
          for comedy."
APR 27   (Thurs.) Elvis finished filming "Clambake."
APR 29   (Sat.) Elvis, Priscilla, Joe Esposito and his wife, and
          George Klein and his wife flew to Palm Springs and
          retired to Elvis' home at 1350 Leadera Way. Vernon
          and Dee had taken the train from Memphis to San Ber-
          nadino, where they were met by Marty Lacker, Jerry
          Schilling and his wife; they drove to Palm Springs.

Judge Zenoff marries Elvis and Priscilla as Michelle Beaulieu looks on.

Wedding day at the Aladdin Hotel in Las Vegas.

APR 30　(Sun.)　Priscilla's mother and stepfather arrived in Palm Springs. Colonel Parker issued a brief statement that there would be a press conference at the Aladdin Hotel the next day at 1:00 p.m.

MAY

MAY 1　(Mon.)　In a rented Lear jet, Elvis, Priscilla, Joe Esposito and his wife, and George Klein flew to Las Vegas, arriving at 3:00 a.m. at McCarran Airport. The rest of the entourage took a DC-3 from Palm Springs to Las Vegas.
At 3:30 a.m., Elvis and Priscilla obtained a marriage license from the Clark County Clerk's office for fifteen dollars. They were accompanied by Joe Esposito.
At 9:41 a.m., in the Aladdin Hotel's second-floor suite of owner Milton Prell, Elvis and Priscilla were married in an eight-minute, double-ring ceremony by the Honorable David Zenoff, a member of the Nevada Supreme Court. Joe Esposito and Marty Lacker were best men, Priscilla's thirteen-year-old sister, Michelle, was the maid of honor, and Joan Esposito was matron of honor.
Following the wedding, there was a press conference in one of the hotel's banquet rooms. This was followed by a $100,000 reception for close friends of Colonel Parker and Elvis in the Aladdin Room. The press was allowed to attend for only a short time.
That afternoon, Elvis, Priscilla, Vernon, Dee, and the Beaulieus returned to Palm Springs for a four-day honeymoon.

MAY 2　(Tues.)　Elvis' honeymoon was cut short as he and Vernon returned to United Artists, so Elvis could finish some last-minute over-dubbing on "Clambake." They returned to Palm Springs that night.

MAY 4　(Thurs.)　Elvis, Priscilla, Vernon and Dee returned to Los Angeles to catch a commercial flight to Memphis. They arrived at Memphis Metropolitan Airport that evening.

MAY 5　(Fri.)　Elvis and Priscilla drove to the Flying Circle G Ranch in Mississippi to look over some repairs.

MAY 6　(Sat.)　*Billboard*, in reviewing *Long Legged Girl (With The Short Dress On)*, said the song was a "strong rhythm entry with traces of his earlier songs." The single was a "Top 60" pick.

MAY 7   (Sun.) Working through agents, Elvis purchased a split-
         level French regency style home at 1174 Hillcrest Road
         in the Trousdale Estates section of Los Angeles. The
         house cost $400,000 and was the first home in the Los
         Angeles area that Elvis purchased, as all the other houses
         had been rented. The length of time Elvis stayed
         in this home is the subject of some controversy.
         (See early DEC 1967.)

MAY 20   (Sat.) *Long Legged Girl* entered the *Billboard* "Hot 100"
         at number 86. It only stayed on the chart five weeks,
         peaking at number 63.

MAY 29   (Mon.) A second wedding reception was held at Graceland
         for Memphis friends, relatives and staff who had not
         been able to attend the Las Vegas ceremony. Elvis and
         Priscilla wore their wedding attire to make the reception
         more meaningful. Elvis' grandmother, Minnie Presley,
         was the guest of honor.

JUNE

JUN 8   (Thurs.) A bridal shower for Priscilla was given by the
         Graceland staff.

JUN 10   (Sat.) RCA Victor ran a full-page ad in *Billboard* as "An
         anniversary salute to Colonel Tom Parker . . . with sin-
         cere thanks for 25 great and profitable years."

         Elvis and Priscilla left Graceland in the motorhome for Los
         Angeles, taking a leisurely trip across the country. Along
         the way, they enjoyed sightseeing at several of the
         scenic areas of the west.

JUN 17   (Sat.) *Billboard*, in reviewing the **Double Trouble** LP said,
         "All his LPs sell like crazy; this one will do the same."

         Elvis and Priscilla arrived in Palm Springs, where Priscilla
         would stay while Elvis was filming "Speedway."

JUN 19   (Mon.) Elvis had a session at M-G-M's recording facility
         for the film "Speedway." Two of the songs were re-
         leased as a single prior to the album release: *Let Your-
         self Go/Your Time Hasn't Come Yet Baby*. All of the
         other songs were issued on the **Speedway** LP: *There
         Ain't Nothing Like A Song, Who Are You, Speedway,
         He's Your Uncle Not Your Dad, Suppose* and *Five
         Sleepy Heads*. The last two songs were cut from final
         prints of the film. Nancy Sinatra also recorded a solo
         effort for the film, *Your Groovy Self*. Musicians in-
         cluded the usual group that backed Elvis in Hollywood.

Background vocals were handled by the Jordanaires, Millie Kirkham and Joe Babcock.

JUN 23   (Fri.) In England, and article in the *New Musical Express* stated that Pyramid Records of England was set to release Elvis' version of *Uncle Penn* (recorded during his days with Sun Records), backed with a medley of Elvis' hits played by the Anthony Hedley Orchestra. (Pyramid soon released a statement that the master of *Uncle Penn* had been "irreparably damaged.")

JUN 24   (Sat.) **Double Trouble** entered the LP charts in *Billboard* at number 179. It stayed nineteen weeks, peaking at number 47.

JUN 26   (Mon.) Production started on "Speedway" for M-G-M Studios in Culver City. The film was released overseas as "California Holiday."

JULY

JUL 13   (Thurs.) M-G-M Studios reported that Priscilla was pregnant, with a due date in February 1968. Elvis had broken the news on the set of "Speedway," when he told co-star Nancy Sinatra and director Norman Taurog.

AUGUST

In mid-August, Elvis and Priscilla vacationed in Las Vegas for a few days following completion of the filming of "Speedway."

AUG 19   (Sat.) *There's Always Me* was a "Top 60" pick in *Billboard*, which nevertheless said the single was "one of Presley's most potent, sensitive and commercial entries."

AUG 26   (Sat.) *There's Always Me* entered *Billboard*'s "Hot 100" chart at number 90. It only stayed six weeks and reached number 56.

Elvis and Priscilla arrived in Memphis aboard a commercial airliner.

LATE AUGUST--EARLY SEPTEMBER

While vacationing in Memphis, Elvis bought a red Cadillac Coupe De Ville and a white Chrysler station wagon. He also bought bicycles for himself and Priscilla. Elvis enjoyed playing badminton and pitching horseshoes at Graceland, and he and Priscilla were often spotted riding his motorcycle.

SEPTEMBER

SEP 10   (Sun.) Elvis, Charlie Hodge, and Joe Esposito flew from Memphis to Nashville, where Elvis had a recording session at RCA Victor's Studio "B." The songs recorded were meant for release as singles and as fillers on soundtrack albums. Along with the usual great Nashville musicians, including Scotty Moore, Harold Bradley, Chip Young on guitar; Bob Moore, bass; D.J. Fontana and Buddy Harmon, drums; Floyd Cramer, piano; Boots Randolph, sax; Pete Drake, steel guitar; Charlie McCoy, harmonica; and the Jordanaires, with Millie Kirkham on background vocals, there was the inspired addition of Jerry Reed on guitar for his own composition, *Guitar Man*, as well as for *Big Boss Man*. Other songs recorded during this all-night session were *Mine*, *Singing Tree* (first version), *Just Call Me Lonesome*, and *High Heel Sneakers*. The session lasted until the early morning hours of the 11th.

SEP 11   (Mon.) Elvis was back in the studio for a second night of recording, but the tone was much more subdued that the night before. Elvis re-recorded *You Don't Know Me* (first attempted in February), *We Call On Him* and *You'll Never Walk Alone* (two gospel numbers), and another version of *Singing Tree*.

The session lasted into the morning of the 12th. Following the recordings, Elvis flew back to Memphis.

SEP 19   (Tues.) Elvis had an altercation at Graceland with a temporary yardman, Troy Ivy, 38. Elvis said that Ivy was "drunk, belligerent, arrogant, cursing loudly and took a swing at me." Elvis said he knocked Ivy down with one blow.

Ivy said that he was leaning against a car when Elvis, "dressed in a red suit came down the driveway in a red car." According to Ivy, Elvis asked him if he was trying to kill Vernon and then struck him twice, but not hard enough to knock him down.

In Nashville, the song *Confidence*, from "Clambake," was overdubbed with a female vocal group: June Page, Priscilla Hubbard, Dolores Edgin, and Millie Kirkham. It is doubtful if Elvis was present.

SEP 29   (Fri.) Governor Buford Ellington declared "Elvis Presley Day" in Tennessee.

OCTOBER

OCT 2   (Mon.) Elvis had a recording session at RCA Victor's studios in Nashville for the film "Stay Away, Joe." The musicians are not known, but they probably included the same ones that backed Elvis during most of his Nashville work. The songs were all recorded for the film: *Goin' Home, Stay Away, All I Needed Was The Rain, Stay Away, Joe,* and *Dominic* (which remains unreleased). *Goin' Home* was cut from final prints of the film and ended up as a filler on the **Speedway** LP. Elvis sang a single line from the nonsense ditty, *Lovely Mamie,* as part of the film, but it was not recorded in the studio.

OCT 4   (Wed.) Elvis left Memphis for Los Angeles.
United Artists Studios turned over the recording tapes from "Clambake" to RCA Victor.

OCT 7   (Sat.) *Big Boss Man/You Don't Know Me* was a "Top 60" pick in *Billboard*, which said: "Presley scores with two equally strong sales items."

OCT 9   (Mon.) Production started on "Stay Away, Joe" at M-G-M Studios in Culver City.

OCT 14   (Sat.) *Big Boss Man* and *You Don't Know Me* entered the "Hot 100" in *Billboard* at numbers 71 and 94 respectively. Both stayed on the chart for six weeks, and *Big Boss Man* peaked at number 38 while *You Don't Know Me* reached number 44.

OCT 18   (Wed.) In its review of "Clambake," the *Hollywood Reporter* said that Elvis can't "continue for long to rely on the same scripts and songs which have become anachronistic in the increasingly sophisticated and ever-changing world of pop music and pulp films."
Elvis started location filming for "Stay Away, Joe" at Cottonwood and Sedona, Arizona. Elvis stayed in Arizona until mid-November.

NOVEMBER

NOV 1   (Wed.) In its review of "Clambake," the *Los Angeles Times* said: "Elvis' songs are as forgettable as ever, and the whole picture has a garish, cluttered look."

NOV 5   (Sun.) Some items from the Flying Circle G Ranch in Mississippi were auctioned off.

NOV 6   (Mon.) Elvis was still on location in Sedona, Arizona.

Elvis in "Clambake."

NOV 19 (Sun.) RCA Victor released the album **Clambake**.

NOV 22 (Wed.) "Clambake" opened in theaters in the United States.

NOV 25 (Sat.) *Billboard*, in reviewing the **Clambake** album said: "Elvis' latest movie track places the singer miles away from his early rock days."

NOV 29 (Wed.) "Clambake" was number 15 in *Variety*'s "National Box Office Survey." The film remained on the chart for only one week.

DECEMBER

DEC 2 (Sat.) **Clambake** entered *Billboard*'s "Top LPs" list at number 188, where it peaked at number 40 and stayed fourteen weeks.

DEC 3 (Sun.) Elvis and Colonel Parker bought time on 3,000 radio stations for a thirty-minute special, "Season's Greetings From Elvis."

early DEC Prior to leaving Los Angeles, Elvis and Priscilla moved into a home at 144 Monovale in the Holmby Hills section of Los Angeles. He paid $400,000 for the house. (Although this is the generally acknowledged date for their move, several later photographs, possibly as late as 1970, show Elvis at the gate of the Trousdale Estate home.)

DEC 7 (Thurs.) Elvis arrived back in Memphis to start his Christmas vacation.

DEC 10 (Sun.) The Christmas special was repeated on many of the original 3,000 radio stations.

Elvis gave Priscilla a Fleetwood Cadillac limousine.

DEC 25 (Mon.) Elvis spent Christmas quietly at Graceland.

The Christmas card from Elvis and the Colonel was the same as the one used in 1966, except that this year it carried no specific date.

DEC 31 (Sun.) Elvis did not attend the New Year's Eve party at the Manhattan Club in Memphis, saying that he was too tired from horseback riding at his ranch in Mississippi. (One account says that the party was at the Thunderbird Lounge and that Elvis and Priscilla partied from 11:00 p.m. to 4:00 a.m. This is doubtful, since Priscilla was eight months pregnant at the time. It is possible that this account was confused with the 1968 New Year's Eve party.)

In 1967, Elvis received the first of his three Grammy awards from the National Academy of Recording Arts and Sciences for the album **How Great Thou Art**. The award was for the "Best Sacred Recording."

ELVIS' HALF-HOUR CHRISTMAS PROGRAM SUNDAY, DEC. 3, 1967

"Seasons Greetings From Elvis" was aired in December 1964 and issued as a reel-to-reel tape for radio use, later appearing as this ten-inch bootleg album.

(Marie's The Name Of)
His Latest Flame

ALL
SHOOK
UP

ELVIS
Day-By-Day,
1968

JANUARY

JAN 3   (Wed.) *Variety*'s annual listing of the past year's biggest films placed "Easy Come, Easy Go" at number 50, with a gross of $1.95 million, and "Double Trouble" at 58 with a gross of $1.6 million.

JAN 15   (Mon.) Elvis traveled to Nashville for a short recording session, which again featured the guitar of Jerry Reed. Only one song was waxed, *Too Much Monkey Business*, the classic originally recorded by Chuck Berry. The other musicians in the studio were the usual members of Elvis' Nashville band.

JAN 17   (Wed.) Elvis returned to the RCA Victor studios in Nashville for another session with Jerry Reed. The only song recorded was *U.S. Male*, a Reed composition.

JAN 20   (Sat.) *Guitar Man/High Heel Sneakers* was a "Top 60" pick in *Billboard*'s "Singles Spotlight" section. The journal said the record "could easily prove one of the top sellers in some time."

JAN 27   (Sat.) *Guitar Man* entered *Billboard*'s "Hot 100" at number 83 where it reached number 43 and stayed only six weeks.

Elvis continued to vacation at Graceland during January.

FEBRUARY

FEB 1   (Thurs.) About 10:30 a.m., Elvis and Priscilla left Graceland in a car driven by Elvis' friend, Charlie Hodge. They arrived at Baptist Memorial Hospital at 10:40 a.m. At 5:01 p.m., Lisa Marie Presley was born. Elvis stayed at the hospital during labor and delivery. Lisa Marie weighed six pounds, fourteen ounces, and measured

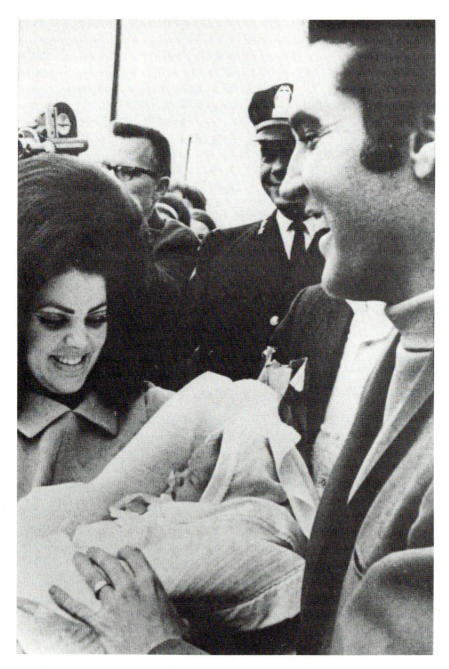

Elvis and Priscilla leave the hospital with Lisa Marie.

fifteen inches long. She was named, in part, for Colonel
Parker's wife, Marie.

FEB 5   (Mon.) Elvis took Priscilla and Lisa Marie home from the
hospital.

FEB 6   (Tues.) Nick Adams, Hollywood actor and friend of Elvis
from 1956 on, died.

FEB 8   (Thurs.) Elvis was elected to *Playboy* magazine's Music
Hall Of Fame.

FEB 17   (Sat.) *Billboard* reviewed **Elvis' Gold Records, Vol. 4**, with
the caustic remark, "To get enough 'gold' to label this
LP, the company had to do some searching."

FEB 25   (Sun.) Elvis flew from Memphis to Los Angeles to start
filming "Live A Little, Love A Little" for M-G-M.

FEB 28   (Wed.) Priscilla and Lisa Marie, accompanied by Joe Esposito, flew from Memphis to Los Angeles. Vernon
Presley drove Elvis' Lincoln Continental Mark IV.

The February issue of *Esquire* magazine carried one of the more
provocative articles on Elvis: "A Hound Dog, To The Manor
Born," by Stanley Booth.

MARCH

MAR 2   (Sat.) **Elvis' Gold Records, Vol. 4** entered the LP chart in
Billboard at number 234 where it stayed twenty-two
weeks, peaking at number 33.

MAR 8   (Fri.) "Stay Away, Joe" opened in the United States.

In its review of "Stay Away, Joe," *Variety* said: "At best,
[the film] is a dim artistic accomplishment; at worst, it
caters to out-dated prejudice . . . [the] thin plot line is
threaded with many forced slapstick situations, in which
the players seem to be having a ball, although the enthu-
siasm rarely transmits from screen to audience."

The *Hollywood Reporter* said: "[The film's] quaint and
patronizing view of American Indians as brawling, ball-
ing, boozing children should rightly offend many."

MAR 9   (Sat.) *Stay Away* was a "Top 60" pick in *Billboard*, which
ambiguously said, "Elvis comes on strong with a folk
flavor in this rhythm number."

MAR 11   (Mon.) *Film Daily*'s review of "Stay Away, Joe" said: "It
doesn't matter that credibility is stretched. What matters
is that the picture evokes a mood of mirth and happy
frenzy that is catching."

Production started on "Live A Little, Love A Little" at
M-G-M's studios in Culver City. Locations for the film

Elvis' 1968 Easter postcard.

included the California coastline near Malibu, Marine-
land of the Pacific, and the Los Angeles Music Center.
Red West can be seen in a fight scene with Elvis in the
press room of a newspaper. Even Vernon Presley had a
small part in the movie, as part of the scene at the
Music Center.

Elvis had a recording session at the Goldwyn Studios for
the soundtrack to "Live A Little, Love A Little." The
exact musicians are not known, but included Scotty
Moore, Bob Moore, D.J. Fontana and Floyd Cramer.
Only four songs were needed for the movie: *Almost
In Love, A Little Less Conversation, Wonderful World,*
and *Edge Of Reality.*

MAR 16 (Sat.) *Stay Away* started up *Billboard*'s "Hot 100" at
number 83, staying only five weeks and peaking at number 67.

MAR 23 (Sat.) *U.S. Male* entered the "Hot 100" chart in *Billboard*,
reaching number 28 and staying nine weeks.

MAR 27 (Wed.) *Variety* reported that **How Great Thou Art** had
been certified a million seller, becoming Elvis' forty-
second gold disk.

APRIL

APR 6   (Sat.) *U.S. Male* entered *Billboard*'s "Hot Country
Singles" chart at number 71. It stayed on the chart for
six weeks, peaking at number 55. This was Elvis' first
single to make the country list since 1961.

Elvis and Priscilla drove from Los Angeles to Las Vegas.
They attended Tom Jones' midnight show at the Fla-
mingo Hotel. Afterward, they visited backstage and in
Jones' penthouse.

APR 13 (Sat.) *We Call On Him/You'll Never Walk Alone* was a
"Top 60" pick in *Billboard*, which commented that
"Presley is in top form."

APR 20 (Sat.) *You'll Never Walk Alone* entered the "Hot 100"
chart in *Billboard*, where it stayed only two weeks,
stalling at number 90.

APR 27 (Sat.) The *Hollywood Citizen—News*, in reviewing "Stay
Away, Joe," said that the picture "marks just another
brilliantly executed step in the making of another Bing
Crosby-like career."

Elvis and Nancy Sinatra in "Speedway."

MAY

MAY 14   (Tues.) M-G-M turned over the recording tapes from "Speedway" to RCA Victor.

MAY 17   (Fri.) *Variety*, in its review of "Speedway," said: "An Elvis Presley film is money in the bank, regardless of the story or who appears with him."
The *Hollywood Reporter* said, "The plot is tissue-thin, [but the film is] bound to make money by merely adhering to the regular distribution schedule."

MAY 24   (Fri.) Elvis and Priscilla arrived in Hawaii for a vacation, following completion of "Live A Little, Love A Little." They stayed at the Ilikai Hotel in Honolulu.

MAY 25   (Sat.) Elvis attended the Karate Tournament of Champions at the Honolulu International Center at 7:30 p.m. Competing for the Mainland against Hawaii were Chuck Norris and Mike Stone, among others.

JUNE

JUN 12   (Wed.) "Speedway" premiered in Charlotte, North Carolina, home of the Charlotte 500 stock car race, which was the setting for the movie. The movie also opened in theaters across the country.

JUN 15   (Sat.) *Let Yourself Go* started up *Billboard*'s "Hot 100" chart at number 94 where it stayed five weeks, peaking at number 71.

mid-JUN   In mid-June, Elvis started rehearsals for his first television special, "Elvis," at NBC-TV's studios in Burbank, California. Musicians working with Elvis included Don Randi, piano; Tommy Tedesco, guitar; Mike Deasy, guitar; and Larry Knectal, bass. (See June 29, 1968.)

JUN 21   (Fri.) Final rehearsals were held for the NBC-TV special.

JUN 22   (Sat.) *Your Time Hasn't Come Yet, Baby* entered *Billboard*'s "Hot 100" chart at number 92. It stayed only seven weeks and stalled at number 72.

JUN 25   (Tues.) Elvis held a press conference for forty-five visiting television editors to explain the upcoming TV special. Also on hand at NBC's Burbank studios were the show's producers, Steve Binder and Bob Finkel.

JUN 27   (Thurs.) Elvis started videotaping his first television special, "Elvis," at NBC-TV's studios in Burbank, California. This night, there were two hour-long mini-concerts

in front of a live audience. Musicians accompanying
Elvis for the "pit" section of the special were Scotty
Moore, guitar; D.J. Fontana, drum pad; Charlie Hodge,
guitar; and Alan Fortas, tambourine. The shows were
at 6:00 and 8:00 p.m.

JUN 28   (Fri.) Elvis continued taping his TV special, working on
the segments which did not require a live audience.

JUN 29   (Sat.) In reviewing the **Speedway** album, *Billboard* said it
"zooms along at a fast clip."

Elvis performed another pair of half-hour concerts with a
live audience for his television special; this segment had
him performing on a small stage in the center of the
audience. Elvis was accompanied by a pre-taped orchestra conducted by W. Earl Brown. The tape was augmented by "live" musicians including Tommy Tedesco,
guitar (of the Fireballs); Mike Deasy, guitar; Don Randi,
piano (session work with the Buffalo Springfield); Larry
Knechtal, bass (later of Bread); Hal Blaine, drums (session work with Phil Spector); The Blossoms, vocals (included Darlene Love of the Phil Spector organization).
The concerts were at 6:00 and 8:00 p.m.

JUN 30   (Sun.) Elvis completed taping the TV special at NBC-TV's
studios in Burbank. Sequences taped this date included
Elvis' singing *If I Can Dream*, the gospel number, and the
Guitar Man dance with the Claude Thomas dancers.

JULY

JUL 1   (Mon.) Following completion of the strenuous taping sessions, Elvis retreated to his home in Palm Springs for a
ten-day vacation.

JUL 4   (Thurs.) Elvis' 1964 Rolls Royce was auctioned off. Proceeds were donated to the charity SHARE, a Hollywood
woman's group aiding mentally retarded children.

JUL 6   (Sat.) **Speedway** entered *Billboard*'s album chart at number 193. It reached only as high as 82 and stayed on the
chart for thirteen weeks.

JUL 7   (Sun.) Elvis recorded the theme song for "Charro." Little
is know about this session except that the song was arranged by Hugo Montenegro, who composed the inci-
dental music for the film. It is probable that the instrumental track was recorded prior to Elvis' vocal track,
and that he was only in the studio for a short time just to
record this song before returning to Palm Springs.

JUL 10   (Wed.) Elvis returned to his home in Los Angeles.

JUL 22   (Mon.) Elvis traveled to Apache Junction, Arizona, which is thirty miles from Phoenix, to begin location filming for National General Productions' "Charro." Most locations were photographed in and around the Apacheland Movie Ranch. While on location, Elvis stayed at the Superstition Inn outside Phoenix.

AUGUST
Shooting continued at Apache Junction on "Charro" for the first few weeks of August. Then the film company moved back to Hollywood, where interior scenes and a few additional exterior scenes were filmed at the Samuel Goldwyn Studios of M-G-M.

SEPTEMBER
In early September, after completing filming on "Charro," Elvis recuperated from a bout with tonsillitis. He stayed at his home in Palm Springs.

SEP 6   (Thurs.) At 1:19 p.m. (EDT), a telephone operator in Louisville, Kentucky, placed a call for an unknown person to Graceland. Shorting thereafter, another call was placed from Louisville to Elvis' uncle in Memphis advising her that Elvis had been killed in an airplane crash near Louisville, and that his body was at a local Louisville funeral home. The entire episode was a hoax, and the perpetrator was not apprehended.

SEP 13   (Fri.) Elvis' cousin, Bobby Smith, died of a heart attack at the age of twenty-six.

SEP 15   (Sun.) RCA Victor released *Almost In Love/A Little Less Conversation*.

SEP 21   (Sat.) *Almost In Love* was a *Billboard* "Top 60" pick. The magazine said the song was a "smooth ballad [that] should hit hard."

SEP 25   (Wed.) After a seven month absence, Elvis returned to Memphis.

LATE SEPTEMBER--EARLY OCTOBER
During his vacation in Memphis, Elvis attended many midnight movies. He and Priscilla also went horseback riding at the Flying Circle G Ranch. Sundays were spent watching the professional football games on television.

From dawn
to darkroom...
from doll to doll...
ELVIS clicks
with the chicks
as a playboy
photographer
who leads a
double-life!

ELVIS PRESLEY
shows you how to
LIVE A LITTLE
LOVE A LITTLE

SEP 28   (Sat.) *Almost In Love* started up *Billboard*'s "Hot 100"
          chart at number 99 but it only stayed two weeks, peak-
          ing at number 95.
          Dewey Phillips, the Memphis DJ who had been most instru-
          mental in helping Elvis in 1954, died.

OCTOBER

OCT 2   (Wed.) In its review of "Live A Little, Love A Little," the
          Motion Picture Herald said: "Audiences may grow a
          little weary of psychological studies of frigidity."
OCT 6   (Sun.) Elvis' uncle, Johnny Smith, died. He had been one
          of the guards at the gate of Graceland.
OCT 9   (Wed.) *Variety* called "Live A Little, Love A Little" one
          of Elvis' "dimmest vehicles . . . [the] songs are full,
          physical values are standard, and mediocrity prevails."
OCT 12   (Sat.) *A Little Less Conversation* entered *Billboard*'s "Hot
          100" chart at number 83 but it only stayed four weeks,
          peaking at number 63.
OCT 13   (Sun.) Elvis flew back to Hollywood to start filming "The
          Trouble With Girls" for M-G-M Studios.
OCT 14   (Mon.) Elvis was in M-G-M's studio for a recording session
          to cut songs for the film, "The Trouble With Girls."
          Musicians included Scotty Moore, D.J. Fontana, and
          Floyd Cramer. The following songs were recorded:
          *Clean Up Your Own Back Yard, Almost, Aura Lee,
          Swing Down Sweet Chariot*, and *Signs Of The Zodiac*
          (a duet with Marilyn Mason). Only the first two were
          released initially by RCA Victor, while the remainder,
          including the duet, became staples for many of the boot-
          leg albums issued in the 1970s. One final song, *We
          Both Went Our Ways*, was rumored to have been recorded
          at this session, but no further information is available.
OCT 15   (Tues.) RCA Victor released *If I Can Dream* b/w *Edge Of
          Reality*. Initially, 175,000 picture sleeves were printed
          for this single.
OCT 18   (Fri.) *Film-TV Daily* said "Live A Little, Love A Little"
          "contains all of the tried-and-true ingredients that go
          into the concoction of a standard Presley opus — ro-
          mance, song, gaiety, a bit of spice, frothiness, a fair
          number of laughs, a simple story."
OCT 23   (Wed.) "Live A Little, Love A Little" opened in movie
          houses in the United States.

Elvis in the 1968 movie "Live A Little, Love A Little."

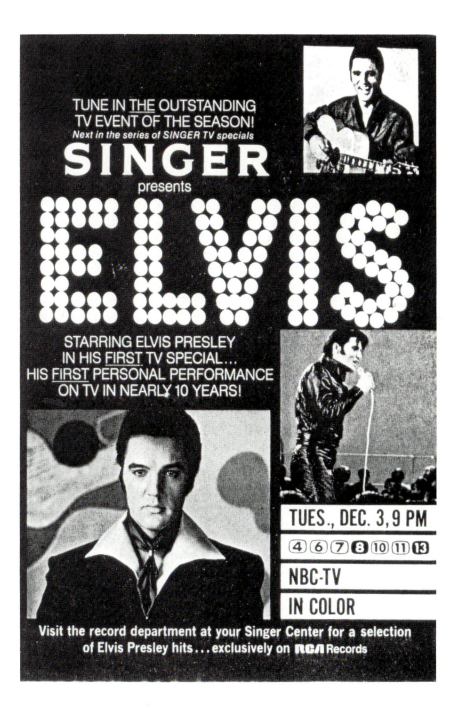

OCT 28   (Mon.) Production started on "The Trouble With Girls (And How To Get Into It)" at M-G-M Studios in Culver City. At this time, the film was known as "The Chautauqua."

NOVEMBER

Elvis continued filming "The Trouble With Girls (And How To Get Into It)."

NOV 23   (Sat.) *If I Can Dream* was a "Top 60" pick in *Billboard*, which noted that this was "one of his strongest commercial entries in a while. Potent and timely lyric message with exceptional production."

NOV 25   (Mon.) RCA Victor started shipping the TV soundtrack album, **Elvis**.

NOV 30   (Sat.) *If I Can Dream* entered *Billboard*'s "Hot 100" at number 100 staying thirteen weeks and reaching number 12. This was the highest any Elvis single had reached since the fall of 1965.

DECEMBER

DEC 3   (Tues.) The special "Elvis" was aired over NBC-TV from 9:00 p.m. to 10:00 p.m. (EST). It received generally favorable reviews and has been credited with restoring credibility to Elvis' career following eight years of increasingly dull movies. The show's producer, Bob Finkel, won a Peabody Award for this special. Ratings for the show placed it in first position for the week, beating "Rowan And Martin's Laugh-In." The special had a Nielsen rating of 32, with a 42 share. In the "Multi-Network Area (MNA)" survey, the Elvis special received a rating of 33.2% of the audience, beating the "Laugh-In" share of 31.1%.

In England, a *New Musical Express* poll named Elvis the "Outstanding Male Singer" of the year.

DEC 5   (Thurs.) Elvis, along with 80,000 other individuals listed in *Who's Who In America*, was asked by President-elect Richard Nixon to recommend exceptional individuals for executive positions in the federal government. In Hollywood, Colonel Parker issued a statement saying that Elvis "doesn't comment on political matters."

DEC 16   (Mon.) Elvis finished filming "The Trouble With Girls
              (And How To Get Into It)."
DEC 19   (Thurs.) Elvis and Priscilla arrived back in Memphis.
late DEC The Nativity scene at Graceland was acknowledged to be
              Memphis' best Christmas decoration.
DEC 21   (Sat.) The album **Elvis** (the soundtrack from the NBC-
              TV special) entered *Billboard*'s LP chart at number 166,
              where it peaked at number 8 and stayed thirty-two
              weeks. This was Elvis' first top ten album in three years.
DEC 24   (Tues.) Christmas Eve was spent at Graceland. This was
              Lisa Marie's first Christmas, and Elvis went all-out to
              please her.
DEC 25   (Wed.) Elvis spent a quiet Christmas at Graceland. Vernon
              dressed up as Santa Claus for Lisa Marie.
DEC 31   (Tues.) Elvis and Priscilla hosted a New Year's Eve party
              at Memphis' Thunderbird Lounge for 250 guests. They
              stayed at the party until 1:30 a.m. Entertainment was
              provided by Flash and the Board of Directors, a local
              Memphis band. Guest artists included Billy Lee Riley,
              B.J. Thomas, and Ronnie Milsap.

   Elvis and Priscilla were superimposed with Frank and Nancy
       Sinatra on the cover of *Movie Mirror*. The accompanying article
       was "What They Whisper About Elvis And Nancy Sinatra!"

Heartbreak Hotel

ALL
SHOOK
UP

ELVIS
Day-By-Day,
1969

JANUARY
Early in the month, Elvis suffered from a sore throat. He recuperated at Graceland.

JAN 8   (Wed.) In *Variety*'s annual year-end review of movies, "Speedway" was number 40, with a gross of $3 million, and "Stay Away, Joe" was number 65 with a gross of $1.5 million.

JAN 13   (Mon.) *Advertising Age* reported that Elvis' December TV special had been watched by more women aged eighteen to forty-nine than any other special in 1968.

Elvis started a marathon recording session at American Studios in Memphis. This was the first time he had recorded in his home town since he left Sun Records in 1955. The sessions started on the 13th and ran every night through the 16th. The recording sessions usually ran from 8:00 p.m. until 5:00 a.m.

For this session, a completely new group of musicians was in the studio. They included Reggie Young, guitar; Tommy Cogbill, bass and guitar; Mike Leech, bass; Gene Chrisman, drums; Bobby Wood, piano; Ronnie Milsap, piano and vocal (on *Don't Cry Daddy*); Bobby Emmons, organ; John Hughey, steel guitar; and Ed Kollis, harmonica.

Songs recorded during these sessions were *Long Black Limousine, This Is The Story* (13th); *Come Out, Come Out* (unreleased), *Wearin' That Loved On Look, You'll Think Of Me* (14th); *I'm Movin' On, A Little Bit Of Green, Don't Cry Daddy, Poor Man's Gold* (unreleased), *Gentle On My Mind* (15th); *Inherit The Wind, Mama Liked The Roses,* and *My Little Friend* (16th). During the last night, Elvis came down with a 100-degree temperature and tonsillitis. He recuperated at Graceland for four days, before returning to the studio.

JAN 20   (Mon.) Elvis was back at American Studios for four days
to finish his recording date. The musicians were the
same as the week before. Songs recorded were *Rubberneckin'* (20th); *In The Ghetto, From A Jack To A King,
Without Love* (21st); *Memory Revival* and *Hey Jude*
(22nd); *I'll Hold You In My Heart, I'll Be There*, and
Suspicious Minds (23rd).
At a later date, the songs were overdubbed with additional
vocals, the Memphis Horns, and the Memphis Strings.

JAN 25   (Sat.) Elvis, Priscilla, and Lisa Marie flew to Aspen,
Colorado, for a few weeks' vacation at a private ski
lodge.

FEBRUARY

FEB 1   (Sat.) Lisa Marie celebrated her first birthday in Aspen.

mid-FEB About the middle of February, Elvis and his family returned
to Memphis.

FEB 17   (Mon.) Elvis started another week-long session at the
American Recording Studio in Memphis. The musicians
were the same as for the January sessions. Ronnie Mil-
sap sang background vocals on *Kentucky Rain*.
Songs recorded were *True Love Travels On A Gravel Road,
Stranger In My Own Home Town* (17th); *And The Grass
Won't Pay No Mind, Power Of My Love, After Loving You*
(18th); *Do You Know Who I Am, Kentucky Rain* (19th);
Only The Strong Survive, It Keeps Right On A-Hurtin'
(20th); *Any Day Now, If I'm A Fool, The Fair's Moving
On* (21st); *Memory Revival* (unreleased), *Who Am I?*
(22nd).
Combined with the January sessions, these recordings were
responsible for two gold albums and three singles which
sold over a million copies each. The unreleased songs
from the January and February sessions are probably only instrumental tracks without Elvis' vocals.

FEB 26   (Wed.) Elvis and Priscilla returned to Aspen, Colorado, to
continue their vacation.
In Las Vegas, a contract was signed with the International
Hotel which would bring Elvis to the town's largest
showroom starting on July 31, 1969. The contract was
signed by Colonel Parker, representing Elvis, and The
International Hotel's director, Bill Miller.

MARCH

Early in the month, Elvis returned to Hollywood to start filming "Change Of Habit" for Universal Pictures. Much of the movie was shot on Stage "D" at Universal City. Exteriors were filmed in and around Los Angeles.

MAR 5   (Wed.) Elvis had a recording session at Universal's facilities in Hollywood. The exact musicians are not known, but they probably differ somewhat from earlier Hollywood sessions. The songs recorded were all intended for the film "Change Of Habit": *Let's Forget About The Stars, Have A Happy, Let's Be Friends, Change Of Habit,* and *Let Us Pray. Let's Be Friends* was cut from the final print in the movie. All songs appeared on RCA Victor's budget Camden albums in the early 1970s.

MAR 8   (Sat.) *Memories* was a "Top 20" pick in *Billboard*. This was his first top twenty pick in three years. The journal said the single was "Presley at his ballad best."

MAR 12   (Wed.) *Variety* called "Charro" a "minor effort. [Elvis] strolls through a tedious role that would have driven any serious actor up the wall."

MAR 13   (Wed.) "Charro" opened in theaters in the United States.

MAR 14   (Fri.) *Film-TV Daily* said of "Charro," "The film is not one of dramatic distinction."

MAR 22   (Sat.) *Memories* entered the "Hot 100" in *Billboard* at number 67. It stayed seven weeks and reached number 35.

APRIL

Elvis continued filming "Change Of Habit."

APR 15   (Tues.) RCA shipped *In The Ghetto/Any Day Now* to distributors. Originally, *In The Ghetto* was subtitled "The Vicious Circle," but RCA released it without this addition. The first 300,000 picture sleeves told fans that Elvis' new **LP, From Elvis In Memphis** was "coming." The second 300,000 sleeves told fans to "ask for" the album.

APR 19   (Sat.) *Billboard*, in its review of the **Elvis Sings Flaming Star** album, noted that this was "a first release for Elvis Presley at this price." This remark referred to the fact that this album was issued on RCA Victor's Camden label, which was a budget line.

Elvis in "Charro."

The photo for Elvis' 1969 promotional Easter postcard.

Elvis Sings Flaming Star entered the LP chart in *Billboard* at number 195. It stayed on the chart for sixteen weeks, reaching number 96.

APR 26   (Sat.) *In The Ghetto* was a "Top 20" pick in *Billboard*, which commented that this was "Elvis at his best . . . could easily prove to be one of his all-time biggest items."

MAY

MAY 2   (Fri.) Elvis completed filming "Change Of Habit."

MAY 3   (Sat.) *In The Ghetto* started climbing the "Hot 100" in *Billboard* at number 79 finally reaching number 3 and staying thirteen weeks. This was Elvis' first top ten single since *Crying In The Chapel* in the spring of 1965.

MAY 4   (Sun.) Elvis and Priscilla flew to Hawaii for a vacation. Lisa Marie was left in the care of Pris' parents. The couple stayed at the Ilikai Hotel.

MAY 13   (Tues.) Elvis and Priscilla attended the opening performance of Tom Jones at the Ilikai Hotel's Pacific Ballroom. They visited backstage after the show.

MAY 14   (Wed.) The *Hollywood Reporter*, in its review of "The Trouble With Girls," commented that "should Presley loyalists be willing to settle for no more than the assurance that their idol is alive and living in Hollywood, the picture will be graced by purpose."

MAY 15   (Thurs.) *Variety* said of "The Trouble With Girls," "With Elvis' songs cut down to a bare three, the film has little to offer."

MAY 18   (Sun.) Elvis and Priscilla flew back to Los Angeles.

MAY 21   (Wed.) Upon returning to Memphis, Elvis negotiated the sale of the Flying Circle G Ranch in Desoto County, Mississippi for $440,100. The ranch was bought by D.L. McClellan, who represented a local gun club; however, the sale apparently fell through, since Elvis resold the ranch in May 1973.

Elvis arranged for the horses to be stabled at Graceland, and the crowds during this time were estimated at 3,000 a day as Elvis rode his horses on the grounds almost daily.

JUNE

JUN 7   (Sat.) In reviewing **From Elvis In Memphis,** *Billboard* said, "He's never sounded better, and the choice of material is perfect."

JUN 10   (Tues.) Elvis was flown to Las Vegas aboard the private jet of Kirk Kerkorian, owner of the International Hotel. He was escorted through the new construction, as the hotel was not set to open for another month.

Elvis went on to Los Angeles for wardrobe fittings for his approaching shows in Las Vegas.

JUN 14   (Sat.) The album, **From Elvis In Memphis** entered *Billboard*'s LP chart at number 29, peaking at number 13 and staying thirty-four weeks.

JUN 21   (Sat.) Elvis returned to Memphis.

JULY

JUL 5   (Sat.) Elvis left Memphis for Los Angeles to begin rehearsals for his upcoming engagement at the International Hotel in Las Vegas. Daily workouts were held at the M-G-M studios in Culver City, where Colonel Parker had a permanent office.

Elvis chose for his backup band some of the finest studio musicians available: James Burton, guitar (formerly with both Dale Hawkins and Rick Nelson); Jerry Scheff, bass (played on some of the last recording sessions of Jim Morrison and the Doors and recorded with Elvis in Hollywood starting in 1966); Ronnie Tutt, drums (a top West Coast session man); John Wilkinson, rhythm guitar (under contract to RCA); Larry Muhoberac, piano (first recorded with Elvis in 1965); and Elvis' close friend since 1958, Charlie Hodge, rhythm guitar and vocals. Bobby Morris would conduct the hotel orchestra. Background vocals would be handled by the Imperials (Jake Hess, Jim Murray, Gary McSpadden, and Armond Morales), who had worked with Elvis in 1966 on the **How Great Thou Art** album; and the Sweet Inspirations (Emily Houston, Myrna Smith, Sylvia Shenwell, and Estelle Brown), a top soul group which had a top 20 hit in 1968 with *Sweet Inspiration*, and had backed Aretha Franklin. The opening comedian was Sammy Shore, a Las Vegas regular.

Clean Up Your Own Backyard started climbing *Billboard*'s "Hot 100" at number 90, peaking at number 35 and staying on the chart eight weeks.

JUL 9   (Wed.) *Variety* reported that Elvis' upcoming Las Vegas engagement was already eighty percent sold out.

JUL 12   (Sat.) Elvis was the cover feature of *Rolling Stone* magazine, with an accompanying article entitled "You Won't Ask Elvis Anything Too Deep?", which told of one reporter's attempt to interview Elvis during the filming of "Change Of Habit."

mid-JUL   Prior to opening at the International Hotel, Elvis and Priscilla, along with Vernon, Dee and Dee's children, vacationed in Hawaii.

JUL 30   (Wed.) Elvis attended Barbra Streisand's closing show at the International Hotel. Afterward, he met with her backstage.

JUL 31   (Thurs.) During the afternoon, Elvis had two dress rehearsals for his opening night at the International Hotel in Las Vegas.

For opening night, there was an invitation-only show in the Showroom Internationale at 10:00 p.m. for celebrities and the press. Among those attending this first show were Wayne Newton, Petula Clark, Ann-Margret, Shirley Bassey, Pat Boone, Paul Anka, Ed Ames, Dick Clark, George Hamilton, Angie Dickinson, and Burt Bacharach.

AUGUST

AUG 1   (Fri.) Elvis held a press conference in the Convention Hall at 12:30 a.m., following the opening night show. On hand were Colonel Parker and Vernon Presley.

Starting this night, Elvis gave two shows per night: a dinner show at 8:15 p.m. and a cocktail show at midnight. The minimum for each show was fifteen dollars, and an average of 2,500 attended each of the two shows per day.

AUG 6   (Wed.) *Variety*'s review of Elvis' Las Vegas opening said, in part, "The Elvis Presley who was a freakish kid curiosity when he was third feature on a New Frontier showbill in 1956, is no more. He has become "ELVIS," not only in huge electric letters on the International's marquee, but also in more publicized and verbalized affirmations of his superstar status."

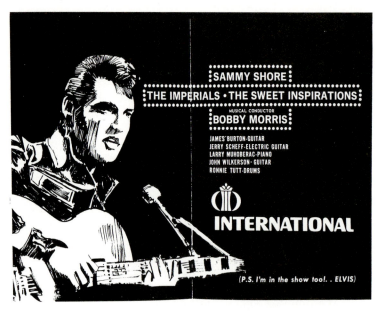

Two-page ad for Elvis' opening at the International Hotel.

Elvis and Vernon following Elvis' opening in Las Vegas.

AUG 8   (Thurs.) In a belated review of "Speedway," the *Los Angeles Times* remarked that the film "has a script that ran out of gas before Elvis Presley was born."

AUG 10   (Sun.) The *Memphis Commercial Appeal* reported that Elvis and Colonel Parker had turned down a $5 million contract in Las Vegas. The *New York Times* ran a generally favorable review of Elvis' opening in Las Vegas by Richard Goldstein, titled "A White Boy With Black Hips."

AUG 11   (Mon.) *Newsweek* ran an article entitled "Return Of The Pelvis," which covered Elvis' opening in Las Vegas.

AUG 15   (Fri.) *Time* magazine published an article titled "Rock 'N' Roll: Return Of The Big Beat," which started with Elvis' Las Vegas opening, and covered other working rock 'n' roll artists such as Chuck Berry, Jerry Lee Lewis, Little Richard, Fats Domino, and the Everly Brothers.

AUG 17   (Sun.) NBC-TV re-ran the special "Elvis" at 9 p.m. (EDT). For this showing, the song *Blue Christmas* was replaced with *Tiger Man*, which had been recorded at the same taping sessions in June 1968.

AUG 22   (Fri.) RCA Victor taped Elvis' dinner show for release on an upcoming album, **From Memphis To Vegas/From Vegas To Memphis**. Felton Jarvis supervised the taping for RCA Victor. Songs recorded during this show which were released on the album were *All Shook Up, Suspicious Minds, Words, Johnny B. Goode,* and *Are You Lonesome Tonight?* *Runaway* was released on the album **On Stage – February 1970**. Several songs were recorded and given matrix numbers, and then were not released: *I Got A Woman* and *Love Me Tender.* A hilarious version of *Are You Lonesome Tonight?* was also recorded. This first appeared on a bootleg album in 1970.

AUG 24   (Sun.) RCA Victor continued taping Elvis' dinner shows. Only two songs from this performance were released on the live portion of **From Memphis To Vegas/From Vegas To Memphis**: *Can't Help Falling In Love* and *My Babe.* Other songs which were recorded but which remain unreleased included *Rubberneckin', This Is The Story, Heartbreak Hotel* and *Funny How The Time Slips Away.*

AUG 25   (Mon.) Another dinner show was taped by RCA Victor with supervision by Felton Jarvis. A medley of *Yesterday/Hey Jude* was recorded, but before it was released on the album **On Stage – February 1970**, the *Hey Jude*

ending was deleted. Two songs were issued on the album **From Memphis To Vegas/From Vegas To Memphis**:
I Can't Stop Loving You and *In The Ghetto*. The remainder of the songs were not released, but they included
Jailhouse Rock/Don't Be Cruel, Memories, What'd I Say
and *Inherit The Wind.*

AUG 26 (Tues.) Yet another dinner show was taped by RCA Vic-
tor. *Blue Suede Shoes, Hound Dog* and *Mystery Train/
Tiger Man* were released on the album **From Memphis
To Vegas/From Vegas To Memphis**. A version of *Baby
What You Want Me To Do* was recorded and given a ma-
trix number, but it was never released.

AUG 27 (Wed.) Elvis received his eleventh gold album for the TV
soundtrack, **Elvis.**

AUG 28 (Thurs.) Elvis closed his first month-long engagement at
the International Hotel. The total attendance had
topped 101,509, a Las Vegas record. The gross receipts
had been $1,522,635, also a Las Vegas record. Although
the showroom only had a capacity of 2,000, this was
increased to over 3,500 on weekends to accommodate
the overflow crowds. Reportedly, Elvis was paid
$100,000 a week. Following the last performance, Elvis
hosted a party for his many friends.

AUG 29 (Fri.) Elvis, Priscilla, Vernon and Dee attended the opening
show of Nancy Sinatra at the International Hotel. Following her show, Elvis and Priscilla, along with Colonel
Parker, attended a party given by Frank Sinatra for his
daughter. Elvis presented Nancy Sinatra with the engrav-
ing plates from the full-page ad he had taken out in a local paper advertising her show.

AUG 30 (Sat.) Elvis and Priscilla traveled to their Palm Springs
home to relax.

SEPTEMBER

SEP 3 (Wed.) "The Trouble With Girls (And How To Get Into
It)" opened in theaters across the country. In many locations, the co-feature was "The Green Slime."

SEP 9 (Sat.) *Billboard*, in reviewing *Suspicious Minds*, predicted "Top 20" action for the single, saying it was an
"outstanding performance."

SEP 13 (Sat.) *Suspicious Minds* started up *Billboard*'s "Hot 100"
at number 77. It stayed on the chart fifteen weeks,

reaching number 1. This was Elvis' first number 1 single since *Good Luck Charm* in April 1962.

SEP 23   (Thurs.) Elvis and Priscilla returned to Memphis.

SEP 27   (Sat.) Elvis attended a midnight showing of "Butch Cassidy And The Sundance Kid" at the Memphian Theater.

OCTOBER

OCT 5   (Sun.) Elvis and Priscilla flew to Honolulu for the start of a three-week vacation. They rented a private home near Kailua on the island of Oahu. Also along for the vacation were Patsy and Gee Gee Gamble.

OCT 11   (Sat.) Elvis and Priscilla attended a show by Al Lopaka at the Surf Lanai Lounge of the Queen's Surf Hotel. They were accompanied by Vernon and Dee, who were staying at the Ilikai Hotel, and ten friends.

OCT 12   (Sun.) The couple flew from Hawaii to Nassau in the Bahama Islands for two more weeks of vacation where they stayed at a private estate.

During their vacation, Graceland was redecorated.

OCT 17   (Fri.) In reviewing "Change Of Habit," the *Hollywood Reporter* said that the film was "something of a departure from the beaten path" for Elvis.

OCT 22   (Wed.) *Variety*, in reviewing "Change Of Habit," said Elvis "displays his customary easy presence."

late OCT At the end of the vacation, Elvis and Priscilla flew to Los Angeles.

NOVEMBER

NOV 1   (Sat.) *Suspicious Minds* peaked at number 1 on *Billboard*'s "Hot 100." It remained at number 1 for only one week, and was his last number 1 single on the "Hot 100."

NOV 7   (Fri.) The *Memphis Commercial Appeal* reported that Elvis had been listed in the current volume of the prestigious *Makers Of The 20th Century.*

NOV 8   (Sat.) In a full-page ad, RCA Victor announced that it was issuing fifteen cassettes containing about half of Elvis' LP material, covering his career from **Elvis' Golden Records** to **From Elvis In Memphis**.

NOV 10   (Mon.) "Change Of Habit" was released to theaters in the United States.

Elvis and Mary Tyler Moore in "Change Of Habit."

NOV 16　(Sun.) RCA Victor released Elvis' first double-album, **From Memphis To Vegas/From Vegas To Memphis**.

NOV 20　(Thurs.) The *Los Angeles Times*, in its review of "Change Of Habit," said: "[Elvis] is especially good, even at times making you forget who you are watching."

NOV 22　(Sat.) *Billboard*, in reviewing **From Memphis To Vegas/ From Vegas To Memphis**, said: "The electricity of his 'live' performance is captured on one disk of this deluxe 2-record set . . . the second disk, cut in Memphis, is equally a powerhouse."

　　　　　In reviewing *Don't Cry Daddy, Billboard* called the song a "compelling rhythm ballad with a potent lyric line."

NOV 26　(Wed.) "Change Of Habit" was number 42 on *Variety*'s "50 Top-Grossing Films" chart for the week ending November 19th. The film remained on the chart for four weeks, peaking at number 17.

NOV 29　(Sat.) *Don't Cry Daddy/Rubberneckin'* started up *Billboard*'s "Hot 100" chart at number 73, peaking at number 6 and staying thirteen weeks. **From Memphis To Vegas/From Vegas To Memphis** entered *Billboard*'s album chart at number 36, where it stayed twenty-four weeks and reached number 12.

　　The fourth issue of *Who's Who In Movies* magazine had a photo of Elvis on the cover, and the article "Elvis Presley – The Sexiest King."

DECEMBER

DEC 10　(Wed.) *Suspicious Minds* became Elvis' forty-eighth gold record.

DEC 18　(Thurs.) Elvis returned to Memphis, accompanied by Priscilla and Lisa Marie.

DEC 20　(Sat.) *Don't Cry Daddy* entered *Billboard*'s country and western singles chart, where it peaked at number 13 and stayed twelve weeks.

DEC 25　(Thurs.) Christmas was spent quietly at Graceland. Lisa Marie was again the center of attention, and Vernon dressed up as Santa Claus in a repeat of the previous year's performance.

DEC 31　(Wed.) Elvis hosted a New Year's Eve party at T.J.'s, a local Memphis nightclub owned by a former member of Elvis' entourage, Alan Fortas. Flash and the Board of

Directors performed, along with special guests Ronnie Milsap and Mark James (composer of *Suspicious Minds*).

Elvis was compared with Tom Jones in the one-time magazine *Elvis & Tom* published in 1969.

If I Can Dream

ALL
SHOOK
UP
ELVIS
Day-By-Day,
1970

JANUARY

JAN 3   (Sat.) Elvis flew from Memphis to Los Angeles to rehearse for his upcoming engagement at the International Hotel.

JAN 7   (Wed.) *Variety*, in its year-end survey of the movie industry ranked "Charro" number 68, with a gross of $1.5 million.

JAN 19 (Mon.) Elvis traveled to Las Vegas, where he continued to rehearse for his approaching second season at the International.

JAN 26 (Mon.) Elvis opened a month-long engagement at the International Hotel in Las Vegas. There was only one show, at 8:00 p.m., on opening night. In the crowd for this performance were Juliet Prowse, George Chakiris, Zsa Zsa Gabor, and Dean Martin. As a special favor to Martin, Elvis sang *Everybody Loves Somebody Sometime*, Martin's number 1 hit in 1964. Elvis' regular back-up band was on hand, except that Glenn D. Hardin had replaced Larry Muhoberac on piano, and Bob Lanning had replaced Ronnie Tutt on drums. The Imperials had a few new faces, too, as Jake Hess had been replaced by Terry Blackwood, and Gary McSpadden had been replaced by Joe Moskeo.

Shows during the remainder of the engagement were at 8:00 p.m. and midnight. During the month, Elvis complained of having a chest cold and sore throat.

FEBRUARY

FEB 4   (Wed.) *Variety*'s review of Elvis' opening said, in part: "Presley's appearance, delivery, and anatomical gestures — the same as he pioneered with 15 years ago — leave no doubt about his influence on present-day Presleys."

315

FEB 7   (Sat.) In reviewing *Kentucky Rain, Billboard* picked it for the top 20, saying the song was a "driving rock-ballad."

FEB 13   (Fri.) *Disc* magazine voted Elvis the award as "Top Male Vocalist."

FEB 14   (Sat.) *Kentucky Rain* started climbing *Billboard*'s "Hot 100" chart at number 96, reaching number 16 and staying nine weeks.
Priscilla and Lisa Marie attended the dinner show.

FEB 16   (Mon.) RCA taped Elvis' dinner show for release on a future album, **On Stage — February 1970**. None of the songs were considered strong enough for release, although *All Shook Up, In The Ghetto,* and *Suspicious Minds* were given matrix numbers by RCA.

FEB 17   (Tues.) RCA continued to tape the dinner shows, this time coming up with three songs for the **On Stage — February 1970** album: *Proud Mary, C.C. Rider,* and *Let It Be Me.* A version of *Don't Cry Daddy* was recorded, but was not released.

FEB 18   (Wed.) Again, RCA taped the dinner show. Songs from this session which were released on the **On Stage — February 1970** album were *Sweet Caroline, Release Me, Walk A Mile In My Shoes*, and *Polk Salad Annie.* Other songs which were recorded, but which remain unreleased, were *Kentucky Rain, Long Tall Sally,* and *I Can't Stop Loving You.*

FEB 19   (Thurs.) One final night of taping captured *The Wonder Of You* for future release.

FEB 23   (Mon.) Elvis closed at the International Hotel. His final show was longer than usual, and Elvis accompanied himself on piano for *Lawdy, Miss Clawdy* and *Blueberry Hill*. During *Love Me Tender*, Priscilla ran on stage and gave Elvis a long kiss.

FEB 24   (Tues.) Colonel Parker and his staff arrived at Houston's Astroworld Hotel to make the final arrangements for Elvis' Thursday through Saturday concerts in the Astrodome.

FEB 25   (Wed.) Elvis arrived in Houston aboard Kirk Kerkorian's private jet during the night. There was a short press conference in the lobby of the Houston Air Center, then Elvis went on to the Astroworld Hotel, where he would stay for the remainder of his engagement.

FEB 27   (Fri.) Elvis had an early afternoon press conference at the hotel.

Following the press conference, Elvis performed shows at 2:00 and 7:45 p.m. at the Astrodome, in conjunction with the Texas Livestock Show. During the matinee, 4,000 handicapped children were the guests of Elvis and the Colonel. Total attendance for the afternoon show was 16,708. According to reports, Elvis appeared nervous and several problems developed with the musicians' equipment and microphones. The total attendance for the evening show was 36,299.

FEB 28 (Sat.) Elvis continued to perform two shows at the Astrodome. The matinee drew a crowd of 34,443; the evening show, however, broke all records for a rodeo performance as 43,614 fans filled the Astrodome.

Kentucky Rain entered *Billboard*'s country and western singles chart where it stayed ten weeks and peaked at number 31.

MARCH

MAR 1 (Sun.) Elvis continued to perform at the Texas Livestock Show, with appearances at 2:00 and 7:00 p.m. A total of 207,494 people saw the six shows. Following the last performance, there was a banquet at the hotel honoring Elvis. Officials from RCA gave Elvis several gold records for recent hits. Both Elvis and Colonel Parker received gold watches from the officials of the Livestock Show And Rodeo.

MAR 2 (Mon.) Elvis, Priscilla and several friends left Houston and flew to Los Angeles.

EARLY–MID MARCH
Elvis and Priscilla vacationed at their home in Palm Springs.

MAR 19 (Thurs.) The *Los Angeles Times* reported that Elvis would appear on a closed-circuit television broadcast to 275 cities. The special would originate in Las Vegas during Elvis' August engagement, and would be produced by Filmways, Inc. Elvis would be paid $1 million.

MAR 20 (Fri.) *Life* magazine ran an article entitled "Elvis Presley At Las Vegas."

APRIL

APR 6   (Mon.) Elvis purchased a six-door, 1969 Mercedes limousine, ID#600001193.

APR 18   (Sat.) *Billboard* said, in reviewing **Let's Be Friends**, that "RCA has repackaged some of Presley's movies' songs into this low-priced LP."

MAY

During May, Elvis and Priscilla visited backstage with Tom Jones at the International Hotel in Las Vegas. They also attended several lounge acts during the early hours of the morning.

MAY 2   (Sat.) *Billboard* picked *The Wonder Of You* to be a "Top 20" single, saying the song was "another top of the chart winner."

MAY 9   (Sat.) **Let's Be Friends** entered *Billboard*'s LP charts at number 108, where it peaked at number 105 and stayed eleven weeks.

MAY 16   (Sat.) *The Wonder Of You/Mama Liked The Roses* started up *Billboard*'s "Hot 100," at number 66, reaching number 9 and staying twelve weeks.

MAY 21   (Thurs.) Elvis and Pris returned to Memphis from Palm Springs.

MAY 22   (Fri.) A new three-picture contract was signed with M-G-M Studios. Included in the deal was a documentary to be filmed against the backdrop of Elvis' summer engagement at the International Hotel in Las Vegas.

MAY 24   (Sun.) Elvis gave Priscilla a surprise birthday party as she turned twenty-five. Dee Presley made peach ice cream, and Elvis gave his three stepbrothers rides on the go-kart, while Lisa Marie stood on the sidelines and laughed.

late MAY During the last week in May, Graceland opened its new air-conditioned guardhouse at the main gate. Elvis frequently came to the gate for lengthy autograph sessions, but he discontinued them when it started getting too hot and humid.

JUNE

JUN 4   (Thurs.) Elvis traveled to Nashville for a recording session at RCA's studios. Over the course of the next five days,

thirty-four songs were waxed. Several were held for re-
lease as singles: *I've Lost You* b/w *The Next Step Is
Love, The Sound Of Your Cry, You Don't Have To Say
You Love Me* b/w *Patch It Up, Life* b/w *Only Believe,*
and *I Really Don't Want To Know* b/w *There Goes My
Everything.*

The remainder of the songs were issued on a succession of
albums. For the **That's The Way It Is** LP, there was
*Twenty Days And Twenty Nights, Bridge Over Troubled
Water* (with added applause), *How The Web Was Woven,
Stranger In The Crowd, Mary In The Morning,* and *Just
Pretend.* For the **Elvis Now** LP, there was *I Was Born
About 10,000 Years Ago* (which was used in part also on
Elvis Country), and *Sylvia.* For the **Elvis Country** LP,
there was *The Fool, Little Cabin On The Hill, It's Your
Baby You Rock It, Faded Love, Tomorrow Never
Comes, Make The World Go Away, Funny How The
Time Slips Away,* and *I Washed My Hands In Muddy
Water.* For the **Love Letters** LP, there was *Cindy Cindy,
Got My Mojo Working, I'll Never Know, It Ain't No Big
Thing, This Is Our Dance, Heart Of Rome, When I'm
Over You, Love Letters,* and *If I Were You.*

Musicians for this session included a different group from
previous Nashville dates: James Burton and Chip
Young, guitar; Norbert Putnam, bass; Jerry Carrigan,
drums; David Briggs, piano; and Charlie McCoy, harmonica.

Background vocals by the Jordanaires, the Imperials, the
Nashville Edition, and soloists Millie Kirkham, Jeannie
Green, Mary Holladay, and Ginger Holladay were added
at a later date.

JUN 6   (Sat.) *The Wonder Of You* started up *Billboard*'s country
and western singles chart, where it peaked at number
37 and stayed ten weeks.

JUN 13   (Sat.) In reviewing **On Stage — February 1970,** *Billboard*
said: "This great package is an illustration of how broad
the artist's versatility is."

JUN 20   (Sat.) *The Wonder Of You* reached number 1 for a week on
Billboard's "Easy Listening Singles" chart.

The **On Stage — February 1970** album entered the LP chart
in *Billboard* at number 31, where it reached number 13
and stayed twenty weeks.

Elvis on stage in August 1970.

JULY

JUL 5   (Sun.) Elvis flew from Memphis to Los Angeles to re-
          hearse at the M-G-M studios for another engagement
          at the International Hotel. Film crews from M-G-M
          were on hand to record the rehearsals for the movie
          "Elvis — That's The Way It Is," which was known
          at the time as "Standing Room Only."
          Songs filmed at the rehearsals were *Words, The Next
          Step Is Love, Polk Salad Annie, Crying Time, That's
          All Right, Little Sister, What'd I Say, Stranger In The
          Crowd, How The Web Was Woven, I Just Can't Help
          Believing,* and *You Don't Have To Say You Love Me.*
early JUL While at M-G-M Studios, Elvis dropped by the set of the
          television show, "The Courtship Of Eddie's Father,"
          which was one of his favorite TV shows.
JUL 18   (Sat.) *Billboard*, in picking *I've Lost You/The Next Step
          Is Love* for the top twenty said the single was "another
          two-sided smash."

AUGUST

AUG 1   (Sat.) *I've Lost You/The Next Step Is Love* entered the
          "Hot 100" chart in *Billboard* at number 85, staying
          nine weeks and reaching number 32.
AUG 10   (Mon.) Elvis opened at the International Hotel in Las
          Vegas. Ronnie Tutt was back on drums, and Joe
          Guercio had taken over as conductor of the twenty-six
          piece hotel orchestra. Millie Kirkham, who had re-
          corded with Elvis since 1957, was added to the backing
          vocalists to sing high soprano.
          There was only one show on opening night, at 8:00 p.m.
          Guests included Sammy Davis, Jr., Cary Grant, Juliet
          Prowse, Sonny Liston, Jack Benny, Nancy Sinatra,
          Xavier Cugat, and his wife Charro. Shows during the
          rest of the month were at 8:00 p.m. and midnight.
          This was the first "Elvis Summer Festival," as later mid-
          year engagements came to be called. Hotel employees
          all wore straw hats with the new catch phrase on the
          hat band.
          One of the songs performed by Elvis was *Tiger Man*, from
          his 1968 "comeback" TV special. During the month,
          Elvis appeared in either a white or black, tailored, one-
          piece suit with gold trim.

Another August 1970 performance shot.

During this week, RCA Victor taped all of Elvis' dinner shows. Also, a film crew from M-G-M was on hand to record the shows for the movie "Elvis — That's The Way It Is." Songs included *That's All Right, I've Lost You, Patch It Up, Love Me Tender, You've Lost That Loving Feeling, Sweet Caroline, I Just Can't Help Believing, Tiger Man, Bridge Over Troubled Water, Heartbreak Hotel, One Night, Blue Suede Shoes, All Shook Up, Polk Salad Annie, Suspicious Minds* and *Can't Help Falling In Love.*

Also, early in the engagement, Elvis was filmed by the M-G-M crew during rehearsals on stage in the International Hotel. Five songs from the rehearsals were included in the film: *Bridge Over Troubled Water, You've Lost That Loving Feeling, Mary In The Morning, Polk Salad Annie,* and *Words.*

AUG 13 (Thurs.) Two of the songs from the dinner show were used by RCA in the album **Elvis — That's The Way It Is**: *I Just Can't Help Believing* and *Patch It Up.*

AUG 14 (Fri.) A paternity suit was filed in Los Angeles Superior Court by Patricia Ann Parker, twenty-one, a Hollywood waitress, against Elvis. She asked the court to award her $1,000 a month in child support. She claimed that the child she was carrying had been fathered by Elvis during his January--February 1970 Las Vegas engagement.

Only two songs from this date were used on the **Elvis — That's The Way It Is** LP: *You've Lost That Loving Feeling* and *I've Lost You.*

AUG 15 (Sat.) *Billboard*, in its review of the four-record boxed set, **Elvis: Worldwide Gold Award Hits, Vol. 1**, astutely noted that this was "a must for collectors."

RCA taped a version of *Bridge Over Troubled Water* from the dinner show, and even assigned a matrix number to it. However, it was not used in the soundtrack album, and another version was substituted from the June 1970 Nashville sessions. This studio version was overdubbed with applause to make it sound as though it had been recorded live.

AUG 19 (Wed.) *Variety*'s review of Elvis' Las Vegas act said, in part, "Presley is cool and very collected all the way through his full hour, knowing just what to do every minute."

AUG 22 (Sat.) **Elvis: Worldwide 50 Gold Hits, Volume 1** entered *Billboard*'s album chart, where it stayed twenty-two weeks and reached number 45.

AUG 26 (Wed.) A security guard at the International Hotel received a telephone call from a man who said that Elvis would be kidnapped that night by two men.

AUG 27 (Thurs.) Colonel Parker received a telephone call from an anonymous individual at 2:55 p.m. The caller said that Elvis would be kidnapped over the weekend.

AUG 28 (Fri.) At 6:15 a.m., Joe Esposito's wife in Los Angeles was telephoned and told that Elvis would be shot by a madman with a silencer. The caller demanded $50,000. An officer from the Los Angeles Police Department was assigned to protect Elvis.

AUG 29 (Sat.) Elvis performed without any problems.

AUG 31 (Mon.) Priscilla and Lisa Marie left Los Angeles for Las Vegas to stay with Elvis during the last week of his engagement.

SEPTEMBER

SEP 7 (Mon.) Elvis closed his month-long engagement at the International Hotel. In addition to the usual 8:00 p.m. and midnight shows, there was one final 3:00 a.m. show added to the schedule on this date to accommodate the final overflow crowd. Later, Elvis attended a farewell party in his honor in the hotel's restaurant. On hand were Nancy Sinatra and Tom Jones.

SEP 8 (Tues.) Elvis attended the opening of Nancy Sinatra's show at the International.

SEP 9 (Wed.) Elvis started his first tour since the 1950s, with a concert in the Veterans' Memorial Coliseum in Phoenix, 8:30 p.m. Tickets throughout this tour were $10, $7.50 and $5. Over 15,000 fans attended, and RCA and M-G-M were on hand to record the show for the movie "Elvis – That's The Way It Is." Only one song from the show made the film, *Mystery Train/Tiger Man*. At one point during the concert, Elvis was so exhausted he lay down in the middle of the stage. At the end of his show, instead of throwing his scarf to the audience as he usually did, Elvis tossed it to Colonel Parker.

During this tour, the Hugh Jarrett Singers replaced the Imperials who were booked into Nashville recording dates.

SEP 10 (Thurs.) Elvis performed in St. Louis' Kiel Auditorium at 8:30 p.m. Over 12,000 fans were on hand. Elvis stayed at the Chase-Park Plaza Hotel.

SEP 11   (Thurs.) Elvis and his entourage of thirty arrived at Detroit's Metro Airport aboard five chartered jets. They stayed at the Detroit-Hilton. That night, at 8:30 p.m., Elvis performed at the Olympia Arena to a capacity crowd of 16,000. According to the *Detroit News* review, "An evening with Elvis Presley will make a television viewer realize how much Tom Jones has copied Elvis' style and that the real product is so much better." During the show, Elvis even sang a few bars of Johnny Cash's early hit, *I Walk The Line.*

SEP 12   (Sat.) Two shows were held in the Miami Beach Convention Center at 3:00 and 9:00 p.m. The attendance for each show topped 12,000. The highlight of the matinee was a very long version of *Polk Salad Annie.*

SEP 13   (Sun.) Two concerts were held in Tampa's Curtis Hixon Hall at 3:00 and 8:30 p.m. Each show had over 7,500 in attendance. During *In The Ghetto*, Elvis transposed the lyrics and sang, "A runny little boy, with a hungry nose." He became so tickled that he could not continue with the song and had to stop the show. The more he tried to become serious, the more he laughed. Elvis introduced his grandmother, who was in the audience. It was only the second time she had been to one of Elvis' shows.

SEP 14   (Mon.) Elvis arrived in Mobile, Alabama, about 4:00 p.m., and went directly to the Admiral Simms Hotel to rest before his 8:30 p.m. show at the Municipal Auditorium. Attendance was pegged at 10,800 for the concert. Elvis sang *Close To You*, a recent hit for the Carpenters, and one of his least performed songs. Following the show, there was a party on the twelfth floor of the hotel.

SEP 15   (Tues.) Following the short tour, Elvis returned to Graceland to rest.

SEP 22   (Tues.) Elvis went to RCA's studios in Nashville for a recording date. Musicians on this session were the same as those used during the marathon June 1970 date, except that Edward Hinton replaced James Burton on lead guitar. Background vocals by the Imperials and the Jordanaires, as well as strings and horns, were overdubbed at a later date under the supervision of Felton Jarvis. Songs recorded were *Snowbird* and *Whole Lotta Shakin' Goin' On*, which first appeared on the **Elvis Country** album, and *Where Did They Go Lord* and *Rags To Riches,* which were released as a single in early 1971.

late SEP   The last week in September, Elvis and Priscilla traveled to Los Angeles. During this week, they also went to Las Vegas where they were ringside at one of Connie Stevens' midnight shows at the Sands Hotel.

OCTOBER

OCT 11   (Sun.) Elvis was named Special Deputy Sheriff of Bel Air, California.

OCT 13   (Tues.) Elvis flew from Los Angeles to Memphis for a few days rest.

OCT 15   (Thurs.) Elvis attended the Gospel Quartet Convention at the Ellis Auditorium in Memphis.

OCT 17   (Sat.) In reviewing "Elvis — That's The Way It Is," the *Hollywood Reporter* said: "[Elvis] is perhaps the only performer today who will bring into movie theaters enough people to make a documentary of himself pay off."

Elvis was back in attendance at the Gospel Quartet Convention. The Imperials, who were one of the groups performing, introduced him from the stage.

You Don't Have To Say You Love Me/Patch It Up was called "another two-sided blockbuster for Elvis," as *Billboard* picked the single for the top twenty.

OCT 18   (Sun.) Elvis flew back to Los Angeles, where he prepared for his second short tour.

OCT 19   (Mon.) A boy was born to Patricia Parker in Presbyterian Hospital in Hollywood. He was named Jason Peter Presley. Miss Parker was involved in a paternity suit against Elvis.

OCT 24   (Sat.) *You Don't Have To Say You Love Me/Patch It Up* entered the "Hot 100" chart in *Billboard* at number 74, staying ten weeks and reaching number 11.

OCT 27   (Tues.) *Variety*, in reviewing "Elvis — That's The Way It Is," said: "Presley is the pied piper of the rock era . . . Presley explodes on screen."

NOVEMBER

NOV 7   (Sat.) In reviewing the Camden release of **Elvis' Christmas Album**, *Billboard* said it "packs all the genius of Elvis in a holiday way."

NOV 10 (Tues.) Elvis started another short concert tour with a
show in the Oakland Coliseum at 8:30 p.m. Ticket
prices for this tour were $10, $7.50 and $5. Attendance
was set at over 14,000.

NOV 11 (Wed.) "Elvis – That's The Way It Is" opened in theaters
in the United States. In many locations, the "B" feature was "Grand Prix," starring James Garner.
Elvis performed at 8:30 p.m. in the Memorial Coliseum
in Portland. Attendance was 11,800.

NOV 12 (Thurs.) Elvis appeared at the Coliseum in Seattle at 8:30
p.m. in front of 15,000 fans.

NOV 13 (Fri.) At 8:30 p.m., Elvis performed at the Cow Palace in
San Francisco to the delight of the 14,300 fans in
attendance.

NOV 14 (Sat.) There were two shows at the Forum in Los Angeles
(Inglewood) at 3:00 and 8:30 p.m. Total attendance
was 37,398, with a gross of $313,464 (18,700 for the
matinee and 18,698 for the evening show). Between
shows, Elvis rested in a Hollywood hotel. While at the
hotel, he was served with some legal papers in the continuing paternity case brought by Patricia Parker. During
the evening show, Elvis was still very irritated, and gave
a long monologue enumerating his achievements.

NOV 15 (Sun.) Elvis held a concert in San Diego's International
Sports Arena at 8:30 p.m. Gross receipts were $114,247
from the 14,659 fans attending.

NOV 16 (Mon.) It was off to Oklahoma City's State Fair Grounds
Arena for an 8:30 p.m. show, with an attendance of
11,000. Elvis did a rousing version of *Blue Christmas* for
the crowd.

NOV 17 (Tues.) The tour moved on to the Denver Coliseum, where
12,000 attended the 8:30 p.m. show. Following this performance, there was a wild "end-of-tour" party at the
Playboy Hotel.

NOV 18 (Wed.) Early in the morning, Elvis flew back to Los
Angeles.

NOV 21 (Sat.) **Back In Memphis** entered the "Hot LPs" chart in
Billboard at number 194. The album was a re-release of
one-half of the previous winter's **From Memphis To
Vegas/From Vegas to Memphis**, and it stayed on the
charts for only three weeks, peaking at number 183. The
budget Camden release, **Almost In Love** fared better, as
it entered the LP chart at number 128 and stayed eighteen
weeks, reaching number 65.

Elvis in the 1970 movie "Elvis – That's The Way It Is."

NOV 25   (Wed.) "Elvis – That's The Way It Is" was number 25 on
         Variety's chart of the "50 Top-Grossing Films" for the
         week ending November 18th. The movie stayed on the
         chart for three of the next five weeks, peaking at num-
         ber 22.

NOV 28   (Sat.) *You Don't Have To Say You Love Me* reached
         number 1 on *Billboard*'s "Easy Listening Singles" chart.
         It was number 1 for only one week.

   The fifth issue of *Who's Who In The Movies* magazine had a photo
   of Elvis on the cover along with an article, "Elvis Presley – Here
   To Stay."

DECEMBER

DEC 3   (Thurs.) Elvis personally delivered a check for $7,000 to
         Los Angeles Police Chief Edward M. Davis to be used
         for the community relations program. Elvis also gave
         Chief Davis a custom-made frontier model Colt .45
         caliber revolver. There was a stipulation at the time that
         there could be no publicity (the event was not reported
         until September 7, 1977). This was the largest single do-
         nation to the program. The money was used to buy toys
         for needy children, uniforms for the LAPD marching
         band, and special flak jackets for explosive-sniffing dogs.

DEC 5   (Sat.) *You Don't Have To Say You Love Me* entered *Bill-
         board*'s country and western singles chart, where it
         stayed five weeks and reached number 56.

DEC 9   (Wed.) The *Los Angeles Herald-Examiner* called "Elvis –
         That's The Way It Is" "a very inadequate documentary.
         Easy exploitation, stock sell stuff. A hack job . . . the
         camera follows but does not penetrate."

DEC 12   (Sat.) **Elvis – That's The Way It Is** started up *Billboard*'s
         LP chart, where it peaked at number 21 and stayed
         twenty-three weeks.

DEC 16   (Thurs.) The Official Elvis Presley Fan Club News Service
         of England reported that Elvis would perform two con-
         certs in Paris on May 27, 1972. The concerts were being
         promoted by the Charles Aznavour Society, and they
         would be held in the open-air Stadium de Colombes.
      In the continuing paternity suit against Elvis brought in
         August by Patricia Parker, there was a new twist. Elvis
         filed a "cross complaint" alleging that her suit was a

Elvis and President Nixon exchange greetings.

conspiracy among herself and ten "John Does" to extort money from him. Elvis formally denounced the charge that he was the father of her child, and stated further that he had never had sexual intercourse with Miss Parker. Elvis asked $1,000 punitive damages, and $1 in other damages and court costs.

DEC 19   (Sat.) *There Goes My Everything/I Really Don't Want To Know* was a "Top 20" pick in *Billboard*, which said the songs were "two country classics."

Elvis, under the pseudonym John Burroughs, boarded an American Airlines flight at Memphis International Airport bound for Washington, D.C. He traveled alone. In Washington, he took a taxi to the Washington Hotel. That night, he flew from Washington to Los Angeles aboard TWA flight number 85.

DEC 20   (Sun.) Elvis arrived in Los Angeles at 1:17 a.m. He went to his home in Holmby Hills. At 10:00 p.m., he took a flight back to Washington with a part-time bodyguard, Jerry Schilling, and California senator George Murphy. Elvis used the alias "Dr. John Carpenter."

DEC 21   (Mon.) The flight landed in Washington at 6:30 a.m. Elvis and Schilling took a limousine to the White House, where Elvis hand-delivered a letter requesting a visit with President Richard M. Nixon. The pair then returned to the Washington Hotel. Senator Murphy telephoned the F.B.I. and made an appointment for Elvis to visit the Bureau of Narcotics and Dangerous Drugs. John Finlator, Deputy Director of the Bureau, called Elvis to set up the appointment. Elvis arrived in a Cadillac limousine. He was wearing a purple, crushed velvet suit and cloak with a large gold belt buckle. Elvis asked Finlator for a federal narcotics officer's badge, but Finlator turned him down. Elvis returned to his hotel.

Shortly thereafter, Elvis, accompanied by Schilling and Sonny West, who had arrived from Memphis, went to the White House for a brief visit with President Nixon. The matter of the narcotics officer's badge came up, and Nixon told his top law enforcement advisor, Egil (Bud) Krogh, to call Finlator and have him bring the badge immediately to the White House. Elvis was so overcome with the gesture, that he gave Nixon a bear hug.

That night, Elvis and West returned to Memphis. Schilling returned to Los Angeles aboard a jet chartered by Elvis.

DEC 25   (Fri.) Following the hectic trip of the week before, Christmas was spent quietly at Graceland. Elvis gave former Shelby County Sheriff William N. Morris a $9,000 foreign car, among the gifts presented this year.

DEC 26   (Sat.) *I Really Don't Want To Know*/*There Goes My Everything* started climbing the *Billboard* "Hot 100" chart at number 56, finally reaching number 21 and staying nine weeks.

DEC 27   (Sun.) The Memphis *Commercial Appeal* reported that Elvis might he a candidate for the Jaycee's "Top 10 Young Men of the Year" award.

DEC 28   (Mon.) Elvis served as best man at the wedding of his bodyguard Sonny West to Judy Morgan. The ceremony was held in Memphis' Trinity Baptist Church. Priscilla served as matron of honor.

DEC 29   (Tues.) Elvis drove to Tupelo to see the work in progress on the "Elvis Presley Center," and to visit friends.

DEC 30   (Wed.) Elvis, accompanied by former Shelby County Sheriff William Morris, returned to Washington, where they stayed at the Washington Hotel. Morris telephoned F.B.I. Assistant Director Casper to set up a tour of the F.B.I. facilities by Elvis, Morris, and six others. In an in-house memorandum, the F.B.I. stated that Elvis "is certainly not the type of individual whom the Director [J. Edgar Hoover] would wish to meet."

DEC 31   (Thurs.) Elvis, Sheriff Morris, and six of Elvis' bodyguards visited F.B.I. Headquarters and were accorded a special tour. The F.B.I.'s memorandum of the visit said Elvis "did give the impression of being a sincere, young man who is conscious of the many problems facing the country."

Upon returning to Memphis, Elvis and Priscilla went to a New Year's Eve party at T.J.'s Club, where Ronnie Milsap was the entertainer for the evening.

The *Memphis Press Scimitar* reported that Elvis had been given a gem-studded badge by the Shelby County Sheriff and others.

In Los Angeles, lawyers representing Elvis asked the Superior Court to order blood tests in the paternity suit against Elvis.

In December, the North Mississippi Gun Club took possession of Elvis' Flying Circle G Ranch on Highway 301 in DeSoto County.

The new catalog of Elvis' records from RCA was issued in December. None of the extended play releases were mentioned, meaning that over twenty songs would be deleted.

Elvis was compared with Glen Campbell in the one-time publication, *Glen Campbell/Elvis Presley*, published in 1970.

Elvis' appearance at the Jaycee's breakfast and banquet in Memphis on January 16, 1971 was the focus of a great deal of press coverage.

Have I Told You Lately That I Love You

ALL
SHOOK
UP
ELVIS
Day-By-Day,
1971

JANUARY

JAN 6   (Wed.) In the Los Angeles Superior Court of Judge
William Hogoboom, Elvis won a court order requiring
a blood test of Patricia Parker in her paternity suit
against him. The tests were to be administered by Dr.
Phillip Sturgeon at his Brentwood clinic. The judge in
the case also ordered each party to take a lie detector
test, to be administered by Police Captain Warren King
of Burbank.

The Official Elvis Presley Fan Club News Service of England reported that Tom Diskin, of Colonel Parker's
office, had said that "everything connected [with the
Paris concert] is false and Elvis will not appear in
Europe in '72."

JAN 9   (Sat.) The national Junior Chamber of Commerce (better
known as the Jaycees) released their list of "The Top
Ten Young Men Of The Year" for 1970, and Elvis was
on the list. The announcement came from Jaycee headquarters in Tucson, Arizona, and the list was accompanied by the following statement: "The United States
Jaycees selects 10 men each year whose exceptional
achievements represent the best efforts in their fields of
endeavor. Each exhibits the dedication, spirit and in-
novation that mark them as advocates of change in a
society becoming progressively unaware of its shortcomings."

I Really Don't Want To Know/There Goes My Everything
entered *Billboard*'s country and western singles chart,
where it reached number 9 and stayed thirteen weeks.
This was Elvis' first top ten country single since *Hard
Headed Woman* in 1958.

JAN 16   (Sat.) Elvis and Priscilla attended a prayer breakfast at
         the Memphis Holiday Inn, sponsored by the United
         States Jaycees. This was followed by a forum. That
         night, at the awards banquet in the Memphis Municipal
         Auditorium, as he was given the award as one of the
         "Top Ten Young Men Of The Year" for 1970, Elvis
         based his short speech upon the words to *Without A
         Song*, ending by saying, "Without a song a man ain't
         got a friend. Without a song the day won't ever end.
         So I'll just keep singing my song . . . " This was the
         first such public function that Elvis had ever attended.
JAN 22   (Fri.) Elvis received the "Guide Dog For The Blind"
         award from England for his generosity; he had sent his
         British fan club personal items which could be auctioned
         off, the proceeds being given to the program to train
         guide dogs.
JAN 23   (Sat.) **Elvis Country** entered *Billboard*'s album chart at
         number 143, where it peaked at number 12 and stayed
         twenty-one weeks.
JAN 24   (Sun.) Elvis flew to Las Vegas for rehearsals prior to his
         opening at the International on the 26th.
JAN 26   (Tues.) Elvis opened another month-long engagement at
         the International Hotel in Las Vegas. There was only
         one show on opening night, at 8:00 p.m. Kathy West-
         moreland had replaced Millie Kirkham as soprano. One
         of the additions to the normal repertoire was *The Im-
         possible Dream*, which Elvis often sang while he accom-
         panied himself on piano.
         During the month, Elvis was plagued with a recurring bout
         of the flu.

FEBRUARY

FEB 1   (Mon.) Priscilla and Lisa Marie attended the dinner show
         for Lisa Marie's third birthday. Later, Elvis had a
         photographer come to their penthouse suite and take
         several family portraits, which later appeared in many
         fan magazines.
FEB 7   (Sun.) Elvis attended a birthday party for his show's resi-
         dent comedian, Sammy Shore. He and Priscilla stayed
         at the party for four hours.
FEB 23   (Tues.) Elvis completed his four-week long stay at the
         International Hotel.

FEB 24 (Wed.) Elvis and Priscilla attended Ann-Margret's opening show at the International Hotel. Afterwards, they chatted backstage with her and her husband, Roger Smith, until 3:00 a.m.

FEB 26 (Fri.) Elvis sneaked into the Stardust Lounge to watch a performance of the Irish Royal Show Band, which featured an impersonation of Elvis by Brendon Bowyer. Elvis joined Bowyer on stage to show how "the real thing" was done.

FEB 28 (Mon.) Elvis and Priscilla left Las Vegas for their home in Palm Springs.

MARCH

Early in the month, Elvis and Priscilla returned to their home in Bel Air.

MAR 5 (Fri.) RCA released another Camden LP, **You'll Never Walk Alone**.

MAR 6 (Sat.) *Billboard* picked *Where Did They Go, Lord/Rags To Riches* for the top twenty, saying it was "certain to ride right into the teens."

MAR 10 (Wed.) Elvis and Priscilla traveled to Memphis.

MAR 13 (Sat.) *Where Do They Go, Lord/Rags To Riches* entered *Billboard*'s "Hot 100" chart at number 60, staying seven weeks and peaking at number 33.

Billboard, in reviewing **You'll Never Walk Alone**, said it "shows Presley in top form."

MAR 15 (Mon.) Elvis flew to Nashville aboard a chartered jet for a recording session at RCA's studio, even though he was complaining of an eye infection. The musicians for this date were the same as those used in September 1970, except that James Burton was back on lead guitar replacing Edward Hinton. Only four songs were completed before the session was cancelled, as Elvis' eye had become more inflamed: *The First Time Ever I Saw Your Face, Amazing Grace, Early Morning Rain*, and *For Lovin' Me.* The studio had been booked for another four days, so James Burton used this time to complete an instrumental album released by A&M Records later in the year.

MAR 16 (Tues.) Following the aborted session, Elvis was taken to a Nashville's Baptist Hospital, where he remained a few days for tests by Dr. Elkin Rippy which determined that Elvis was suffering from secondary glaucoma. While in

the hospital, he was visited by Tennessee Governor Winfield Dunn.

MAR 19   (Fri.) Elvis was released from the hospital. He wore a
black eyepatch for the next several weeks.

MAR 20   (Sat.) **You'll Never Walk Alone** started up the *Billboard*
LP chart at number 190, where it peaked at number 69
and stayed twelve weeks.

late MAR Back in Memphis, Elvis was examined at the Memphis Eye
and Ear Hospital, 1060 Madison.

Late in March, Elvis, Priscilla, and some friends flew to
Hawaii for a vacation.

APRIL

Elvis returned to Memphis early in the month. He was still wearing
an eyepatch on his left eye for protection.

APR 21   (Wed.) Elvis and Priscilla flew to Mt. Holly, New Jersey,
to surprise her brother, Don, who was on leave from
Vietnam, where he was a helicopter pilot.

late APR Late in April, Elvis and Priscilla traveled to Las Vegas,
where they attended shows by Sammy Shore and the
Sweet Inspirations in the Casino Lounge of the International Hotel. They also saw Bobbie Gentry at the
Landmark Hotel, and Tom Jones at Caesar's Palace.

In April, Elvis ordered the first of the TCB (Takin' Care
Of Business) necklaces, for his close friends and associ-
ates, from Schwartz-Ableser Jewelers in Beverly Hills.

MAY

MAY 1   (Sat.) Elvis and Priscilla celebrated their fourth wedding
anniversary in Las Vegas.

A few days later, they flew back to Memphis.

MAY 4   (Tues.) Elvis was featured on the cover of *Look* magazine
in conjunction with the publication of the first part of
a two-part excerpt of the Jerry Hopkins' book, *Elvis.*

MAY 8   (Sat.) In picking *Only Believe/Life* for the top sixty, *Billboard* said the "A" side was a "gospel oriented ballad
that builds into a heavy production."

MAY 11   (Tues.) *Look* published part two of the excerpt from
Elvis, without a cover photo of Elvis.

MAY 15   (Sat.) *Life/Only Believe* started climbing the "Hot 100"
chart in *Billboard* at number 87, but it only reached as

high as number 53 and stayed but seven weeks.

Elvis started a marathon week-long recording session at RCA's studios in Nashville. The musicians were the same as for the past few Nashville dates, except that Kenneth Buttery was added as a second drummer, a practice that Elvis had used during the 1960s. Also, Elvis' friends Charlie Hodge and Joe Esposito played guitar on several on the songs.

The main reasons for this session were to produce a Christmas album, a few new singles, and material for a studio album. The Christmas songs were released on the album **Wonderful World Of Christmas**, and were recorded on the dates indicated: *It Won't Seem Like Christmas, If I Get Home On Christmas Day, Holly Leaves And Christmas Trees, Merry Christmas Baby*, and *Silver Bells* (15th); *I'll Be Home On Christmas Day, On A Snowy Christmas Night, Winter Wonderland, O Come All Ye Faithful, The First Noel*, and *The Wonderful World Of Christmas* (16th).

Several of the songs were held for release on the 1973 album **Elvis**, also referred to as the "Fool" album after its title song: *Padre* (15th); *Don't Think Twice, It's All Right* (16th); *It's Still Here, I'll Take You Home Again Kathleen*, and *I Will Be True* (20th); and *Love Me, Love The Life I Lead* (21st). The album **Elvis Now** used some of the songs from these sessions: *Miracle Of The Rosary* (15th); *Help Me Make It Through The Night* (16th); and *Fools Rush In* (18th). Several religious songs were used on the LP **He Touched Me**: *Lead Me, Guide Me* (17th); *I've Got Confidence* and *An Evening Prayer* (18th); *Seeing Is Believing* and *A Thing Called Love* (19th).

The remainder of the songs were released as singles: *Until It's Time For You To Go* (17th); *He Touched Me* (18th); *I'm Leavin', We Can Make It In The Morning*, and *It's Only Love* (20th).

In all, thirty songs were recorded from May 15th through May 21st.

MAY 21   (Fri.) At the first annual Memphis Music Awards banquet at the Holiday Inn--Rivermont, Elvis was voted the "Founder's Award," and *Suspicious Minds* received the award as the "Outstanding Single Recorded In Memphis." Vernon and Dee made an appearance to accept the awards for Elvis.

late MAY In late May, Elvis flew to Los Angeles.

In May, Elvis was negotiating to lease a jet and a full-time pilot for $470,000 a year.

JUNE

JUN 1   (Tues.) Elvis' birthplace on Old Saltillo Road in Tupelo was opened to the public. It had been restored by the East Heights Garden Club.

JUN 5   (Sat.) *Life* entered the *Billboard* country and western singles chart, where it stayed eight weeks and reached number 34.

JUN 7   (Mon.) Elvis returned to Memphis.

JUN 8   (Tues.) Elvis returned to RCA's studios in Nashville to complete work on the religious album, **He Touched Me**. The musicians on hand were essentially the same as those used during the week-long session in May. Songs recorded this night were *Put Your Hand In The Hand, Reach Out To Jesus*, and *He Is My Everything*. An attempt was made to re-record *Until It's Time For You To Go*, but it was not as good as the version recorded in May.

JUN 9   (Wed.) Elvis was back in the studio for another evening session. More gospel songs were recorded, including *There Is No God But God, I John,* and *Bosom Of Abraham*. Elvis attempted another version of *I'll Be Home For Christmas*, but, again, the May version was released instead. During this session, Elvis lost his temper at one of the background singers, and stalked out of the studio before the session was completed.

JUN 10   (Thurs.) The local press reported that an ordinance supported by Memphis Mayor Henry Loeb would re-name a twelve-mile portion of Highway 51 south from the Memphis city limits to the Mississippi border (which passed in front of Graceland) as "Elvis Presley Boulevard."

JUN 19   (Sat.) The album **Love Letters From Elvis** was "sure to prove another top seller," according to *Billboard*'s review.

JUN 26   (Sat.) **Love Letters From Elvis** started climbing *Billboard*'s album chart at number 40. It reached number 33 and stayed fifteen weeks.

JUN 29   (Tues.) The Memphis City Council officially renamed the twelve-mile stretch of Highway 51 South, known as

South Bellevue Boulevard, as the "Elvis Presley Boulevard." The actual change took place in January 1972.

JULY

JUL 4   (Fri.) Elvis arrived at his Holmby Hills home.
JUL 7   (Mon.) Elvis began evening rehearsals at RCA's studios,
            on the third floor of the RCA building on Sunset Strip.
            Rehearsals continued for several days.
JUL 10   (Sat.) *Billboard* picked *I'm Leavin'* for the top sixty, say-
            ing the song was a "driving rock ballad." Of the album,
            C'mon Everybody, *Billboard* said: "The repackaging of
            Presley on the low priced Camden line has consistently
            proven a hot chart item."
            I'm Leavin' entered *Billboard*'s "Hot 100" chart at num-
            ber 82, staying nine weeks and peaking at number 36.
JUL 14   (Wed.) Elvis left his home in Bel Air for Lake Tahoe. He
            and his entourage drove in a caravan led by Elvis' rented
            Mercedes Benz. At Lake Tahoe, he continued afternoon
            rehearsals at the Sahara Tahoe Hotel.
JUL 20   (Tues.) Elvis opened his first engagement in the High
            Sierra Room of the Sahara Tahoe Hotel located in
            Stateline, Nevada. Comedian Nipsy Russell opened the
            show, replacing Sammy Shore. Elvis performed two
            shows each night, at 8:00 p.m. and midnight. The mini-
            mum for each show was fifteen dollars.
            Elvis broke Tahoe showroom records with an attendance
            of 3,400 for two shows in the High Sierra Room of the
            Sahara Tahoe. The next month, Elvis would set the record
            for all showrooms.
            According to a review in *Billboard*, Elvis "left a capacity
            crowd of 1,500 in the High Sierra Room almost as ex-
            huasted (emotionally, if not physically) as he was."
            Fans who attended the opening night show were given a
            special tote bag containing Elvis' **C'mon Everybody** al-
            bum, a hat, scarf, button, photo album, and a teddy bear.
            During his shows, one of the highlights came during *You've
            Lost That Lovin' Feelin'*, when he would turn his back
            to the audience, then slowly turn around wearing a
            monkey mask!
            During the engagement, Elvis complained about not feeling
            well, and that the high altitude bothered him.

JUL 24   (Sat.) **C'mon Everybody** entered the LP chart in *Billboard*
          at number 144, where it stayed eleven weeks, peaking at
          number 70.

The July issue of the British magazine *Films And Filming*, in reviewing "Elvis – That's The Way It Is," said: "If [Dennis]
Sanders [the film's director] has wished to show the Presley
followers as morons he has succeeded admirably."

AUGUST

AUG 1   (Sun.) Singer Paul Anka attended Elvis' show at the
          Sahara Tahoe Hotel. He and Elvis exchanged a few
          friendly words about their singing styles.
AUG 2   (Mon.) Elvis closed his two weeks engagement at the
          Sahara Tahoe Hotel.
AUG 3   (Tues.) Elvis left Lake Tahoe for Las Vegas to ready him-
          self for his month-long engagement at the newly re-
          named Las Vegas Hilton International.
AUG 9   (Mon.) Elvis opened at the Las Vegas Hilton International
          Hotel. Due to the overwhelming demand for his shows,
          several performances were added at 3:00 a.m., in addi-
          tion to his regular shows at 8:00 p.m. and midnight.
          During the first part of his engagement, Elvis complained
          of a mild case of laryngitis.
          Bob Melvin replaced Nipsy Russell as the opening comedian
          for this series of shows.
          One of the highlights of each show came during Elvis' sing-
          ing of *Teddy Bear*, when he would toss stuffed toy bears
          into the audience.
          Another "new" song for Elvis during this engagement was
          It's Impossible.
AUG 14   (Sat.) During the midnight show, Elvis attempted to sing
          It's Over, which he would not record for another two
          years. He started three times but could not get through
          it. Then he tried *Rip It Up*, but the orchestra was caught
          completely off-guard, so Elvis stopped singing. This was
          followed by *I Need Your Loving Everyday*, a song almost
          never performed live. All of this makes this performance
          much more memorable than the usual Vegas show.
AUG 21   (Sat.) The four-LP boxed set, **Elvis: The Other Sides –
          Worldwide Gold Award Hits, Volume 2** was reviewed by
          Billboard, which said the set would "prove a sales mon-
          ster via his fans."

AUG 23   (Mon.) Elvis complained of having the flu, but gave a great show nonetheless.

AUG 24   (Tues.) As the curtain closed following the midnight show, Elvis completely surprised everyone by suddenly appearing on the left side of the stage for a few seconds. He was chased by several women who tried to follow him backstage, but they were too late.

AUG 25   (Wed.) At the end of the midnight show, several women rushed the stage and were able to grab Elvis and Charlie Hodge. Red West and Joe Esposito came on stage to rescue Elvis, and they were grabbed by several more women. It took several minutes to restore order.

AUG 28   (Sat.) **Elvis: The Other Sides — Worldwide Gold Award Hits, Volume 2** entered *Billboard*'s album chart at number 144. It only stayed on the chart seven weeks and peaked at number 120.

During a brief ceremony between shows in his dressing room, Elvis was given a large ebony-and-gold plaque representing the Bing Crosby Award. The plaque was presented by Bing's son, Chris, and by William Cole, an officer of the National Academy Of Recording Arts And Sciences. Originally known as the Golden Achievement Award, and renamed in honor of its first recipient, the award had been given to only five other persons, Crosby, Frank Sinatra, Duke Ellington, Ella Fitzgerald, and Irving Berlin.

The citation on the plaque read: "To Elvis Presley in recognition of your artistic creativity and your influence in the field of recorded music upon a generation of performers and listeners whose lives and musical horizons have been enriched and expanded by your unique contributions."

SEPTEMBER

SEP 3   (Fri.) Over the Labor Day weekend, ninety radio stations throughout the United States aired "The Elvis Presley Story," a twelve-part special marketed by Watermark, Inc. and narrated by Wink Martindale.

RCA hired a photographer to film Elvis' shows for possible use on album covers or in a new photo album.

During the midnight show, Elvis surprised the audience, as well as the orchestra, by attempting to sing *(Marie's The Name Of) His Latest Flame*. After four lines, with only

Glenn Hardin attempting to keep up with Elvis, the song collapsed. Then Elvis started *Treat Me Nice*, but switched to *Wooden Heart*, in which he sang the German verse. All three songs were not performed live by Elvis very often.

SEP 6   (Mon.) Elvis closed his month-long engagement at the Las Vegas Hilton International Hotel. During the month, Elvis had broken his own record for attendance in a showroom with 4,428 for two shows. This record would stand for years, since fire codes were violated to allow overflow crowds into a room designed to hold 2,000 per performance.

SEP 10 (Fri.) Elvis bought the first Stutz Blackhawk Coupe automobile manufactured. It cost about $35,000, and was a custom-made Italian/US sportscar with I.D. number 276571A139060.

The second Stutz Blackhawk went to Frank Sinatra.

late SEP Elvis and Priscilla returned to Memphis.

OCTOBER

OCT 2   (Sat.) *It's Only Love* was a top sixty pick in *Billboard*, which said the song was a "strong rock ballad."

OCT 8   (Fri.) Elvis purchased a customized $90,000 Mercedes Benz automobile.

OCT 9   (Sat.) *It's Only Love* started up *Billboard*'s "Hot 100" chart at number 90, but it only reached as high as number 51 and stayed a short six weeks.

OCT 17 (Sun.) During a special television salute to Ed Sullivan on CBS-TV, Elvis was featured from his 1956--57 performances.

In October, Simon & Schuster published Jerry Hopkins' book, *Elvis: A Biography*. The initial printing was 25,000 copies. Portions of the book had appeared in two issues of *Look* magazine in May.

NOVEMBER

NOV 5   (Fri.) Elvis started a longer than usual tour, with J.D. Sumner and the Stamps Quartet replacing the Imperials. Jackie Kahane became the resident comedian. Tickets for the concerts were $10, $7.50 and $5. The tour was promoted by Management III of Seattle.

The first concert was held before 17,600 fans in Minneapolis' Metropolitan Sports Center. Gross receipts from
this show were $125,000. Elvis was on stage for an
hour and ten minutes.

NOV 6   (Sat.) Elvis performed at 2:30 and 8:30 p.m. in the Cleveland Public Hall Auditorium. Attendance for both shows
was pegged at 20,000 total, with gross receipts of
$146,000.

NOV 7   (Sun.) In Louisville, Kentucky, Elvis gave a matinee show
at 2:30 p.m. at the State Fair and Expo Center's Freedom Hall. Among the 18,550 fans (a Louisville record
for a single performance) were Jesse D. Presley and his
wife, Elvis' grandfather and step-grandmother. During
the show, Elvis had the house lights turned up so he
could say hello to them.

NOV 8   (Mon.) In Philadelphia's Spectrum, 16,601 fans paid
$113,173 for Elvis' 8:30 p.m. performance. Elvis was in
fine voice, and startled many of his Yankee fans with a
superb rendition of *How Great Thou Art.*

NOV 9   (Tues.) Elvis entertained a crowd of 12,228 at the Baltimore Civic Center for fifty-five minutes before closing
with *Can't Help Falling In Love.* During the show,
several young women tried to jump up on the stage, but
they were quickly subdued by the police.

NOV 10   (Wed.) Elvis arrived at Logan Airport in Boston during
the afternoon. He stayed on his Fairchild 28 jet until
shortly before the 8:30 p.m. show at the Boston Garden.
One of the "new" songs for this appearance was *I'm
Leavin'*, a recent release. Elvis was on stage for fifty-two
minutes. Following the show, he was driven back to the
airport where he flew to Cincinnati. Attendance was
15,509 and receipts topped $150,000, a Boston record
for a one-nighter.

NOV 11   (Thurs.) The tour traveled to Cincinnati for an 8:30 p.m.
show at the Gardens, with 13,272 attending.

NOV 12   (Fri.) The Elvis show traveled to Houston's Hofheinz
Pavillion for an 8:30 p.m. show. Attendance was set at
over 12,000. Elvis was on stage for nearly an hour. Toward the end of the show, as Elvis was singing *Funny
How The Time Slips Away*, he started to put on his cape,
which was a signal that the show was almost over. The
crowd reacted so negatively, that he flung off his cape

and said, "Hell, I ain't goin' nowhere!" Then he ran
through a wild version of *Mystery Train/Tiger Man* before closing the show with *Can't Help Falling In Love.*

NOV 13   (Sat.) Still in Texas, Elvis gave a matinee and evening show
in Dallas' Memorial Auditorium. Attendance was estimated at 10,000 for each performance. During Elvis'
singing of *How Great Thou Art*, the audience punctu-
ated Elvis' singing by shouting "Hallelujah" throughout.

NOV 14   (Sun.) Elvis performed at the University of Alabama Field
House in Tuscaloosa at 8:30 p.m. Over 12,000 fans
were on hand.

NOV 15   (Mon.) The tour dropped in at the Municipal Auditorium
in Kansas City, where 10,400 fans attended an 8:30 p.m.
show. Elvis was in a great mood and performed for over
an hour and a half.

NOV 16   (Tues.) The tour wound up in the Salt Palace in Salt Lake
City for an 8:30 p.m. concert. The show was delayed
fifteen minutes to accommodate the many fans who had
been caught in a large traffic jam in front of the auditorium. The 13,000 fans on hand for the show received
a treat when Elvis sang *Blue Christmas*, one of his least
frequently performed songs. Elvis was on stage for an
hour and fifteen minutes.

Following the performance, Elvis returned to his home in
Bel Air.

NOV 17   (Wed.) Elvis and Vernon chartered a plane to fly back to
Memphis to congratulate Billy Stanley on his engagement
to be married.

NOV 19   (Fri.) Elvis returned to Los Angeles.

RCA released **The Wonderful World Of Christmas** album
and the single *Merry Christmas, Baby* b/w *O Come All
Ye Faithful.*

NOV 20   (Sat.) As a reflection of Elvis' slipping popularity as a recording artist, he had no charted records in *Billboard*
this week. He newest releases were the budget LP, **I Got
Lucky**, and the new Christmas album and single, none
of which were big sellers.

NOV 21   (Sun.) Elvis' stepbrother, Billy Stanley, married his high
school sweetheart, Angelia Payne. Elvis did not attend,
but Vernon was best man.

NOV 24   (Wed.) In the continuing paternity case against Elvis
brought by Patricia Parker, the results of the blood tests
ordered by the court the previous January were

Elvis, with Vernon and Priscilla, backstage before a show.

presented. The results were kept confidential, but one source confirmed that in the three specific areas checked for compatibility, Elvis could not have fathered Miss Parker's baby. The case was continued to January 26, 1972.

late NOV In Los Angeles, Elvis visited a doctor to have his eye examined. He was told to wear an eyepatch for a few days.

NOV 27 (Sat.) **I Got Lucky** started up *Billboard* LP chart at number 122, where it only reached number 104 and stayed eight weeks.

NOV 29 (Mon.) WHBQ radio in Memphis had a twelve-hour tribute to Elvis.

DECEMBER

In early December, Elvis returned to Memphis. During his vacation, Elvis frequently rented a local movie theater for private showings of the latest movies, including the current James Bond epic, "Diamonds Are Forever," "Dirty Harry," and "Straw Dogs."

late DEC A few days before Christmas, Elvis hosted a party at Graceland. It was obvious to all present that Priscilla and Elvis were not getting along.

DEC 25 (Sat.) In *Billboard*'s year-end review, Elvis ranked number 26 in "Top Male Singles Artists" and number 11 in "Top Male Albums Artists."
As a Christmas gift, Elvis gave Priscilla ten $1,000 bills instead of the limousine he had planned, since she did not need a new car.

late DEC The week following Christmas, Priscilla and Lisa Marie left Elvis to return to their Bel Air home.

DEC 31 (Fri.) Elvis hosted a New Year's Eve party at Graceland. Over $1,000 worth of fireworks were set off at midnight.

During 1971, Elvis was the subject of the magazine, *Elvis: 1971 Presley Album.*

In 1971, Elvis was the subject of *Meet Elvis Presley* by Favius Friedman. The book was distributed throughout the nation's school systems.

In 1972, the reincarnated Sun Records Company issued a mysterious version of *That's All Right/Blue Moon Of Kentucky* . . .

. . . which immediately suspicious Elvis fans soon determined was an effort by vocalist Jimmy "Orion" Ellis.

Separate Ways

JANUARY

JAN 8   (Sat.) During a birthday party at Graceland, Elvis disclosed that Priscilla had moved into her own apartment
in Los Angeles with Lisa Marie. It was evident that this
was only the beginning of a long separation.

JAN 15   (Sat.) *We Can Make It In The Morning/Until It's Time For
You To Go* was only a "Top 60" pick in *Billboard*,
which, nevertheless, called it a "strong coupling."

JAN 19   (Wed.) Mayor Wyeth Chandler and Vernon Presley raised
the first of the "Elvis Presley Boulevard" signs at a ceremony in front of Graceland.

JAN 26   (Wed.) Elvis opened at the Las Vegas Hilton International
Hotel. Jackie Kahane was now firmly entrenched as the
resident comedian, and J.D. Sumner and the Stamps
had formally replaced the Imperials as Elvis' male backing vocal group. Only one show was held on this date;
thereafter, there were 8:00 p.m. and midnight performances for the remainder of the month.

New songs for this engagement were *Never Been To Spain,
An American Trilogy, I'll Remember You, The First
Time Ever I Saw Your Face*, and *You Gave Me A
Mountain.*

Elvis' shows usually ran forty to forty-five minutes long,
and there was little chatter from Elvis between songs,
as he hardly waited for the applause to end before he
started another song.

The 145 billboards featuring Elvis which were put up
throughout southern Nevada represented yet another
record-breaker, as the single largest piece of display advertising in the state's history.

In the paternity suit brought against Elvis by Miss Patricia
Parker in August 1970, the court found against her

charge that Elvis had fathered her child. Elvis was ab-
solved of all guilt.

JAN 27   (Thurs.) Columnist Jack Anderson told his readers in the
Washington Post of Elvis' December 1970 trip to the
F.B.I. and the White House in an article entitled "Pres-
ley Gets Narcotics Bureau Badge."

JAN 29   (Sat.) *Until It's Time For You To Go* entered *Billboard*'s
"Hot 100" chart at number 80, where it stayed nine
weeks and reached number 40.

In January, the rumors that Elvis would perform in Europe continued, with the most likely venue being Paris or England. It
was even reported that Elvis' uncles, who were gate guards at
Graceland, were telling fans that such a trip was planned.

FEBRUARY

FEB 8   (Tues.) In a telephone interview, Tom Diskin, Colonel
Parker's right-hand man, flatly denied all of the rumors
that Elvis might be coming to Europe in 1972.

FEB 9   (Wed.) *Variety*'s review of Elvis' Las Vegas act said, in
part, "Other than gimmickry to sell a superstar, who
needs none of it in the real sense, this time out is the
best yet for Presley. His format is taut, he pays attention to his songs and audience, the karate exercises are
quite vigorous and his ringside kissing technique is like a
dozen midway attractions rolled into one."

FEB 10   (Thurs.) The *Memphis Commercial Appeal* reported that
Elvis had been named the "Top Male Singer" by *Disc
Magazine.*

FEB 12   (Sat.) In reviewing **Elvis Now**, *Billboard* commented that
"Presley is very much 'now.' " The album entered *Billboard*'s chart at number 175, staying nineteen weeks and
peaking at number 43.

FEB 14   (Mon.) RCA began taping Elvis' dinner shows for an upcoming album project, entitled **Standing Room Only**.
The album was never released, and several of the songs
ended up on bootleg albums, including *Never Been To
Spain* from the show this night.

FEB 15   (Tues.) Two songs from RCA's taping of the dinner show
which ended up being released on bootleg albums were
You Gave Me A Mountain and *A Big Hunk O' Love.*

FEB 16   (Wed.) RCA continued taping Elvis' dinner shows, and the

song *It's Impossible* actually was released in June 1973
on the album **Elvis** (also known as the "Fool" LP). *The
Impossible Dream* had to wait until 1978 to be released
on the album **He Walks Beside Me.**

FEB 17   (Thurs.) The dinner shows continued to be taped by RCA.
An American Trilogy, from this date, was released as a
single in April 1972.

FEB 19   (Sat.) In reviewing Elvis' current Las Vegas engagement,
Billboard mentioned that Elvis was "considerably
slimmer . . . Elvis Presley got it all together and did a
no-nonsense superb show that would have pleased even
a non-Presley fan."

FEB 23   (Wed.) Elvis closed at the Las Vegas Hilton International.
Before he returned to the house in Holmby Hills, Priscilla had moved out with Lisa Marie, renting a two-
bedroom apartment near the Pacific Ocean.

MARCH

MAR 27   (Mon.) Elvis had a recording session for the first time in
RCA's studios in Hollywood. Camera crews from
M-G-M were on hand to film the session for the new
documentary movie, "Elvis On Tour." (Working title
for the movie at this time: "Elvis On Tour In The
USA.") Elvis used his concert band for this session,
with the exception of Jerry Scheff on bass, who
was replaced by Emory Gordy.
Songs from this date were *Separate Ways*, an unreleased
version of *For The Good Times*, and *Where Do I Go
From Here.*

MAR 28   (Tues.) Elvis was back in RCA's studios for another recording session. Songs recorded on this date were
Burning Love, Fool, Always On My Mind, and *It's A
Matter Of Time.* The session lasted into the early morning hours of the 29th.

In March, the rumors that Elvis would tour Europe were again
widespread, apparently coming from the President of Management III, the promoters of Elvis' last two tours.

In March, it was reported that Elvis and Kirk Kerkorian, previous
owner of the International Hotel before he sold it to the Hilton
chain, were working out a deal which would put Elvis at Kerkorian's as-yet-to-be-built M-G-M Grand Hotel. According to

the report, Colonel Parker and Elvis were putting in $6 million for an active interest in the project.

APRIL

APR 5   (Wed.) Elvis started a concert tour with a show at 8:30
         p.m. in the Memorial Auditorium in Buffalo, New York,
         which was attended by 17,340 fans. Tickets were
         $10, $7.50 and $5. Elvis stayed at the Statler Hotel.
         A camera crew from M-G-M filmed the show, and Elvis'
         karate demonstration became part of the film "Elvis On
         Tour." The only "new" song added for this tour was
         For The Good Times.
         During the tour, Elvis traveled in his Lear jet, while the re-
         mainder of the troupe went in a caravan of other air-
         planes.

APR 6   (Thurs.) In Detroit's Olympia Stadium, 16,216 fans at-
         tended Elvis' 8:30 p.m. show. This was the largest
         audience ever to witness a concert in the forty-four-year
         old arena. During *An American Trilogy* someone from
         the audience tossed a blue suede shoe onstage. At the
         song's dramatic finish, Elvis reached down and threw the
         shoe back into the crowd. People fought over it!

APR 7   (Fri.) Elvis set a record for both attendance and ticket
         sales for his 8:30 p.m. concert at the University of Day-
         ton (Ohio) Arena. Attendance was 13,788, and a news-
         paper article published the next day said that the Colonel
         stopped counting the money when he got to $120,000
         (actual gross was close to $157,000).

APR 8   (Sat.) Elvis' chartered Lear jet arrived at McGhee-Tyson
         Airport in Knoxville, Tennessee, at 11:45 a.m. Elvis
         was greeted by Mrs. Kyle Testerman, wife of the local
         mayor. Elvis then motored to the Sheraton Campus Inn.
         That afternoon, Elvis gave a 2:30 p.m. matinee performance
         at the University of Tennessee's Stokley Athletics Center.
         The show was about thirty minutes late in starting due
         to problems with the sound system, which continued to
         plague the afternoon performance.
         That evening, there was an 8:30 p.m. concert. Attendance
         was 10,500 in the afternoon and 13,300 at night.
         Originally, there had been no Tennessee show on the tour
         schedule, but after Governor Winfield Dunn and Senator
         Howard Baker were asked to intercede, Colonel Parker

set up the shows in Knoxville.

There was one nasty incident as a local photographer, Terry Moore, approached Elvis in the parking lot under the hotel. He was told by Sonny West not to take any pictures. When Moore continued, he was detained by West and off-duty Police Lt. Jim Rowan. During the shoving match, Moore allegedly tried to kick West. An investigation was conducted by the Knoxville Safety Department.

APR 9   (Sun.) Elvis arrived at Patrick Henry Airport in Hampton Roads, Virginia, about 2:00 p.m. He was rushed to the Coliseum for a 2:30 p.m. concert. Elvis' 8:30 p.m. show was filmed by a crew from M-G-M for the movie, which was to be titled "Elvis On Tour." Attendance was 11,000 for the matinee, and 10,650 for the evening concert.

A brief interview with Colonel Parker revealed that Elvis was filming a new movie, "Remnants Of The Old West." The Colonel also mentioned that Priscilla and Lisa Marie had been with Elvis on this tour but had returned to Los Angeles about three days before.

APR 10   (Mon.) M-G-M also filmed the 8:30 p.m. show in the Coliseum in Richmond, Virginia. Over 11,500 fans attended the show. *Polk Salad Annie*, usually a crowd-pleaser, was rushed so fast that the orchestra could not keep up. During the singing of *Bridge Over Troubled Water*, several female fans became hysterical as the camera crew filmed them. Elvis stopped the song, and waited for the audience to calm down before going on.

APR 11   (Tues.) Elvis' Lear jet landed at Woodrum Field in Roanoke, Virginia, at 6:00 p.m. Before disembarking, Elvis was given the key to the city by Roanoke Mayor Roy Webber. This was filmed by the M-G-M crew for "Elvis On Tour." Elvis shook a few hands and threw kisses to the crowd at the airport before leaving for the Civic Center Holiday Inn on Orange Avenue. At 7:00 p.m., at the Roanoke Civic Center Coliseum, there was a bomb threat which caused the evacuation of the 6,500 fans. No bomb was found, and the show started a little after 8:30 p.m.

While Elvis was singing *Release Me*, a group of women stormed the stage and nearly succeeded in pulling one of the backup musicians off the stage. The show was stopped for five minutes to restore order.

After the show, Elvis left for Indianapolis, while the rest of the troupe stayed at the Holiday Inn. Attendance was 10,436, and the gross was $90,000, a record for the Civic Center.

APR 12 (Wed.) Elvis' 8:30 p.m. show at the Indianapolis Fair Ground's Coliseum broke a local record. Even thundershowers could not keep over 11,000 fans away. Elvis was on stage for fifty minutes. He stayed overnight at the Indianapolis Hilton Hotel.

APR 13 (Thurs.) Elvis arrived in Charlotte, North Carolina, aboard his private jet in the afternoon, five hours behind the rest of his troupe. He was driven to the Coliseum Downtowner Motel, arriving at 2:52 p.m., where he was booked into the entire top floor.

That night, 12,000 fans attended Elvis' 8:30 p.m. concert in the Coliseum.

APR 14 (Fri.) Elvis' charted Gulfstream Two flew from the Charlotte Airport at 4:30 p.m., arriving at the Greensboro-High Point charter strip at 5:11 p.m. The crew on the plane was Pilot Ed Hahn, First Officer Tom Brougham, and Flight Engineer Bob Cupery.

In Greensboro, North Carolina, 16,300 fans spent $150,000 to attend Elvis' concert in the Coliseum at 8:30 p.m. M-G-M filmed this show, and the song *Burning Love* was included in "Elvis On Tour." Following the show, Elvis flew to Macon, Georgia.

APR 15 (Sat.) In reviewing **He Touched Me**, *Billboard* said: "The great sahib of rock, Elvis Presley, has another winning album."

There were two shows, at 2:30 and 8:30 p.m., in the Coliseum in Macon, Georgia. The total gross was over $200,000, as over 23,000 attended the two shows.

APR 16 (Sun.) Elvis performed another pair of shows in the Veteran's Memorial Coliseum in Jacksonville, Florida. At the 2:30 p.m. show, the attendance was 9,258, and at the 8:30 p.m. show, attendance was 9,500.

In a review by JoAnna Moore in the Jacksonville *Times-Union*, she said: "His extremely physical presentation was alive in each song and the audience reaction never subsided."

APR 17 (Mon.) Elvis traveled to Little Rock for an 8:30 p.m. show at the T.H. Barton Coliseum. Attendance was pegged at over 10,000.

APR 18 (Tues.) M-G-M was back to film the 8:30 p.m. show in San Antonio's Convention Center Arena, where 10,500 fans spent over $100,000, a local record for tickets. The city of San Antonio also jumped on the "Elvis" bandwagon as several record stores had special "Elvis" promotions, and one radio station aired "The Elvis Presley Story" in the complete twelve-hour form on the day of the show. The highlight of the concert was *Burning Love*, a song which had yet to be released on record.

APR 19 (Wed.) The final show of the tour was held in the Tingley Coliseum in Albuquerque, New Mexico, at 8:30 p.m. During intermission, Elvis met with Denise Sanchez, age eight, in a small trailer outside of the coliseum. She was terminally ill with cancer. Elvis autographed a poster for her. A touching photo of Elvis and Denise appeared in a local newspaper the next day. Elvis dedicated *You Gave Me A Mountain* to her during the concert. Attendance for the performance was 11,847. Following the show, Elvis flew back to Memphis.

APR 22 (Sat.) **He Touched Me** entered *Billboard*'s album chart at number 122, where it stayed ten weeks and peaked at number 79. (See March 1, 1975.)

MAY

MAY 6 (Sat.) *An American Trilogy* started up the "Hot 100" chart in *Billboard*, but it peaked at number 66 and stayed only six weeks. One of the reasons for the poor sales of Elvis' version of *An American Trilogy* may have been that Mickey Newbury had a hit with the song only six months earlier.

MAY 8 (Mon.) Tickets for Elvis' June concerts at Madison Square Garden went on sale in New York. All four shows were sold out within a day.

MAY 11 (Thurs.) A newspaper in Honolulu ran the following: "Elvis reportedly in town, resting from the rigors of the mainland showbiz routine." Elvis was in Hawaii for a vacation with Priscilla, Lisa Marie and twelve friends. They stayed at the Rainbow Towers, part of the Hilton Hawaiian Village. While in Honolulu, Elvis attended a karate demonstration. It was also reported that Elvis purchased $5,000 worth of opals from one of the hotel's shops.

Elvis meets with Denise Sanchez before his show in Albuquerque.

Press conference prior to starting the historic Madison Square Garden appearances.

MAY 28   (Sun.) Elvis was in Las Vegas to attend a show by Glen
         Campbell at the International Hotel. Campbell intro-
         duced Elvis, who was in the audience. As might be ex-
         pected, the crowd turned their attention completely to-
         ward Elvis, and Campbell lost control of his own show.
         To restore order, Elvis had to leave. After the show,
         Elvis attended a special party in Campbell's honor at
         the hotel.

JUNE

JUN 9   (Fri.) Elvis started another tour with a 4:00 p.m. press
         conference in the Mercury Ballroom of the New York
         Hilton. Each date on this tour was guaranteed for
         $70,000 against seventy percent of the gate ($980,000
         total for the fourteen shows). Tickets for this tour
         were the usual $10, $7.50 and $5.
         Elvis made entertainment history over the next three days
         with a total of four sold-out concerts in Madison Square
         Garden (8:30 p.m. on the 9th, 2:30 and 8:30 p.m. on
         the 10th, and 8:30 p.m. on the 11th). He was the first
         performer to do so. A total of 80,000 fans attended
         the shows, which grossed $730,000. RCA recorded both
         of the shows on the 10th for the album **Elvis As Re-
         corded At Madison Square Garden**, but only the evening
         show was included on the LP. *I Can't Stop Loving You*,
         from the matinee, turned up on the album **Welcome To
         My World** in 1977. Two other songs, *Reconsider Baby*
         and *I'll Remember You*, were issued in 1983 on **Elvis –
         A Legendary Performer, Volume 4**.
         Well-known celebrities who were spotted at the concerts
         included John Lennon, George Harrison, Bob Dylan,
         David Bowie, and Art Garfunkel.
         While in New York, Elvis stayed at the Hilton Hotel.
JUN 12   (Mon.) The tour continued with an 8:30 p.m. concert at
         the Memorial Coliseum in Ft. Wayne, Indiana.
JUN 13   (Tues.) Elvis performed at 8:30 p.m. in the Robert's
         Memorial Stadium in Evansville, Indiana, in front of
         11,500 fans.
JUN 14   (Wed.) Elvis moved on to the Milwaukee Auditorium
         Arena for a show at 8:30 p.m. Attendance was pegged
         at 10,500.
JUN 15   (Thurs.) Still in Milwaukee, the 8:30 p.m. concert was
         attended by 11,000 fans.

On stage at New York's Madison Square Garden.

JUN 16   (Fri.) The tour stopped in Chicago for a concert at 8:30
p.m. at the Chicago Stadium. Attendance topped
22,000. Elvis took to the stage at 9:28 p.m. and performed for fifty-one minutes.

JUN 17   (Sat.) Elvis remained in Chicago for two more shows, at
2:30 and 8:30 p.m. There were over 20,000 fans on
hand for each show. The total receipts for all three of
the Chicago concerts was reported to be over $500,000.

JUN 18   (Sun.) Elvis flew into Ft. Worth's Greater Southwest
Airport in the afternoon in his executive jet, accompanied by another small jet and a turboprop airliner.
He checked into the Sheraton Towers Hotel at 4:45
p.m., where he stayed on the thirteenth floor. Elvis'
8:30 p.m. concert was attended by 14,122 fans, a record
for the Tarrant County Convention Center Arena.

JUN 19   (Mon.) RCA "rush-released" the album **Elvis As Recorded
At Madison Square Garden**, only nine days after the
concert was recorded.

About a dozen fans were waiting as Elvis arrived at the Air-
craftco Hangar at Municipal Airport in Wichita, Kansas,
at 7:00 p.m. He stayed on board the chartered jet until
8:30 p.m., when he traveled to the Henry Levitt Arena
where over 10,000 fans were ready for his portion of the
show to begin. Following the concert, Elvis flew to
Tulsa, Oklahoma, arriving about midnight.

JUN 20   (Tues.) Elvis stayed at the Fairmont Mayo Hotel in Tulsa,
occupying the top three floors, including the eighteenth,
where his suite was located. Over 9,500 fans attended
his 8:30 p.m. concert in the Civic Assembly Center.
Following the show, Elvis returned to the hotel.

JUN 21   (Wed.) Elvis departed the Mayo Hotel at 3:55 p.m. for the
airport, where he flew back to Memphis.

late JUN During Elvis' stay in Memphis, rumors foretold of an im-
minent divorce between Elvis and Priscilla.

In late June, there was a foreclosure auction on the property owned by the North Mississippi Gun Club, which had
formerly been Elvis' Flying Circle G Ranch. The only
bidders were the club's president, D.L. McClellan, and
Vernon Presley. McClellan bid $338,973.62 which was
$1 more than Vernon, but he could not come up with
the money, so Vernon ended up with the ranch. At the
time, there were seven lawsuits against the club for
money owed for materials and services. Because of pro-

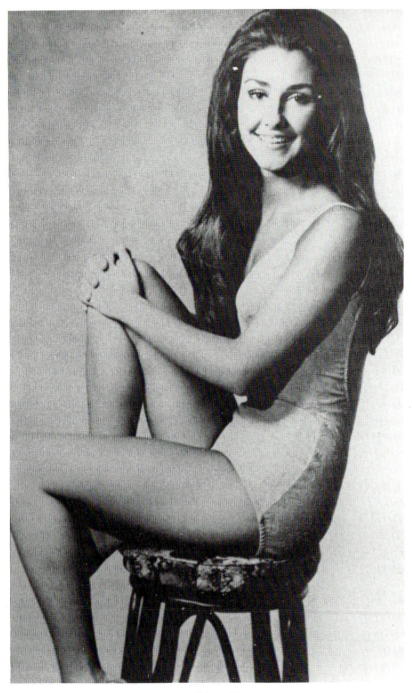

Beauty queen Linda Thompson.

tests from neighbors, the club had never been issued a permit for shooting.

In June, Australian promoter James McKay offered Elvis $900,000 for one appearance in Melbourne and two in Sidney. He also offered Elvis the use of a private jet, a personal pilot, and a secret hideaway villa for a vacation.

JULY

JUL 1   (Sat.) The *New Yorker* magazine published a review of Elvis' Madison Square Garden concerts.

JUL 4   (Tues.) Elvis attended a demonstration at the Tennessee Karate Institute, where he gave a ninety-minute lecture-demonstration with Ed Parker.

JUL 5   (Wed.) During midnight movies at the Memphian Theater, Elvis was introduced to Linda Diane Thompson by George Klein, Elvis' friend since their days at Humes High School. She was a former Miss Memphis State and Miss Liberty Bowl (an annual football game played in Memphis). She was the current Miss Tennessee in the Miss U.S.A. (part of the Miss Universe) pageant system.

JUL 6   (Thurs.) Elvis was back at the Memphian Theater, but this time, he made sure that Linda Thompson was seated next to him. So started a relationship that lasted until 1976.

JUL 8   (Sat.) The *Memphis Commercial Appeal* reported that plans were underway for Elvis to perform on a worldwide sixty-minute television program to be broadcast live from Honolulu in October or November 1972. The program would be seen in the Far East and Europe.
The album **Elvis As Recorded At Madison Square Garden** entered *Billboard*'s LP chart at number 96, where it reached number 11 and stayed thirty-four weeks. Also on the LP chart, **Elvis Sings His Hits From The Movies** started its climb at number 161, but it peaked at number 87 and stayed fifteen weeks.

mid-JUL   In the middle of July, while Linda Thompson was away on a vacation, Elvis' houseguest was Sandra Zancan, a Las Vegas showgirl. She and Elvis were seen together for about two weeks.

JUL 21   (Mon.) Elvis made the cover story in *Rolling Stone* magazine.

JUL 24   (Mon.) Buddah Records started distribution of "Current Audio Magazine, Vol. 1 No. 1 August--September 1972." The package came with a ten-page magazine and a twelve-inch record containing portions of Elvis' press conference in New York in June, along with an interview with Mick Jagger and other "audio" news items. List price for the package was $2.49.

JUL 27   (Thurs.) Pricilla formally separated from Elvis. She had moved out of their Holmby Hills home into an apartment in Newport Beach in January.

JUL 28   (Fri.) Elvis flew from Memphis to Las Vegas to prepare for his next month-long engagement.

The Associated Press reported that Elvis and Priscilla had separated but were trying for a reconciliation. Although Elvis' attorney, Ed Gregory Hookstraten, would not give details of the separation, the *Memphis Commercial Appeal* had recently reported that Elvis and Priscilla had been living in separate homes since January 8th. The AP also reported that if the couple did not reconcile, Priscilla would retain custody of Lisa Marie and receive a generous settlement.

AUGUST

AUG 4   (Fri.) **Elvis As Recorded At Madison Square Garden** was certified "gold" by the RIAA.

Elvis opened at the Las Vegas Hilton Hotel, which had dropped the "International" name altogether, although they retained the Showroom Internationale. Opening night, there was only one show, at 8:00 p.m. Guests included Richard Harris, Paul Anka, and Sammy Davis, Jr. Elvis was only on stage for thirty minutes, and he did not sing any rock songs. He complained that he had a headache.

Shows for the rest of the engagement were at 8:00 p.m. and midnight.

Elvis had added a few new songs to his act, including *What Now My Love* and *My Way*. The main complaint among the fans was that Elvis did not move very much, having eliminated most of the karate routines. His voice was said to be stronger than before. There was almost no interplay between Elvis and the audience, and it was reported that Elvis hardly said a word except to introduce his band.

It was reported that camera crews from M-G-M were on hand to record the opening show for "Elvis On Tour."

AUG 5   (Sat.) Elvis flew to Los Angeles to meet Linda Thompson, who arrived from Memphis at 11:00 a.m. They returned to Las Vegas that afternoon.

During the month, Elvis' steady companions were Linda Thompson for opening week, Cybill Shepherd for four days, Sandra Zancan for a week, and Linda Thompson, again, to close out the month.

AUG 6   (Sun.) The *Memphis Commercial Appeal* reported that Elvis would perform on the West Coast in November, and that there would be a worldwide television show broadcast from Honolulu as part of the tour.

AUG 18 (Fri.) A petition for divorce was filed in Los Angeles Superior Court in Santa Monica by Ed Gregory Hookstraten on behalf of Elvis. The reason for the divorce was listed as "irreconcilable differences." The divorce was not contested by Priscilla, and neither she nor Elvis made an appearance in court. Hookstraten told reporters the reason for the divorce was "that Elvis has been spending six months a year on the road which put a tremendous strain on the marriage."

AUG 19 (Sat.) *Burning Love* entered *Billboard*'s "Hot 100" chart at number 90 where it stayed fifteen weeks and reached number 2. This was the highest any Elvis single had reached since *Suspicious Minds* topped the chart in 1969. It was also Elvis' last top ten single in the "Hot 100."

AUG 21 (Mon.) During the midnight show, Elvis split the inseam in his pants during *Proud Mary*, the third song in the set. With some help from Charlie Hodge, Elvis changed behind the curtain and came out holding the pants while singing *Until It's Time For You To Go*. Up to that night, he had been wearing a two-piece suit. The next night, and for the remainder of the engagement, Elvis wore jumpsuits brought out from Los Angeles.

AUG 22 (Tues.) Tom Jones attended Elvis' midnight show.

AUG 23 (Wed.) *Variety*'s review of Elvis' Las Vegas act said, in part, "Showing more discipline this time than last, he has a smoother running turn with a welcome absence of horseplay and inside gags with his musicians. It's a pleasant party with the legend at his best."

AUG 26   (Sat.) RCA Records filed a suit against Buddah Records in New York's Supreme Court for distribution of the "Current Audio Magazine" (see July 24, 1972).

Judge Harry Frank denied RCA's petition for an injunction of the sale of the "magazine." RCA had contended that they had exclusive rights to Elvis' performances and image. The judge, in his remarks, stated that he did not feel that Elvis' press conference statements constituted "a performance." It was noted that the right to *print* reports of what a celebrity said is protected under the First Amendment, but whether or not that same right allows a party to use a recording of the voice was yet to be adjucated.

AUG 27   (Sun.) Priscilla and Lisa Marie traveled from Los Angeles to Las Vegas, where they attended several of Elvis' performances during his last week at the Hilton.

During the month, there was a telethon over a Los Angeles TV station. Colonel Parker called from Las Vegas to say that Elvis would donate half of the amount on the tote board at the end. The amount which Elvis donated was $85,000.

During the engagement at the Hilton, Elvis was awarded a gold record for the album **Elvis As Recorded Live At Madison Square Garden**. He was presented with the award by RCA executive George Parkhill in his dressing room between shows.

SEPTEMBER

SEP 2   (Sat.) Elvis performed a special 3:00 a.m. show (on the morning of the 3rd). Celebrities attending included Tom Jones, Shirley MacLaine, and Marty Allen.

SEP 4   (Mon.) Elvis closed at the Las Vegas Hilton. He stayed in Las Vegas for three weeks, attending several shows, before returning to his home in Holmby Hills. Among the shows that he attended was the Rowan and Martin review at the Tropicana, with Vernon, Joe Esposito, Charlie Hodge, and two others.

SEP 5   (Tues.) In the early morning hours, there was a press conference at the Las Vegas Hilton to announce that the proposed worldwide television concert had been changed from November to January. The venue was still to be Honolulu. The announcement was made by Rocco Laginestra, President of RCA Records. Elvis was present, and said that he hoped that he wouldn't let his fans down.

The hour-long concert on January 14, 1973 would be broadcast via satellite to Southeast Asia, including Japan and Australia. The following night it would be seen in twenty-eight European countries. That performance, plus an additional thirty minutes added at a later date, would constitute "Aloha From Hawaii," to be seen over NBC-TV at a later date. It was predicted that the program would reach the largest audience in the history of television.

In the press release from RCA, it was announced that for the first time ever, the album from the concert would be marketed on a global basis simultaneously. It was predicted that the album would have an advance order of one million copies worldwide.

late SEP In late September, Elvis returned to Memphis for a week before flying back to Los Angeles.

Late in September, Elvis recorded the spoken dialog for the movie "Elvis On Tour" at the M-G-M studios in Culver City.

OCTOBER

In October, the Warner Paperback Library published a paperback version of Jerry Hopkins' book, *Elvis: A Biography*.

During October, Elvis vacationed in Las Vegas.

OCT 20 (Fri.) NBC-TV aired "Change Of Habit" on "Friday Night At The Movies."

OCT 28 (Sat.) *Burning Love* peaked at number 2 on *Billboard*'s "Hot 100" chart. It remained in the number 2 position for only one week.

NOVEMBER

NOV 1 (Wed.) "Elvis On Tour" opened in theaters in the United States. In most locations, the "B" feature was "Elvis — That's The Way It Is." "Elvis On Tour" won the Golden Globe award as the best documentary of 1972.

In its review of "Elvis On Tour," *Variety* called the picture "a bright entertaining pop music documentary."

NOV 2 (Thurs.) The *Hollywood Reporter* said "Elvis On Tour" was "little more than an ambitious public relations tract."

| early | Early in November, Elvis returned to Los Angeles, where he attended a karate demonstration held by Ed Parker, one of Elvis' bodyguards. He also rehearsed for his next tour, which would begin in less than a week. |

NOV 6 (Mon.) The *Las Vegas Sun* reported that Elvis would not be switching from the Hilton to the new M-G-M Grand Hotel in 1974. The paper quoted Colonel Parker as saying that such a move was out of the question. After all, the Colonel pointed out, the M-G-M Grand seated 600 fewer people in its showroom, and what hotel could match the Hilton's generous offer.

NOV 8 (Wed.) Elvis began a new tour with a concert in the Lubbock, Texas, Municipal Coliseum at 8:30 p.m. Ticket prices for this tour remained at $10, $7.50 and $5. Over 10,000 fans turned out for the show.

NOV 9 (Thurs.) Elvis moved on to the Tucson, Arizona, Community Center Arena for an 8:30 p.m. show, with 9,700 attending.

NOV 10 (Fri.) In the afternoon, Elvis' private jet landed at the Southwest Air Rangers strip in El Paso. Elvis stayed on the second floor of the Hilton Hotel. That night, at 8:30 p.m., Elvis appeared at the Coliseum in front of a crowd of 9,000.

NOV 11 (Sat.) The album **Burning Love And Hits From His Movies** entered *Billboard*'s LP chart at number 65, where it stayed twenty-five weeks and reached number 22.

The tour moved on to the West Coast for an 8:30 p.m. concert in the Oakland Coliseum. Attendance was over 14,000. Backstage, Nancy Laity Parker was led to Elvis' dressing room, where she received a big kiss from Elvis and Vernon. (See February 23, 1957.) The story made the front page of the *San Francisco Chronicle* again!

Elvis stayed at the Oakland Hilton. During the "party" that generally followed Elvis' shows, he complained of not feeling well and he went to bed early.

NOV 12 (Sun.) Elvis performed a 5:00 p.m. show in San Bernadino's Swing Auditorium. Over 7,200 fans were on hand.

NOV 13 (Mon.) Still in San Bernadino, Elvis gave a concert at 8:30 p.m. Again, over 7,200 were in attendance.

NOV 14 (Tues.) Elvis appeared at the Long Beach Arena at 8:30 p.m. Attendance was pegged at over 14,000.

NOV 15 (Wed.) "Elvis On Tour" entered *Variety*'s "50 Top-Grossing Films" at number 18 for the week ending

November 8th. It stayed on the chart for two weeks, peaking at number 13.

Lisa Marie and Linda Thompson were Elvis' guests for the second concert in Long Beach at 8:30 p.m. Again, the attendance was reported at 14,000.

NOV 16 (Thurs.) Elvis flew from Los Angeles to Honolulu. During the next five days, he stayed in the penthouse of the Hawaiian Village Hotel's Rainbow Towers, part of the Hilton chain.

NOV 17 (Fri.) Elvis gave a show at 8:30 p.m. in the Honolulu International Center. Attendance was 8,500. Elvis was on stage for an hour and ten minutes. Among the songs that he sang was *I'll Remember You*, composed by Hawaiian Kui Lee. Approximately 3,000 fans from Japan were on hand for the concert. They had chartered eight to ten jets for the trip.

NOV 18 (Sat.) There were two more shows at the International Center. The 2:30 p.m. matinee drew a crowd of 8,400, and Elvis was on stage for an hour. The evening show at 8:30 p.m. had an attendance of over 9,000 and Elvis performed for an hour and five minutes.

NOV 19 (Sun.) Elvis rested from the tour in Hawaii. He remained in seclusion in his penthouse suite at the Hawaiian Village Hotel.

NOV 20 (Mon.) Elvis attended a press conference in the Rainbow Rib Room of the Hilton's Hawaiian Village Hotel. It was announced that the upcoming concert, planned for world-wide telecast on January 14, 1973, would be a benefit for the Kui Lee Cancer Fund. Lee was Hawaii's most prolific singer-composer, and he was a victim of cancer. Elvis and the Colonel started the benefit by donating a check for $1,000.

late NOV Elvis returned to Los Angeles shortly after the 20th.

The November issue of *Hi-Fi* magazine published an article on the "Merchandising Of Elvis."

According to the cover story in *TV Radio Show* magazine, "Elvis To Wed Dancer," Sandra Zancan was in Elvis' future.

DECEMBER

DEC 1 (Fri.) A "limited pre-seizure hearing" was set for December 22nd on a suit brought against Elvis in connection

with $23,676 in furnishings that had been removed
from the gun club which had occupied the Flying Circle
G Ranch site between the time Elvis sold it to the club
in May 1969, and then obtained it again in late June
1972 in a foreclosure auction. The suit was filed November 29th by D.L. McClellan, former head of the gun
club.

DEC 2   (Sat.) *Separate Ways* started up the "Hot 100" chart in
            Billboard at number 72 where it stayed twelve weeks
            and reached number 20.

early-mid   Early in the month, Elvis traveled to Las Vegas, where he
DEC   was spotted at a Paul Anka show at Caesar's Palace.
            By the middle of December, he was back in Memphis.

DEC 21   (Thurs.) The *Memphis Press-Scimitar* noted that Elvis
            had donated thousands of dollars to local charities.

DEC 22   (Fri.) U.S. District Court Judge William C. Keady ordered
            that D.L. McClellan be allowed to take some furnishings
            from Elvis' Flying Circle G Ranch. McClellan had pur-
            chased the ranch from Elvis, then lost it in a foreclo-
            sure auction, and he claimed that he had installed over
            $25,000 worth of fixtures and furnishings at the ranch.
            The judge allowed a portion to be removed, and the rest
            was tagged until a determination could be made as to
            the owner.

late DEC   Lisa Marie arrived at Graceland a few days before Christmas
            to spend the holidays with Elvis.

DEC 25   (Mon.) Elvis gave Linda Thompson a mink coat for a
            Christmas present, and then had her model it for those
            present.
            The Christmas card from Elvis and the Colonel had a shot
            of Elvis performing, superimposed with two St. Ber-
            nards and Colonel Parker in a Santa suit standing beside
            a Christmas tree.

DEC 30   (Sat.) In *Billboard*'s annual year-end review of music,
            Elvis was the number 41 singles artist, and the number
            23 album artist.

DEC 31   (Sun.) Elvis hosted a New Year's Eve party at Graceland.

In 1972, Elvis received his second of three Grammy awards for the
album **He Touched Me**. The award from the National Academy
of Recording Arts and Sciences was for "Best Sacred Recording."

Elvis was the December cover story in *Hit Parader* magazine,
which covered his press conference in New York City in June,
and featured a four-page section of color photos of him.

Elvis: The Hollywood Years was the title of a one-shot magazine
that reached the stands during 1972.

In 1972, Elvis was given the *Photoplay* magazine's "Special Editor's Award."

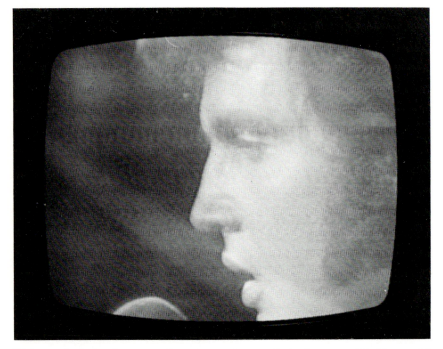

Elvis reached the largest audience ever for a televised event with his special "Elvis: Aloha From Hawaii" on January 14, 1973.

I'm Left, You're Right, She's Gone

ALL
SHOOK
UP
ELVIS
Day-By-Day,
1973

JANUARY

JAN 7   (Sun.) Elvis departed Memphis for Los Angeles.
         Tickets went on sale at the International Center Arena
         box office in Honolulu for Elvis' January 14th concert.
         Mail orders had been accepted for about two weeks pre-
         viously, and 4,000 of the 5,500 available seats had been
         taken. Seating was cut by 3,000 due to the large
         amount of television gear installed in the Center. Tickets
         were obtainable by making a donation to the Kui Lee
         Cancer Fund, with no minimum being set. The dress re-
         hearsal was to be opened for ticket sales as soon as the
         main show sold out. By 6:00 p.m., only 100 tickets re-
         mained in the box office for the January 14 concert.

JAN 8   (Mon.) In anticipation of the live broadcast of Elvis' show,
         "Elvis Presley Week" was declared in Japan.

JAN 9   (Tues.) Elvis flew from Los Angeles to Honolulu. He
         arrived at the International Airport at 4:00 p.m. He
         took a helicopter to the Hilton's Hawaiian Village Hotel,
         where his landing was filmed for use in the upcoming
         TV special.

JAN 10   (Wed.) Elvis rehearsed for the upcoming TV satellite
         special.

JAN 11   (Thurs.) Rehearsals continued.

JAN 12   (Fri.) At 8:30 p.m., there was a full-dress rehearsal with
         an audience. Almost six thousand fans jammed the In-
         ternational Convention Center.

JAN 13   (Sat.) The mayor of Honolulu declared "Elvis Presley
         Day."

JAN 14   (Sun.) At 12:30 a.m., Elvis again made entertainment
         history with his concert at the Honolulu International
         Convention Center, which was beamed via Globecom
         Satellite live to most of the countries in the Far East,

including Australia, South Korea, Japan, Thailand, the Philippines, and South Vietnam. Ratings for the show were among the highest ever recorded: Japan, 37.8% of all viewers; the Philippines, 91.8% of the viewing audience; Hong Kong, 70% of all viewers; Korea, 70-80% of viewers. The show was beamed from Hong Kong to Macao on the Chinese mainland, where it was viewed by thousands in Communist China itself. The show was seen on a delayed basis later in thirty countries in Europe. The total estimated audience was over one billion. It was the most expensive entertainment special up to that time, with costs estimated at $2.5 million.

At the end of the performance, Elvis removed his jeweled cape and hurled it into the audience. It was caught by Bruce Spinks, sports writer for the *Honolulu Advisor*.

Admission fees for the main concert and the dress rehearsal came to $75,000, which was donated to the Kui Lee Cancer Fund. The original estimate had only come to $25,000.

Following the live show, Elvis recorded several "studio" songs, which would be included in the United States version of "Elvis: Aloha From Hawaii."

Following all of this, Elvis returned to his hotel and slept for twenty-four hours straight.

JAN 15   (Mon.) Elvis returned to Los Angeles.

JAN 17   (Wed.) The *Los Angeles Times*, in a belated review of "Elvis On Tour," said: "Both off stage and on, Presley comes across as an assured, relaxed, thoroughgoing pro who knows exactly what he's doing and enjoys it immensely."

JAN 26   (Fri.) Elvis opened at the Las Vegas Hilton. He gave a single show on this date, but there were the usual two shows a night, at 8:15 p.m. and midnight, for the remainder of the engagement. In the audience for opening night was Redd Foxx.

JAN 27   (Sat.) The **Separate Ways** LP entered *Billboard*'s album chart at number 117. It stayed on the chart for eighteen weeks, peaking at number 46.

JAN 28   (Sun.) "Elvis On Tour" won the Golden Globe award as the "Best Documentary" of 1972. The ceremony was televised from New York over the Metromedia Group's TV stations from 9 to 10:30 p.m. (EST).

Priscilla outside her boutique "Bis & Beau."

JAN 31 (Wed.) Because of the flu, Elvis spent one night in the Sunrise Hospital in Las Vegas, where he underwent treatment for a throat ailment. Both shows were cancelled for this night.

Elvis was featured on the cover of the *Harrison Tape Guide* magazine's January-February issue.

In January, Priscilla opened a clothing boutique on Robertson Avenue in Hollywood with Olivia Bis. It was called "Bis & Beau," and the establishment was an immediate hit with the Beverly Hills crowd. Priscilla helped by designing many of the clothes for the shop.

FEBRUARY

FEB 1 (Thurs.) Elvis returned to the Hilton to do the dinner show at 8:00 p.m., but he was unable to go back on stage at midnight, and he returned to the hospital for treatment. Lisa Marie attended the show to celebrate her fifth birthday.

FEB 7 (Wed.) *Variety*, in its review of Elvis' Las Vegas engagement, said, in part, "Colonel Tom Parker has returned to the Hilton, hawking his elixir of unbottled sex and satisfaction, Elvis Presley . . . Presley returns with one of his better programs, inserting many of his primitive rockers juxtaposed with hits along the way to the current 'Burning Love.' He may be merchandised beyond belief, yet possesses too much musicality to become the colonel's mechanized doll — at least onstage."

FEB 13 (Tues.) Just prior to the 8:00 p.m. show, it was announced to the awaiting audience "that due to an illness, Elvis had been advised by his doctors not to perform that night, but that Elvis had decided he would perform, even though it was against his doctor's orders. The show would start thirty minutes late and would be the only show that evening." Considering the announcement, Elvis put on a fine show. (Later, Elvis gave Dr. Sidney Boyers a white Lincoln Continental as a gift.)

FEB 14 (Wed.) Again, Elvis performed only the dinner show. It was apparent that he had a bad case of laryngitis, as his voice was very hoarse.

FEB 15 (Thurs.) In the middle of the dinner show, Elvis had to leave the stage while the Stamps sang *Walk That*

Lonesome Road, Sweet Sweet Spirit, When It's My Time, How Great Thou Art, and *I Should Have Been Crucified.* After about twenty minutes, Elvis returned to the stage, just as the orchestra was beginning the opening notes of *Can't Help Falling In Love.* Before the curtain dropped, Elvis stopped it and started the show in the middle. He sang four songs before ending with *Can't Help Falling In Love*, again.

FEB 17 (Sat.) Just before the dinner show, Elvis was presented with a trophy from the American Cancer Society in recognition of his benefit show the previous January in Honolulu.

FEB 18 (Sun.) During the midnight show, in the early morning hours of the 19th, first one man, then three others, came on stage. The first man was subdued by Red West and taken backstage. The remaining three men were met by Sonny West, Jerry Schilling, Jerry Scheff, as well as Vernon Presley and Tom Diskin of Colonel Parker's office. In the short melee that ensued, Elvis knocked one of the men off the stage into the audience, where he smashed a table. Brothers Roberto and Kenneth McKenzie, Jr., and Mario Martinez, all from Peru, and Marcello Jose Filas of Nicaragua, were arrested on charges of public intoxication.

Elvis' comments to the crowd after the fight were "I'm sorry ladies and gentlemen . . . I'm sorry I didn't break his goddamned neck is what I'm sorry about! . . . If he wants to shake my hand, that's fine. If he wants to get tough, I'll whoop his ass!" Elvis received a seven minute standing ovation.

FEB 19 (Mon.) At 3:00 a.m., following the midnight show, Elvis decided that he wanted Priscilla's boyfriend, Mike Stone, killed. This decision was apparently made when Priscilla told Elvis that she was not going to allow Lisa Marie to come visit Elvis in Las Vegas. Elvis was finally sedated by Dr. Elias Ghanem, but his rage lasted several days.

FEB 20 (Tues.) *Variety* reported that Elvis had been offered $500,000 for six concerts in the 18,000-seat Earl's Court Stadium in London. The concerts would be relayed via closed circuit television to most of England.

FEB 23 (Fri.) Elvis closed at the Hilton.

Souvenir sales of $27,000 were donated by Elvis and

Colonel Parker to the Southern Nevada Society For The Aurally Handicapped.

Elvis stayed at the Hilton as a guest until early March.

FEB 24 (Sat.) **Elvis: Aloha From Hawaii** entered the "Top LPs" chart in *Billboard* at number 99. It remained on the chart for thirty-five weeks, peaking at number 1. It was Elvis' first number 1 album in nine years, since **Roustabout** reached the top spot in January 1965. It was also Elvis' last number 1 album.

Elvis and Linda Thompson attended Ann-Margret's opening night show at the Hilton, and met with her backstage between shows. Later, they went out to catch a few other shows on the Strip.

FEB 26 (Mon.) Elvis and Linda Thompson returned to watch Ann-Margret's show at the Hilton.

MARCH

MAR 1 (Thurs.) Elvis signed a new seven-year contract with RCA Victor even though his current contract did not expire until December 31, 1974. Under the terms of the new contract, Elvis was to provide RCA with two LPs and four singles each year, for which he would receive a royalty of ten cents per single and fifty cents per album (one-half of the royalty would be paid to Elvis and one-half to All Star Shows, owned by Colonel Parker). RCA agreed to pay Elvis and All Star Shows $100,000 each at the end of the seven-year contract. RCA also agreed to pay All Star Tours, also owned by Colonel Parker, $675,000 over the course of the seven years, while RCA Records Tours would match that amount. This payment to Colonel Parker was for his assistance in "planning, promotion, and merchandising." Colonel Parker would also get ten percent of RCA Records Tours profits.

RCA agreed to pay Colonel Parker a $50,000 consultancy fee payable over five years. RCA also agreed to pay another $350,000 over seven years to All Star Tours for Colonel Parker's services for "planning, promotion and merchandising in connection with the operation of the tour agreement."

In addition, RCA paid $5 million (to be split equally between Elvis and the Colonel) to buy back the royalty rights on Elvis' entire catalog up to 1973. After taxes, Elvis would end up with about $1.25 million.

MAR 3   (Sat.) Elvis was reportedly still staying at the Hilton Hotel in Las Vegas. Among the shows which he attended was that of comedian Marty Allen and Mama Cass Elliot at the Flamingo. Both stars were invited back to Elvis' suite, and Elvis and Miss Elliot sang gospel songs all night.

late MAR In late March, Elvis started rehearsals in Los Angeles (probably at RCA's studios) prior to starting his spring tour.

The March issue of *Films And Filming*, the distinguished British film magazine, said of "Elvis On Tour," "It's difficult to distinguish between the public Elvis and the personal Elvis, if indeed anything of the personal is presented, if indeed it exists." *Screen Stories*' cover story was "Elvis Gets Priscilla Back Home Again!"

APRIL

APR 4   (Wed.) The TV special, "Elvis: Aloha From Hawaii" was broadcast at 8:30 p.m. (EST) over NBC-TV. The Nielsen ratings placed the show at number 1 for the night and the week with 33.8% of homes with TV tuned in, and 51% of those watching TV viewing Elvis.

APR 7   (Sat.) Elvis, along with Linda Thompson, Joe Esposito, Charlie Hodge, Gee Gee and Patsy Gamble, Jerry Schilling, and King Rhee, Elvis' karate instructor, flew from Los Angeles to San Francisco. They stayed at the Hyatt Hotel.

APR 8   (Sun.) Elvis attended the California Karate Championships at the Civic Auditorium. Advance publicity said that Elvis would perform a demonstration in brick breaking prior to the 7:30 p.m. championship matches. However, there was a problem with Elvis' scheduled appearance, in that Elvis had a contract with the Sahara Tahoe Hotel which forbade any "personal appearances" within a radius of 300 miles and within thirty days of his engagements at Lake Tahoe. Elvis did attend and watched the final bouts from the stands.

APR 14   (Sat.) *Steamroller Blues/Fool* entered the "Hot 100" chart in *Billboard* at number 80, where it stayed twelve weeks and reached number 17.

APR 20   (Fri.) In Philadelphia, Elvis purchased a custom-made
         Cadillac station wagon.
APR 22   (Sun.) Elvis started a new tour with a concert in the
         Veterans Memorial Coliseum in Phoenix at 3:00 p.m.
         Tickets for this tour were the usual $10, $7.50 and $5.
         Over 15,000 fans attended the show, which grossed over
         $120,000. Jerry Scheff was no longer the bass player,
         having been replaced by Emory Gordy. Scheff had re-
         portedly returned to his native Vancouver, Canada, to
         live on his island.
APR 23   (Mon.) Attendance was 8,500 at the Anaheim Conven-
         tion Center for Elvis' 8:30 p.m. show. Lisa Marie was
         in the audience, along with Linda Thompson and two
         other women.
APR 24   (Tues.) Still in Anaheim, Elvis had another 8:30 p.m. con-
         cert with about 8,500 attending.
APR 25   (Wed.) There were two shows at Fresno's Selland Arena,
         one at 3:30 and one at 8:30 p.m. A total of $120,000
         was grossed as 7,500 attended each show. Once again,
         Lisa Marie and Linda Thompson were part of the audi-
         ence, this time for both performances.
APR 26   (Thurs.) Elvis appeared at the San Diego International
         Sports Arena at 8:30 p.m. Again, the total gross was
         set at $120,000 as 15,000 fans attended.
APR 27   (Fri.) Still on the West Coast, Elvis traveled to Portland
         for an 8:00 p.m. concert in the Coliseum. All reports
         place this show as the best of the tour, with Elvis on
         stage for an hour-and-five minutes. Attendance was
         pegged at 14,000 and the show grossed over $100,000.
APR 28   (Sat.) There were two shows in Spokane in the Coliseum
         at 3:00 and 8:00 p.m. During the matinee, Elvis had a
         lot of trouble with the sound system and the show was
         not up to par. Neither show was a complete sell out,
         with less than 100 tickets remaining. There were over
         6,500 fans present for each performance and the gross
         receipts came to $100,000 for both shows.
APR 29   (Sun.) Another pair of concerts was held at 3:00 and
         8:00 p.m. in the Seattle Center Arena. Elvis mentioned
         that he had been in Seattle filming "It Happened At
         The World's Fair" when he was "young . . . really
         young." Attendance was 8,000 for each show with a
         total gross of $130,000.

APR 30   (Mon.) Over 13,000 fans were on hand for Elvis' 8:00
            p.m. concert in Denver's Coliseum.

    Elvis shared the cover of *Screen Stars* magazine with Steve
    McQueen and Ali McGraw. The accompanying story, "Elvis
    Warns Steve: You'll Lose Ali, Too!", reported that Ali Mc-
    Graw was taking karate lessons from Chuck Norris, who had
    introduced Priscilla to Mike Stone.

MAY

MAY 4   (Fri.) Elvis opened in the High Sierra Theatre at the
            Sahara Tahoe Hotel in Stateline, Nevada. Emory Gordy
            was now a regular on bass, and the Al Tronti Orchestra
            replaced Joe Guercio and the band from the Las Vegas
            Hilton. The Sahara Tahoe had badly overbooked the
            showroom, and there were reports of near riots as hun-
            dreds of fans who had reservations could not get in
            to the show.
MAY 5   (Sat.) **Elvis: Aloha From Hawaii** peaked at number 1 on
            Billboard's "Top LPs" chart. It remained at number 1
            for only one week.
            It was reported that Elvis had sold his Flying Circle G
            ranch in DeSoto County, Mississippi, to Boyle Invest-
            ment Company.
MAY 13 (Sun.) A special Mother's Day show was given by Elvis
            at 3:00 a.m., with the proceeds going to the Barton
            Memorial Hospital at Lake Tahoe in Elvis' mother's
            name.
            In Great Britain, the radio announced that Elvis was being
            detained at Heathrow Airport by customs officials. It
            turned out that the person was an Elvis imitator named
            Eli Culbertson and the entire episode was a hoax. But
            not before many fans had rushed to the airport for a
            glimpse of their idol.
MAY 16 (Wed.) *Variety*'s review of Elvis' Sahara Tahoe act said, in
            part, "Elvis is neither looking or sounding good. Some
            30 pounds overweight, he's puffy, white faced and
            blinking against the light. The voice sounds weak,
            delivery is flabby with occasional dynamic great effort
            and no enthusiasm."
MAY 17 (Thurs.) Following the midnight show on the 16th, Elvis
            cancelled the remainder of his engagement at the Sahara

Tahoe Hotel due to the flu and a chest infection. He was scheduled to continue through the 20th. Elvis flew back to his Los Angeles home to recuperate.

MAY 29 (Tues.) Priscilla filed a motion in Santa Monica Superior Court to set aside her initial concurrence in the original property settlement in the divorce case with Elvis. Originally, she had settled for a lump sum payment of $100,000 and a few cars.

JUNE

JUN 17 (Sun.) In a belated review of "Elvis On Tour," the *New York Times* said: "The film strips away the storybook myth to find underneath a private person who is indistinguishable from the public one, except for the fact he dresses with somewhat less flamboyance."

JUN 19 (Tues.) Elvis arrived in Mobile, Alabama.

JUN 20 (Wed.) Elvis started another tour with a concert at the Mobile Municipal Auditorium at 8:30 p.m. Over 11,000 fans attended. While in Mobile, Elvis read an article about a summer camp in New Orleans that had been ransacked by thieves. He had Colonel Parker call the Louisiana State Police to tell them that he would restock the camp. A check was forthcoming on July 11th.

JUN 21 (Thurs.) There was a concert in Atlanta at the Omni at 8:30 p.m. The gross receipts were $170,000, as over 17,200 fans were on hand. Following the show, Elvis went directly to the Atlanta International Airport for departure to New York.

JUN 22 (Fri.) Elvis had the first of four shows at the Nassau Veterans Memorial Coliseum in Uniondale, New York. The 8:30 p.m. show was attended by 16,500 fans. Elvis was in fine form, and his medley of rock 'n' roll songs, including *Flip, Flop And Fly*, was a big hit with the audience.

JUN 23 (Sat.) There were two shows, at 3:00 and 8:30 p.m. in Uniondale. Again, over 16,500 were on hand for each show. During the matinee, several pieces of underwear were thrown on stage, prompting Elvis to remark, "We've got a lot of naked people out there, man!" The evening show was very close to his Las Vegas act, with little interplay between Elvis and the crowd.

JUN 24   (Sun.) There was a 3:00 p.m. show in Uniondale, which
          again drew 16,500 fans. The total gross for the four
          shows was set at $600,000. Being Sunday, Elvis ob-
          liged the audience by singing the climactic ending to
          How Great Thou Art through twice.
JUN 25   (Mon.) Elvis performed at 8:30 p.m. in the Pittsburgh
          Civic Arena. Attendance was set at 14,000.
JUN 26   (Tues.) Another show in Pittsburgh drew over 14,000
          fans. The total take for the pair of shows was over
          $250,000.
JUN 27   (Wed.) Attendance was reported to be 13,060 for Elvis'
          8:30 p.m. concert at the Cincinnati Gardens. Total re-
          ceipts topped $125,000.
JUN 28   (Thurs.) Elvis appeared at the Kiel Auditorium in St.
          Louis at 8:30 p.m. Over 12,000 attended for a total
          gross of $100,000. Elvis stayed at the Chase-Park Plaza
          Hotel.
JUN 29   (Fri.) Elvis returned to Atlanta's Omni for an 8:30 p.m.
          show with 17,200 attending.
JUN 30   (Sat.) There were two more shows in Atlanta, at 3:00 and
          8:30 p.m. Again, 17,200 attended each show and the
          total gross for all three shows was set at $500,000.

   Elvis and Linda Thompson made the cover of *Screen Stars* magazine with the accompanying story, "We Find The Woman Elvis
   Will Marry!"

JULY

JUL 1   (Sun.) Elvis continued to tour with two concerts at the
          Municipal Auditorium in Nashville, at 3:00 and 8:30
          p.m. There were 10,000 fans at each show, with a
          total gross of $180,000.
JUL 2   (Mon.) There was a show at Oklahoma City's Myriad
          Center Arena at 8:30 p.m. Attendance was reported at
          15,400, with a total gate of $140,000.
JUL 3   (Tues.) Elvis traveled back to Atlanta for an 8:30 p.m.
          show in the Omni. Again, over 17,000 fans attended,
          for a box office gross of $170,000. Elvis sang *Memphis*,
          one of his least performed songs. Also, Elvis' version of
          Suspicious Minds was equal to his shows of three years
          ago.
          Following the concert, Elvis flew back to Memphis.

JUL 11   (Wed.) Elvis donated a check for $1,000 to a New Orleans boys camp that had lost equipment to vandals. He first heard about the problem on June 20th while in Mobile.

mid-JUL In mid-July, Lisa Marie arrived at Graceland for her month-long summer vacation.

In July, RCA announced that it was releasing a new album, **Elvis**, also known as the "Fool" album. Songs, according to the original order form, were: *Fool, Where Do I Go From Here, It's Impossible, A Blues Jam, I'll Take You Home Again Kathleen, Blue Hawaii, Ku-U-I-Po, No More, Hawaiian Wedding Song*, and *Early Mornin' Rain*. The last five songs had been part of the April "Elvis: Aloha From Hawaii" TV special, which was broadcast in the U.S. The actual songs on the album as it was finally released were: *Fool, Where Do I Go From Here, Love Me Love The Life I Lead, It's Still Here, It's Impossible, (That's What You Get) For Lovin' Me, Padre, I'll Take You Home Again Kathleen, I Will Be True*, and *Don't Think Twice It's All Right*. (The last song was probably the *Blues Jam* mentioned in the first release, as this was later released in an eight-and-a-half-minute version, although the song in this album is only two minutes and forty-five seconds long.)

JUL 21   (Sat.) The album **Elvis** entered the "Top LPs" chart in *Billboard* at number 130. It only stayed on the list for thirteen weeks, peaking at number 52.

Elvis started a recording session at the Stax Studios in Memphis. Musicians for this date were James Burton, guitar; and Ronnie Tutt, drums (both from Elvis' concert band); along with Tommy Cogbill, bass; Bobby Wood, piano; Bobby Emmons, organ; Jerry Carrigan, drums; Charlie Hodge, guitar; and Joe Esposito, percussion. (Hodge and Esposito were regular members of Elvis' "Memphis Mafia.")

Songs recorded on this date were *If You Don't Come Back* and *Three Corn Patches* which appeared on the album **Raised On Rock/For Ol' Times Sake**, and *Take Good Care Of Her*, which was released as a single in January 1974.

JUL 22   (Sun.) Elvis was back at the Stax Studios, where he recorded *Find Out What's Happening* and *Just A Little Bit* for the **Raised On Rock/For Ol' Times Sake** album, and *I've Got A Thing About You Baby*, which would be released as the B-side of the single *Take Good Care Of Her* in January 1974.

JUL 23   (Mon.) Still at the Stax Studios, Elvis recorded another single, *Raised On Rock* and *For Ol' Times Sake*.

JUL 24   (Tues.) Apparently, several of the musicians hired for the Stax sessions, including Burton and Tutt from Elvis' show band, had other commitments, so new replacements were brought in to fill out the last two days of recording: Bobby Manuel and Johnny Christopher joined Charlie Hodge on guitar; Donald Dunn and Al Jackson (of Booker T. & the M.G.'s) sat in on bass and drums. Jerry Carrigan, Joe Esposito, Bobby Wood and Bobby Emmons remained from the previous sessions. Background vocals were handled by J.D. Sumner and the Stamps with Kathy Westmoreland, Jeannie Green, Mary and Ginger Holladay.

There must have been some problem between Elvis and the new musicians because only one track was completed, *Girl Of Mine*, which was released on the **Raised On Rock/For Ol' Times Sake LP.** Elvis then departed the studio, and the musicians laid down an instrumental track to *Good Bad, But Beautiful* which was never overdubbed by Elvis.

JUL 25   (Wed.) Elvis did not show up for this night's session, and producer Felton Jarvis had the musicians record backing tracks to *Color My Rainbow, Sweet Angeline* and *The Wonders You Perform*. Elvis never returned to the studio to overdub these songs. *Sweet Angeline* was overdubbed by Elvis in September, while on vacation in Palm Springs.

JUL 29   (Sun.) Elvis flew from Memphis to Los Angeles to prepare for his August opening at the Las Vegas Hilton.

In July, Elvis received his seventh degree black belt in karate.

AUGUST

AUG 6   (Mon.) Elvis opened at the Las Vegas Hilton for his usual month-long summer engagement. Liza Minelli and Petula Clark were among the opening night guests. Shows were at 8:00 p.m. and midnight.

early   During this engagement, it was reported that Elvis and
AUG   Colonel Parker had a falling out. Although both men were apparently sincere in their anger, the matter was resolved within a day.

AUG 17   (Fri.) Elvis' uncle died. He was one of the gatekeepers
          at Graceland.
AUG 19   (Sun.) During a party in Elvis' penthouse suite, Beverly
          Albreco was allowed to get Elvis in a "full nelson"
          wrestling hold. He kicked her in the ankle while at-
          tempting to break the hold. She allegedly suffered a
          broken ankle. In August 1975, she filed suit for
          damages.
AUG 22   (Wed.) *Variety*'s review of Elvis' Las Vegas act said, in
          part, "Lines are long waiting to get inside . . . What
          audiences see in the flesh is a rather somnolent, lacka-
          daisical superstar attired in bejeweled jumpsuit and
          who, with almost sleepwalking fervor, makes his rounds
          kissing little girls and throwing sweat-stained scarves out
          to eager hands."

Elvis was the cover story in the August issue of *Coronet* magazine.
   The accompanying article was titled "Elvis: The Unhappy Man
   Behind The Myth."
The August issue of *Ladies Home Journal* carried a lengthy inter-
   view with Priscilla titled "My Life With And Without Elvis
   Presley." This was the first time that Priscilla had granted an
   interview.
The third issue of *Playgirl* magazine published a cartoon that pre-
   sented a nude Elvis, discretely covered by a hand-held teddy
   bear. The caption had Elvis singing, "I want to be your teddy
   BARE . . . . "

SEPTEMBER

SEP 2   (Sun.) Elvis gave a special 3:00 a.m. show, during which
          he got a case of the "sillies" (as Tom Diskin called them).
          Elvis burst into laughter throughout the show and had
          to ad lib his way through most of the songs. The Hilton
          Hotel presented Elvis with a special gold chain as
          thanks for doing the show.
SEP 3   (Mon.) Elvis closed at the Las Vegas Hilton. Among the
          many guests at the "wrap" party in Elvis' suite was
          singer Bobbie Gentry.
early SEP Elvis stayed in Las Vegas for over a week attending several
          of the shows on the "Strip," including that of Tom
          Jones.

SEP 11   (Sat.) While practicing karate in his Las Vegas suite, Elvis fractured his wrist and had to be treated at a local hospital's emergency ward.

Elvis, Linda Thompson, and several of his entourage flew to Memphis, where Elvis bought a few cars. Then it was off to Los Angeles to buy jewelry.

SEP 13   (Wed.) Elvis was the cover story in *Zoo World* magazine (a music journal).

mid-SEP   By mid-September, Elvis was resting at his home in Palm Springs. It was during this visit to Palm Springs that a teenager nearly overdosed on Hycodan cough syrup. Although this story received much attention when it was repeated in *Elvis — What Happened?*, at least one person who was present at the time had a different version of what happened. In an article published in the fanzine "Teddy Bear" in May 1980, it was reported that Elvis was not present in the same room as the girl when she was taking the medicine; and, both Red and Sonny West were asleep during the whole incident. According to the article, Red West later admitted that the story was "falsely" related in the book.

SEP 22   (Sat.) *Raised On Rock/For Ol' Times Sake* started climbing *Billboard*'s "Hot 100" chart at number 81, only staying nine weeks and peaking at number 41.

SEP 24   (Mon.) A recording session was held at Elvis' Palm Springs home. This was an attempt to salvage the remains of the July sessions, using the instrumental tracks laid down at the Stax Studios. Elvis was aided by Voice, a vocal group from Nashville, made up of Donnie Sumner, Tim Baty, and Sherrill Nielsen. The pianist on this session was probably Per-Erik Hallin, who worked with Voice. Other musicians were James Burton and probably some of Elvis' friends. *Sweet Angeline* from the July session was successfully overdubbed. New songs recorded at this time were *I Miss You* and *Are You Sincere*. All three pieces ended up as part of the album **Raised On Rock/For Ol' Times Sake.**

SEP 29   (Sat.) *Billboard* reported that Elvis would star in a kung fu/adventure movie to be filmed that year in Hawaii.

SEP 30   (Sun.) In Las Vegas, Baron Hilton, owner of the Hilton Hotel chain, announced that Elvis would remain at the Las Vegas Hilton as an attraction through 1975. Although it was not mentioned, it was generally believed

Leaving court after the divorce is finalized.

at the time that the contract was for $150,000 a week
for eight weeks a year. A non-hotel source said Elvis
could split up the engagement into four two-week group-
ings instead of two four-week engagements, as in the
past.

OCTOBER

OCT 9   (Tues.) Elvis' petition for divorce from Priscilla was
finalized. A modified property settlement was granted
in the Santa Monica Superior Court by Judge Lawrence
J. Rittenband. In the settlement, Elvis agreed to leave
in Priscilla's hands all property conceded in the original
agreement, plus $725,000 to discharge any further
claims on community property, plus one-half of the
proceeds of the sale of the couple's Holmby Hills home,
plus five percent of the total outstanding stock in Elvis
Presley Music, Inc. and White Haven Music, Inc., plus
$4,200 a month for twelve months alimony, plus $4,000
a month for Lisa Marie until maturity or marriage, plus
$6,000 for ten years, plus joint custody of Lisa Marie.
Upon leaving the courthouse, Elvis kissed Priscilla and
drove away in his customized automobile.

OCT 12   (Fri.) Elvis flew back to Memphis.

OCT 15   (Mon.) Fire Engine House No. 29, on Elvis Presley
Boulevard, dispatched an ambulance to Graceland, and
Elvis was rushed to Baptist Hospital where he was admitted for "recurring pneumonia and pleurisy." Additional symptoms were an enlarged colon and toxic
hepatitis. (On August 16, 1977, the official report
stated "hypertension and headaches.")

NOVEMBER

NOV 1   (Thurs.) Elvis was released by Baptist Hospital. He returned to Graceland to rest.

NOV 9   (Fri.) Elvis flew to Palm Springs to continue to recuperate.

NOV 10   (Sat.) The repeat of NBC-TV's "Elvis: Aloha From
Hawaii" special (on the 14th) was cause for *TV Guide*
magazine to feature Elvis on its cover, along with seven
other specials to be aired during the week.

NOV 14   (Wed.) NBC-TV repeated the special, "Elvis: Aloha From
Hawaii," at 8:30 p.m. (EST).

mid-NOV In mid-November, Elvis went to Los Angeles to visit with Lisa Marie and Priscilla.

NOV 19 (Mon.) Elvis returned to Memphis to prepare for an upcoming recording session.

NOV 24 (Sat.) **Raised On Rock/For Ol' Times Sake** entered the *Billboard* LP chart at number 176. It stayed on the chart for thirteen weeks, peaking at number 51.

Mainliner, the magazine of United Air Lines, ran an article entitled "America: 1955--1960," which was accompanied by an artist's rendering of Elvis above such 1950s luminaries as Martin Luther King, Jr., "I Love Lucy," a 1955 Thunderbird, and "Sgt. Bilko."

DECEMBER

DEC 10 (Mon.) Elvis started a week-long series of recording sessions at the Stax Studio in Memphis. This time, there were no "new" musicians on hand to confuse things, and eighteen songs were recorded over the next seven days. James Burton and Johnny Christopher were on guitar; Norbert Putnam played bass; David Briggs and Per-Erik Hallin were on piano and organ; Ronnie Tutt played drums. Background vocals were handled by J.D. Sumner and the Stamps, Kathy Westmoreland, Jeannie Green, Mary Holladay and Susan Pinkington. Also on hand was Voice, the vocal group from Nashville. Songs recorded during the week included *I Got A Feeling In My Body* and *It's Midnight* (10th); *You Asked Me To* and *If You Talk In Your Sleep* (11th); *Mr. Songman, Thinking Of You, Love Song Of The Year,* and *Help Me* (12th); *My Boy, Loving Arms,* and *Good Time Charlie's Got The Blues* (13th); *Talk About The Good Times* (14th); *Promised Land, Your Love's Been A Long Time Coming* and *There's A Honky Tonk Angel* (15th); *If That Isn't Love, Spanish Eyes* and *She Wears My Ring* (16th). There were three singles released from this session, and all three went into the top 20. This was also the last studio session for Elvis for the next fourteen months.

DEC 16 (Sun.) Lisa Marie arrived to spend three days of her Christmas vacation with Elvis at Graceland.

DEC 18 (Tues.) Governor Jimmie Carter of Georgia signed a proclamation naming January 8, 1974, as "Elvis Presley Day" throughout the state. Elvis had performed at the

For The Good Times

JANUARY

JAN 8   (Tues.) For Elvis' thirty-ninth birthday, Georgia celebrated
         "Elvis Presley Day," which had been proclaimed by
         Governor Jimmie Carter the month before.
         In Memphis, fans, led by the mayors of both Memphis
         and Tupelo, paraded down Elvis Presley Boulevard to
         Graceland, where the Humes High School band played
         "Happy Birthday." Elvis appeared on his front porch
         and waved to the crowd.

JAN 12   (Sat.) The *Los Angeles Times* published a story by
         Robert Hilburn which quoted Joel Whitburn's refer-
         ence book, "Top Pop Records 1955--1972." Elvis was
         ranked as the most successful recording artist over the
         period, far outdistancing the Beatles by a two-to-one
         margin in the book's point structure.
         Elvis flew from Memphis to Los Angeles. He started re-
         hearsals for his upcoming engagement in Las Vegas.

JAN 15   (Tues.) Elvis' March tour was announced in the press.

JAN 19   (Sat.) In reviewing **Elvis — A Legendary Performer,
         Volume 1**, *Billboard* called the album "perhaps the
         most significant Presley disk from a historic standpoint."

JAN 22   (Tues.) Elvis traveled to Las Vegas to continue rehearsals.

JAN 26   (Sat.) Elvis opened at the Las Vegas Hilton for the first of
         his newly structured two-week engagements. Shows
         were at 8:00 p.m. and midnight. The original date for
         the opening had been the 25th, but it was set back so
         as not to conflict with Frank Sinatra's "comeback" at
         Caesar's Palace. On opening night, there were two
         shows instead of the usual one, because it was a Satur-
         day. Celebrities included Jack Lord, Ernest Borgnine,
         Lorne Greene, Mike Connors, and Elvis' original come-
         dian, Sammy Shore. Elvis' usual group of backing

vocalists were augmented by Voice, made up of Tim Batey, Donnie Sumner, and Sherrill Nielsen (whom Elvis mistakenly labeled Sean Nielsen). Souvenir sales were handled by the sisters of the Home of the Good Shepherd, who received all monies. During the engagement, Elvis was seen with both Linda Thompson and Shelia Ryan. It was during this engagement that Elvis fired a .22 caliber pistol at a wall light switch in his penthouse. The bullet passed through the wall and nearly hit Linda Thompson, who was in the bathroom on the other side. Fortunately, she was unhurt.

JAN 27   (Sun.) There was only one show on this night. This was the usual "opening night" show, which had been delayed from the night before.

FEBRUARY

FEB 1   (Fri.) Lisa Marie missed her usual birthday trip to see Elvis perform, because she was hospitalized in Los Angeles with tonsillitis.

FEB 2   (Sat.) **Elvis — A Legendary Performer, Volume 1** entered the "Top LPs" chart in *Billboard* at number 130. It stayed on the chart fourteen weeks and peaked at number 43. In reviewing the single *I've Got A Thing About You Baby, Billboard* said the song represented "a good changing sound for him."

FEB 6   (Wed.) *Variety*'s review of Elvis' Las Vegas engagement read, in part, "Despite the thickening around the middle and rather puffy countenance, Presley is the center of attention for femmes who squeal, writhe and grab for his neck scarves whenever he cruises ringside. Certainly the extra poundage doesn't interfere with his familiar type of belting or mooing ballads."

FEB 9   (Sat.) *I've Got A Thing About You Baby* entered *Billboard's* "Hot 100" chart at number 90. It stayed twelve weeks and reached number 39.

Elvis closed his engagement at the Las Vegas Hilton. At a party in Elvis' suite following the last night's show, he played piano and sang *Softly As I Leave You, Early Morning Rain,* and *I'm So Lonesome I Could Cry.*

MARCH

MAR 1   (Fri.) Elvis started a new tour with a concert at the Tulsa, Oklahoma, Oral Roberts University Special Events Center at 8:30 p.m. Over 11,000 fans were on hand. Tickets for this tour remained at $10, $7.50 and $5.

MAR 2   (Sat.) Elvis remained in Tulsa for a second concert at 1:30 p.m. Again, attendance was reported to be over 11,000. The gross receipts for both shows were near $200,000.

MAR 3   (Sun.) Alabama Governor George Wallace proclaimed "Elvis Presley Week" throughout the state in celebration of Elvis' forthcoming appearances, set for Auburn on the 5th and Montgomery on the 6th.

        Meanwhile, Elvis continued to tour, with a pair of concerts in the Astrodome in Houston at 2:00 and 8:00 p.m. A total of 88,149 people attended for an all-time one-day attendance record (up to that time). Elvis stayed on the sixteenth floor of the Shamrock Hotel. Elvis' appearance was part of the Houston Livestock Show and Rodeo.

MAR 4   (Mon.) Elvis was greeted by the mayor of Monroe, Louisiana, when he arrived in his Lear jet at the local airport. That evening, over 8,000 fans were on hand at the Civic Center for his 8:30 p.m. performance.

MAR 5   (Tues.) There was an 8:30 p.m. show at the Auburn, Alabama, University Memorial Coliseum. Attendance was pegged at 13,239, with a gross of $125,000. During the show, Elvis drew the largest applause when he said that he was a fan of the Auburn football team. As he sang *An American Trilogy*, the crowd gave out with a loud rebel yell during the "Dixie" portion of the song.

        After the show, Elvis flew on to Montgomery, Alabama.

MAR 6   (Wed.) Elvis arrived at the Downtowner Motor Inn in Montgomery after midnight; 400 fans were awaiting. The 8:30 p.m. show at the Garrett Coliseum was attended by 11,328 fans for a box office gross of $104,000. Just before the performance, Elvis met briefly with Alabama Governor George Wallace and his wife, who stayed for the entire concert.

MAR 7   (Thurs.) Elvis returned to Monroe, Louisiana, for another concert at the Civic Center. Again, the attendance was over 8,000.

Elvis meets backstage with Alabama Governor George Wallace.

MAR 9   (Sat.) There were a pair of shows at the Charlotte, North Carolina, Coliseum at 2:30 and 8:30 p.m. Attendance for each show was set at 11,960, although one report placed attendance at above 13,000. The total receipts were $250,000. Elvis stayed on the twelfth floor of the Sheraton Motor Inn, where he and his troupe booked twenty-six rooms.

MAR 10   (Sun.) Elvis arrived in the early afternoon at Woodrum Field in Roanoke, Virginia, aboard his Convair 880. The plane made two passes before landing, since the first attempt to land was too fast for the short runway. Elvis went straight to the Civic Center Holiday Inn. The 8:30 p.m. concert at the Roanoke Civic Center drew 10,640 and grossed $95,925. Following the concert, Elvis returned to his hotel room. In the middle of the night, he flew to Hampton Roads, Virginia.

MAR 11   (Mon.) There was a show at the Hampton Roads Coliseum at 8:30 p.m. The gate was $100,000 and a total of 10,957 attended. At one point during the show. Elvis tossed a scarf into the crowd and caused an instant fist fight between two women. A security guard solved the problem by tearing the scarf down the middle.

MAR 12   (Tues.) Elvis appeared at the Richmond, Virginia, Coliseum at 8:30 p.m. The total attendance was 11,791, and the ticket receipts were $109,250.

MAR 13   (Wed.) Over 16,200 attended Elvis' show at the Greensboro, North Carolina, Coliseum at 8:30 p.m. The gross receipts were above $151,000. Elvis arrived at the Coliseum at 9:10 p.m. in one of three limousines. During the concert, Elvis spotted a young boy dressed in a sequined jumpsuit. Elvis motioned to have the boy brought forward, and a scarf was draped around the boy's neck. Then Elvis said jokingly, "Get him outta here . . . he's dressed better than I am!"

MAR 14   (Thurs.) Still in the mid-Atlantic states, Elvis appeared in Murfreesboro, Tennessee, at the Middle Tennessee State University Murphy Athletic Center at 8:30 p.m. Over 12,500 fans were on hand, and the gross receipts topped $112,500. The high point of the evening was Elvis' moving rendition of *Why Me, Lord?*

MAR 15   (Fri.) There were two concerts at the University of Tennessee's Stokley Athletic Center in Knoxville at 2:30 and 8:30 p.m. A total of 13,305 attended each show.

Midway through the show, a little girl was hoisted to the
stage to give Elvis a lei of roses. This was immediately
followed by two women who broke through the security
guards to present Elvis with more leis made of paper.
Elvis commented, "We must be in Hawaii."

MAR 16 (Sat.) Elvis returned to Memphis for four shows in two
        days, at 2:30 and 8:30 p.m. at the Mid-South Coliseum.
        This was Elvis' first appearance in his home town since
        February 1961. Attendance was reported to be 12,300
        for each show.

MAR 17 (Sun.) Elvis continued to perform at the Mid-South Coli-
        seum. The total for the four shows was set at $586,000.

MAR 18 (Mon.) Elvis traveled back to Richmond, Virginia, for an-
        other show at 8:30 p.m. at the Coliseum. The atten-
        dance was 11,791, with a gross of $109,250.

MAR 19 (Tues.) Elvis returned to Murfreesboro, Tennessee, for
        a show at the Middle Tennessee State University Murphy
        Athletic Center at 8:30 p.m. Attendance was 12,500
        for a total gate of $112,500.

MAR 20 (Wed.) Elvis wound up this tour by returning to the Mid-
        South Coliseum in Memphis for an 8:30 p.m. show in
        front of 12,300 fans. RCA was on hand to record this
        show for the album **Elvis As Recorded Live On Stage In
        Memphis.** Elvis was on stage for an hour and a half.

Elvis made the cover of *TV Radio Mirror*, but was barely men-
tioned in the accompanying story, "Don't Marry Your Lover –
Dean Martin's Wife Cathy Warns Linda Thompson."
In *Screen Stories*, Elvis was superimposed with Bobbie Gentry
on the cover, and an article featured the revelation: "Behind
Elvis' Hometown Wedding" (to Miss Gentry).
Elvis was the cover story in the March issue of *Pageant* magazine.

APRIL

APR 4   (Thurs.) The *Memphis Commercial Appeal* reported that
        Elvis had rejected $1 million to tour Australia. Accord-
        ing to legend, Colonel Parker told the promoter that $1
        million was plenty for him, but what about Elvis?

APR 6   (Sat.) **Good Times** started climbing *Billboard*'s album
        chart at number 125. It stayed on the chart for only
        eight weeks, peaking at number 90.

Elvis was superimposed with Cher on the cover of *Movie Mirror*, which carried the story, "Elvis Tells Cher: 'If You Want A Divoce, I'll Pay The Alimony.' "

MAY

MAY 10 (Fri.) Elvis began another tour with a concert in San Bernadino at the Swing Auditorium at 8:30 p.m. Tickets for this tour were $10, $7.50 and $5. Attendance was reported to be above 7,200. Elvis sang *Why Me*, a recent hit for Kris Kristofferson, which Elvis said was his favorite gospel song. He also performed his latest single, *Help Me*, which was due to be released in a week.

MAY 11 (Sat.) There were two shows at the Forum in Inglewood near Los Angeles. Attendance was above 18,500 for both the 2:30 and 8:30 p.m. concerts. Elvis stayed at a hotel across the street from the Forum between shows. Members of the rock band Led Zeppelin attended the evening show.

MAY 12 (Sun.) Elvis appeared at 3:00 p.m. in the Selland Arena in Fresno, California. Over 7,500 fans were present for the show.

MAY 13 (Mon.) Elvis returned to the Swing Auditorium in San Bernadino at 8:30 p.m., where 7,200 attended the show.

MAY 14 (Tues.) Elvis few from Los Angeles to Lake Tahoe to prepare for his upcoming engagement.

MAY 16 (Thurs.) Elvis opened for a ten-day run at the Sahara Tahoe Hotel in Stateline, Nevada. During this engagement, he missed two shows due to the flu. The Al Tronti Orchestra replaced Joe Guercio during this engagement.

MAY 20 (Mon.) In a lawsuit filed on October 11, 1974, Edward L. Ashley claimed that he was beaten by Elvis, Delbert "Sonny" West, David Stanley, and Dick Grob outside of Elvis' penthouse suite at the Sahara Tahoe Hotel on this date. He claimed he had been invited to an after-show party, and then been refused admittance.

MAY 22 (Wed.) *Variety*'s review of Elvis' Lake Tahoe show read, in part, "Looking good this time (though about 10 pounds overweight) and performing with an engaging air of humor and self deprecation, the Elvis appeal hasn't waned."

MAY 23 (Thurs.) Elvis hosted a 2:30 a.m. party to celebrate Linda Thompson's twenty-third birthday. The party was held

in Elvis' fourteenth floor penthouse suite at the Sahara Tahoe Hotel. Elvis complained of being hoarse, and he went to bed about 4:00 a.m.

MAY 26   (Sun.) This is the official date for Elvis' closing at the Sahara Tahoe Hotel, however:

MAY 27   (Mon.) Elvis added one last performance, at 3:00 a.m., to accommodate the crowds who wanted to see him.

JUNE

JUN 8   (Sat.) *If You Talk In Your Sleep* started up the "Hot 100" chart in *Billboard* at number 77, staying thirteen weeks and reaching number 17.

JUN 15   (Sat.) Elvis began his third tour of 1974 by arriving at Meecham Field in Fort Worth at 3:30 a.m. with three jets full of musicians and a turbo-prop full of equipment. Ticket prices for this tour remained at $10, $7.50 and $5. Elvis stayed at the Green Oaks Inn, but the remainder of the troupe stayed at the Holiday Inn several miles away. There were two shows at the Tarrant County Convention Center at 3:00 and 8:30 p.m. Attendance for each show was 14,000.

JUN 16   (Sun.) There were two additional shows in Ft. Worth. Total receipts for the four concerts were $518,417.

JUN 17   (Mon.) Elvis traveled to Baton Rouge for an 8:30 p.m. show at the University of Louisiana's Assembly Center. Attendance was over 15,000.

JUN 18   (Tues.) Elvis stayed in Baton Rouge for another 8:30 p.m. show. Another 15,000 fans attended, and the total receipts for the two days were $290,000.

JUN 19   (Wed.) In Amarillo, Texas, 14,000 fans attended Elvis' concert in the Civic Center at 8:30 p.m. The gate was reported to be over $90,000.

JUN 20   (Thurs.) Elvis arrived in Des Moines during the afternoon and went to the Ramada Inn, where he and his entourage had booked all sixty-seven rooms on the top floor. At 8:30 p.m., over 11,000 fans attended his concert at the Veterans Memorial Auditorium. During the show's closing number, *Can't Help Falling In Love*, seventy-five women stormed the stage for one last scarf or a touch of Elvis' hand. Instead of leaving the stage as soon as the song was finished, Elvis continued to hand out scarves and kiss a lucky few.

JUN 21   (Fri.) The tour stopped at the Cleveland Convention Center Public Hall for an 8:30 p.m. show, attended by 10,000 fans who spent $90,000 for their tickets.

JUN 22   (Sat.) There were two performances at the Civic Center Auditorium in Providence, Rhode Island, at 3:00 and 8:30 p.m. Attendance was 13,113 for each show. Elvis and his entourage flew from Providence to Philadelphia after the show.

JUN 23   (Sun.) The tour arrived at Eppley Airport in Philadelphia shortly after midnight. Elvis then went to the Hilton's Smuggler's Inn. There were two shows in the Spectrum at 3:00 and 8:30 p.m. Total attendance was almost 40,000, and the gate was $360,000.

JUN 24   (Mon.) Elvis and the troupe moved on for another pair of shows at the Niagara Falls International Convention Center at 3:00 and 8:30 p.m. A total of $200,000 was taken in on ticket sales. During the matinee, Elvis had to rescue an usherette from in front of the stage, where she had been pinned by the crush of the crowd. During the evening show, a fist fight broke out in the audience. Elvis stayed at the Parkway Ramada Inn.

JUN 25   (Tues.) Elvis appeared at the St. John's Arena in Columbus, Ohio, at 8:30 p.m. Attendance was 14,000, with a total take of $125,000.

JUN 26   (Wed.) Elvis performed in front of 20,000 fans at an 8:30 p.m. show at the Fair and Expo Center's Freedom Hall in Louisville, Kentucky. Ticket sales were reported to be in excess of $180,000. The din of noise from the audience was so great that the show was stopped several times. At one point, Elvis said, "If this is all I have to do, I've got it made."

JUN 27   (Thurs.) Sixteen thousand attended a performance at 8:30 p.m. at the Indiana University Assembly Hall in Bloomington. The total take was $150,000. Elvis was on stage for sixty-seven minutes.

JUN 28   (Fri.) Elvis' show was attended by 11,800 fans at the Milwaukee Arena at 8:30 p.m. Ticket sales totaled $100,000.

JUN 29   (Sat.) There were two shows, at 3:00 and 8:30 p.m., at the Municipal Auditorium in Kansas City, Missouri. Attendance was 10,400 for each show, for a total gross of $200,000. The evening show was one of Elvis' best. At one point, two girls raised a five-foot tall stuffed toy gorilla on the stage as a gift for Elvis. He stood very still and finally said, "That son of a bitch better not move!" The audience went wild.

JUN 30   (Sun.) There were also two performances by Elvis at the Civic Auditorium Arena in Omaha at 3:00 and 8:30 p.m. Attendance was 10,246 for the matinee and 10,311 for the evening show. Total receipts were $180,000.

JULY

JUL 1   (Mon.) Still in Omaha, Elvis gave an 8:30 p.m. show for 10,440 fans, who paid $90,000 for tickets.

JUL 2   (Tues.) There was one final show of this tour at the Salt Palace in Salt Lake City at 8:30 p.m. Thirteen thousand fans attended.

Following the show, Elvis flew back to Memphis.

JUL 4   (Thurs.) Elvis, who had recently received his seventh-degree black belt in karate, put on a ninety-minute demonstration with Ed Parker at the Tennessee Karate Institute in Overton Park. The TKI was owned by Red West.

JUL 10   (Wed.) Elvis attended the opening game of the new World Football League, as the Memphis Southmen hosted the Portland Storm. During the television broadcast of the game, the announcer mentioned that Elvis was seated in the owner's box. Accompanying Elvis to the Mid-South Coliseum were Red and Sonny West.

JUL 27   (Sat.) **Elvis Recorded Live On Stage In Memphis** entered the "Top LPs" chart in *Billboard* at number 82. It peaked at number 33 and stayed thirteen weeks.

In July, Elvis and several friends vacationed in Hawaii for a couple of weeks. This trip was kept very private, and almost no word of Elvis leaked to the local press.

AUGUST

Elvis returned to Memphis from Hawaii early in the month.

AUG 10   (Sat.) Elvis attended a midnight movie in Memphis.

AUG 12   (Mon.) Elvis left Memphis for Los Angeles to rehearse for his next engagement in Las Vegas.

mid-AUG In mid-August, Elvis traveled to Las Vegas, where he continued to rehearse.

Elvis with fellow performer Jackie Wilson.

AUG 18 (Sun.) Elvis and nineteen of his friends attended a performance of Dick Clark's "Good Ol' Rock 'n' Roll Review," in the casino lounge of the Hilton Hotel. Later, he met with Jackie Wilson, one of the stars of the review.

AUG 19 (Mon.) Elvis opened at the Las Vegas Hilton. For opening night, there was only one show at 10:00 p.m. During the remainder of the engagement, shows were at 8:00 p.m. and midnight. Opening night, Elvis started the show without the "2001" orchestral introduction, and his first song was *Big Boss Man*. He did not do many of his older songs, relying on mostly new material. The audience was caught off guard, and the applause was polite but not overwhelming.

It was during this engagement that Elvis met in his dressing room with Barbra Streisand. They discussed the possibility of Elvis co-starring with her in a remake of "A Star Is Born." Elvis, at first, seemed to welcome the chance to prove his acting ability, but negotiations with Colonel Parker broke down over salary demands.

The souvenir booth was operated to aid the Aurally Handicapped Children. One of the hot items was a special album titled **Having Fun With Elvis On Stage**, which was issued by Elvis and the Colonel on their Boxcar label.

AUG 20 (Tues.) It was back to "2001" and the old songs for the rest of the engagement. Reaction from the crowd was much better. Elvis did have a few new songs which were included in most shows: *Softly As I Leave You, Help Me*, and *If You Talk In Your Sleep*.

AUG 22 (Thurs.) About 3:30 a.m., there was a fire on the twenty-sixth floor of the Hilton, and six fire engines responded. The fire was quickly extinguished, and when the sun came up, all that could be seen was a charred section on the outside of the hotel.

AUG 26 (Mon.) The two performances this night were cancelled because Elvis had the flu. He spent the day with an upset stomach, dressed in black silk pajamas, lying on a couch in his suite.

AUG 27 (Tues.) Elvis was well enough to continue with his performances.

AUG 28 (Wed.) *Variety*'s review of Elvis' Las Vegas opening said, in part, "Presley is in good voice, looks fairly trim and seems to be having a ball."

AUG 29 (Thurs.) Elvis was awarded his eighth-degree black belt
        in karate during a ceremony which was part of his
        evening show. Elvis wore a karate gi and did a demon-
        stration on stage for the audience.

AUG 30 (Fri.) An Evangelical minister was having a telethon from
        a local Las Vegas hotel to raise money for his church.
        J.D. Sumner and the Stamps were guests on the show,
        and the group sang a few songs. When interviewed by
        the minister, J.D. was asked if Elvis might drop by the
        telethon. J.D. responded that he would jump in the
        swimming pool if Elvis did. Elvis called the station and
        pledged $2,500 if J.D. and the Stamps would jump in
        the pool. They did, and Elvis pledged another $1,000
        if the minister would jump in the pool. The minister
        had to be thrown in, but the telethon from a local Las
        Vegas hotel raised $3,500 from Elvis that day.

SEPTEMBER

SEP 2   (Mon.) Elvis closed his two-week engagement at the Hilton
        with a two-hour show, which was among the best he ever
        gave. The highlight had to be a jam session with Voice,
        which included *Without You, Bringing It Back* and
        Aubrey. Priscilla and Lisa Marie were in the audience
        and they shared their booth with Shelia Ryan, Elvis'
        latest girlfriend.
        During this engagement, Elvis and two of his bodyguards
        went into the showroom after the midnight performance
        and painted one of the decorative cherubs black as a
        joke. (One version of this story mentions Sonny West
        and Dave Hebler. Another, Red West and Jerry Schill-
        ing. A third has Sonny West, Jerry Schilling and David
        Stanley, Elvis' stepbrother.)

SEP 3   (Tues.) Elvis and Shelia Ryan attended Tom Jones' mid-
        night show at Caesar's Palace. During Jones' final num-
        ber, a fast gospel-type, Elvis came on stage and did his
        karate routine, much to the delight of the audience.

SEP 4   (Wed.) Elvis, Shelia Ryan, and sixteen friends attended
        Vicki Carr's opening at the Tropicana Hotel. He
        walked on stage during her monolog, and the two stars
        compared diamond rings. Hers was a gift from Elvis.

SEP 5   (Thurs.) Elvis left for Los Angeles about 10:00 p.m.

SEP 8   (Sat.) Elvis was a spectator at Evel Knievel's attempt to rocket over the Snake River Canyon in Idaho. Other celebrities included John Wayne, Steve McQueen, Dustin Hoffman, and President Ford's two sons.

mid-SEP In September, Elvis took delivery of his fourth Stutz Blackhawk in Beverly Hills. The car was valued at $60,000. He also gave a Stutz to Dr. Elias Ghanem, his Las Vegas physician.

By mid-September, Elvis had returned to Memphis.

SEP 17   (Tues.) Photos of Elvis at a karate demonstration appeared in the local Memphis papers. It was reported that he was involved in producing a film on karate, which he would narrate.

SEP 23   (Mon.) Elvis bought the entire stock of Lincoln Continental Mark IV's from Schilling Lincoln-Mercury in Memphis for $60,000. The cars were red, aqua, silver, black, and blue. Salesman Raymond Surber said Elvis drove one of them off the lot. The Continentals were given to Billy Smith (Elvis' cousin), Red West, Marty Lacker (an Elvis aide), Richard Davis (Elvis' valet), and Linda Thompson. Elvis also bought five Cadillacs. He kept two and give the others to Vester Presley (his uncle), Gee Gee Gamble (an aide), and Mrs. George Kline (wife of Elvis' close friend since his days at Humes High).

SEP 27   (Fri.) Elvis started his fourth tour of 1974 with a concert at 8:30 p.m. in the College Park (Baltimore) University of Maryland Fieldhouse. Attendance was reported at 15,000. Ticket prices for this tour remained at $10, $7.50 and $5. Elvis' weight had increased dramatically in the three weeks since closing in Las Vegas. Much of this show, Elvis seemed to be holding on to the microphone for support. For this tour, Elvis had booked the "Playboy" jet, which was owned by the magazine and leased to celebrities.

SEP 28   (Sat.) Elvis remained in College Park for another 8:30 p.m. show, with 15,000 attending. He seemed to be in better health for this show, but his weight was still a problem and seemed to limit his movements on stage.

SEP 29   (Sun.) There was a 2:30 p.m. show in Detroit's Olympia Stadium, attended by 17,105 fans. This was one of Elvis' poorest concerts, and he was reportedly suffering with a temperature of a hundred and two degrees. Elvis

was only on stage for thirty minutes, but he sang fourteen songs before he brought out the backing group,
Voice, to sing three songs while he stood at the back of
the stage.

SEP 30   (Mon.) Elvis performed in South Bend, Indiana, at the
Notre Dame Athletic and Convention Center, at 8:30
p.m. Attendance was 12,301. By all reports, this show
was one of the best Elvis had performed in years. Highlights included a powerful *You Gave Me A Mountain*
and *Let Me Be There*. Elvis was on stage for an hour
and twenty minutes.

In September, Vernon and Dee Presley formally separated.

OCTOBER

OCT 1   (Tues.) Elvis remained at Notre Dame for another show at
8:30 p.m. Again, the sold out audience totaled 12,301.

OCT 2   (Wed.) Elvis traveled to St. Paul for an 8:30 p.m. concert
in the Civic Center. Attendance was 17,163.

OCT 3   (Thurs.) There was another show in St. Paul at 8:30 p.m.
Again, the total paid attendance was 17,163.

OCT 4   (Fri.) Elvis returned to Detroit's Olympia Stadium for another 8:30 p.m. concert, with 17,105 attending.

OCT 5   (Sat.) There were a pair of shows in Indianapolis at the
Expo Convention Center. Attendance was 14,000 for
both the 2:30 and 8:30 p.m. concerts. The matinee was
another of Elvis' poorer shows, but the evening concert
was a complete turnaround. Elvis even performed a version of *That's All Right*, on which he accompanied himself on guitar.

OCT 6   (Sun.) Another pair of concerts were held at the University of Dayton Arena. The attendance for both the 2:30
and 8:30 p.m. show was set at 13,500. Immediately
following this show, Elvis was taken to Cox Airport,
where he flew directly to Kansas City.

OCT 7   (Mon.) There was an 8:30 p.m. concert at the Levitt Arena
in Kansas City. There were over 10,000 fans on hand.

OCT 8   (Tues.) Over 10,500 attended the performance in the San
Antonio Convention Center at 8:30 p.m.

OCT 9   (Wed.) Still in Texas, Elvis performed at the Abilene Expo
Center at 8:30 p.m. in front of 8,604 fans. Vernon flew
from Memphis with Lisa Marie and Linda Thompson for

the concert. Reportedly, he was so upset with Elvis'
appearance that he had the family physician, Dr. George
Nichopoulos, come out from Memphis as well.

After the show, Elvis and his crew flew to Lake Tahoe.

OCT 11   (Fri.) Edward L. Ashley, a real estate developer from
Grass Valley, California, filed a $6.3 million suit against
Elvis and several of his bodyguards for an alleged beating
that took place at the Sahara Tahoe Hotel on May 20,
1974.

Elvis opened at the Sahara Tahoe Hotel in Stateline,
Nevada. He performed at 8:15 p.m. and midnight
through the weekend. This was the first time that tickets had been sold for shows in the High Sierra Theatre,
and no dinner show was offered. The eight shows were
to make up for the cancelled performances the previous
May.

OCT 14   (Mon.) Elvis closed at the Sahara Tahoe Hotel.

mid-OCT Elvis traveled back to Los Angeles, where his home at 144
Monovale was up for sale. It was sold to Telly Savalas
in March 1975. One account had Elvis staying in Santa
Monica. He divided his time between Los Angeles, Palm
Springs, and Memphis until mid-November.

OCT 26   (Sat.) *Promised Land* entered the "Hot 100" in *Billboard*
at number 86 where it stayed thirteen weeks and
reached as high as number 14.

late OCT Elvis' English fan club reported that in late October Elvis
had been in a fight with a service station manager, and
that Elvis had been exonerated. (No further information
is available.)

The October issue of *Pageant* magazine featured Elvis on the cover.
The accompanying article was entitled "Elvis At 40."

NOVEMBER

It was rumored that Elvis had showered Priscilla with gifts and had
asked her to remarry him.

NOV 2   (Sat.) **Having Fun With Elvis On Stage** started up the "Top
LPs" chart in *Billboard* at number 163. It only stayed
on the chart seven weeks, peaking at number 130.

NOV 19   (Tues.) Elvis flew from Memphis to Palm Springs to relax.

Photoplay featured Elvis on the cover in tribute to his twentieth
anniversary in show business.

DECEMBER

DEC 5   (Thurs.) The Las Vegas Hilton announced, "Elvis Presley's
            next appearance in our Showroom is from January 26th
            to February 9th, 1975."
mid-DEC   By the middle of the month, Elvis was back in Memphis
            preparing for the holiday season.
DEC 20   (Fri.) The *Memphis Press-Scimitar* reported that Elvis had
            given donations to twenty-three charities.
DEC 25   (Wed.) Elvis spent a quiet Christmas at Graceland.
DEC 28   (Sat.) In *Billboard*'s annual "Talent In Action" review,
            Elvis was ranked number 67 as a singles artist and number
            35 as an album artist.

   In 1974, Elvis received the *Photoplay* magazine award as the "Most
   Popular Variety Star," based on a poll of the magazine's reader-
   ship.
   Elvis' income for 1974 was reported by his Memphis accountants
   to be $7,273,622, with over $6 million coming from appearances
   in Las Vegas, Lake Tahoe and in concert. The rest was divided
   between record royalties and publishing rights, and movie ren-
   tals to theaters and television. But, Elvis spent all of that and
   more on "expenses" of both a business (over $4 million) and
   personal (over $3 million) nature.
   Elvis was the cover artist of the second volume of *The Story of
   Rock*, a hardcover series of books on rock-and-roll.

Elvis' fortieth birthday generated these two magazine cover stories.

For The Heart

JANUARY

JAN 8   (Wed.) Elvis celebrated his fortieth birthday quietly at Graceland. There was a private dinner party with his constant companion, Linda Thompson, around 9:00 p.m. Among other things, Elvis was suffering from the flu. Newspapers reported that Elvis was "fat and forty," and that he spent a "lonely day fighting a weight problem." Nevertheless, the number of visitors to the gates of Graceland exceeded 2,000. The *Memphis Press-Scimitar* reported that Elvis' Las Vegas engagement of January 26th to February 9th had been cancelled so Elvis could fight his weight problem. (The Las Vegas Hilton quickly put out a news release stating that the reason for the cancellation was so that Elvis could be the first to appear at the grand opening of the new $20 million addition, scheduled for April 1st.)

JAN 13   (Mon.) *People* magazine featured Elvis on its cover, accompanied by an article titled "Elvis The Pelvis Turns 40, But He Isn't All Shook Up." The cover photo was from Elvis' June 1972 press conference in New York.

JAN 17   (Fri.) In Memphis, Elvis went on one of his car-buying sprees. By days' end, he had purchased eleven Cadillacs for his friends.

       Two co-eds from Mississippi, Patsy Haynes, nineteen, and Areecia "Honeybee" Benson, seventeen, had themselves shipped to Graceland in a crate marked "Russian Wolfhounds." R.E.A. Express delivered the box to the gatehouse at Graceland, but when Uncle Vester called the mansion, he was told that Elvis did not need any more dogs. The crate was loaded back on the truck, at which point the girls were discovered. They never got to see Elvis.

JAN 18   (Sat.) Watermark, Inc. started soliciting clients for its ex-
          panded, thirteen-part version of "The Elvis Presley
          Story" radio special.
          Billboard, in reviewing the **Promised Land** LP, said: "This
          record shows his ability to sing country or pop together
          or separately."

JAN 21   (Thurs.) Elvis put in a $1.5 million bid for the plush Boeing
          707 jet which had belonged to Robert L. Vesco. The
          plane had been empounded after Vesco, a fugitive finan-
          cier, defaulted on payments. Vesco had been indicted
          by former U.S. Attorney General John Mitchell for
          allegedly trying to influence an inquiry by the Securities
          and Exchange Commission in exchange for a large con-
          tribution to President Richard Nixon's 1972 campaign
          for re-election.
          The jet had a gym, sauna and discotheque. At this time, it
          was parked at the Newark, New Jersey, International
          Airport. Elvis made a down payment of $75,000 to se-
          cure his bid.

JAN 25   (Sat.) *My Boy* started up *Billboard*'s "Hot 100" chart at
          number 82, reaching number 20 and staying eleven
          weeks.
          The current issue of *Now* magazine in Las Vegas had Elvis
          on the cover, and announced that he would be playing
          the Hilton Hotel from January 26th through February
          9th. The engagement had been cancelled two weeks
          earlier.

JAN 29   (Wed.) Elvis was admitted to the Baptist Memorial Hospi-
          tal in Memphis at 4:00 a.m. He stayed on the eighteenth
          floor of the Madison East Wing. It was reported that
          Elvis would receive a "general medical workup," and that
          he had a "liver problem." (On August 16, 1977, the
          official reason for the hospitalization was given as "hy-
          pertension and an impacted colon.")

JAN 30   (Thurs.) A hospital spokesman said that Elvis was feeling
          rather well, that he was up, and that he was undergoing
          a series of tests.

FEBRUARY

FEB 1   (Sat.) **Promised Land** entered the "Top LPs" chart in *Bill-
          board* at number 102. It stayed on the chart twelve
          weeks and peaked at number 47.

FEB 5   (Wed.) Vernon Presley suffered a major heart attack and
           was admitted to Baptist Memorial Hospital.
FEB 13   (Thurs.) Lawyers for Elvis sought to withdraw Elvis'
           offer to buy the Vesco jet. In the Newark, New Jersey,
           Superior Court, Judge Irwin I. Kimmelman ordered
           Elvis' down payment of $75,000 be held until the issue
           could be decided at a later hearing. The *New York
           Times* reported that the sale of the Boeing 707 had
           been "snagged" by a telegram, allegedly sent by agents
           of Vesco, threatening to have the jet seized if it landed
           outside the U.S.
FEB 14   (Fri.) Between midnight and 1:00 a.m., Elvis was released
           from Baptist Memorial Hospital. He was taken back to
           Graceland to rest.
mid-FEB   During his recovery, Elvis was frequently seen driving his
           yellow Panterra sports car in Memphis. During this
           time, Elvis bought five new horses and played racquet-
           ball for exercise.
FEB 20   (Thurs.) Elvis went to the Memphian Theater with Linda
           Thompson, Joe Esposito, Red West, and Jerry Schilling
           for midnight movies.
FEB 23   (Sun.) Elvis left Graceland about 9:00 a.m. and returned
           after 8:00 p.m. His whereabouts for the day were un-
           known.
FEB 24   (Mon.) About 9:30 p.m., Elvis went to the Memphian
           Theater with Linda Thompson and Red West. They
           stayed until after 2:00 a.m.

MARCH

In March, British boxing promoter Jack Solomons offered £1
million for Elvis to sing at Earl's Court in London. Colonel
Parker objected to the ticket prices, which would have to be
£20 to £60, which he felt were too high for the average fan.
Another promoter, Arthur Howes, offered £2 million for Elvis
to play Wembley Stadium in London. Colonel Parker said that
Elvis was not interested in playing ball parks.

MAR 1   (Sat.) Elvis was awarded his third of three Grammy awards
           from the National Academy of Recording Arts and Sciences
           during a CBS-TV show. He had been nominated in the
           "Best Sacred Recording" category for *How Great Thou
           Art*, which was included on the album **Elvis Recorded In
           Memphis**. The album **How Great Thou Art** won a Grammy
           in 1967.

MAR 10 (Mon.) Elvis went into RCA's Hollywood studios for a recording session. Musicians were members of his touring
band: James Burton, guitar; Charlie Hodge, guitar; John
Wilkinson, guitar; Duke Bardwell, bass; Ronnie Tutt,
drums; Glenn Hardin, piano; and David Briggs, electric
piano. Backing vocals by Voice and several female vocalists, including Kathy Westmoreland, were added at a
later date by producer Felton Jarvis.
The songs from these sessions were to make up the heart
of Elvis' album, **Today**: *Fairytale, Green Green Grass
Of Home, I Can Help, And I Love You So, Susan When
She Tried,* and *T-R-O-U-B-L-E.*
The session lasted into the early morning hours of the 11th.

MAR 11 (Tues.) Elvis was back in RCA's Hollywood studios for another day of recording. More songs were completed for
the **Today** LP: *Woman Without Love, Shake A Hand,
Bringing It Back,* and *Pieces Of My Life.*

MAR 18 (Tues.) Elvis opened at the Las Vegas Hilton for two
weeks to make up for the engagement in January, which
had been postponed. This opening coincided with the
opening of the Hilton's new thirty-story, 620-room addition, which made it the largest resort and convention hotel in the world. These were the first of the "Elvis In
Concert" engagements in Las Vegas with tickets priced
at twenty dollars. There were no dinner or cocktail
shows in the usual sense. Shows were scheduled for
8:00 p.m. and midnight. Some of the new material for
this engagement included *Fairytale, Green Green Grass
Of Home* and *Promised Land.*
The souvenir stand was operated for the "Aid To Adoption
Of Special Kids." Linda Thompson was not seen with
Elvis, and it was rumored that they had parted company
after she had allowed a photographer inside Graceland.

MAR 20 (Thurs.) The *Memphis Press-Scimitar* ran an article entitled "Presley Carries More Weight At Opening Night In
Vegas."

MAR 26 (Wed.) *Variety*'s review of Elvis' Las Vegas act said, in part:
"He looks healthy and sounds good . . . . Once he gets
onstage he carries the singing load and minimizes the
patter, a wise departure from several previous visits."

During March, Elvis sold his home at 144 Monovale in the Holmby
Estates section of Los Angeles to Telly Savalas for $650,000.

418

APRIL

APR 1   (Tues.) Elvis' closing night at the Hilton was the occasion of a special "invitation only" dinner show to celebrate the opening of the Hilton's new wing. Conrad Hilton and many of the officers of the Hilton organization were on hand, and Elvis gave a fairly straight performance. It was rumored that between shows, Elvis had been seen in the hotel's lobby dressed in a turban with long, flowing robes. The midnight show was very wild. Elvis played many April Fool's jokes on his band, and Colonel Parker came on stage dressed in a Santa Claus outfit. Even Elvis' pet chow, Get-Lo, was brought on stage.

It was announced that, to date, sales of souvenirs had raised $250,000 for Nevada charities. Over $13,000 had been raised during this season for the Adoption of Special Kids Fund.

Following the last night's show, Elvis hosted a party in his thirtieth floor suite, but he refused to see Conrad Hilton's son, who showed up at the door expecting to be admitted.

APR 2   (Wed.) Elvis returned to Memphis.

APR 24   (Thurs.) Elvis started his first tour of 1975 with a concert in Macon, Georgia, at the Coliseum at 8:30 p.m. Attendance was 10,242, with a total gross of $100,000. Tickets for this tour were $10, $7.50 and $5. Elvis stayed at the Macon Hilton Hotel, occupying the entire seventeenth floor.

Throughout this tour, the reviews mentioned that Elvis was overweight and pale. Toward the end of the tour, it was mentioned that he looked "tired." One reviewer, however, noted that Elvis seemed to lose twenty pounds between the concerts in Macon and Atlanta, just a week later.

Elvis' companion on this tour was Shelia Ryan, a twenty-two-year-old model.

APR 25   (Fri.) Elvis performed at the Veterans Memorial Coliseum in Jacksonville, Florida, at 8:30 p.m. Another $100,000 was taken in ticket receipts from the 10,532 attending. Elvis stayed at the Hilton Hotel. A local radio station tried to give away ten pairs of tickets in a contest, and the response was so overwhelming that the central telephone system was out of order for hours. One ticket scalper was arrested outside of the concert selling $10 tickets for as much as $200 each.

APR 26 (Sat.) Elvis performed a pair of shows at Tampa's Curtis-Hixon Auditorium. There were 7,500 fans on hand for both the 2:30 and 8:30 p.m. shows. The total gross was $150,000 for the day. Elvis introduced his new single, *T-R-O-U-B-L-E*, but since he was unfamiliar with the words, he had to read them off a piece of sheet music.

APR 27 (Sun.) The tour continued in Florida with another pair of concerts at the Lakeland Civic Center at 2:30 and 8:30 p.m. Over 8,200 fans attended each show. Sound problems in the amplification system failed to detract from Elvis' fine performance. One girl threw a pair of panties on stage, and Elvis put them on J.D. Sumner's head as he asked the girl, "Aren't you cold, honey?"

APR 28 (Mon.) Elvis remained in Lakeland for an 8:30 p.m. show, with another 8,200 attending. The total gross for both days was set at $226,500. One woman got hold of Elvis' arm and nearly dragged him off stage into the waiting arms of hundreds of screaming females.

APR 29 (Tues.) Elvis traveled to Middle Tennessee State University's Athletic Center in Murfreesboro for an 8:30 p.m. show, with 12,000 attending.

APR 30 (Wed.) The 8:30 p.m. concert in Atlanta's Omni was attended by 17,228 fans for a total of $180,000. Elvis started giving away scarves almost as soon as he came on stage, and the light from the flashbulbs was almost blinding. At one point, an ardent fan threw a green bra on stage. Elvis stopped the show to find the culprit, who brazenly stood up to be identified.

MAY

MAY 1 (Thurs.) Still at the Omni, Elvis pulled in another 17,228 for his 8:30 p.m. show.

MAY 2 (Fri.) In a rare third day's appearance in the same town, Elvis easily filled the Omni again with 17,228 fans for his 8:30 p.m. concert. The total for all three days was above $520,000.

MAY 3 (Sat.) There were a pair of shows at the Monroe, Louisiana, Civic Center. Over 8,000 fans attended both the 2:30 and 8:30 p.m. shows, which grossed a total of $150,000.

MAY 4   (Sun.) Elvis remained in Louisiana for another pair of shows at the Civic Center in Lake Charles. Attendance was put at 10,000 for both the 2:30 and the 8:30 p.m. shows, and the total box office receipts were over $250,000. Just prior to taking the stage for the evening concert, Elvis was greeted backstage by Mayor Ronnie Black, who gave Elvis the key to the city.

MAY 5   (Mon.) Elvis performed a special benefit in Jackson, Mississippi, for the victims of a tornado in McComb. The 8:30 p.m. show at the Mississippi State Fair Coliseum was attended by 10,242 fans. A check for $108,860 was presented by Elvis to Governor Bill Waller.

MAY 6   (Tues.) Elvis returned to Murfreesboro and the Middle Tennessee State University Murphy Athletic Center for an 8:30 p.m. concert attended by 12,000 fans.

MAY 7   (Wed.) Elvis closed out the tour with another show in Murfreesboro at 8:30 p.m. Again, 12,000 attended.

MAY 9   (Fri.) The *Memphis Press-Scimitar* reported that Elvis had been freed from his contract to purchase the Vesco jet airliner.

MAY 10 (Sat.) *T-R-O-U-B-L-E* started climbing the "Hot 100" chart in *Billboard* at number 87, staying nine weeks and reaching number 35.
        In Indianapolis, the J.J.B.B.F.A., an association dedicated to martial arts, voted Elvis "The Outstanding Achievement in Martial Arts" award. Elvis was not on hand for the group's tenth annual dinner.

MAY 30 (Fri.) Elvis began his second tour of 1975, with a show in Huntsville, Alabama, at the Von Braun Civic Center. There were 8,000 on hand for the 8:30 p.m. concert. Elvis stayed at the Huntsville Hilton Hotel.

MAY 31 (Sat.) *Billboard* gave a favorable review to Elvis' **Today** album, calling it "the most versatile and energetic album Presley has come up with in several releases."
        Elvis stayed in Huntsville for a pair of performances at 2:30 and 8:30 p.m. Attendance was 8,000 for each show.

JUNE

JUN 1   (Sun.) Elvis performed another two shows in Huntsville. Again, there were 8,000 for both the 2:30 and 8:30 p.m. performances.

JUN 2   (Mon.) Still in Alabama. Elvis appeared for another pair
        of shows in Mobile's Municipal Auditorium. The at-
        tendance was pegged at 10,620 for both the 4:30 and
        8:30 p.m. shows, and the total gate was $197,000.

JUN 3   (Tues.) Remaining in Alabama, Elvis appeared at the
        University of Alabama's Memorial Auditorium in
        Tuscaloosa at 8:30 p.m. Attendance was reported at
        15,400.

JUN 4   (Wed.) There was an 8:30 p.m. performance at Houston's
        Hofheinz Pavillion. Over 12,000 attended.

JUN 5   (Thurs.) Another 12,000 were on hand in Houston for
        Elvis' 8:30 p.m. show.
        NBC-TV broadcast "Elvis: That's The Way It Is" at 9:00
        p.m. as part of "Wednesday Night At The Movies." The
        movie received a "Close-Up" review in *TV Guide.*

JUN 6   (Fri.) Still in Texas, Elvis performed at the Dallas Conven-
        tion Center's Memorial Auditorium at 8:30 p.m. It was
        reported that over 10,000 attended. RCA recorded this
        show, and it was issued in 1980 as part of the eight-
        record set **Elvis Aron Presley**.

JUN 7   (Sat.) **Today** started up the "Top LPs" chart in *Billboard*
        at number 129. It stayed thirteen weeks and peaked at
        number 57.
        There were two concerts in Shreveport's Hirsch Coliseum.
        Over 11,000 fans attended the 2:30 and 8:30 p.m.
        shows.

JUN 8   (Sun.) Another pair of shows was held at the State Fair
        Coliseum in Jackson, Mississippi. Over 11,000 fans were
        on hand for both the 2:30 and 8:30 p.m. performances.
        While on stage, Elvis was given, among other things, a
        lei of roses and a group photo of the sixth grade class of
        East Tupelo.

JUN 9   (Mon.) Another 11,000 fans were on hand as Elvis stayed
        in Jackson for an 8:30 p.m. concert.

JUN 10 (Tues.) Elvis closed this tour by returning to his home
        town of Memphis for an 8:30 p.m. show, with 12,367
        attending at the Mid-South Coliseum. While leaning over
        to kiss an adoring female fan, Elvis split his pants, but
        he continued to perform.

JUN 11 (Wed.) Elvis purchased a Delta Airlines Convair 880 jet,
        which he promptly re-named the "Lisa Marie." The
        blue-and-white four-engine plane was given the identifi-
        cation number of N880EP, and the call sign "Hound

Dog." The jet was purchased through Nigel Winfield in Florida for $1.2 million, and Elvis ordered a $750,000 remodeling, which included a queen size bed in the rear compartment. The plane was remodeled in Ft. Worth, and Elvis often shuttled friends from Memphis to watch the progress.

JUN 16   (Mon.) Elvis was hospitalized in Memphis at the Mid-South Hospital to undergo eye tests. For several years he had complained of what had been diagnosed as glaucoma.

(It is not confirmed, but it is reported that Elvis underwent surgery to remove the bags under his eyes, and to tighten the facial tone — commonly referred to as a facelift. This was first reported in the *Memphis Press-Scimitar* on February 17, 1977, followed by the *National Enquirer* on April 26, 1977. The date given for the facelift is June 18, 1975.)

JUN 17   (Tues.) Elvis was released from Mid-South Hospital.

JULY

JUL 4   (Fri.) Lisa Marie arrived at Graceland to spend the Fourth of July weekend.

JUL 8   (Tues.) Elvis started his third tour of 1975 with a concert in Oklahoma City's Myriad Convention Center, where 15,291 attended the 8:30 p.m. show. Gross receipts were $140,000.

Elvis was accompanied on this tour by Diana Goodman, the current Miss Georgia in the Miss USA contest.

JUL 9   (Wed.) In Terra Haute, Indiana, Elvis performed at the Hulman Civic Center at 8:30 p.m. Attendance was reported at 10,244.

JUL 10   (Thurs.) Elvis traveled to Richfield, Ohio, (near Cleveland) for an 8:30 p.m. concert in the Cleveland Coliseum. Attendance was pegged at 21,000.

JUL 11   (Fri.) Over 8,400 attended Elvis' 8:30 p.m. performance at the Charleston, West Virginia, Civic Center. Elvis stayed at the Daniel Boone Hotel. During his stay in the hotel, Elvis and his entourage ran up a room service bill of $6,000.

JUL 12   (Sat.) There were two additional shows in Charleston at 2:30 and 8:30 p.m. Attendance was 8,200 for each show, and the total receipts for both days topped $253,000.

JUL 13 (Sun.) Elvis traveled to Niagara Falls, New York, for two concerts at the International Convention Center. There were 11,500 on hand for both the 2:30 and 8:30 p.m. shows. The total receipts were put at $210,000 for the day. Elvis stayed at the Parkway Ramada Inn. During the concerts, at least two people required medical attention. A female fan was crushed against the stage, and a security guard had difficulty breathing. Over 150 buses full of fans from Canada were on hand for the shows.

JUL 14 (Mon.) Elvis performed at 8:30 p.m. at the Springfield, Massachusetts, Civic Center Hockey Arena. Attendance was reported to be above 9,000. The high point of the show was reported to be a "stunning rendition of the gospel song, 'How Great Thou Art.' "

JUL 15 (Tues.) Remaining in Springfield, Elvis gave another concert attended by 9,000 fans at 8:30 p.m.

JUL 16 (Wed.) Elvis performed at the Veterans Memorial Coliseum in New Haven, Connecticut, at 8:30 p.m. Attendance was about 10,000. As Elvis started singing *C.C. Rider* about 100 screaming female fans stormed the stage, but Elvis continued without pausing. He gave away a few kisses and scarves to calm the crowd. In turn, he was given many bouquets and a bottle of champagne.

JUL 17 (Thurs.) Elvis stayed in New Haven for another 8:30 p.m. show. Another 10,000 attended. The total gross for the two days was $206,000.

JUL 18 (Fri.) Total receipts of $190,000 were taken from Elvis' 8:30 p.m. show at the Cleveland Coliseum in Richfield, Ohio. Attendance was over 21,000. Elvis performed for an hour and fifteen minutes. He sang *Little Darlin'* and *Let Me Be There*, and introduced Vernon in the audience.

JUL 19 (Sat.) Elvis gave a pair of concerts at the Nassau Coliseum in Uniondale, New York, near Long Island. Attendance was 16,500 for the 2:30 matinee and the 8:30 evening shows, and the total box office gate was $260,000. One of the highlights of the show was *You'll Never Walk Alone*, which featured Elvis accompanying himself on piano. One reviewer said the song showed "the power and emotion that established him as the King of Rock and Roll."

JUL 20 (Sun.) In Norfolk, Virginia, Elvis gave two shows at 2:30 and 8:30 p.m. Over 11,300 attended each show, and the total take was over $200,000. During the evening

show, Elvis made some comments to the audience about what it was like having 11,000 persons breathing on him. He said that he smelled green peppers and onions, and that his backup singers had been eating catfish. Two of the Sweet Inspirations took the comments personally and walked off the stage. Following the show, Elvis flew directly to Greensboro, North Carolina.

JUL 21   (Mon.) Elvis arrived at the Hilton Hotel in Greensboro shortly after midnight. He made a visit to a local dentist to have a toothache cared for. Upon returning to the hotel, he dined on a tray of cantaloupe, honeydew melon, apple slices, banana chunks, grapes, and cottage cheese before retiring. He had breakfast at 5:00 p.m. which consisted of more fruit and an omelet. During the 8:30 p.m. show at the Coliseum, Elvis apologized to the Sweet Inspirations for his remarks of the night before. Attendance for the show was 16,300. Later that night, Elvis returned to the dentist for more work on the problem tooth.

JUL 22   (Tues.) Elvis performed at 8:30 p.m. in the Ashville, North Carolina, Civic Center. Attendance was 7,437. Elvis was on stage for two hours, nearly twice as long as usual. During the show, a fan presented Elvis and several members of the troupe with boxer shorts which had their names down one leg. Elvis stopped the show and had a lot of fun with this novel gift. Also, Elvis gave J.D. Sumner his diamond ring, valued at $40,000, during this show. Elvis stayed at the Rodeway Inn. During the stay in Ashville, Elvis shot out the TV set in his motel room; the nearly-spent bullet ricocheted, hitting Dr. Nichopoulos in the chest under the heart but causing no physical damage.

JUL 23   (Wed.) Still in Ashville, Elvis gave another show at 8:30 p.m. attended by 7,437. Elvis introduced his father, who was in the audience, saying how sick Vernon had been for the past six months.

JUL 24   (Thurs.) During Elvis' 8:30 p.m. concert in Asheville, he gave away his guitar to a man in the audience. He also gave away two diamond rings worth $6,500. Attendance, again, was 7,437. The total receipts for the three days came to $223,917. Throughout his stay in Asheville, Elvis did not receive a single standing ovation, even though his shows were among the best of the tour. On

this date, he was on stage for an hour and a half.
Following the concert, Elvis returned to Memphis.

JUL 27   (Sun.) It was reported that Elvis had purchased a $1.2
million twin-engine turbo prop plane for Colonel
Parker, who refused the gift on the grounds that it
was too extravagant, even for Elvis.
While at the Madison Cadillac dealer's lot on Union Avenue
in Memphis, Elvis gave away an $11,500 gold-and-white
Cadillac to Minnie Person, a teller at a local bank. She
had been admiring Elvis' customized Cadillac. When
Elvis discovered that her birthday was the 29th, he told
one of his aides to write out a check so she could treat
herself to some new clothes. In addition to the Cadillac
for Mrs. Person, Elvis bought another thirteen Cadillacs
for his friends.

late JUL In late July, Elvis dated Melissa Blackwood, a former
Queen of the Memphis Southmen professional football
team. Elvis bought her a white Pontiac Grand Prix the
day of their first meeting. That night, they flew in his
Jetstar to Fort Worth to check out the renovation of
the 880 Convair, which he had purchased the previous
June.

AUGUST

AUG 6   (Wed.) Elvis was offered $2.5 million to play silent film
star Rudolph Valentino in "Ciao Rudy," which was
opening for four weeks on January 30, 1976, at Radio
City Music Hall in New York.

AUG 7   (Thurs.) Elvis' stepbrother, Rick Stanley, was arrested at
Methodist Hospital in Memphis while trying to pass a
forged prescription for Demerol. Elvis personally bailed
him out of the Shelby County Jail that night.

AUG 9   (Sat.) Elvis paid a surprise visit to the press booth at the
Mid-South Coliseum during a Memphis Southmen foot-
ball game. The Southmen were part of the now-defunct
World Football League.

AUG 12   (Tues.) Elvis' pet dog, Get-Lo, was flown from Memphis to
Boston at 3:00 a.m. The purebred chow had become ill
with a kidney ailment. Get-Lo was treated for two days
at the Copely Plaza Hotel before being transferred to a
central Massachusetts veterinary clinic. The dog returned
to Memphis in November.

AUG 16   (Sat.) Elvis left Graceland around midnight. He flew from Memphis to Las Vegas to prepare for his next engagement. Over Texas, Elvis had trouble breathing and a forced landing was made in Dallas. Elvis was taken to a motel to rest. Five hours later, he was well enough to continue the trip to Las Vegas.

AUG 18   (Mon.) Elvis opened at the Las Vegas Hilton for a two-week engagement. The opening night show was at 8:00 p.m. only, with the remainder of the shows at 8:00 p.m. and midnight. Elvis appeared to tire about halfway through the opening night's performance, and he frequently sat down while his backing vocalists entertained the crowd. Linda Thompson was back with Elvis, and Jerry Scheff was back on bass in the band.

AUG 19   (Tues.) Elvis was sued in Clark County (Nevada) district court by Beverly Albreco, who claimed that he had broken her ankle during a party in his suite on August 19, 1973. She was seeking $10,000 in damages.

AUG 20   (Wed.) Elvis' midnight performances were filled with laughter as he played with two water pistols, which had been given to him by two girls with front row seats. He sprayed everyone on stage and seemed to be having a wonderful time.

AUG 21   (Thurs.) Elvis left the hotel through the front lobby at 6:00 a.m. He was taken to the airport and flown back to Memphis, accompanied by Dr. Nichopoulos. By mid-morning, all traces that Elvis had been at the hotel were gone, and notices were placed in the foyer stating, "The remainder of the Elvis Presley engagement has been cancelled due to illness." In a statement from the hotel, the reason for the cancellation was given as a "fatigue state which developed in recent weeks." Elvis had been scheduled to appear through September 1st.
Upon arriving in Memphis, Elvis was admitted to Baptist Memorial Hospital for treatment of "fatigue and for tests." He stayed on the eighteenth floor of the Madison Wing in the hospital. (On August 16, 1977, the official report stated that Elvis had been hospitalized for hypertension and an impacted colon.)

AUG 26   (Tues.) Elvis was allowed to leave the hospital for five hours so he could go to Graceland. For the remainder of his stay in the hospital, Elvis was allowed to leave for a few hours each day.

AUG 27 (Wed.) *Variety*'s review of Elvis' Las Vegas opening said, in part: "Presley may be suffering from a continuing physical disability. His overweight condition and lack of stamina, poor vocal projection may spring from such a malady. It is difficult for him to maintain any credible vocal lines. [He is] spending more time in playing with his ringside romps with femmes, but tosses nearly every member of his backup quintet a lengthy solo. In addition he lumbers around in travesties of his earlier karate moves."

AUG 29 (Sat.) Elvis' physician, Dr. George C. Nichopoulos, said that his patient would stay put for another week, but that tests showed that the trouble with Elvis was "severe exhaustion" and not due to any "serious medical problem." Dr. Nick predicted that Elvis should be back in full form in three to five months.

AUG 30 (Sat.) Elvis donated $5,000 to the Jerry Lewis Muscular Dystrophy Telethon.

SEPTEMBER

SEP 5 (Fri.) Elvis was released from the hospital about 9:30 p.m. Two nurses, Marion Cocke and Kathy Seaman, were assigned duty at Graceland. Seaman worked from 9:00 a.m. to 2:00 p.m. and Cocke worked from 11:00 p.m. to 7:00 a.m. Seaman only worked at Graceland for two months, but Cocke remained until January 1976.

early SEP Following his release from the hospital, Elvis bought three super-cycles (three-wheeled vehicles). Elvis could be seen with Linda Thompson riding through the Memphis neighborhoods on the new cycles.

Elvis supervised the building of an addition to the trophy room at Graceland. He was also adding a sauna bath to the estate.

SEP 10 (Sat.) Elvis was ticketed by Patrolman Robert T. Logan in Memphis.

SEP 26 (Fri.) Elvis ran an ad in the *Wall Street Journal* which offered his twin engine jet Commander 1121 for $550,000, and his Lockheed twin engine prop jet for $750,000. (He still kept his $750,000 Lockheed Jetstar and the $1.2 million Convair 880.)

OCTOBER

OCT 25   (Sat.) *Bringing It Back* entered *Billboard*'s "Hot 100"
staying only five weeks and reaching number 65.

NOVEMBER

NOV 18   (Tues.) Elvis played racquetball at Graceland, and welcomed back his pet chow, Get-Lo, who had returned
from a two-month stay at an animal hospital.

NOV 27   (Thurs.) Elvis flew from Memphis to Las Vegas. This was
the maiden flight of the "Lisa Marie." The remodeling
had cost Elvis $1 million. The plane was finished in
white, with red and blue trim, and the name "Lisa Marie"
on the side near the cockpit. On the tail was the "TCB"
(Takin' Care of Business) insignia with the lightning
bolt. The interior contained a complete bedroom in
royal blue. There was a stereo and video system, and
a complete communications system. The crew at this
time consisted of Elwood David, pilot; Ron Strauss, co-
pilot; Jim Manny, flight engineer; and two stewardesses
who worked part-time.

The November issue of *Country Music* magazine ran a cover story
on Elvis entitled "Elvis And America."

DECEMBER

DEC 2   (Tues.) Elvis opened at the Las Vegas Hilton. This was another of the "Elvis In Concert" engagements, with Elvis
appearing only once each day, at 10:15 p.m., except on
Saturdays when he gave an 8:00 p.m. and midnight show.
The engagement was billed as the "Elvis Pre-Holiday
Jubilee." The concerts were rescheduled for the cancelled
Hilton shows the past August. Tickets were $22.50 per
person. Throughout the two-week engagement, it was
apparent to all that Elvis was in great spirits and very
much recovered after three months away from touring.
During several of the shows he took requests and performed many songs which were not part of his regular
routine, including *Little Sister, Blue Christmas, Help Me
Make It Through The Night*, and *Little Darlin'*. The vocal group Voice had disbanded, but Sherrill Nielsen was
still part of Elvis' backing group.

Elvis, surrounded by his backstage security: Jerry Schilling (left), Vernon and Red West (right) and Dick Grob (lower).

DEC 5   (Fri.) Lisa Marie arrived for an extended stay with Elvis
            at the Hilton.
DEC 6   (Sat.) Elvis was late for the dinner show, explaining that
            he had been trapped in the elevator which brought him
            down from his penthouse suite. Later, he said "I really
            panicked."
DEC 10   (Wed.) *Variety*'s review of Elvis' Las Vegas performance
            read, in part, "Elvis Presley, looking healthy and sound-
            ing cheerful after his recent hospitalization is presenting
            a show which will delight his fans."
DEC 15   (Mon.) Elvis closed at the Hilton. During the engagement,
            Elvis had performed before 32,000 fans for a total take
            of $800,000 in ticket sales. The Hilton presented Elvis
            with a gold medallion with his name in diamonds. De-
            cember is traditionally a slow time in Las Vegas, but for
            Elvis' closing show, there were more people in the Hilton
            showroom than for all the showrooms on the "Strip"
            put together.
DEC 17   (Wed.) Elvis returned to Memphis.
DEC 25   (Thurs.) Elvis spent a quiet Christmas at Graceland with
            Linda Thompson.
            The Christmas card from Elvis and the Colonel had a shot
            of Elvis in concert superimposed with a photo of Colonel
            Parker in a Santa suit in front of a Christmas tree.
DEC 26   (Fri.) Elvis flew from Memphis to Pontiac, Michigan, to
            prepare for his New Year's Eve concert. He stayed a few
            days and then returned to Memphis by the 30th.
DEC 30   (Tues.) Elvis was the cover story in *Faces* magazine's sec-
            ond issue. The accompanying article was entitled "The
            'King' Comes Back." The article told of Elvis' continuing
            fight against weight and depression.
DEC 31   (Wed.) Elvis departed Memphis early in the morning with
            Linda Thompson. They flew to Pontiac, Michigan, where
            Elvis performed a special New Year's Eve concert, which
            started at 9:00 p.m. Elvis took the stage about 11:00
            p.m. Over 62,500 fans attended, which set a world's
            record for a single performance. Tickets were scaled up
            to fifteen dollars, and the total receipts were reported to
            be $816,000. According to *Newsweek*, Elvis split his
            pants during the performance and had to change outfits.
            Vernon and Lisa Marie were on hand for the show.

It was reported in December that "not long ago" an emotionally unstable boy entered Graceland and shot up the library. (No other information is available.)

Elvis was the subject of four books published during 1975: *Elvis Presley — An Illustrated Biography* by W.A. Harbinson, *Elvis In Hollywood* by Paul Lichter, *The Elvis Presley Scrapbook* by James Robert Parish, and *Elvis Presley*, an educational booklet published by Creative Education.

Elvis was the subject of *The Elvis Years* and *Elvis — Yesterday . . . Today*, two magazines devoted entirely to his career, which were published during 1975.

Elvis was awarded the 1975 *Photoplay* Gold Medal Award as the "Most Popular Variety Star" based on a poll of the magazine's readers.

ALL
SHOOK
UP
ELVIS
Day-By-Day,
1976

JANUARY

JAN 1 (Thurs.) Elvis and Linda Thompson arrived back in Memphis at 5:00 a.m.

JAN 5 (Mon.) Elvis, Linda and about a dozen friends flew from Memphis to Denver, Colorado. From the airport, he took a caravan of cars to Vail, Colorado, for a vacation. He rented three condominiums to house his entourage. For amusement, many of the nights were spent riding snowmobiles.

JAN 8 (Thurs.) It was reported that Elvis was househunting. To keep the owner from knowing who he was, Elvis wore a ski mask and a jump suit.

JAN 14 (Wed.) An associate of Elvis called Kumpf Lincoln-Mercury salesman Bob Suber in Denver late in the afternoon to make an appointment. Elvis and several friends arrived at the dealership about 9:00 p.m. in a caravan of several cars. Elvis told Denver Police Captain Jerry Kennedy, of the Vice Squad, to pick out a Lincoln. He chose a white and blue one. Then Elvis gave Police Doctor Gerald Starkey a brown-on-brown Lincoln. Kennedy's wife also was given a Lincoln, as well as Private Detective Ron Pietrofeso. In all, five Lincolns were purchased at a total cost of $70,000. Elvis paid with a personal check and a company check.

Dr. Starkey had been called to Vail to treat an itch that Elvis had developed from wearing the ski mask to keep from drawing crowds. Both he and Kennedy had first met Elvis in Las Vegas around 1970.

One of the cars went to Robert Cantwell, a member of Colorado's Organized Crime Strike Force. Cantwell commented that he had never "gotten anything for nothing." Elvis overheard the remark and became very irritated.

JAN 19   (Mon.) RCA released **Elvis — A Legendary Performer, Volume 2**.

JAN 21   (Wed.)   Denver broadcaster Don Kinney of KOA-TV was given a Cadillac by Elvis, after he complained on the air about the gifts to members of the police department.

late JAN Linda Thompson left Elvis and flew to Los Angeles. By the end of the month, it was reported that she was trying to become an actress, having landed jobs on "The Rookies" and "Starsky And Hutch" TV series.

JAN 23   (Sat.) Elvis and his entourage returned to Memphis, arriving at 9:00 p.m.

JAN 24   (Sat.) In reviewing **Elvis — A Legendary Performer, Volume 2**, *Billboard* said the album was "another fun set for the collector, young fans who may not have the older things, and fans in general."

FEBRUARY

FEB 2   (Mon.) Elvis started a week-long series of recording sessions in a studio which RCA had set up in the den at Graceland. The musicians on hand were the regular members of Elvis' touring band, including Jerry Scheff on bass and David Briggs on electric piano. Songs recorded the night of February 2nd were *Bitter They Are Harder They Fall, She Thinks I Still Care*, and *The Last Farewell*. The sessions lasted from 10:00 p.m. to 7:00 a.m. each day.

FEB 3   (Tues.) Again, in the evening hours, Elvis was in the Graceland studio recording, even though only one track was completed, *Solitaire*.

FEB 4   (Wed.) On this night, Elvis completed two more songs: *Moody Blue* and *I'll Never Fall In Love Again*.

FEB 5   (Thurs.) Three more songs were completed on this night: *For The Heart, Hurt* and *Danny Boy*.

FEB 6   (Fri.) *Never Again* and *Love Comin' Down* were the only two songs finished this evening.

FEB 7   (Sat.) **Elvis — A Legendary Performer, Volume 2** entered *Billboard*'s "Top LPs And Tapes" chart at number 76. It stayed on the chart for seventeen weeks, peaking at number 46.

FEB 8   (Sun.) Apparently Elvis' band had other engagements over the weekend, so a mostly new group was brought in for this final session: John Wilkinson, Charlie Hodge, Ronnie

Tutt, and David Briggs remained, and they were augmented by Bill Sanford, guitar; Norbert Putnam, bass; and Bobby Emmons, electric piano. The only song completed was *Blue Eyes Crying In The Rain*. All of the songs recorded during this week were later overdubbed by Felton Jarvis, using several Nashville musicians and vocalists.

FEB 16   (Mon.) Elvis had a meeting with Memphis hypnotist, William Foote, who was to teach Elvis to relax through mind control.

FEB 20   (Fri.) Elvis and his friends flew to Denver and motored to Vail, where a local real estate agent later reported that Elvis was there to buy a house that he had looked at in January. Elvis did not purchase the home.

LATE FEBRUARY-EARLY MARCH
Elvis stayed in Colorado for a few weeks before returning to Memphis.

MARCH

MAR 17   (Wed.) Back on the concert circuit for the first time since July 1975, Elvis opened a very short tour with an 8:30 p.m. performance in Johnson City, Tennessee's Freedom Hall. Attendance was pegged at 7,000. Elvis stayed at the Holiday Inn in Bristol, Tennessee, about fifteen miles from the auditorium. Tickets for this tour were raised to $12.50, $10, and $7.50. This was the first raise in ticket prices since Elvis started touring in 1970. The show stoppers were *Hurt, America*, and the usual *How Great Thou Art*. When Elvis sang *For The Heart*, he had to read the words from a cue sheet. Linda Thompson and Vernon were along for the tour.

MAR 18   (Thurs.) There was another 8:30 p.m. concert in Johnson City, with attendance of 7,000.

MAR 19   (Fri.) Elvis closed his three days in Johnson City with another 8:30 p.m. show before 7,000 fans. The total gate for the three days was set at $240,000. As Elvis was leaving his motel, a well-endowed female fan rushed forward and tore open her blouse, revealing her bare breasts. She shouted, "Here it is, honey. You can have it all." Elvis turned to Red West, commenting, "It's tempting."

MAR 20   (Sat.) There were a pair of shows in Charlotte, North Carolina, at the Coliseum. Attendance was over 12,000

437

for both the 2:30 and 8:30 p.m. shows, and the total box office take was about $260,000. During the matinee while Elvis was singing *Steamroller Blues*, a girl broke through the security forces and was able to make it to Elvis for a quick kiss, which cut his lip. Elvis was so rattled that he forgot the words to his next song, *Burning Love*.

Following the show, Elvis flew to Cincinnati, where he occupied the twenty-fourth floor of the Netherland Hilton Hotel. Colonel Parker's staff was on the twenty-third floor.

MAR 21 (Sun.) There were shows at 2:30 and 8:30 p.m. in Cincinnati's Riverfront Coliseum. Over 17,500 fans were on hand for each show, and the total box office gross was reported to be $407,274. While singing *Polk Salad Annie* during the matinee, Elvis split the seam in his show pants, again. He had J.D. Sumner introduce the Stamps, while he left the stage with Charlie Hodge using a towel to cover his bottom. Elvis returned quickly in another jumpsuit and performed for a total of sixty-five minutes.

MAR 22 (Mon.) Elvis left Cincinnati in the afternoon and flew to St. Louis for an 8:30 p.m. performance at the Kiel Auditorium, before 10,546 fans. When the concert tickets went on sale the previous February, they sold out in seven hours, which was a record for over-the-counter sales for this facility.

Following the show, Elvis flew back to Memphis.

While at home, Elvis practiced racquetball almost daily on the court at Graceland. He also frequently rode his three-wheel motorcycle around Memphis. At night, he attended late movies at the Crosstown Theater. On one occasion, he even took a joy-ride in his small jet and circled over Graceland, to the enjoyment of his fans.

MAR 26 (Fri.) Elvis stopped at a traffic accident in Memphis and offered his assistance as a U.S. Deputy Marshall.

MAR 27 (Sat.) *Hurt/For The Heart* entered the "Hot 100" in *Billboard* at number 85, staying eleven weeks and reaching number 28.

APRIL

APR 7   (Wed.) A widow with four children in Athens, Alabama, announced that Elvis was going to show up and marry her. Apparently she had been hoodwinked by an anonymous person who said he was Elvis. No matter how improbable it sounded, hundreds of people waited at the church in vain for a glimpse of the groom, who never arrived.

APR 10   (Sat.) In reviewing **The Sun Sessions** album, *Billboard* said: "This could become a landmark LP."

APR 12   (Mon.) Elvis Presley Center Courts, Inc. broke ground for a new racquetball court in Memphis. Elvis was the Chairman of the Board. Other members of the corporation were Elvis' doctor, George Nichopoulos; Elvis' chief of staff, Joe Esposito; and Michael McMahon, a long-time friend of Elvis. The project folded after only a year.

APR 17   (Sat.) **The Sun Sessions** started up the *Billboard* album chart at number 144. It stayed on the chart for only eleven weeks, peaking at number 76.

APR 21   (Wed.) Elvis started the second tour of 1976, which was also a very short one, with a concert in the Kemper Arena in Kansas City. Attendance was 17,600, and the gate was $120,000. This was one of Elvis' best shows of the tour, and he stayed on stage for an hour and a half.

APR 22   (Thurs.) Elvis jetted into Omaha just as his 8:30 p.m. show was beginning. He arrived at the City Auditorum Arena during the intermission. He was on stage for eighty minutes, performing a show which had changed little since his last trip to Omaha in 1974. The attendance was 10,546.

APR 23   (Fri.) Over 19,000 attended Elvis' show at Denver's McNichols Arena at 8:30 p.m.

APR 24   (Sat.) Foregoing the usual two concerts on a Saturday, there was only an 8:30 p.m. performance at the Sports Arena in San Diego. Attendance was over 17,500. Elvis was on stage for an hour, and included one of his least performed songs, *My Woman, My Woman, My Wife*, while Linda Thompson looked on attentively.

APR 25   (Sun.) There were two shows in Long Beach at the Arena. There were 14,000 fans on hand for both the 2:30 and 8:30 p.m. shows.

APR 26   (Mon.) Still on the West Coast, Elvis traveled to Seattle, where 14,687 were on hand for his 8:30 p.m. concert in the Coliseum.

APR 27   (Tues.) Elvis closed out this short tour with a final show at 8:30 p.m. in the Coliseum in Spokane. The total receipts were above $80,000 from the 7,500 fans attending. Elvis performed for fifty minutes.
Following the concert, Elvis flew to Lake Tahoe.

APR 30   (Fri.) Elvis opened at the Sahara Tahoe Hotel in Stateline, Nevada. He performed only one show per day at 10:00 p.m. in the "Elvis In Concert" format, except on Friday and Saturday, when he had an 8:00 p.m. and a midnight show. Tickets were twenty dollars per person.

MAY

MAY 9   (Sun.) Elvis closed at the Sahara Tahoe Hotel. His final show at Lake Tahoe was a special Mother's Day performance, and Elvis and the Colonel gave orchids to all the ladies. Elvis was on stage for two hours and five minutes as he gave one of his longest concerts ever.
Following the engagement, Elvis returned to Memphis.

MAY 19   (Wed.) Elvis gave Linda Thompson a Lincoln Continental Mark IV.

MAY 27   (Thurs.) Elvis was off on another ten-day tour, his third of 1976, with a show in Bloomington, at the University of Indiana's Assembly Hall at 8:30 p.m. Attendance was over 16,000.

MAY 28   (Fri.) The tour moved on to the University of Iowa in Ames, where Elvis gave an 8:30 p.m. concert in the James W. Hilton Coliseum. There were 14,750 fans on hand for the show.

MAY 29   (Sat.) Elvis' next stop was in Oklahoma City at the Myriad Center Arena, where 15,300 fans paid $176,278 for the 8:30 p.m. show.

MAY 30   (Sun.) There were two shows, at 2:30 and 8:30 p.m., at the Odessa, Texas, Ector County Coliseum. Total attendance was 16,000.

MAY 31   (Mon.) Still in Texas, Elvis performed in Lubbock's Municipal Coliseum at 8:30 before 9,600 fans.

In May, *The National Tattler* published a special magazine, *Elvis.*

441

A ticket for Elvis' last show at Lake Tahoe.

JUNE

JUN 1   (Tues.) Over 10,000 attended Elvis' 8:30 p.m. show at the Tucson Community Center Arena.

JUN 2   (Wed.) Back to Texas, Elvis performed before 7,050 fans at 8:30 p.m. in El Paso's Grand Hall of the Civic Center.

JUN 3   (Thurs.) Elvis remained in Texas for a concert in Ft. Worth's Tarrant County Convention Center at 8:30 p.m. Attendance was pegged at over 14,000.

JUN 4   (Fri.) Elvis started a weekend series of shows in the Omni in Atlanta with an 8:30 p.m. show, attended by 17,200 fans. Elvis stayed at the Hyatt Regency Hotel over the weekend.

JUN 5   (Sat.) **From Elvis Presley Boulevard** entered *Billboard*'s album chart at number 183. It stayed on the chart for seventeen weeks, peaking at number 41.

There were a pair of shows, at 2:30 and 8:30 p.m., in the Omni. Attendance at each was 17,200, again.

JUN 6   (Sun.) Elvis closed out this tour with a final show in the Omni at 8:30 p.m. Attendance was 17,200.

Following this concert, Elvis returned to Memphis for a brief three-week rest before the next series of shows.

JUN 25   (Sat.) Elvis' fourth tour in three months started with an early morning trip to Buffalo, New York, where he stayed in the Statler Hotel before his 8:30 p.m. show at the Memorial Auditorium. Attendance was set at 17,500. Following the concert, Elvis flew on to Providence, Rhode Island.

JUN 26   (Sat.) It was back to the two shows on a Saturday regimen in Providence, Rhode Island, as Elvis performed at 2:30 and 8:30 p.m. at the Civic Center. There were 13,500 fans on hand for each show, and the total gate was reported to be above $300,000.

JUN 27   (Sun.) Elvis appeared at 2:30 and 8:30 p.m. in the Capitol Center at Largo, Maryland, near Landover and Washington, D.C. A total of 40,000 fans attended the concerts. During intermission in the evening show, Elvis met backstage with Elton John.

JUN 28   (Mon.) Elvis arrived in Philadelphia during the afternoon and went to the Hilton Hotel to rest. The 8:30 p.m. performance at the Spectrum was attended by over 19,000 fans. Elvis sang one of his least performed songs, *Love*

Letters. He also sang *Hurt* twice, something he did only when he was in a good mood.

JUN 29   (Tues.) The tour traveled to Richmond, Virginia, for a show in the Coliseum at 8:30 p.m., with 11,900 in attendance.

JUN 30   (Wed.) There was a concert in Greensboro, North Carolina, at the Coliseum at 8:30 p.m., with 16,000 on hand.

JULY

JUL 1   (Thurs.) Dropping into the deep South, Elvis appeared in the Hirsch Coliseum in Shreveport, Louisiana. The 8:30 p.m. show drew a crowd of 11,000.

JUL 2   (Fri.) Moving further south in Louisiana, Elvis appeared in Baton Rouge at the Louisiana State University's Assembly Center. There were 16,000 fans on hand for the 8:30 p.m. concert.

JUL 3   (Sat.) There was only one show on this Saturday in Ft. Worth, as Elvis returned to the Tarrant County Convention Center for an 8:30 p.m. appearance. There were 14,000 on hand.

JUL 4   (Sun.) There was also only a single show on this Sunday in Tulsa at the Oral Roberts University's Mabee Center. The 2:30 p.m. matinee drew a crowd of 11,974, and a box office gross of $129,000. For this Fourth of July show, Elvis wore his Bicentennial outfit, complete with the Presidential seal on the face of his belt buckle. The studs on his shirt made the designs of the Liberty Bell, the Presidential Seal, and the American flag. Elvis sang *Hurt* twice, and surprised the audience with *Little Darlin'*. The next to last song was a beautiful rendition of *America*.

JUL 5   (Mon.) Elvis departed Tulsa at 4:30 p.m., arriving just before showtime in Memphis, where Mayor Wythe Chandler had proclaimed "King Of Rock 'N' Roll Day." Elvis' 8:30 p.m. concert in the Mid-South Coliseum was attended by 11,999 fans, who paid a total of $146,450 for their tickets.

JUL 7   (Wed.) Elvis traveled to Palm Springs for a vacation.

JUL 11   (Fri.) In conjunction with an Elvis Fan Club Convention in Memphis, Vernon received a plaque and a trophy on Elvis' behalf.

JUL 12   (Mon.) Colonel Parker's office at the M-G-M Studios in Culver City, California, took receipt of three oil paintings by Loxi Sibley, of Sacramento. These paintings were reproduced and sold as souvenirs during Elvis' tours in late 1976 and 1977.

            It was extensively reported in the press that Elvis was to marry Alexis Skylar in Las Vegas. Hundreds of fans jammed the chapel, only to be disappointed when Elvis did not show up.

JUL 13   (Tues.) Vernon Presley notified Red and Sonny West and Dave Hebler that they were fired as Elvis' bodyguards. Red had been with Elvis since the early days with Sun Records. Sonny, cousin of Red, had worked for Elvis since the 1960s. Hebler had been on Elvis' payroll since 1974.

JUL 23   (Fri.) With less than three weeks rest, Elvis was off on his fifth tour of 1976. The opening show was at 8:30 p.m. in the Freedom Hall in Louisville, Kentucky. The attendance was reported to be 19,400.

JUL 24   (Sat.) There were a pair of performances in Charleston, West Virginia, at 2:30 and 8:30 p.m. in the Civic Center. The total gate was $206,052, as 8,500 fans attended each show. During the matinee, the electricity went off during Elvis' closing number, *Can't Help Falling In Love*, as the result of a thunderstorm. By the evening show, everything was back to normal.

JUL 25   (Sun.) In Syracuse, New York, Elvis appeared at 8:30 p.m. at the Onondaga War Memorial Auditorium. There were 8,550 fans in attendance.

JUL 26   (Mon.) Elvis flew from Syracuse to Rochester in his Viscount jet, leaving the "Lisa Marie" behind because the runway in Rochester was too short to accommodate the larger plane. The show that night at 8:30 p.m. in the Community War Memorial Auditorium was attended by 10,000 fans.

JUL 27   (Tues.) It was back to Syracuse again for another show at the Onondaga War Memorial Auditorium. The total gross was $103,000 from the 8,500 fans attending the 8:30 p.m. show.

JUL 28   (Wed.) The tour moved on to Hartford, Connecticut's Civic Center for an 8:30 p.m. show. The gate was reported to be $136,000, as 12,314 fans were on hand. By this concert, Elvis had developed a sore throat which was to bother him for the remainder of the tour.

445

JUL 29   (Thurs.) Elvis appeared in Springfield, Massachusetts'
         Civic Center at 8:30 p.m. Attendance was over 10,000.
JUL 30   (Fri.) The gross was $100,000 from Elvis' concert in the
         New Haven, Connecticut, Veteran's Memorial Coliseum.
         The 8:30 p.m. show drew a crowd of 9,600.
JUL 31   (Sat.) Dropping down the Eastern seaboard. Elvis gave an
         8:30 p.m. concert in the Hampton Coliseum in Hampton
         Roads, Virginia, for 11,000 fans.

The *National Lampoon* magazine featured a parody of Elvis on its
July cover. There was no accompanying article.

AUGUST

AUG 1   (Sun.) Elvis remained in Hampton Roads for another 8:30
         p.m. show with a crowd of 11,000.
AUG 2   (Mon.) Elvis arrived at Woodrum Field in Roanoke, Vir-
         ginia, at 5:20 p.m. aboard his jet, the "Lisa Marie."
         Elvis went to the Sheraton Inn, where he stayed in suite
         214--216 with his traveling companion, Linda Thomp-
         son. The show that night at the Roanoke Civic Center
         was ticketed at $12.50, $10, and $7.50, and 10,598 fans
         paid $126,440 to see the concert. The promoter kept
         $111,995 of the gate. Elvis seemed very tired throughout
         most of the show.
AUG 3   (Tues.) Elvis flew out of Roanoke in the afternoon des-
         tined for Fayetteville, North Carolina, and another con-
         cert at the Cumberland County Memorial Auditorium
         at 8:30 p.m., with 7,000 in attendance.
AUG 4   (Wed.) Elvis stayed in Fayetteville for another 8:30 p.m.
         show. Again, the total attendance was pegged at 7,000.
AUG 5   (Thurs.) Elvis performed in Fayetteville for a third day.
         Again, the 8:30 p.m. show drew an audience of 7,000.
mid-AUG Following the show, Elvis returned to Memphis. Lisa
         Marie came out from Los Angeles for a visit.
AUG 21   (Sat.) RCA announced that the sales of Elvis' records had
         passed the 400 million mark.
AUG 27   (Fri.) Tour number six for 1976 started with an 8:30 p.m.
         show in the Convention Center in San Antonio. The
         crowd was estimated at over 11,000.
AUG 28   (Sat.) Elvis gave a matinee performance at the Hofheinz
         Pavillion in Houston. There were over 12,000 fans in
         attendance.

AUG 29 (Sun.) A crowd of 10,720 was on hand for Elvis' 8:30 p.m. performance at the Municipal Auditorium in Mobile, Alabama.

AUG 30 (Mon.) Elvis departed Mobile in the afternoon, flying on to Tuscaloosa, Alabama. That night, he performed at 8:30 p.m. at the University of Alabama's Memorial Coliseum in front of 12,000 fans.

AUG 31 (Tues.) The tour moved on to Macon, Georgia, for an 8:30 p.m. show at the Coliseum that drew 10,200.

SEPTEMBER

SEP 1 (Wed.) The Jacksonville, Florida, Coliseum held 9,500 for Elvis' 8:30 p.m. show.

SEP 2 (Thurs.) Over in Tampa, Elvis filled the Curtis Hixon Hall at 8:30 p.m. with 7,500 fans.

SEP 3 (Fri.) Still in Florida, Elvis appeared at 8:30 p.m. in the St. Petersburg Bay Front Center. The crowd was measured at over 8,000.

SEP 4 (Sat.) There were two shows in Lakeland, Florida, at the Civic Center at 2:30 and 8:30 p.m. Over 8,000 attended each performance.

SEP 5 (Sun.) Elvis traveled on to Jackson, Mississippi, for an 8:30 p.m. show at the Mississippi State Fair Civic Center, where 12,000 were in attendance. During the intermission, before Elvis took to the stage, he met with Governor Cliff Finch, who gave Elvis a plaque naming him to the Mississippi Hall Of Fame.

SEP 6 (Mon.) In Huntsville, Alabama, Elvis appeared at the Von Braun Civic Center, where 8,000 turned out for both the 2:30 and 8:30 p.m. shows.

SEP 7 (Tues.) Elvis stopped at the Pine Bluffs, Arkansas, Convention Center for an 8:30 p.m. appearance in front of 7,500. Although he was supposed to stay at the local Holiday Inn, there were so many fans hanging around the motel that Elvis flew home to Memphis for the night.

SEP 8 (Wed.) Elvis returned to Pine Bluff for another 8:30 p.m. show with 7,500 fans present to close out the tour.

late SEP Following the concert, Elvis returned to Memphis.
Work progressed on a widening of Elvis Presley Boulevard in front of Graceland. Elvis had donated 12,530 square feet of his property so that the city could put in a dozen parking spaces and a turn-lane to accommodate the many

fans who were always outside the main gates of Elvis' home.

After a few days rest in Memphis, Elvis flew to Palm Springs for a vacation. He was visited frequently by Priscilla and Lisa Marie.

Elvis returned to Memphis in late September.

The September issue of *In The Know* magazine featured Elvis and six other recording artists on its September cover. The accompanying article was entitled "At Home With Elvis: Catering To The King."

OCTOBER

OCT 4   (Mon.) Elvis was spotted coming out of Graceland about 2:00 a.m. on a new Harley Davidson show bike. He was followed by over a dozen fans, and when he stopped at Vicker's gas station, he chatted with his fans for about thirty minutes.

OCT 10   (Tues.) Elvis flew from Memphis for parts unknown.

OCT 14   (Thurs.) Elvis' seventh tour of 1976 began with an 8:30 p.m. concert in the Chicago Stadium. Attendance was reported to be over 19,000. Elvis stayed at the Arlington Hilton Hotel, on the eleventh floor.

Elvis had lost so much weight since the last tour that he could again wear stage outfits that he had originally used in 1973.

OCT 15   (Fri.) Elvis remained in Chicago for another 8:30 p.m. show. Again, the attendance was pegged at 19,000.

OCT 16   (Sat.) Elvis performed at 8:30 p.m. in the Duluth, Minnesota, arena.

OCT 17   (Sun.) Elvis remained in Minnesota for a show in Minneapolis' Metropolitan Sports Center at 8:30 p.m. Attendance was reported at 15,800 with a total gate of $190,000. He brought the house down with a wild version of *Mystery Train/Tiger Man*. As Elvis left the stage, the crowd became hysterical and surged onto the stage, overrunning the twenty-four security guards, but Elvis escaped into a waiting limousine.

Following the concert, Elvis flew on to Sioux Falls, South Dakota.

OCT 18   (Mon.) Elvis' appearance in Sioux Falls, South Dakota, was an 8:30 p.m. concert in the Arena.

OCT 19 (Tues.) Elvis' show stopped in Madison, Wisconsin, at the Dane County Coliseum for an 8:30 p.m. performance. Attendance was 10,211. Mayor Paul Soglin had proclaimed "Elvis Day."

OCT 20 (Wed.) Over 12,000 attended the 8:30 p.m. concert at the Notre Dame University Athletic and Convention Center in South Bend, Indiana.

OCT 21 (Thurs.) Elvis performed at the Wings Stadium in Kalamazoo, Michigan, at 8:30 p.m. He was on stage for seventy minutes, and, among other songs, he performed *Blue Christmas.*

OCT 22 (Fri.) The attendance was reported to be over 17,000 for Elvis' concert in Champaign, Illinois, at the University of Illinois Assembly Hall at 8:30 p.m.

OCT 23 (Sat.) The total box office receipts were over $225,000 as 20,000 fans were on hand for the 8:30 p.m. show at the Coliseum in Richfield, Ohio, just outside Cleveland. Following *Polk Salad Annie*, a fan gave Elvis a "stick pony" toy, which he rode around the stage. Elvis stayed at the Keg and Quarter Hotel in Cleveland, while the remainder of the troupe stayed in the Holiday Inn near the Coliseum.

OCT 24 (Sun.) The tour stopped in Evansville, Indiana, for an 8:30 p.m. concert in Roberts Stadium, where 13,500 attended. The highlights of the show were Elvis' accompaniment on his guitar while he sang *Blue Christmas* and *That's All Right.*

OCT 25 (Mon.) Elvis stayed in Indiana for an 8:30 p.m. show in the Ft. Wayne Memorial Coliseum, with 8,500 in attendance.

OCT 26 (Tues.) Over 13,000 were on hand for Elvis' 8:30 p.m. show in Dayton at the University of Ohio.

OCT 27 (Wed.) Elvis performed at the Southern Illinois University's Arena at 8:30 p.m. in Carbondale, Illinois.
Following the concert, Elvis flew back to Memphis.

OCT 29 (Fri.) RCA again set up a recording studio at Graceland. The musicians on hand included most of the members of Elvis' traveling band plus Chip Young, guitar; Tony Brown, piano; and David Briggs, electric piano. Background vocals were handled by J.D. Sumner and the Stamps, Kathy Westmoreland, Myrna Smith of the Sweet Inspirations, and Sherrill Nielsen of Voice. During the evening session, Elvis recorded *It's Easy For You, Way Down* and *Pledging My Love.* The last two tracks were

overdubbed on January 22, 1977. This session ran into
the morning hours.

OCT 30   (Sat.) During a second night of recording, only two tracks
          were attempted: *There's A Fire Down Below* and *He'll
          Have To Go*. Elvis did not record any vocals on these
          tracks at this time, although, according to session notes,
          both were completed at a later date. The first track has
          not been released. The session lasted into the early
          morning hours of the 31st.

OCT 31   (Sun.) Elvis gave his white Lincoln Continental limousine
          to J.D. Sumner.

NOVEMBER

Early in the month, Elvis vacationed in Vail, Colorado. Upon his
return to Memphis, he brought along Lisa Marie.

early   During the first week in November, Linda Thompson called
NOV   it quits and left Elvis. She wrote a "Dear John" letter to
          explain her feelings, then charged $30,000 on his Master
          Charge card in one final spending spree.

NOV 10   (Wed.) In the afternoon, Elvis bought a new Chevrolet
          Corvette at Jim Ellis Chevrolet in Whitehaven. The car
          cost $10,403.99, and Elvis wrote out a personal check
          on the National Bank of Commerce in Memphis (account
          number 01-143875-0210). The car was a gift for Lamar
          Fike, a long-time member of Elvis' inner circle.

NOV 16   (Tues.) The New Jersey Supreme Court agreed to review
          a breach of contract suit brought against Elvis in the
          aborted attempt to purchase Robert Vesco's jet in
          January 1975. The suit resulted when Vesco sold the jet
          to a third party for $650,000. Agents for Vesco then
          tried to get Elvis to make up the difference between the
          selling price and Elvis' offer of $1.5 million ($850,000).
          (On February 16, 1978, the New Jersey Supreme Court
          ruled that Elvis may have improperly backed out of his
          agreement to purchase the jet.)

NOV 19   (Fri.) Elvis met Ginger Alden at a party at Graceland. By
          coincidence, her father had been a sergeant in the Army
          and had been present when Elvis was inducted in 1958.
          Her older sister, Terry, was the reigning Miss Tennessee.
          Ginger had been a runner-up in the Miss Tennessee
          pageant, which was part of the Miss Universe pageant.

NOV 20   (Sat.) Elvis and Ginger flew to Las Vegas late at night.

Ginger Alden, Elvis' last girlfriend.

NOV 21   (Sun.) They arrived at Hughes Airport at dawn, and were chauffeured to the Hilton Hotel. After sleeping most of the day, they flew back to Memphis that evening.

NOV 23   (Tues.) At 3:07 a.m., Graceland security guard Robert Lloyd telephoned the Memphis Police Department to report a disturbance at the front gate. Patrolman B.J. Kirkpatrick responded and arrested Jerry Lee Lewis outside of Graceland for causing a disturbance. Jerry Lee was also booked for carrying a concealed weapon, a .38 caliber derringer. According to Jerry Lee, he had been asked to come to Graceland to see Elvis, but he had been refused admittance when he arrived at the gate. He was found not guilty in court, with Judge Albert Boyd presiding.

NOV 24   (Wed.) Elvis' eighth tour of 1976 started with an 8:30 p.m. show at the Centennial Coliseum in Reno, Nevada.

NOV 25   (Thurs.) Elvis performed at 8:30 p.m. in Eugene, Oregon, at the McArthur Court.

NOV 26   (Fri.) Still in Oregon, Elvis appeared at the Memorial Coliseum in Portland at 8:30 p.m. Attendance was over 11,000. Elvis stayed at the Sheraton Inn.

NOV 27   (Sat.) Back in Eugene, Elvis performed again at 8:30 p.m.

NOV 28   (Sun.) Elvis traveled to San Francisco for an 8:30 p.m. performance at the Cow Palace. Attendance was pegged at 14,300 with a reported gross of $158,115. Elvis stayed at the Hilton Towers. He was joined by Ginger Alden, who arrived from Memphis.

NOV 29   (Mon.) There was another show in the Cow Palace at 8:30 p.m. Again, the reported attendance was 14,300 with receipts of $158,115.

NOV 30   (Tues.) Elvis wrapped up this short tour with a concert in Anaheim's Convention Center at 8:30 p.m. Attendance was reported at 8,500.
Following the concert, Elvis flew to Las Vegas.

DECEMBER

DEC 2   (Thurs.) Elvis opened at the Las Vegas Hilton. He performed "in concert" at 9:00 p.m. each day with 1:00 a.m. shows Friday and Saturday nights. Tickets were twenty-nine dollars per person. A few of the many celebrities who attended one of the shows were Glen Campbell, Vickie Carr, Wayne Newton, Liza Minelli,

Tanya Tucker, and Merv Griffin. Priscilla came for opening night and stayed for the weekend. Also on hand for each show was Elvis' latest girlfriend, Ginger Alden. During this engagement Elvis included *Blue Christmas* and *The Hawaiian Wedding Song* in the show line-up. The opening night show was an hour and forty minutes long. Elvis seemed to have his weight under control during this engagement.

DEC 4   (Sat.) Lisa Marie attended the early show with Priscilla.

DEC 5   (Sun.) Lisa Marie was again in the audience for Elvis' concert. Elvis was late coming on stage, and said he had sprained his ankle in his suite by falling down a step in the dark on the way to the bathroom. He performed several songs while seated in a chair.

DEC 6   (Mon.) Elvis shortened his show, complaining of the sprained ankle.

early   During the second week of this engagement, Ginger Alden's
DEC   parents flew in to attend several shows.

DEC 8   (Wed.) Even though Elvis was still bothered by a sprained ankle, he was on stage for an hour and a half. Vernon was admitted to a Las Vegas hospital with chest pains following the show.

DEC 10   (Fri.) At 4 a.m., Elvis called Gerald Peters, owner of the limousine service that Elvis used in Los Angeles. Peters was told to deliver a white-on-white Lincoln Mark IV to Las Vegas that night. After several frantic phone calls, Peters located such a car in Glendale, which he picked up and drove to Las Vegas. The midnight show was plagued by technical problems and had to be stopped while sound engineers came on stage to attempt to check the microphones. Following the show, Elvis gave the Mark IV to Ginger Alden.

DEC 12   (Sun.) Elvis closed at the Las Vegas Hilton. His final show lasted an hour and a half. Vernon was back in the audience after his recent hospitalization. The souvenir sales had been handled by the American Heart Association, which had raised $17,000 during the two weeks.

mid-DEC Elvis returned to Memphis shortly after closing at the Hilton. Gerald Peters and his son drove the Lincoln Mark IV non-stop from Las Vegas to Memphis, but when they arrived, Elvis told them they needn't have hurried. He had bought Ginger a Cadillac Seville in the meantime.

DEC 15 (Wed.) *Variety*'s review of Elvis' recent Las Vegas engagement said, in part, "Presley, trimmed down somewhat,
seems to have enough energy to get through his nightly
ordeal. The current aim of much of his vocalizing is
for hotdogging effects."

DEC 23 (Thurs.) Vernon apologized for being late with the usual
donations to local Memphis charities, which was a
Christmas ritual with Elvis.

DEC 25 (Sat.) *Moody Blue/She Thinks I Still Care* entered *Billboard*'s "Hot 100" at number 82, staying thirteen weeks
and reaching number 31. In *Billboard*'s year-end music
review, Elvis did not rank among the top 100 singles'
artists and was only number seventy-two as an album
artist.

Christmas was celebrated quietly at Graceland. Elvis gave
Lisa Marie a golf cart, which she used to ride around the
grounds of their home.

DEC 27 (Mon.) Elvis began his ninth tour of 1976 with a concert
in Wichita Falls at the Texas State University Henry
Levitt Arena. Over 10,000 attended the 8:30 p.m. show.

DEC 28 (Tues.) Elvis' 8:30 p.m. show in the Dallas Memorial
Auditorium was attended by 9,800 fans, who paid
$144,214 for tickets.

DEC 29 (Wed.) Elvis traveled to Birmingham for an 8:30 p.m.
concert in the Civic Center. Attendance was 18,056.

DEC 30 (Thurs.) Over 17,000 fans were on hand for Elvis' 8:30
p.m. concert in Atlanta's Omni.

DEC 31 (Fri.) Elvis gave a special New Year's Eve show in Pittsburgh, Pennsylvania, at the Civic Center Arena at
9:30 p.m. There were 16,049 fans in attendance. The
highlights of the show were many, and included a soulful
version of *Reconsider Baby*, and two songs on which he
accompanied himself on piano, *Rags To Riches* and *Unchained Melody*. Vernon, Lisa Marie, and Ginger were in
the audience. The temperature outside was nine degrees,
but inside, Elvis kept his fans warm.

In 1976, Elvis won the *Photoplay* Gold Medal Award as the "Most
Popular Variety Star," based on a poll of *Photoplay* readers.

Elvis' photo was on the cover of the December issue of *Pageant*
magazine. The accompanying article was entitled "Whatever
Happened to Elvis Presley?"

As in 1975, Elvis was again the subject of four books published

throughout the year: *The Films And Career of Elvis Presley* by
James and Boris Zmijewsky, *Elvis* by Dick Tatham, *All Ameri-can Elvis* by Ron Barry, and *On Stage – Elvis Presley* issued by
Creative Education.
In 1976, Elvis was the subject of several magazines devoted to his
career, including *Elvis – The Hollywood Years, Elvis – The
Trials And Triumphs Of The Legendary King Of Rock & Roll,*
and *Elvis* (a *Story Of Rock* special). Elvis was also featured on
the cover of the children's magazine, *Dynomite*, issue twenty-four.

ALL
SHOOK
UP
ELVIS
Day-By-Day,
1977

JANUARY

JAN 3   (Mon.) Elvis, Ginger Alden, and fifteen members of Elvis' security staff flew to Harrison, Arkansas, to attend the funeral of William Spencer, Ginger's grandfather. After the 10:00 a.m. funeral, the party went to the Ramada Inn for lunch. Later that afternoon, Elvis, Ginger, and her parents drove to the airport in Elvis' Lincoln Continental, which had been driven to Harrison by Lamar Fike. They flew back to Memphis, arriving at dusk.

JAN 5   (Wed.) Elvis and Ginger flew to Palm Springs for a week's vacation. During this time, Elvis' dentist, Dr. Max Shapiro, was married at Elvis' home at 1350 Leadera Circle.

JAN 8   (Sat.) Lisa Marie was Elvis' guest in Palm Springs.

JAN 12   (Wed.) Elvis and his entourage returned to Memphis aboard the "Lisa Marie."

JAN 20   (Thurs.) Dr. Nichopoulos filled out prescriptions for Elvis totaling the following: 20 tablets of Biphetamine, 130 tablets of Dexedrine, 50 tablets of Dilaudid, 100 tablets each of Amytal and Quaalude.

JAN 22   (Sat.) Elvis flew from Memphis to Nashville's Jet Center Airport in the morning. He was accompanied by Ginger Alden. A waiting Cadillac Brougham took the couple to the Sheraton South Inn, where Elvis had reserved the entire top floor for an indefinite stay.

Meanwhile, a 9:00 a.m. recording session had been scheduled at Creative Workshop. Elvis did not attend the session, but stayed in the hotel with his producer, Felton Jarvis, listening to demonstration tapes. At the studio, additional rhythm tracks were recorded by the musicians, J.D. Sumner and the Stamps, and the Sweet Inspirations for *Way Down* and *Pledging My Love.*

JAN 23   (Sun.) Elvis remained in seclusion at the hotel while the musicians and backup singers reported back to Creative Workshop.

JAN 24   (Mon.) Without ever attending the recording session, Elvis flew back to Memphis.

JAN 26   (Wed.) Elvis gave an eleven-and-a-half carat diamond engagement ring, valued at $70,000, to Ginger Alden. The couple decided to wait to announce their engagement until the fall, with a Christmas wedding planned.

FEBRUARY

In early February, RCA set up a recording studio in the racquetball court at Graceland. After keeping the musicians and backup vocalists waiting in a local motel for three days, Elvis let them return to their homes. He complained of a sore throat. This was to be the last attempt to record Elvis in a studio situation.

FEB 12   (Sat.) Elvis started his first tour of 1977 with a concert at the Sportatorium in Hollywood, Florida, near Miami. The 8:30 p.m. show drew a crowd of 15,500, with a total gross of $206,350. Fans reported that Elvis had lost some of the weight which had plagued him during the past year.

FEB 13   (Sun.) Up the Florida coast at West Palm Beach, Elvis appeared at the auditorium for an 8:30 p.m. concert, with 5,981 fans attending. The gate was reported to be $87,400.

FEB 14   (Mon.) Still in Florida, Elvis' tour stopped for an 8:30 p.m. show at the Bayfront Center in St. Petersburg. The attendance was 8,355. During the opening number, *C.C. Rider*, his guitar strap broke, and Elvis gave the guitar to a shocked fan in the front row. Many fans laid handsome Valentines on the stage to commemorate the holiday.

FEB 15   (Tues.) Elvis arrived in Orlando at noon and went directly to the Hilton Inn West, where he had reserved the third floor penthouse suite. That night, he appeared in the Sports Stadium at 8:30 p.m.

FEB 16   (Wed.) Elvis traveled to Montgomery, Alabama, for a show at the Garrett Coliseum at 8:30 p.m.

FEB 17   (Thurs.) The *Memphis Press-Scimitar* reported that Elvis had undergone a facelift during his stay at Methodist Hospital in June 1975.

Elvis' next concert was at 8:30 p.m. in the Savannah, Georgia Civic Center.

FEB 18   (Fri.) Over 20,000 fans attended Elvis' 8:30 p.m. show in Columbia, South Carolina, at the Carolina Coliseum. Elvis dedicated *Release Me* to "chicken-neck," and then laughed so hard he could barely sing the song.

FEB 19   (Sat.) Elvis appeared at the Civic Center Freedom Hall in Johnson City, Tennessee. The 8:30 p.m. performance drew 7,000 fans. In the middle of the show, someone handed Elvis a coconut with an ugly face carved on it. Elvis thought this was very funny, and he handed the "gift" to Ginger who was sitting to the right of the stage. Elvis also sang *Where No One Stands Alone*, while accompanying himself on the piano. This song apparently was never performed by Elvis anywhere else.

FEB 20   (Sun.) Over 12,000 fans attended Elvis' show at the Charlotte, North Carolina, Coliseum at 8:30 p.m. Elvis introduced Ginger's sister, Terry Alden, who was the reigning Miss Tennessee. She came on stage and played a classical piece on the piano, much to the amusement of Elvis. He tried to sing *Moody Blue* several times, but he said the note was too high. Finally he ripped up the lyric sheet, and that was the end of *Moody Blue* for that evening.

FEB 21   (Mon.) Still in Charlotte, another 12,000 fans were on hand for Elvis' 8:30 p.m. concert. Although he kidded around during the first half of the concert, kissing many of his female fans and accepting various gifts, it was during the second half of the show that Elvis proved he was still the King of Rock and Roll with dramatic versions of *How Great Thou Art* and *Hurt*. During the latter song, Elvis sang the powerful ending twice. And, to many fans' delight, Elvis finally did sing *Moody Blue*.
Following the concert, Elvis returned to Memphis.

The February issue of *Preview* magazine featured Elvis on the cover, with an accompanying article entitled "Elvis Presley: Who Can Protect Him Now," which reported that his ex-bodyguards were writing an explosive book and that his relationship with Colonel Parker was on the wane.

MARCH

MAR 3   (Thurs.) Elvis signed his Last Will And Testament. The document was witnessed by Ginger Alden and Charlie Hodge. That night, at 8:30 p.m., Elvis and his entourage departed from Memphis for Oakland where they picked up some more friends. At 11:00 p.m., the group, now numbering thirty-one, flew from Oakland to Honolulu.

MAR 4   (Fri.) Elvis and his friends arrived in Honolulu during the early morning hours. The party stayed at the Hilton Rainbow Towers for two days. During this time, Elvis attended a show at the Polynesian Cultural Center with Ed Parker and Ginger Alden, and her sisters Terry and Rosemary.

MAR 6   (Sun.) Elvis and his group moved into the rented Bender House at Kailua, on the west side of Oahu Island, to swim and relax.

MAR 12   (Sat.) Elvis was scheduled to visit the USS Arizona Memorial in Pearl Harbor, but the trip was cancelled after news was received that Vernon had suffered a mild heart attack back in Memphis.

MAR 13   (Sun.) Elvis flew from Honolulu to the mainland, eventually arriving back in Memphis.

MAR 18   (Fri.) Lisa Marie arrived at Graceland to spend the weekend.

MAR 20   (Sun.) In preparation for Elvis' upcoming tour, Dr. Nichopolous had several prescriptions filled under Elvis' name, though he later said that the drugs were to be used by all of the members of the entourage. He also erroneously said, at a later date, that the drugs were also for the Hawaiian holiday.

MAR 22   (Tues.) At 11:30 p.m., Elvis departed Memphis aboard the "Lisa Marie," enroute to Phoenix, Arizona.

MAR 23   (Wed.) Elvis' second concert tour of 1977 started near Phoenix, with a show at the Arizona State University Activities Center in Tempe. The 3:30 p.m. show was attended by 14,047 fans, who paid $198,390 for tickets.

Most reports indicated that Elvis had lost a lot of weight for this tour when compared with the summer of 1976. It was also reported that Elvis appeared to tire on stage.

MAR 24   (Thurs.) The gross receipts were $100,242, as 7,389 fans were on hand for Elvis' 8:30 p.m. show at the Amarillo,

Texas, Civic Center.

MAR 25   (Fri.) The tour moved on to the University of Oklahoma's Lloyd Noble Center in Norman, near Oklahoma City, for an 8:30 p.m. show. Attendance was 11,415.

MAR 26   (Sat.) Elvis remained in Norman for another 8:30 p.m. show. Attendance was 11,500. The total gross for both days was $325,460. Prior to the start of the show, Elvis chipped a tooth.

MAR 27   (Sun.) Elvis appeared at 8:30 p.m. in the Taylor County Coliseum in Abilene, Texas. Attendance was pegged at 7,500.

MAR 28   (Mon.) Over 6,000 fans were in attendance for Elvis' 8:30 p.m. performance at the Municipal Auditorium in Austin, Texas.

MAR 29   (Tues.) Elvis appeared in Alexandria, Louisiana, at the Rapides Parish Coliseum. The 8:30 p.m. show brought out 15,000 fans.

MAR 30   (Wed.) Elvis remained in Alexandria for a second concert, attended by 15,000.

MAR 31   (Thurs.) There were 13,000 fans on hand at the Louisiana State Assembly Center in Baton Rouge when it was announced, during intermission, that the remainder of the show had been cancelled because Elvis had the flu. At that moment, Elvis was bound for Memphis aboard the "Lisa Marie" under the care of Dr. Nichopoulos.

The March issue of *Ladies Home Journal* published an article entitled "Arthritis Update" which said, in part, "Elvis Presley has been hospitalized repeatedly in the past few years because of arthritis. He is said to suffer from Reiter's Syndrome, an ailment characterized by inflammation of the urinary tract, eye irritation, and severe joint pain."

APRIL

APR 1   (Fri.) About 3:00 a.m., Elvis was admitted to Baptist Memorial Hospital's Madison East Wing, sixteenth floor, for intestinal flu and fatigue. (On August 16, 1977, a hospital spokesman reported that Elvis had "gastroenteritis, a strained back, and mild anemia.") Elvis' concert in Mobile, Alabama, was cancelled.

APR 2   (Sat.) **Welcome To My World** started climbing *Billboard*'s "Top LPs and Tapes" chart at number 100. It stayed

on the chart for eleven weeks, peaking at number 44.
Elvis' concert in Macon, Georgia, was cancelled.

APR 3 (Sun.) Elvis' concert in Jacksonville, Florida, was cancelled.

APR 5 (Tues.) About 4:00 a.m., Elvis was discharged from Baptist Memorial Hospital. He was taken back to Graceland to relax.

Priscilla and Lisa Marie arrived for a short visit. It was rare that both she and Elvis were together with their child. Since the divorce, Lisa Marie had usually vacationed with Elvis alone.

APR 21 (Thurs.) With two weeks rest, Elvis was back on the tour circuit for the third time in 1977. His first show was in Greensboro, North Carolina, Coliseum at 8:30 p.m. Attendance was 16,565, and gross receipts were $235,045.

APR 22 (Fri.) The tour traveled to Detroit for an 8:30 p.m. show in Olympia Stadium. There were 15,600 fans on hand, and tickets brought in $229,800. During *Are You Lonesome Tonight*, Elvis and Charlie Hodge got the giggles, and the more they tried to get serious, the worse it got. As Elvis was singing a medley of his hits, a small girl handed him a homemade "Elvis doll," which he found very interesting. The critics, on the other hand, were not amused. Elvis was described as "old," "either high or stiff," "fat and virtually immobile." According to one critic, the show "stunk."

APR 23 (Sat.) Elvis appeared at the University of Toledo's Centennial Hall at 8:30 p.m. There were 9,322 fans on hand, and the total gate was $134,450. Elvis was on stage for an hour and ten minutes.

APR 24 (Sun.) Elvis' concert in Ann Arbor's Crisler Arena at 8:30 p.m. brought in 12,000 fans.

APR 25 (Mon.) RCA recorded the concert at the Saginaw Civic Center at 8:30 p.m. Attendance was 7,197. *If You Love Me, Little Darlin'*, and *Unchained Melody* were recorded for the **Moody Blue** album.

APR 26 (Tues.) Elvis appeared at the Wings Stadium in Kalamazoo, Michigan, at 8:30 p.m. He made his getaway from the stadium in a rusted blue Pontiac to fool the many fans who had waited at the back entrance.

APR 27 (Wed.) Elvis' 8:30 p.m. show in the Milwaukee Arena brought in 11,854 fans.

APR 28 (Thurs.) The tour moved on to Green Bay's Brown County

Veteran's Memorial Coliseum for an 8:30 p.m.

APR 29   (Fri.) Elvis appeared in Duluth, Minnesota, and the Arena at 8:30 p.m.

APR 30   (Sat.) The long-time rumor of a split between Elvis and Colonel Parker resurfaced in the nation's newspapers. According to the press reports, Colonel Parker was in poor health and needed money to cover gambling losses. As a result, Elvis' contract was supposedly up for sale. Colonel Parker immediately responded by calling the *Nashville Banner*, the newspaper where the story had originated, from St. Paul, Minnesota, where he was busy with Elvis' current tour. Colonel Parker completely denied that any of the report was true. The original *Banner* article claimed that Colonel Parker had lost over $1 million in December, while Elvis was playing Las Vegas, and that Elvis and Colonel Parker had not spoken to each other in two years. In a second telephone call, this time from Elvis' Chief of Staff, Joe Esposito, everything was again denied.

Remaining in Minnesota, Elvis appeared at St. Paul's Civic Center at 8:30 p.m. Over 17,000 fans attended for a total gross of $200,527.

MAY

MAY 1   (Sun.) Elvis' 8:30 p.m. concert in the Chicago Stadium drew over 20,000 fans.

MAY 2   (Mon.) Staying in Chicago, Elvis' second night drew 19,600. Total receipts were reported at $264,050.

MAY 3   (Tues.) In Memphis, Elvis was sued by his Chief of Staff, Joe Esposito, Dr. George Nichopoulos, and Michael McMahon, because Elvis had withdrawn his support for Elvis Presley Center Courts, Inc.

Elvis appeared at the Saginaw Center at 8:30 p.m. The gross was $102,598, as 7,197 attended.

Following the concert, Elvis returned to Memphis.

MAY 5   (Thurs.) In Memphis, Vernon Presley filed for divorce from Dee, his wife of almost seventeen years. They were granted a divorce on November 15, 1977, by Judge Euripides Matos Medina in Santo Domingo in the Dominican Republic.

mid-MAY Elvis visited Tupelo during May.

MAY 20 (Fri.) Elvis began his fourth tour of 1977 with a concert at the University of Tennessee's Stokley Athletics Center in Knoxville. The 8:30 p.m. performance was attended by 13,000 fans. It was so hot on stage that Elvis, who was sweating profusely, said at one point, "When the show's over I'll only be three feet tall."

MAY 21 (Sat.) Elvis appeared at 8:30 p.m. in Louisville, Kentucky, at the Freedom Hall. Attendance was reported at 18,000.

MAY 22 (Sun.) The tour moved on to Landover, Maryland, for an 8:30 p.m. show at the Capitol Center, near Washington, D.C. Over 19,000 fans were in attendance.

MAY 23 (Mon.) The 8:30 p.m. concert at the Providence, Rhode Island, Civic Center was attended by 13,500 fans.

MAY 24 (Tues.) Elvis appeared at the Augusta, Maine, Civic Center at 8:30 p.m.

MAY 25 (Wed.) Over 10,000 attended Elvis' 8:30 p.m. concert at Rochester, New York, Community War Memorial. Elvis sang *Little Sister*, one of the songs he sang less frequently. The best songs during the show were *Tryin' To Get To You* and *One Night*.

MAY 26 (Thurs.) Elvis gave a concert at 8:30 p.m. in Binghampton, New York.

MAY 28 (Sat.) Elvis' 8:30 p.m. show at the Philadelphia Spectrum drew a crowd of 18,850, and a total gate of $259,117.

MAY 29 (Sun.) Elvis' 8:30 p.m. concert in the Baltimore Civic Center was marred by his illness during the middle of the show, which forced him to leave the stage for thirty minutes while he was attended to by a physician. Some news reports said that Elvis looked like he was high on drugs and that Elvis fell while on stage. *Variety*, in its review of the show, said, in part, "Presley was heavy-lidded and appeared to most observers to be weak and tired. [He was] paunchy and apparently pained. [The first thirty minutes were] marked by anemic singing, a few stilted attempts at his patented gyrations, bewildered patter, and awkward stage movements." Interestingly, one review of this concert did not mention anything out of the ordinary.

MAY 30   (Mon.) There were no problems during Elvis' 8:30 p.m.
                 concert in Jacksonville, Florida's Coliseum, which had
                 an attendance of 10,300.
MAY 31   (Tues.) Elvis returned to Baton Rouge to make up for the
                 March show, which had been cancelled. There were
                 15,000 fans on hand for his 8:30 p.m. concert.

JUNE

JUN 1   (Wed.) The *Memphis Commercial Appeal* reported that
                 Elvis had signed with CBS-TV for an "anniversary"
                 special.
                 Elvis performed in Macon, Georgia, to make up for the
                 March show, which had been cancelled. The 8:30 p.m.
                 concert in the Coliseum drew 10,242 fans. The high
                 point during the evening was Elvis' rendition of *Fairy-
                 tale*. During the middle of the show, Elvis developed a
                 "frog" in his throat. He did not sing *How Great Thou
                 Art* or *Hurt*, for fear of further straining his voice.
JUN 2   (Thurs.) Making up the final show of the three that had
                 been cancelled in March, Elvis appeared at the Municipal
                 Auditorium in Mobile, Alabama, at 8:30 p.m. where
                 over 11,000 fans were in attendance.
                 Following the show, Elvis returned to Memphis.
JUN 4   (Sat.) The *Memphis Press-Scimitar* reported that Elvis
                 had recently given a luxury automobile to Ginger Alden.
JUN 10   (Fri.) Jeanne Dixon, seeress, predicted that Elvis would
                 have "recurring problems with his health." She said
                 that his ailments would make it difficult for him to ful-
                 fill his contracts for personal appearances.
JUN 17   (Fri.) Elvis' fifth tour of 1977 began with an 8:30 p.m.
                 show at the Southwestern Missouri State University's
                 Hammons Center. Over 9,000 attended. Elvis stayed
                 at the local Howard Johnson's Inn.
JUN 18   (Sat.) Elvis appeared at the Kemper Arena in Kansas City,
                 Missouri. The total take was $225,000, as 17,000 fans
                 attended. Elvis flew to Lincoln, Nebraska, where he
                 checked into the Hilton's Plaza Lincoln Hotel.
JUN 19   (Sun.) RCA and CBS-TV were on hand to record the 8:30
                 p.m. show at the Civic Auditorium Arena in Omaha, as
                 10,604 fans were in attendance. The only song from this
                 concert to be included in the TV special, "Elvis In
                 Concert" was *My Way*. The rest of the special came from

a show in Rapid City, South Dakota. RCA would also
issue part of this concert on its album of the same name.

JUN 20   (Mon.) RCA and CBS-TV were also on hand to record the
concert at the Pershing Municipal Auditorium in Lincoln,
Nebraska. Over 7,500 attended the 8:30 p.m. show.
Elvis stayed at the Hilton's Plaza Lincoln Hotel.

JUN 21   (Tues.) Once again, RCA and CBS-TV were on hand to
record Elvis' 8:30 p.m. show at the Rushmore Plaza
Civic Center in Rapid City. Elvis drew a crowd estimated at 10,000. He stayed at the Holiday Inn. With
the exception of *My Way* mentioned above, all of the
October TV special "Elvis In Concert" came from this
show.

JUN 22   (Wed.) Elvis stayed at the local Holiday Inn prior to his
8:30 p.m. show at the Arena in Sioux City, South
Dakota.

JUN 23   (Thurs.) Elvis arrived in Des Moines, Iowa, and stayed at
the Holiday Inn prior to his 8:30 p.m. concert at the
Veteran's Memorial Auditorium. The turnout for the
show was 11,000. Following the show, Elvis flew to
Madison, Wisconsin.

JUN 24   (Fri.) Elvis arrived in Madison, Wisconsin, shortly after
midnight. Enroute from the airport, Elvis had the limousine stop at a service station when he saw two youths
gang up on the attendant, Keith Lowry, Jr. Elvis assumed
a karate stance and said he would take both of them on.
The fight was averted, and the entire incident lasted less
than five minutes. After tempers cooled, Elvis even
posed for pictures with all concerned. Elvis stayed at
the Sheraton Inn prior to performing at the Cane County
Coliseum at 8:30 p.m. Over 10,000 fans attended the
show.

JUN 25   (Sat.) *Way Down* entered *Billboard*'s "Hot 100" chart at
number 70 where it reached number 21 and stayed
eighteen weeks.

Elvis arrived in Cincinnati in the early morning hours. At
3:00 p.m., disgusted that the air-conditioning was not
working properly, he marched out of his hotel and
walked down the street to the Netherland Hotel, where
he booked two rooms, one for himself and one for his
bodyguards. He appeared at 8:30 p.m. at the Riverfront
Coliseum, and 17,140 fans attended. Elvis was late in
starting his half of the show because of a "technical

hitch." After taking to the stage, he explained that he had to have a tooth filled. Elvis accompanied himself on piano during *Unchained Melody*. Following the show, Elvis flew back to Memphis to spend the night.

JUN 26   (Sun.) Elvis left Memphis in the afternoon and flew to Indianapolis, Indiana, arriving about 6:00 p.m. He was filmed by the CBS-TV crew as he left the "Lisa Marie." Prior to the show, Elvis rested at the Stouffers Indianapolis Inn. Backstage, before the show, Elvis was given a special plaque by RCA which commemorated his 2 billionth record pressed by RCA. The plaque had a copy of the **Moody Blue** LP, along with an inscription. The 8:30 p.m. show at the Market Square Arena was one of Elvis' best on this tour, even though he was obviously very tired. Over 18,000 fans watched, not knowing that this was the last farewell.

After the performance, Elvis returned to Memphis, arriving before dawn on the 27th.

JULY

JUL 23   (Sat.) The **Moody Blue** album entered *Billboard*'s "Top LPs And Tapes" chart at number 58. It peaked at number 3 and stayed on the chart thirty weeks.

In July, Elvis received two *Photoplay* awards for "Favorite Variety Performer" and for "Favorite Rock Star."
In July, Lisa Marie arrived at Graceland for her summer visit.

AUGUST

AUG 8   (Mon.) Elvis rented "Libertyland" amusement park in Memphis for an all-night party (1:15 a.m. to dawn) with Lisa Marie and members of his staff.

AUG 10   (Wed.) Elvis went to the Southbrook Theater for a round of late night movies. One of the films that night was "The Spy Who Loved Me," the latest James Bond movie.

AUG 13   (Sat.) About 3:30 a.m., Elvis, Ginger, Lisa Marie, Billy Smith and his wife Jo left Graceland for a few hours of "midnight movies." They returned to Graceland about 5:30 a.m.

AUG 14   (Sun.) Elvis started a "pre-tour" fast, limiting his intake to fruits and other light foods. His weight had reached almost 250 pounds, but the tour was only three days away.

AUG 15   (Mon.) In preparation for the upcoming tour, Dr. Nicho-poulos ordered the following amounts of prescription drugs from Irving Jack Kirsch's The Prescription House in Memphis: Amytal, 100 three-gram capsules and 12 half-gram ampules; Quaalude, 150 three-hundred-milligram tablets; Dexedrine, 100 five-milligram tablets; Bipheta-mine, 100 twenty-milligram spansules; Percodan, 100 tablets; and Dilaudid, 50 four-milligram tablets, and 20 ccs of two-milligram solution.

Elvis and Ginger took a motorcycle ride through the Memphis suburbs in the late afternoon. Al Strada, Billy Smith, and his wife Jo went along for company. About 10:30 p.m., Elvis, accompanied by Ginger, Charlie Hodge and Billy Smith, visited his dentist, Dr. Lester Hoffman, on Estate Drive.

AUG 16   (Tues.) Shortly after midnight, Elvis returned to Grace-land. He played racquetball on his private court from 4:30 to 6:30 a.m. with Billy Smith. He retired to his bedroom with Ginger, but complained that he could not get to sleep. After taking medication to make him drowsy, he retired to his bath/dressing room at 9:00 a.m. He took along a book to read, Frank Adams' *The Face Of Jesus*, about the Shroud of Turin.

In Chicago, syndicated columnist Bob Greene interviewed Sonny West by telephone concerning the book, *Elvis: What Happened?* The interview would appear in many newspapers the next day, fueling the controversy about Elvis' drug habits and personal life. The interview was completed about noon.

Shortly after 2:00 p.m., Ginger awoke and upon investiga-tion, discovered Elvis slumped over onto the dressing room floor. She called Al Strada on the house intercom. After only a brief look at Elvis, Strada called Joe Es-posito, who had just arrived at Graceland. Esposito started CPR in an attempt to revive Elvis. The Memphis Fire Engine House No. 29 on Elvis Presley Boulevard was notified at 2:33 p.m. Paramedics Charlie Crosby and Ulysses S. Jones, Jr., arrived at Graceland just as Dr. Nichopolous drove in from his office. The ambu-lance with Dr. Nichopoulos, David Stanley, and Joe Es-posito accompanying Elvis rushed to Baptist Memorial

B U L L E T I N

(ELVIS)

(MEMPHIS, TENNESSEE)---ELVIS PRESLEY---THE 42-YEAR-OLD KING OF

ROCK N' ROLL---DIED TODAY IN MEMPHIS, TENNESSEE. POLICE SAY HE DIED,

OF RESPIRATORY FAILURE IN BAPTIST HOSPITAL.

---END REPEAT---

UPI 08-16 02:40 PPD

Hospital. All efforts to revive Elvis failed and his death was announced at 3:30 p.m.

That night, following an autopsy supervised by Dr. Jerry T. Francisco, Tennessee's chief medical examiner, Elvis' body was removed from Baptist Hospital and taken to the Memphis Funeral Home.

In a statement issued to the press, Dr. Nichopoulos said that Elvis had been taking appetite suppressant drugs and drugs to control his hypertension and colon problem.

AUG 17 (Wed.) During a press conference, Dr. Francisco listed three causes that could have led to Elvis' death: an enlarged heart, clogging of the coronary arteries, and moderately severe high blood pressure. He reported that there were no new or old needle marks on the body. The official cause of death was listed as cardiac arrhythmia (an irregular heartbeat, during which the heart ceases to pump effectively).

Shortly after noon, Elvis' body was taken to Graceland. There was a short, informal, open-coffin service for his family and friends at 2:00 p.m. in the music room. Beginning at 3:00 p.m., an estimated 75,000 mourning fans attempted to file past Elvis' open casket. The number that actually made it inside was estimated between 10,000 and 20,000. The original cut-off time had been set for 5 p.m., but Vernon agreed to extend the time until 6:30 p.m.

There were 3,166 floral wreaths sent to Graceland by fans and celebrities. The U.S. Navy laid a wreath in Elvis' name at the memorial to the USS Arizona at Pearl Harbor. It was Elvis' 1961 benefit concert that had insured the memorial would be built.

President Jimmy Carter issued a proclamation which read in part, Elvis was a symbol of "the vitality, rebelliousness and good humor" of the United States. "Elvis' death deprived our country of a part of itself."

AUG 18 (Thurs.) At 3:30 a.m., a car driven by Treatsie Wheeler, III and carrying three female juvenile passengers plowed into the crowd of 350 fans outside of the gates to Graceland, killing Juanita Joanne Johnson and Alice Marie Hovartar of Monroe, Louisiana, and injuring Tammy J. Baiter of St. Clair, Missouri. Wheeler was charged with second-degree murder, leaving the scene of an accident,

public drunkenness, and reckless driving. He registered
1.6 on the Breathalyzer shortly after being taken into
custody.

At 2:00 p.m., a private funeral service for Elvis was held
at Graceland. Kathy Westmoreland, backing soprano for
Elvis on tour, sang a hymn. Jake Hess and the Statesmen Quartet, James Blackwood, and J.D. Sumner and
the Stamps also sang hymns. Rev. C.W. Bradley, pastor
of the Wooddale Church of Christ; Rev. Rex Humbard,
television evangelist; and Jackie Kahane, comedian on
Elvis' tours, all gave their parting remarks. Many celebrities were reported to have paid their respects at
Graceland, including John Wayne, Burt Reynolds,
Sammy Davis, Jr., and Jacqueline Kennedy Onassis,
but only Ann-Margret and her husband Roger Smith,
Chet Atkins, and Caroline Kennedy were spotted for
certain.

The coffin was sealed and transported to a waiting white
hearse. The funeral caravan began leaving Graceland at
3:28 p.m. It consisted of the white hearse and sixteen
white Cadillac limousines. In all, forty-nine cars were in
the procession from Graceland to Forest Hills Cemetery,
located three miles north on Elvis Presley Boulevard.
Elvis' body was emtombed in a mausoleum about 100
yards from the grave of his mother.

AUG 19   (Fri.) At the request of Vernon Presley, all of the flowers
from the 3,166 floral displays were given away to fans
at Forest Hills Cemetery.

AUG 20   (Sat.) The *Billboard* charts for the week Elvis died read as
follows: *Way Down/Pledging My Love* was number 1 on
the "Hot Country Singles" chart, *Way Down* was number
47 and fading on the "Hot 100," and **Moody Blue** was
number 24 and climbing on the "Hot LPs And Tapes"
chart.

AUG 22   (Mon.) Elvis' thirteen-page will was filed for probate before
Judge Joseph W. Evans in a twenty-minute ceremony in
Memphis. Vernon Presley was named executor, and the
estate was to be split between him, Grandma Minnie,
and eventually, everything would go to Lisa Marie in a
trust. Neither Priscilla, Linda Thompson, or Ginger
Alden were mentioned in the will. There was a provi-
sion for Elvis' relatives to get assistance for health, education, support, comfortable maintenance, and welfare.

AUG 23   (Tues.) RCA reported Elvis' total sales up to that time of

600 million singles. He had been awarded fifty-five
gold singles, twenty-four gold albums, and his thirty-
three movies had grossed $150 million. It was estimated
that Elvis' total lifetime gross exceeded $4.3 billion.

AUG 24 Weds.) At a Memphis press conference, Dr. Nichopoulos
denied that Elvis' had a "drug problem," although he did
report that Elvis had accidently taken too many prescribed medications on several occasions. He also said that,
as far as he knew, the only medications available in Graceland at the time of Elvis' death were a few sleeping pills
and medications for Elvis' colon discomfort and for a
recurring sinus problem.

AUG 25 (Thurs.) In an interview with Linda Thompson, she dis-
counted Ginger Alden's claim that Elvis and Ginger
would be married. According to Miss Thompson, neither
she, Priscilla, or Elvis' father, nor any of Elvis' entourage
were aware of any pending marriage.

AUG 27 (Sat.) This is the date that Elvis and Ginger Alden had
planned to announce their engagement during Elvis' concert in Memphis.

AUG 29 (Mon.) Three men, Ronnie Lee Adkins, twenty-six, Raymond M. Green, twenty-five, and Bruce Nelson, twenty,
were charged with attempting to steal Elvis' body
from the mausoleum at Forest Hills Cemetery.

AUG 31 (Weds.) Dr. Nichopoulos called another press conference
in Memphis to again deny reports that Elvis' death had
been drug induced.

SEPTEMBER

SEP 7 (Weds.) In Memphis, Beecher Smith, an attorney for the
Presley estate, filed an application for a zoning variance
with the Board of Adjustment which would allow both
Elvis' and Gladys' bodies to be moved from Forest Hill
cemetary to a plot inside the walls of Graceland. The
request was placed on the agenda of the board's next
meeting on September 28th.
NBC-TV aired a one-hour version of "Elvis On Tour," the
1972 documentary, at 10:00 p.m. (EST).

SEP 10 (Sat.) Two of Elvis' earlier albums entered *Billboard*'s
"Top LPs'And Tapes" chart: **Elvis' Golden Records,
Volume 3** entered at number 130 and peaked at num-
ber 64, staying twenty-two weeks; and **Elvis' Golden**

Records entered at number 136, peaked at number 63, and stayed twenty-three weeks.

SEP 11   (Sun.) Three men, Nicholas W. Baldwin, Thomas J. Kamphais, and Marcus Worth Logue, were charged with vandalism in the ripping of the Graceland fence.

SEP 15   (Thurs.) During the "Third Rock Music Award Show," Elvis was inducted into the Hall Of Fame. The previous inductees were Chuck Berry and the Beatles.

SEP 17   (Sat.) Three more albums entered the LP chart in *Billboard:* **Welcome To My World** started at number 122, peaked at number 71, and stayed fourteen weeks; **Elvis — A Legendary Performer, Volume 1** entered at number 122, peaked at number 62, and stayed fourteen weeks; and **Elvis' Worldwide Gold Award Hits, Volume 1** entered at number 126, peaked at number 83 and stayed fourteen weeks.

SEP 28   (Weds.) At the regular meeting of the Memphis Board of Adjustment, a variance in the zoning ordinance was approved which would allow Elvis and Gladys to be reburied at Graceland.

OCTOBER

OCT 2   (Sun.) Elvis and his mother were reburied in the Meditation Garden at Graceland.

OCT 3   (Mon.) Elvis' final TV show, "Elvis In Concert," was shown over CBS-TV at 8:00 p.m. (EDT). The program was taken from Elvis' June 1977 tour, and consisted mainly of the concerts in Omaha, Nebraska, and Rapid City, South Dakota.

OCT 4   (Tues.) Charges were dropped in the case that resulted from the August 29th arrest of three men in an apparent attempt to steal Elvis' body and hold it for $10 million ransom. Authorities admitted that one of the men, Ronnie Adkins, was a police informant, and the whole plan may have been a hoax. The trio were charged with misdemeanor trespassing.

OCT 19   (Wed.) The Mississippi State Legislature voted to rename that portion of Highway 78 from Tupelo to Memphis the "Elvis Presley Memorial Highway."

At a Memphis press conference, Dr. Jerry Francisco refused to comment on a local newspaper report that as many as ten drugs had contributed to Elvis' death. Vernon, when

reached by reporters, deferred all questions to Dr.
Francisco.

OCT 21   (Fri.) At a press conference, Dr. Francisco confirmed that
eight prescription drugs had been found in Elvis' blood
samples, taken during the autopsy on the day of his death.
Four of these drugs were found in "significant amounts."
These included three sedatives and codeine. The other
drugs included Demoral and Valium. Dr. Francisco
said that the drugs might have been taken up to seven
days before Elvis died.

OCT 29   (Sat.) **Elvis In Concert** started up *Billboard*'s "Top LPs
And Tapes" chart at number 18. It peaked at number
5 and stayed seventeen weeks.

NOVEMBER

NOV 12   (Sat.) *My Way* entered *Billboard*'s "Hot 100" chart at
number 75. It peaked at number 22 and stayed on the
chart twelve weeks.

NOV 23   (Weds.) An inventory of Elvis' personal estate was filed in
the Memphis probate court by attorneys representing
the Presley family. According to the inventory, Elvis
had a checking account at the National Bank of Commerce
with a balance of $1,055,173; several savings accounts
with balances ranging from $39 to $35,000; $150 million
due from RCA in royalties from record sales; fifty guns,
including three machineguns; two Stutz Blackhawks, a
black Ferrari, a pink 1955 Cadillac and four other vehicles,
six golf carts and six motorcycles; a Convair 880 (the
"Lisa Marie") and a nine-passenger Jetstar. There was a
room-by-room listing of all furniture in Graceland, including a collection of Louis XIV and Louis XV sofas and
dining room pieces and many television sets, including
two in the ceiling above his nine-by-nine foot bed. Among
his jewelry was a gold cross pendant inlaid with 236
round diamonds and other stones.

NOV 27   (Sun.) Thousands of fans who had waited in a near freezing
downpour were allowed to enter the grounds of Graceland for the walk up to the Meditation Garden to view
Elvis' gravesite. Thereafter, fans would be allowed to
visit the grave on a daily basis, Tuesday through Sundays.

DECEMBER

DEC 4 (Fri.) NBC-TV broadcast the "Las Vegas Entertainment Awards" show at 8:00 p.m. (EST). Elvis was overwhelmingly voted the top male musical star of the year by the Academy of Variety and Cabaret Artists.

DEC 18 (Sun.) At the end of a revival at the Tanner Apostolic Church in Decatur, Alabama, two dozen youths burned copies of Elvis' records as Evangelist Eddie Jones urged them to "burn them before they burn you in hell." Jones later said that he objected to Elvis' records because many of the songs contained suggestive lyrics. Jones said that records by other "marijuana-smoking, pot-smoking, drug-using groups" were also burned.

DEC 24 (Sat.) Elvis was voted the "Number 1 Box Office Award" for 1977 for arenas seating 6,000 to 20,000. In *Billboard's* annual year-end survey of the music scene, Elvis was voted the number six "Pop Male Artist." He was number forty-five in "Pop Singles" and number eighteen in "Pop Albums." The single *Way Down* was number 64 for the year.

DEC 25 (Sun.) Christmas was spent quietly at Graceland.

It matters not how a man dies, but how he lives. The act of dying is not of importance, it lasts so short a time. — *Samuel Johnson, circa 1775*

A Discussion Of Elvis' Place
In The Memphis Music Scene
Prior To July 1954

One of the most often asked, and least answered, questions surrounding the life of Elvis Presley is: just how involved was he as a teenager in the music scene in Memphis before his first professional recording session at Sun Records on July 5, 1954? It is unfortunate that this important question will never be completely answered. There are two basic reasons why.

First, many of the individuals directly involved with Elvis and/or the Memphis music scene during the period before Elvis achieved national popularity have died, taking their recollections to the grave with them. Among those who knew Elvis during this period and never committed their recollections to paper were Elvis' parents, Johnny and Dorsey Burnette, Bob Neal, Dewey Phillips, Bill Black, and several of Elvis' aunts, uncles and cousins.

The second complicating factor is no less troublesome: human nature. Elvis made his first recording for Sun Records in July 1954. Within three weeks, one local newspaper was already reporting that this record was "getting an amazing number of plays on all Memphis radio stations." By November 1954, Elvis had appeared on both the "Grand Ole Opry" and the "Louisiana Hayride," arguably the two biggest country and western radio shows in the world. By December 1954, Elvis was being called the "hottest" thing on the "Louisiana Hayride" in a long time. A year later, in November 1955, Elvis was an unprecedented success in the country market, and RCA Victor records was eager to pay Sun Records the unheard of sum of $35,000, with a bonus of $5,000 to Elvis, for his contract. By July 1956, Elvis was a nationwide phenomenon, the likes of which may never be seen again. It was precisely the suddenness of Elvis' rise to fame that left many people who had been close to him during the early days hungry for a piece of the glory. In his hometown of Tupelo, thousands of people, forgetting that the Presley's lived among the city's poor . . . forgetting that Elvis had been just another nondescript child in the local school . . . and forgetting that the Presley's had fled from Tupelo's poverty in the fall of 1948 when Elvis was only thirteen . . . these thousands were eager to claim that they had been close friends with the Presley family, had in fact lived next door to Elvis, been Elvis' closest friend, had made a mental note of Elvis' seemingly inborn talent for singing. Many more, in fact, than could have possibly done so. In Memphis, the Presley's adopted home, the phenomenon of "friendship with the famous" was just as strong. By July 1956, Elvis had thousands of classmates from Humes High who remembered this shy, quiet teen-ager quite vividly. There were an equal number of neighbors, employers, and close friends offering their reminiscences. Any musician, white or black, country singer or blues shouter, who had passed through Memphis during the previous ten years had seemingly met and jammed with this boy, whom they all knew would become a star. Such is human nature.

Through the more than thirty years since Elvis first recorded *That's All Right*, there have been dozens of people who have come forth and claimed that they either sat in on jam sessions with Elvis, introduced him to nightclub owners who alternately loved/hated Elvis' act, or who managed him before he got to Sam Phillips' studios. Several of these stories deserve close scrutiny. First, it should be noted from the outset that I am not questioning the truthfulness of any of the people involved. I am only reviewing the facts in the specific stories related.

The incident that has received the most notoriety was the announcement, in 1978, that Elvis' "earliest known recording" had been unearthed in, of all places, Arizona. The song, *Tell Me Pretty Baby*, was supposedly made in early 1954, while Elvis was passing through Phoenix. Affidavits were produced confirming that Elvis had been paid fifteen dollars to sit in with a local group, The Red Dots, who had booked a session at Audio Studios. The recording had apparently remained under wraps for the next twenty-four years. The participants later admitted that the entire episode was a fraud, but not until untold thousands of Elvis' fans had sent in five dollars for a copy of the single. This story should have raised an immediate question in the minds of most fans, who should have known that the Presley's were too poor to afford the luxury of a vacation in the Southwest in early 1954. On closer inspection, the record does not even sound as though it could have been produced as early as 1954. The use of a backing vocal group similar to that used on the recordings of Buddy Holly in 1957, and the inclusion of a Fender bass in the group, should have immediately warned any music critic that this song was a phony. Still, that didn't stop the story from wide circulation.

Blues singer Roy Brown has stated, in an article published in *Blues Unlimited* magazine in 1977, that whenever he played Tupelo, Elvis would come around to see him. This is highly unlikely, considering the strict segregation in Mississippi at that time, and the fact that Elvis moved from Tupelo to Memphis when he was thirteen. It is doubtful that any pre-teen white boy would have been allowed in any establishment in Tupelo where Roy Brown might have performed. Brown also figures in several other stories involving Elvis. One, in which Elvis would drop by any of the several Memphis nightclubs where Brown was appearing and buy wine for the band, seems very questionable. Due to the age restrictions on liquor buying in Tennessee, it is doubtful that such things occurred until after Elvis turned twenty-one in 1956, if then. Brown also claimed that he saw Elvis performing at the airport in Memphis in the mid-1960s. Brown was reportedly down on his luck at the time, and Elvis reached into his pocket and give Brown several hundred dollars. While the story does sound like an example of Elvis' generosity, it should be remembered that Elvis didn't play the airport lounge in Memphis after 1954, a time during which it is doubtful if Elvis ever had a hundred dollars in his pocket at one time.

Another famed blues singer who remembers Elvis is Lowell Fulson. Fulson says they met at the Club Handy in June 1954, during a set by B.B. King. This is hard to disprove but, again, most clubs in Memphis at that time would have been segregated and not allowed a nineteen-year-old through the doors. King, on the other hand, is certain that he remembers first meeting the young Elvis in a Beale Street pawn shop. Who knows?

A remembrance of another kind comes from George Klein, a lifelong friend of Elvis. According to Klein, during the eighth grade, the homeroom teacher, Elsie Marmann, told Elvis he was singing off-key in the class choir. The next day, Elvis returned to school with his guitar and sang *Cold Icy Fingers* for the class. Elvis told Mrs. Marmann that she just didn't appreciate his type of singing. She agreed! This story sounds a little like the well-known Christmas revue story, which reportedly took place in 1950 while Elvis was in the tenth grade.

The Elvis fanzine "Teddy Bear" published a most interesting article in March 1980: one George Owens, who reportedly lived at 27 N. Bellvue in an apartment building shared by Elvis' uncle, Vester Presley, allegedly took Elvis to a "little country and western club in Memphis to try to get him a booking." There they met Sleepy Eyed John, but the pair was chased out of the club. They went to another club, where Elvis "did a song of two. There were a couple of musicians playing there and they were real jealous of Elvis and the way people were screaming and carrying on when they heard him." Then, the duo went to the Palms Club on Summer Avenue, where Elvis "did one hell of a show . . . he just drove them wild. He was about 16 or 17 at the time." This wonderful anecdote supposedly took

483

place in August 1950 (Elvis would have actually been fifteen). Everyone who knew Elvis at this time remembers a basically shy boy, not yet two years in the big city, whose mother walked him to and from school daily. If Elvis really had the talent to "drive them wild" at fifteen, he would have been discovered much earlier than he was. In August 1950, children just did not act in this fashion.

Johnny Burnette and the Rock 'N Roll Trio, a popular Memphis band which would gain national fame in 1956, figure in a number of stories centered around the year before Elvis' first professional recording session. In the spring of 1953, Elvis reportedly "jammed" with the group at a jamboree in West Memphis. In August of the same year, Elvis supposedly sat in with the trio during a promotion at a used car lot on Airways Boulevard in Memphis. *The New Musical Express*, an English music journal, reported that Johnny Burnette remembered first seeing Elvis singing at the fire station near his home on Alabama Street (the Presleys moved into the Alabama Street apartment in April 1953). According to an interview published in *Goldmine* magazine in 1982, Paul Burlison, guitar with the Rock 'N Roll Trio, stated that Elvis lived across the street from him and that Elvis was close friends with Johnny Black, Bill Black's brother. On Saturday evenings, Elvis, Johnny Black, and Dorsey Burnette (Johnny Burnette's brother and the third member of the Rock 'N Roll Trio) would play at a teen canteen dance. Also, according to Burlison, Johnny Black was Elvis' original choice to play at his first recording session, but Johnny was in Texas at the time, so Bill Black took his place. Burlison finally reports that, while he was playing at a Memphis shopping center with Jerry Fowler (in a show broadcast over KWEM radio on Saturdays), Elvis came out of the audience to sing *Take Your Finger Out Of It, It Don't Belong To You* and *Talking 'Bout Your Birthday*. Most of this information appears to be factually based, and it would certainly indicate that Elvis was already musically active in Memphis before he was offered the opportunity to make a professional recording in July 1954. The part about Johnny Black, though, does not fit the facts. Scotty Moore and Bill Black were regular members of Doug Poindexter and His Starlight Wranglers, and it is doubtful if Scotty would have called anyone other than Bill Black to play bass at the session.

Author Vince Staten, in *The Real Elvis: Good Old Boy*, reports that Elvis' first paid appearance was in October 1953 at the Eagle's Nest Club. The house band at the time was the Johnny Long's Orchestra, and Elvis was introduced by Dewey Phillips during an intermission break. Elvis chose to sing *That's Amore*, a current hit for Dean Martin, and several other similar ballads. Elvis was paid five dollars to fill in for the orchestra during the week, but he was not renewed because the club owner was not impressed. This is an interesting story in light of the three photographs in Vester Presley's book, *A Presley Speaks*, which show a teenaged Elvis at the Eagle's Nest. However, it is actually quite doubtful that Dewey Philips met Elvis before interviewing him on his radio show the Saturday night after that first recording session in 1954.

Another club owner who reportedly was not bowled over by the early Elvis was Clyde Leopard, who refused to allow Elvis to sing at the Cotton Club in West Memphis in January 1954. In another item printed in a 1982 issue of *Goldmine* magazine, it is reported that Roy Hall auditioned Elvis for a spot at his Nashville nightclub, The Music Box. Elvis did not get the job because, as Hall related, "He weren't no damn good." These last two items should be taken with a grain of salt.

Finally, it has been well known for some time that Elvis was very interested in the Memphis gospel music scene prior to July 1954. He frequently attended the all-night gospel sings at Ellis Auditorium, and he was enough of a gospel music fan to have wangled his way backstage on several occasions so that his face, if not his name, was familiar to many of the members of the groups that performed in Memphis. J.D. Sumner, who was a member of the Sunshine Boys Quartet and later led the Stamps Quartet when they were Elvis' regular background male vocalists in the 1970s, remembers seeing Elvis backstage at many of the gospel shows. In fact, Elvis was so close to joining the Blackwood Brothers' junior group, The Songfellows, that only a matter of a few days stood between his choice of a career as a popular singer or a gospel group member.

All of this leads one to speculate that either an awful lot of people are mistaken (remembering our cautions regarding human nature); or that they were all subject to some sort of mass delusion; or that Elvis was really actively involved in the music scene in Memphis prior to July 1954. I'll allow for the possibility that some of the first and some of the last alternatives are creditable choices. It is certain that Elvis was searching for some sort of musical identity during the year after he graduated from Humes High School and his first recording session. It would be naive to assume that Elvis had no experience prior to singing *That's All Right* and *Blue Moon Of Kentucky*. One listen, and it is apparent that Elvis could not have simply "absorbed" his performing style from possibly watching others and listening to the radio. There were musical undercurrents in Memphis in the early 1950s in both blues and country music, and it was as logical a place as any to have nurtured the sound that eventually became identified as the music of Elvis Presley.

Appendix II

The Sun Records Sessions

Scenario No. 1: Sam Phillips' Story

Several months prior to July 1954, Sam Phillips, owner of Memphis' Sun Records, which doubled as the Memphis Recording Service, received a demonstration record from Peer Music in Nashville. The song on the disk, *Without You*, was sung by a soulful black singer whose whereabouts — indeed, whose very name — could not be determined when Phillips inquired about the possibility of releasing the record "as is." Realizing that he would have to re-record the song, Phillips searched his files for the name of a ballad singer who could do the job. The name of Elvis Presley did not come immediately to mind. Phillips had met Elvis only once before, on Elvis' second trip to the 706 Union Avenue recording studios of the Memphis Recording Service to make a two-sided demonstration disk of his own. That meeting, on January 4th, about four months before the arrival of the demo of *Without You*, had left Phillips with less than a clear idea of just exactly what type of singer Elvis wanted to be. It was only after some prodding by Marion Keisker, Phillips' secretary, that Elvis was summoned to the studio and an attempt was made to record *Without You*. The result was unsatisfactory, but Phillips was not completely disappointed. He asked Elvis just what type of song he could sing. Elvis proceeded to run through a series of pop ballads, which he sang in the style of Dean Martin. Sensing that there was enough talent in the boy to warrant further work, Phillips contacted Scotty Moore, lead guitarist with Doug Poindexter And His Starlight Wranglers, a local country and western band which would make its only recording a month later for Phillips' Sun Records. Moore took Elvis under his tutelage and together with fellow Wrangler, bassist Bill Black, they worked diligently for the next two months developing Elvis' vocal style to a point, in early July, where both Phillips and Moore felt that Elvis was ready to record.

487

Scenario No. 2: Scotty Moore's Story

Scotty Moore was an up-and-coming electric guitarist who was playing the local country and western clubs with Doug Poindexter And His Starlight Wranglers. He also worked days at his brother's dry cleaning establishment, where he was adept at blocking hats. In his off hours, he frequently stopped by Miss Taylor's coffee shop, located next door to Sun Records on Union Avenue. There he became friendly with Sun Record's owner, Sam Phillips, and with several of the other local acts who were trying to persuade Phillips to record them. Up to this time, Sun Records had been known as a company that issued records only by black artists, but Phillips was aware of the demand for country music and was always open to the prospects of recording other talent. After some persuading, Moore convinced Phillips to use the Starlight Wranglers as a studio group backing singers who required additional instrumentation. Moore also persuaded Phillips to issue a record of the Poindexter band, and a session was held on May 25, 1954. Unfortunately, no one felt the subsequent record, *My Kind Of Carrying On* backed with *Now She Cares No More For Me*, (Sun 202), had even the remotest possibility of being a local hit. More importantly, however, it had opened the door for Moore to pursue his business relationship with Phillips. Moore envisioned himself as a talent scout for Sun Records. The name of Elvis Presley came up during their talks over coffee at Miss Taylor's, and through some prompting by Moore, Phillips put Elvis in touch with Moore. A meeting was arranged for Sunday, July 4th, at Moore's apartment. Also on hand was Bill Black, bassist with the Poindexter band. After an afternoon of rehearsal, Moore called Phillips and said he felt Elvis was ready for a studio session. Arrangements were made for the trio to come to Sun Records the next night.

Scenario No. 3: Who's Right?

There was indeed a demonstration disk of *Without You* sent to Sam Phillips by Peer Music. And it was impossible to locate the singer on the record. This part of the story is substantiated by Phillips' secretary, Marion Keisker. She remembers calling Elvis on the telephone to come to the studio on a Saturday for the ill-fated audition. The first point in the Phillips' version that really does not jibe with Moore's is the timing. Was Elvis' audition in April or June? And, following the audition, did Elvis work with Moore, Phillips, and Bill Black for months before hitting on the right combination with *That's All Right* on July 5th, or was there only a single afternoon's rehearsal at Scotty Moore's apartment on Sunday, July 4th?

Prior to the May 25th recording session for the Poindexter band, several sources place Moore and Phillips together. All sources confirm, however, that it was only after this session that the name of Elvis was raised between the two. If the demonstration record of *Without You* arrived in late May or early June, this would fit the known facts. Also, just at this time, Phillips was working with several new recording acts, each of which required attention on his part. During June 1954, Sun Records released no less than six new singles, which is a large number for an operation this small.

So, who is to be believed? On the one hand, we have the memories of a busy man, submerged in the recording of several acts, whose office was filled daily with drugstore cowboys wanting him to record them. On the other hand, there are the recollections of an aspiring artist who worked days as a hatter and dreamed nights of success; a musician who was being offered his first big break. Sorry, there is no contest. I have to go with Scotty's recollections.

Which leads to the night of July 5, 1954, in Sun Records' studios at 706 Union Avenue, Memphis, Tennessee.

Steve Sholes' Sun Sessions Notes

It is unfortunate that Sam Phillips did not keep a complete log of the activities at Sun Records. There are no session notes for the historian to draw from. There is no known ledger which accounts for the number of records pressed or sold. There are only the memories of those present at the time and, as we have seen, those recollections are not always compatible. There is, however, one piece of paper which has survived for almost thirty years, but one which raises as many new questions as it answers.

In November 1955, following RCA Victor's purchase of Elvis' recording contract from Sam Phillips and Sun Records, fifteen boxes of Scotch-brand recording tape were turned over to Steve Sholes, head of Specialty Singles for RCA Victor. After receiving these boxes of tape, Sholes reviewed each tape and made a brief note covering each box. These notes were handwritten on a single piece of notebook paper which reads, verbatim, as follows:

WORK PARTS ON
1. F2WW   8000, 8001, 8039 only
2.   "   8040 & two other selections ?
3.   "   8043 & "Just Because"
4.   "   8046 & "I Got A Woman" and "Baby, Trying To Get To You"
5.   "   8047 only
6.   "   "   "

```
 7.  F2WB  8115   "
               8116   "
 8.     "      8117   "
 9.     "      8118
        "      8116 & F2WB
10.     "      8118 only  8043
11.     "      "When It Rains It Really Pours" N.G.
12.     "      8116 & "Satisfied" N.G.
13.     "      8040
               G2WB – "I Love You Because"
14.  F2WB  8041 only not so hot
15.  "Harbor Lights" N.G.
```

These cryptic comments offer a wealth of material for the researcher, but first it is necessary to break down the code into understandable English.

The "F2" notation denotes that the songs were mastered by RCA Victor in 1955. The next letter, "W," indicates that RCA Victor considered Elvis a "western" performer. The reason for the change from "F2WW" to "F2WB" in the middle of the sheet is unclear. The "B" notation was used by RCA Victor at this time for all master recordings, and it appeared on all 78 r.p.m. records issued at this time. The "W" was used on 45 r.p.m. records, probably to differentiate them from the 78s in RCA Victor's bookkeeping system. The lone "G2WB" for the version of *I Love You Because* in box thirteen denotes a 1956 matrix number. The four-digit numbers are more important. These are the specific master numbers assigned by RCA Victor to each song on a given tape. As you can see, not all of the songs were given master numbers; some were noted by title. It is also clear that the same number appears more than once, indicating that several versions of the same song existed on different tapes.

Now, let me present another listing based on the song titles involved:

1. "I Forgot To Remember To Forget," "Mystery Train," "Trying To Get To You" only
2. "That's All Right" + 2 other selections*
3. "Good Rockin' Tonight," "Just Because"*
4. "Baby Let's Play House," "I Got A Woman,"* "Trying To Get To You"*
5. "I'm Left, You're Right, She's Gone"
6. "I'm Left, You're Right, She's Gone"
7. "Tomorrow Night,"* "I'll Never Let You Go"
8. "Blue Moon"
9. "Just Because," "I'll Never Let You Go" and F2WB(?)

10. "Just Because," only "Good Rockin' Tonight"
11. "When It Rains It Really Pours"* N.G.
12. "I'll Never Let You Go," "Satisfied"* N.G.
13. "That's All Right," "I Love You Because"*
14. "Blue Moon Of Kentucky"
15. "Harbor Lights"* N.G.

I have indicated those versions of specific songs which were originally listed by title and not number with an asterisk (*). These versions most probably were outtakes or rehearsals. The notation "N.G." which appears for boxes eleven, twelve, and fifteen means "no good," and was Sholes' personal comment, after listening to the tape, that the song was not commercial enough for release.

Several sheets of ruled paper, also handwritten by Sholes but with a more expanded analysis of each box of tape, have been reproduced as part of the packaging for several of the **Elvis — A Legendary Performer** albums. These sheets give timings and other information concerning the songs on tapes eleven through fifteen. Although not of specific significance to this appendix, it is important to note that on the single sheet referred to at the beginning of this section, the songs for box thirteen are reversed from the way they actually appear on the tape. Since the remainder of the timing sheets were not available from RCA Victor, I can only assume that the songs on the remainder of the tapes are in the order listed.

Looking at the list above, it becomes immediately apparent that unless the two selections referred to in box two are *Milkcow Blues Boogie* and *You're A Heartbreaker* (F2WW 8044 and 8045), then these two songs, which were issued as Elvis' third Sun Records single, are missing. Also missing is *I Don't Care If The Sun Don't Shine* (F2WW 8042), the B-side of Elvis' second release, *Good Rockin' Tonight*; more about this song in a moment.

It is also interesting to note that *I Got A Woman*, box four, appears to have been recorded during the same session that produced *Baby Let's Play House* and an unreleased version of *Trying To Get To You*. A live version of *I Got A Woman* from a March 1955 show has been available for several years, and the song was the first one recorded by Elvis for RCA Victor in January 1956, probably at Steve Sholes' urging after listening to this tape.

When It Rains It Really Pours remained a hidden mystery for nearly thirty years. Although listed by Sholes, both the tape and the box were reported missing from RCA Victor's storage vault. In 1982, the tape and the original Scotch box were found inside of another tape box. It was only this stroke of dumb luck that saved the tape from the same end which befell most of the remaining tapes from Elvis' Sun Records sessions, virtually all of which have been misplaced or stolen over the years.

Finally, *Satisfied*, in box twelve, has never surfaced, and appears to have been attempted only once — unsuccessfully. Again, RCA Victor reports that this tape has been either stolen or misplaced.

As part of an attempt to relate the above information to other known, and sometimes legendary, facts surrounding Elvis' recording sessions at Sun Records, it was necessary to come up with what I felt was a probable recording sequence for the tapes. Here is what I believe is the correct sequence for the fifteen known boxes:

15. "Harbor Lights"
13. "I Love You Because" and "That's All Right"
 2. "That's All Right" + 2 selections
14. "Blue Moon Of Kentucky"
 8. "Blue Moon"
 7. "Tomorrow Night" and "I'll Never Let You Go"
12. "I'll Never Let You Go," "Satisfied" and "I'll Never Let You Go"
 9. "Just Because," "I'll Never Let You Go" and F2WB (?)
 3. "Good Rockin' Tonight" and "Just Because"
10. "Just Because" and "Good Rockin' Tonight"
 5. "I'm Left, You're Right, She's Gone"
 6. "I'm Left, You're Right, She's Gone"
 4. "Baby Let's Play House," "I Got A Woman" and "Trying To Get To You"
 1. "I Forgot To Remember To Forget," "Mystery Train," and "Trying To Get To You"
11. "When It Rains It Really Pours"

Looking at this rearranged list, I feel that the missing song title in box nine is probably *I Don't Care If The Sun Don't Shine*. This would fit the pattern and fill the gap at the right point in time. It also fits with the material which was issued in 1974 on the bootleg album, **Good Rocking Tonight**. On that LP, there are portions of four Sun Records outtakes sung by Elvis: *I Don't Care If The Sun Don't Shine, Blue Moon Of Kentucky, I'll Never Let You Go*, and *My Baby Is Gone* (a slow version of *I'm Left, You're Right, She's Gone*).

If this song sequence is correct, linking the session information to an approximate recording date now becomes a little easier.

Elvis' first professional recording session took place on the night of July 5, 1954. That night, he attempted *Harbor Lights, I Love You Because*, and *That's All Right*. The next night he was back to record *Blue Moon Of Kentucky*, and possibly *Blue Moon*.

On September 10, 1954, Elvis' second recording session was

almost a disaster. Starting with *Tomorrow Night*, the session disintegrated as the trio tried over and over to record an acceptable version of either *I'll Never Let You Go* or *Just Because*, then picked up with *Good Rockin' Tonight* and *I Don't Care If The Sun Don't Shine*.

On December 10, 1954, Elvis recorded *Milkcow Blues Boogie* and *You're A Heartbreaker* (two of the "lost" songs). He also spent a lot of time trying out different versions of *I'm Left, You're Right, She's Gone*. This final song was the first to feature a drummer.

On February 5, 1955, *Baby Let's Play House* was waxed. Two other songs from the session, *I Got A Woman* and *Trying To Get To You*, were less than successful.

On July 11, 1955, Elvis' second session with drums started with *I Forgot To Remember To Forget*, followed by *Mystery Train* and a re-recording of *Trying To Get To You*. Only the first and last song used the drummer, whose style is completely different from the person at the December 20th session. This last song is also the only one from Elvis' Sun period that uses a pianist, which may or may not have been Elvis himself. One final song, *When It Rains It Really Pours*, was also apparently recorded on this date. Knowledge of this song's existence, like that of *Harbor Lights*, was kept a secret until RCA chose to issue it after it had languished for years in a vault.

All of the above sessions may have lasted more than one evening.

Additional Comments

Elvis' version of *Tomorrow Night* is based completely on the recording issued in 1948 by Lonnie Johnson. It was coincidental that LaVerne Baker released a version of this song in late 1954 as the B-side of *Tweedle Dee*. Elvis' effort does not sound as though he was at all aware of Miss Baker's styling.

Carl Perkins can be heard in the studio during the July 1955 recording session, which produced *When It Rains It Really Pours*. It is known that Perkins also had a recording session on July 11, 1955, which produced his versions of *Gone, Gone Gone* and *Let The Jukebox Keep On Playing*.

Although it is probable that all versions of *I Love You Because* were recorded at the same time, they do not sound like it. The two versions released in the 1970s by RCA Victor sound very different, both in terms of Elvis' vocal styling and in Scotty Moore's guitar picking.

What About the Mystery Songs?

Fans have heard for years about the possibility that Elvis may have recorded another dozen songs during his days at Sun Records. Specifically, a number of titles have been bandied about with some regularity. This mystery started in 1955 with the publication of *The Elvis Presley Album Of Juke Box Favorites*, a folio containing the words and music to fifteen songs. Included, along with four songs actually recorded by Elvis, were eleven which appear to have been included by the publisher, Hill and Range Songs, Inc., to fill out the booklet. These songs probably were never recorded by Elvis and it is doubtful that he ever even performed most of them while touring in 1954 and 1955: *Blue Guitar, Always Late (With Your Kisses), Tennessee Saturday Night, Gone, Give Me More More More (Of Your Kisses), Oakie Boogie, That's The Stuff You Gotta Watch, Rag Mop, I Almost Lost My Mind, Cryin' Heart Blues,* and *I Need You So.*

There is another song, *Uncle Pen*, also referred to as *Uncle Penn*, which is mentioned frequently as a possible recording by Elvis. The song had been around for years, having been written and recorded by Bill Monroe in the 1940s. (Monroe also wrote and recorded *Blue Moon Of Kentucky* about the same time.) There was another hit version of *Uncle Pen* recorded, coincidentally, in 1956 by Porter Wagoner on the RCA Victor label. A version by Elvis was reportedly bootlegged in 1956, but I have never seen a copy, nor have I ever met with anyone who has.

Other songs mentioned as having been recorded by Elvis during his sixteen months with Sun Records include *Night Train To Memphis* (also listed erroneously as *Last Train To Memphis*), *Mean Heart Blues* (see *Crying' Heart Blues* above), *Down The Line, Tennessee Partner, Long Journey,* and *Rocking Little Sally,* and *Sunshine.* Again, none of these songs have ever surfaced and it is doubtful if they were ever recorded by Elvis.

The two songs recorded by Elvis at the Memphis Recording Service in July 1953, *My Happiness* and *That's When Your Heartaches Begin,* and the two songs recorded in January 1954, *Casual Love Affair* and *I'll Never Stand In Your Way,* were never meant for release and although portions of these songs may have been recorded on tape, the only complete versions were the acetates that Elvis took home with him.

Without You, sometimes referred to as *Without Love,* which Elvis tried to sing for Sam Phillips in the weeks before July 1954, also appears to have never been committed to tape.

Cold Icy Fingers and *Til I Waltz Again With You,* sung by Elvis during the high school Christmas talent show in December, 1950,

494

were never recorded by Elvis.

On the other hand, there are two songs that were definitely performed by Elvis during 1955 and which do not appear to have ever been recorded by him: *Tweedle Dee* and *Maybelline*.

Does this mean that all of the Sun Records material is accounted for? Not necessarily. RCA Victor has released two Sun songs during the past eight years which were previously unknown to even the most dedicated of Elvis' fans: *Harbor Lights* and *When It Rains It Really Pours*. More of the "lost" Sun tapes may yet turn up in RCA Victor's vaults.

A Chronological List Of
Elvis' Personal Appearances, 1954-1977

Late July 1954 – Memphis, Bon Air Club

July 30, 1954 – Memphis, Overton Park Shell

August 7, 1954 – Memphis, Eagle's Nest Club

August 21, 1954 – Gladewater, TX

August 22, 1954 – Houston, TX

August 27, 1954 – Memphis, Eagle's Nest Club

August 1954 – Memphis, Bel Air Club

August 1954 – Memphis, Kennedy Hospital Benefit Show

September 4, 1954 – Nashville, TN, "Grand Ole Opry"

September 9, 1954 – Memphis, Lamar-Airways Shopping Center Opening

September 18, 1954 – Memphis, Eagle's Nest Club

September 24, 1954 – Memphis, Eagle's Nest Club

September 25, 1954 – Memphis, Eagle's Nest Club

October 1, 1954 – Memphis, Eagle's Nest Club

October 6, 1954 – Memphis, Eagle's Nest Club

October 9, 1954 – Memphis, Eagle's Nest Club

October 13, 1954 – Memphis, Eagle's Nest Club

October 15, 1954 – Memphis, Eagle's Nest Club

October 16, 1954 – Shreveport, "Louisiana Hayride"

October 22, 1954 – New Orleans, LA

October 23, 1954 – Shreveport, "Louisiana Hayride"

October 29, 1954 – Memphis, Eagle's Nest Club

October 30, 1954 – Memphis, Eagle's Nest Club

October 1954 – Shreveport, Lake Cliff Club

October 1954 – Houston, TX

October 1954 – Gladewater, TX

Fall 1954 – Sweetwater, TX

Fall 1954 – Boston, TX

Fall 1954 – Lufkin, TX

Fall 1954 – Longview, TX

Fall 1954 – Odessa, TX

Fall 1954 – Memphis, Airport Inn

November 6, 1954 – Shreveport, "Louisiana Hayride"

November 13, 1954 – Shreveport, "Louisiana Hayride"

November 17, 1954 – Memphis, Eagle's Nest Club

November 20, 1954 – Shreveport, "Louisiana Hayride"

November 27, 1954 – Shreveport, "Louisiana Hayride"

December 4, 1954 – Shreveport, "Louisiana Hayride"

December 11, 1954 – Shreveport, "Louisiana Hayride"

December 18, 1954 – Shreveport, "Louisiana Hayride"

December 28, 1954 – Houston, TX

January 1, 1955 – Houston, TX

January 8, 1955 – Shreveport, "Louisiana Hayride"

January 12, 1955 – Clarksdale, MS

January 13, 1955 – Helena, AR

January 15, 1955 – Shreveport, "Louisiana Hayride"

January 16, 1955 – Booneville, MS

January 17, 1955 – Sheffield, AL

January 18, 1955 – Leachville, AR

January 19, 1955 – Sikeston, MO

January 22, 1955 – Shreveport, "Louisiana Hayride"

January 23, 1955 – Week-long tour of East Texas (possibly including Midland, Boston, Lubbock, Gladewater, and Mobile, AL)

January 29, 1955 – Houston, TX

February 4, 1955 – New Orleans, LA

February 5, 1955 – Shreveport, "Louisiana Hayride"

February 6, 1955 – Memphis Auditorium

February 12, 1955 – Shreveport, "Louisiana Hayride"

February 14, 1955 – Carlsbad, NM

February 15, 1955 – Albuquerque, NM*

February 16, 1955 – Odessa, TX

February 18, 1955 – Monroe, AL

February 19, 1955 – Shreveport, "Louisiana Hayride"

February 22, 1955 – Hope, AR

February 24, 1955 – Bastrop, LA

February 26, 1955 – Cleveland, OH, "Circle Theater Jamboree"

March 5, 1955 – Shreveport, "Louisiana Hayride" (TV)
March 6, 1955 – Five-day tour: TN, AR, MS, LA, MO
March 12, 1955 – Shreveport, "Louisiana Hayride"
March 14, 1955 – Washington, DC; interview on WMAL-TV
Mid-March – New York, NY, audition for "Arthur Godfrey's Talent Scouts"
March 19, 1955 – Houston, TX
March 1955 – Other dates in Houston area
March 26, 1955 – Shreveport, "Louisiana Hayride"
March 28, 1955 – Cleveland, OH, "Circle Theater Jamboree"
March 1955 – Madison, TN
April 1, 1955 – Odessa, TX
April 2, 1955 – Shreveport, "Louisiana Hayride"
April 9, 1955 – Shreveport, "Louisiana Hayride"
April 16, 1955 – Dallas, "Big D Jamboree"
April 23, 1955 – Waco, TX, "Louisiana Hayride"
April 30, 1955 – Gladewater, TX, "Louisiana Hayride"
April 1955 – El Dorado, AR
April 1955 – Helena, AR
April 1955 – Texarkana, AR
May 1, 1955 – New Orleans, LA
May 4, 1955 – Mobile, AL
May 5, 1955 – Mobile, AL
May 6, 1955 – Birmingham, AL
May 7, 1955 – Daytona Beach, FL
May 8, 1955 – Tampa, FL
May 9, 1955 – Macon, GA
May 10, 1955 – Ocala, FL
May 13, 1955 – Jacksonville, FL
May 14, 1955 – Shreveport, "Louisiana Hayride"
May 16, 1955 – Richmond, VA
May 17, 1955 – Norfolk, VA
May 18, 1955 – Roanoke, VA
May 19, 1955 – New Bern, NC*
May 20, 1955 – Chattanooga, TN
May 21, 1955 – Shreveport, "Louisiana Hayride"
May 22, 1955 – Houston, TX
Late May 1955 – Kilgore, TX
Late May 1955 – Gainesville, TX
May 25, 1955 – Meridian, MS, "Jimmie Rodgers Day"
May 28, 1955 – Dallas, "Big D Jamboree"
May 29, 1955 – Ft. Worth (afternoon)
May 29, 1955 – Dallas (evening)
May 30, 1955 – Abilene, TX
May 31, 1955 – Midland, TX (afternoon)
May 31, 1955 – Odessa, TX (evening)

June 1, 1955 – Guymon, OK
June 2, 1955 – Amarillo, TX
June 3, 1955 – Lubbock, TX
June 4, 1955 – Shreveport, "Louisiana Hayride"
June 1955 – Marianna, AR
June 9, 1955 – Lawton, OK
June 10, 1955 – Lawton, OK
June 11, 1955 – Shreveport, "Louisiana Hayride"
June 13, 1955 – Bruce, MS
June 14, 1955 – Tupelo, MS
June 15, 1955 – Gobler, MO
June 16, 1955 – El Dorado, AR
June 17, 1955 – Stamford, TX
June 18, 1955 – Dallas, "Big D Jamboree"
June 19, 1955 – Houston, TX
June 20, 1955 – Beaumont, TX
June 21, 1955 – Beaumont, TX
June 22, 1955 – Vernon, TX
June 23, 1955 – Lawton, OK
June 24, 1955 – Altus, OK
June 25, 1955 – Shreveport, "Louisiana Hayride"
June 26, 1955 – Biloxi, MS
June 27, 1955 – Keesler, AFB, MS
June 28, 1955 – Keesler AFB, MS
June 29, 1955 – Mobile, AL
June 30, 1955 – Mobile, AL
July 1, 1955 – Baton Rouge, LA
July 2, 1955 – Shreveport, "Louisiana Hayride"
July 3, 1955 – Corpus Christi, TX
July 4, 1955 – Stephenville, TX
July 22, 1955 – Odessa, TX
July 23, 1955 – Dallas, "Big D Jamboree"
July 25, 1955 – Tampa, FL
July 26, 1955 – Orlando, FL
July 27, 1955 – Orlando, FL
July 28, 1955 – Jacksonville, FL
July 29, 1955 – Jacksonville, FL
July 30, 1955 – Daytona Beach, FL
July 31, 1955 – Sheffield, AL
August 1, 1955 – Little Rock, AR
August 2, 1955 – Little Rock, AR
August 3, 1955 – Tupelo, MS
August 4, 1955 – Camden, AR
August 5, 1955 – Memphis, TN
August 6, 1955 – Shreveport, "Louisiana Hayride"
August 8, 1955 – Gladewater, TX, area
August 9, 1955 – Gladewater, TX, area
August 10, 1955 – Gladewater, TX, area
August 11, 1955 – Dallas, TX
August 12, 1955 – San Antonio, TX
August 13, 1955 – Houston, TX
August 20, 1955 – Cleveland, OH
August 27, 1955 – Shreveport, "Louisiana Hayride"

498

September 1, 1955 — New Orleans, LA
September 2, 1955 — Texarkana, AR
September 3, 1955 — Dallas, "Big D Jamboree"
September 5, 1955 — Forrest City, AR
September 6, 1955 — Bono, AR
September 7, 1955 — Sikeston, MO
September 8, 1955 — Clarksdale, MS
Spetember 9, 1955 — McComb, MS
September 10, 1955 — Shreveport, "Louisiana Hayride"
September 11, 1955 — Norfolk, VA
September 12, 1955 — Norfolk, VA
September 14, 1955 — Asheville, NC
September 15, 1955 — Roanoke, VA
September 16, 1955 — New Bern, NC
September 17, 1955 — Wilson, NC
September 18, 1955 — Raleigh, NC
September 19, 1955 — Thomasville, NC
September 20, 1955 — Richmond, VA
September 21, 1955 — Danville, VA
September 22, 1955 — Kingsport, TN
September 24, 1955 — Shreveport, "Louisiana Hayride"
September 26, 1955 — Wichita Falls, TX
September 27, 1955 — Bryan, TX
September 28, 1955 — Conroe, TX
September 29, 1955 — Austin, TX
September 30, 1955 — Gonzales, TX
October 1, 1955 — Shreveport, "Louisiana Hayride"
October 8, 1955 — Shreveport, "Louisiana Hayride"
October 9, 1955 — Lufkin, TX*
October 10, 1955 — Brownwood, TX*
October 11, 1955 — Abilene, TX
October 12, 1955 — Midland, TX
October 13, 1955 — Amarillo, TX
October 14, 1955 — Odessa, TX
October 15, 1955 — Lubbock, TX
October 16, 1955 — Lubbock, TX
October 17, 1955 — El Dorado, AR
October 19, 1955 — Cleveland, OH
October 20, 1955 — Cleveland, OH
October 21, 1955 — St. Louis, MO
October 22, 1955 — St. Louis, MO
October 26, 1955 — Prichard, AL
October 27, 1955 — Prichard, AL
October 28, 1955 — Prichard, AL
October 29, 1955 — Shreveport, "Louisiana Hayride"
November 5, 1955 — Shreveport, "Louisiana Hayride"
November 6, 1955 — Biloxi, MS
November 6, 1955 — Keesler AFB, MS
November 8, 1955 — Keesler AFB, MS
November 12, 1955 — Carthage, TX (afternoon)
November 12, 1955 — Shreveport, "Louisiana Hayride" (evening)
November 13, 1955 — Memphis, TN
November 14, 1955 — Forrest City, AR
November 15, 1955 — Sheffield, AL
November 16, 1955 — Camden, AR
November 17, 1955 — Texarkana, AR
November 18, 1955 — Longview, TX
November 19, 1955 — Gladewater, TX, "Louisiana Hayride"
November 25, 1955 — Port Arthur, TX
November 26, 1955 — Shreveport, "Louisiana Hayride"
December 2, 1955 — Atlanta, GA
December 3, 1955 — Montgomery, AL
December 10, 1955 — Shreveport, "Louisiana Hayride"
December 17, 1955 — Shreveport, "Louisiana Hayride"
December 1955 — Memphis, "Humes High benefit"
December 31, 1955 — Shreveport, Louisiana Hayride"
January 7, 1956 — Shreveport, "Louisiana Hayride"
January 14, 1956 — Shreveport, "Louisiana Hayride"
January 21, 1956 — Shreveport, "Louisiana Hayride"
January 28, 1956 — New York, "Stage Show"
January 29, 1956 — Richmond, VA
February 4, 1956 — New York, "Stage Show"
February 5, 1956 — Norfolk, VA
February 6, 1956 — Greensboro, NC
February 11, 1956 — New York, "Stage Show"
February 18, 1956 — New York, "Stage Show"
February 21, 1956 — Sarasota, FL
February 25, 1956 — Shreveport, "Louisiana Hayride"
March 3, 1956 — Shreveport, "Louisiana Hayride"
March 10, 1956 — Shreveport, "Louisiana Hayride"
March 14, 1956 — Atlanta, GA
March 15, 1956 — Atlanta, GA
March 17, 1956 — New York, "Stage Show"
March 22, 1956 — Richmond, VA
March 24, 1956 — New York, "Stage Show"
April 3, 1956 — San Diego, "The Milton Berle Show"
April 4, 1956 — San Diego, CA
April 5, 1956 — San Diego, CA
April 7, 1956 — Shreveport, "Louisiana Hayride"
April 13, 1956 — Wichita Falls, TX*
April 15, 1956 — San Antonio, TX

499

April 16, 1956 — Corpus Christi, TX
April 17, 1956 — Oklahoma City, OK*
April 18, 1956 — Tulsa, OK
April 19, 1956 — Amarillo, TX*
April 20, 1956 — Ft. Worth, TX
April 21, 1956 — Dallas, TX
April 23–May 6, 1956 — Las Vegas, New Frontier Hotel
May 13, 1956 — St. Paul, MN
May 14, 1956 — LaCrosse, WI
May 15, 1956 — Memphis, TN
May 16, 1956 — Little Rock, AR
May 17, 1956 — Springfield, MO
May 18, 1956 — Des Moines, IA
May 19, 1956 — Lincoln, NE
May 20, 1956 — Omaha, NE
May 24, 1956 — Kansas City, MO
May 25, 1956 — Detroit, MI
May 26, 1956 — Columbus, OH
May 27, 1956 — Dayton, OH
June 3, 1956 — Oakland, CA
June 5, 1956 — Los Angeles, "The Milton Berle Show"
June 6, 1956 — San Diego, CA
June 7, 1956 — Long Beach, CA
June 8, 1956 — Los Angeles, CA
June 22, 1956 — Atlanta, GA
June 23, 1956 — Atlanta, GA
June 24, 1956 — Atlanta, GA
June 25, 1956 — Savannah, GA
June 26, 1956 — Charlotte, NC
June 27, 1956 — Augusta, GA
June 28, 1956 — Charlotte, NC
June 30, 1956 — Richmond, VA
July 1, 1956 — New York, "The Steve Allen Show"
August 3, 1956 — Miami, FL
August 4, 1956 — Miami, FL
August 5, 1956 — Tampa, FL
August 6, 1956 — Lakeland, FL
August 7, 1956 — St. Petersburg, FL
August 8, 1956 — Orlando, FL
August 9, 1956 — Daytona Beach, FL
August 10, 1956 — Jacksonville, FL
August 11, 1956 — Jacksonville, FL
August 12, 1956 — New Orleans, LA
September 9, 1956 — Los Angeles, "The Ed Sullivan Show"
September 26, 1956 — Tupelo, MS
October 11, 1956 — Dallas, TX
October 12, 1956 — Waco, TX
October 13, 1956 — San Antonio, TX
October 14, 1956 — Houston, TX
October 28, 1956 — New York, "The Ed Sullivan Show"
November 23, 1956 — Toledo, OH
November 24, 1956 — Cleveland, OH

November 25, 1956 — Louisville, KY
December 16, 1956 — Shreveport, "Louisiana Hayride"
December 22, 1956 — Memphis, (non-singing appearance, WDIA Review)
January 6, 1957 — New York, "The Ed Sullivan Show"
March 28, 1957 — Chicago, IL
March 29, 1957 — St. Louis, MO
March 30, 1957 — Ft. Wayne, IN
March 31, 1957 — Detroit, MI
April 1, 1957 — Buffalo, NY
April 2, 1957 — Toronto, Canada
April 3, 1957 — Ottawa, Canada
April 4, 1957 — Philadelphia, PA
April 5, 1957 — Philadelphia, PA
April 9, 1957 — Wichita Falls, TX
August 30, 1957 — Spokane, WA
August 31, 1957 — Vancouver, Canada
September 1, 1957 — Tacoma, WA
September 2, 1957 — Seattle, WA
September 3, 1957 — Portland, OR
September 27, 1957 — Tupelo, MS
October 26, 1957 — San Francisco, CA
October 27, 1957 — Oakland, CA
October 28, 1957 — Los Angeles, CA
October 29, 1957 — Los Angeles, CA
November 10, 1957 — Honolulu, HI
November 11, 1957 — Pearl Harbor, HI
December 31, 1957 — St. Louis, MO
March 15, 1958 — Memphis, TN
March 26, 1960 — Miami, "The Frank Sinatra Special"
February 25, 1961 — Memphis, TN
March 25, 1961 — Honolulu, HI
June 27, 1968 — Burbank, CA; NBC-TV Studios; 2 shows
June 29, 1968 — Burbank, CA; NBC-TV Studios; 2 shows
July 31–August 28, 1969 — Las Vegas, NV; International Hotel; 57 shows
January 26–February 23, 1970 — Las Vegas, NV; International Hotel; 57 shows
February 27–March 1, 1970 — Houston, TX; 6 shows
August 10–September 7, 1970 — Las Vegas, NV; International Hotel; 58 shows
September 9, 1970 — Phoenix, AZ‡
September 10, 1970 — St. Louis, MO
September 11, 1970 — Detroit, MI
September 12, 1970 — Miami, FL; 2 shows
September 13, 1970 — Tampa, FL; 2 shows
September 14, 1970 — Mobile, AL
November 10, 1970 — Oakland, CA
November 11, 1970 — Portland, OR
November 12, 1970 — Seattle, WA

‡All individual concerts for the remainder of this section are evening unless noted.

November 13, 1970 – San Francisco, CA
November 14, 1970 – Los Angeles, CA; 2 shows
November 15, 1970 – San Diego, CA
November 16, 1970 – Oklahoma City, OK
November 17, 1970 – Denver, CO
January 26--February 23, 1971 – Las Vegas, NV ; International Hotel; 57 shows
July 20--August 2, 1971 – Stateline, NV; Sahara Tahoe Hotel; 28 shows
August 9–September 6, 1971 – Las Vegas, NV; Hilton International Hotel; 57 shows
November 5, 1971 – Minneapolis, MN
November 6, 1971 – Cleveland, OH; 2 shows
November 7, 1971 –Louisville, KY; matinee
November 8, 1971 – Philadelphia, PA
November 9, 1971 – Baltimore, MD
November 10, 1971 – Boston, MA
November 11, 1971 – Cincinnati, OH
November 12, 1971 – Houston, TX
November 13, 1971 – Dallas, TX; 2 shows
November 14, 1971 – Tuscaloosa, AL
November 15, 1971 – Kansas City, MO
November 16, 1971 – Salt Lake City, UT
January 26--February 23, 1972 – Las Vegas, NV; Hilton International Hotel; 57 shows
April 5, 1972 – Buffalo, NY
April 6, 1972 – Detroit, MI
April 7, 1972 – Dayton, OH
April 8, 1972 – Knoxville, TN; 2 shows
April 9, 1972 – Hampton Roads, VA; 2 shows
April 10, 1972 – Richmond, VA
April 11, 1972 – Roanoke, VA
April 12, 1972 – Indianapolis, IN
April 13, 1972 – Charlotte, NC
April 14, 1972 – Greensboro, NC
April 15, 1972 – Macon, GA; 2 shows
April 16, 1972 – Jacksonville, FL; 2 shows
April 17, 1972 – Little Rock, AR
April 18, 1972 – San Antonio, TX
April 19, 1972 – Albuquerque, NM
June 9, 1972 – New York; matinee
June 10, 1972 – New York, NY; 2 shows
June 11, 1972 – New York, NY; matinee
June 12, 1972 – Ft. Wayne, IN
June 13, 1972 – Evansville, IN
June 14–15, 1972 – Milwaukee, WI; 2 shows
June 16, 1972 – Chicago, IL
June 17, 1972 – Chicago, IL; 2 shows
June 18, 1972 – Ft. Worth, TX
June 19, 1972 – Wichita, KS
June 20, 1972 – Tulsa, OK

August 4--September 4, 1972 – Las Vegas, NV; Hilton Hotel; 63 shows
November 8, 1972 – Lubbock, TX
November 9, 1972 – Tucson, AZ
November 10, 1972 – El Paso, TX
November 11, 1972 – Oakland, CA
November 12--13, 1972 – San Bernadino, CA; 2 shows
November 14--15, 1972 – Long Beach, CA; 2 shows
November 17, 1972 – Honolulu, HI
November 18, 1972 – Honolulu, HI; 2 shows
January 12, 1973 – Honolulu, HI; dress rehearsal
January 14, 1973 – Honolulu, HI; "Elvis: Aloha From Hawaii" satellite TV special; 12:30 am. show
January 26--February 23, 1973 – Las Vegas, NV; Hilton Hotel (scheduled closing date: February 26, 1973); 54 shows
April 22, 1973 – Phoenix, AZ; matinee
April 23--24, 1973 – Anaheim, CA; 2 shows
April 25, 1973 – Fresno, CA; 2 shows
April 26, 1973 – San Diego, CA
April 27, 1973 – Portland, OR
April 28, 1973 – Spokane, WA; 2 shows
April 29, 1973 – Seattle, WA; 2 shows
April 30, 1973 – Denver, CO
May 4--16, 1973 – Stateline, NV; Sahara Tahoe Hotel (scheduled closing date: May 20, 1973); 25 shows
June 20, 1973 – Mobile, AL
June 21, 1973 – Atlanta, GA
June 22, 1973 – Uniondale, NY
June 23, 1973 – Uniondale, NY; 2 shows
June 24, 1973 – Uniondale, NY
June 25--26, 1973 – Pittsburgh, PA; 2 shows
June 27, 1973 – Cincinnati, OH
June 28, 1973 – St. Louis, MO
June 29, 1973 – Atlanta, GA
June 30, 1973 – Atlanta, GA; 2 shows
July 1, 1973 – Nashville, TN; 2 shows
July 2, 1973 – Oklahoma City, OK
July 3, 1973 – Atlanta, GA
August 6–September 3, 1973 – Las Vegas, NV; Hilton Hotel; 59 shows
January 26--February 9, 1974 – Las Vegas, NV; Hilton Hotel. 29 shows
March 1–2, 1974 – Tulsa, OK; 2 shows
March 3, 1974 – Houston, TX; 2 shows
March 4, 1974 – Monroe, LA
March 5, 1974 – Auburn, AL
March 6, 1974 – Montgomery, AL
March 7--8, 1974 – Monroe, LA; 2 shows
March 9, 1974 – Charlotte, NC; 2 shows
March 10, 1974 – Roanoke, VA
March 11, 1974 – Hampton Roads, VA

March 12, 1974 — Richmond, VA
March 13, 1974 — Greensboro, NC
March 14, 1974 — Murfreesboro, NC
March 15, 1974 — Knoxville, TN; 2 shows
March 16–17, 1974 — Memphis, TN; 4 shows
March 18, 1974 — Richmond, VA
March 19, 1974 — Murfreesboro, NC
March 20, 1974 — Memphis, TN
May 10, 1974 — San Bernadino, CA
May 11, 1974 — Los Angeles, CA
May 12, 1974 — Fresno, CA; matinee
May 13, 1974 — San Bernadino, CA
May 16–26, 1974 — Stateline, NV; Sahara Tahoe Hotel; 22 shows
June 15–16, 1974 — Ft. Worth, TX; 4 shows
June 17–18, 1974 — Baton Rouge, LA; 2 shows
June 19, 1974 — Amarillo, TX
June 20, 1974 — Des Moines, IA
June 21, 1974 — Cleveland, OH
June 22, 1974 — Providence, RI; 2 shows
June 23, 1974 — Philadelphia, PA; 2 shows
June 24, 1974 — Niagara Falls, NY; 2 shows
June 25, 1974 — Columbus, OH
June 26, 1974 — Louisville, KY
June 27, 1974 — Bloomington, IN
June 28, 1974 — Milwaukee, WI
June 29, 1974 — Kansas City, KS; 2 shows
June 30, 1974 — Omaha, NE; 2 shows
July 1, 1974 — Omaha, NE
July 2, 1974 — Salt Lake City, UT
August 19–September 2, 1974 — Las Vegas, NV; Hilton Hotel; 27 shows
September 27–28, 1974 — College Park, MD; 2 shows
September 29, 1974 — Detroit, MI; matinee
September 30–October 1, 1974 — South Bend, IN; 2 shows
October 2–3, 1974 — St. Paul, MN; 2 shows
October 4, 1974 — Detroit, MI
October 5, 1974 — Indianapolis, IN; 2 shows
October 6, 1974 — Dayton, OH; 2 shows
October 7, 1974 — Wichita, KS
October 8, 1974 — San Antonio, TX
October 9, 1974 — Abilene, TX
October 11–14, 1974 — Stateline, NV; Sahara Tahoe Hotel: 8 shows
March 18–April 1, 1975 — Las Vegas, NV; Hilton Hotel; 29 shows
April 24, 1975 — Macon, GA
April 25, 1975 — Jacksonville, FL
April 26, 1975 — Tampa, FL; 2 shows
April 27, 1975 — Lakeland, FL; 2 shows
April 28, 1975 — Lakeland, FL
April 29, 1975 — Murfreesboro, NC
April 30–May 2, 1975 — Atlanta; 3 shows

May 3, 1975 — Monroe, LA; 2 shows
May 4, 1975 — Lake Charles, LA; 2 shows
May 5, 1975 — Jackson, MS
May 6–7, 1975 — Murfreesboro, NC; 2 shows
May 30, 1975 — Huntsville, AL
May 31, 1975 — Huntsville, AL; 2 shows
June 1, 1975 — Huntsville, AL; 2 shows
June 2, 1975 — Mobile, AL; 2 shows
June 3, 1975 — Tuscaloosa, AL
June 4–5, 1975 — Houston, TX; 2 shows
June 6, 1975 — Dallas, TX
June 7, 1975 — Shreveport, LA; 2 shows
June 8, 1975 — Jackson, MS; 2 shows
June 9, 1975 — Jackson, MS
June 10, 1975 — Memphis, TN
July 8, 1975 — Oklahoma City, OK
July 9, 1975 — Terre Haute, IN
July 10, 1975 — Richfield, OH
July 11, 1975 — Charleston, WV
July 12, 1975 — Charleston, WV; 2 shows
July 13, 1975 — Niagara Falls, NY; 2 shows
July 14–15, 1975 — Springfield, MA; 2 shows
July 16–17, 1975 — New Haven, CT; 2 shows
July 18, 1975 — Cleveland, OH
July 19, 1975 — Uniondale, NY; 2 shows
July 20, 1975 — Norfolk, VA; 2 shows
July 21, 1975 — Greensboro, NC
July 22–24, 1975 — Asheville,NC; 3 shows
August 18–20, 1975 — Las Vegas, NV; Hilton Hotel (Scheduled closing date: September 1, 1975; 5 shows
December 2–15, 1975 — Las Vegas, NV; Hilton Hotel; 17 shows
December 31, 1975 — Pontiac, MI
March 17–19, 1976 — Johnson City, TN; 3 shows
March 20, 1976 — Charlotte, NC; 2 shows
March 21, 1976 — Cincinnati, OH; 2 shows
March 22, 1976 — St. Louis, MO
April 21, 1976 — Kansas City, MO
April 22, 1976 — Omaha, NE
April 23, 1976 — Denver, CO
April 24, 1976 — San Diego, CA
April 25, 1976 — Long Beach, CA; 2 shows
April 26, 1976 — Seattle, WA
April 27, 1976 — Spokane, WA
April 30–May 9, 1976 — Stateline, NV; Sahara Tahoe Hotel; 15 shows
May 27, 1976 — Bloomington, IN
May 28, 1976 — Ames, IA
May 29, 1976 — Oklahoma,City, OK
May 30, 1976 — Odessa, TX; 2 shows
May 31, 1976 — Lubbock, TX
June 1, 1976 — Tucson, AZ
June 2, 1976 — El Paso, TX
June 3, 1976 — Ft. Worth, TX

June 4, 1976 – Atlanta, GA
June 5, 1976 – Atlanta, GA; 2 shows
June 6, 1976 – Atlanta, GA
June 25, 1976 – Buffalo, NY
June 26, 1976 – Providence, RI; 2 shows
June 27, 1976 – Largo, MD; 2 shows
June 28, 1976 – Philadelphia, PA
June 29, 1976 – Richmond, VA
June 30, 1976 – Greensboro, NC
July 1, 1976 – Shreveport, LA
July 2, 1976 – Baton Rouge, LA
July 3, 1976 – Ft. Worth, TX
July 4, 1976 – Tulsa, OK; matinee
July 5, 1976 – Memphis, TN
July 23, 1976 – Louisville, KY
July 24, 1976 – Charleston, WV; 2 shows
July 25, 1976 – Syracuse, NY
July 26, 1976 – Rochester, NY
July 27, 1976 – Syracuse, NY
July 28, 1976 – Hartford, CT
July 29, 1976 – Springfield, MA
July 30, 1976 – New Haven, CT
July 31–August 1, 1976 – Hampton Roads, VA; 2 shows
August 2, 1976 – Roanoke, VA
August 3–5, 1976 – Fayetteville, NC; 3 shows
August 27, 1976 – San Antonio, TX
August 28, 1976 – Houston, TX; matinee
August 29, 1976 – Mobile, AL
August 30, 1976 – Tuscaloosa, AL
August 31, 1976 – Macon, GA
September 1, 1976 – Jacksonville, FL
September 2, 1976 – Tampa, FL
September 3, 1976 – St. Petersburg, FL
September 4, 1976 – Lakeland, FL
September 5, 1976 – Jackson, MS
September 6, 1976 – Huntsville, AL
September 7–8, 1976 – Pine Bluffs, AR; 2 shows
October 14–15, 1976 – Chicago, IL; 2 shows
October 16, 1976 – Duluth, MN
October 17, 1976 – Minneapolis, MN
October 18, 1976 – Sioux Falls, SD
October 19, 1976 – Madison, WI
October 20, 1976 – South Bend, IN
October 21. 1976 – Kalamazoo, MI
October 22, 1976 – Champaign, IL
October 23, 1976 – Richfield, OH
October 24, 1976 – Evansville, IN
October 25, 1976 – Ft. Wayne, IN
October 26, 1976 – Dayton, OH
October 27, 1976 – Carbondale, IL
November 24, 1976 – Reno, NV
November 25, 1976 – Eugene, OR
November 26, 1976 – Portland, OR
November 27, 1976 – Eugene, OR

November 28–29, 1976 – San Francisco, CA; 2 shows
November 30, 1976 – Anaheim, CA
December 2–12, 1976 – Las Vegas, NV; Hilton Hotel; 15 shows
December 27, 1976 – Wichita Falls, TX
December 28, 1976 – Dallas, TX
December 29, 1976 – Birmingham, AL
December 30, 1976 – Atlanta, GA
December 31, 1976 – Pittsburgh, PA
February 12, 1977 – Hollywood, FL
February 13, 1977 – West Palm Beach, FL
February 14, 1977 – St. Petersburg, FL
February 15, 1977 – Orlando, FL
February 16, 1977 – Montgomery, AL
February 17, 1977 – Savannah, GA
February 18, 1977 – Columbia, SC
February 19, 1977 – Johnson City, TN
February 20–21, 1977 – Charlotte, NC; 2 shows
March 23, 1977 – Tempe, AZ
March 24, 1977 – Amarillo, TX
March 25–26, 1977 – Norman, OK; 2 shows
March 27, 1977 – Abilene, TX
March 28, 1977 – Austin, TX
March 29–30, 1977 – Alexandria, LA; 2 shows
March 31, 1977 – Baton Rouge, LA (cancelled)
April 1, 1977 – Mobile, AL (cancelled)
April 2, 1977 – Macon, GA (cancelled)
April 3, 1977 – Jacksonville, FL (cancelled)
April 21, 1977 – Greensboro, NC
April 22, 1977 – Detroit, MI
April 23, 1977 – Toledo, OH
April 24, 1977 – Ann Arbor, MI
April 25, 1977 – Saginaw, MI
April 26, 1977 – Kalamazoo, MI
April 27, 1977 – Milwaukee, WI
April 28, 1977 – Green Bay, WI
April 29, 1977 – Duluth, MN
April 30, 1977 – St. Paul, MN
May 1–2, 1977 – Chicago, IL; 2 shows
May 3, 1977 – Saginaw, MI
May 20, 1977 – Knoxville, TN
May 21, 1977 – Louisville, KY
May 22, 1977 – Largo, MD
May 23, 1977 – Providence, RI
May 24, 1977 – Augusta, ME
May 25, 1977 – Rochester, NY
May 26–27, 1977 – Binghampton, NY; 2 shows
May 28, 1977 – Philadelphia, PA
May 29, 1977 – Baltimore, MD
May 30, 1977 – Jacksonville, FL
May 31, 1977 – Baton Rouge, LA
June 1, 1977 – Macon, GA

June 2, 1977 — Mobile, AL
June 17, 1977 — Springfield, MO
June 18, 1977 — Kansas City, MO
June 19, 1977 — Omaha, NE
June 20, 1977 — Lincoln, NE
June 21, 1977 — Rapid City, SD
June 22, 1977 — Sioux City, SD
June 23, 1977 — Des Moines, IA
June 24, 1977 — Madison, WI
June 25, 1977 — Cincinnati, OH
June 26, 1977 — Indianapolis, IN

The following tour was scheduled and sold out at the time of Elvis's death:

August 17–18, 1977 — Portland, ME; 2 shows
August 19, 1977 — Utica, NY
August 20, 1977 — Syracuse, NY
August 21, 1977 — Hartford, CT
August 22, 1977 — Uniondale, NY
August 23, 1977 — Lexington, KY
August 24, 1977 — Roanoke, VA
August 25, 1977 — Fayatteville, TN
August 26, 1977 — Ashville, NC
August 27–28, 1977 — Memphis, TN; 2 shows

Billboard Memphis'
Country & Western Singles Charts

MEMPHIS' COUNTRY AND WESTERN SINGLES CHARTS COMPILED FROM
BILLBOARD – (8/54–4/56). (Dates are those for the chart, not the date of the magazine.)[1]

1954

	AUG		SEP					OCT			
	18	25	1	8	15	22	29	6	13	20	27
Blue Moon Of Kentucky	3	4	1	4	1	4	6	6	2	4	6
That's All Right			7	6	4	5	7				
Good Rockin' Tonight									5		

	NOV			
	3	10	17	24
Good Rockin' Tonight	3	5	8	
Blue Moon Of Kentucky			5	6

1955

	MAY	JUN	
	18	22	29
I'm Left, You're Right, She's Gone	5	4	5

	JUL	AUG	SEP			
	27	31	7	14	21	28
I'm Left, You're Right, She's Gone	6					
I Forgot To Remember To Forget		2		1	1	
Mystery Train					2	8

	OCT		DEC
	5	12	7
I Forgot To Remember To Forget	2	1	4

1956

	MAR			
	7	14	21	28
I Was The One	3	2	4	3
Heartbreak Hotel			3	2

	APR		
	4	11	18
I Was The One	3	4	5
Heartbreak Hotel	5	2	2

----

[1] Chart positions are taken from the "Country and Western Territorial Best Sellers" chart which varied from seven to ten positions.

Billboard Country & Western Singles Charts

COUNTRY AND WESTERN SINGLES CHARTS COMPILED FROM *BILLBOARD*. (Dates given are those for the chart, not the date of the magazine).[1]

1955

	JUL				AUG					SEP			
	6	13	20	27	3	10	17	24	31	7	14	21	28
Baby Let's Play House (*w/I'm Left, You're Right, She's Gone)	15	15	14	10	14	12*	11*	14	15	15		15	
Mystery Train (*w/I Forgot To Remember To Forget)										14	11*	14*	9*

	OCT				NOV					DEC			
	5	12	19	26	2	9	16	23	30	7	14	21	28
I Forgot To Remember To Forget (*w/Mystery Train)	8*	7*	7*	7*	3*	6*	7	4*	5	4	4*	5	4

1956

	JAN				FEB					MAR			
	4	11	18	25	1	8	15	22	29	7	14	21	28
I Forgot To Remember To Forget (*w/Mystery Train)	3*	3*	5*	4*	4*	2*	1	1*	2*	2*	2*	3*	3*
Heartbreak Hotel/I Was The One)								9*	3*	1*	1*	1*	1*
Baby Let's Play House											12		

	APR				MAY					JUN			
	4	11	18	25	2	9	16	23	30	6	13	20	27
Heartbreak Hotel/I Was The One	1	1	1	1	1	1	1	1	1	1	1	1	1
I Forgot To Remember To Forget (*w/Mystery Train)	3*	3*	3*	3*	3*	3*	5	9	11*	15			
Baby Let's Play House			13	12	15								
My Baby Left Me/I Want You, I Need You, I Love You								13					
I Want You, I Need You, I Love You/My Baby Left Me									6	3	3	2	2

---

[1] In 1955, the chart was called "Country Best Sellers In Stores" and was limited to 15 places.

1956

	JUL				AUG					SEP			
	4	11	18	25	1	8	15	22	29	5	12	19	26
*I Want You, I Need You, I Love You (*w/My Baby Left Me)*	1*	4*	2*	2*	2*	3*	5*	5*	5*	6	8	11	13
*Heartbreak Hotel (*w/I Was The One)*	2*	7	4	5	8	7	10	12					
Hound Dog/Don't Be Cruel						5	4	3	2	2	2		
Don't Be Cruel/Hound Dog												1	1

	OCT					NOV				DEC			
	3	10	17	24	31	7	14	21	28	5	12	19	26
Don't Be Cruel/Hound Dog	1	1	1	2	3	4	3	3	13	5	5	6	6
I Want You, I Need You, I Love You	12												
*Love Me Tender (*w/Any Way You Want Me)*		9	6	5	5*	5	5*	5	5	3*	3*	5	5

1957

	JAN					FEB				MAR			
	2	9	16	23	30	6	13	20	27	6	13	20	27
*Love Me Tender (*w/Any Way You Want Me)*	5*	8	7	7	10								
Don't Be Cruel/Hound Dog	8	6		9	13		11‡						
Too Much				15	9	14	9	7	5	5	5	5	6

	APR				MAY					JUN			
	3	10	17	24	1	8	15	22	29	5	12	19	22²
Too Much	6	9	12	14									
All Shook Up	12	5	5	5	4	3	5	5	4	5	5	8	9
Teddy Bear													15

	JUN	JUL				AUG				
	29	6	13	20	27	3	10	17	24	31
*Teddy Bear (*w/Loving You)*	9*	8*	6	7	1*	2*	2*	2*	2*	2*
All Shook Up	11	11	14							

	SEP				OCT				NOV				
	7	14	21	28	5	12	19	26	2	9	16	23	30
*Teddy Bear (*w/Loving You)*	3*	5*	6	12	14								
*Jailhouse Rock (*w/Treat Me Nice)*						6	2	2	2*	2*	2*	1*	2*

	DEC			
	7	14	21	28
*Jailhouse Rock (*w/Treat Me Nice)*	2*	2*	4	3*

---

²Effective with the July 1, 1957 issue, *Billboard* changed the effective date of its charts to the Saturday of the week before the publication date.

‡Erroneously listed as having been on the chart 29 weeks.

1958

	JAN				FEB				MAR				
	4	11	18	25	1	8	15	22	1[3]	8	15	22	29
Jailhouse Rock	4	4	5	7	8	7	9	15	18	20	20		
I Beg Of You/Don't				8	4								
Don't/I Beg Of You							3	2	2	2	2	3	3

	APR				MAY					JUN			
	5	12	19	26	3	10	17	24	31	7	14	21	28
Don't (*w/I Beg Of You)	3*	5*	6*	9	9	10	18	19					
Wear My Ring Around Your Neck (*w/Doncha' Think It's Time)		8	4	3	3*	3*	3	4	4	5	5	6	8
Hard Headed Woman												16	9

	JUL			AUG				SEP			
	5	12	19	10[4]	17	24	31	7	14	21	28
Hard Headed Woman (*w/Don't Ask Me Why)	4	2*	2*	3*	3	3	4	6	12	11	10
Wear My Ring Around Your Neck	11	15	19								

	OCT				NOV					DEC			
	5	12	19	26[5]	2	9	16	23	30	7	14	21	28
Hard Headed Woman	15	18	20										
One Night													29

1959

	JAN	
	4	11
One Night	24	28

NO CHARTED C&W SINGLES UNTIL JUNE 5, 1960

1960

	JUN		DEC		
	5	12	18	25	31
Stuck On You	27	30			
Are You Lonesome To-night?			28	23	24

1961

	JAN		
	8[6]	15	22
Are You Lonesome To-night?	24	†	†

NO CHARTED C&W SINGLES UNTIL APRIL 6, 1968.
By 1968, the country chart had expanded to 100 places.

---

[3] *Billboard* expanded the chart to 20 places.

[4] Effective with the August 4, 1958 issue, *Billboard* changed the effective date of its charts to the following Sunday.

[5] Effective with the October 20, 1958 issue, *Billboard* expanded the C&W chart from 20 to 30 places and changed the name to "Hot C&W Sides."

[6] Effective with the December 31, 1960 issue, *Billboard* moved the date of its charts to the following Sunday.

† Microfilm issues for these dates not available.

1968

	APR				MAY	
	6	13	20	27	4	11
U.S. Male	71	67	67	62	58	55

	JUN	JUL				AUG		
	29	6	13	20	27	3	10	17
Your Time Hasn't Come Yet, Baby	61	60	58	56	55	50	50	53

1969

	APR	
	19	26
Memories	61	56

	JUN			JUL				AUG		
	14	21	28	5	12	19	26	16	23	30
In The Ghetto	72	69	68	61	61	60	60			
Clean Up Your Own Backyard								75	74	74

	DEC	
	20	27
Don't Cry Daddy/ Rubberneckin'	51	41

1970

	JAN					FEB				MAR			
	3	10	17	24	31	7	14	21	28	7	14	21	28
Don't Cry Daddy/ Rubberneckin'	36	31	25	21	17	13	13	15	18	39			
Kentucky Rain										75	61	49	36	32

	APR				MAY					JUN			
	4	11	18	25	2	9	16	23	30	6	13	20	27
Kentucky Rain	31	32	32	32	47								
The Wonder Of You										73	65	61	50

	JUL				AUG					SEP			
	4	11	18	25	1	8	15	22	29	5	12	19	26
The Wonder Of You	50	44	40	37	40	42							
I've Lost You/The Next Step Is Love										63	61	60	57	64

	OCT					NOV				DEC			
	3	10	17	24	31	7	14	21	28	5	12	19	26
I've Lost You/The Next Step Is Love	62												
You Don't Have To Say You Love Me										57	56	59	59

1971

	JAN					FEB				MAR			
	2	9	16	23	30	6	13	20	27	6	13	20	27
You Don't Have To Say You Love Me	65												
I Really Don't Want To Know/There Goes My Everything (*listed with titles reversed)		50	45*	36	30	23	15	11	9*	9*	10	14	18
Where Did They Go, Lord													67

510

1971

	APR				MAY					JUN			
	3	10	17	24	1	8	15	22	29	5	12	19	26
I Really Don't Want To Know/There Goes My Everything	39												
Where Did They Go Lord	67	66	66	55	55	60	60						
Life											67	50	40

	JUL			
	3	10	17	24
Life	37	36	34	40

1972

	MAR	
	4	11
Until It's Time For You To Go	68	68

	SEP				OCT				NOV				DEC
	9	16	23	30	7	14	21	28	4	11	18	25	2
It's A Matter Of Time	68	65	60	54	52	48	43	41	40	38	38	36	45

	DEC			
	9	16	23	30
Always On My Mind/Separate Ways	74	63	53	48

1973

	JAN				FEB				MAR				
	6	13	20	27	3	10	17	24	3	10	17	24	31
Always On My Mind/Separate Ways	42	35	30	27	23	19	16	21	25				

	APR				MAY				JUN				
	7	14	21	28	5	12	19	26	2	9	16	23	30
Fool/Steamroller Blues				66	55	49	44	42	37	34	32	31	34

	OCT				NOV				DEC	
	6	13	20	27	3	10	17	24	1	8
For Ol' Times Sake	76	71	69	65	60	54	44	42	56	59

1974

	FEB		MAR					APR				MAY	
	16	23	2	9	16	23	30	6	13	20	27	4	11
I've Got A Thing About You Baby/Take Good Care Of Her	67	42	32	21	17	10	5	4	7	10	16	30	44

	JUN				JUL				AUG				
	8	15	22	29	6	13	20	27	3	10	17	24	31
Help/If You Talk In Your Sleep	90	80	57	37	22	18	13	9	7	6	8	10	33

	SEP	
	7	14
Help/If You Talk In Your Sleep	41	55

1974

	OCT	NOV					DEC			
	26	2	9	16	23	30	7	14	21	28
It's Midnight (*w/ Promised Land)	88	75	61	50	38	26	21	18	14	11*

1975

	JAN				FEB				MAR				
	4	11	18	25	1	8	15	22	1	8	15	22	29
It's Midnight/Promised Land	10	9	23	49									
My Boy						88	75	58	34	20	16	14	22

	APR				MAY					JUN			
	5	12	19	26	3	10	17	24	31	4	14	21	28
My Boy	45	59											
T-R-O-U-B-L-E							61	50	45	35	28	22	14

	JUL				AUG	
	5	12	19	26	2	9
T-R-O-U-B-L-E	12	11	15	47	53	74

	OCT		NOV					DEC		
	18	25	1	8	15	22	29	6	13	20
Pieces Of My Life	90	73	63	53	45	39	35	33	33	56

1976

	APR			MAY					JUN				JUL
	10	17	24	1	8	15	22	29	5	12	19	26	4[7]
Hurt/For The Heart	68	45	27	19	15	11	9	7	6	9	10	35	78

	DEC
	25
Moody Blue/She Thinks I Still Care	72

1977

	JAN					FEB				MAR			
	1	8	15	22	29	5	12	19	26	5	12	19	26
Moody Blue/She Thinks I Still Care	72	55	40	21	14	8	3	1	2	4	13	30	42

	APR	
	2	9
Moody Blue/She Thinks I Still Care	54	63

	JUN	JUL					AUG				SEP		
	25	2	9	16	23	30	6	13	20	27	3	10	17
Way Down/She Thinks I Still Care	66	44	29	21	12	6	4	2	1	3	5	3	4

	OCT					NOV				DEC			
	1	8	15	22	29	5	12	19	26	3	10	17	24
Way Down/She Thinks I Still Care	34	44	53	83									
My Way							58	32	19	11	8	6

[7] Issue dated July 4, 1976 to coincide with the nation's 200th birthday.

512

1977
DEC
31

My Way | ‡

1978

	JAN				FEB			
	7	14	21	28	4	11	18	25
My Way	3	3	2	8	27	39	60	74

‡_Billboard_ issue for this date not available.

513

Appendix VI
Billboard Singles Charts

POPULAR SINGLES CHARTS COMPILED FROM *BILLBOARD*. (Dates given are for the chart, not the issue date of the magazine. In 1956, the chart was called "The Top 100.")

1956

	FEB		MAR				APR			
	22	29	7	14	21	28	4	11	18	25
Heartbreak Hotel	68	28	21	11	9	8	6	2	2	1
I Was The One		84	31	29	25	23	23	23	23	32
Blue Suede Shoes						88	57	54	28	24

	MAY					JUN				JUL			
	2	9	16	23	30	6	13	20	27	4	11	18	25
Heartbreak Hotel	1	1	1	1	1	1	4	5	11	17	19	28	38
Blue Suede Shoes	27	37	41	38	68	66			88				
I Was The One	40	40	58	52	67			70	79				
Money Honey	84	80	76	95		93							
My Baby Left Me			68	72	34	31	37	48	42	42	63	50	59
I Want You, I Need You, I Love You			90	31	19	16	11	7	5	4	4	3	3
Hound Dog													24

	AUG					SEP				OCT		
	1	8	15	22	29	5	12	19	26	3	10	17
I Want You, I Need You, I Love You	6	7	8	10	11	20	22	19	32	60	46	47
Hound Dog	11	6	3	2	2	3	3	3	2	6	9	9
Don't Be Cruel	28	17	6	4	3	1	1	1	1	1	1	1
My Baby Left Me	63	77			100							
Heartbreak Hotel	65	92	96	94								
Blue Moon								87	61	55	64	84
I Don't Care If The Sun Don't Shine										77	74	87
Love Me Tender											12	6

	OCT		NOV				DEC			
	24	31	7	14	21	28	5	12	19	26
Don't Be Cruel	2	3	4	5	7	8	14	15	26	24
Love Me Tender	3	1	2	1	1	2	2	1	2	3
Hound Dog	12	13	19	19	31	27	35	36	54	62
Any Way You Want Me	56	40	33	35	27	42	43	59	70	
Blue Moon	65	66	93	93	94	92		89	93	60
I Don't Care If The Sun Don't Shine	77	76	82							
I Want You, I Need You, I Love You	96									
Love Me, **Elvis Vol. 1 (EP)**			84	41	24	17	9	8	7	6
When My Blue Moon Turns To Gold Again, **Elvis Vol. 1, (EP)**				94	61	49	36	38	41	
Old Shep, **Elvis Vol. 2 (EP)**									47	
Poor Boy, **Love Me Tender (EP)**									54	40
Paralyzed, **Elvis Vol. 1 (EP)**									78	74

515

1957

	JAN 2	9	16	23	30	FEB 6	13	20	27	MAR 6	13	20	27
Love Me Tender	3	6	10	11	13	26	27	41	74	58			
Love Me, **Elvis Vol. 1** (EP)	6	6	8	10	11	11	17	40	62	58			93
Don't Be Cruel	41	55	51	58	83								
When My Blue Moon Turns To Gold Again, **Elvis Vol. 2** (EP)	46	31	27	38	44	83	62	100	85				
Poor Boy, **Love Me Tender** (EP)	50	46	35	35	48	49	98	75	75				
Hound Dog	53	93			85								
Paralyzed, **Elvis Vol. 1** (EP)	63	59	67	78	92								
Too Much			30	17	7	4	3	2	2	2	2	8	13
Playing For Keeps				41	40	34	36	37	57	61	65	91	
Blue Moon	88		97			97							
Old Shep, **Elvis Vol. 2** (EP)						99							
Any Way You Want Me								92					
All Shook Up													25

	APR 3	10	17	24	MAY 1	8	15	22	29	JUN 5	12	19	22[1]
All Shook Up	6	1	1	1	1	1	1	1	1	2	2	4	6
Too Much	18	28	35	56									71
Peace In The Valley (EP)	58	49	58	39	46	70	57	64	90	86			
That's When Your Heartaches Begin	59	73	58	60	83		97						
Teddy Bear												47	4
Loving You												81	51
Hound Dog													85

	JUN 29	JUL 6	13	20	27	AUG 3	10	17	24	31
Teddy Bear	4	1	1	1	1	1	1	1	3	3
All Shook Up	6	10	15	18	22	32	38	39	46	48
Loving You	39	35	31	31	37	32	28	33	34	34
Too Much	83									
Hound Dog	92									

	SEP 7	14	21	28	OCT 5	12	19	26	NOV 2	9	16	23	30
Teddy Bear	5	6	8	12	20	26	32	43	54	75	82		
Loving You	39	46	38	38	48	51	66	85					
All Shook Up	46	63	82	74	88	97							
Jailhouse Rock					15	3	2	1	1	1	1	1	1
Treat Me Nice						61	36	27	30	46	63	82	84

	DEC 7	14	21	28
Jailhouse Rock	2	2	6	6
Treat Me Nice	86		93	
Loving You			97	93
Teddy Bear				87

---

[1] Effective with the July 1, 1957 issue, *Billboard* changed its effective date for the charts to Saturday of the week before publication.

1958

	JAN				FEB				MAR				
	4	11	18	25	1	8	15	22	1	8	15	22	29
Jailhouse Rock	7	6	14	21	28	40	64	76	66	76	94	90	76
Teddy Bear	91												
Don't			40	10	4	3	3	2	1	3	8	5	7
I Beg Of You			56	13	8	14	22	30	40	50	59	90	

	APR				MAY					JUN			
	5	12	19	26	3	10	17	24	31	7	14	21	28
Don't	17	25	32	39	43	44	81	88	83				
Jailhouse Rock	86												
I Beg Of You	100		87										
Wear My Ring Around Your Neck		7	4	5	5	3	3	3	10	12	15	24	24
Doncha' Think It's Time		74	53	21	44	86			87				
Hard Headed Woman												15	3
Don't Ask Me Why													58

	JUL			AUG				SEP				
	5	12	19	10[2]	17	24	31	7	14	21	28	
Hard Headed Woman	3	2	3	4	7	13	21	26	56	78	94	
Wear My Ring Around Your Neck	27	57	73									
Don't Ask Me Why	37	28	33	34	54	55	54	70				

	NOV				DEC				
	9	16	23	30	7	14	21	28	
I Got Stung	65	18	11	8	9	9	9	11	
One Night		30	14	7	5	5	4	6	

1959

	JAN				FEB				MAR				
	4	11	18	25	1	8	15	22	1	8	15	22	29
One Night	4	5	8	13	17	28	35	61	79	92			
I Got Stung	14	14	18	22	31	46	66	100‡					
A Fool Such As I													64

	APR				MAY					JUN			
	5	12	19	26	3	10	17	24	31	7	14	21	28
A Fool Such As I	26	13	8	5	2	6	5	8	11	19	27	43	71
I Need Your Love Tonight	33	12	10	4	7	7	10	17	20	29	46	59	76

	JUL				AUG				SEP			
	5	12	19	26	2	9	16	23	30	6	13	20	27
A Fool Such As I	95												
A Big Hunk O' Love		43	25	9	8	2	1	1	4	7	13	20	42
My Wish Came True			39	27	22	14	14	12	16	21	22	36	49

	OCT		
	4	11	
A Big Hunk O' Love	63	96	

LAST "HOT 100" SINGLE UNTIL APRIL 10, 1960.

----

[2] Effective with the August 4, 1958 issue, *Billboard* changed the date of its singles chart to the next Sunday. The name was also changed to "The Hot 100."
‡Chart erroneously says *I Got Stung* and was listed for 15 weeks.

1960

	APR			MAY					JUN			
	10	7	24	1	8	15	22	29	5	12	19	26
Stuck On You	84	17	6	1	1	1	1	2	2	2	8	10
Fame And Fortune		71	44	20	20	17	20	20	23	25	67	

	JUL					AUG				SEP			
	3	10	17	24	31	7	14	21	28	4	11	18	25
Stuck On You	22	39	50	93									
It's Now Or Never					44	14	3	3	1	1	1	1	3
A Mess Of Blues					53	40	51	32	46	63	55	52	59

	OCT					NOV				DEC			
	2	9	16	23	30	6	13	20	27	4	11	18	25
It's Now Or Never	6	7	11	10	16	27	32	47	70	99			
A Mess Of Blues	64	73											
Are You Lonesome To-Night?								35	2	1	1	1	1
I Gotta Know								63	56	34	27	20	30

1961

	JAN					FEB				MAR			
	1	8	15	22	29	5	12	19	26	5	12	19	26
Are You Lonesome To-night?	‡	1	2	2	6	10	11	21	58	62			
I Gotta Know	‡	33	32	37	43								
Surrender									24	4	2	2	1
Lonely Man										84	44	35	32

	APR					MAY				JUN			
	2	9	16	23	30	7	14	21	28	4	11	18	25
Surrender	1	3	7	10	19	25	42						
Lonely Man	63												
Flaming Star (EP)				85	34	19	16	14	27	47			
I Feel So Bad								43	17	9	5	7	14
Wild In The Country											73	48	27

	JUL					AUG				SEP			
	2	9	16	23	30	6	13	20	27	3	10	17	24
I Feel So Bad	15	35	86										
Wild In The Country	26	54											
Little Sister									61	26	15	9	13
(Marie's The Name Of) His Latest Flame										66	32	22	4

	OCT					NOV				DEC			
	1	8	15	22	29	5	12	19	26	3	10	17	24
Little Sister	6	5	8	17	34	34	48	70					
(Marie's The Name Of) His Latest Flame	10	26	21	22	41	55	57						
Can't Help Falling In Love										57	41	18	
Rock-a-Hula Baby										62	47	32	

	DEC
	31
Can't Help Falling In Love	10
Rock-a-Hula Baby	25

‡This issue was unavailable on microfilm.

1962

	JAN 7	13[3]	20	27	FEB 3	10	17	24	MAR 3	10	17	24	31
Can't Help Falling In Love	5	4	4	4	2	4	8	12	29	40			
Rock-a-Hula Baby	23	31	30	43	49								
Good Luck Charm											51	14	9
Anything That's Part Of You											70	58	48

	APR 7	14	21	28	MAY 5	12	19	26	JUN 2	9	16	23	30
Good Luck Charm	3	2	1	1	5	5	11	17	26	43			
Anything That's Part Of You	36	33	31	35	40								
Follow That Dream (EP)							58	38	30	24	22	15	15	26

	JUL 7	14	21	28	AUG 4	11	18	25	SEP 1	8	15	22	29
Follow That Dream (EP)	54	64											
She's Not You					57	26	13	8	6	5	6	10	16
Just Tell Her Jim Said Hello						80	70	66	55	58			
King Of The Whole Wide World, **Kid Galahad** (EP)												69	53

	OCT 6	13	20	27	NOV 3	10	17	24	DEC 1	8	15	22	29
She's Not You	32												
King Of The Whole Wide World, **Kid Galahad** (EP)	37	35	30	39	58								
Return To Sender			68	20	10	4	2	2	2	2	2	3	6
Where Do You Come From				99									

1963

	JAN 5	12	19	26	FEB 2	9	16	23	MAR 2	9	16	23	30
Return To Sender	6	13	21	34	59								
One Broken Heart For Sale							59	25	19	16	11	11	13
They Remind Me Too Much Of You								74	67	53	60		

	APR 6	13	20	27	MAY 4	11	18	25	JUN 1	8	15	22	29
One Broken Heart For Sale	29	48											
(You're The) Devil In Disguise													84

	JUL 6	13	20	27	AUG 3	10	17	24	31	SEP 7	14	21	28
(You're The) Devil In Disguise	49	15	9	7	4	3	3	9	17	42			

	OCT 5	12	19	26	NOV 2	9	16	23	30	DEC 7	14	21	28
Bossa Nova Baby			77	41	25	9	8	8	10	29	37	56	
Witchcraft			72	57	45	36	32	39	43				

---

[3]With the January 13, 1962 issue, *Billboard* changed the date of its charts to coincide with the publication date.

1964

	JAN 4	11	18	25	FEB 1	8	15	22	29	MAR 7	14	21	28
Kissin' Cousins								63	45	21	16	12	12
It Hurts Me									78	44	35	33	29

	APR 4	11	18	25	MAY 2	9	16	23	30	JUN 6	13	20	27
Kissin' Cousins	17	34	39										
It Hurts Me	29	41											
Kiss Me Quick					79	66	43	34	34	50			
Viva Las Vegas						87	54	46	33	33	29	40	
What'd I Say								50	29	24	21	21	35

	JUL 4	11	18	25	AUG 1	8	15	22	29	SEP 5	12	19	26
Viva Las Vegas (EP)	92												
Such A Night					82	56	35	28	16	16	21	33	

	OCT 3	10	17	24	31	NOV 7	14	21	28	DEC 5	12	19	26
Ain't That Lovin You, Baby		76	47	32	23	18	17	16	25	27	‡		
Ask Me		88	73	53	31	26	22	14	12	12	15	27	50

1965

	JAN 2	9	16	23	30	FEB 6	13	20	27	MAR 6	13	20	27
Do The Clam									68	49	39	28	23

	APR 3	10	17	24	MAY 1	8	15	22	29	JUN 5	12	19	26
Do The Clam	21	21	34										
Crying In The Chapel				79	51	39	20	10	6	4	3	4	6
(Such An) Easy Question												70	47
It Feels So Right												81	71

	JUL 3	10	17	24	31	AUG 7	14	21	28	SEP 4	11	18	25
Crying In The Chapel	8	15	20	41									
(Such An) Easy Question	27	20	15	11	11	35							
It Feels So Right	65	59	55	69									
Tickle Me (EP)		98	88	84	83	73	70	82					
I'm Yours									83	66	51	32	21

	OCT 2	9	16	23	30	NOV 6	13	20	27	DEC 4	11	18	25
I'm Yours	16	11	11	17	26	50							
Puppet On A String							80	56	46	27	22	19	14

----

‡This issue is missing from the microfilm. It was the last date on the chart, making it impossible to backtrack from the next issue.

1966

	JAN					FEB				MAR			
	1	8	15	22	29	5	12	19	26	5	12	19	26
Puppet On A String	14	21	44										
Tell Me Why	75	64	47	37	33	35	47						
Blue River	95												
Frankie And Johnny												74	60
Please Don't Stop Loving Me												85	69

	APR					MAY
	2	9	16	23	30	7
Frankie And Johnny	50	39	28	28	25	28
Please Don't Stop Loving Me	58	48	46	45	45	66

	JUL					AUG	
	2	9	16	23	30	6	13
Love Letters	87	40	26	19	19	21	55

	OCT				NOV			
	8	15	22	29	5	12	19	26
Spinout	78	57	47	44	40	40	68	
All That I Am	82	62	52	42	42	42	41	60

1967

	JAN	FEB				MAR		
	28	4	11	18	25	4	11	18
Indescribably Blue	77	58	47	35	33	33	38	54

	MAY		JUN		
	20	27	3	10	17
Long Legged Girl	86	71	68	63	‡
That's Someone You'll Never Forget		92			

	AUG	SEP					OCT				NOV		
	26	2	9	16	23	30	7	14	21	28	4	11	18
There's Always Me	90	74	58	56	56	62							
Judy			89	88	82	78	78						
Big Boss Man								71	55	48	38	38	48
You Don't Know Me							94	57	56	45	45	44	

1968

	JAN	FEB				MAR					APR		
	27	3	10	17	24	2	9	16	23	30	6	13	20
Guitar Man	83	67	50	44	43	43							
Stay Away								83	81	73	67	77	
U.S. Male									75	63	47	42	32
You'll Never Walk Alone													90

---

‡This copy of the "Hot 100" was not available.

1968

	APR 27	MAY 4	11	18	25	JUN 1	8	15	22	29
U.S. Male	32	31	28	41						
You'll Never Walk Alone	90									
Let Yourself Go							94	94	92	
Your Time Hasn't Come Yet, Baby								92	85	

	JUL 6	13	20	27	AUG 3	10	17	24	31	SEP 7	14	21	28
Let Yourself Go	81	71											
Your Times Hasn't Come Yet, Baby	82	72	72	72	72								
Almost In Love													99

	OCT 5	12	19	26	NOV 2	9	16	23	30	DEC 7	14	21	28
Almost In Love	95												
A Little Less Conversation		83	69	69	77								
If I Can Dream						100	63	40	36	30	26	17	17

1969

	JAN 4	11	18	25	FEB 1	8	15	22	MAR 1	8	15	22	29
If I Can Dream	16	12	12	16	36								
Memories												67	52

	APR 5	12	19	26	MAY 3	10	17	24	31	JUN 7	14	21	28
Memories	48	35	35	41	41								
In The Ghetto						79	41	23	17	9	6	3	4	7

	JUL 5	12	19	26	AUG 2	9	16	23	30	SEP 6	13	20	27
In The Ghetto	12	16	17	26									
Clean Up Your Own Backyard	90	65	54	47	37	35	35	38					
Suspicious Minds											77	36	19

	OCT 4	11	18	25	NOV 1	8	15	22	29	DEC 6	13	20	27
Suspicious Minds	14	11	6	5	1	2	7	9	16	17	28	57	
Don't Cry Daddy/ Rubberneckin'										73	41	36	25	23

1970

	JAN 3	10	17	24	31	FEB 7	14	21	28	MAR 7	14	21	28
Don't Cry Daddy/ Rubberneckin'	15	11	7	7	6	14	17	25					
Kentucky Rain							96	40	26	24	17	16	16

	APR 4	11	18	25	MAY 2	9	16	23	30	JUN 6	13	20	27
Kentucky Rain	25	31											
The Wonder Of You/Mama Liked The Roses					66	36	33	29	15	18	9		

1970

	JUL 4	11	18	25	AUG 1	8	15	22	29	SEP 5	12	19	26
The Wonder Of You/Mama Liked The Roses	9	9	13	17	24								
I've Lost You/The Next Step Is Love					85	47	44	36	32	32	41	47	52

	OCT 3	10	17	24	NOV 31	7	14	21	28	DEC 5	12	19	26
You Don't Have To Say You Love Me/Patch It Up				74	49	38	20	20	11	11	14	29	31
I Really Don't Want To Know/There Goes My Everything													56

1971

	JAN 2	9	16	23	30	FEB 6	13	20	27	MAR 6	13	20	27
I Really Don't Want To Know/There Goes My Everything	35	29	25	24	22	21	28	31					
Where Did They Go, Lord/Rags To Riches											60	49	36

	APR 3	10	17	24	MAY 1	8	15	22	29	JUN 5	12	19	26
Where Did They Go, Lord/Rags To Riches	35	33	40	61									
Life/Only Believe							87	69	60	57	53	53	60

	JUL 3	10	17	24	AUG 31	7	14	21	28	SEP 4
I'm Leavin'		82	59	52	45	44	38	36	63	78

	OCT 9	16	23	30	NOV 6	13
It's Only Love	90	58	56	52	51	58

1972

	JAN 29	FEB 5	12	19	26	MAR 4	11	18	25
Until It's Time For You To Go	80	60	56	50	44	43	40	49	56

	MAY 6	13	20	27	JUN 3	10
An American Trilogy	97	76	71	66	70	71

	AUG 19	26	SEP 2	9	16	23	30	OCT 7	14	21	28
Burning Love	90	68	58	40	22	18	9	7	4	3	2

	NOV 4	11	18	25	DEC 2	9	16	23	30
Burning Love	5	10	19	22					
Separate Ways					72	53	47	39	34

1973

Song	JAN 6	13	20	27	FEB 3	10	17	24	MAR 3	10	17	24	31
Separate Ways	28	26	23	21	20	24	44						

Song	APR 7	14	21	28	MAY 5	12	19	26	JUN 2	9	16	23	30
Steamroller Blues/Fool	80	60	44	30	26	23	19	17	21	28	50	53	

Song	SEP 22	29	OCT 6	13	20	27	NOV 3	10	17
Raised On Rock/For Ol' Times Sake	81	58	46	46	45	41	44	49	68

1974

Song	FEB 9	16	23	MAR 2	9	16	23	30	APR 6	13	20
I've Got A Thing About You Baby (*w/Take Good Care Of Her)	90	72	53	47	45	42	39*	39*	44*	61*	72*‡

Song	JUN 8	15	22	29	JUL 6	13	20	27	OCT 3	10	17	24	31
If You Talk In Your Sleep	77	62	46	34	32	25	21	21	17	34	54	73	95

Song	OCT 26	NOV 2	9	16	23	30	DEC 7	14	21	28
Promised Land	86	48	37	29	23	18	17	14	28	26

1975

Song	JAN 4	11	18	25	FEB 1	8	15	22	MAR 1	8	15	22	29
Promised Land	36	49	64										
My Boy				82	69	42	33	27	23	20	20	38	57

Song	APR 5	12	19	26	MAY 3	10	17	24	31	JUN 7	14	21	28
My Boy	60												
T-R-O-U-B-L-E					87	71	48	44	40	35	35	44	

Song	JUL 5
T-R-O-U-B-L-E	68

Song	OCT 25	NOV 1	8	15	22
Bringing It Back	88	78	70	65	65

‡Chart mistakenly said record had been listed for twelve weeks.

1976

	JAN					FEB				MAR			
	3	10	17	24	31	7	14	21	28	6	13	20	27
Hurt													85

	APR				MAY					JUN
	3	10	17	24	1	8	15	22	29	5
Hurt/For The Heart	75	64	53	42	38	34	30	30	28	54

	DEC
	25
Moody Blue/She Thinks I Still Care	82

1977

	JAN					FEB				MAR			
	1	8	15	22	29	5	12	19	26	5	12	19	26
Moody Blue/She Thinks I Still Care	82	59	56	46	42	39	37	35	33	31	44	56	

	JUN	JUL					AUG				SEP		
	25	2	9	16	23	30	6	13	20	27	3	10	17
Way Down	70	49	44	40	36	35	31	31	47	53	35	24	21

	SEP	OCT					NOV				DEC		
	24	1	8	15	22	29	5	12	19	26	3	10	17
Way Down	18	18	27	28	45	44	61	96					
My Way								75	60	48	38	30	28

	DEC	
	24	31
My Way	22	(no issue)

1978

	JAN			
	7	14	21	28
My Way	22	35	65	86

Billboard Album Charts

ALBUM CHARTS COMPILED FROM *BILLBOARD*. (Dates given are those for the chart, not the date of the magazine.)[1]

1956

	MAR	APR				MAY				JUN		
	31	7	14	21	28	5	12	19	26	2	9	16
Elvis Presley	11	3	3	3	2	1	1	1	1	1	1	1

	JUN		JUL				AUG				SEP	
	23	30	7	14	21	28	4	11	18	25	1	8
Elvis Presley	1	1	1	2	2	3	3	3	3	4	4	4

	SEP			OCT				NOV			
	15	22	29	6	13	20	27	3	10	17	24
Elvis Presley	5	5	5	6	6	6	6	6	6	6	7
Elvis										7	3

	DEC				
	1	8	15	22	29
Elvis	2	1	1	1	1
Elvis Presley	7	7	7	6	6

1957

	JAN				FEB				MAR				
	5	12	19	26	2	9	16	23	2	9	16	23	30
Elvis	1	2	2	2	2	2	2	2	2	2	2	3	3
Elvis Presley	7	9	9	10	12	14	15	15					

	APR					MAY				JUN				
	6	13	20	27	29[2]	6	13	20	27	3	10	17	22[3]	24
Elvis	5	5	9	10	13			15						
Peace In The Valley (EP)						14						4		3

---

[1] In 1956, the chart was called "Best Selling Packaged Records – Popular Albums," and it consisted of fifteen to twenty spaces.

[2] On April 29, 1957, *Billboard* changed from a Saturday to Monday publication date.

[3] Effective with the July 1, 1957 issue, *Billboard* tabulated albums the same as singles, with a nine-day delay. The title of the chart was also changed to "Best Selling Pop Albums."

1957

	JUN 29	JUL 6	13	20	27	AUG 3	10	17	24[4]	31
Peace In The Valley (EP)	12				10	8	13			
Loving You		11	1	1	1	1	1	1	1	1
Elvis Presley									20	
Love Me Tender (EP)									22	
Elvis									23	18

	SEP 7	14	21	28	OCT 5	12	19	26	NOV 2	9	16	23	30
Loving You	1	1	1	4	5	4	3	9	11	8	6	6	13
Elvis	19	20	20										
Just For You (EP)			16										
Peace In The Valley (EP)	23												
Elvis' Christmas Album												23	3

	DEC 7	14	21	18
Elvis' Christmas Album	1	1	1	2
Loving You	10	15	17	16

1958

	JAN 4	11	18	25	FEB 1	8	15	22	MAR 1	8	15	22	29
Elvis' Christmas Album	1												
Loving You	17	13	20									24	

	APR 5	12	19	26	MAY 3	10	17	24	31	JUN 7	14	21	28
Elvis' Golden Records		9	3	3	7	8	7	10	5	5	6	9	12

	JUL 5	12	19	26	AUG 2	9	16	23	30	SEP 6	13	20	27
Elvis' Golden Records	13	14	17		22	19	15	12	21			19	10
King Creole										11	4	3	2

	OCT 4	11	18	25	NOV 1	8	15	22	29	DEC 6	13	20	27
King Creole	3	4	8	5	6	8	8	9	17	17	19		
Elvis' Golden Records	13	11	15	19								26	20

1959

	JAN 3	10	17	24	31	FEB 7	14	21	28	MAR 7	14	21	28
Elvis' Golden Records	13	16	19										
For LP Fans Only											20	19	25

	APR 4	11	18	25	MAY 31[5]	JUN 7	14	14[6]	21	28
For LP Fans Only	25		24	23	41	33				
Elvis' Golden Records					42	36	38	21	33	45

---

[4] On September 2, 1957, *Billboard* increased its popular album chart to twenty-five places.

[5] Effective with the May 25, 1959 issue, *Billboard* changed the effective date of the LP chart to the following Sunday. The chart was split into 50 places for monophonic LPs and 30 places for stereophonic LPs.

1959

JUL

	5
Elvis' Golden Records	50

	SEP		OCT				NOV	DEC	
	20	27	4	11	18	25	1	20	20[7]
A Date With Elvis	39	39	32	33	34	45	48		
Elvis' Golden Records								39	43

1960

JAN FEB

	29	19
A Date With Elvis	36	
50 Million Fans Can't Be Wrong, Elvis' Gold Records, Vol. 2		34

	APR				MAY				JUN			
	8	15	22	29	6	13	20	27	5	12	19	26
Elvis' Gold Records, Vol. 2	37	34	32	32								
Elvis Is Back					35	4	3	3	2	3	2	

	JUL					AUG					SEP	
	1	10	17	24	31	7	7[8]	14	21	28	4	11[9]
Elvis Is Back	2	3	3	3	3	3	4	4	4	5	8	10[25]

	SEP		OCT				
	18	23	2	9	16	23	30
Elvis Is Back	8[20]	11[10]	10[17]	16[14]	14[11]	27[12]	17[9]
G.I. Blues							6x

	NOV				DEC			
	6	13	20	27	4	11	18	25
G.I. Blues	4[x]	4[x]	3[13]	2[10]	1[13]	2[11]	1[6]	1[5]
Elvis Is Back	33[17]	x[17]	x[18]	x[21]	34[22]	x[23]		

1961

	JAN				FEB				MAR			
	8	15	23	30	6	13	18	27	4	13	20	27
G.I.Blues	1[2]	‡	+	+	+	+	+	+	+	+	+	+
His Hand In Mine		‡	14[x]	15[x]	18[x]	14[x]	13[x]	13[x]	16[x]	15[x]	+	+
Elvis Is Back		‡	+	+	+	+	+	+	+	+	+	+
Elvis Christmas Album	33	‡										

[6] With the June 15, 1959 issue, *Billboard* moved the LP chart to the day prior to publication, resulting in two charts with a June 14th date.

[7] With the Dec. 28, 1959 issue, *Billboard* moved the LP chart back a week, resulting in two charts having a Dec. 20th date.

[8] With the Aug. 8, 1960 issue, *Billboard* again moved the LP chart to the date prior to publication, resulting in two charts with an Aug. 7th date.

[9] First number is monaural; superscript is stereo.

‡ No microfilm exists for this date.

+ On January 9, 1961, *Billboard* eliminated its usual album charts in favor of listing the "Best Selling LP's By Category" with no numerical ranking. In addition, there was a list of "Action Albums" which contained 25 places for monaural and 15 places for stereo albums which were new to the chart. Albums marked + were listed in the "Best Selling" chart.

1961

	APR					MAY				JUN			
	2	9^{10}	16	23	30	7	14	21	28	4	11	18	25
His Hand In Mine	+	97^x	87^x	104^x	95^x	135^x	131^x	140^x	145x				
G.I. Blues	+	1^2	2^{11}	2^{14}	2^{15}	2^{12}	2^{14}	1^{15}	1^{19}	1^{19}	2^{22}	2^{23}	3^{33}
Elvis Is Back	+	83x	93x	76x	76x	77x	77x	78x	99x	120x	123x	134x	141x

	JUL					AUG				SEP			
	2	9	16	23	30	6	13	20	27	3	10	17	24
G.I. Blues	4^{37}	5^{27}	7^{26}	8^{36}	10^{34}	11^{30}	14^{46}	15x	1^{19}	14^{48}	18^{26}	16^{31}	19^{35}
Something For Everybody		136x	98x	61^{37}	30^{23}	15^{22}	2^{22}	14x	1^{18}	1^{14}	6^{18}	5^{14}	

	OCT					NOV			
	1	8	15	22	29	5	12	19	26
Something For Everybody	5^{16}	5^{19}	9^{25}	14^{45}	11^{36}	18^{36}	35^{31}	37^{41}	53^{49}
G.I. Blues	26^{32}	24^{37}	29^{42}	31^{35}	27^{44}	23^{46}	41^{42}	55^{44}	60^{50}
Blue Hawaii				75x	10^{48}	5^{35}	3^{32}	2^{26}	

	DEC				
	3	10	17	24	31
Blue Hawaii	3^{17}	2^7	1^6	1^7	1^6
G.I. Blues	52^{39}	54^{33}	46^{39}	60^{45}	49^{45}
Something For Everybody	64x	77x	82x	90x	128x

1962

	JAN				FEB				MAR				
	7	13^{11}	20	27	3	10	17	24	3	10	17	24	31
Blue Hawaii	1^2	1^2	1^1	1^1	1^1	1^2	1^2	1^2	1^2	1^2	1^2	1^2	1^2
G.I. Blues	67^{49}	70x	57x	61x	86x	105x	105x	114x	105x	104x	85x	92x	105x
Elvis' Christmas Album	149x	120x											

	APR				MAY				JUN				
	7	14	21	28	5	12	19	26	2	9	16	23	30
Blue Hawaii	1^1	1^2	1^2	1^4	2^3	3^4	3^3	3^4	3^4	4^4	4^8	5^7	5^8
G.I. Blues	120x	113x	142x	138x	134x	125x	118x	106x	92x	90x	82x	69x	90x

	JUL				AUG				SEP				
	7	14	21	28	4	11	18	25	1	8	15	22	29
Blue Hawaii	7^{18}	10^{26}	6^{19}	7^{13}	12^{23}	16^{35}	12^{33}	11^{31}	25^{27}	36^{27}	37^{21}	39^{24}	89^{39}
G.I. Blues	104x	123x	142x	127x	119x	127x	136x	121x	124x	97x	76x	69x	74x
Pot Luck		116^{33}	57^{15}	21^9	15^8	4^{14}	4^{13}	4^{15}	5^{18}	6^{32}	7^{17}	7^{20}	8^{22}

	OCT				NOV				DEC				
	6	13	20	27	3	10	17	24	1	8	15	22	29
Pot Luck	10^{14}	11^{28}	14^{36}	17^{49}	29^{35}	46x	40x	53x	46x	47x	70x	84x	81x
Blue Hawaii	52^{29}	33^{30}	28^{28}	40^{33}	40^{44}	50x	86x	122x	139x	118x	103x	116x	138x
G.I. Blues	60x	50x	69x	75x	82x	115x							
Girls! Girls! Girls!									27^{36}	7^7	6^{10}	5^5	
Elvis' Christmas Album									143x	143x	77x	59x	

---

[10] On April 3, 1961, *Billboard* initiated the "Hot LPs" chart which listed 150 mono and 50 stereo albums.

[11] On January 13, 1962, *Billboard* changed the effective date of its LP chart to coincide with the publication date.

1963

	JAN 5	JAN 12	JAN 19	JAN 26	FEB 2	FEB 9	FEB 16	FEB 23	MAR 2	MAR 9	MAR 16	MAR 23	MAR 30
Girls! Girls! Girls!	5[14]	3[14]	6[15]	6[11]	8[11]	8[17]	8[33]	9[22]	10[16]	12[26]	15[27]	13[26]	17[32]
Pot Luck	70x	113x	138x	117x	132x	148x							
Blue Hawaii	95x	66x	86x	108x	115x	92x	87x	67x	57x	59x	74x	65x	63x
G.I. Blues					117x	90x	105x	116x	146x				

	APR 6	APR 13	APR 20	APR 27	MAY 4	MAY 11	MAY 18	MAY 25	JUN 1	JUN 8	JUN 15	JUN 22	JUN 29
Girls! Girls! Girls!	32[26]	31[29]	43[49]	40x	35x	46x	52x	99x	133x	114x	101x	91x	128x
Blue Hawaii	96x	117x	114x	128x									
It Happened At The World's Fair			90[43]	12[29]	6[18]	6[18]	6[23]	4[15]	4[15]	5[25]	9[39]	10[27]	11[33]

	JUL 6	JUL 13	JUL 20	JUL 27	AUG 3	AUG 10	AUG 17[12]	AUG 24	AUG 31	SEP 7	SEP 14	SEP 21	SEP 28
It Happened At The World's Fair	16[45]	28[47]	24[41]	20[39]	‡	‡	32	45	48	39	68	118	144
Girls! Girls! Girls!	120x	122x											
Elvis' Golden Records, Vol. 3											119	48	17

	OCT 5	OCT 12	OCT 19	OCT 26	NOV 2	NOV 9	NOV 16	NOV 23	NOV 30	DEC 7	DEC 14	DEC 21	DEC 28
Elvis' Golden Records, Vol. 3	12	9	7	7	4	4	3	3	6	6	5	5	6
It Happened At The World's Fair	149	141											
Fun In Acapulco												63	41

1964

	JAN 4	JAN 11	JAN 18	JAN 25	FEB 1	FEB 8	FEB 15	FEB 22	FEB 29	MAR 7	MAR 14	MAR 21	MAR 28
Elvis' Golden Records, Vol. 3	4	19	16	21	22	33	49	65	60	52	93	81	77
Fun In Acapulco	18	4	3	3	3	7	11	9	7	11	12	12	13

	APR 4	APR 11	APR 18	APR 25	MAY 2	MAY 9	MAY 16	MAY 23	MAY 30	JUN 6	JUN 13	JUN 20	JUN 27
Fun In Acapulco	23	28	38	43	48	49	53	80	146				
Elvis' Golden Records, Vol. 3	63	57	76	118	127	126	123	128	127	144	142		
Kissin' Cousins		96	23	10	6	6	6	7	11	12	14	15	21

	JUL 4	JUL 11	JUL 18	JUL 25	AUG 1	AUG 8	AUG 15	AUG 22	AUG 29	SEP 5	SEP 12	SEP 19	SEP 26
Kissin' Cousins	33	42	44	39	30	30	47	47	53	66	81	73	65

	OCT 3	OCT 10	OCT 17	OCT 24	OCT 31	NOV 7	NOV 14	NOV 21	NOV 28	DEC 5	DEC 12	DEC 19	DEC 26
Kissin' Cousins	74	86	117	131	142								
Roustabout						100	47	14	5	4	2	2	

‡Copies of *Billboard* for these dates not available on microfilm.
[12] With the August 24, 1963 issue, *Billboard* combined its stereo and mono album charts into a single LP chart, again. The new chart listed 150 positions.

531

1965

	JAN 2	9	16	23	30	FEB 6	13	20	27	MAR 6	13	20	27
Roustabout	1	2	6	8	8	10	9	10	11	13	20	20	22

	APR 3	10	17	24	MAY 1	8	15	22	29	JUN 5	12	19	26
Roustabout	27	30	44	50	62	71	101						
Girl Happy			140	82	54	25	14	10	9	9	8	8	9

	JUL 3	10	17	24	31	AUG 7	14	21	28	SEP 4	11	18	25
Girl Happy	11	16	17	17	21	27	30	35	39	44	49	53	59
Elvis For Everyone							149	102	63	50	43	37	29

	OCT 2	9	16	23	30	NOV 6	13	20	27	DEC 4	11	18	25
Elvis For Everyone	24	15	11	10	13	15	17	28	38	45	47	47	41
Girl Happy	55	61	65	66	77	95	106						
Harum Scarum							122	94	33	16	11	10	10

1966

	JAN 1	8	15	22	29	FEB 5	12	19	26	MAR 5	12	19	26
Harum Scarum	8	8	12	20	35	37	46	50	62	66	66	73	76
Elvis For Everyone	43	52	58	61	78	86	104						

	APR 2	9	16	23	30	MAY 7	14	21	28	JUN 4	11	18	25
Harum Scarum	84	107	130										
Frankie And Johnny				103	80	55	24	21	20	21	29	32	32

	JUL 2	9	16	23	30	AUG 6	13	20	27	SEP 3	10	17	24
Frankie And Johnny	31	31	47	50	66	76	109	120	126				
Paradise – Hawaiian Style			132	117	59	40	27	21	17	15	15	19	22

	OCT 1	8	15	22	29	NOV 5	12	19	26	DEC 3	10	17	24
Paradise – Hawaiian Style	38	60	70	70	71	78	83	123					
Spinout					135	91	80	57	52	30	21	18	18

	DEC 31
Spinout	18

1967

	JAN 7	14	21	28	FEB 4	11	18	25	MAR 4	11	18	25
Spinout	28	40	43	43	38	32	38	46	49	50	57	69
How Great Thou Art											147	

1967

	APR					MAY				JUN			
	1	8	15	22[13]	29	6	13[14]	20	27	3	10	17	24
Spinout	74	73	76	81	86	143	153	172	174	174			
How Great Thou Art	132	89	67	50	31	21	19	18	20	33	33	32	40
Double Trouble													179

	JUL					AUG				SEP			
	1	8	15	22	29	5	12	19	26	2	9	16	23
How Great Thou Art	43	56	61	66	74	90	92	92	91	99	112	116	132
Double Trouble	161	143	86	76	60	59	49	47	47	49	99	120	119

	SEP	OCT				NOV			
	30	7	14	21	28	4	11	18	25
Double Trouble	112	112	125	175	175	175			
How Great Thou Art	138	143							

	DEC				
	2	9	16	23	30
Clambake	188	102	79	61	56

1968

	JAN				FEB				MAR				
	6	13	20	27	3	10	17	24	2	9	16	23	30
Clambake	55	50	50	41	41	40	42	62	64				
Elvis' Gold Records, Vol. 4										134	119	94	83	72

	APR				MAY				JUN				
	6	13	20	27	4	11	18	25	1	8	15	22	29
Elvis' Gold Records, Vol. 4	68	57	52	52	47	39	38	34	33	42	55	59	70

	JUL				AUG				SEP			
	6	13	20	27	3	10	17	24	31	7	14	21	28
Elvis' Gold Records, Vol. 4	91	103	147	162									
Speedway	193	174	157	156	96	94	83	82	87	88	88	108	115

	DEC	
	21	28
Elvis (TV Special)	166	106

1969

	JAN				FEB				MAR				
	4	11	18	25	1	8	15	22	1	8	15	22	29
Elvis (TV Special)	93	73	55	22	11	8	8	8	13	20	30	29	29

	APR				MAY				JUN				
	5	12	19	26	3	10	14	24	31	7	14	21	28
Elvis (TV Special)	40	39	37	40	53	53	52	61	79	79	87	102	123
Elvis Sings Flaming Star			195	193	194	194	160	148	145	98	96	106	106
From Elvis In Memphis											29	18	16

---

[13] Chart expanded to 175 places.
[14] Chart expanded to 200 places.

1969

	JUL 5	12	19	26	AUG 2	9	16	23	30	SEP 6	13	20	27
From Elvis In Memphis	15	14	13	13	18	23	23	32	32	38	38	40	46
Elvis Sings Flaming Star	116	119	130	136	170								
Elvis (TV Special)	146	135	149	158									

	OCT 4	11	18	25	NOV 1	8	15	22	29	DEC 6	13	20	27
From Elvis In Memphis	44	50	83	83	82	88	111	111	107	105	105	93	94
From Memphis To Vegas/ From Vegas To Memphis									36	16	15	14	12

1970

	JAN 3	10	17	24	31	FEB 7	14	21	28	MAR 7	14	21	28
From Memphis To Vegas/ From Vegas To Memphis	18	12	12	22	22	36	37	44	44	56	64	87	97
From Elvis In Memphis	98	110	122	124	140								

	APR 4	11	18	25	MAY 2	9	16	23	30	JUN 6	13	20	27
From Memphis To Vegas/ From Vegas To Memphis	108	124	124	139	169	169							
Let's Be Friends					108	106	105	115	129	113	113	106	
On Stage – February 1970												31	21

	JUL 4	11	18	25	AUG 1	8	15	22	29	SEP 5	12	19	26
On Stage – February 1970	14	14	14	13	18	18	24	24	23	48	54	54	50
Let's Be Friends	195	143	152										
Elvis: Worldwide Gold Award Hits, Vol. 1								117	90	84	71	71	55

	OCT 3	10	17	24	31	NOV 7	14	21	28	DEC 5	12	19	26
Elvis: Worldwide Gold Award Hits, Vol. 1	47	45	72	70	74	72	94	103	115	109	107	126	147
On Stage – February 1970	56	53	106	118	164								
Almost In Love								128	122	66	65	74	80
Back In Memphis								194	189	183			
Elvis–That's The Way It Is											63	37	25

1971

	JAN 2	9	16	23	30	FEB 6	13	20	27	MAR 6	13	20	27
Elvis–That's The Way It Is	21	21	34	33	46	58	57	54	65	70	77	78	72
Almost In Love	80	95	107	117	116	141	136	134	139	166	162	160	
Elvis: Worldwide Gold Award Hits, Vol. 1	150	168	173										
Elvis Country				143	23	19	16	13	12	22	22	20	29
You'll Never Walk Alone												190	87

	APR 3	10	17	24	MAY 1	8	15	22	29	JUN 5	12	19	26
Elvis Country	32	45	45	59	69	70	102	112	112	162	160		
Elvis–That's The Way It Is	78	84	91	116	118	130	152						
You'll Never Walk Alone	75	73	69	69	87	123	136	133	135	165			
Love Letters From Elvis													40

1971

	JUL					AUG				SEP			
	3	10	17	24	31	7	14	21	28	4	11	18	25
Love Letters From Elvis	35	33	33	40	50	51	51	61	69	74	82	99	145
C'mon Everybody				144	135	80	78	70	78	87	93	108	127
Elvis: The Other Sides — Worldwide Gold Award Hits, Volume 2									144	134	120	120	146

	OCT					NOV				DEC			
	2	9	16	23	30	6	13	20	27	4	11	18	25
Love Letters From Elvis	156												
C'mon Everybody	168												
Elvis: The Other Sides— Worldwide Gold Award Hits, Volume 2	185	176							122	155	106	104	154

1972

	JAN					FEB				MAR			
	1	8	15	22	29	5	12	19	26	4	11	18	25
I Got Lucky	160	178	178										
Elvis Now							175	91	56	48	44	43	50

	APR					MAY				JUN			
	1	8	15	22	29	6	13	20	27	3	10	17	24
Elvis Now	65	70	91	82	98	104	104	108	123	140	163	183	
He Touched Me				122	87	84	79	88	92	101	107	127	166

	JUL					AUG				SEP			
	1	8	15	22	29	5	12	19	26	2	9	16	23
Elvis As Recorded At Madison Square Garden		96	30	21	18	16	14	13	12	12	11	11	13
Elvis Sings Hits From His Movies, Volume 1		161	125	110	94	91	87	91	103	109	114	124	124

	SEP	OCT				NOV			
	30	7	14	21	28	4	11	18	25
Elvis As Recorded At Madison Square Garden	13	18	20	19	28	28	32	52	63
Elvis Sings Hits From His Movies, Volume 1	128	135	162						
Burning Love And Hits From His Movies, Volume 2							65	50	39

	DEC				
	2	9	16	23	30
Elvis As Recorded At Madison Square Garden	65	79	99	100	105
Burning Love And Hits From Hit Movies, Volume 2	30	27	25	25	24

1973

	JAN				FEB				MAR				
	6	13	20	27	3	10	17	24	3	10	17	24	31
Burning Love And Hits From His Movies, Volume 2	22	22	22	28	32	47	59	60	62	65	67	74	79
Elvis As Recorded At Madison Square Garden	111	122	140	176	176	180	189	194					
Separate Ways				117	87	75	63	53	50	49	46	57	58
Elvis: Aloha From Hawaii								99	58	31	20	13	11

	APR				MAY				JUN				
	7	14	21	28	5	12	19	26	2	9	16	23	30
Elvis: Aloha From Hawaii	11	10	4	2	1	3	7	8	14	17	31	30	31
Separate Ways	77	81	98	115	117	148	165	190					
Burning Love And Hits From His Movies, Volume 2	103	107	121	129									

	JUL				AUG				SEP				
	7	14	21	28	4	11	18	25	1	8	15	22	29
Elvis: Aloha From Hawaii	33	37	46	50	67	77	86	90	91	93	99	114	121
Elvis (Including *Fool*)		130	74	60	55	52	56	58	64	82	110	141	

	OCT				NOV				DEC				
	6	13	20	27	3	10	17	24	1	8	15	22	29
Elvis: Aloha From Hawaii	137	151	151										130
Elvis	151	155											
Raised On Rock							176	159	110	52	51	51	

1974

	JAN				FEB				MAR				
	5	12	19	26	2	9	16	23	2	9	16	23	30
Raised On Rock	50	64	74	81	102	153	181						
Elvis: Aloha From Hawaii	114	87	80	77	80	81	83	87	88	104	119	137	138
Elvis — A Legendary Performer, Volume 1					130	70	50	45	43	48	60	72	91

	APR				MAY				JUN				
	6	13	20	27	4	11	18	25	1	8	15	22	29
Elvis — A Legendary Performer, Volume 1	98	130	164	165	182								
Good Times	125	108	104	92	90	113	146	196					
Elvis: Aloha From Hawaii	144	160	184										

	JUL				AUG					SEP			
	6	13	20	27	3	10	17	24	31	7	14	21	28
Elvis Recorded Live On Stage In Memphis				83	50	40	36	33	35	49	59	79	100

	OCT				NOV					DEC			
	5	12	19	26	2	9	16	23	30	7	14	21	28
Elvis Recorded Live On Stage In Memphis	125	138	167										
Having Fun With Elvis On Stage					163	148	136	130	130	150	198		

1975

	JAN				FEB				MAR				
	4	11	18	25	1	8	15	22	1	8	15	22	29
Promised Land					102	84	73	62	52	48	47	48	86

	APR				MAY					JUN			
	5	12	19	26	3	10	17	24	31	7	14	21	28
Promised Land	132	152	161										
Today										129	116	98	85

	JUL				AUG				
	5	12	19	26	2	9	16	23	30
Today	74	64	64	60	57	76	80	115	141

(NO CHARTED ALBUM UNTIL FEBRUARY 7, 1976.)

1976

	FEB				MAR				APR				MAY
	7	14	21	28	6	13	20	27	3	10	17	24	1
Elvis – A Legendary Performer, Volume 2	76	65	54	49	46	46	62	82	109	105	110	121	117
The Sun Sessions											144	120	109

	MAY				JUN				JUL				
	8	15	22	29	5	12	19	26	4[15]	10	17	24	31
The Sun Sessions	92	82	79	76	116	116	196	191					
Elvis – A Legendary Performer, Volume 2	127	147	147	150									
From Elvis Presley Boulevard					183	91	72	60	48	44	41	68	68

	AUG				SEP			
	7	14	21	28	4	11	18	25
From Elvis Presley Boulevard	85	91	128	128	128	126	173	173

1977

	APR			MAY				JUN			
	16	23	30	7	14	21	28	4	11	18	25
Welcome To My World	100	90	78	68	56	46	44	60	81	130	177

	JUL		AUG				SEP			
	23	30	6	13	20	27	3	10	17	24
Moody Blue	58	40	28	26	24	24	5	5	3	3
Elvis' Gold Records, Volume 3								130	76	65
Elvis' Golden Records								136	99	78
Welcome To My World									120	105
Elvis – A Legendary Performer, Volume 1									122	110
Elvis: Worldwide Gold Award Singles, Volume 1									126	114

---

[15] Issue dated July 4, 1976 to coincide with the nation's 200th birthday.

1977

	OCT					NOV				DEC			
	1	8	15	22	29	5	12	19	26	3	10	17	24
Moody Blue	3	5	4	8	11	15	17	33	58	108	108	108	180
Elvis' Golden Records	63	71	71	92	102	109	125	125	119	164	162	167	189
Elvis' Gold Records, Volume 3	72	68	68	64	68	71	95	95	112	169	169	178	178
Welcome To My World	94	83	73	71	71	81	116	126	121	170	166	173	
Elvis — A Legendary Performer, Volume 1	89	78	65	62	67	65	98	98	98	126	188	188	
Elvis: Worldwide Gold Award Singles, Volume 1	99	89	85	83	110	127	138	142	137	174	167	174	
Elvis In Concert					18	9	7	5	5	17	40	70	136

1978

	JAN				FEB			
	7	14	21	28	4	11	18	25
Elvis In Concert	136	136	126	116	114	112	112	191
Elvis' Gold Records, Volume 3	177	169	159	149	149	196		
Moody Blue	182	173	166	161	160	156	199	
Elvis' Golden Records	189	181	172	167	169	169	171	

Billboard EP Charts

EXTENDED PLAY SINGLES CHARTS COMPILED FROM *BILLBOARD*. (Dates are those for the chart, not the date of the magazine.)[1]

1957

	SEP	OCT				NOV				
	28	5	12	19	26	2	9	16	23	30
Loving You, Vol. 1	1	1	1	1	1	2	2	2	3	4
Just For You	3	3	2	4	3	3	4	4	5	6
Peace In The Valley	9			10	6	9	6	7	8	
Loving You, Vol. 2	10	6	4	5	5	6	7			
Jailhouse Rock						1	1	1	1	1
Elvis, Vol. 1							9		9	
Elvis Sings Christmas Songs									2	2

	DEC			
	7	14	21	28
Jailhouse Rock	1	1	1	1
Elvis Sings Christmas Songs	2	2	2	2
Loving You, Vol. 1	4	4	6	6
Just For You	10			
Peace In The Valley			9	
Loving You, Vol. 2			10	

1958

	JAN				FEB				MAR				
	4	11	18	25	1	8	15	22	1	8	15	22	29
Jailhouse Rock	1	1	1	1	1	1	1	1	1	1	1	1	1
Elvis Sings Christmas Songs	2												
Loving You, Vol. 1	4	3	3	6	9		7	4				8	6
Love Me Tender	10												9
Elvis, Vol. 1		8	9	9	10		9		10	7	9	7	8
Elvis Presley, EPB-1254		9											
Just For You			7	7									
Peace In The Valley									6	9			

---

[1] The chart was known throughout its existence as "Best Selling Pop EPs" and was limited to ten places.

1958

	APR				MAY					JUN			
	5	12	19	26	3	10	17	24	31	7	14	21	28
Jailhouse Rock	2	1	1	1	1	1	1	2	3	4	3	3	4
Loving You, Vol. 1	4	5			7	5	4						
Elvis, Vol. 1	10	2	2	4	5	9	6	1	1	2	4	8	6
Heartbreak Hotel		10	5	6									
Peace In The Valley					4	3					10	9	
Just For You										7	5		
The Real Elvis										8	6		
Love Me Tender											10	9	

	JUL				AUG					SEP			
	5	12	19	26	2	9	16	23	30	6	13	20	27
Elvis, EPA 992	7	6	4	5		7	6			9			
King Creole, Vol. 1		1	1	1	1	1	1	1	1	1	1	1	1
Jailhouse Rock		10	5	6			9		7	6	6	8	
King Creole, Vol. 2							2	2	2	2	2	2	2
Loving You								10	4				
Elvis Presley, EPA 747									10				

	OCT				NOV					DEC			
	4	11	18	25	1	8	15	22	29	6	13	20	27
King Creole, Vol. 1	1	1	1	1	1	1	1	1	1	1	1	3	5
King Creole, Vol. 2	1	2	2	2	2	2	2	2	2	2	2	5	8
Elvis Presley, EPB 1254	9												
Elvis, EPA 992		5											
Jailhouse Rock			8		10	7	6						
Loving You							8						

1959

	JAN					FEB				MAR			
	3	10	17	24	31	7	14	21	28	7	14	21	28
King Creole, Vol. 1	1	1	2	5	5	5	4	6	6	9	9	6	7
The Real Elvis	8	7	5										
Elvis Sails	9	4	3	2									
Jailhouse Rock				6	6								
King Creole, Vol. 2				7	7								
Elvis Presley, EPB-1254				9									
Elvis, EPA-992							10		8	10		10	

	APR				MAY		JUN				
	4	11	18	25	2	9	31²	7	14	21	28
Elvis Sails	6	4	4	5	6	3	7	8			
King Creole, Vol. 1			7	6	3	7	2	2	1	1	1

---

²Effective with the May 25, 1959 issue, *Billboard* changed the date of the EP chart to the following Sunday.

1959

	JUL				AUG		
	5	12	19	26	2	9	16
King Creole, Vol. 1	1	2	2	3	7	9	9

(ELVIS HAD NO EPs ON THIS CHART UNTIL DECEMBER 28, 1959.)

	DEC
	28
Elvis Sings Christmas Songs	1

1960

	JAN
	4
Elvis Sings Christmas Songs	1

(THIS WAS ELVIS' LAST EXTENDED PLAY ON THE "BEST SELLING EPs" CHART. *BILLBOARD* DISCONTINUED THIS LIST IN MID-1960.)

Variety's
"Top-Grossing Films" Charts

MOTION PICTURE CHARTS COMPILED FROM *VARIETY*. (Dates are for the issue of the magazine.)[1]

1956
NOV	DEC							
28*	5	12	19					

Love Me Tender	2	4	9	12				

1957
JUL	AUG				NOV			
31	7	14	21		13	20	27

Loving You	8	7	14	14			
Jailhouse Rock					4	3	11

1958
JUL			
9	16	23	30

King Creole	5	5	12	14

1960
NOV	DEC			
30	7	14	21	28

G.I. Blues	2	4	13	
Flaming Star				12

1961
NOV	DEC			
29	6	13	20	

Blue Hawaii	2	2	5	12

1962
MAY	JUN		SEP		NOV	DEC	
30	6		5		28	5	12

Follow That Dream	5	6					
Kid Galahad			9				
Girls! Girls! Girls!					6	9	12

1963
DEC		
4	11	18

Fun In Acapulco	5	7	10

---

[1] In 1956, the title of the chart was "The National Box Office Survey."

1964

	APR		JUL			DEC	
	1		1	8		2	9
Kissin' Cousins	11						
Viva Las Vegas			14	8			
Roustabout						8	10

1965

	DEC
	1
Harum Scarum	11

1967

	NOV
	29
Clambake	15

1969[2]

	NOV		DEC	
	19	26	3	10
Change Of Habit	42	17	40	50

1970

	NOV		DEC		
	18	25	2	9	16
Elvis – That's The Way It Is	25		28		22

1972

	NOV		
	8	15	22
Elvis On Tour	18		13

----

[2] Title of *Variety*'s chart changed to "50 Top-Grossing Films." Number of films expanded from 15 to 50.

Bibliography

Adler, Bill *Love Letters to Elvis*
Barlow, Roy *The Elvis Presley Encyclopedia*
Barris, George *Stars And Their Cars*
Barry, Ron *All American Elvis*
Belz, Carl *The Story Of Rock*
Berman, Jay *The Fifties Book*
Berry, Peter E. *...And The Hits Just Keep On Comin'*
Bowser, James W. *Starring Elvis*
Brooks, Tim and Erle Marsh *The Complete Dictionary of Prime-time TV Shows*
Busnar, Gene *It's Rock 'n' Roll*
Canada, Lena *To Elvis With Love*
Canady, Barbara *Elvis Memoribilia Catalogue And Price Guide*
Carpozi, George, Jr. *The Johnny Cash Story*
Carr, Roy and Mick Farren *Elvis: The Illustrated Record*
Cash, Johnny *Man In Black*
Chapman, Bruce L. (editor) *Hardening Rock*
Chapple, Steve and Reebee Garofalo *Rock 'n' Roll Is Here To Pay*
Clark, Alan *Elvis Presley Memories No. 4*
Clark, Alan *Elvis Presley Memories No. 8*
Clark, Alan *Rock And Roll Legends*
Clark, Dick and Richard Robinson *Rock, Roll And Remember*
Cocke, Marion J. *I Called Him Babe: Elvis Presley's Nurse Remembers*
Cohn, Nik *A WopBopaLooBopALop-BamBoom*
Cohn, Nik *Rock From The Beginning*
Cortez, Diego *Private Elvis*
Corvino, Nick *Elvis: The Army Years*
Cotten, Lee *Elvis: His Life History*
Cotten, Lee and Howard A. DeWitt *Jailhouse Rock*
Cranor, Rosalind *Elvis Collectibles*
Crumbaker, Marge with Gabe Tucker *Up And Down With Elvis Presley*
DeWitt, Howard A. *Chuck Berry: Rock 'N' Roll Music*
Eisen, Johnathan (editor) *The Age of Rock*
Escott, Colin and Martin Hawkins *Sun Records: The Brief History Of The Legendary Record Label*
Farren, Mick and Pearce Marchbank *Elvis* (compilers) *Elvis In His Own Words*
Flip Magazine *Flip's Groovy Guide To The Guys*
Fong-Torres, Ben (editor) *The Rolling Stone Rock 'N' Roll Reader*
Fox, Sharon R. *Elvis: He Touched My Life*
Friedman, Favius *Meet Elvis Presley*
Gillett, Charlie *The Sound Of The City*
Goldman, Albert *Elvis*
Goldstein, Stewart and Alan Jacobson *Oldies But Goodies*
Gregory, James (editor) *The Elvis Presley Story*
Gregory, Neal and Janice Gregory *When Elvis Died*
Grove, Martin A. *Elvis - The Legend Lives*
Grove, Martin A. *The King Is Dead*
Guralnick, Peter *Feel Like Going Home: Portraits In Blues And Rock 'N' Roll*
Guralnick, Peter *Lost Highway: Journeys And Arrivals Of American Musicians*
Hamblett, Charles *Elvis: The Swinging Kid*
Hand, Albert *A Century Of Elvis*
Hand, Albert (editor) *Elvis Special* (annual from 1963 thru 1983)
Hand, Albert (editor) *The Elvis Pocket Handbook*
Hanna, David *Elvis: Lonely Star At The Top*
Harbinson, W.A. *Elvis: A Tribute To Elvis, King Of Rock*
Harbinson, W.A. *The Illustrated Elvis*
Harbinson, W.A. *The Life And Death Of Elvis Presley*
Harms, Valerie *Tryin' To Get To You*
Harper, Betty *Newly Discovered Drawings Of Elvis Presley*
Hatcher, Harley *Elvis, Is That You?*
Hawkins, Martin and Colin Escott *Elvis: The Illustrated Discography*
Hill, Wanda June *We Remember Elvis*
Holum, Torben; Ernst Jorgensen and Erik Rasmussen *Recording Sessions, 1954-1974*
Holzer, Hans *Elvis Presley Speaks*
Hopkins, Jerry *Elvis*

Hopkins, Jerry *Elvis: The Final Years*
Hopkins, Jerry *The Rock Story*
Hudson, James A. *Johnny Cash Close-Up*
James, Anthony *Presley: Entertainer Of The Century*
Jenkinson, Phillip and Alan Warner *Celluiod Rock*
Jones, Peter *Elvis*
Jorgensen, Ernst; Erik Rasmussen, and Johnny Mikkelsen *Recording Sessions*
Lacker, Marty; Patsy Lacker and Leslie S. Smith *Elvis: Portrait Of A Friend*
Langbroek, Hans *The Hillbilly Cat*
Levy, Alan *Operation Elvis*
Lichter, Paul *Elvis In Hollywood*
Lichter, Paul *The Boy Who Dared To Rock: The Definitive Elvis*
Lichter, Paul (editor) with S.K. Scott *Elvis: The Legend Lives On*
Loyd, Harold and George Baugh *The Graceland Gates*
Mann, May *Elvis And The Colonel*
Mann, May *Elvis, Why Won't They Leave You Alone*
Mann, May *The Private Elvis*
Mann, Richard *Elvis*
Marcus, Greil *Mystery Train*
Marcus, Greil *Rock And Roll Will Stand*
Marsh, Dave *Elvis*
Matthew-Walker, Robert *Elvis Presley: A Study In Music*
Meltzer, R. *The Aesthetics Of Rock*
Miller, Jim (editor) *The Rolling Stone Illustrated History Of Rock & Roll*
Murrells, Joseph *The Book Of Golden Discs*
Nash, Bruce M. *The Elvis Presley Quiz-book*
Nite, Norm N. *Rock On*
Nugent, Steven and Charlie Gillett *Rock Almanac*
O'Grady, John *The Life And Times Of Hollywood's Number One Private Eye*
Osborne, Jerry *Elvis Presley Record Price Guide*
Osborne, Jerry and Bruce Hamilton *Presleyana*
Page, Betty *I Got Ya, Elvis, I Got Ya!*
Parish, James Robert *The Elvis Presley Scrapbook*
Parker, Ed *Inside Elvis*
Pascall, Jeremy (editor) *The Stars And Superstars Of Rock*
Pascall, Jeremy *The Story Of Rock* (Vol. 1-3)
Pleasents, Henry *The Great American` Popular Singers*
Pollock, Bruce *When Rock Was Young*
Presley, Dee; Billy Stanley; Rick Stanley & David Stanley *Elvis: We Love You Tender*

Presley, Vester *A Presley Speaks*
Propes, Steve *Those Oldies But Goodies*
Reed, Bill and David Ehrenstein *Rock On Film*
Reggero, John *Elvis In Concert*
Rhode, H. Kandy *The Gold Of Rock & Roll, 1955-1967*
Rolling Stone Magazine *The Rolling Stone Record Review*
Rosenbaum, Helen *The Elvis Presley Trivia Quiz Book*
Roxon, Lillian *Rock Encyclopedia*
Salisbury, Harrison E. *The Shook-up Generation*
Sauers, Wendy *Elvis Presley: A Complete Reference*
Schultheiss, Tom *The Beatles: A Day In The Life*
Shapiro, Angela and Jerome Shapiro (editors) *Candidly Elvis*
Shaver, Sean *The Life Of Elvis Presley*
Shaw, Arnold *The Rock Revolution*
Shaw, Arnold *The Rockin' 50's*
Shaw, Arnold *The World Of Soul*
Slaughter, Todd *Elvis A-Z*
Slaughter, Todd (editor) *Elvis Presley*
Stambler, Irwin *Encyclopedia of Pop, Rock & Soul*
Stambler, Irwin and Grelun Landon *Encyclopedia of Folk, Country And Western Music*
Staten, Vince *The Real Elvis: Good Old Boy*
Stearn, Jess and Larry Geller *The Truth About Elvis*
Sullivan, Ed *1000 Sundays*
Tatham, Dick *Elvis*
Tobler, John and Richard Wooten *Elvis: The Legend And His Music*
Torgoff, Martin (editor) *The Complete Elvis*
Tosches, Nick *Country: The Biggest Music In America*
Unknown *Elvis (An Unauthorized Biography)*
Unknown *The Life And Death Of Elvis Presley*
Wallraf, Ranier and Heinz Plehn *Elvis Presley: An Illustrated Biography*
Walter, Claire *The Book Of Winners*
Wertheimer, Alfred *Elvis '56*
West, Red; Sonny West and Dave Hebler *Elvis: What Happened?*
Whisler, John A. *Elvis Presley Reference Guide And Discography*
Whitburn, Joel *Top Country and Western Records, 1949-1971* (and supplements)
Whitburn, Joel *Top Easy Listening Records, 1961-1974* (and supplements)

Whitburn, Joel *Top LP's, 1945-1972* (and supplements)
Whitburn, Joel *Top Pop, 1955-1982*
Whitburn, Joel *Top Rhythm And Blues Records, 1949-1972* (and supplements)
Whitcomb, Ian *Rock Odyssey*
Worth, Fred L. and Steve Tamerius *All About Elvis*
Yancey, Becky and Cliff Linedecker *My Life With Elvis*
Yorke, Ritchie *The History Of Rock 'N' Roll*
Zmijewsky, Steven and Boris Zmijewsky *The Films And Career Of Elvis Presley*

FANZINES

The following is a partial list of Elvis fan club publications researched for *All Shook Up:*

Always Elvis
Blue Hawaiians Fan Club
Canada Calling
Completely Elvis
Elvis Country
Elvis Mail
Elvis Monthly
Elvis News Service Weekly
Elvis The Record
Elvis Voice
For Elvis Fans Only
Hound Dogs Newsletter
Memphis Flash
Reflections
Specialists Elvis Fan Club
Spring Fever
Strictly Elvis
Taking Care Of Elvis
Teddy Bear
World-wide Elvis News Service

Index

550

552

553

555

movie) 246
Harlin, Howard 134
Harmon, Murray "Buddy" 151,181,188,202,205,246, 263
Harmony, Dottie (photo) 116,117,119
Harpers (magazine) 129,146
Harris, Becky 9
Harris, Curley 23
Harris, Richard 366
Harris, Mrs. Weir 15
Harris, Wynonie 26
Harrison Tape Guide (magazine) 378
Harrison, George 361
Hart, Delores 123, (photo) 132, (photo) 153
"Harum Scarum" (film) (production) 246,247, (reviews) 255,257, (national release) 257, (chart action) 257, (other) 259
Harum Scarum (album) (review) 255, (chart action) 255
Harville, Sonny 23
Haskell, Jimmie 184
Have A Happy (recording session) 303
Have I Told Your Lately That I Love You (recording session) 123, (other) 138
Having Fun With Elvis On Stage (album) 407, (chart action) 412
Hawaiian Sunrise (recording session) 199
Hawaiian Sunset (recording session) 199
Hawaiian Wedding Song (recording session) 199, (other) 386, (performance) 454
Hawk, Buddy 60
Hawkins, Dale 228,306
Hawkins, Hoyt 88
Haynes, Patsy 415
Hayworth, Rita 188
He Is My Everything (recording session) 342
He Knows Just What I Need (recording session) 188
He Touched Me (recording session) 341
He Touched Me (album) 341, 342, (review) 358, (chart action) 359, (other) 372
He Walks Beside Me (album) 355
He'll Have To Go (recording session) 451
He's Your Uncle Not Your Dad (recording session) 278
Hearn, Barbara (photo) 104,

105,117
Heart Of Rome (recording session) 319
Heartbreak Hotel (recording session) 63, (release) 65, (performance) 67,71, 73,74,84,85,103,119, (review) 67, (chart action) 69,71,74,78,79, 84, (other) 60,69,75,77, 78,97,110,111,117,124, 130,131, (live recording) 309,323
Heartbreak Hotel (extended play) (release) 75, (chart action) 79,81,82, 83, (other) 162
Heartbreak Hotel, The, Kenansville, FL 65
Hebler, Dave 408,445
Hedley, Anthony 279
Helm, Anne (photo) 212
Help Me (recording session) 392, (performance) 401,407
Help Me Make It Through The Night (recording session) 341, (performance) 431
Henderson, Marcia 141
Henderson, Mike 267
Henderson, Skitch (photo) 88,88
Hep Cats (magazine) 125, 144
Herald, The (yearbook) 15
Herald-Tribune, The (newspaper) 88
Here Comes Santa Claus (recording session) 137
Herman's Hermits 246, 254
Herndon, Curley see Hoot and Curley
Hess, Jake 306,474
Heustis, Chief Carl 111
Hey, Hey, Hey (recording session) 272
Hey Jude (live recording) 309
Hey, Little Girl (recording session) 246
Hi-Fi (magazine) 371
Hi-Lo Music 59
Hicks, Jeanette 32,59
High Heel Sneakers (recording session) 280, (review) 285
Hilburn, Robert 395
Hill and Range Publishing Company 59,60,179
Hill, Eddie 17,26
Hill, Marianna 252,253, (photo) 264

Hilton Hotel, Las Vegas, NV 366,376,387,395,407, 413,415,418,429,431,453, (show reviews) 367,378, 388,396,407,418,430,433, 455
Hilton International Hotel, Las Vegas, NV 345,353, (show reviews) 354,355
Hilton, Baron 389
Hilton, Conrad 420
Hinton, Edward 325,338
His Hand In Mine (recording session) 188
His Hand In Mine (album) 188, (review) 193,194, (chart action) 197, (other) 247
His Latest Flame see *(Marie's The Name Of) His Latest Flame*
Hit Parader (magazine) 124,373
Hodge, Charlie 158,183, 188,265,273,280,285,292, 306,341,346,367,368,381, 386,387,418,436,439,461, 464,471
Hoffman, Dustin 409
Hoffman, Dr. Lester 471
"Holiday On Ice" 181
Holifield, Cecil 44
Holladay, Ginger 319,387
Holladay, Mary 387,392
Holly Leaves And Christmas Trees (recording session) 341
Holly, Buddy (Charles Hardin Holley) 55,56, 482 (see also Buddy and Bob)
Hollywood Citizen News (newspaper) 242,257, 289
"Hollywood Or Bust" (Martin and Lewis movie) 77
Hollywood Reporter, The (newspaper) 131,140, 194,202,215,221,225,235, 236,242,245,255,265,275, 281,287,291,305,311,326
Hollywood Screen Parade (magazine) 146
"Hollywood Star Hunt" 135
Home Is Where The Heart Is (recording session) 205
HOMES:
(Tupelo, 1935-1948)
306 Old Saltillo Road 1, (photo) 2, 342
Old Saltillo Road (J.D. Presley's house) 7
Kelly Street 7

456

On Stage-February 1970
(album) 309,316, (review)
319, (chart action) 319
On Top Of Old Smokey
(recording session) 203
Onassis, Jacqueline Kennedy
474
Once Is Enough (recording
session) 230
One Boy, Two Little Girls
(recording session) 230
One Broken Heart For Sale
(recording session) 217,
(review) 225, (chart action)
225
One More Day (sung by Mickey
Shaughnessey) 129
One Night (recording session) 123, (release) 161,
(review) 161, (chart
action) 161, (live recording)
323, (performance) 466
One Sided Love Affair (recording session) 66, (single
release) 96, (review) 97
1000 Sundays (Ed Sullivan's
autobiography) 88
One Track Heart (recording
session) 235
Only Believe (recording session) 319, (review) 339,
(chart action) 339
Only The Strong Survive
(recording session) 302
Only You (performance)
79
Operation Elvis (book) 195
Otis, Johnny 107
Owen, Larry 198
Owens, George 483
Owens, Shelia 96
"Ozark Jubilee" 71

Padre (recording session)
341, (other) 386
Page, Frank 29
Page, June 263,280
Pageant (magazine) 400,412,
455
Paget, Debra 84,114,124
Painters Local No. 49, Memphis, TN 128
"Paradise-Hawaiian Style"
(film) 251, (production)
253,254, (reviews) 265,
(Memphis opening) 265,
(national release) 266,
(other) 271
Paradise-Hawaiian Style
(recording session) 252
Paradise-Hawaiian Style
(album) 252, (chart
action) 266
Paralyzed (recording session)

96, (chart action, **Elvis,
Volume 1** extended play)
117, (other) 115
Paramount Pictures 73,74,
122,123,125,144,145,
147,167,170,183,187,
199,204,211,213,219,
225,230,234,235,240,
245,254,267
Parchman Farm Prison 4,
7
Parish, James Robert 434
Parker Machinists see JOBS
(held by Elvis)
Parker, Butch 267
Parker, Ed 365,370,405,
461
Parker, Herman "Little
Junior" 48,117
Parker, Marie 287
Parker, Nancy Laity 370
Parker, Patricia Ann see
Paternity Suits
Parker, Col. Thomas A.
31,41,43,47,49,51,60,67,
71,81,88,91,93,99,102,
103,107,109,114,133,
143,147,149,151,163,
166,173,174,177,179,
181,182,183,185,194,
200,202,208,209,210,
234,240,242,253,254,
270,271,277,278,283,
287,298,302,306,307,
309,310,315,317,324,
335,354,356,357,368,
370,371,372,378,379,
380,384,387,394,400,
407,417,420,428,433,
439,441,445,460,465
Parker, Willard 193
Parkhill, George 368
Party (recording session)
124
Patch It Up (recording
session) 319, (live re-
cording) 323, (review)
326, (chart action) 326
Paternity Suits:
Mississippi Teenager
(name unknown) 33
Patricia Ann Parker
323,327,329,332,335,
349,353
Patricia Stevens Finishing
School, Memphis, TN
228
Patterson, Sara Ann (pho-
to) 100
Paul, LeFawn 40
Payne, Angela 349
Payne, Leon 45
Peace In The Valley (performance) 119, (record-
ing session) 122

Peace In The Valley (ex-
tended play) (release)
126, (chart action) 130,
138, (other) 162
"Peanuts" (cartoon strip)
85
Peer Music Company, Nash-
ville, TN 18,487,488
People (magazine) 415
Pepper, Gary 259,262,269,
271
Perfect For Parties (promo-
tional extended play)
(release) 106
Perkins, Carl 44,48,57,66,
71,87, (photo) 113,114,
493
Perkins, Millie 190
"Perry Como Show, The"
(TV show) 66
Perryman, Tom 36
Person, Minnie 428
Personalities (magazine)
135
Peter Cottontail (song) 125
Peters, Gerald 454
Peterson, James B. 149
*Petunia, The Gardener's
Daughter* (recording
session) 247
Phillips, Dewey 20, (pho-
to) 21,90,295,481,484,
485
Phillips, Sam 16,17,18,19,
20,25,26,27, (photo) 34,
56,114,482,487,488,489,
494
Photoplay (magazine) 134,
161,412,413,434,455,470
Pickins, Slim (Louis Bert
Lindley, Jr.) 20
Pieces Of My Life (record-
ing session) 418
"Pied Piper Of Cleveland, Or
A Day In The Life Of A
Disk Jockey" (movie) 51
Pietrofeso, Ron 435
Pinkington, Susan 392
"Pioneer, Go Home" (work-
ing title for "Follow That
Dream movie) 203
Plantation Rock (recording
session) 211
Plastics Products Company,
Memphis, TN 21
Platters, The 79
Playboy (magazine) 287
Playing For Keeps (record-
ing session) 96, (release)
119, (review) 122,123,
(chart action) 124
Playing With Fire (recording
session) 199
*Please Don't Drag That
String Around* (recording

568

570

572

session) 302, (review) 310, (chart action) 310,311, (other) 213,313,314,341, 367, (live recording) 310, 316,323, (performance) 385

Suzore's No. 2 Theater, Memphis, TN   20

Sweet Angeline   (recording session) 387,389

Sweet Inspiration (song)   386

Sweet Inspirations, The (Emily Houston, Myrna Smith, Sylvia, Shenwell, and Estelle Brown)   306,339,427,450, 457

Sweet, Sweet Spirit (sung by J.D. Sumner and the Stamps Quartet)   379

Swing Down, Sweet Chariot (recording session) 188,295

Sylvia   (recording session) 319

TCB necklaces   339

T-R-O-U-B-L-E   (recording session) 418, (performance) 421, (chart action) 422

TV And Movie Screen (magazine)   129,161,185

TV And Radio Mirror (magazine)   118

TV Film Stars (magazine)   187

TV Guide (magazine)   92,97, 391,423

TV Headliners (magazine)   127,144

TV Radio Mirror (magazine)   182,400

TV Radio Show (magazine)   371

TV Star Parade (magazine)   102,129,155,167

TV World (magazine)   118

TV-Movie Fan (magazine)   118

Tagore, Dr. J.N.   275

Take Good Care Of Her   (recording session) 386, (other) 387

Take Me, Please (sung by Stella Stevens)   211

Take Me To The Fair   (recording session) 217

Take My Hand, Precious Lord (recording session) 122

Take Your Finger Out Of It, It Don't Belong To You (performance) 484

Talk About The Good Times (recording session) 392

Talking 'Bout Your Birthday (performance) 484

"Tamahine" (Nancy Kwan movie)   237

Tatham, Dick   456

Taurog, Norman   279

Tavares, Fred   199

Taylor, Elizabeth   185

Teague, Albert   15

Teal Record Company   240

Teddy Bear   (recording session) 123, (release) 130, (review) 130, (chart action) 131,133, (other) 133,134,143, (performance) 345

Teddy Bear (fanzine)   389, 483

Tedesco, Tommy   291, 292

Teen (magazine)   211

Teen Life (magazine)   129

Teen Records Company   88

Teenage Rock And Roll Review (magazine)   109, 144

Tell Me Pretty Baby   (non-Elvis recording) 482

Tell Me Why   (recording session) 122, (review) 257, (chart action) 259

"Ten Commandments" (Charlton Heston movie)   262

Tender Feeling   (recording session) 230

Tennessee Employment Security Office   15

Tennessee Highway Patrol   158

Tennessee Partner (song)   494

Tennessee Saturday Night (recording session) 19, (song) 60,494

Tennessee State Legislature   198

Termini, Joe   135

Tarran, Anthony   223,267

Terry, Al   87

Testerman, Mrs. Kyle   356

Texas State Fair, Dallas, TX   51,103

Texas Stompers, The   44, 45

Thanks To The Rolling Sea (recording session) 211

That's All Right   (recording session) 19, (demonstration record) 20, (first release) 21, (review) 23, (performance) 26,29,51, 84,410,450, (re-release) 60, (other) 52,59,69, 482,485,488,490,491, 492, (live recording) 321, 323

That's All Right   (record-

ing by Marty Robbins)   32

That's Amore   (performance) 484

That's Someone You'll Never Forget   (recording session) 202

That's The Stuff You Gotta Watch (song)   60,494

That's The Way It Is (album) see **Elvis-That's The Way** (album)

That's When Your Heartaches Begin (song)   16, 494, (recording session) 122, (release) 126, (review) 126, (chart action) 128

That's What You Gotta Watch   (recording session) 29

There Ain't Nothing Like A Song   (recording session) 278

There Goes My Everything (recording session) 319, (review) 331, (chart action) 332,335

There Is No God But God (recording session) 342

There Is So Much World To See   (recording session) 266

There She Goes   (recording by Carl Smith) 53

There's A Brand New Day On The Horizon   (recording session) 235

There's A Fire Down Below (recording session) 451

There's A Honky Tonk Angel (recording session) 392

There's Always Me   (recording session) 198, (review) 279, (chart action) 279

There's Gold In The Mountains   (recording session) 230

They Remind Me Too Much Of You   (recording session) 217, (review) 225

Thing Called Love, A   (recording session) 341

Thinking About You   (recording session) 392

This Is Living   (recording session) 205

This Is My Heaven   (recording session) 252

This Is Our Dance   (recording session) 319

This Is The Story   (recording session) 301, (live recording) 309

Thomas, Billy Joe "B.J."   299

573

575

About The Author

Lee Cotten, although born in Philadelphia, is a product of Southern upbringing. He arrived in Newton, Mississippi, about 130 miles south of Tupelo, with his parents in 1948, about the same time that Elvis was moving north to Memphis. Lee lived in Mississippi, Georgia, and Tennessee for the next sixteen years, finally graduating from the University of Georgia with a B.A. in Journalism. His first recollections of Elvis center around the summer of 1956 and the community swimming pool in Monroe, Georgia. It was nighttime, and someone dropped a nickel in the jukebox. *My Baby Left Me* came popping out of the speakers with that hard drum riff and the slapping bass line, followed by Scotty Moore's unique rockabilly guitar lead. And then there was the vocal . . . that high, demanding, wailing, pleading vocal as Elvis intoned: "was it something I done, something that she heard?" Lee spent a week's allowance that night, playing the record over and over. He had heard Elvis before, but this was the turning point. He became fascinated by the fact that another person, a performer, could touch the inner parts of his being in the way Elvis and his song had done that night. To this day, *My Baby Left Me* remains Lee's personal favorite of the more than 600 songs recorded by Elvis.

Following college, Lee was a member of the U.S. Air Force's elite strategic reconnaissance program stationed first in Wyoming and then Alaska over a period of five years. Following his tour of duty, he settled in Sacramento, California to study professional photography under world-renowned photographer Glen Fishback. In the midst of a successful career as a freelance photographer in Sacramento, Lee started a retail record business dealing in the hits from the past. His store, Golden Oldies, is one of the most unique record stores in the country, specializing as it does in 45 rpm singles. His reputation as an expert in the field of collectable records has spread around the world. His expertise has led to numerous appearances on both radio and television. Lee was also the producer of one of the finest Elvis Fan Festivals ever presented in this country, which took place in Sacramento in January 1979. In addition to his outstanding collection of Presleyana, Lee is also the author of *Elvis: His Life History* (self-published, 1980) and the co-author of *Jailhouse Rock* (Pierian Press, 1983). *Jailhouse Rock* has received overwhelmingly high praise from both critics and fans as the first major work to cover the many bootleg recordings of Elvis from 1970-1983. At this time, Lee is starting work on a major project, a multi-volume chronological history of rock 'n' roll music, which Pierian Press is proud to announce that they will publish.